The Structure
of Argument

SEVENTH EDITION

The Structure of Argument

Annette T. Rottenberg

Donna Haisty Winchell
Clemson University

Bedford/St. Martin's
Boston • New York

For Bedford/St. Martin's

Executive Editor: John E. Sullivan III
Production Editor: Kerri A. Cardone
Senior Production Supervisor: Jennifer Peterson
Senior Marketing Manager: Molly Parke
Editorial Assistant: Alyssa Demirjian
Copyeditor: Helen van Loon
Indexer: Steve Csipke
Permissions Manager: Kalina K. Ingham
Senior Art Director: Anna Palchik
Text Design: Glenna Collett
Cover Design: Donna Lee Dennison
Cover Photo: Courtesy of Veer
Composition: Achorn International, Inc.
Printing and Binding: RR Donnelley and Sons

President: Joan E. Feinberg
Editorial Director: Denise B. Wydra
Editor in Chief: Karen S. Henry
Director of Marketing: Karen R. Soeltz
Director of Production: Susan W. Brown
Associate Director, Editorial Production: Elise S. Kaiser
Managing Editor: Elizabeth M. Schaaf

Library of Congress Control Number: 2011927768

Manufactured in the United States of America.

6 5 4 3 2 1
f e d c b a

For information, write: Bedford/St. Martin's, 75 Arlington Street, Boston, MA 02116 (617-399-4000)

ISBN-13: 978–0–312–65069–8

Acknowledgments

Acknowledgments and copyrights appear at the back of the book on pages 497–500, which constitute an extension of the copyright page. It is a violation of the law to reproduce these selections by any means whatsoever without the written permission of the copyright holder.

Praise for *The Structure of Argument*

"*The Structure of Argument* is thorough without being dry, challenging while remaining accessible. It is the only text I would consider using for my argument class."

—Dan Chelotti, *Elms College*

"*The Structure of Argument* is well organized, comprehensive, thoughtful, and clear."

—Rossana Lhota, *Arizona State University*

"*The Structure of Argument* is a well-written, comprehensive, accessible text. Students get their money's worth."

—Rick Rivera, *Columbia College*

"I appreciate the comprehensive offerings in *The Structure of Argument*."

—Ann Smith, *Modesto Junior College*

Preface

Purpose

Where do our students — some of our youngest voters and our future leaders — get their take on current events? Where do they get their news? Probably not from sitting down and watching network broadcasts or listening to the radio like their parents and grandparents did. Probably not from reading a newspaper regularly either. More likely they get it from a computer or a cell phone, which means they get it in bits and pieces, and on the run. Where do they read or hear arguments? Again, probably in short digital bursts. Their idea of debate may come from the most recent presidential debates. More likely, it comes from comments made online in response to YouTube videos or Facebook postings. They may get today's political news from Jon Stewart or Glenn Beck, from the cover of *Time* or *Newsweek*, or from skits on *Saturday Night Live*. Their most consistent source of headlines may be cnn.com, fox.com, or Twitter.

In order to get our students to really think about argument, we have to get them to slow down and practice the art of critical reading — and listening. We have to get them to analyze sustained argumentative discourse, and we have to give them a vocabulary to be able to talk about it. The vocabulary we use in *The Structure of Argument* is primarily that of Stephen Toulmin, whose model of argument is based on three principal elements: claim, support, and warrant. These three elements answer the questions "What are you trying to prove?" "What have you got to go on?" and "How did you get from evidence to claim?" These questions are precisely the ones that students must ask and answer in analyzing arguments.

We also have to get our students to write sustained argumentative discourse. They have to learn to apply their knowledge of claim, support, and warrant. They have to understand that successful arguments require a blend of *logos*, *pathos*, and *ethos*. Logic is not always enough; it must usually be used in conjunction with legitimate appeal to emotion, and it must come from a trusted speaker or writer. In addition to grounding our text in Toulmin's model of argumentation, we also introduce students to the basics of Aristotle's classical theories of rhetoric and to Carl Rogers's theories of nonconfrontational communication. We stress the significance of audience as a practical matter. In the rhetorical or audience-centered approach to argument, to which we subscribe in this text, success is defined as acceptance of the claim by an audience. Arguers in the real world recognize intuitively that their primary goal is not to demonstrate the purity of their logic, but to win the adherence of their audiences.

To do so, students must read critically and reflect on what others have to say. The Internet has redefined what research means to our students. A large part of the challenge now is not to find sources but to eliminate the thousands of questionable ones. Faced with the temptation to cut and paste instead of read and understand, students need more help than ever with accurate and fair use of sources. We provide that help in the context of an increasingly digital world.

Organization

Part One of *The Structure of Argument* introduces Aristotelian, Rogerian, and Toulmin approaches to argumentation, then critical reading and analytical writing. It is rich in readings that support these approaches.

Part Two devotes one chapter apiece to definition and to the chief elements of argument — claim, support, and warrant. The examples are drawn from both print and online sources — essays, articles, speeches, blogs, cartoons, and advertisements. Chapter 8 teaches students to identify and avoid errors in logic, and Chapter 9 deals with the power of word choice in arguing effectively. Each chapter in this section includes examples, readings, discussion questions, and writing suggestions, as well as a selection of readings for analysis and a debate that shows contrasting perspectives on the same controversial issue.

Part Three takes up the process of researching, writing, and presenting arguments. Chapter 10 focuses on planning and research. Chapter 11 covers writing and documentation and provides two sample research papers, one employing the Modern Language Association (MLA) documentation system and the other employing the American Psychological Association (APA) documentation style. Chapter 13 provides guidelines for presenting arguments orally.

New to This Edition

As is the case with each edition of *The Structure of Argument*, we have updated readings throughout to keep information current and subjects interesting. In this seventh edition, over half of the readings are new. Three new debates examine derogatory use of the word "retard," the environmental costs of recycling plastic, and the social responsibility of business.

We are pleased to offer students more support in researching and documenting research than we have in any previous edition. The research paper in MLA style, on competitive foods and obesity, is new to this edition, and in Chapters 10 and 11 students will be able to follow its author through the research process as she responds to an assignment, and researches, writes, and revises her paper, providing a real-world model of the research process. Chapters 1 through 9 now end with a "Research Readiness" exercise that prepares students for investigating and documenting an independent research topic, helping them practice skills such as narrowing down a list of possible digital sources or writing a summary. Additional sentence templates in Chapter 3 help students understand the effective use of summary and response in argument. And *The Structure of Argument* is also more visual than ever before. A fresh new design provides a reinvigorated look and improves navigation in the text, and many new photographs provide visual examples and opportunities for analysis. We are particularly proud of our new blog *Argument Update*. Here, we will add weekly comments and examine world events using the theories and terminology introduced in the text. See *Bits* entry on page x for more information.

An electronic edition of *The Structure of Argument* is available at about half the price of the print book. See coursemart.com for details.

You Get More Digital Choices for *The Structure of Argument*

The Structure of Argument doesn't stop with a book. Online, you'll find both free and affordable premium resources to help students get even more out of the book and your course. You'll also find convenient instructor resources, such as downloadable sample syllabi, classroom activities, and even a nationwide community of teachers. To learn more about or order any of the products below, contact your Bedford/St. Martin's sales representative, e-mail sales support (sales_support@bfwpub.com), or visit the Web site at bedfordstmartins.com.

Companion Web site for *The Structure of Argument*
bedfordstmartins.com/rottenberg

Send students to free and open resources, choose flexible premium resources to supplement your print text, or upgrade to an expanding collection of innovative digital content.

Free and open resources for *The Structure of Argument* provide students with easy-to-access reference materials, visual tutorials, and support for working with sources.

- Appendix on Writing about Literature
- *TopLinks* with reliable online sources
- *Research and Documentation Online* by Diana Hacker
- *Bedford Bibliographer*: a tool for collecting source information and making a bibliography in MLA, APA, and *Chicago* styles

VideoCentral is a growing collection of videos for the writing class that captures real-world, academic, and student writers talking about how and why they write. *VideoCentral* can be packaged with *The Structure of Argument* at a significant discount. An activation code is required. To order *VideoCentral* packaged with the print book, use ISBN 978–1–4576–0452–2.

Re:Writing Plus gathers all of Bedford/St. Martin's premium digital content for composition into one online collection. It includes hundreds of model documents, the first ever peer review game, and *VideoCentral*. *Re:Writing Plus* can be purchased separately or packaged with the print book at a significant discount. An activation code is required. To order *Re:Writing Plus* packaged with the print book, use ISBN 978–1–4576–0453–9.

i-series on CD-ROM

Add more value to your text by choosing one of the following CD-ROMs, free when packaged with *The Structure of Argument*. This popular series presents multimedia tutorials in a flexible format — because there are things you can't do in a book. To learn more about package options or any of the products below, contact your Bedford/St. Martin's sales representative or visit bedfordstmartins.com.

ix visual exercises helps students put into practice key rhetorical and visual concepts. To order *ix visual exercises* packaged with the print book, use ISBN 978–1–4576–0435–5.

i-claim: visualizing argument offers a new way to see argument — with 6 tutorials, an illustrated glossary, and over 70 multimedia arguments. To order *i-claim: visualizing argument* packaged with the print book, use ISBN 978–1–4576–0427–0.

Instructor resources

You have a lot to do in your course. Bedford/St. Martin's wants to make it easy for you to find the support you need — and to get it quickly.

Resources for Teaching The Structure of Argument 7e is available in PDF that can be downloaded from bedfordstmartins.com/rottenberg. In addition to chapter overviews and teaching tips, the instructor's manual includes sample syllabi and suggestions for classroom activities.

Teaching Central (bedfordstmartins.com/teachingcentral) offers the entire list of Bedford/St. Martin's print and online professional resources in one place. You'll find landmark reference works, sourcebooks on pedagogical issues, award-winning collections, and practical advice for the classroom — all free for instructors.

Bits (bedfordbits.com) collects creative ideas for teaching a range of composition topics in an easily searchable blog. A community of teachers — leading scholars, authors, and editors — discuss revision, research, grammar and style, technology, peer review, and much more. Take, use, adapt, and pass the ideas around. Then, come back to the site to comment or share your own suggestion.

Content cartridges for the most common course management systems — Blackboard, WebCT, Angel, and Desire2Learn — allow you to easily download digital materials for your course. To find the cartridges available with *The Structure of Argument* visit bedfordstmartins.com/rottenberg.

Teaching Argument in the Composition Course, by Timothy Barnett, is also available. It offers a range of perspectives, from Aristotle to the present day, on argument and on teaching argument. The twenty-eight readings — many of them classic works in the field — present essential insights and practical information. For ordering information, contact your local sales representative or e-mail us at sales_support@bfwpub.com.

Also Available

A longer edition, *Elements of Argument*, Tenth Edition, is available for instructors who prefer a text with more readings. It includes not only Chapters 1 through 12, but also eight Multiple Viewpoints and Classic Arguments. See bedford stmartins.com for details.

Acknowledgments

This book has profited by the critiques and suggestions of instructors who responded to a questionnaire: Leandra Binder, Chemeketa Community College; Dan Chelotti, Elms College; Jeannie Chiu, Diablo Valley College; Marcia B. Dinneen, Bridgewater State University; H. George Hahn, Towson University; William Levine, Middle Tennessee State University; Rossana Lhota, Arizona State University; Chad McLane, North Iowa Area Community College; Steven R. Mohr, Terra State Community College; Dan Morgan, Scott Community College; Daniel Powell, Florida State Community College at Jacksonville; Rick Rivera, Columbia College; Sharon Russell, Pierce College; Ann Smith, Modesto Junior College; Barbara Schwarz Wachal, St. Louis Community College-Florissant Valley. We also thank those reviewers who chose to remain anonymous.

We are grateful to those at Bedford/St. Martin's who have helped in numerous ways large and small: Joan Feinberg, Denise Wydra, Karen Henry, Steve Scipione, Shannon Walsh, Alyssa Demirjian, Kalina Ingham, Martha Friedman, Linda Zielke, Connie Gardner, Sue Brown, Elizabeth Schaaf, Elise Kaiser, Kerri Cardone, Helen van Loon, Anna Palchik, and, most especially, John Sullivan.

A Note on the Council of Writing Program Administrators' (WPA) Outcomes

The Structure of Argument is coauthored by former writing program directors, and the WPA outcomes are espoused and reinforced throughout the book. Below, the outcomes are outlined, and italic references link the outcomes to particular chapters.

Rhetorical Knowledge. By the end of first-year composition, students should:

- Focus on a purpose.
- Respond to the needs of different audiences.
- Respond appropriately to different kinds of rhetorical situations.
- Use conventions of format and structure appropriate to the rhetorical situation.
- Adopt appropriate voice, tone, and level of formality.
- Understand how genres shape reading and writing.
- Write in several genres. *See especially Chapters 1, 2, and 9.*

Critical Thinking, Reading, and Writing. By the end of first-year composition, students should:

- Use writing and reading for inquiry, learning, thinking, and communicating.
- Understand a writing assignment as a series of tasks, including finding,evaluating, analyzing, and synthesizing appropriate primary and secondary sources.
- Integrate their own ideas with those of others.
- Understand the relationships among language, knowledge, and power. *See especially Chapters 2, 3, and 8.*

Processes. By the end of first-year composition, students should:

- Be aware that it usually takes multiple drafts to create and complete a successful text.
- Develop flexible strategies for generating, revising, editing, and proofreading.
- Understand writing as an open process that permits writers to use later invention and re-thinking to revise their work.
- Understand the collaborative and social aspects of writing processes.
- Learn to critique their own and others' works.

Knowledge of Conventions. By the end of first-year composition, students should:

- Learn common formats for different kinds of texts.
- Develop knowledge of genre conventions ranging from structure and paragraphing to tone and mechanics.
- Practice appropriate means of documenting their work.
- Control such surface features as syntax, grammar, punctuation, and spelling. *See especially Chapters 10 and 11.*

Composing in Electronic Environments. By the end of first-year composition, students should:

- Use electronic environments for drafting, reviewing, editing, and sharing texts.
- Locate, evaluate, organize, and use research material collected from electronic sources, including scholarly library databases; other official databases; and informal electronic networks and Internet sources.
- Understand and exploit the differences in the rhetorical strategies and in the affordances available for both print and electronic texts. *See especially Chapters 1, 2, 10, and 11.*

Brief Contents

Contents

3 Analytical Writing 76

11 The Argumentative Paper: Writing and
Documentation   439

The Structure
of Argument

Understanding Argument

CHAPTER 1

Approaches to Argument

Because of the First Amendment, Americans have the freedom to speak —
and they do, sometimes loudly, sometimes offensively, sometimes movingly.
Give a nation with America's diversity freedom of speech, and its people will
use it, and they will often disagree. But that, after all, is the point of the First
Amendment: Americans can express disagreement without fear of reprisal.

Public education has been a part of America since its beginning because
in a country where the citizens choose their leaders, an educated citizenry is
in the best interest of all except those who would silence dissenting voices.
For centuries, from a time long before thirteen colonies became a country,
young men — and eventually young women — have been trained to let their
voices be heard. They have been taught the art of rhetoric. You have probably grown up letting your voice be heard, some of you more than others.
This course is designed to teach you to be more proficient in expressing your
ideas about controversial issues, to argue more effectively in speech, but more
so in writing.

Of course, not all arguments end in clear victories for one side or another. Nor should they. In a democratic society of competing interests and
values, a compromise between two or more extreme points of view may be
the only viable solution to a vexing problem. Although formal debates under
the auspices of a debating society, such as those that take place on many college
campuses, usually end in winners and losers, real-life problems — both public and private — are often resolved through negotiation. Courtroom battles
may result in compromise, and the law itself allows for exemptions and ex-
tenuating circumstances.

Most of the argumentative writing in this book will deal with matters of
public controversy, an area traditionally associated with the study of argument. As the word *public* suggests, these matters concern us as members of
a community. In the arguments you will read, human beings are engaged in
explaining and defending their own actions and beliefs and opposing or compromising with those of others. They do this for at least two reasons: (1) to

3

justify what they do and think, both to themselves and to their audiences, and (2) in the process to solve problems and make decisions. In the arguments you will write in this course, you will be doing the same.

A distinction is sometimes made between argument and persuasion. Argument, according to most authorities, gives primary importance to logical appeals. Providing abundant evidence and making logical connections, however, may not be enough to win agreement from an audience. A writer or speaker must take into account an audience's emotional response to the subject matter and the way in which it is presented. Also, success in convincing an audience is almost always inseparable from the audience's belief in the writer's trustworthiness. In this book, we use the term *argument* to represent forms of discourse that attempt to persuade readers or listeners to accept a claim, whether acceptance is based on logical or emotional appeals or, as is usually the case, on both.

In this chapter we will discuss the approaches to argument proposed by the Greek philosopher Aristotle, the American psychologist Carl Rogers, and the British philosopher Stephen Toulmin.

Aristotelian Rhetoric

Aristotle, who wrote a treatise on argument that has influenced its study and practice for well over two thousand years, defined rhetoric as all available means of persuasion. He used the term *logos* to refer to logical appeals and the term *pathos* to refer to emotional appeals. He believed that, in an ideal world, logic alone would be enough to persuade. He acknowledged, however, that in the less-than-ideal real world, effective arguments depend not only on *logos* and *pathos*, but also on the writer's or speaker's credibility, which he called *ethos*. In fact, he considered *ethos* to be the most important element in the arguer's ability to persuade the audience to accept a claim.

Aristotle named intelligence, character, and goodwill as the attributes that produce credibility. Today we might describe these qualities somewhat differently, but the criteria for judging a writer's credibility remain essentially the same. First, writers must convince the audience that they are knowledgeable and as well informed as possible about the subject. Second, they must persuade their audience that they are not only truthful in the presentation of evidence but also morally upright and dependable. Third, they must show that, as arguers with good intentions, they have considered the interests and needs of others as well as their own.

As an example in which the credibility of the arguer is at stake, consider a wealthy Sierra Club member who lives on ten acres of a magnificent oceanside estate and who appears before a community planning board to argue against future development of the area. The board, acting in the interests of all the citizens of the community, will ask themselves: Has the arguer proved that his informa-

Aristotle (384–322 BCE) had ideas about argument that are important and useful to this day.

tion about environmental impact is complete and accurate? Has he demonstrated that he sincerely desires to preserve the wilderness, not merely his own privacy and space? And has he made clear that he has considered the needs and desires of those who might want to live in a housing development by the ocean? If the answers to all of these questions are yes, then the board will hear the arguer with respect, and the arguer will have begun to establish his credibility.

A reputation for intelligence, character, and goodwill is not often earned overnight. And it can be lost more quickly than it is gained. Once writers or speakers have betrayed an audience's belief in their character or judgment, they may find it difficult to persuade an audience to accept subsequent claims, no matter how sound the data and reasoning are.

For Aristotle, *logos, ethos,* and *pathos* constituted the elements of argument. With this triad, he laid the foundation for classical or traditional rhetoric and for all rhetorical theories to follow.

In Aristotle's day, one of the chief goals of rhetorical training was to learn to argue successfully in a court of law on judicial matters or in another public forum on political ones. The primary goal of rhetoric itself was to win — either to win a court case concerning what had happened in the past or to win approval for a political proposal about what should happen in the future.

Beyond what Aristotle teaches us about credibility, how does ancient rhetoric translate to our digital world? It gives us a vocabulary and also gives us a systematic way of thinking about a rhetorical situation. A writer or speaker is always preparing a text *about* something (the subject) and *for* someone (the audience). Since the texts produced in this course will be written, we will use the term *writer* instead of *speaker* in discussing rhetorical situations, although in Aristotle's world, the texts would have been primarily oral.

Rhetoric is largely a study of relationships. The relationship between writer and audience is the rhetorical relationship. That between writer and subject is the referential.[1]

Writers — but more commonly speakers — in Aristotle's world of the fourth century BCE were very limited in audience and in subject matter. As far as the rhetorical relationship is concerned, inventions like the printing press, and later the telegraph, gave the writer access to a wider and wider range of audiences; the computer in general and the Internet in particular have increased exponentially the audiences a writer can reach. The audiences available to a writer are now almost endless, not bound in size or in geographic location.

On a developmental level, individuals used to learn to write for increasingly distant audiences, starting in childhood with writing primarily for a parent or for one teacher, with an occasional letter to someone well known to them. Only later did they sometimes write to people they didn't know personally and to larger groups and, in a few cases, go on to publish their writing. Now elementary students, for good or ill, converse online with others a world away and completely unknown to them on a personal level. The Internet provides everyone a voice on almost any subject.

The amount of information available at the click of a mouse has also exploded with the advent of the Internet. That means that the relationship between writer and subject — the referential relationship — has also changed with the times. Research used to mean going to the library to work with hard copies of texts or using a set of encyclopedias and a small number of reference books available at home. Now a world of information is accessible in a matter of seconds, literally.

If the latest news is as close as your remote control, it is also as close as your computer mouse or even your cell phone. Aristotle gave us a vocabulary for talking about communication (such as the syllogism, treated on p. 26, and logic,

---

[1] These two terms come from James Moffett, *Teaching the Universe of Discourse* (Boston: Houghton Mifflin, 1968), p. 18. He illustrates the two with a grid crossing rhetorical and referential.

In Aristotle's time, the audience was simply those people in front of the speaker. Today, with electronic media, unless the presentation is live, as in this photograph, the audience may be broader and unknown.

treated in Chapter 8), and changes in culture and in technology have led us to redefine that vocabulary for a world vastly different from his.

In the proscribed world of ancient Greece, it was relatively easy to predict what an audience would know about a subject of discourse. There was more of a shared world view than has existed in more recent times. In ancient Greece, rigid rules dictated the organization of a speech, and the examples were drawn from well-known narratives, true or fictional. Today it is much more difficult for a writer to place himself or herself in someone else's position and try to see from that person's point of view.

It is in addressing this relationship between audience and subject that rhetorical theories differ the most in their approach, as we will discuss.

SAMPLE ESSAY WITH ANALYSIS   Aristotelian

Don't Mourn *Brown v. Board of Education*
JUAN WILLIAMS

L et us now praise the *Brown* decision. Let us now bury the *Brown* decision. With yesterday's Supreme Court ruling ending the use of voluntary schemes to create racial balance among students, it is time to acknowledge that *Brown's* time has passed. It is worthy of a send-off with fanfare for setting off the civil rights movement and inspiring social progress for women, gays, and the poor. But the decision in *Brown v. Board of Education* that focused on outlawing segregated schools as unconstitutional is now out of step with American political and social realities.

Desegregation does not speak to dropout rates that hover near 50 percent for black and Hispanic high school students. It does not equip society to address the so-called achievement gap between black and white students that mocks *Brown's* promise of equal educational opportunity.

And the fact is, during the last 20 years, with *Brown* in full force, America's public schools have been growing more segregated — even as the nation has become more racially diverse. In 2001, the National Center for Education Statistics reported that the average white student attends a school that is 80 percent white, while 70 percent of black students attend schools where nearly two-thirds of students are black and Hispanic.

By the early '90s, support in the federal courts for the central work of *Brown* — racial integration of public schools — began to rapidly expire. In a series of cases in Atlanta, Oklahoma City, and Kansas City, Mo., frustrated parents, black and white, appealed to federal judges to stop shifting children from school to school like pieces on a game board. The parents wanted better neighborhood schools and a better education for their children, no matter the racial make-up of the school. In their rulings ending court mandates for school integration, the judges, too, spoke of the futility of using schoolchildren to address social ills caused by adults holding fast to patterns of residential segregation by both class and race.

The focus of efforts to improve elementary and secondary schools shifted to magnet schools, to allowing parents the choice to move their children out of fail-

5

Juan Williams is a former senior correspondent for National Public Radio and a political analyst for Fox News Channel. His books include *Enough: The Phony Leaders, Dead-End Movements, and Culture of Failure That Are Undermining Black America* (2006) and *Thurgood Marshall: American Revolutionary* (1998). The article was published June 29, 2007, on nytimes.com.

The effects of the *Brown* decision are still being dealt with today.

ing schools and, most recently, to vouchers and charter schools. The federal No Child Left Behind plan has many critics, but there's no denying that it is an effective tool for forcing teachers' unions and school administrators to take responsibility for educating poor and minority students.

It was an idealistic Supreme Court that in 1954 approved of *Brown* as a race-conscious policy needed to repair the damage of school segregation and protect every child's 14th-Amendment right to equal treatment under law. In 1971, Chief Justice Warren Burger, writing for a unanimous court still embracing *Brown*, said local school officials could make racial integration a priority even if it did not improve educational outcomes because it helped "to prepare students to live in a pluralistic society."

But today a high court with a conservative majority concludes that any policy based on race — no matter how well intentioned — is a violation of every child's 14th-Amendment right to be treated as an individual without regard to race. We've come full circle.

In 1990, after months of interviews with Justice Thurgood Marshall, who had been the lead lawyer for the N.A.A.C.P. Legal Defense Fund on the *Brown* case, I sat in his Supreme Court chambers with a final question. Almost 40 years later, was he satisfied with the outcome of the decision? Outside the courthouse, the failing Washington school system was hypersegregated, with more than 90 percent of its students black and Latino. Schools in the surrounding suburbs, meanwhile, were mostly white and producing some of the top students in the nation.

Had Mr. Marshall, the lawyer, made a mistake by insisting on racial integration instead of improvement in the quality of schools for black children? 10

His response was that seating black children next to white children in school had never been the point. It had been necessary only because all-white school boards were generously financing schools for white children while leaving black students in overcrowded, decrepit buildings with hand-me-down books and underpaid teachers. He had wanted black children to have the right to attend white schools as a point of leverage over the biased spending patterns of the segregationists who ran schools — both in the 17 states where racially separate schools were required by law and in other states where they were a matter of culture.

If black children had the right to be in schools with white children, Justice Marshall reasoned, then school board officials would have no choice but to equalize spending to protect the interests of their white children.

Racial malice is no longer the primary motive in shaping inferior schools for minority children. Many failing big city schools today are operated by black superintendents and mostly black school boards.

And today the argument that school reform should provide equal opportunity for children, or prepare them to live in a pluralistic society, is spent. The winning argument is that better schools are needed for all children — black, white, brown and every other hue — in order to foster a competitive workforce in a global economy.

Dealing with racism and the bitter fruit of slavery and "separate but equal" legal segregation was at the heart of the court's brave decision 53 years ago. With *Brown* officially relegated to the past, the challenge for brave leaders now is to deliver on the promise of a good education for every child.

15

Analysis

Viewed from an Aristotelian perspective, Juan Williams uses all three types of appeal: *logos, pathos,* and *ethos.* Williams assumes from the beginning that his audience will be familiar with the 1954 case *Brown v. Board of Education* because it is a significant part of American history. He balances the opening of his essay by equally praising the *Brown* decision and welcoming its demise: It is time for *Brown* to go, but its end should be viewed with respect. He anticipates the negative emotional response that some might have to the end of what many saw and still see as a major step toward racial equality by praising it as "worthy of a send-off with fanfare for setting off the civil rights movement and inspiring social progress for women, gays and the poor." He is appealing to the emotions of his audience and is also presenting himself as an ethical man by acknowledging both the good and the bad of the decision. The thesis that he is trying to support is stated at the end of the second paragraph: "But the decision in *Brown v. Board of Education* that focused on outlawing segregated schools as unconstitutional is now out of step with American political and social realities."

Consider the logical support that Williams offers for this thesis. In paragraph 3, he summarizes the problems with desegregation and then in paragraphs 4–7 looks back in more detail at how the ruling has failed America's children over the last twenty years. In spite of all the promise Americans saw in the ruling, the reality, according to Williams, "mocks *Brown*'s promise of equal educational opportunity." He uses statistics in two places, giving his source in one case but not in the other. He gives less specific information about parents' response, but by that point in the essay, he has established himself as a reasonable man who is fair in his presentation of his case. In an emotional appeal at the end of paragraph 5, he skillfully expresses the futility that parents were feeling and that the judges also expressed in justifying their ruling: "the futility of using schoolchildren to address social ills caused by adults holding fast to patterns of residential segregation by both class and race."

Williams gives his readers no reason to question his logic when, in the second half of the essay, he argues that we have come full circle. We have gone from a "race-conscious policy needed to repair the damage of school segregation and protect every child's 14th-Amendment right to equal treatment under the law" to a Supreme Court decision "that any policy based on race — no matter how well intentioned — is a violation of every child's 14th-Amendment right to be treated as an individual without regard to race."

Some readers will know Juan Williams as a correspondent for National Public Radio and/or as a political analyst for Fox News and may have a preconceived notion of his *ethos*, or character. Those who come to the essay with some knowledge of its author will most likely know that Williams is African American. In the second half of his essay, he contributes significantly to the image of himself as an authority on the subject of racial desegregation when he says that he interviewed Justice Thurgood Marshall over a series of months and had the chance to sit in Marshall's Supreme Court chambers and ask him whether he was satisfied with the outcome of the *Brown* decision. Here is *pathos* as Williams reports Marshall's response. He is appealing to his audience's values when he explains that Marshall, as the lead lawyer for the NAACP Legal Defense Fund on the case, was not concerned primarily with gaining black children the right to sit next to white ones, but with forcing whites to equalize spending for both. Most readers today want to see children treated fairly, and some will be angered that it took such lengths to gain even some progress toward that goal.

Williams's plea at the end of the essay is for a good education for every child. Few in his audience could argue with that goal.

Rogerian Argument

Carl Rogers was a twentieth-century humanistic psychologist who translated his ideas about therapy into communication theory. As a therapist, he believed that the experience of two people meeting and speaking honestly to each other would have a healing effect. In later years he became convinced that the same principles of nondirective, nonconfrontational therapy that emphasized attentive listening could work not only for couples and small groups, but also for large groups, even nations, to create more harmonious relationships.

Carl Rogers (1902–1987), second from right, leads a panel in 1966.

Such nonconfrontational communication between individuals or among groups is hampered, Rogers believed, by the fact that there is no longer anything approaching a shared world view. He wrote:

> From time immemorial, the tribe or the community or the nation or the culture has agreed upon what constitutes the real world. To be sure, different tribes and different cultures might have held sharply different world views, but at least there was a large, relatively unified group which felt assured in its knowledge of the world and the universe, and knew that this perception was *true*.[2]

Those like Copernicus and Galileo who saw reality differently were often condemned or even killed. Rogers wrote, "Although society has often come around eventually to agree with its dissidents . . . there is no doubt that this insistence upon a known and certain universe has been part of the cement that holds a culture together" (103).

That cement is now missing, to the world's peril. Because of the "ease and rapidity of worldwide communication" that Rogers described as early as 1980, there were already as many realities as there were people:

> The only reality I can possibly know is the world as *I* perceive and experience it at this moment. The only reality you can possibly know is the

---

[2] "Do We Need 'a' Reality?" *A Way of Being* (New York: Houghton Mifflin 1980), pp. 102–03.

world as *you* perceive and experience it at this moment. And the only
certainty is that those perceived realities are different. (102)

In the Rogerian approach to argumentation, effective communication requires
both understanding another's reality and respecting it.

Rogers explained his theories of communication in an essay entitled "Communication: Its Blocking and Its Facilitation," which was originally presented as
a speech in 1951.[3] An emotionally maladjusted person suffers from the inability to
communicate effectively with others and with himself. In Rogers's experience,
one of the most potent means of improving such a patient's relationships and
communication with others sounds simple: Just listen with understanding. It is
not that simple, however, because of a very human tendency to listen judgmentally. We tend to respond to an opinion by stating an opinion. Maxine Hairston
was a leader in applying Rogers's theories to composition, and in 1976 she explained how the human rush to judgment hampers communication:

> Value judgments tend to freeze people into the status quo and make them
> commit themselves to a stand, and almost inevitably once a person takes
> a position on an issue, even one as trivial as the merits of a movie or of
> daylight-saving time, the possibility of his listening to a dissenting point
> of view with an open mind diminishes. Instead of wanting to hear both
> sides, he goes on the defensive and becomes more concerned about justifying his own opinion than understanding someone else's point of view.[4]

According to Rogers, "Real communication occurs, and this evaluative tendency
is avoided, when we listen with understanding. What does this mean? It means
to see the expressed idea and attitude from the other person's point of view, to
sense how it feels to him, to achieve his frame of reference in regard to the thing
he is talking about (331–32)."

The tendency to evaluate is most intense when feelings and emotions are
most deeply involved, "so the stronger our feelings, the more likely it is that there
will be no mutual element in the communication. There will be just two ideas,
two feelings, two judgments, missing each other in psychological space" (331).

Rogers's approach to communication is based on this idea of mutual elements or common ground. A writer or speaker and an audience who have very
different opinions on a highly charged emotional issue need a common ground
on which to meet if any communication is going to take place. In the midst
of all of their differences, they have to find a starting point on which they
agree. In 1977 Hairston summed up five steps for using Rogerian argumentation
that incorporate the two essentials of the approach — being able to summarize

---

[3] "Communication: Its Blocking and Its Facilitation," reprinted in Carl Rogers, *On Becoming
a Person* (Boston: Houghton Mifflin, 1961), pp. 329–37.
[4] "Carl Rogers's Alternative to Traditional Rhetoric," *College Composition and Communication,*
December, 1976, p. 374.

The Rogerian approach tries to bridge the gap between positions held by each party.

another's position with understanding and clarity and to locate common ground between two different positions:

1. Give a brief, objective statement of the issue under discussion.
2. Summarize in impartial language what you perceive the case for the opposition to be; the summary should demonstrate that you understand their interests and concerns and should avoid any hint of hostility.
3. Make an objective statement of your own side of the issue, listing your concerns and interests, but avoiding loaded language or any hint of moral superiority.
4. Outline what common ground or mutual concerns you and the other person or group seem to share; if you see irreconcilable interests, specify what they are.
5. Outline the solution you propose, pointing out what both sides may gain from it. (375–76)

PRACTICE

Read the following article by Joe Sharkey and then Chris Kapper's blog posting in response to it. What steps in the process described by Hairston do you find in Kapper's
response to Sharkey?

Airport Screeners Could See X-rated X-rays

JOE SHARKEY

I am looking at a copy of an ad that ran in the back of comic books in the 1950s
and early 1960s.

"X-Ray Specs! See Thru Clothing!" blares the copy, which is illustrated with
a cartoon of a drooling geek wearing the amazing toy goggles and leering at a
shapely woman.

Now, any kid with half a brain knew that X-Ray Specs were a novelty gag that
didn't really work. But time marches on and technology makes the impossible possible. Stand by, air travelers, because the Homeland Security Department is preparing to install and test high-tech machines at airport checkpoints that will, as the
comic-book ads promised, "See Thru Clothing!"

Get ready for electronic portals known as backscatters, expected to be tested
at a handful of airports this year, that use X-ray imaging technology to allow a
screener to scan a body. And yes, the body image is detailed. Let's not be coy here,
ladies and gentlemen:

"Well, you'll see basically everything," said Bill Scannell, a privacy advo-   5
cate and technology consultant. "It shows nipples. It shows the clear outline of
genitals."

The Homeland Security Department's justification for the electronic strip
searches has a certain logic. In field test after field test, it found that federal airport
screeners using metal-detecting magnetometers did a miserable job identifying
weapons concealed in carry-on bags or on the bodies of undercover agents.

In a clumsy response late last year, the department instituted intrusive pat-
downs at checkpoints after two planes in Russia blew up from nonmetallic explosives that had apparently been smuggled into the aircraft by female Chechen
terrorists. But it reduced the pat-downs after passengers erupted in outrage at the
groping last December.

"The use of these more thorough examination procedures has been protested
by passengers and interest groups, and have already been refined" by the Transportation Security Administration, Richard Skinner, the acting inspector general of
the Homeland Security Department, told a Senate committee in January. Skinner

---

Joe Sharkey is a columnist writing frequently about business travel for the *New York Times*,
where the article appeared on May 24, 2005.

said then that the TSA was ramping up tests of new technologies like backscatter imaging.

Last month, Michael Chertoff, the Homeland Security secretary, told a Senate subcommittee that "technology is really what we ultimately have to use in order to get to the next level" in security.

The technology is available, he said. "It's a question of the decision to deploy it and to try to balance that with legitimate privacy concerns," he added. "We haven't put it out yet because people are still hand-wringing about it."

Steve Elson isn't exactly hand-wringing. Let's just say he is mighty skeptical. A former Federal Aviation Administration investigator, Elson led the agency's red team of undercover agents who poked around airports looking for — and finding — holes in security.

"Backscatting has been around for years," he said. "They started talking about this stuff back during the protests when they were grabbing women. Under the right circumstances, the technology has some efficacy and can work. That is, provided we're willing to pay the price in a further loss of personal privacy."

He isn't. "I have a beautiful 29-year-old daughter and a beautiful wife, and I don't want some screeners to be looking at them through their clothes, plain and simple," he said.

Like many security experts, Elson argues for a sensible balance between risk management and risk reduction. On numerous occasions since the 2001 terrorist attacks, he has led reporters on test runs at airports, showing how easy it is to penetrate security throughout the airport.

Thwarting body-scanning technology would be simple, he argues. Because of concerns about radiation, body scanners are designed not to penetrate the skin. All that's needed is someone heavily overweight to go through the system, he said. I won't quote him directly on the details; suffice it to say he posits that a weapon or explosives pack could be tucked into flabby body folds that won't be penetrated by the scanner.

Homeland Security has not identified the airports that will test backscatters. More than a dozen have been selected to test various new technologies.

One maker of backscatters is Rapiscan Security Products, a unit of OSI Systems. "Since the Russian plane tragedy, which is suspected due to suicide bombers, the interest has heightened for these needs, especially for the body scanner," Deepak Chopra, the chief executive of OSI Systems, recently told analysts.

Scannell, the privacy advocate, scorns that reasoning as alarmist nonsense. He does see one virtue, though, for some airport screeners if backscatting technology becomes the norm.

"They'll be paid to go to a peep show," he said. "They won't even need to bring any change."

Freedom to Live Trumps All!

CHRIS KAPPER

I have read many different comments to this story.

The opinions against the technology seem to boil down to this:

1. It is offensive to be viewed naked.
2. Being viewed naked is an affront to personal freedom.
3. This is a slippery slope and once allowed here it will be allowed everywhere until there are virtually no personal freedoms left.

The opinions for the technology seem to boil down to this:

1. Who cares if one is viewed naked?
2. It is better to be seen naked and alive than be dead.
3. This will make the airplanes safer.
4. This is a less obtrusive way to search passengers.

I have to agree — for the most part — with the latter. Here is why:

1. In the demonstration I saw, the screeners could not see the people — all they could see were the images. Therefore, they never saw a person walk up, through, and then leave. The point is that if their own mother walked through, they would have no idea since you can't tell who it is.
2. Nobody else can see your image other than the security operator. That includes other passengers and employees of the airports.
3. This is much less obtrusive than removing shoes, clothing, and emptying out all of your pockets — in front of everyone.
4. The fundamental liberty is the right to life. One's right to live trumps others' rights.
5. It is not only the liberty of the passengers and crew that must be considered here. It is their lives as well as the lives of all the people on the ground as that airplane flies over. Additionally, it is the nation's and even the world's economy and peace that must be considered. Remember what 9/11 did to the economy and the peace in the world?
6. Air travel is not a required means of travel. You can use other public transportation. You can travel by car or even by boat. Air travel is a convenience — and a choice. When you buy your ticket, you agree to be bound by their rules and policies.

Chris Kapper posted this response to Joe Sharkey's article, "Airport Screeners Could See X-rated X-rays," on CNET's TalkBack, on May 27, 2005.

7. For the person who quoted Benjamin Franklin — "They who would give up an essential liberty for temporary security, deserve neither liberty or security." IMHO, this technology does not cause you to give up any ESSENTIAL liberty and there is nothing TEMPORARY about DEATH!

Rogerian argument places more emphasis on the relationship between audience and subject than other rhetorical theories. It emphasizes the audience's view of the subject. In order to understand another's ideas with the clarity and lack of a judgmental attitude that Rogers proposed requires taking on, temporarily, that other's point of view — walking a mile in his shoes — and seeing the subject with his eyes.

Classical oratory did not require that level of identification with an opponent's perspective, as is suggested by the very fact that classical oratory assumed an *opponent*. A speaker composing a speech in the classical or Aristotelian tradition could make certain assumptions about the world in which his audience lived and therefore about his audience's knowledge of his subject. He would certainly try to anticipate his audience's logical and emotional response to the subject. In fact, an expected part of a classical oration was the refutation of opposing positions, but the purpose was to prove others wrong, not to be conciliatory. He would not acknowledge the strengths of his opponent's argument to the extent of compromising his own. The product of his endeavors was a formal speech, not an analysis of a rhetorical situation.

Therein lies another primary difference between Rogerian rhetoric and all other rhetorical theories. An essay can be written using the Rogerian approach to argumentation, and its thesis or claim will be one reconciling opposing positions — at least as far as that is possible with the sorts of emotionally charged subjects that call for a nonconfrontational approach in the first place. The approach is more useful, however, in analyzing a rhetorical situation than in producing formal prose.

Consider the example of management and striking union members. The situation can quickly degenerate into shouting matches and violence with little progress toward resolution. The union can make demands, which the management turns down, and the shouting matches begin again. Rogers would advocate the seemingly simple method of the two sides listening to each other with understanding. Management has to be able to explain the union's position in a way that the union members feel is fair before it can present its own. And then the reverse. This approach is time consuming, but it can keep the discussion from dissolving into anger and impasse. Rogers even suggests that arguing spouses should have to sum up each other's position *in a manner acceptable to the other spouse* before responding to it.

A text using the Rogerian approach merely to record the steps of the process can be rather formulaic. Done well, it can provide an excellent example of analytical writing. Therefore, we will discuss writing based on the Rogerian model primarily in Chapter 3, Analytical Writing. Another use is as a response to an earlier text, as was the case with Kapper's response to Sharkey's essay earlier in this chapter, so you will also see references to Rogers in Chapter 2, Critical Reading.

SAMPLE ESSAY WITH ANALYSIS   Rogerian

Racial Profiling at the Airport: Discrimination We're Afraid to Be Against

MICHAEL KINSLEY

When thugs menace someone because he looks Arabic, that's racism. When airport security officials single out Arabic-looking men for a more intrusive inspection, that's something else. What is the difference? The difference is that the airport security folks have a rational reason for what they do. An Arab-looking man heading toward a plane is statistically more likely to be a terrorist. That likelihood is infinitesimal, but the whole airport rigmarole is based on infinitesimal chances. If trying to catch terrorists this way makes sense at all, then Willie-Sutton logic says you should pay more attention to people who look like Arabs than to people who don't. This is true even if you are free of all ethnic prejudices. It's not racism.

But that doesn't make it OK. Much of the discrimination that is outlawed in this country — correctly outlawed, we (almost) all agree — could be justified, often sincerely, by reasons other than racial prejudice. Without the civil rights laws, employers with nothing personal against blacks might well decide that hiring whites is more cost-efficient than judging each jobseeker on his or her individual merits. Universities could base their admissions policies on the valid assumption that whites, on average, are better-prepared for college. Even though this white advantage is the result of past and present racism, these decisions themselves might be rational and not racially motivated.

All decisions about whom to hire, whom to admit, whose suitcase to ransack as he's rushing to catch a plane are based on generalizations from observable characteristics to unobservable ones. But even statistically valid generalizations are wrong in particular instances. (Many blacks are better prepared for college than

---

Michael Kinsley is a political journalist and commentator who has written for the *Los Angeles Times* and the *Wall Street Journal*; has been an editor of the *New Republic*, *Harper's*, and the *Washington Monthly*; and founded the online journal *Slate*, where this essay was posted on September 28, 2001. He is a columnist for the *Washington Post* and is perhaps best known for having been cohost of CNN's *Crossfire* for six years.

many whites. Virtually every Arab hassled at an airport is not a terrorist.) Because even rational discrimination has victims, and because certain generalizations are especially poisonous, America has decided that these generalizations (about race, gender, religion, and so on) are morally wrong. They are wrong even if they are statistically valid, and even if not acting on them imposes a real cost.

Until recently, the term "racial profiling" referred to the police practice of pulling over black male drivers disproportionately, on the statistically valid but morally offensive assumption that black male drivers are more likely to be involved in crime. Now the term has become virtually a synonym for racial discrimination. But if "racial profiling" means anything specific at all, it means rational discrimination: racial discrimination with a non-racist rationale. The question is: When is that OK?

The tempting answer is never: Racial discrimination is wrong no matter what   5
the rationale. Period. But today we're at war with a terror network that just killed 6,000 innocents and has anonymous agents in our country planning more slaughter. Are we really supposed to ignore the one identifiable fact we know about them? That may be asking too much.

And there is another complication in the purist view: affirmative action. You can believe (as I do) that affirmative action is often a justifiable form of discrimination, but you cannot sensibly believe that it isn't discrimination at all. Racial profiling and affirmative action are analytically the same thing. When the cops stop black drivers or companies make extra efforts to hire black employees, they are both giving certain individuals special treatment based on racial generalizations. The only difference is that in one case the special treatment is something bad and in the other it's something good. Yet defenders of affirmative action tend to deplore racial profiling and vice versa.

The truth is that racial profiling and affirmative action are both dangerous medicines that are sometimes appropriate. So when is "sometimes"? It seems obvious to me, though not to many others, that discrimination in favor of historically oppressed groups is less offensive than discrimination against them. Other than that, the considerations are practical. How much is at stake in forbidding a particular act of discrimination? How much is at stake in allowing it?

A generalization from stereotypes may be statistically rational, but is it necessary? When you're storming a plane looking for the person who has planted a bomb somewhere, there isn't time to avoid valid generalizations and treat each person as an individual. At less urgent moments, like airport check-in, the need to use ethnic identity as a shortcut is less obvious. And then there are those passengers in Minneapolis last week who insisted that three Arab men (who had cleared security) be removed from the plane. These people were making a cost, benefit, and probability analysis so skewed that it amounts to simple racism. (And Northwest Airlines' acquiescence was shameful.)

So what about singling out Arabs at airport security checkpoints? I am skeptical of the value of these check-in rituals in general, which leads me to suspect that the imposition on a minority is not worth it. But assuming these procedures do work, it's hard to argue that helping to avoid another Sept. 11 is not worth the imposition, which is pretty small: inconvenience and embarrassment, as opposed to losing a job or getting lynched.

A colleague says that people singled out at airport security should be consoled   10
with frequent flier miles. They're already getting an even better consolation: the huge increase in public sensitivity to anti-Muslim and anti-Arab prejudice, which President Bush — to his enormous credit — has made such a focal point of his response to Sept. 11. And many victims of racial profiling at the airport may not need any consolation. After all, they don't want to be hijacked and blown up either.

Analysis

In this essay from September 2001, Kinsley seems to be having an argument with himself. He is, in that two conflicting positions are battling for acceptance in his mind. Each represents a position held by countless others for whom he speaks. This is in keeping with Rogers's belief that conflict can be resolved if those on each side can fairly summarize the position of the other side before summarizing their own. Kinsley is not trying to win an argument but rather to look objectively at the subject from different perspectives. His goal is to decide when each of two ways of looking at the situation is appropriate.

Notice how skillfully Kinsley balances different perspectives. He quickly dismisses as racism the situation where thugs threaten someone who looks Arabic. However, it is perfectly logical, he argues, when Arab-looking men are singled out at airports for additional screening because they are statistically more likely to be terrorists. That, he states bluntly, is not racism.

The other side chimes in: It may not be racism, but it is not okay. Decisions about such things as hiring and college admissions can be rational and not racially motivated. However, as Kinsley writes, "Because even rational discrimination has victims, and because certain generalizations are especially poisonous, America has decided that these generalizations (about race, gender, religion, and so on) are morally wrong. They are wrong even if they are statistically valid, and even if not acting on them imposes a real cost." Racial profiling equals rational discrimination — "racial discrimination with a non-racist rationale." The question that Kinsley raises at the end of paragraph 4 is, "When is that OK?"

Notice how Kinsley once again balances two perspectives: "Racial profiling is wrong no matter what the rationale," but given the events of 9/11, it may be asking too much to ignore "the one identifiable fact we know about [the terrorists]." He uses the term *purist* to describe those who think discrimination is always wrong. That would suggest, though, that racial discrimination is wrong even when it favors the group or individual being discriminated against, as with affirmative action. Kinsley most clearly reveals his own personal perspective when he slips into use of the first person singular in discussing affirmative action.

Kinsley calls both racial profiling and affirmative action "dangerous medicines that are sometimes appropriate." What determines when "sometimes" is appropriate is what is at stake. If airport security measures really work, the safety is worth the small imposition on a minority. If they don't, it is not.

Where is the common ground that is a key component of Rogers's communications theory? What everyone wants — with the exception of terrorists — is safety on the world's commercial flights. Those singled out for additional security screening may not need any other consolation than the fact that they are less likely to be blown up.

The Toulmin Model

Although Aristotle and Rogers, centuries and worlds apart, have both made significant contributions to rhetorical theory, we made the decision to organize this text around an argumentative model that we believe is more helpful in reading and writing arguments in a systematic manner: the Toulmin Model. The late Stephen Toulmin provided the vocabulary about argumentation that gives this book its structure.[5]

Toulmin's model, proposed in 1958 in *The Uses of Argument*, was designed to analyze courtroom arguments. Only after his model had been introduced to rhetoricians by Wayne Brockriede and Douglas Ehninger did he discuss its rhetorical implications in *Introduction to Reasoning* (1979). Of the six key terms in Toulmin's model, we draw heavily on three: claim, support, and warrant.

Stephen Toulmin (1922–2009) developed the model of argumentation that structures this book.

[5] *The Uses of Argument* (Cambridge: Cambridge University Press, 1958).

The Terms of Toulmin Argument

The Claim

The claim (also called a proposition) answers the question "What are you try-ing to prove?" It will generally appear as the thesis statement of your essay, although in some arguments, it may not be stated directly. There are three prin-cipal kinds of claim (discussed more fully in Chapter 5): claims of fact, of value, and of policy. *Claims of fact* assert that a condition has existed, exists, or will exist and are based on facts or data that the audience will accept as being objectively verifiable.

- The diagnosis of autism is now far more common than it was twenty years ago.
- Fast foods are contributing significantly to today's epidemic of child-hood obesity.
- Global warming will affect the coastlines of all continents.

All these claims must be supported by data. Although the last example is an inference or an educated guess about the future, a reader will probably find the prediction credible if the data seem authoritative.

Claims of value attempt to prove that some things are more or less desirable than others. They express approval or disapproval of standards of taste and mo-rality. Advertisements and reviews of cultural events are one common source of value claims, but such claims emerge whenever people argue about what is good or bad, beautiful or ugly.

- Mel Gibson's *Apocalypto* is marred by its excessive violence.
- Abortion is wrong under any circumstances.
- The right to privacy is more important than the need to increase secu-rity at airports.

Claims of policy assert that specific policies should be instituted as solutions to problems. The expression *should, must,* or *ought to* usually appears in the statement.

- The electoral college should be replaced by popular vote as the means of electing a president.
- Attempts at making air travel more secure must not put in jeopardy the passengers' right to privacy.
- Backscatter x-raying ought to be implemented at every American air-port as soon as possible as a means of detecting concealed weapons.

Policy claims call for analysis of both fact and value.

PRACTICE

1. Classify each of the following as a claim of fact, value, or policy.

    a. Solar power could supply 20 percent of the energy needs now satisfied by fossil and nuclear power.

    b. Violence on television produces violent behavior in children who watch more than four hours a day.

    c. Both intelligent design and evolutionary theory should be taught in the public schools.

    d. Some forms of cancer are caused by viruses.

    e. Dogs are smarter than cats.

    f. The money that our government spends on the space program would be better spent solving domestic problems like unemployment and homelessness.

    g. Wherever the number of illegal aliens increases, the crime rate also increases.

    h. Movie sequels are generally inferior to their originals.

    i. Tom Hanks is a more versatile actor than Tom Cruise.

    j. Adopted children who are of a different race than their adoptive parents should be raised with an understanding of the culture of their biological parents.

    k. Average yearly temperatures in North America are already being affected by global warming.

    l. Human activity is the primary cause of global warming.

2. Which claims listed above would be most difficult to support?

3. What type or types of evidence would it take to build a convincing case for each claim?

The Support

Support consists of the materials used by the arguer to convince an audience that his or her claim is sound. These materials include evidence and motivational appeals. The *evidence* or data consist of facts, statistics, and testimony from experts. The *motivational appeals* are the ones that the arguer makes to the values and attitudes of the audience to win support for the claim. The word *motivational* points out that these appeals are the reasons that move an audience to accept a belief or adopt a course of action. (See Chapter 6 for a detailed discussion of support.)

The Warrant

Certain assumptions underlie all the claims we make. In the Toulmin model, the term *warrant* is used for such an assumption, a belief or principle that is taken for granted. It may be stated or unstated. If the arguer believes that the audience shares the assumption, it may be unnecessary to express it. But if the audience seems doubtful or hostile, the arguer may decide to state the assumption to emphasize its importance or argue for its validity. The warrant, stated or not, allows the reader to make the same connection between the support and the claim that the author does. In other words, you have to accept the warrant in order to accept the author's claim based on the evidence provided.

This is how the warrant works. Before he posted on the blog about the proposed x-raying of airline passengers, Kapper had read earlier postings discussing the issue. He considered the arguments he had heard in favor of and against the x-ray technique and actually went so far as to summarize them in his posting. The conclusion he reached, which became the claim of his piece of writing, was that he agrees for the most part with those who argue in favor of the new screening technique. In outline form, a portion of his argument looks like this:

Claim: Backscatter screening should be implemented in America's airports.

Support: Backscatter screening will make planes safer.

Warrant: Any screening technique that will make planes safer should be implemented.

The following example demonstrates how a different kind of warrant, based on values, can also lead an audience to accept a claim.

Claim: Backscatter screening should be implemented in America's airports.

Support: Being seen naked by a security screener is better than dying.

Warrant: Being safe is worth a small loss of privacy.

The warrant — or underlying assumption — behind increased security is that safety is more important than privacy.

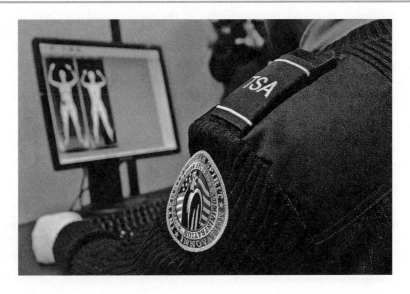

Writer's Guide: Learning the Key Terms

Claim — the proposition that the author is trying to prove. The claim may appear as the thesis statement of an essay but may be implied rather than stated directly.

• *Claims of fact* assert that a condition has existed, exists, or will exist and are based on facts or data that the audience will accept as being objectively verifiable.

• *Claims of value* attempt to prove that some things are more or less desirable than others; they express approval or disapproval of standards of taste and morality.

• *Claims of policy* assert that specific plans or courses of action should be instituted as solutions to problems.

Support — the materials used by the arguer to convince an audience that his or her claim is sound; those materials include evidence and motivational appeals.

Warrant — an inference or assumption; a belief or principle that is taken for granted in an argument.

Kapper's title shows how strongly he feels about this warrant: "Freedom to Live Trumps All!"

Let us suppose that the reader agrees with the supporting statement, that being seen naked by a security screener is better than dying. But to accept the claim, the reader must also agree with the principle expressed in the warrant, that being safe is worth a small loss of privacy. He or she can then agree that backscatter screening should be implemented. Notice that this warrant, like all warrants, certifies that the relationship between the support and the claim is sound.

One more important characteristic of the warrant deserves mention. In many cases, the warrant is a more general statement of belief than the claim. It can, therefore, support many claims, not only the one in a particular argument. For example, the warrant you have just read — being safe is worth a small loss of privacy — is a broad assumption or belief that we take for granted and that can underlie claims about many other practices in American society. (For more on warrants, see Chapter 7.)

Toulmin and the Syllogism

You will see some similarities between Toulmin's three-part structure of claim, support, and warrant and the classical deductive syllogism articulated by Aristotle. In fact, a comparison of the two may help in understanding the warrant.

The syllogism is useful for laying out the basic elements of an argument, and lends itself more readily to simple arguments. It is a formula that consists of three elements: (1) the major premise, (2) the minor premise, and (3) the conclusion, which follows logically from the two statements. The following syllogism summarizes a familiar argument.

Major Premise:	Advertising of things harmful to our health should be legally banned.
Minor Premise:	Cigarettes are harmful to our health.
Conclusion:	Therefore, advertising of cigarettes should be legally banned.

Cast in the form of a Toulmin outline, the argument looks like this:

Claim:	Advertising of cigarettes should be legally banned.
Support (Evidence):	Cigarettes are harmful to our health.
Warrant:	Advertising of things harmful to our health should be legally banned.

Or in diagram form:

Support ———————————————→ *Claim*
Cigarettes are harmful   Advertising of cigarettes
to our health.   should be legally banned.

Warrant
Advertising of things harmful to our
health should be legally banned.

In both the syllogism and the Toulmin model the principal elements of the argument are expressed in three statements. You can see that the claim in the Toulmin model is the conclusion in the syllogism — that is, the proposition that you are trying to prove. The evidence (support) in the Toulmin model corresponds to the minor premise in the syllogism. And the warrant in the Toulmin model resembles the major premise of the syllogism.

In the Toulmin model, the use of the term *warrant* indicates that the validity of the proposition must be established to *guarantee* the claim or make the crossing from support to claim. It makes clear that the arguer must ask *why* such advertising must be banned.

While the syllogism is essentially static, with all three parts logically locked into place, the Toulmin model suggests that an argument is a *movement* from support to claim by way of the warrant, which acts as a bridge. Toulmin introduced the concept of warrant by asking, "How do you get there?" (His first two questions, introducing the claim and support, were "What are you trying to prove?" and "What have you got to go on?")

In addition to the three basic elements, the Toulmin model offers supplementary elements of argument. The *qualifier,* in the form of words like "probably" or "more likely," shows that the claim is not absolute. The *backing* offers support for the validity of the warrant. The *reservation* suggests that the validity of the warrant may be limited. These additional elements, which refine and expand the argument itself, reflect the real flexibility and complexity of the argumentative process.

PRACTICE

1. Report on an argument you have heard or read recently. Identify the parts of that argument — claim, support, warrant — as they are defined in this chapter. What were the strengths and weaknesses of the argument?

2. Choose one of the more controversial claims from the list on page 23. Explain why it is controversial. Would it be difficult to support? Impossible? Are the warrants unacceptable to many people? If there has been a change in recent years in public acceptance of the claim, offer what you think may be an explanation for the change.

No matter what the subject, there are certain basic steps that a writer can take to ensure that not only the proposition, or claim, but the whole argument is worthy of credence. You are not yet an expert in many of the subjects you will deal with in assignments, although you are knowledgeable about many other things, including your cultural and social activities. But there are several ways in which you can develop confidence in your discussion of topics derived from academic disciplines, such as political science, psychology, economics, sociology, and art. The following steps that every writer of argumentative texts should follow will be the basis for Chapters 4–9.

Steps for Writing Argumentative Texts

Defining Key Terms (CHAPTER 4)

Many of the controversial questions you will read or write about are primarily arguments of definition. Such terms as *abortion, pornography, racism, poverty, freedom of speech,* and *terrorism* must be defined before useful solutions to the problems they represent can be formulated. Even if the primary purpose of your essay is not definition, you can successfully communicate with an audience only if that audience understands how you are using key terms. That is true whether you are using the Rogerian approach or a more traditional approach. With the Rogerian method you may have to stipulate a definition that both sides can accept if you are to achieve successful communication about strongly held beliefs.

Choosing an Appropriate Claim (CHAPTER 5)

It must be clear to the individual or group that constitutes your audience what change in thought or what action you hope to achieve by presenting your case.

If you are seeking a change in your reader's thinking on a subject, you will have a much greater chance of accomplishing your goal if you consider the audience's current thinking on the subject and are realistic about the extent to which you might hope to change that thinking. The Rogerian approach emphasizes this need to assess fairly your audience's position in order to accommodate that position in writing your claim. If there is something you want your audience to do, that action must be realistically within the power of that audience.

Choosing and Documenting Appropriate Sources (CHAPTER 6)

You must present evidence of careful research, demonstrating that you have been conscientious in finding the best authorities, giving credit, and attempting to arrive at the truth.

Analyzing Assumptions (CHAPTER 7)

You must consider the warrant or assumption on which your argument is based. A warrant need not be expressed if it is so widely accepted that you can assume any reasonable audience will not need proof of its validity. You must be prepared to defend any other warrant. In Rogerian argument, more than in other rhetorical approaches, you must understand both your assumptions and your audience's in order to reconcile the two and establish common ground.

Analyzing Logical Errors (CHAPTER 8)

Understanding the ways in which inductive and deductive reasoning processes work can help you to determine the truth and validity of your arguments, as well as other arguments, and to identify and correct faulty reasoning.

Editing for Appropriate Language (CHAPTER 9)

Another important resource is the careful use of language, not only to define terms and express personal style but also to reflect clarity of thought, to avoid the clichés and outworn slogans that frequently substitute for fresh ideas, and to avoid word choices that would make your audience unwilling to consider your ideas.

Now let's turn to an example of argumentative writing and an analysis based on the Toulmin model.

The Hard Truth of Immigration

ROBERT J. SAMUELSON

Immigration is crawling its way back onto the national agenda — and not just as a footnote to keeping terrorists out. Earlier this year, Congress enacted a law intended to prevent illegal aliens from getting state drivers' licenses, the volunteer "minutemen" who recently patrolled the porous Arizona border with Mexico attracted huge attention, and members of Congress from both parties are now crafting proposals to deal with illegal immigration. All this is good. But unless we're brutally candid with ourselves, it won't amount to much. Being brutally candid means recognizing that the huge and largely uncontrolled inflow of unskilled Latino workers into the United States is increasingly sabotaging the assimilation process.

Americans rightly glorify our heritage of absorbing immigrants. Over time, they move into the economic, political, and social mainstream; over time, they become American rather than whatever they were — even though immigrants themselves constantly refashion the American identity. But no society has a boundless capacity to accept newcomers, especially when many are poor and unskilled. There are now an estimated 34 million immigrants in the United States, about a third of them illegal. About 35 percent lack health insurance and 26 percent receive some sort of federal benefit, reports Steven Camarota of the Center for Immigration Studies. To make immigration succeed, we need (paradoxically) to control immigration.

Although this is common sense, it's common sense that fits uneasily inside our adversarial political culture. You're supposed to be either pro-immigrant or anti-immigrant — it's hard to be pro-immigrant and pro tougher immigration restrictions. But that's the sensible position, as any examination of immigration trends suggests.

Consider a new study of Mexican immigrants by Harvard economists George Borjas and Lawrence Katz. Mexicans are now the single largest group of U.S. immigrants, 30 percent of the total in 2000. Indeed, the present Mexican immigration "is historically unprecedented, being both numerically and proportionately larger than any other immigrant influx in the past century," note Borjas and Katz. In 1920, for example, the two largest immigrant groups — Germans and Italians — totaled only 24 percent of the immigrant population.

Some Mexican-Americans have made spectacular gains, but the overall picture is dispiriting. Among men, about one in 20 U.S. workers is now a Mexican

5

Robert J. Samuelson, a contributing editor at *Newsweek*, has written a column for the *Washington Post* since 1977. This essay appeared in the June 13, 2005, issue of *Newsweek*.

immigrant; in 1970, that was less than one in 100. The vast majority of Mexican workers lacked a high-school diploma in 2000 (63 percent for men, 57 percent for women). Only a tiny share had college degrees (3 percent for men, 5 percent for women). By contrast, only 7 percent of native-born U.S. workers were high-school dropouts and 28 percent were college graduates in 2000. Mexican workers are inevitably crammed into low-wage jobs: food workers, janitors, gardeners, laborers, farm workers. In 2000, their average wages were 41 percent lower than average U.S. wages for men and 33 percent lower for women.

What's particularly disturbing about the Borjas-Katz study is that children of Mexican immigrants don't advance quickly. In 2000, Americans of Mexican ancestry still had lower levels of educational achievement and wages than most native-born workers. Among men, the wage gap was 27 percent; about 21 percent were high-school dropouts and only 11 percent were college graduates. Borjas and Katz can't explain the lags. "What's the role of culture vs. lousy [U.S.] schools?" asks Katz. "It's hard to say." Borjas doubts that the cause is discrimination. Low skills seem to explain most of the gap, he says. Indeed, after correcting for education and age, most of the wage gap disappears. Otherwise, says Borjas, "I don't know."

But some things we do know — or can infer. For today's Mexican immigrants (legal or illegal), the closest competitors are tomorrow's Mexican immigrants (legal or illegal). The more who arrive, the harder it will be for existing low-skilled workers to advance. Despite the recession, immigration did not much slow after 2000, says Camarota. Not surprisingly, a study by the Pew Hispanic Center found that inflation-adjusted weekly earnings for all Hispanics (foreign and American-born) dropped by 2.2 percent in 2003 and 2.6 percent in 2004. "Latinos are the only major group of workers whose wages have fallen for two consecutive years," said the study. Similarly, the more poor immigrants, the harder it will be for schools to improve the skills of their children. The schools will be overwhelmed; the same goes for social services.

We could do a better job of stopping illegal immigration on our southern border and of policing employers who hire illegal immigrants. At the same time, we could provide legal status to illegal immigrants already here. We could also make more sensible decisions about legal immigrants — favoring the skilled over the unskilled. But the necessary steps are much tougher than most politicians have so far embraced, and their timidity reflects a lack of candor about the seriousness of the problem. The stakes are simple: will immigration continue to foster national pride and strength or will it cause more and more weakness and anger?

Analysis

Immigration is still on the national agenda, as it was when Samuelson wrote this essay in 2005. At that time, Congress was drafting legislation to deal with problems associated with immigration.

To analyze the piece using the Toulmin model, you must think in terms of claim, support, and warrant. At the end of the first paragraph, Samuelson makes this statement: "Being brutally candid means recognizing that the huge and largely uncontrolled inflow of unskilled Latino workers into the United States is increasingly sabotaging the assimilation process." This is a factual statement that his readers must accept in order to accept his claim, but the claim itself is a claim of policy — a statement of what needs to be done about immigration. That statement comes at the end of paragraph 2: "To make immigration succeed, we need (paradoxically) to control immigration." He rewords his claim in the next paragraph when he points out that the sensible position is to be both pro-immigrant and pro-tougher immigration restrictions. His goal in the essay, then, is to support this assertion.

Support consists of evidence and appeals to needs and values. Samuelson is appealing to his readers' American values when he starts his second paragraph by noting that America's "heritage of absorbing immigrants" is something to be proud of. He goes on, though, to counter that with the point that "no society has a boundless capacity to accept newcomers, especially when many are poor and unskilled." He offers statistical evidence regarding the numbers of immigrants America is trying to absorb and the percentage of the immigrant population that are Mexicans. Here he draws on Harvard economists George Borjas and Lawrence Katz for his information.

Samuelson also provides statistical evidence that Mexican immigrants are poorly educated and thus relegated to low-wage jobs — and their children are not progressing very rapidly. When it comes to earnings, Hispanics are losing ground. The more poor immigrants, the more overwhelmed the schools and social services.

The warrant of an essay is what a reader must believe in order to accept that the support offered justifies the claim. What is our understanding of the way the world works that makes us accept, based on the support Samuelson provides, that in order to make immigration succeed, we must control it? Think in terms of a broad statement that might serve as the major premise of a syllogism. In this case, such a statement might be "To be successful, a program needs restrictions controlling it."

Samuelson suggests what could be done to improve the situation, such as making our southern border more secure, favoring skilled over unskilled workers for legal entry, providing legal status to immigrants already here, and enforcing laws about hiring illegal immigrants. In his closing sentence, he again appeals to his readers' values: "The stakes are simple: Will immigration continue to foster national pride and strength or will it cause more and more weakness and anger?"

Assignments for Understanding the Structure of Argument

READING AND DISCUSSION QUESTIONS

1. Consider at what point news stations cross the line between reporting the news and analyzing the news. Think of some examples from recent news stories that illustrate the argumentative nature of today's news coverage.

2. Do you believe that presidential debates are good examples of argumentation? Explain.

3. What are some of the controversial issues in the field of your major or a major that you are considering? Analyze one or more of them using Toulmin's terms: claim, support, and warrant.

4. When you write essays and reports for your classes, how do you establish your credibility? On the other hand, how do students lose their credibility with the instructors who read their work?

WRITING SUGGESTIONS

5. Write an essay in which you support your opinion about whether backscatter screening should be implemented at America's airports.

6. Write an essay in which you discuss how technological advances have changed an audience's ability to evaluate a speaker's *ethos*.

7. Write an essay in which you discuss how both Aristotelian and Rogerian argument are useful in contemporary politics.

8. Write an essay in which you identify some of the issues about which it is most difficult to achieve common ground, and explain why.

Research Readiness: Using Databases

What is the first step you take when you need to do some research?

If your response is to go to Google, the answer is yes and no. In your daily life, if you need to look up some factual information, you can find it quickly on Google or another similar search engine. For most assignments for your classes, the answer is no.

For one thing, remember that Google finds *any* reference to your search term and doesn't discriminate based on quality. Anyone can post on the Internet, so there is no control over accuracy. You will also be inundated with far more sources than you could ever look at.

If you had checked Google for information about Aristotle when this book went to press, you would have found these numbers:

"Aristotle" — 39,600,000 results

"Aristotle" and "argument" — 2,940,000 results

"Aristotle's argument" — 688,000 results

"Aristotle" and "rhetoric" — 195,000 results

"Aristotle's rhetoric" — 120,000 results

Wikipedia will be near the top of the list for many subjects, but don't plan to use Wikipedia as a source for college work. It lacks the authority your professors will expect.

Where, then, do you start? Prowling the shelves of the library? Don't rule out electronic sources. Instead, find out what databases your school has access to and which of those databases are most appropriate for your research.

For example, a good general database for academic subjects is Expanded Academic ASAP. There, a search for information about Aristotle yields these results:

"Aristotle" — subject search 1869 results
            keyword search 3370 results

"Aristotle" and "argument" — 79 results

"Aristotle's argument" — 79 results

"Aristotle" and "rhetoric" — 15 results

"Aristotle's rhetoric" — 15 results

As you can see, by the end of this search, you are reaching a manageable number of sources to explore. Even with 79 results, a quick look at the titles will eliminate some and let you know which ones are worth investigating.

The numbers refer to articles in academic journals, generally the ones most widely accepted by college faculty. Available in separate listings are citations for 615 magazines, 4 books, and 445 newspaper articles.

You will learn more about finding sources in Chapter 10, but as a starting point, do the following.

ASSIGNMENT

1. Every library will have access to different databases for student use. Find a list of the databases available to you and do a search for articles about how Carl Rogers's theories about therapy relate to argument. You will have to try different combinations of terms to find the best information. Write down what you discover about sources available to you.

2. What are two specialized databases that might be a starting point for information related to your major or a major that you might choose?

2

Critical Reading

$\mathbf{A}$ full response to any argument means more than understanding the message. It also means evaluating, deciding whether the message is successful, and then determining *how* it succeeds or fails in persuading us. In making these judgments about the arguments of others, we learn how to deliver our own. We try to avoid what we perceive to be flaws in another's arguments, and we adapt the strategies that produce clear, honest, forceful arguments.

Critical reading is essential for mastery of most college subjects, but its importance for reading and writing about argument, where meaning is often complex and multilayered, cannot be overestimated. The ability to read arguments critically is essential to advanced academic work—even in science and math—since it requires the debate of multifaceted issues rather than the memorization of facts. Just as important, learning to read arguments critically helps you develop the ability to *write* effective arguments, a process valued at the university, in the professional world, and in public life.

Prereading

In the last chapter, you read an essay by Juan Williams entitled "Don't Mourn *Brown v. Board of Education.*" You probably were familiar with the court case Williams was writing about. If not, you could discover from the context that he was referring to a famous case that made its way to the Supreme Court in 1954, making school segregation unconstitutional in the United States. You will frequently confront texts dealing with subjects unfamiliar to you, and you should have a plan of action for prereading them; that is, for getting an overview of a piece before you read. Here are a few strategies, illustrated by references to "Don't Mourn *Brown v. Board of Education*":

1. Pay attention to the title, as it may state the purpose of the argument in specific terms. Williams's title immediately announces the "death" of *Brown v. Board of Education*. It also establishes that that death should not be mourned. The reference is clearly to a legal case. If it were one that you were not familiar with, you could either stop and look it up or read on and hope to learn about it as you read. The title captures the reader's desire to read on and find out what happened to alter this famous ruling.

2. Work hard to understand the kind of text you are reading. Was it published recently? Is it a response to another text, or perhaps to an event? Certainly if it is argumentative writing, it is at least a response to a perceived problem. Was there something specific that led an author to write about this subject in this way at this particular time? What background about the subject are you familiar with?

> A quick look at the first few sentences of Williams's article establishes that he is writing in response to a ruling by the Supreme Court the day before that has "killed" the *Brown* decision by "ending the use of voluntary schemes to create racial balance among students."
>
> A note at the bottom of the first page of each article in this textbook gives the article's date and tells you both when and where the article was published. Otherwise, most titles can be looked up on *Google* or another search engine to get a date and place of publication. Often you can find the whole article online.
>
> The *Brown v. Board of Education* decision was issued in 1954; Williams's article was published in 2007. The immediate context in which he was writing was a decision by the Supreme Court that had in some way significantly altered the historic ruling.

3. As a rule, the more information you know about an author, the easier and more productive your reading will be. You should learn to read in a way that allows you to discover not just meaning in the text itself but information about the author's point of view, background, motives, and ideology. Such understanding comes from close analysis of a text but also from background reading on the author and/or the subject and discussion with your classmates and instructors on the material.

If you read the analysis that accompanied the article in Chapter 1, you know that Juan Williams is a political commentator for the Fox News Channel and was then a senior correspondent for National Public Radio. These credentials establish him as a respected political journalist, even if the television network for which he works is well known to have a conservative bias. (On the other hand, some accuse NPR of having a liberal bias but not evenly so on all issues.)

The fact that Williams has written a book on Thurgood Marshall, the lead attorney in the *Brown* case and later a Supreme Court justice, would suggest that he is quite knowledgeable on the subject and that he might approach it with sympathy for the side of the plaintiffs, six African American children from Kansas. The fact that Williams is African American may or may not be relevant.

4. Imagine the context in which the author was writing and the target audience. Was it a specific or general audience? Does the text come from a journal that publishes primarily conservative or liberal writers? What values and ideals are shared by the author and the audience most likely to agree with the argument? How might these values help make sense of the context? What sort of audience might be most strongly opposed to the argument and why?

> The racial animosity that existed in the American South 1954 is almost inconceivable to young adults in the early twenty-first century who grew up in racially and culturally diverse schools. Williams, writing for the general audience of the *New York Times* in 2007, would be writing to many who could remember quite well a time of segregated buses, water fountains, restrooms, and restaurants, in addition to schools. The mention of the death of *Brown v. Board of Education* would still strike a nerve with that generation. A title that suggested *not* mourning the death of a ruling that was a landmark in the history of the civil rights movement was risky, so he has to address a potentially hostile response in the opening sentences.
>
> Young readers would respond to the subject as a historical reference rather than as a personal memory. However, in some cases, they would be approaching it from the perspective of students attending schools still marred by racial tension.

Research Skill: Examining Author, Subject, and Context

Williams's essay is a good example of the value of pre-reading. It is also a good place to start thinking about some of the earliest stages of research. Some background knowledge is essential to understanding the full significance of Williams's argument. If you wanted to refresh your memory of the *Brown* decision, you might go back to a textbook you studied in the past or to class notes, but you are far more likely to go to *Google* or a similar search engine.

Wonderful as our search engines can be—and as much time as they save—us they are not at all discriminating. They are a quick way to get factual information, but when it comes to opinions, you have to do the discriminating yourself.

—If you search Williams's title, for example, the first entry tells you place and date of publication.

—If you search *Brown v. Board of Education*, the first entry is likely to be Wikipedia.

We all know that Wikipedia is an online encyclopedia but also that the authors of its articles are not necessarily experts on their subjects. Often there is even a note that indicates that sources need authentication or that more information is needed. Wikipedia can be useful to get a general idea about a subject but should be used with caution. More authoritative would be an online encyclopedia by a reputable company like Britannica.

Watch closely the URLs for any online sources that you find. As you know, *.com* represents commercial site, *.gov* represents a government site, and *.edu* represents, for the most part, a college or university site. Don't be fooled by an .edu site that also has a tilde (~) followed by a username, though, because that indicates that you are on an individual's site and not the institution's. That individual could be an expert, but he or she may also be a student just like you who is not a specialist in the area.

Organizational sites, those that end in *.org*, must also be used with care. One of the first sites a search engine will list for the *Brown* decision is brownboard .org, which was founded in honor of the plaintiffs and attorneys in the case but may for that reason have a particular bias. A site called nationalcenter.org is a national public policy research institute that could also have its biases that would have to be investigated, but in this case it proves to be a handy source for a copy of the decision rendered by the Supreme Court in 1954.

If you search for Juan Williams, you will find Wikipedia again, then sites for the places that Williams is employed, where you can most likely get good factual information about him and his career. With later entries, you start to

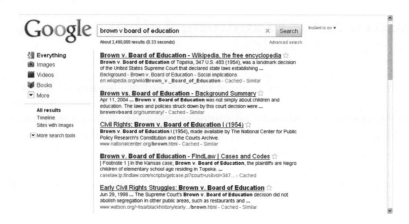

find writing done by Williams himself, such as an article in the online version of the *Wall Street Journal,* another reputable source.

Whenever you move into *.com* sources, keep in mind that you have moved into the commercial realm and must be alert to whatever interests the company or group may have in the way information is presented.

PRACTICE

Apply the Prereading Strategies to the folowing essay.

Let's Have No More Monkey Trials

CHARLES KRAUTHAMMER

The half-century campaign to eradicate any vestige of religion from public life has run its course. The backlash from a nation fed up with the A.C.L.U. kicking crèches out of municipal Christmas displays has created a new balance. State-supported universities may subsidize the activities of student religious groups. Monuments inscribed with the Ten Commandments are permitted on government grounds. The Federal Government is engaged in a major antipoverty initiative that gives money to churches. Religion is back out of the closet.

But nothing could do more to undermine this most salutary restoration than the new and gratuitous attempts to invade science, and most particularly evolution, with religion. Have we learned nothing? In Kansas, conservative school-board members are attempting to rewrite statewide standards for teaching evolution to make sure that creationism's modern stepchild, intelligent design,

Charles Krauthammer, winner of the 1987 Pulitzer Prize for distinguished commentary, writes a nationally syndicated column for the *Washington* Post Writers Group. He also writes for the *Weekly Standard* and the *New Republic.* This piece appeared in Time on August 1, 2005.

infiltrates the curriculum. Similar anti-Darwinian mandates are already in place in Ohio and are being fought over in 20 states. And then, as if to second the evangelical push for this tarted-up version of creationism, out of the blue appears a declaration from Christoph Cardinal Schönborn of Vienna, a man very close to the Pope, asserting that the supposed acceptance of evolution by John Paul II is mistaken. In fact, he says, the Roman Catholic Church rejects "neo-Darwinism" with the declaration that an "unguided evolutionary process—one that falls outside the bounds of divine providence—simply cannot exist."

Cannot? On what scientific evidence? Evolution is one of the most powerful and elegant theories in all of human science and the bedrock of all modern biology. Schönborn's proclamation that it cannot exist unguided—that it is driven by an intelligent designer pushing and pulling and planning and shaping the process along the way—is a perfectly legitimate statement of faith. If he and the Evangelicals just stopped there and asked that intelligent design be included in a religion curriculum, I would support them. The scandal is to teach this as science—to pretend, as does Schönborn, that his statement of faith is a defense of science. "The Catholic Church," he says, "will again defend human reason" against "scientific theories that try to explain away the appearance of design as the result of 'chance and necessity,'" which "are not scientific at all." Well, if you believe that science is reason and that reason begins with recognizing the existence of an immanent providence, then this is science. But, of course, it is not. This is faith disguised as science. Science begins not with first principles but with observation and experimentation.

In this slippery slide from "reason" to science, Schönborn is a direct descendant of the early 17th century Dutch clergyman and astronomer David Fabricius, who could not accept Johannes Kepler's discovery of elliptical planetary orbits. Why? Because the circle is so pure and perfect that reason must reject anything less. "With your ellipse," Fabricius wrote Kepler, "you abolish the circularity and uniformity of the motions, which appears to me increasingly absurd the more profoundly I think about it." No matter that, using Tycho Brahe's most exhaustive astronomical observations in history, Kepler had empirically demonstrated that the planets orbit elliptically.

This conflict between faith and science had mercifully abated over the past four centuries as each grew to permit the other its own independent sphere. What we are witnessing now is a frontier violation by the forces of religion. This new attack claims that because there are gaps in evolution, they therefore must be filled by a divine intelligent designer.   5

How many times do we have to rerun the Scopes "monkey trial"? There are gaps in science everywhere. Are we to fill them all with divinity? There were gaps in Newton's universe. They were ultimately filled by Einstein's revisions. There are gaps in Einstein's universe, great chasms between it and quantum theory. Perhaps they are filled by God. Perhaps not. But it is certainly not science to merely declare it so.

To teach faith as science is to undermine the very idea of science, which is the acquisition of new knowledge through hypothesis, experimentation, and evidence. To teach it as science is to encourage the supercilious caricature of America as a nation in the thrall of religious authority. To teach it as science is to discredit the welcome recent advances in permitting the public expression of religion. Faith can and should be proclaimed from every mountaintop and city square. But it has no place in science class. To impose it on the teaching of evolution is not just to invite ridicule but to earn it.

Comprehension

The first step in the critical reading process is comprehension—understanding what an author is trying to prove. Comprehending academic arguments can be difficult because they are often complex and often challenge accepted notions. Academic writing also sometimes assumes that readers already have a great deal of knowledge about a subject and therefore can require further research for comprehension.

Readers sometimes fail to comprehend a text they disagree with or that is new to them, especially in dealing with essays or books making controversial, value-laden arguments. Some research even shows that readers will sometimes remember only those parts of texts that match their points of view.[1] The study of argument does not require you to accept points of view you find morally or otherwise reprehensible, but to engage with these views, no matter how strange or repugnant they might seem, on your own terms.

Reading arguments critically requires you to at least temporarily suspend notions of absolute "right" and "wrong" and to intellectually inhabit gray areas that do not allow for simple "yes" and "no" answers. Of course, even in these areas, significant decisions about such things as ethics, values, politics, and the law must be made, and in studying argument you shouldn't fall into the trap of simple relativism: the idea that all answers to a given problem are equally correct at all times. We must make decisions about arguments with the understanding that reasonable people can disagree on the validity of ideas. Read others' arguments carefully and consider how their ideas can contribute to or complicate your own. Remember Carl Rogers's approach and look for common ground between your beliefs and those of the author. Also recognize that what appears to be a final solution will always be open to further negotiation as new participants, new historical circumstances, and new ideologies become involved in the debate.

To comprehend difficult texts you should understand that reading and writing are linked processes, and use writing to help your reading. This can mean writing comments in the margins of the book or essay itself or in a separate notebook; highlighting passages in the text that seem particularly important; or freewriting about the author's essential ideas after you finish reading. For complex arguments, write down the methods the author uses to make the argument:

---

[1]See, for example, Patrick J. Slattery, "The Argumentative, Multiple-Source Paper: College Students Reading, Thinking, and Writing about Multiple Points of View," *Journal of Teaching Writing* 10, Fall/Winter 1991, pp. 181–99.

- Did the text use historical evidence or rely on experts?
- Were emotional appeals made to try to convince readers, or did the text rely on scientific or logical forms of evidence?
- Did the author use analogies or comparisons to help readers understand the argument?
- Was some combination of these or other strategies used? Writing down the author's methods for argumentation can make even the most complex arguments understandable.

Strategies for Comprehending Arguments

1. Skim the article or book for the main idea and overall structure. At this stage, avoid concentrating on details.

   a. Make a skeleton outline of the text in your mind or on paper. From this outline and the text itself, consider the relationship between the beginning, middle, and end of the argument. How has the author divided these sections? Are there subheadings in the body of the text? If you are reading a book, how are the chapters broken up? What appears to be the logic of the author's organization?

   b. From your overview, what is the central claim or argument of the essay? What is the main argument against the author's central claim and how would the author respond to it?

2. Remember that the claim is usually in one of the first two or three paragraphs (if it is an essay) or in the first chapter (if it is a book). The beginning of an argument can have other purposes, however; it may describe the position that the author will oppose or provide background for the whole argument.

3. Pay attention to topic sentences. The topic sentence is usually but not always the first sentence of a paragraph. It is the general statement that controls the details and examples in the paragraph.

4. Don't overlook language signposts, especially transitional words and phrases that tell you whether the writer will change direction or offer support for a previous point — words and phrases like *but, however, nevertheless, yet, moreover, for example, at first glance, more important, the first reason,* and so on.

5. When it comes to vocabulary, you can either guess the meaning of an unfamiliar word from the context and go on or look it up immediately. The first method makes for more rapid reading and is sometimes recommended by teachers, but guessing can be risky. Keep a good dictionary handy. If a word you don't understand seems crucial to meaning, look it up before going on.

6. If you use a highlighter to mark main points, use it sparingly. Marking passages in color is meant to direct you to the major ideas and reduce the necessity for rereading the whole passage when you review. Look over the marked passages and do a five-minute freewrite to sum up the central parts of the argument.

7. Once you are done reading, think again about the original context the text was written in: Why did the author write it and for whom? Why might an editor have published it in a book or journal, and why did your instructor assign it?

Sex and the Cinema

EDWARD JAY EPSTEIN

Contrast with early days

In the early days of Hollywood, nudity—or the illusion of it—was considered such an asset that director Cecil B. DeMille famously made bathing scenes an obligatory ingredient of his biblical epics. Nowadays, nudity is a decided liability when it comes to the commercial success of the movie. In 2004, none

Examples of Top 25 movies with no sex

of the six major studios' top 25 grossing films, led by *Spider-Man 2*, *Shrek 2*, *Harry Potter and the Prisoner of Azkaban*, and *The Incredibles*, contained any sexually oriented nudity; only one had a restrictive R rating—Warner Bros.' *Troy*—and that was mainly due to the film's gory violence, not its sexual content.

Claim

The absence of sex — at least graphic sex — is key to the success of Hollywood's moneymaking movies. Directors may consider a sex scene artistically integral to their movie, but studios, which almost always have the right to exercise the final cut, also have to consider three factors.

Three factors to consider
I-The rating system

First, there is the rating system. For a film to play in movie theaters belonging to the National Association of Theater Owners—which includes all the multiplexes in America—it first needs to obtain a rating from a board organized by the Motion Picture Association of America—the trade association of the six major studios. All the expenses for rating movies are paid to the MPAA by the studio out of a percentage deducted from box-office receipts. As it presently works, a movie that contains sexually oriented nudity gets either an NC-17 or an R rating, depending

Topic sentence: NC-17 = box-office failure

on how graphically sex is depicted. The NC-17 rating, which forbids theaters from admitting children under the age of 18, is the equivalent of a death sentence as far as the studios are concerned. In fact,

---

Edward Jay Epstein is an investigative reporter who has written over a dozen books, most recently *The Hollywood Economist: The Hidden Financial Reality Behind the Movies* (2010). This essay appeared on August 15, 2005, in *Slate*, a daily online magazine affiliated with the *Washington Post*.

Claudette Colbert in *The Sign of the Cross* (1932), directed by Cecil B. DeMille

Old movies with sex that wouldn't be made today

since the financial disaster of Paul Verhoeven's NC-17 *Showgirls* in 1995, no studio has attempted a wide release of a NC-17 film. As one Paramount executive suggested, because of their sexually related nudity, movies such as Louis Malle's *Pretty Baby*, Bernardo Bertolucci's *Last Tango in Paris*, and Stanley Kubrick's *A Clockwork Orange* would not even be considered by a major studio today. So far this year there has been only one limited release of an NC-17 film by a studio: the documentary *Inside Deep Throat*, which yielded Universal less from the box-office—$330,000—than it cost to wrangle media stars and others to free screenings and dinners to promote it.

If a movie contains less explicit nudity, it earns an R rating, which merely prohibits youth unaccompanied by an adult. Even though this option means that some number of multiplex employees—who might otherwise be selling popcorn—are required to check the identity documents of the teenage audience, theaters accept R rated films, especially when, as was the case with *Troy*, the R is for the sort of graphic violence that is also the principal attrac-

Topic sentence:
R-rated movies may get a
wide showing, but the rating
complicates marketing them.

tion. But even if an R doesn't prevent studios from
staging a wide opening of a movie at the multiplexes,
it complicates the movie's all-important marketing
drive. For one thing, if a film receives an R rating,
many television stations and cable networks, particularly teenage-oriented ones, are not allowed
to accept TV ads for the movies. In addition, an R
rating—especially for sexual content—will preclude
any of the fast-food chains, beverage companies, or
toy manufacturers that act as the studios' merchandise tie-in partners from backing the movie with tens
of millions of dollars in free advertising. As a result,
it becomes much more expensive to alert and herd
audiences to R rated films.

II-The Wal-Mart consideration

Second, there is the Wal-Mart consideration. In
2004, the six studios took in $20.9 billion from home-
video sales, according to the studios' own internal
numbers. Wal-Mart, including its Sam's Club stores,
accounted for over one-quarter of those sales, which
means that Wal-Mart wrote more than $5 billion in
checks to the studios in 2004. Such enormous buying
power comes dangerously close to constituting what
the Justice Department calls a monopoly—control
of a market by a single buyer—and it allows the giant retailer to effectively dictate the terms of trade.
Internet mythology aside, Wal-Mart doesn't use its
clout to advance any political agenda or social engineering objective, according to a studio executive
involved in the process; it is "strictly business." Wal-
Mart uses DVDs, especially the weekly released hits,
to lure in customers who, while they pass through
the store, may buy more profitable items, such as
toys, clothing, or electronics.

New DVDs = more customers,
who buy other products

Wal-Mart's main concern with the content of the
DVDs is that they not offend important customers—especially mothers—by containing material
that may be inappropriate for children. It guards
against this risk with a "decency policy" that con-
signs DVDs containing sexually related nudity to
"adult sections" of the store, which greatly reduces
their sales. (Wal-Mart is less concerned with vulgar
behavior and language.) These guidelines, in turn,
put studios under tremendous pressure to sanitize
their films of sexual content. The Wal-Mart buyer
would merely have to order for their stores the

Wal-Mart's "decency policy"
forces studios to avoid sexual
content

5

"in-flight entertainment" version of DVDs, from which studios expunge nudity and other sexually explicit scenes for airline passengers (censorship that almost all directors quietly accept). In light of such leverage, studios have to weigh the Wal-Mart factor with great care.

Topic sentence: Studios have to take the Wal-Mart factor seriously

III Nudity: a problem for television

Finally, movies with nudity are a problem for the studios' other main moneymaker: television. As became abundantly clear in the controversy surrounding Janet Jackson's wardrobe malfunction at Superbowl XXXVIII, broadcast television is a government-regulated enterprise. When the government grants a free license to a station to broadcast over the public airwaves, it does so under the condition that it conform to the rules enforced by the Federal Communications Commission. Among those rules is the standard of "public decency," which among other things specifically prohibits salacious nudity—which is why CBS had to pay a fine for Ms. Jackson's brief exposure. Because the FCC regulates broadcast television (though not cable television), television stations run similar risks—and embarrassments—if they show movies that include even partial nudity. So, before a studio can license such a movie to a broadcast network, it first has to cut out all the nudity and other scenes that run afoul of the decency standard. Aside from the expense involved, it requires the hassle of obtaining the director's permission, which is contractually required by the Directors Guild of America. The same is true in studio sales to foreign television companies, which have their own government censorship. Since graphic sex in movies is a triple liability, the studios can be expected to increasingly find that the artistic gain that comes from including it does not compensate for the financial pain and greenlight fewer and fewer movies that present this problem. We may live in an anything-goes age, but if a studio wants to make money, it has to limit how much of "anything"— at least anything sexually explicit—it shows on the big screen. As one studio executive with an MBA lamented, "We may have to leave sex to the independents."

Movies on TV must meet standards of "public decency"

Conclusion restates claim

PRACTICE

1. Choose from your school paper or another newspaper an editorial of at least two paragraphs on a controversial subject that interests you. The title will probably reveal the subject. Annotate the editorial as you read, using the Writer's Guide as a set of guidelines and the annotations on "Sex and the Cinema" as a model. Then read the article again. You should discover that annotating the article caused you to read more carefully, more critically, with greater comprehension and a more focused response.

2. Summarize the claim of the editorial in one sentence. Has the author proved his or her point?

3. Annotate Krauthammer's "Let's Have No More Monkey Trials," pages 39–41, keeping all of your marginal notes in the left margin.

Writer's Guide: Annotating a Text

One purpose of annotating a text is to comprehend it more fully. Another is to prepare to write about it.

1. If you use a highlighter as you read a text, use it sparingly. Highlighting too much of a text is not very useful when it comes time to review what you have marked. You might consider a more targeted approach to highlighting, focusing only on thesis statement and topic sentences in an essay, for example, or on conclusions in a report.

2. More useful than highlighting is making marginal notes, perhaps underlining the portion of the text that each note refers to. However, with underlining, as with highlighting, increased quantity equals decreased usefulness. Some of the most useful marginal notes will be those that summarize key ideas in your own words. Such paraphrases force you to understand the text well enough to reword its ideas, and reading the marginal notes is a quick way to review the text when you do not have time to reread all of it.

3. It will be useful to make notes both on what a piece of writing says and how it says it. Notations about how a piece is written can focus on structural devices such as topic sentences, transitional words or phrases, and the repetition of ideas or sentence structure but also on rhetorical concerns such as identifying the claim, support, and warrant; the tone; and the types of appeal.

4. As you annotate a text, you may also want to make note of questions you still have after having read the text. These questions may be the basis for class discussion.

5. You may also find it useful to note similarities that you see between the text you are reading and others you have read or between the text and your own experience.

Research Skill: Summarizing

One skill required by the Rogerian approach to communication is the ability to summarize another's ideas fairly and objectively, just as in more confrontational forms of argumentation a writer or speaker cannot build a successful case on a misunderstanding or misinterpretation of an opponent's position. At least, such a case will not hold up under careful scrutiny. The ability to summarize is also a basic research skill used in writing research papers, as discussed in Chapter 10. Summarizing is the cornerstone on which all other critical reading and writing tasks are built.

When summarizing long or difficult texts, try some of the following strategies to help you comprehend the essential points of the text.

1. Reread the introduction and conclusion after you have read the text once or twice. These two sections should complement each other and offer clues to the most significant issues of the text. An introduction or conclusion is often more than one paragraph; therefore, it is important that you read the first and last few paragraphs of a text to understand what the author is trying to impress upon the reader. If you are summarizing a book, look especially at the preface, the first and last chapters, and any reviewers' comments. These sections won't tell you everything you need to know to summarize an entire book, but they will help you decide which points matter.

2. For a difficult text, you may want to list all the subheadings (if they are used) or the topic sentence of each paragraph. These significant guideposts will map the piece as a whole: What do they tell you about the central ideas and the main argument the author is making? After reviewing the subheads or topic sentences, can you reread the text and engage more easily with its finer points? For a book, you can do the same thing with chapter headings to break down the essential ideas. Remember that when you summarize, you must put another's words into your own (and cite the original text as well), so do not simply let a list of the subheadings or chapter titles stand as your summary. They likely won't make sense when put together in paragraph form, but they will provide you with valuable ideas regarding the central points of the text.

3. Remember that summarizing requires attention to overall meanings and not to specific details. Therefore, avoid including many specific examples or concrete details from the text you are summarizing and try to let your reader know what these examples and details add up to. Some of the specificity and excitement of the original text will be lost, but when summarizing, the goal is to let the reader know the essential meaning of the original text in a clear, straightforward way. Of course, if you need to respond, as part of your argument, to specifics in the essay, you should do so, but you will most likely do so in the form of a paraphrase or a direct quotation.

There are two types of summaries, rhetorical and referential. The two share some characteristics. Both types should

- Be objective instead of expressing opinions.
- Identify the author and the work.
- Use present tense.
- Summarize the main points of the whole work or passage, not just part of it.

A *rhetorical* summary summarizes the text in terms of rhetorical choices the author made. An example:

> In "Let's Have No More Monkey Trials," Charles Krauthammer celebrates the end of the separation of religion from public life at the local, state, and federal levels but argues that the progress made will be undermined by those trying to replace the teaching of evolution with the teaching of intelligent design, a new form of creationism. He notes that Christoph Cardinal Schönborn of Vienna . . .

The other type of summary, a *referential* summary, focuses on ideas rather than on the author's actions and decisions.

> According to Charles Krauthammer in his article "Let's Have No More Monkey Trials," a fifty-year trend toward removing religion from public life is now being reversed. This positive movement, however, is threatened by those who are trying to replace the teaching of evolution with the teaching of intelligent design, a new form of creationism. Christoph Cardinal Schönborn of Vienna has asserted that . . .

PRACTICE

Complete either the rhetorical summary or the referential summary of Krauthammer's essay.

When you try to comprehend an argument, try to imagine other readers' response to it. A writer needs to be able to represent fairly others' views rather than ignoring, demeaning, or misrepresenting them. Carl Rogers taught us to sum up objectively someone else's point of view and to look for common ground in order to make communication about emotionally charged subjects possible. Sometimes you will read an argument, and whether you agree with it or not, you will know that others with strongly held beliefs on the other side of the issue will not even give it a hearing. It may totally ignore their position or represent it unfairly, which blocks communication and makes compromise impossible. There is a tendency to write for those who already agree with us, but they are not the ones who need convincing. At times the best you can do falls short of the ideal solution, but getting the audience to hear your position may be as much as you can hope for.

Evaluation

The second step in the critical reading of arguments involves evaluation—careful judgment of the extent to which the author has succeeded in making a point—which can be difficult because some readers who do not thoroughly engage with an author's point of view may immediately label an argument they disagree with as "wrong," and some readers believe they are incapable of evaluating the work of a published, "expert" author because they do not feel expert enough to make such judgments.

Critically evaluating an argument means not simply reading a text and agreeing or disagreeing with it, but doing serious analytical work that addresses multiple viewpoints before deciding on the effectiveness of an argument.

The following essay supports a claim of value in which, as the title suggests, the author claims that competitive sports are destructive. In arguments about values, the author may or may not suggest a solution to the problem caused by the belief or behavior. If so, the solution will be implicit—that is, unexpressed or undeveloped—as is the case here, and the emphasis will remain on support for the claim.

Notice the difference between the annotations a student made in response to the following essay and those another student made earlier in response to "Sex and the Cinema" (p. 43). In the earlier example, the student was making marginal notes primarily on the ideas presented in the essay. Here the annotations focus on how successfully Kohn argues his case.

Strategies for Evaluating Arguments

1. As you read the argument, don't be timid about asking questions of the text. No author is infallible, and some are not always clear. Disagree with the author if you feel confident of the support for your view, but first read the whole argument to see if your questions have been answered. If not, this may be a signal to read the article again. Be cautious about concluding that the author hasn't proved his or her point.

2. Reading an assigned work is usually a solitary activity, but what follows a reading should be shared. Talk about the material with classmates or others who have read it, especially those who have responded to the text differently than you did. Consider their points of view. You probably know that discussion of a book or a movie strengthens both your memory of details and your understanding of the whole. And defending or modifying your evaluation will mean going back to the text and finding clues that you may have overlooked. Not least, it can be fun to discuss even something you didn't enjoy.

3. Consider the strengths of the argument and examine the useful methods of argumentation, the points that are successfully made (and those which help the reader to better understand the argument), and what makes sense about the author's argument.

4. Consider the weaknesses of the argument and locate instances of faulty reasoning, unsupported statements, and the limitations of the author's assumptions about the world (the warrants that underlie the argument).

5. Consider how effective the title of the reading is and whether it accurately sums up a critical point of the essay. Come up with an alternative title that would suit the reading better, and be prepared to defend this alternative title.

6. Evaluate the organizational structure of the essay. The author should lead you from idea to idea in a logical progression, and each section should relate to the ones before and after it and to the central argument in significant ways. Determine whether the writer could have organized things more clearly, logically, or efficiently.

7. Look at how the author follows through on the main claim, or thesis, of the argument. The author should stick with this thesis and not waver throughout the text. If the thesis does waver, there could be a reason for the shift in the argument, or perhaps the author is being inconsistent. The conclusion should drive home the central argument.

8. Evaluate the vocabulary and style the author uses. Is it too simple or too complicated? The vocabulary and sentence structure the author uses could relate to the audience the author was initially writing for.

SAMPLE ANNOTATED ESSAY

No-Win Situations

ALFIE KOHN

I learned my first game at a birthday party. You remember it: X players scramble for X-minus-one chairs each time the music stops. In every round a child is eliminated until at the end only one is left triumphantly seated while everyone else is standing on the sidelines, excluded from play, unhappy . . . losers.

Good example.

This is how we learn to have a good time in America.

Good use of sarcasm.

Competition

Several years ago I wrote a book called *No Contest*, which, based on the findings of several hundred studies, argued that competition undermines self-esteem, poisons relationships, and holds us back from doing our best. I was mostly interested in the win/lose arrangement that defines our workplaces and classrooms, but I found myself nagged by the

This establishes his expertise on the subject.

This article by Alfie Kohn, author of *No Contest: The Case Against Competition* (1986) and *The Homework Myth: Why Our Kids Get Too Much of a Bad Thing* (2006), appeared in *Women's Sports and Fitness Magazine* (July–August 1990).

The comparison is flawed because those who compete during the week are mostly spectators on weekends.

following question: If competition is so destructive and counterproductive during the week, why do we take for granted that it suddenly becomes benign and even desirable on the weekend?

This is a particularly unsettling line of inquiry for athletes or parents. Most of us, after all, assume that competitive sports teach all sorts of useful lessons and, indeed, that games by definition must produce a winner and a loser. But I've come to believe that recreation at its best does not require people to try to triumph over others. Quite to the contrary.

Is recreation the same as sports?

An appropriate authority to use.

Terry Orlick, a sports psychologist at the University of Ottawa, took a look at musical chairs and proposed that we keep the basic format of removing chairs but change the goal; the point becomes to fit everyone on a diminishing number of seats. At the end, a group of giggling children tries to figure out how to squish onto a single chair. Everybody plays to the end; everybody has a good time.

5

Not much fun as spectator sports. Our most popular sports draw huge crowds.

Aristotelian versus Rogerian?

This suggests that football, baseball, and basketball offer no advantages. Many would disagree.

At one extreme is cooperative activity. At the other is "war minus the shooting." Competition seems to be a happy medium.

We may be able to do without them, but should we have to?

It might not be the same if it were adults.

Orlick and others have devised or collected hundreds of such games for children and adults alike. The underlying theory is simple: All games involve achieving a goal despite the presence of an obstacle, but nowhere is it written that the obstacle has to be someone else. The idea can be for each person on the field to make a specified contribution to the goal, or for all the players to reach a certain score, or for everyone to work with her partners against a time limit.

Note the significance of an "opponent" becoming a "partner." The entire dynamic of the game shifts, and one's attitude toward the other players changes with it. Even the friendliest game of tennis can't help but be affected by the game's inherent structure, which demands that each person try to hit the ball where the other can't get to it. You may not be a malicious person, but to play tennis means that you try to make the other person fail.

I've become convinced that not a single one of the advantages attributed to sports actually requires competition. Running, climbing, biking, swimming, aerobics—all offer a fine workout without any need to try to outdo someone else. Some people point to the camaraderie that results from teamwork, but that's precisely the benefit of cooperative activity, whose very essence is that *everyone* on the field is working together for a common goal. By contrast, the distinguishing feature of team competition is that a given player works with and is encouraged to feel warmly toward only half of those present. Worse, a we-versus-they dynamic is set up, which George Orwell once called "war minus the shooting."

The dependence on sports to provide a sense of accomplishment or to test one's wits is similarly misplaced. One can aim instead at an objective standard (How far did I throw? How many miles did we cover?) or attempt to do better than last week. Such individual and group striving—like cooperative games—provides satisfaction and challenge without competition.

If large numbers of people insist that we can't do without win/lose activities, the first question to ask is whether they've ever tasted the alternative. When Orlick taught a group of children noncompetitive games, two-thirds of the boys and all of the girls preferred them to the kind that require opponents.

10

If our culture's idea of fun requires beating someone else, it may just be because we don't know any other way.

It may also be because we overlook the psychological costs of competition. Most people lose in most competitive encounters, and it's obvious why that causes self-doubt. But even winning doesn't build character. It just lets us gloat temporarily. Studies have shown that feelings of self-worth become dependent on external sources of evaluation as a result of competition. Your value is defined by what you've done and who you've beaten. The whole affair soon becomes a vicious circle: The more you compete, the more you *need* to compete to feel good about yourself. It's like drinking salt water when you're thirsty. This process is bad enough for us; it's a disaster for our children.

> It's a bit excessive to rule out completely the possibility that sports do build character.

While this is going on, competition is having an equally toxic effect on our relationships. By definition, not everyone can win a contest. That means that each child inevitably comes to regard others as obstacles to his or her own success. Competition leads children to envy winners, to dismiss losers (there's no nastier epithet in our language than "loser!"), and to be suspicious of just about everyone. Competition makes it difficult to regard others as potential friends or collaborators; even if you're not my rival today, you could be tomorrow.

> It's not clear if he has been talking about just children or everyone.

This is not to say that competitors will always detest one another. But trying to outdo someone is not conducive to trust—indeed it would be irrational to trust a person who gains from your failure. At best, competition leads one to look at others through narrowed eyes; at worst, it invites outright aggression.

> He hasn't supported this idea.

Changing the Structure of Sports

But no matter how many bad feelings erupt during competition, we have a marvelous talent for blaming the individuals rather than focusing on the structure of the game itself, a structure that makes my success depend on your failure. Cheating may just represent the logical conclusion of this arrangement rather than an aberration. And sportsmanship is nothing more than an artificial way to try to limit the damage of competition. If we weren't set against each other on the court or the track, we wouldn't

> If he has support for this, he should provide it.

need to keep urging people to be good sports; they might well be working *with* each other in the first place.

As radical or surprising as it may sound, the problem isn't just that we compete the wrong way or that we push winning on our children too early. The problem is competition itself. What we need to be teaching our daughters and sons is that it's possible to have a good time—a better time—without turning the playing field into a battlefield.

15

This seems a bit extreme.

"No-Win Situations." Copyright © 1990 by Alfie Kohn. Reprinted from *Women's Sports & Fitness* with the author's permission. For more on this topic, please see www.alfiekohn.org <http://www.alfiekohn.org> or Alfie Kohn's book *No Contest: The Case Against Competition.*

Analysis

The pattern of organization in this essay is primarily a *defense of the main idea*—that competitive sports are psychologically unhealthy. But because the author knows that competitive sports are hugely popular, not only in the United States but in many other parts of the world, he must also try to *refute the opposing view*—that competition is rewarding and enjoyable. In doing so, Kohn fails to make clear distinctions between competitive sports for children, who may find it difficult to accept defeat, and for adults, who understand the consequences of any competitive game and are psychologically equipped to deal with them. Readers may therefore share Kohn's misgivings about competition for children but doubt that his criteria apply equally to adults.

The *claim,* expressed as the *thesis statement* of the essay, appears at the end of paragraph 4: "recreation at its best does not require people to try to triumph over others. Quite to the contrary." The three-paragraph introduction recounts a relevant personal experience as well as the reasons that prompted Kohn to write his essay. Because we are all interested in stories, the recital of a personal experience is a popular device for introducing almost any subject.

The rest of the essay, until the last two paragraphs, is devoted to summarizing the benefits of cooperative play and the disadvantages of competitive sport. The emphasis is overwhelmingly on the disadvantages as stated in the third paragraph: "competition undermines self-esteem, poisons relationships, and holds us back from doing our best." This is the *warrant,* the assumption that underlies the claim. In fact, here Kohn is referring to a larger study that he wrote about competition in workplaces and classrooms. We must accept this broad generalization, which applies to many human activities, before we can agree that the claim about competition in sports is valid.

Kohn relies for support on examples from common experience and on the work of Terry Orlick, a sports psychologist. The examples from experience are ones that most of us will recognize. Here we are in a position to judge for ourselves, without the mediation of an expert, whether the influence of competition in sports is as hurtful as Kohn insists. Orlick's research suggests a solution—adaptations of familiar games that will provide enjoyment but avoid competition. On the other hand, the results from studies by one psychologist whose work we aren't able to verify and the mention of "studies" in paragraph 3 without further attribution are probably not enough to answer all the arguments in favor of competition. Critics may also ask if Kohn has offered support for one of his contentions—that competition "holds us back from doing our best" (para. 3). (Support for this may appear in one of Kohn's books.)

The last two paragraphs sum up his argument that "the problem is competition itself" (para. 15)—the structure of the game rather than the people who play. Notice that the conclusion does not merely repeat the main idea. It also offers a new idea about good sportsmanship that confirms his conclusion.

The language is clear and direct. Kohn's article, which appeared in a women's sports magazine, is meant for the educated general reader, not the expert. This is also the audience for whom most student papers are written. But the written essay need not be unduly formal. Kohn uses contractions and the personal pronouns *I* and *you* to establish a conversational context. One of the particular strengths of his style is the skillful use of transitional expressions, words like *this* and *also* and clauses like *This is not to say that* and *Note the significance of* to make connections between paragraphs and new ideas.

The tone is temperate despite the author's strong feelings about the subject. Other authors, supporting the same argument, have used language that borders on the abusive about coaches and trainers of children's games. But a less inflammatory voice is far more effective with an audience that may be neutral or antagonistic.

You will find it helpful to look back over the essay to see how the examples we've cited and others work to fulfill the writer's purpose.

PRACTICE

Using the annotations on Epstein's "Sex and the Cinema" and Kohn's "No-Win Situations" as models, annotate the following essay.

The Gay Option

STEPHANIE FAIRYINGTON

I came out to my mother in a letter. I was 28. "I was born this way," I wrote, following with the most shattering high note of self-loathing I can think of: "If there were a straight pill," I lamented, "I'd swallow it faster than you can say the word *gay*."

I didn't mean either of these things. I said them because I knew they would elicit pity and absolve my mother of the belief that her parenting was to blame for my same-sex attractions. It worked. Five years later, my mother continues to talk about my lesbianism as if it were a genetic defect like Down syndrome—a parallel she's actually drawn—because clearly, in her mind, no one would choose such a detestable and challenging state of being.

This is not a message I'm proud to have sent. Contrary to how I actually feel about my sexuality, it suggests that I'm drowning in a sea of self-disgust, desperately grasping for a heterosexual lifeboat to sail my way out of it. But would my mother have been as sympathetic and tolerant if she thought I had a choice in the matter? Would conservative allies support us if they believed we could help it?

If the answer is no, and I believe it is, what does it say about our self-worth and status in society if we, as gay people, must practice a politics of pity to secure our place in the world? It says, for one, that we don't have a place at the table. It says that we are tolerated, but not accepted. It says, ultimately, that it's time to change our rhetoric.

Until homosexuality is cast and understood as a valid choice, rather than a biological affliction, we will never rise above our current status. We will remain Mother Nature's mistake, tolerable (to some) because our condition is her fault, not ours.

By choice, I don't mean that one can choose one's sexual propensities any more than one can choose one's personality. What I mean is that it's a choice to act on every desire we have, and that acting on our same-sex attractions is just as valid as pursuing a passion for the Christian faith or Judaism or any other spiritual, intellectual, emotional, or physical craving that does not infringe on the rights of others. And it should be respected as such.

As a firm Kinsey 6—with 6 being the gayest ranking on sexologist Alfred Kinsey's 1-to-6 scale of sexual orientation—I understand the resistance to putting *choice* and *homosexuality* in the same sentence. My same-sex attractions were awakened in me at such a young age that they felt as much a part of me as my limbs. In the late 1990s, when I was coming out, had someone told me that I had

5

Stephanie Fairyington is a research editor for Hachette Filipacchi Media US and a freelance journalist who writes about gender issues. A version of this article appeared in the Winter 2010 issue of *Dissent* as "Choice as Strategy: Homosexuality and the Politics of Pity"; the excerpt here appeared in the *Utne Reader*, May–June 2010.

chosen my deepest, most tender and passionate affections, it would have been like telling me that I had chosen the arms and legs I have.

But I have plenty of desires, like throwing my fists in the faces of conservative Republicans, which for one reason or another, I don't act on; my desire for women is not one of them. Biology is not destiny, and I am the architect of my own life, as is everyone. My point is not to challenge or even enter the debate about whether or not some combination of nature and nurture contributes to the formation of an inclination toward one's own sex. My point is that most inquiries into the origins of homosexuality are suspect, and their service to us is limited, if not perilous.

A politics of *choice* would be one that regards same-sex desire enough to announce it as a conscious decision rather than a predetermined abnormality. No matter how bumpy the ride or long the journey, *choice* as a political strategy is the only ride out of Freaksville.

Forty years ago, gay activists had a similar view, taking their cues from radical lesbian feminists who believed that heterosexuality and homosexuality were products of culture, not nature. "In the absence of oppression and social control," writes historian John D'Emilio, gay liberationists believed that "sexuality would be polymorphous"—fluid, in other words. Back then they talked about "sexual preference," which implies choice, as opposed to "sexual orientation," which does not.

It wasn't until the 1970s that the mental health establishment and its gay allies put forth the view that homosexuality is a permanent psychological condition and debunked the notion that it was a mental illness in need of a cure. Then came the 1980s and 1990s and a slew of shoddy and inconclusive scientific research on the biological origins of gayness, reinforcing the belief that sexuality is predestined. Both psychological and medical discourses formed today's dominant paradigm, which insists that sexuality is inborn and immutable.

The LGBT activists who have helped construct this sexual framework are neither lazy nor naive in their thinking, as D'Emilio points out in his essay "Born Gay?," a crisp case against the politics of biological determinism. As a political strategy, it has helped reap enormous benefits, from antidiscrimination legislation to adoption rights in some states and civil unions in others. The reasons this model of sexuality is politically expedient and effective are threefold.

First, if sexuality is understood as predestined and therefore fixed, it poses less of a challenge to the hetero monolith than does a shifting spectrum of desire. It protects straight people, in other words, from the threat of homosexuality. Second, by presenting homosexuality as a biological fact as firm and absolute as race or sex, gay activists have formed an identity the law can recognize and can follow in the footsteps of civil rights legislation. Third, it's conceptually easier to understand sexuality as a permanent trait rather than the complex, ever-morphing mess that it often is.

But for all the success this politics has had, in the end, it's not only shortsighted but rife with limitations—and dangers. As lesbian activist Joan Nestle told me, it's not good politics to cling to the "born gay" edict because "the use of biological 'abnormalities' was used by the Nazis when they measured the nostril thickness of imprisoned Jews to prove they were an inferior race; and when colo-

10

nizers measured the brains of Africans to make a case for their enslavement; and when doctors at the turn of the century used the argument that the light weight of women's brains proved their inferiority to men. I do not want to enter into this sad history of biological dehumanization as the basis for gay rights."

All the studies that gay sympathizers and activists invoke to justify our right   15
to same-sex love cast homosexuality as a loud hiccup at the dinner table of nor-
mality. As such, we're put on par with other undesirable deviations from nature's norm, taunting eugenics with the keys to eliminating us. This is the ugly under-belly of our biology-centered claims to human rights.

The typical conservative assault on homosexuality casts it as a sinful choice that can be unchosen through a commitment to God and reparative therapy. And the left usually slams into this simplistic polemic by taking up the opposite stance: Homosexuality is not a choice, and because we can't help it, it's not sinful.

By affirming that homosexual practice and identity *are* a choice, we can attach an addendum—it's a good choice—and open the possibility of a more nuanced argument, one that dismantles the logic of the very premise that whom we choose to love marks us as sinful and immoral and interrogates the assumption that het-erosexuality is somehow better for the individual and society as a whole.

In my conservative Republican family, signs already point to a kind of readi-ness to engage homosexuality as a legitimate decision. Recently, I called my mother in California to throw out my "born-gay-pity-me" garbage. She didn't swallow my pill of choice with ease, but managed to cough up an exasperated, "Well, whatever makes you happy." That's one down and a nation to go.

Critical Listening

Of course, not all public arguments are written. Today the art of listening has become an indispensable tool for learning about the world we live in. We watch the news on television and occasionally hear it on the radio. We may be more likely to learn the latest via a video clip on our computer or BlackBerry than to read it in a newspaper.

Most relevant to the kinds of written arguments you will read and write about in this course are television and radio shows that examine social and political problems. The most intelligent and responsible programs usually con-sist of a panel of experts—politicians, journalists, scholars—led by a neutral moderator (or one who at least allows guests to express their views). Some of these programs are decades old; others are more recent—*Meet the Press, Face the Nation, Hardball with Chris Matthews, The McLaughlin Group, PBS NewsHour.* An outstanding radio show, *Talk of the Nation* on National Public Radio, invites listeners, who are generally informed and articulate, to call in and ask questions of, or comment on remarks made by, experts on the topic of the day.

Several enormously popular radio talk shows are hosted by people with strong, sometimes extreme ideological positions. They may use offensive language and insult their listeners in a crude form of theater. Among the most influential shows are those of Don Imus and Howard Stern. In addition, elections and political crises bring speeches and debates on radio and television by represen- tatives of a variety of views. Some are long and formal, written texts that are simply read aloud, but others are short and impromptu.

Whatever the merits or shortcomings of individual programs, significant general differences exist between arguments on radio and television and argu- ments in the print media. These differences include the degree of organization and development and the risk of personal attacks.

First (excluding for the moment the long, prepared speeches), contributions to a panel discussion must be delivered in fragments, usually no longer than a single paragraph, weakened by time constraints, interruptions, overlapping speech, memory gaps, and real or feigned displays of derision, impatience, and disbelief by critical panelists. Even on the best programs, the result is a lack of both co- herence—or connections between ideas—and solid evidence that requires de- velopment. Too often we are treated to conclusions with little indication of how they were arrived at.

The following brief passage appeared in a newspaper review of "Resolved: The flat tax is better than the income tax," a debate on *Firing Line* by an im- pressive array of experts. It illustrates some of the difficulties that accompany programs attempting to capture the truth of a complicated issue on television or radio.

> "It is absolutely true," says a proponent. "It is factually untrue," coun- ters an opponent. "It's factually correct," responds a proponent. "I did my math right," says a proponent. "You didn't do your math right," says an opponent. At one point in a discussion of interest income, one of the experts says, "Oh, excuse me, I think I got it backward."

No wonder the television critic called the exchange "disjointed and at times perplexing."[2] And these are polished productions compared to the vast majority of the millions of *YouTube* videos available online.

In the sensational talk shows the participants rely on personal experience and vivid anecdotes, which may not be sufficiently typical to prove anything.

Second, listeners and viewers of all spoken arguments are in danger of eval- uating them according to criteria that are largely absent from evaluation of written texts. It is true that writers may adopt a persona or a literary disguise, which the tone of the essay will reflect. But many readers will not be able to identify it or recognize their own response to it. Listeners and viewers, however, can hardly avoid being affected by characteristics that are clearly definable: a speaker's voice, delivery, bodily mannerisms, dress, and physical appearance. In addition, listeners may be adversely influenced by clumsy speech containing more slang, colloquialisms, and grammar and usage errors than written texts that have had the benefit of revision.

---

[2]Walter Goodman, "The Joys of the Flat Tax, Excluding the Equations," *New York Times*, December 21, 1995, sec. C, p. 14.

But if listeners allow consideration of physical attributes to influence their judgment of what the speaker is trying to prove, they are guilty of an ad hominem fallacy—that is, an evaluation of the speaker rather than the argument. This is true whether the evaluation is favorable or unfavorable. (See p. 311 for a discussion of this fallacy.)

Talk shows may indeed be disjointed and perplexing, but millions of us find them both instructive and entertaining. Over time we are exposed to an astonishing variety of opinions from every corner of American life, and we also acquire information from experts who might not otherwise be available to us. Then there is the appeal of hearing the voices, seeing the faces of people engaged in earnest, sometimes passionate, discourse—a short, unrehearsed drama in which we also play a part as active listeners in a far-flung audience.

Strategies for Critical Listening

Listening is hearing with attention, a natural and immensely important human activity, which, unfortunately, many people don't do very well. The good news is that listening is a skill that can be learned and, unlike some other skills, practiced every day without big investments of money and effort.

Here are some of the characteristics of critical listening most appropriate to understanding and responding to arguments.

1. Above all, listening to arguments requires concentration. If you are distracted, you cannot go back as you do with the written word to clarify a point or recover a connection. Devices such as flow sheets and outlines can be useful aids to concentration. In following a debate, for example, judges and other listeners often use flow sheets — distant cousins of baseball scorecards — to record the major points on each side and their rebuttals. For roundtable discussions or debates you can make your own simple flow chart to fill out as you listen, with columns for claims, different kinds of support, and warrants. Leave spaces in the margin for your questions and comments about the soundness of the proof. An outline is more useful for longer presentations, such as lectures. As you listen, try to avoid being distracted by facts alone. Look for the overall pattern of the speech.

2. Listeners often concentrate on the wrong things in the spoken argument. We have already noted the distractions of appearance and delivery. Research shows that listeners are likely to give greater attention to the dramatic elements of speeches than to the logical ones. But you can enjoy the sound, the appearance, and the drama of a spoken argument without allowing these elements to overwhelm what is essential to the development of a claim.

3. Good listeners try not to allow their prejudices to prevent careful evaluation of the argument. This doesn't mean accepting everything or even most of what you hear. It means trying to avoid premature judgments about what is actually said. This precaution is especially relevant when the speakers and their views are well known and the listener has already formed an opinion about them, favorable or unfavorable.

Reading a Visual Argument

> Man has been communicating by pictures longer than he has been using
> words. With the development of photography in this century we are using
> pictures as a means of communication to such an extent that in some
> areas they overshadow verbal language.[3]

Paul Wendt wrote these words long before the digital age. Now we can snap
pictures with our cell phones and send them to the other side of the world.
Most elementary school children know how to use *Google* or another search
engine to find pictures of almost anything imaginable, and by middle school
they know how to go to *YouTube* to see thousands of amateur videos or to submit their own.

Wendt was writing, however, about the persuasive power of pictures, or
pictures as argument. The nation saw the power of the visual in the 2008 presidential campaign when questions for the candidates came for the first time in
the form of video clips submitted via *YouTube*—and campaigns may never be
the same. Questions were not merely read by a moderator or asked by a panel
of journalists. They didn't come in the form of disembodied voices over a telephone line. They came from real people who were visible on the screen to the
candidates and to the whole country. Two women looked straight into the camera and asked the candidates if they would let them get married to each other.
A snowman asked about global warming and what it would mean to his son's
future. A young man asked what they could do to protect his "baby" and held
up an assault rifle. The visual images did not replace the verbal language, but
complemented it. They were an integral part of the argument.

You've probably seen similarly powerful still images in photographic journalism: soldiers in battle, destruction by weather disasters, beautiful natural
landscapes, inhumane living conditions, the great mushroom cloud of early
atomic explosions. These photographs and thousands of others encapsulate arguments of fact, value, and policy. We often don't need to read their captions to
understand what they tell us: *The tornado devastated the town. The Grand Canyon
is our most stupendous national monument. We must not allow human beings to live
like this.*

An exception would be a pair of pictures that gained wide circulation in the
aftermath of Hurricane Katrina in 2005. They seemed innocuous enough when
seen without commentary, except to show the extent of the flooding. One shows
a young black man wading through the chest-deep floodwaters carrying a black
garbage bag. Another shows a young white man also wading through chest-
deep water, wearing a backpack and accompanied by a young white woman
wearing a backpack and dragging a bag. The text accompanying the pictures,

---

[3]Paul Wendt, "The Language of Pictures," in S. I. Hayakawa, ed., *The Use and Misuse of Language* (Greenwich, CT: Fawcett, 1962), p. 175.

"Looting" and "finding"

however, shows the bias of those who described the pictures. Next to the picture of the black youth are these words: "A young man walks through chest deep water after looting a grocery store in New Orleans on Tuesday, August 30, 2005." Notice the difference in the words accompanying the other picture: "Two residents wade through chest deep flood water after finding bread and soda from a local grocery store after Hurricane Katrina came through the area in New Orleans, Louisiana." The wording produced such a response that *Yahoo!* offered this statement:

> News photos are an especially popular section of Yahoo! News. In part, this is because we present thousands of news photos from some of the leading news services, including The Associated Press, Reuters, and Agence France Press. To make this volume of photos available in a timely manner, we present the photos and their captions as written, edited and distributed by the news services with no additional editing at Yahoo! News.
>
> In recent days, a number of readers of Yahoo! News have commented on differences in the language in two Hurricane Katrina-related photo captions (from two news services). Since the controversy began, the supplier of one of the photos has asked all its clients to remove the photo from their databases. Yahoo! News has complied with the AFP request. . . . Yahoo! News regrets that these photos and captions, viewed together, may have suggested a racial bias on our part. We remain committed to bringing our readers the full collection of photos as transmitted by our wire service partners.[4]

Other images provided additional glimpses into the aftermath of Katrina. The photograph of Milvertha Hendricks was striking enough that David Dante Troutt, Charles Ogletree, and Derrick Bell used a color version of it for the cover photo of their book, *After the Storm: Black Intellectuals Explore the Meaning of Hurricane Katrina* (2007).

PRACTICE

1. Look closely at the photograph of a flag-draped woman taken following Hurricane Katrina (Fig. 1). Who is pictured? What sort of expression does she have on her face? Then consider why the elderly woman might have a blanket that looks like an American flag draped over her. What do you know about the rescue of Katrina victims that might be relevant to how you "read" the picture as an argument? Under the circumstances, how might the flag blanket be seen as symbolic? What claim might you infer from the picture?

2. Now compare the picture to the next photo, "At the Time of the Louisville Flood," taken in 1937 by Margaret Bourke-White (Fig. 2). Do you see any similarity in the message being conveyed by each? Explain.

3. Finally, look at the third picture (Fig. 3) and decide if you feel it conveys a similar or a very different message.

---

[4]The Yahoo! News statement can be found at http://news.yahoo.com/page/photostatement.

Figure 1   Eric Gay, "Milvertha Hendricks, 84, waiting in the rain outside the New Orleans Convention Center on September 1, 2005"

Figure 2   Margaret Bourke-White, "At the Time of the Louisville Flood" (1937)

Figure 3   Bruce Chambers, "Edgar Hollingsworth rescued from his home after Hurricane Katrina" (2005)

Edgar Hollingsworth, the seventy-four-year-old man shown being rescued in the third picture, snapped by Bruce Chambers of the *Orange County Register*, survived the hurricane but was found near death in his home fourteen days after the storm. He died four days later in the hospital.

The reactions this third picture has elicited provide an excellent illustration of varied responses to the same visual image. Not every viewer will "read" a picture in the same way. Not every viewer will see it as support for the same argument. These are some of the responses that the picture of Hollingsworth's rescue has produced:

- A typical headline accompanying the photo called the discovery of Hollingsworth a "miracle rescue." According to a report from Post-Gazette.com, "The rescue was a bright spot on a day in which the owners of a nursing home were charged in the deaths of dozens of patients killed by hurricane floodwaters, the death toll in Louisiana jumped to 423 and the New Orleans mayor warned that the city is broke."[5] And according to Keith Sharon of the *Orange County Register*, "The rescue pumped up the spirits of [California] Task Force 5, which has been mostly marking the locations of dead bodies for the last week."[6]

- *USA Today* termed the photo "iconic."[7] Marcia Prouse, director of photography at the *Orange County Register*, had a similar view: "This man's story needs to be told. He's an important symbol of the hurricane. . . . It's anybody's father or grandfather."[8]

- Chambers's picture (p. 66) has become known through the Internet as the *Katrina Pietá*. The *Pietá* alluded to is Michelangelo's famous sculpture of Mary holding the body of Christ after his crucifixion. The way that the National Guardsman is holding Hollingsworth is reminiscent of Mary's pose, and the link to the loving mother of Jesus leads to a positive interpretation of the scene.

- For some, the sight of two white aid workers and one Hispanic one aiding a black man provides a sharp contrast to other images that stress the racial tension that grew out of Katrina's aftermath.

- Others were enraged by rules that could have kept the rescue team from entering Hollingsworth's home to rescue him. Keith Sharon wrote, "In the past few days, the Federal Emergency Management Agency has ordered searchers not to break into homes. They are supposed to look in through a window and knock on the door. If no one cries out for help, they are supposed to move on. If they see a body,

[5]See http://www.post-gazette.com/pg/05257/570999.stm.
[6]See http://www.ocregister.com/blog/rescue/.
[7]See http://www.usatoday.com/news/nation/2005-11-10-hollingsworth-katrina_x.htm.
[8]See http://www.editorandpublisher.com/eandp/news/article_display.jsp?vnu_content_id=1001137369.

they are supposed to log the address and move on." The rescue team went against orders in breaking down the door to reach Hollingsworth. Sharon added that earlier "they had been frustrated when FEMA delayed their deployment for four days, housing them in the Hyatt Regency in Dallas."[9] The Sharon quotes are referenced on DailyKOS.com, under the title "American Shame: The Edgar Hollingsworth Story."[10]

Just as readers bring to an argument their biases and their own personal store of experiences, so do viewers bring the same to a visual argument.

Photographs, of course, function everywhere as instruments of persuasion. Animal-rights groups show pictures of brutally mistreated dogs and cats; children's rights advocates publish pictures of sick and starving children in desolate refugee camps. On a very different scale, alluring photographs from advertisers—travel agencies, restaurants, sporting goods manufacturers, clothiers, jewelers, movie studios—promise to fulfill our dreams of pleasure.

But photographs are not the only visual images we respond to. We are also susceptible to other kinds of illustrations and to signs and symbols which over the years have acquired connotations, or suggestive significance. The flag or bald eagle, the shamrock, the crown, the cross, the hammer and sickle, and the swastika can all rouse strong feelings for or against the ideas they represent. These symbols may be defined as abbreviated claims of value. They summarize the moral, religious, and political principles by which groups of people live and often die. In commercial advertisements we recognize symbols that aren't likely to enlist our deepest loyalties but, nevertheless, have impact on our daily lives: the apple with a bite in it, the golden arches, the Prudential rock, the Nike swoosh, and a thousand others.

In fact, a closer look at commercial and political advertising, which is heavily dependent on visual argument and is something we are all familiar with, provides a useful introduction to this complex subject. We know that advertisements, with or without pictures, are short arguments, often lacking fully developed support, whose claims of policy urge us to take an action: Buy this product or service; vote for this candidate or issue. The claim may not be directly expressed, but it will be clearly implicit. In print, on television, or on the Internet, the visual representation of objects, carefully chosen to appeal to a particular audience, can be as important as, if not more important than, any verbal text.

In a political advertisement we often see a picture of the candidate surrounded by a smiling family. The visual image is by now a cliché, suggesting traditional values—love and security, the importance of home and children. Even if we know little or nothing about his or her platform, we are expected to make a sympathetic connection with the candidate.

---

[9]Keith Sharon, "Survivor Rescued 16 Days after the Hurricane," *Orange County Register*, September 14, 2005.

[10]See www.dailykos.com/story/2005/9/14/12516/3649.

In a commercial advertisement the image may be a picture of a real or fictitious person to whom we will react favorably. Consider the picture on a jar of spaghetti sauce. As a famous designer remarked, "When you think about it, sauce is mostly sauce. It's the label that makes the difference."[11]And what, according to the designer, does the cheerful face of Paul Newman on jars of his spaghetti sauce suggest to the prospective buyer? "Paul Newman. Paul Newman. Paul Newman. Blue eyes. All the money goes to charity. It's humanitarian, funny, and sexy. Selling this is like falling off a log." Not a word about the quality of the sauce.

Even colleges, which are also selling a product, must think of appropriate images to attract their prospective customers—students. Today the fact that more women than men are enrolled in college has caused some schools to rethink their images. One college official explained:

> We're having our recruiting literature redesigned, and we've been thinking about what's a feminine look and what's a masculine look. We have a picture of a library with a lot of stained glass, and people said that was kind of a feminine cover. Now we're using a picture of the quadrangle.[12]

In addition to the emblem itself, the designer pays careful attention to a number of other elements in the ad: colors, light and shadow, foreground and background, relative sizes of pictures and text, and placement of objects on the page or screen. Each of these contributes to the total effect, although we may be unaware of how the effect has been achieved. (In the ad that follows, you will be able to examine some of the psychological and aesthetic devices at work.)

When there is no verbal text, visual images are less subject to analysis and interpretation. For one thing, if we are familiar with the objects in the picture, we see the whole image at once, and it registers immediately. The verbal message is linear and takes far longer to be absorbed. Pictures, therefore, appear to need less translation. Advertisers and other arguers depend on this characteristic to provide quick and friendly acceptance of their claims, although the image may, in fact, be deceptive.

This expectation of easy understanding poses a danger with another visual ally of the arguer—the graph or chart. Graphics give us factual information at a glance. In addition to the relative ease with which they can be read, they are "at their best . . . instruments for reasoning about quantitative information. . . . Of all methods for analyzing and communicating statistical information, well-designed data graphics are usually the simplest and at the same time the most powerful."[13]

---

[11]Tibor Kalman, "Message: Sweet-Talking Spaghetti Sauce," *New York Times Magazine*, December 13, 1998, p. 81.

[12]*New York Times*, December 6, 1998, p. 38.

[13]Edward R. Tufte, *The Visual Display of Quantitative Information* (Cheshire, CT: Graphics Press, 1983), introduction.

Nevertheless, they may mislead the quick reader. Graphics can lie. "The lies are told about the major issues of public policy—the government budget, medical care, prices, and fuel economy standards, for example. The lies are systematic and quite predictable, nearly always exaggerating the rate of recent change."[14]

Visual images, then, for all their apparent immediacy and directness, need to be read with at least the same attention we give to the verbal message if we are to understand the arguments they represent.

Consider these questions as you analyze images:

1. What does the arguer want me to do or believe? How important is the visual image in persuading me to comply?

2. Has the visual image been accompanied by sufficient text to answer questions I may have about the claim?

3. Are the visual elements more prominent than the text? If so, why?

4. Is the visual image representative of a large group, or is it an exception that cannot support the claim?

5. Does the arrangement of elements in the message tell me what the arguer considers most important? If so, what is the significance of this choice?

6. Can the validity of this chart or graph be verified?

7. Does the visual image lead me to entertain unrealistic expectations? (Can using this shampoo make hair look like that shining cascade on the television screen? Does the picture of the candidate for governor, shown answering questions in a classroom of eager, smiling youngsters, mean that he has a viable plan for educational reform?)

Sample Analysis of an Advertisement

We have pointed out that a commercial advertisement is a short argument that makes an obvious policy claim, which may or may not be explicit: *You should buy this product.* Depending on the medium—television, print, radio, or Internet—an ad may convey its message through language, picture, or sound.

Here is how one analyst of advertising sums up the goals of the advertiser: (1) attract attention, (2) arouse interest, (3) stimulate desire, (4) create conviction, and (5) get action.[15] Needless to say, not every ad successfully fulfills all these objectives. If you examine the ad reproduced on page 71, you can see how the advertiser brings language and visual image together in an attempt to support the claim.

---

[14]Tufte, *The Visual Display*, p. 76.
[15]J. V. Lund, *Newspaper Advertising* (New York: Prentice-Hall, 1947), p. 83.

The image in the ad appeals to our common knowledge as Americans. We have probably all heard the story of how George Washington, as a boy, chopped down a cherry tree. The clothes that the young boy in the ad is wearing—particularly the tricorner hat—along with the architecture, suggest a colonial setting. The hatchet hidden behind the boy's back combined with the exclamation

"Oops!" calls to mind the specific story about Washington. Upon hearing the story, you may have envisioned a much smaller tree and less substantial damage, but it is critical to the ad's effect that in this rendering of the story of our first president's youth, the tree has fallen on someone's house, possibly the Washingtons'. The ad appears to have been reproduced on parchment, another detail that helps to place the incident historically, and each corner is subtly decorated with a cherry.

What has made the cherry tree story a classic for teaching morals is what the young Washington is said to have done after he chopped down the tree. All of us are familiar with the words "I can not tell a lie," Washington's response when questioned about what he had done. It was a fitting reply for a man who would later be chosen to lead the new nation. The largest text on the page—and the text most likely therefore to catch the attention of a reader casually flipping through *Newsweek*—is a play on this famous quote that changes *I* to *we*. The identification with Washington and his famous words is particularly critical for a company whose name may not be a household word. The designers of the ad, having captured the attention of the reader with the image and the quote, go on in the smaller text to build on the foundation they have established.

Like most ads, this one is a claim of policy asking the audience to buy a product. In this case the product is Encompass Insurance. One of the frustrations of dealing with an insurance company is that not every possible type of loss is covered by the standard policy. Unfortunately, the homeowner often does not find this out until the damage has already been done. The ad is designed to sell the company's *Elite* policy, which "covers many of life's unexpected perils," unlike most insurance companies, which "only cover things that are specifically listed in your policy." The text continues, "It covers pretty much everything that befalls your household, even if something like 'damage caused by child chopping down cherry tree' isn't specifically listed." Two examples of the sorts of damage that the company might cover are Worker's Compensation for an employee in your household and the recovery of lost computer data.

The support for the claim is not specific. The writer carefully avoided absolute statements, using instead such qualifiers as *many, pretty much*, and *most everything*. The last two are colloquial expressions that are designed to suggest that those who work for Encompass are simple folks with whom the average reader could identify. And if you want any more specifics about what the policy actually says—after all, the legal document that is an insurance policy can hardly use such qualifiers—you can call toll-free or visit the company's Web site.

The underlying warrant is that it is better to buy an insurance policy that covers you against damages that are not specifically listed on the policy than one that does not. A person in the market for insurance would certainly want to read the fine print and know the cost of the insurance compared to that offered by other companies before accepting the warrant and thus the claim.

The colloquial language and even the name of the policy—The Encompass Universal Security Policy—Elite—are designed to appeal to the reader's need to feel secure. The word choice also adds a subtle humor, from the cartoonlike "Oops!" to the final echo of the Pledge of Allegiance: "Liberty, Justice, and Really Good Insurance."

Assignments for Critical Reading

READING AND DISCUSSION QUESTIONS

1. Listen to a recording of Martin Luther King Jr.'s "I Have a Dream" and discuss how the language of the speech adds power to the ideas.

2. Watch (and *listen to*) one of the afternoon television talk shows in which guests discuss a controversial social problem. (The *TV Guide*, daily newspapers, and online listings often list the subject. Past topics include when parents abduct their children, when children kill children, and when surgery changes patients' lives.) Analyze the discussion, considering the major claims, the most important evidence, and the declared or hidden warrants. How much did the oral format contribute to success or failure of the arguments?

3. Watch one episode of either the *Daily Show with Jon Stewart* or the *Colbert Report* and discuss how the show, successfully or not, tries to use humor to make serious points about political and/or social issues.

4. Steven Johnson, author of *The Ghost Map* (2006), writes, "It has become a cliché to say that we now live in a society where image is valued over substance, where our desires are continually stoked by the illusory fuel of marketing messages." Do you believe that we live in the society Johnson describes? Explain.

5. Locate an advertisement that you find visually and verbally interesting. Using as a model the analysis of the ad for Encompass Insurance (p. 71), what sorts of observations can you make about your ad? Exchange ads with a classmate and discuss whether the two of you respond in the same way to each ad.

6. Find two articles on opposing sides of a controversial issue such as abortion, gay marriage, or off-shore drilling. Determine what common ground the two authors share. Then share paired articles with classmates and discuss other examples of common ground.

WRITING SUGGESTIONS

7. Write an essay analyzing "Sex and the Cinema" (p. 43). You may choose to support an evaluative claim that analyzes how effective the essay is or one that objectively analyzes how the essay is written.

8. Write an essay evaluating "The Gay Option" (p. 57).

9. Do you agree with Alfie Kohn in "No-Win Situations" (p. 51) that games and sports should not be so competitive? Write an essay explaining why or why not.

10. Choose an editorial from your school newspaper or a local newspaper and write an evaluation of it.

11. Watch one of the television talk shows that features experts on social and political issues, such as the *The O'Reilly Factor, Hannity and Colmes,* or *The McLaughlin Group.* Write a review, telling how much you learned about the subject(s) of discussion. Be specific about the features of the show that were either helpful or not helpful to your understanding.

12. Choose an advertisement, taking into consideration both the visual and the verbal. Turn your observation into the thesis of an essay explaining the ad's argument.

13. Find a picture that you believe makes a political statement and write an analysis, making clear what you believe that statement is.

14. Find two pictures that present either complementary or conflicting arguments. Write an essay explaining the arguments.

15. Write an essay explaining what visual images represent your school and why.

Research Readiness: Skimming and Summarizing

What if you find good sources of information about your research subject, but there is just too much to read and take notes on?

One possibility, of course, is that your subject is too broad, something that you may need to discuss with your instructor. Even if your topic is appropriate for the length of paper you have been assigned, you may find texts that are too long to read in their entirety, and you may want to skim them to find material relevant to your topic. That is a legitimate research technique as long as you do not distort ideas by taking them out of context.

If you are not careful, you can spend too much time taking notes that you will not use. Unless the wording of an idea is particularly striking or significant, you can often summarize an author's ideas while taking notes. It should be very clear in your notes which information is in the author's exact words and which is paraphrase or summary.

In this chapter you have practiced summarizing. Now practice skimming to find relevant information by doing one or more of the following. Do not use any direct quotations (a skill you will learn more about in the next chapter).

ASSIGNMENT

1. Read Barbara Spellman's "Could Reality Shows Become Reality Experiments?" (p. 114). Write a paragraph explaining why Spellman suggests that some reality television shows would be considered unethical if they were run as experiments in psychology.

2. Write a paragraph summarizing Newman P. Birk and Genevieve B. Birk's thoughts in "Selection, Slanting, and Charged Language" (p. 347) about the variety of ways that language is selected and slanted and why word choice is so important.

3. Write a paragraph based on Jacob Neusner's "The Speech The Graduates Didn't Hear" (p. 374) that explains Neusner's position on how well — or poorly — college prepares students for the outside world.

4. Explain in a paragraph or two what Martin Luther King Jr. meant in his speech, "I Have A Dream" (p. 492).

CHAPTER 3

Analytical Writing

Anytime the press cover a major speech, whether by the president, the chairman of the Federal Reserve, or the accused party in the most recent sex scandal, their next step is an analysis of every detail of the speaker's words and manner. People not only like to listen to arguments but they also like to argue about them. Political pundit Bill O'Reilly even has an analyst come in regularly to critique the body language of political and media headliners.

An understanding of the elements of argument provides you not only with the ability to write your own arguments but also with the vocabulary to write about those of others. When you write an essay about an argument that you have read, listened to, or seen, you have two major options. You may choose to make a factual, nonjudgmental statement about the argument, or you may choose to evaluate it.

Writing the Claim

If you examined the most recent McDonald's commercial and wrote an essay explaining what tactics were used to try to persuade consumers to eat at McDonald's or to try McDonald's newest sandwich, you would be supporting a *factual claim*, or a claim of fact. On the other hand, if you evaluated the ad's effectiveness in attracting adult consumers, you would be supporting an *evaluative claim*, or a claim of value. It's the difference between *explaining* Geico's use of a talking gecko in its ads and *praising* that marketing decision. What this means, of course, is that what you write about a commercial or any other type of argument that you see or read will itself have a claim of fact or a claim of value as its thesis.

What about a *claim of policy*, the third type of claim introduced in Chapter 1? In analyzing an argument, it would be rare to have a thesis that expressed what should or should not be done. Claims of policy are future oriented. They do not look back and express what should have been done in the past, but instead look forward to what should be done in the future. You might write an essay about what McDonald's should do in its future ads, but you would not really be writing an analysis.

Think how claims of fact and claims of value might serve as thesis statements for essays *about* written arguments. Charles Adams's essay "Lincoln's Logic" is a criticism of Abraham Lincoln's Gettysburg Address and thus supports a claim of value:

> Lincoln's address did not fit the world of his day. It reflected his logic, which was based on a number of errors and falsehoods.

An objective analysis of the speech, based on a claim of fact, might explain the oration in the context of its time or Lincoln's use of poetic language.

Consider how your thesis would look different if you were making a *statement* about a document instead of making a *judgment*:

Claims of Fact:	The Declaration of Independence bases its claim on two kinds of support: factual evidence and appeals to the values of its audience.
	As a logical pattern of argument, the Declaration of Independence is largely deductive.
Claims of Value:	Jefferson's clear, elegant, formal prose remains a masterpiece of English prose and persuades us that we are reading an important document.
	The document's impact is lessened for modern readers because several significant terms are not defined.

What type of thesis does Roger Kaplan support in the following analysis?

Enabling Ignorance

ROGER KAPLAN

B arack Obama's version of the "No Child Left Behind Act" (NCLB) easily made it through Congress this year. Originally passed at the instigation of George W. Bush in 2002, NCLB shows what happens when "expertise" and political huckstering replace common sense and experience. Fortunately, Diane Ravitch has

---

Roger Kaplan was a high school English teacher in New York City and is now a writer in Washington, D.C. He is a contributor to the *American Spectator*, where this article appeared in September 2010.

published a new book showing why the ideas driving NCLB promote the weaknesses in American public schools without doing anything for their strengths. *The Death and Life of the Great American School System* stands as a cautionary tale on the delusion that something as complex as education can be reformed with quick fixes and federal dollars.

The declining quality of instruction in American public schools became a perennial political issue in 1983 when the Reagan administration issued its "Nation at Risk" report, which called attention to the declining standards and the steady erosion of meaningful, content-rich curricula in many if not most districts.

Ravitch, a Columbia PhD who had earned widespread admiration as a critical historian of American public education, became a prolific leader of the reform movement. She insisted that without attention to the substance of what is taught in schools — the curriculum — change under any name is mere cosmetics.

Ravitch shows that, just when it thought it had reached its goals with the passage of NCLB, the reform movement was subverted by the throw-money-at-it artists in the political and policy-making classes, encouraged by all manner of snake-oil salesmen who saw the get-rich opportunities of school reform (and, for the pinheads, of writing about reform without understanding the public schools' complex social conditions). Instead of restoring guts to education, NCLB, in effect, gutted instruction. At the center of the racket: "testing."

Tests have inherent pedagogical functions beyond their usefulness in assessing students' learning. But in the NCLB scheme, testing became the link to everything — most ruinously, federal money. Districts and schools raised test scores or lost money and eventually were shut down. By corollary, principals and teachers got merit pay, or pending that, strongly favorable evaluations, according to their kids' test performance. Never had corruption been introduced so brazenly into American schools. 5

Since the easiest actors to blame for failure in this shoddy program were the teachers, they and their unions were turned into the culprits of America's educational shortcomings. Neither the administrators, who usually knew nothing about anything; nor the politicians, like New York City's Mayor Bloomberg, who were thinking only in terms of administrative efficiency; nor the chancellors, like New York's Joel Klein or Washington, D.C.'s Michelle Rhee, who were thinking only in terms of meaningless test numbers: none could conceive of anything more intelligent than to tell teachers they were not doing their jobs properly. This resonated with one of the stupider slogans of the NCLB era, which was that "the kids" deserved "excellent teachers." What were they supposed to have — mediocre teachers?

On the other hand, NCLB diminished accountability at the leadership level. While embroiled in disputes with the teachers' union on how to introduce merit pay — a dubious idea — into the school system, it became evident that Ms. Rhee either did not understand or chose to fudge her own budget numbers, and this in a relatively small school system (by big-city standards). Nor has anyone in the D.C. school system ever explained how one of the two or three richest districts in the country, if you count the amount of money nominally available per pupil, is one of the most run-down and under-achieving.

"Not my job" is the usual response of employees of the education industry, most of whom are not teachers, when confronted with their own failure. Teachers, who tend to be sweet souls even if prone to *kvetching*, are not finger-pointers by nature, and they take responsibility for what goes on in their classrooms. But what they often tell you is that they are required (by stuffed shirts who are never in classrooms) to concentrate on teaching kids "how to learn."

You cannot, however, teach kids "how to learn" if you do not give them *learning* — facts, substance: what the education writer E. D. Hirsch Jr. calls a content-rich curriculum. History, complete with dates, events, and heroes; math, complete with formulae, equations, and systems of computation; foreign languages, complete with vocabulary drills and verb declensions; music, complete with scales and sheet music; physical education, complete with fitness drills and sports rules — all this has been replaced by "learning to learn" and math-problem and reading-comprehension "strategies." And Hirsch, whose devastating critiques of these trends are supported not only by common sense but by hard science (and by visible results), is viewed as a marginal crank by an education establishment that blocks any real reform by invoking "kids first" slogans the same way the Communists used to invoke the "working class."

Teachers know content must come first, but are advised to stop wasting time   10
transmitting knowledge when they should be showing kids how to think for themselves and ace a test. When a teacher observes that you cannot think for yourself if you have nothing to think about, the principal, superintendent, school counselor, or Department of Education specialist responds that this represents an example of "teacher-centered" learning, sort of like being called a Trotskyist in Stalin's Moscow,[1] and insists students working in small groups can educate themselves.

Undermining teachers' authority in the classroom erodes the democratic and egalitarian premises of public education, since it undercuts the opportunity schools are supposed to provide.

Arguably Ravitch should have explored this theme more deeply, by examining the specific flaw that renders the educational establishment incapable of defending the public service role of public schools. The establishment includes the teachers' unions, whose disputes with district leaderships all too often look like shadow boxing. That unions invariably support liberal Democratic candidates at every election strengthens the sense that they are committed to a status quo amounting to a kind of plantation system for poor and disadvantaged children. Nobody can object to a labor union trying to get better pay and benefits for its members, just as no one should object to criticizing a union for undermining its own industry's economic viability or public credibility.

Of course, one should never ask an author to write the book she did not set out to write, but *The Death and Life of the Great American School System* leaves the

[1]Leon Trotsky (1879–1940) was a leader of the Russian Revolution of 1917. He opposed the rise of Joseph Stalin (1879–1953), longtime dictator of the Soviet Union, whose brutal policies led to the extermination of millions of Russians. [EDS. note]

impression that the kind of teachers' union Ravitch pines after has its source in her one, untypical indulgence in historical romanticism, which in turn grows out of the author's admiration for the late Albert Shanker and his successors at the American Federation of Teachers, Sandy Feldman and Randi Weingarten. These are exceptional figures in American education and in American labor history. Too many education union leaders talk the talk of serious reform, then walk the walk of the failed and failing policies Ravitch criticizes so eloquently.

Ravitch passionately lays out the argument that public school teachers are, or should be, missionaries of social advancement and opportunity. They fulfill their role by imbuing children and adolescents with love of learning — a corny idea, maybe, but not a cynical one. They do this not by teaching them "how to learn," but by giving them real knowledge. Teachers must be counselors, pastors, coaches, and community leaders, but knowing and loving what they teach comes first.

The simplicity of this idea is deceptive. Of course, the layman thinks, a teacher   15
has to know his stuff and love it. But the reform movement, as it was hijacked in the '90s and implemented in the '00s under the guise of NCLB, does not know this. By its lights, an excellent teacher is one who raises scores on tests designed to assess not knowledge learned but "skills" in fill-the-bubble exercises that require the same level of talent as choosing lottery numbers. It is only partly whimsical to observe that state-sponsored lotteries became widespread in our nation around the same time as public schools became driven by bubble-tests rather than curricular content.

It is small consolation to observe that the cynicism and corruption introduced by NCLB's testing requirements — which include lowering the bar on tests and laundering their results — reflect a larger rot in American society. It is unfortunate the teachers' unions have not denounced this trend, but they cannot if they trade professional integrity for the American mania for "getting yours." However, pursuing this question would take us beyond the scope that Ravitch wants to cover in *The Death and Life of the Great American School System.*

One of Ravitch's most sensible and profound prescriptions is to know our own history. It comes as no surprise to see how little American history the "experts" know or care for, even as they happily go about burning billions in tax dollars to inflict further damage on our public schools.

Schools are not businesses but civic and neighborhood institutions, and pedagogy is not a how-to-succeed program, but the hard, incremental, frustrating, and exhilarating work of turning savages into civilized citizens. It is not rocket science, but it is a vocation.

The teachers represented by the UFT, the New York teachers' union, know this. So does the author of *The Death and Life of the Great American School System.*

In Kaplan's essay and in the earlier examples based on the Gettysburg Address and the Declaration of Independence, we were looking at one document at a time and thus at a single argument. At times you will want to compare two (or more) arguments, synthesizing their ideas. Again, there are two basic types of thesis that you might choose to support, those that *objectively analyze* the points of comparison or contrast between the two and those that *evaluate* the two in relationship to each other. If you wrote claims about how the two pieces compare, they might look like these:

Claims of Fact: Where Jefferson based his argument primarily on logical appeal, Lincoln depended primarily on emotional appeal.

Because Lincoln's purpose was to dedicate a cemetery, he left implicit most of his references to the political situation that was on the minds of his listeners. Because Jefferson knew he was justifying rebellion for King George III but also for the future, he spelled out explicitly why the colonies were breaking with England.

Claims of Value: Lincoln's address is a period piece that recalls a dark chapter in American history, but Jefferson's Declaration has had a much greater impact as an inspiration for other reform movements worldwide.

Different as the two historical documents are, both the Gettysburg Address and the Declaration of Independence were effective in achieving their respective purposes.

Planning the Structure

When your purpose in writing about an argument is to support a factual claim, you will most likely use a very simple and direct form of organization called *defending the main idea*. In all forms of organization, you need to defend your main idea, or claim, with support; in this case, the support will come from the argument or arguments you are writing about.

At times, your claim may set up the organization of your essay, as was the case with the first example about the Declaration of Independence:

The Declaration of Independence bases its claim on two kinds of support: factual evidence and appeals to the values of its audience.

The body of an essay with this thesis would most likely have two main divisions, one about factual evidence, providing examples, and the other about appeals to values, also providing examples. The other thesis about the Declaration of Independence does not suggest such an obvious structure. An essay based on that thesis would need to explain how the Declaration is an example of deductive reasoning, most likely by first establishing what generalization the document is based on and then what specifics Jefferson uses to prove that the colonists' situation fits that generalization.

Remember that when you compare or contrast two arguments, there will be two basic patterns to choose from for structuring the essay. One, often called *point-by-point* comparison, discusses each point about Subject A and Subject B together before moving on to the second point, where again both subjects are discussed:

    I. Introduction
   II. Context
      A. Jefferson
      B. Lincoln
 III. Implicitness/explicitness
      A. Jefferson
      B. Lincoln
 IV. Language
      A. Jefferson
      B. Lincoln
   V. Conclusion

The second, often called *parallel order* comparison, focuses in roughly half the essay on Subject A and then in the other half on Subject B. The points made in each half should be parallel and should be presented in the same order:

    I. Introduction
   II. Jefferson
      A. Context
      B. Implicitness/explicitness of references to politics
      C. Language
 III. Lincoln
      A. Context
      B. Implicitness/explicitness of references to politics
      C. Language
 IV. Conclusion

Using Sentence Forms to Construct an Argument

When you present an argument that responds to an essay or that uses research, it is important to clearly explain how the previous writer approached the topic, and then explain how your view differs. There's no point in quoting or paraphrasing an author and ending with "and I agree." Indeed, academic writing means explaining current thinking on a topic and showing how it is different from what you believe. Sometimes the points of difference are large, sometimes small. But in writing for college, it is crucial that you explain your own understanding of a situation *and* that you express your own point of view.

It is easier to think about how you might summarize the argument of others and present your own if you have a model from which to work. This kind of model is called a *sentence form*, and it can help you to organize the presentation of others' views and your own responses to them. Here are some basic sentence forms for this kind of work.

PRESENTING ANOTHER'S VIEW

In _____, X claims that _____.

X's conclusion is that _____.

On the topic of _____, X attempts to make the case that
_____.

These sentence forms are useful for presenting a brief summary of another's views on an issue. Note that the final sentence form implies that the writer has failed to make a convincing argument. (You would then go on to explain X's failure.)

PRESENTING ANOTHER'S VIEW USING DIRECT QUOTATIONS

In _____, X writes, "_____."

After discussing the topic of _____, X's conclusion is that
"_____."

X attempts to make the case that "_____."

Quotations are a powerful way to present another's views when the language is particularly striking, clear, and succinct. (For more on using quotations, including a list of alternatives to the verb "writes," see the Writer's Guide: "Incorporating Quotations into Your Text" on p. 88.) These templates help you to employ a key skill in making an argument: showing the work others have done on the issue. The next step is to introduce your own voice.

PRESENTING ANOTHER'S VIEW AND RESPONDING TO IT

She claims _____. It is actually true that _____.

In his essay _____, X writes that _____.
However, _____.

In her essay, X implies _____. However, careful consideration shows
that _____.

The formula for this kind of template introduces what the author has to say and then has you take your turn with your own view of the matter.

As this suggests, writing in college means taking part in an ongoing conversation. You need to be respectful of what others say and write, and you need to account for their positions accurately. You'll want to be sure to clearly summarize the author's presentation. We have more to say about summary shortly, but, briefly put, in writing arguments, you must show the author's point before you explain how your ideas differ. You'll need to be able to sum up in a neutral, fair way what the writer says. Then, when you respond, you can agree on some points, but you'll need to focus on the points of disagreement.

Where you agree with some of what a writer says, but not all of it, you must distinguish between the parts you think are correct and those parts that are not. Sentence forms for this kind of response include the following.

AGREEING IN PART

Although most of what X writes about _____ is true, it is not true that _____.

X is correct that _____. But because of _____ it is actually true that _____.

X argues that _____. While it is true that _____ and _____ are valid points, _____ is not. Instead, _____.

These sentence templates ask you to identify those parts of the argument that are valid. Keep in mind that it is rare to disagree totally with every view expressed in an essay. A careful arguer will separate out what is correct and what is not. The writer can then focus energy on showing why these parts are not correct.

At times you'll need to correct a distortion or misstatement of fact. Statistics, for instance, can be and often are manipulated to present the arguer's viewpoint in the best light. You may wish to propose an alternative interpretation or set the statistics in a different context, one more accurate and favorable to your own point of view. Of course, you'll want to be certain that you do not distort statistics. (For more on the importance of using statistics fairly, see the full discussion on pp. 212–13.) Here's a sentence form for correcting factual information in an argument.

CORRECTING A FACTUAL MISTAKE

While X claims _____, it is actually true that _____.

Although X states _____, a careful examination of _____ and _____ indicate that _____.

These templates allow you to identify a mistaken claim of fact in an argument and present evidence opposing it.

More often, rather than correcting clear mistakes of fact, you'll need to refine the argument of a writer. You may find that much of the argument makes
sense to you, but that the writer does not sufficiently anticipate important objections. In those cases, a sentence form such as one of the following can help
you refine the argument to make a stronger conclusion.

REFINING ANOTHER'S ARGUMENT

Although it is true, as X shows, that _____, the actual result is
closer to _____ because _____.

While X claims _____ and _____, he fails to consider
the important point _____. Therefore, a more accurate conclusion
is _____.

Such sentence forms allow you to clarify and amplify an argument.

At times you'll need to distinguish between the views of two different writers and then weigh in with your own assessment of the situation. When two
authors write on the same topic, they will most likely share similar views on
some of the points. They will, however, disagree on other points. Similarly, you
may find that you agree with some of what each writer has to say, but disagree
with some other parts. Your job is to identify the points of contrast between the
two authors and then explain how your own position differs from one or both.
In those cases, you may find the following sentence forms helpful.

EXPLAINING CONTRASTING VIEWS AND ADDING YOUR POSITION

X says _____. Y says _____. However,_____.

On the topic of _____, X claims that _____.
In contrast, Y argues that _____. However, _____.

A careful writer makes sure the reader understands fine distinctions. The forms
above help make those distinctions clear.

While sentence forms may be rather simple — perhaps even simplistic —
good writers use them all the time. Once you have tried them out a few times,
you'll begin to use them automatically, perhaps without even realizing it. They
are powerful tools for incorporating others' views into your own work and then
helping you to make careful distinctions about various parts of arguments.

Providing Support

In writing about any argument, you will need to understand the argument and
to make it clear to your readers that you do. You cannot write a clear explanation or a fair evaluation if you do not have a clear understanding of your subject.

You will need to look closely at the piece to recall what specific words or ideas led you to the thesis statement that you have chosen to support.

Your support for your thesis will come from the text or texts you are writing about in the form of summary, paraphrase, or quotations. The ability to summarize, paraphrase, and quote material from your source is necessary in writing about arguments, but it is also essential in writing your own arguments, especially those that require research.

Summarizing

A summary involves shortening the original passage as well as putting it into your own words. It gives the gist of the passage, including the important points, while leaving out details. What makes summarizing difficult is that it requires you to capture often long and complex texts in just a few lines or a short paragraph. To summarize well, you need to imagine yourself as the author of the piece you are summarizing and be true to the ideas the author is expressing, even when those ideas conflict with your point of view. You must then move smoothly from being a careful reader to being a writer who, in your own words, recreates another's thoughts.

We summarize for many reasons: to let our boss know the basics of what we have been doing or to tell a friend why she should or should not see a movie. In your classes you are often asked to summarize articles or books, and even when this is not an explicit part of an assignment, the ability to summarize is usually expected. That is, when you are instructed to analyze an essay or to compare and contrast two novels, central to this work is the ability to carefully comprehend and recreate authors' ideas. See pages 48–50 in Chapter 2 for a more detailed treatment of summarizing.

Paraphrasing

Paraphrasing involves restating the content of an original source in your own words. It differs from summarizing in that a paraphrase is roughly the same length as the passage it paraphrases instead of a condensation of a longer passage. You will use paraphrasing when you want to capture the idea but there is nothing about the wording that makes repeating it necessary. You may also use it when the idea can be made clearer by rephrasing it or when the style is markedly different from your own. Here is an example drawn from a student paper:

> Randolph Warren, a victim of the thalidomide disaster himself and founder and executive director of the Thalidomide Victims Association of Canada, reports that it is estimated 10,000 to 12,000 deformed babies were born to mothers who took thalidomide. (40)

There is no single sentence on page 40 of the Warren article that both provides the estimate of number of affected babies and identifies Warren as one of them. Both the ideas were important, but neither of them was worded in such a unique way that a direct quote was needed. Therefore, a paraphrase was the logical choice. In this case, the writer correctly documents the paraphrase using Modern Language Association (MLA) style.

Quoting

You may want to quote passages or phrases from your sources if they express an idea in words more effective than your own. In reading a source, you may come across a statement that provides succinct, irrefutable evidence for an issue you wish to support. If the author of this statement is a professional in his or her field, someone with a great deal of authority on the subject, it would be appropriate to quote that author. A student research paper in Chapter 11 is Angela Mathers' about women in combat. Suppose, during the course of Angela's research for her paper, she found several sources that agree that women in the military who are denied combat experience are, as a result, essentially being denied a chance at promotion to the highest ranks. Others argue that such considerations should not be a deciding factor in assigning women to combat. To represent the latter of these two positions, Angela chose to use a quotation from an authority in the field, using APA style:

> Elaine Donnelly, president of the Center for Military Readiness, says, "Equal opportunity is important, but the armed forces exist to defend the country. If there is a conflict between career opportunities and military necessity, the needs of the military must come first" (as qtd. in "Women in the Military," 2000).

It is especially important in argumentative writing to establish a source's authority on the subject under discussion. The most common way of doing this is to use that person's name and position of authority to introduce the quotation, as in the previous example. It is correct in both MLA and APA styles to provide the author's name in parentheses at the end of the quoted material, but that type of documentation precludes lending to the quote the weight of its having come from an authority. It is likely that those readers not in the military — and even some who are — will not know who Donnelly is just by seeing her name in parentheses. Your writing will always have more power if you establish the authority of each author from whose work you quote, paraphrase, or summarize. To establish authority, you may refer to the person's position, institutional affiliation, publications, or some other similar "claim to fame."

Another example, also using APA style:

> According to the late Ulysses S. Seal III (1982), founder of the Conservation Breeding Specialist Group and of a "computer dating service" for mateless animals, "None of these [zoo] budgets is allocated specifically for species preservation. Zoos have been established primarily as recreational institutions and are only secondarily programs in conservation, education, and research" (p. 74).

Notice that once the name of the author being cited has been mentioned in the writer's own text, it does not have to be repeated in the parentheses.

Writer's Guide: Incorporating Quotations into Your Text

There are three primary means of linking a supporting quotation to your own text. Remember that in each case, the full citation for the source will be listed alphabetically by the author's name in the list of works cited at the end of the paper, or by title if no author is given. The number in parentheses is the page of that source on which the quotation appears. The details of what appears in parentheses will be covered later in the discussion of APA (American Psychological Association) and MLA (Modern Language Association) documentation styles.

- You may choose to make a brief quotation a grammatical part of your own sentence. In that case, you do not separate the quotation from your sentence with a comma, unless there is another reason for the comma, and you do not capitalize the first word of the quotation, unless there is another reason for doing so. In this sort of situation, there may be times when you have to change the tense of a verb, in brackets, to make the quotation fit smoothly into your text or when you need to make other small changes, always in brackets.

    Examples:

    APA style

    James Rachels (1976), University Professor of Philosophy at the University of Alabama at Birmingham and author of several books on moral philosophy, explains that animals' right to liberty derives from "a more basic right not to have one's interests needlessly harmed" (p. 210).

    MLA style

    James Rachels, University Professor of Philosophy at the University of Alabama at Birmingham and author of several books on moral philosophy, explains that animals' right to liberty derives from "a more basic right not to have one's interests needlessly harmed" (210).

- You may use a traditional speech tag such as "he says" or "she writes." This is the most common way of introducing a quotation. Be sure to put a comma after the tag and to begin the quotation with a capital letter. At the end of the quotation, close the quotation, add the page number and any other necessary information in parentheses, and then add the period.

    Examples:

    APA style

    James Rachels (1976), University Professor of Philosophy at the University of Alabama at Birmingham and author of several books on moral philosophy, writes, "The right to liberty — the right to be free of external constraints on one's actions — may then be seen as derived from a more basic right not to have one's interests needlessly harmed" (p. 210).

MLA style

James Rachels, University Professor of Philosophy at the University of Alabama at Birmingham and author of several books on moral philosophy, writes, "The right to liberty — the right to be free of external constraints on one's actions — may then be seen as derived from a more basic right not to have one's interests needlessly harmed" (210).

Students are sometimes at a loss as to what sorts of verbs to use in these tag statements. Try using different terms from this list or others like them. Remember that in writing about a printed or electronic text, it is customary to write in present tense unless there is a compelling reason to use past tense.

argues	continues	implores	replies
asks	counters	insists	responds
asserts	declares	proclaims	states
concludes	explains	questions	suggests

- You may vary the way you introduce quotations by at times using a colon to separate the quotation from a *complete sentence* that introduces it.

Examples:

APA style

For example, the Zurich Zoo's Dr. Heini Hediger (1985) protests that it is absurd to attribute human qualities to animals at all, but he nevertheless resorts to a human analogy: "Wild animals in the zoo rather resemble estate owners. Far from desiring to escape and regain their freedom, they are only bent on defending the space they inhabit and keeping it safe from invasion" (p. 9).

MLA style

The late Ulysses S. Seal III, founder of the Conservation Breeding Specialist Group and of a "computer dating service" for mateless animals, acknowledges the subordinate position species preservation plays in budgeting decisions: "Zoos have been established primarily as recreational institutions and are only secondarily developing programs in conservation, education, and research" (74).

PRACTICE

Write a summary of Alan Dershowitz's "Is There a Torturous Road to Justice?" (p. 110) using either the rhetorical method, which explains what the author is doing in the piece, or using the referential method, which focuses instead on the ideas. Be sure to remain objective. Include at least one direct quotation in your summary. Identify the author and the title in your first sentence and provide in parentheses the page number for the quotation(s).

Documenting Your Sources

Chapter 11 will provide additional information about documenting sources, but you should start now documenting your use of others' work, even when the only sources you use are essays from this textbook. The single most important thing to remember is why you need to inform your reader about your use of sources. Once it is clear from your writing that an idea or some language came from a source and thus is not your own original thought or language, full documentation provides the reader with a means of identifying and, if necessary, locating your source. If you do not indicate your source, your reader will naturally assume that the ideas and the language are yours. It is careless to forget to give credit to your sources. It is dishonest to intentionally take credit for what is not your own intellectual property. Note, though, that the convention is for authors of magazine articles not to provide page numbers for their sources in the way that you will be expected to do.

The following Writer's Guide provides the general guidelines for documenting your use of sources.

Writer's Guide: Documenting Use of Summary, Paraphrase, and Quotation

1. One of the most common mistakes that student writers make is to think that material needs to be documented only if they use another author's words. In fact, you must give credit for *any ideas* you get from others, not only for wording you get from them.

2. You must identify the author and the location of ideas that you summarize. A *summary* is the condensing of a longer passage into a shorter one, using your own words. You will use summary often in your academic writing when you want to report briefly on an idea covered at greater length in your source.

3. You must identify the author and the location of ideas that you paraphrase. A *paraphrase* is a rewording of another author's idea into your own words. A paraphrased passage is roughly the same length as the original.

4. You must identify the author and the location of language that you quote. A *quotation* is the copying of the exact wording of your source and is placed in quotation marks. Remember that *exact* means just that. You cannot change anything inside quotation marks, with these exceptions: (a) If there is a portion of the quotation that is not relevant to the point that you are making and *that can be omitted without distorting the author's meaning*, you may indicate an omission of a portion of the quotation with an ellipsis (. . .). If there is a sentence break within the portion you are omitting, add a fourth period to the ellipsis to so indicate. (b) If you need to make a very slight change in the quote to make the quote

fit grammatically into your own text or to avoid confusion and if the change does not distort the author's meaning, you may make that slight change and place the changed portion in square brackets ([ ]). This method is used primarily to change the tense of a quoted passage to match that of your text or to identify a person identified in the quotation only by a pronoun.

5. Both the MLA and the APA systems make use of in-text or parenthetical documentation. That means that while a complete bibliographical listing for each work summarized, paraphrased, or quoted in your text is included in a Works Cited or References list at the end of your paper, each is also identified exactly at the point in the text where you use the source. If you are using the MLA system of documentation, the system most commonly used in the humanities, immediately following the sentence in which you use material from a source, you need to add in parentheses the author's name and the page number on which the material you are using appeared in the original source. However, since the credibility of your sources is critical in argumentative writing, it is even better to name the source in your own sentence and to identify the position or experience that makes that person a reliable source for the subject being discussed. In that case, you do not need to repeat the author's name in the parentheses. In fact, any time the author's name is clear from the context, you do not need to repeat it in the parentheses.

Acceptable: The mall has been called "a common experience for the majority of American youth" (Kowinski 3).

Better: According to William Severini Kowinski, author of *The Malling of America*, "The mall is a common experience for the majority of American youth" (3).

In the APA system, the system most commonly use in the social sciences, in-text or parenthetical documentation is handled a bit differently because the citation includes the year of publication. The most basic forms are these:

The mall has been called "a common experience for the majority of American youth" (Kowinski, 1985, p. 3).

Kowinski (1985) writes, "The mall is a common experience for the majority of American youth" (p. 3).

6. Remember that these examples show only the most basic forms for documenting your sources. Some works will have more than one author. Sometimes you will be using more than one work by the same author. Usually Web sites do not have page numbers. Long quotations need to be handled differently from short ones. For all questions about documenting your use of sources not covered here, see Chapter 11.

Note: If you are writing about an essay in this book, you have a slightly more complicated situation than if you were looking at the essay in its original place of publication. Unless your instructor indicates otherwise, use the page numbers on which the essay appears in this textbook when summarizing, paraphrasing, or quoting from it instead of going back to the page numbers of the original. Also, unless your instructor indicates otherwise, use this model for listing in your Works Cited page an essay reprinted here:

Quindlen, Anna. "A New Look, an Old Battle." *Newsweek* April 9, 2001: 72–73. Rpt. in *Elements of Argument: A Text and Reader*. Donna Haisty Winchell and Annette T. Rottenberg. 10th ed. Boston: Bedford/St. Martin's, 2011. 333–35.

Avoiding Plagiarism

Plagiarism is the use of someone else's words or ideas without adequate acknowledgment — that is, presenting such words or ideas as your own. Putting something into your own words is not in itself a defense against plagiarism; the source of the ideas must be identified as well. Giving credit to the sources you use serves three important purposes: (1) it reflects your own honesty and seriousness as a researcher; (2) it enables the reader to find the source of the reference and read further, sometimes to verify that the source has been correctly used; and (3) it adds the authority of experts to your argument. Plagiarism is nothing less than cheating, and it is an offense that deserves serious punishment. You can avoid accidentally slipping into plagiarism if you are careful in researching and writing your papers.

Taking care to document sources is an obvious way to avoid plagiarism. You should also be careful in taking notes and, when writing your paper, indicating where your ideas end and someone else's begin. When taking notes, make sure either to quote word for word or to paraphrase — one or the other, not both. If you quote, enclose any language that you borrow from other sources in quotation marks. That way, when you look back at your notes days or weeks later, you won't mistakenly assume that the language is your own. If you know that you aren't going to use a particular writer's exact words, then take the time to summarize that person's ideas right away. That will save you time and trouble later.

When using someone else's ideas in your paper, always let the reader know where that person's ideas begin and end. Here is an example from a student paper that uses APA style:

> When zoo animals do mate successfully, the offspring is often weakened by inbreeding. According to geneticists, this is because a population of 150 breeder animals is necessary in order to "assure the more or less permanent survival of a species in captivity" (Ehrlich & Ehrlich, 1981, p. 211).

The phrase "according to geneticists" indicates that the material to follow comes from another source, cited parenthetically at the end of the borrowed material. If the student had not included the phrase "according to geneticists," it might look as if she only borrowed the passage in quotation marks, and not the information that precedes that passage.

Examining Some Models

Now that you have read about writing an analytical essay, it will help to see some examples. The first pair of essays are an argument about reality television and an analysis of it. The analysis gives you a model of the type of analytical writing that is the focus of this chapter. This particular analytical essay supports a claim of fact.

You'll note that parenthetical documentation is missing from the analysis essay. Normally when the author's name is clear from the context, as it is in this case, all you need to put in the parentheses is the page number. Because the source is an online magazine, there are no page numbers.

SAMPLE ESSAY AND ANALYTICAL RESPONSE Claim of Fact

Reality Check

ERIC JAFFE

See: the world of reality television. The cast members bear little resemblance to your usual television actors (but they also seem quite unlike you and me). In exotic settings and high-stakes competitions, strangers are stranded and banded together, elevated to star status as long as they are willing to do and say things we could never imagine. Video editors whirl through raw footage, past the mundane, in search of incidental lusts or brawls. Promises are bound and broken in a single breath. Triumph is declared over enemies who, moments before, were friends who, days before, were strangers. True love may or may not be found, depending on whether the check is real.

Such is the world that has advertisers flocking, Juilliard graduates panhandling, and psychologists wondering whether life could ever come to imitate this peculiar art.

Eric Jaffe has written on behavioral science issues for the *Los Angeles Times, Smithsonian, Slate, Science News,* and the A[ssociation for] P[sychological] S[cience] *Observer*. This article appeared in the *Observer* in March 2005. Jaffe writes the Headcase blog for *Psychology Today*.

Reality television has been criticized for humiliating its cast members.

Reality television has been vilified as the lowest form of entertainment, a threat to intelligence, and catering to (and rising from) the most prurient of human instincts. As such, the shows would seem to offer a bounty of possible examinations from a behavioral perspective. But until recently, the effects of reality television remained sparsely explored. Bryant Paul, Indiana University, offers two explanations for the dearth of literature. First, reality TV is perpetually changing, making it difficult for researchers to collect and analyze data that remain relevant. The other reason is that some researchers do not think it will last. "It's been around three to five years, which is a blink in the bigger scheme," Paul said. "The novelty is wearing off."

If that is the case, losing popularity has never been so popular. Fifty-one million people tuned in to the first-season finale of *Survivor* in August 2000.[1] In January 2003, reality shows accounted for 85 percent of the most valuable TV advertising space in the United States, according to the Cable News Network. Competing plans for entire reality networks — Reality 24-7 and Fox Reality Channel — are in the works. The craze has even reached the classroom. James Hay, University of Illinois at Urbana-Champagne, recently began teaching a course called The Reality TV Syndrome. "I'm often asked, 'Why would you want to teach in higher education the lowest form of television?'" Hay said. "But it's an important matter in everyday life."

And not all researchers believe the fad is fading. "I don't see any signs that it's going away any time soon," said Brad Waite, Central Connecticut State University, who presented reality television research at the American Psychological Society's 16th Annual Convention. "Something so ubiquitous must have an effect on behavior."

5

Passion for Peeping

Flip back to that first *Survivor* finale. As a frame of reference, 51 million viewers is more than watched the 1983 *M*A*S*H* special — the top Nielson-rated show of all time. (Nielson officially ranks shows by time-share and household percentage, however, so *M*A*S*H* still holds the top spot, and *Survivor* doesn't even crack the top 100.) By watching in such high numbers, viewers told network executives to dump their high-priced writers and lovely actors in favor of identifiable people in familiar conflicts. All we really wanted to see was the same thing we saw in the mirror every morning — ourselves. Only different.

According to Waite, a writers' strike loomed in Hollywood around this time. The airwaves were ripe for inexpensive replacements. After *Survivor*, previously impossible profits became, well, a reality.

"It is not difficult to imagine the difference in cost between a whole series where one person wins $1 million and producing a series of *Friends*, where each cast member earns that much each episode," said James Wiltz, Ohio State University. "One big hit in this genre is worth many attempts."

Network executives thought the same thing. The new strain of television soon spread throughout the viewing community, plagiarizing and mutating into myriad subgenres. But as the number of shows grew, so did the media criticism. A month before the *Survivor* finale, *Time* said we had a passion for peeping and that we enjoyed the suffering, mean-spiritedness, and humiliation endured by others. The *New Statesman* blamed not only reality viewers but also participants for the culture of voyeurism. Nearly a year later, a *Newsweek* headline read: "Another reality show, another IQ point disappears."

It was all the negative publicity that motivated Robin Nabi to conduct some   10
of the earliest research on why people watch. "The press suggested we'd reached an all-time low in taste," said Nabi, a communications professor at University of California, Santa Barbara who takes a social-psychological approach to research. "It's frustrating to see these claims not based on any data. I wanted to know if the claims were reflected in the general public."

Why We Watch

The roots of reality television appear in the 1950s show *Queen for a Day*, in which women in dire circumstances competed for the studio audience's sympathy to win fur coats and appliances. Prior to the end of the twentieth century, most reality television research centered on the show *Cops* which follows law enforcement officers on their daily beats. But unlike newer reality shows, people on *Cops* were not removed from their natural setting, and the research mostly addressed the show's violence. *The Real World*, a pioneer of modern reality TV, has aired since 1992, but for years there were too few shows like it to merit a study.

Researching after the turn of the millennium, it did not take Nabi long to debunk some of the criticism. In her *Media Psychology* report, "Reality-Based Television Programming and the Psychology of Its Appeal,"[2] Nabi found the notion of reality watchers as voyeurs questionable at best.

"The idea of voyeurism didn't bear itself out in the data. Viewers wanted to watch other people, but not to see something the characters didn't want them to see," Nabi said, noting that voyeuristic pleasure is undermined when the subject knows he or she is being watched. Besides, said Nabi, viewers are well aware that illicit activity is certain to be censored even if it occurs.

A year later, Ohio State University psychologist Steven Reiss confirmed the absence of voyeurism, though what he found instead was debatably worse. He and collaborator James Wiltz based their research on Reiss's sensitivity theory, which says that most complex human motives can be reduced to 16 basic desires. Each time a desire is realized, a related joy is experienced. Though the motives are universal, they are individually prioritized to reflect our unique comportments, our personal Desire Profiles. Reiss has used these profiles to accurately predict spirituality, underachievement, teamwork — even organ donation.

According to Reiss, media events repeatedly allow people to experience the   15
16 desires and joys. Drawing on the uses and gratification theory — which suggests that people select media to fulfill certain needs — as well as the sensitivity theory, Reiss predicted that reality viewers would display a collective Desire Profile. Finding any difference from the normal profile would have been intriguing. What he and Wiltz found about the basic needs of reality viewers proved that truth is sometimes scarier than fiction.

Reiss's data showed that the largest significant motive for watching reality television was social status, which leads to the joy of self-importance. Only slightly less strong was the need for vengeance, which leads to vindication. "Some people may watch reality TV partially because they enjoy feeling superior to the people being portrayed," Reiss said. "People with a strong need for vengeance have the potential to enjoy watching people being humiliated."

In a content analysis of the five most popular reality shows and the five top scripted dramas and comedies, Waite and collaborator Sara Booker confirmed that reality shows might reflect a desire for viewing humiliation. Using show raters to code character behaviors, they found that reality shows rated higher in humiliation than scripted dramas. (This even after data from "The Swan" — a reality show on which a homely woman receives a makeover, only to then compete in a beauty pageant — was omitted.)

Humilitainment

Waite and Booker call this phenomenon "humilitainment," the tendency for viewers to be attracted to spectacular mortification. Since their study, similarly indecorous shows have popped up like pockmarks on the genre. *Temptation Island* placed dating couples on opposite ends of an island resort and introduced tempters and temptresses whose main purpose, it seems, was to initiate philandering while wearing as little clothing as possible. Some titles alone are enough to evoke disgust: *I Want a Famous Face, Trading Spouses: Meet Your New Mommy, The Virgin,* and the ever-popular font of humiliation: *Who's Your Daddy?*

Humilitainment has a more graceful and precise cousin — the German word *schadenfreude*, which translates to the pleasure one receives at the suffering of others. Colin Wayne Leach and Russell Spears studied schadenfreude as it related to an even more real type of reality contest — World Cup soccer matches. Looking at soccer fans' reactions to their team's losses and rival team's victories, Leach and Spears found that schadenfreude was the result of threatened inferiority. In the wake of losing a competition, schadenfreude is "a covert form of prejudice that is used in the maintenance of self-worth," the authors wrote in the *Journal of Personality and Social Psychology.*

If reality viewers are in fact tuning in to feel better at another person's expense, Waite predicts a maladaptive future for heavy watchers. "They expect it's OK to humiliate and to be humiliated by others, instead of thinking there's something wrong with this behavior," Waite said. "The world they're living in is different from others." In this world according to Waite, the borders separating on-screen from off-screen blend indistinguishably. It is this seamless convergence of fiction and reality that psychologists fear could have a severe behavioral impact.

20

Real People, Real Problems

Each semester, Bryant Paul demonstrates the power of media to his psychology students. He asks how many of them have been to New York. Half raise their hands. He then asks how many of them perceive New York as a dangerous place. The students draw no connection to the previous response, and nearly all the hands are raised.

The theory Paul sets into action is not a new one. It has been around since the late 1960s, when media psychologist George Gerbner stated that exposure to cultural imagery can shape a viewer's concept of reality. Simply put, the more TV a person watches, the more that person believes in the world of TV. Using his "cultivation theory," Gerbner showed that heavy news viewers believed they resided in a "meaner" world, to the point where they might even approve stricter violence interventions.

"In general, one of the negative things about television is that it gives a distorted image of what the rest of the world is like," said APS Fellow and Charter Member Craig A. Anderson, Iowa State University, who focuses mostly on violent media but sees some overlap with reality shows. "TV changes the perception of what is normative."

Mary Beth Oliver, a communications professor at Pennsylvania State University who researches the psychological effects of media on viewers, also wondered what happens when this mean world is a real world.

"I thought the perceived reality would have a strong impact on viewers' social-reality judgments," said Oliver, who studied *Cops* long before the reality boom. Her analysis of crime shows found that African Americans and Latinos were overwhelmingly cast as criminals and whites as police officers. In addition, police were using aggression frequently, particularly if the criminals were minorities.

25

"Reality television requires viewers to disengage from the suffering of other people or to derive enjoyment from it," Oliver said.

To test how greatly these shows were actually influencing worldviews, Oliver asked regular watchers to estimate the prevalence of crime in the real world.

Startlingly, reality crime watchers gave increased crime estimates, particularly for the amount of black crimes. Yet Oliver's most unsettling realization came from a phone call she received from an officer in charge of training at a Roanoke, Virginia, police department. The man had read her research and was very nervous, because every trainee who wanted to sign up for the force was addicted to these reality crime shows.

"He told me it wasn't just for the enjoyment," Oliver recalled. "That's what they thought policing would really be like."

The blurry line between fiction and reality should come as less of a surprise considering that the godmother of reality television, Mary-Ellis Bunim, was an executive producer for the soap opera *As the World Turns* before creating *The Real World* with partner Jonathan Murray. Bunim's obituary in the December 26, 2004, *New York Times Magazine* said her idea was to "craft soap-opera storylines with actual people."

Fulfilling this idea requires a luxury unavailable to normal reality — heavy   30
editing. *The Apprentice* and *Survivor* each shoot for almost a month and a half, turning 1,000 hours of life into about 15 hours of programming. *The Real World*, reality's longest shoot, tapes for five months before producing two dozen episodes. Many researchers, including Paul, find this manipulation problematic.

"Reality TV is just as real as anything else on TV — it's not," Paul said. "They can create any impression they want. One-eighth of an hour one time a week is all viewers get to construct an opinion about a character."

Douglas Gentile, director of research at the National Institute on Media and the Family and psychology professor at Iowa State University, agreed that reality TV's presentation has a large influence on viewers. "One of the things we know from media violence research is that the more realistic the presentation is, the media violence effect seems to be stronger," Gentile said. "Reality TV is claiming it's real, even though there's a striking lack of resemblance to what's really happening in the world. But the average viewers, who aren't as savvy to know how the shows are being produced, are being told that what they're seeing is true."

In addition to how the shows are marketed, rumors linger that cast members exaggerate their behavior and that producers instigate conflict. According to Booker, the character Toni from *Paradise Hotel* admitted letting her rage get the best of her on camera. The villainy of Omarosa from *The Apprentice* seems nothing more than shrewd self-promotion — she still frequents gossip-columns a year after the show's end. Gentile has a clinical term for the insults and antics that come so naturally to reality characters: relational aggression.

"A lot of reality television is very relationally aggressive," he said, describing the term as *I'm having a party and you're not invited*. "Not only do the characters interact unpleasantly to each other, they also spread rumors. This is a classic example of relational aggression — trying to gang up, enhancing one's own status by bringing others down."

Anderson has seen some evidence that relational aggression does not always   35
stop with words. "Relational aggression frequently escalates into physical aggres-

sion," he said. "Many assaults occur between acquaintances, when name-calling escalates beyond saying nasty things."

Waite fears such consistent, ignominious behavior will lead to a modified re-creation of Gerbner's "mean world."

"Is the world of the heavy viewer of modern reality TV a 'mean world' but in a different sense?" he asked. "Is this 'mean world' one in which embarrassment, disrespect, and degradation are common? This to me is one of the most interesting reasons why we study this type of programming."

Improving Reality

If reality television does persist, psychologists may in time grow to understand more about its allure. Waite and Gentile both said that video game users have been recently hooked up to functional Magnetic Resonance Imaging machines; whether for marketing or empirical purposes, reality viewers might not be far behind. Until then, Waite speculates that younger generations are simply accustomed to being on screen. Digital cameras now come standard with most cell phones, and Web cams televise daily adventures, from the quotidian to the erotic, around the clock. "Expectations of privacy have been eroded," Waite said. "Public disclosure, even of formerly private behaviors and feelings, are the expectation."

This intimacy entitlement might explain why 37 million people tuned in after the "Survivor" finale to watch the reunion. Miles away from the island of Pulau Tiga, plain-clothed cast members discussed their feelings and opinions on the experience. To Reiss, this suggests that these once-regular people now hovered somewhere between the celebrity and pedestrian echelons.

"If you pay attention to ordinary people then you're saying ordinary people are important," he said. "People can watch reality TV shows and see ordinary people like themselves become famous, win cash prizes, and move up in their status." 40

Paul disagrees that a desire to be famous attracts viewers — after all, he says, these people can be famous for you. Rather, the fact that these people were not groomed for celebrity in the traditional sense, that friends of friends invariably went to camp with someone on one of the shows, is the great draw. "The closer someone is to you, the easier it is to empathize," Paul said, "and really good empathy equals really good television."

Nabi stumbled onto this possibility when she found almost as much variety among preference for reality subgenres as she did preference between reality and fiction. In some cases, the very quality that defined one show's enjoyment was anathema to another's — suspense was a draw for reality talent shows, but for a reality crime show it was a major detractor, perhaps because the viewer wondered if the criminal remained at large. To Nabi, this could mean that watching real people, whatever the circumstance, is the real attraction.

"Watching real people on TV is fascinating, just like watching people in the airport is fascinating," she said. "Viewers are interested in people — not pain."

This leads her to think that some of the negativity directed toward reality TV may be unjustified, but it does not solve the riddle of why viewing real people is such an attraction. "Something deeper is happening here that we haven't gotten to."

For the time being, Nabi sees a positive side to viewer malleability and the scientific evidence supporting it. "It is possible that the way producers put their programs together may be influenced by the academic research," she said. In fact, she has already seen an improvement in the way some reality shows depict real events. Previously, "Extreme Makeover" was criticized for making plastic surgery seem beneficial, rapid, and risk-free. In its current season, however, Nabi said the show more clearly depicts the multiple, intensive steps involved in surgical procedures.

An altruistic show even lurks on the horizon — "The Scholar," in which 10 exceptional and financially needy high school seniors from around the country will compete for a full scholarship. "Imagine this concept," wrote Booker at the end of her second study, "using reality television to actually improve reality." Given the genre's impact on behavior, that might not be too unrealistic.

45

The Reiss Profile

In their 2004 report "Why People Watch Reality TV," published in *Media Psychology*, lead authors Steven Reiss and James Wiltz used the Reiss Profile to explain why certain people watched reality television. Validated by responses from over 10,000 people, the Reiss Profile measures how basic motives result in a particular joy. Reality viewers were found to have significantly higher motives for status and vengeance.

MOTIVE	JOY
ACCEPTANCE: Desire for approval	**SELF-CONFIDENCE**
CURIOSITY: Desire for knowledge	**WONDERMENT**
EATING: Desire for food	**SATIATION**
FAMILY: Desire to raise own children	**LOVE**
HONOR: Desire to obey a traditional moral code	**LOYALTY**
IDEALISM: Desire to improve society (including altruism, justice)	**COMPASSION**
INDEPENDENCE: Desire for autonomy	**FREEDOM**
ORDER: Desire to organize (including desire for ritual)	**STABILITY**
PHYSICAL EXERCISE: Desire to exercise muscles	**VITALITY**
ROMANCE: Desire for sex (including courting)	**LUST**
POWER: Desire to influence (including leadership)	**EFFICACY**
SAVING: Desire to collect	**OWNERSHIP**

SOCIAL CONTACT: Desire for peer companionship   **FUN**
             (and desire to play)

STATUS: Desire for prestige   **SELF-IMPORTANCE**
             (including desire for attention)

TRANQUILITY: Desire for inner peace   **SAFE, RELAXED**
             (prudence, safety)

VENGEANCE: Desire to get even (including desire to win)   **VINDICATION**

REFERENCES AND NOTES

Reiss, S., & Wiltz, J. (2004). Why people watch reality TV. *Media Psychology, 6*, 363–378.

1. Nielsen Media Research. (2000). *Report on television.*

2. Nabi, R. L., Biely, E. N., Morgan, S. J., Stitt, C. R. (2003). Reality-based television programming and the psychology of its appeal. 2003. *Media Psychology, 5*, 303–330.

STUDENT ANALYTICAL RESPONSE   Claim of Fact

Psychoanalyzing Reality TV

DEION MOORE

In his article "Reality Check," which appeared on the Association for Psychological Science Web site in March of 2005, behavioral science writer Eric Jaffe looks at the phenomenon that is reality television from the psychologist's perspective. He weaves together the history of reality television, the history of research on reality television, and the various possible answers to the question why we watch it.

Jaffe traces the evolution — or devolution — of reality television to its roots in the 1950s show *Queen for a Day*, which featured ordinary women in competition for prizes, and to *Cops*, which filmed police officers on the job. The real boom began with the first season of *Survivor*, when a writers' strike left the networks looking for cheap replacements for their breadwinners — and they realized how profitable reality shows could be. Jaffe explains how this "new strain of television soon spread throughout the viewing community, plagiarizing and mutating into myriad subgenres." He writes of how "indecorous shows have popped up like pockmarks on the genre." He points to *Temptation Island*, which "placed dating couples on opposite ends of an island resort and introduced tempters and temptresses whose main purpose, it seems, was to initiate philandering while wearing

At the time he wrote this analysis, Deion Moore was a student at Clemson University.

as little clothing as possible," and other shows whose "titles alone are enough to evoke disgust: *I Want a Famous Face, Trading Spouses: Meet Your New Mommy, The Virgin*, and the ever-popular font of humiliation: *Who's Your Daddy?*"

Until this recent proliferation of reality shows, there were not enough on which to do any substantial research. Besides, some psychologists believe they are not worth the trouble anyway since reality television won't be around for long. Jaffe quotes Bryant Paul of Indiana University, who explains, "It's been around three to five years, which is a blink in the bigger scheme. . . . The novelty is wearing off."

Jaffe points out, though, that an increase in the number of studies being done on reality television shows suggests otherwise, as does their continued popularity. He traces some of the research studies that since 2000 have served to debunk common misconceptions about why people tune in and have offered other explanations.

Robin Nabi at the University of California, Santa Barbara, was one of the first   5
to insist on some data to back up all of the negative press the shows were getting. One common criticism has been that watching reality shows is voyeuristic. Nabi's data, however, do not support this hypothesis about why we watch. She writes, "The idea of voyeurism didn't bear itself out in the data. Viewers wanted to watch other people, but not to see something the characters didn't want them to see." There is not much pleasure in voyeurism anyway if the subjects know they are being watched.

Jaffe next introduces the research of Ohio State University psychologist Steven Reiss, who supports Nabi's conclusion that viewers are not primarily voyeurs. He and his collaborator James Wiltz analyzed viewers' motives in terms of the desires the shows fulfilled for them. The two most common motives they discovered were desire for social status and need for vengeance. The first indicates that viewers want to feel superior to the people they are watching, and the second that they "have the potential to enjoy watching people being humiliated." Brad Waite of Central Connecticut State University and his colleague Sara Booker have called this second desire "humilitainment." They go so far as to predict "a maladaptive future for heavy watchers" who enjoy seeing others being mortified. Mary Beth Oliver, a communications professor at Penn State, agrees with their concern: "Reality television requires viewers to disengage from the suffering of other people or to derive enjoyment from it." The amount of relational aggression exhibited is also a concern.

Jaffe also touches on other less ominous reasons viewers tune in: They like to believe that what they are seeing is real, in spite of the heavy editing that goes on behind the scenes (although this also is alarming if their perception of the real world becomes distorted). They like to see people like themselves become famous and win prizes. They like to see people like themselves, but different. He ties the strands of his argument together in the end by quoting Nabi: "It is possible that the way producers put their programs together may be influenced by the academic research." That is, if reality shows are around long enough.

SAMPLE ESSAY AND ANALYTICAL RESPONSE Claim of Value

The next pair of essays are another article about reality television and an analysis of it, this time one supporting a claim of value, or an evaluative claim. Again the source is an online source, so there are no page numbers.

The Meaning of Reality (TV)

NOAM SHPANCER

Channel surfing requires "no commitment or concentration."

I don't watch much TV. When I do, I mostly channel surf. Channel surfing, like ocean wave noise, soothes because it requires no commitment or concentration. It provides a relief from the commitments and concentrations that mark the work day.

Channel surfing has other advantages. While I can't tell you the plot line of any particular show, I know something about the TV landscape as a whole; the color palette; the thematic preoccupations.

I have noticed, for example, that those "reality" shows that pack the TV schedule come in two main formats. One involves people who compete for some prize while showing off a skill

Noam Shpancer is a clinical psychologist and professor of psychology at Otterbein College in Westerville, Ohio. He is also a clinician with the Center for Cognitive and Behavioral Psychology in Columbus, Ohio, where he specializes in the treatment of anxiety disorders. He has written a novel called *The Good Psychologist* (2010). His essay appeared on psychologytoday .com on August 10, 2010.

or dealing with a novel situation. The other depicts people who are just followed around, having the minutiae of their lives aired out in public.

The contestants, I find, also fall into two groups. One is made of "performers" — aspiring artists and actors desperate for a stage and assorted odd characters instructed to act up, carnival sideshow-style; those dominate the judgment and novelty shows.

The second, more interesting group is the so-called regular people — housewives, families, high school buddies — who possess no unique skill, no thespian claims, no glaring oddities. These are just asked to be themselves rather than compete or perform.

Psychological research, of course, has been "staging reality shows" for years. Placing people in novel situations and asking them to deal, carrying out fly-on-the-wall naturalistic observations of daily life, and judging people's skill levels are staple psychology research designs. And anyone involved in this field knows their inherent fascination. Look at the grainy videos of Zimbardo's prison experiment, Milgram's obedience studies, Mischel's marshmallow kids; watch the infants attempting to negotiate Ainsworth's "strange situation" and you'll see compelling human drama.[1]

One difference is that in research, the participants do not become stars, public icons, role models, or fodder for water cooler conversations; they usually remain unknown by design, to protect them, and the research. The star of research is not "self," but "truth." In reality shows, "self" is the star while "truth" is inconsequential; the subjects do become known, by design. In fact, getting known is the participants' prime motive.

And that's the other reason these shows are watched: they reflect the cultural dictum that being on TV elevates you, marks you as special and important.

This TV-Special Merit link has a long history, of course. Historically, however, the causal arrow led from Merit to TV. First, you acquired some special value, talent, or achievement in the world; then, by virtue of that accomplishment, you were elevated, via TV, onto the public pedestal. Being on TV rewarded achievement. This causal structure is natural and organic. When things are in proper

5

[1]In 1971, Philip Zimbardo, a psychology professor at Stanford University, led researchers in conducting an experiment in which students were randomly assigned roles as prisoners or prison guards in a mock prison. Both "prisoners" and "guards" took their roles to such extremes that the experiment was halted after only six days. In 1961, psychologist Stanley Milgram at Yale tested the willingness of student subjects to inflict electric shocks on other student subjects. No shocks were really administered, but far more subjects than predicted inflicted up to the maximum voltage even when they believed they were inflicting severe pain. In the 1960s, Walter Mischel at Stanford tested the concept of delayed gratification on four-year-olds by giving each a marshmallow and seeing if they could wait twenty minutes before eating it in order to get a second one. Canadian psychologist Mary Ainsworth studied infants' emotional attachment by filming their reactions as a parent and a stranger went in and out of their presence.

order, quality rises to the top. The fastest swimmer gets to climb the medal stand. Appreciating this logic is part of our nature.

But our nature is complex, and reality TV reflects another aspect of that archi- 10 tecture. After all, laboring in the world to gain special skill or achievement is hard and time consuming. It's a burden. And part of our nature is to seek relief from burden. People are always looking for easier, quicker ways to get the good stuff. And you don't have to be super clever to imagine that the TV-Special Merit connection may work both ways; that instead of laboring to become special and thus get on TV, you can get on TV first, and have that make you special.

This latter route, which is currently gaining in America, represents a cunning, even rational, short-term strategy, akin to that used by the ambitious "helicopter mother" who does her daughter's homework in secret, to boost the daughter's chances of getting into Harvard. The mother knows that just as super ability causes admission to Harvard, so does being at Harvard make you appear super able, with all the attendant benefits.

But in the long run, this strategy is risky, because it results in one of two bad outcomes: either the audience realizes the ruse and abandons the show, having wasted precious time and energy for naught (the girl fails at Harvard and flunks out, but not before thwarting the dreams of another, truly deserving applicant); or the audience buys the ruse and takes the mediocrity on offer as truly special, thus narrowing its own horizon (the girl's half-baked ideas are taken as gospel by a culture mesmerized by her Harvard credentials).

You can see variations of the same principle at work throughout the culture. For example, competence naturally breeds self esteem. However, educators and psychologists in the 80s and early 90s, particularly in California, responded to research results showing the competence-self esteem link by concluding that self esteem can cause competence. A whole movement flourished trying to teach children self esteem, in the hope that they would become successful as a result. This of course ended in a waste of time and money, and a betrayal of children. Putting someone on the medal stand is unlikely to turn her into a good swimmer.

The same dynamic can be seen underlying America's troubled relations with food. The work of our biological architect, natural selection, made good things sweet. Our cultural food architects have realized they could exploit the sweet-is-good natural link and make people buy a lot of really bad stuff by just making it sweet. So we are now consuming a lot of bad sweet stuff. And by the time the ruse is discovered, we already weigh 350 pounds and our hearts have exploded.

Which of course makes us ideal contestants for the next big reality show, 15 where the winner of all the challenges gets a heart transplant surgery while the losers are cast away to die.

Live, on TV, it's *Survivor: Mt. Sinai!*

The Meaning of Shpancer (Really)

ASHLEY WILSON

Noam Shpancer opens his essay "The Meaning of Reality (TV)" with the image of him relaxing in front of the TV after a hard day at work, remote in hand, no commitments, no need to concentrate. As he points out, though, he has learned enough from watching the channels flash by to gain some fairly good insights into the nature of reality television. Unfortunately, the essay peaks in the middle with some thought-provoking ideas but comes to a confusing and disappointing conclusion.

Shpancer begins with a simple but workable classification scheme for reality shows: They are about either "people who compete for some prize while showing off a skill or dealing with a novel situation" or "people who are just followed around, having the minutiae of their lives aired out in public." These people themselves, the contestants, also fall into two categories, those who perform and those who simply go about being themselves. Unfortunately, Shpancer offers no examples to support his classification, and he drops this idea to move on to the next.

One of the most important points that Shpancer makes relates reality shows to psychological research. There is certainly validity to his point that psychologists have been conducting their own "reality shows" for years: "Placing people in novel situations and asking them to deal, carrying out fly-on-the-wall naturalistic observations of daily life, and judging people's skill levels are staple psychology research designs." He mentions specific psychological studies that are "compelling human drama" and mentions the scientists' last names, but assumes his audience will know their work. That may be enough for some readers of psychologytoday .com, but others are not given enough information to accept his assertion that they are compelling.

The most original and thought-provoking idea that Shpancer offers is what he refers to as the TV-Special Merit link. That is, the reality shows "reflect the cultural dictum that being on television elevates you, marks you as special and important." The equation generally works the other way: if you proved that you had special value, "you were elevated, via TV, onto the public pedestal." Logic would dictate that hard work helps one win recognition, but reality shows are a way to avoid the hard work but get the recognition anyway. The analogy that Shpancer provides is the "helicopter" mother who helps her daughter get into Harvard by doing her homework for her. A certain level of recognition comes to the daughter by virtue

---

At the time she wrote this analysis, Ashley Wilson was a student at Clemson University.

of being at Harvard, and she may actually get by on her Harvard credentials — or she may flunk out. By analogy, the reality show's audience may accept mediocrity, or they may give up on the show.

Shpancer points out that the same logic led teachers in the 1980s and 1990s to try to guide students to competence by elevating their self-esteem, but the experiment was a failure: "Putting someone on the medal stand is unlikely to turn her into a good swimmer."

The essay loses its coherence, however, when Shpancer next tries to link his theory to "America's troubled relations with food" and ends by envisioning a new reality show with 350-pound contestants "where the winner of all the challenges gets a heart transplant surgery while the losers are cast away to die." Dr. Shpancer must have gotten hungry as he sat there in his recliner channel surfing, or maybe TV requires a little more concentration than he thought.

SAMPLE ESSAY WITH ANALYSIS | Rogerian Argument

In Chapter 1 we discussed how Carl Rogers's theory of communication can serve as a useful approach to resolving a conflict. It can also be a useful approach to analyzing, in writing, the two sides of an argument. The following essay is not a response to another piece of writing but to conflicting ideas.

The first step to resolving a conflict, of course, is to recognize that there is a conflict. The next step is to analyze *both sides* in the conflict. Before you begin, refer back to Maxine Hairston's guidelines for Rogerian argument from "Carl Rogers's Alternative to Traditional Rhetoric" on page 14.

Experienced writers may not adhere strictly to these guidelines, as is the case in the following essay, but as you read, notice where Whitehead includes the steps in a Rogerian analysis of an argument.

Parents Need Help: Restricting Access to Video Games
BARBARA DAFOE WHITEHEAD

A century ago, Jane Addams and other progressive reformers in Chicago responded to the dangers of the industrial age by creating laws and institutions that would protect children from the unwholesome lures of the city streets. Her work is rightly honored. A similar, and equally important, struggle is being waged in Illinois today. On the surface, it's about the sale of video games to kids. It's also

Barbara Dafoe Whitehead is the author of *The Divorce Culture: Rethinking Our Commitments to Marriage and Family* (1998) and *Why There Are No Good Men Left: The Romantic Plight of the New Single Woman* (2003). The column appeared in *Commonweal* on January 28, 2005.

a debate about a deeper question: To what degree does the responsibility for teaching good values to children fall solely on parents? Should some of that responsibility be shared by the state?

Those who make and sell video games say parents alone should bear the responsibility. On the other side is Illinois Governor Rod Blagojevich. He's trying to outlaw the sale of excessively violent or sexually explicit video games to children under eighteen. In his effort to restrict such sales he's making the argument that raising children is a shared responsibility: "Parenting is hard work and the state has a compelling interest in helping parents raise their children to be upstanding men and women."

The governor firmly believes that parents have the primary responsibility for teaching their children right from wrong. He believes just as firmly that parents should not have their efforts subverted by the avalanche of "amusements" that tell kids it is fun to blow people up. "Too many of the video games marketed to our children teach them all of the wrong lessons and all of the wrong values," Blagojevich writes in a "letter to Illinois parents" posted on the state's informational Web site (www.safegamesIllinois.com). "These games use violence, rage, and sexual aggression as play. That is not acceptable. When kids play, they should play like children, not like gangland assassins."

The governor's reference to gangland assassins is not an overstatement. One video game, the top-selling, industry-award-winning Grand Theft Auto: San Andreas, features gang warfare and the killing of prostitutes. Another, released on the forty-first anniversary of the Kennedy assassination, gets players to step into the shoes of Lee Harvey Oswald and to aim at the president's head as his motorcade rolls by. "Content descriptors" for video games also suggest how lurid the violence can be. These games include depictions of "blood and gore (mutilation of body parts)," "intense violence (human injury or death)," and "sexual violence (depictions of rape and other sexual acts)."

No sooner had Blagojevich unveiled his proposal than he faced powerful organized opposition from the entertainment industry. The Illinois Retail Merchants Association, the National Association of Theater Owners, the Entertainment Software Rating Board, and the Motion Picture Association of America took strong exception to the legislation. Imposing a curb on the free market is not the way to protect kids, these critics argued. Instead, parents should screen what their kids are buying and playing. As one lobbyist put it: "Retailers can't be held accountable for lack of oversight by parents."

This is a distortion of the governor's position, and of the problem. No one denies that parents have the primary responsibility for monitoring their kids. Blagojevich points out, though, that the sophisticated technology of video games makes that very hard to do. Consequently, it's up to the state to step in on the side of parents and children to help them cope.

The industry argument would be plausible if it were still 1955. Back then, it was easier for parents to exercise strict oversight. The big, boxy home entertainment technologies of that era — radio, television, and record players — produced images and sounds that parents could see and hear. They came with OFF buttons

5

for parents to push and plugs for parents to pull. All that has changed. The new entertainment technologies include a dizzying and ever-multiplying array of small, portable, individual, kid-friendly devices that defy close parental supervision. It was easy for parents to check on a half-hour TV show. It's much harder to review a video game. The games feature successive levels of difficulty; players must qualify at a lower level before earning the right to move to a higher level. So it takes time and practice before acquiring the skill to progress to the highest level of the game — which may also be its highest level of violence. To ensure that a video game isn't excessively violent, a parent would have to be looking over a child's shoulder until the highest level of play was finally revealed. This could take days.

Moreover, it isn't as if parents and the video-game industry meet each other on a level playing field. This is a multibillion-dollar industry that spends all its time and money devising ever more ingenious ways to market to kids over the heads of their parents and to deliberately undermine the ability of parents to regulate what their children are seeing. And in a tactic called "age compression," the marketers target their appeals to ever-younger kids. Like the youth sex revolution, the youth marketing revolution has migrated down the age scale. Even four-year-olds know what is cool.

To be sure, the industry's Entertainment Software Rating Board has voluntarily established its own ratings system. The trouble is: It isn't enforced. A study by the Federal Trade Commission found that early teens were able to buy games rated M (Mature 17+) 69 percent of the time.

It is telling that the makers and sellers of video games have responded so quickly and vigorously to Governor Blagojevich's very modest proposal. Clearly the corporate sector finds it in its interest to prompt kids to engage in fantasy rape, beheadings, and mass murder. And why should we expect otherwise? Its interest is the bottom line. Violence sells. But isn't it in the compelling interest of the community to curb such violent play?

10

Analysis

In her first paragraph, Whitehead makes clear what is at issue: the sale of video games to children. The larger question is whether parents are solely responsible for values education or whether the state should share some of the burden. In the second paragraph, she establishes the two sides in the controversy: those who make and sell video games and then governor of Illinois, Rod Blagojevich, who wanted to outlaw the sale of extremely violent or sexually explicit video games to those under the age of eighteen. Rogerian guidelines indicate that usually the next step is to present the side that the writer does not agree with, but this time, after a quick reference to the producers and marketers of the games, she focuses on Blagojevich's position. She then turns to the industry's position. Whitehead concedes under what circumstances the industry's claims might be valid: if we were still living in 1955. The closest the two sides come to common ground is Whitehead's acknowledging that the Entertainment Software Rating Board has voluntarily created a rating system for games. Unfortunately, it is not enforced. By the end, she still sees Blagojevich's proposal as very modest and his opponents' as driven by the bottom line. Her thesis comes in the form of a question at the end of the piece and hints at a shared concern for the good of the community: "But isn't it in the compelling interest of the community to curb such violent play?"

READINGS FOR ANALYSIS

The two essays below are an argument written by Alan Dershowitz shortly after the terrorist attacks of September 11, 2001, and an evaluation of it written by Seth Finkelstein approximately three months later. Notice what Finkelstein says about Dershowitz's article but also how each author organizes his essay.

Is There a Torturous Road to Justice?
ALAN M. DERSHOWITZ

The FBI's frustration over its inability to get material witnesses to talk has raised a disturbing question rarely debated in this country: When, if ever, is it justified to resort to unconventional techniques such as truth serum, moderate physical pressure, and outright torture?

The constitutional answer to this question may surprise people who are not familiar with the current U.S. Supreme Court interpretation of the 5th Amendment privilege against self-incrimination: Any interrogation technique, including the use of truth serum or even torture, is not prohibited. All that is prohibited is the introduction into evidence of the fruits of such techniques in a criminal trial against the person on whom the techniques were used. But the evidence could be used against that suspect in a non-criminal case — such as a deportation hearing — or against someone else.

If a suspect is given "use immunity" — a judicial decree announcing in advance that nothing the defendant says (or its fruits) can be used against him in a criminal case — he can be compelled to answer all proper questions. The issue then becomes what sorts of pressures can constitutionally be used to implement that compulsion. We know that he can be imprisoned until he talks. But what if

Alan M. Dershowitz is the Felix Frankfurter Professor of Law at Harvard Law School and a civil liberties attorney who defends the indigent as well as the famous. One of his many works of fiction and nonfiction is *The Case for Moral Clarity: Israel, Hamas, and Gaza* (2009). His article appeared in *Commentary* on November 8, 2001.

Are there circumstances under which we should allow torture?

imprisonment is insufficient to compel him to do what he has a legal obligation to do? Can other techniques of compulsion be attempted?

Let's start with truth serum. What right would be violated if an immunized suspect who refused to comply with his legal obligation to answer questions truthfully were compelled to submit to an injection that made him do so?

Not his privilege against self-incrimination, since he has no such privilege now that he has been given immunity.

What about his right of bodily integrity? The involuntariness of the injection itself does not pose a constitutional barrier. No less a civil libertarian than Justice William J. Brennan rendered a decision that permitted an allegedly drunken driver to be involuntarily injected to remove blood for alcohol testing. Certainly there can be no constitutional distinction between an injection that removes a liquid and one that injects a liquid.

What about the nature of the substance injected? If it is relatively benign and creates no significant health risk, the only issue would be that it compels the recipient to do something he doesn't want to do. But he has a legal obligation to do precisely what the serum compels him to do: answer all questions truthfully.

What if the truth serum doesn't work? Could the judge issue a "torture warrant," authorizing the FBI to employ specified forms of non-lethal physical pressure to compel the immunized suspect to talk?

Here we run into another provision of the Constitution — the due process clause, which may include a general "shock the conscience" test. And torture in general certainly shocks the conscience of most civilized nations.

But what if it were limited to the rare "ticking bomb" case — the situation in which a captured terrorist who knows of an imminent large-scale threat refuses to disclose it?

Would torturing one guilty terrorist to prevent the deaths of a thousand inno-cent civilians shock the conscience of all decent people?

To prove that it would not, consider a situation in which a kidnapped child had been buried in a box with two hours of oxygen. The kidnapper refuses to dis-close its location. Should we not consider torture in that situation?

All of that said, the argument for allowing torture as an approved technique, even in a narrowly specified range of cases, is very troubling.

We know from experience that law enforcement personnel who are given lim-ited authority to torture will expand its use. The cases that have generated the cur-rent debate over torture illustrate this problem. And, concerning the arrests made following the September 11 attacks, there is no reason to believe that the detainees know about specific future terrorist targets. Yet there have been calls to torture these detainees.

I have no doubt that if an actual ticking bomb situation were to arise, our law   15 enforcement authorities would torture. The real debate is whether such torture should take place outside of our legal system or within it. The answer to this seems clear: If we are to have torture, it should be authorized by the law.

Judges should have to issue a "torture warrant" in each case. Thus we would not be winking an eye of quiet approval at torture while publicly condemning it.

Democracy requires accountability and transparency, especially when extraor-dinary steps are taken. Most important, it requires compliance with the rule of law. And such compliance is impossible when an extraordinary technique, such as torture, operates outside of the law.

Alan Dershowitz's Tortuous Torturous Argument

SETH FINKELSTEIN

It's torture. Literally. That is, whether or not the United States government should use torture as a method of interrogation for suspected terrorists is now a subject of debate.

Surprisingly, long-time civil-libertarian Alan Dershowitz has been writing unexpectedly in favor of the legal basis for torture. On November 8, 2001, in a commentary for [the] *Los Angeles Times* "Is There a Torturous Road to Justice?" he discusses a proposal for a "torture warrant."

Much of the reaction to Alan Dershowitz's advocacy has blurred over a subtle point. Given that torture is such an incendiary subject, he's been accused of ad-vocating torture itself ("Dershowitz: Make Torture an Option" reads a headline on cbsnews.com). However, a careful reading of his commentary makes it clear that he isn't putting forth an argument in favor of torture *per se*. Rather, he postulates

---

Seth Finkelstein is a computer programmer who has worked extensively doing anticensorware research. He is the winner of an Electronic Frontier Foundation Pioneer Award. This article was posted to the Ethical Spectacle Web site in February 2002.

it will occur (*"I have no doubt that if an actual ticking bomb situation were to arise, our law enforcement authorities would torture."*). His point is then almost tangential from that perspective, a professorial concern with the due process of torture! To wit:

> *The real debate is whether such torture should take place outside of our legal system or within it. The answer to this seems clear: If we are to have torture, it should be authorized by the law.*

In this piece, I will not take up the arguments against torture. That's been done far better elsewhere, by other civil-libertarians such as Harvey Silverglate, or Amnesty International. Rather, I stand in awe of Dershowitz's focus on legal authorization of torture as the *"real debate."* All the moral and practical questions are swept away by his assumption of inevitability. We are left only to consider how to deal with what, if any, judicial procedures should surround torture.

He goes on to assert: 5

> *Democracy requires accountability and transparency, especially when extraordinary steps are taken. Most important, it requires compliance with the rule of law. And such compliance is impossible when an extraordinary technique, such as torture, operates outside of the law.*

While this sounds stirring, on reflection, the meaning of the call for "accountability and transparency" is not at all clear to me. If torture is illegal, then by definition it's operating outside the law. So if a torture warrant is created, obviously torture *with warrant* would be within the law. But there seems to be a tail-wagging-the-dog situation here. Torture doesn't comply with the rule of law because it's against the law. If the law is changed so that torture is permitted (*with warrant*), then it's only become compliant with the rule of law because that rule has been changed to accept it.

What is the *purpose* of the torture warrant? Is it an anti-hypocrisy measure, to force us, as a society, to confront what we are doing? To have a public record of the event, that the defense attorney can use in a trial? To allow the torture to be supervised, with proper medical monitoring, to guard against it becoming life-threatening? To officially provide for doctors to treat the torturee during and after the ordeal?

Perhaps the idea is the simple belief that we can have legal torture, which is bad, but illegal torture would be worse. However, the obvious rebuttal is that we would end up having both legal and illegal torture, feeding off each other. Dershowitz even explicitly takes this into account (*"We know from experience that law enforcement personnel who are given limited authority to torture will expand its use."*).

So, in the face [of] this expansion of authority to torture, what is gained by making it "accountable"? The anti-hypocrisy basis seems to be Dershowitz's rationale, as he justified the above by saying:

> *Judges should have to issue a "torture warrant" in each case. Thus we would not be winking an eye of quiet approval at torture while publicly condemning it.*

Overall, Dershowitz's reasoning seems shockingly convoluted. We end up re-   10
solving the conflict between torture and the rule of law by changing the rule of law to accommodate torture. Then an admitted following expansion in torture

(both from legal and illegal sources) is brushed aside with the argument that the legal torture would somehow possess accountability and transparency (accountable for what? transparent how?). Suppose Dershowitz is correct that there will be illegal torture under desperate circumstances, and without issuing a torture warrant, as a society we will be "winking an eye" to it. Is he really arguing that it's better to have more torture (due to the admitted effects of the tendency [to] "expand its use"), but at least some of the torture will then be *authorized* torture? That is, judicial process is regarded as so sacred that it's worth **torturing more people** in order to preserve it in the merest formal sense? That's both tortuous and torturous.

READING AND DISCUSSION QUESTIONS

1. What does Dershowitz mean when he says that no interrogation techniques are prohibited? What is?
2. What techniques of compulsion does Dershowitz discuss?
3. What are his main points about torture?
4. What about Dershowitz's argument does Finkelstein find so objectionable?
5. Do you agree with Dershowitz's argument? Why, or why not?

WRITING SUGGESTIONS

6. Dershowitz's article appeared approximately two months after the terrorist attacks of September 11, 2001. Were his ideas logical, considering the circumstances? Explain in an essay.
7. Write an essay explaining under what circumstances you might be willing to accept that torture is appropriate.
8. What are Finkelstein's main criticisms of Dershowitz?

Could Reality Shows Become Reality Experiments?

BARBARA A. SPELLMAN

The first question is, why *don't* reality game shows have to get Institutional Review Board approval? The answer: They are not research. According to the Code of Federal Regulations, research studies are "systematic investigations designed to develop or contribute to generalizable knowledge."

Barbara Spellman is a professor of psychology at the University of Virginia and founder of the Association for Psychological Science Committee on Human Subject Protection. This article was published in the APS *Observer* in March 2005.

But certainly many reality shows touch on issues that could make great questions for behavioral researchers. So, if you were an experimenter with an unlimited budget, could you get IRB approval to run one of these reality shows as "research" and then publish your results in a leading psychology journal? For the most part, probably not. Here's why.

The Reality Review

IRBs are charged with ensuring that research is conducted ethically, and one of the core values of ethical research is respect for the autonomy of the research participants. Participants must be told everything that might "reasonably be expected to influence willingness to participate." That includes the goals of the research, what they will be doing, whether there are any risks or benefits of the study (both physical and psychological), and whether and how much they will be paid. The participants need to know that participation in the research is voluntary and that they can withdraw at any time without penalty.

Usually, this information is communicated with a consent form that the participant reads and signs before engaging in the study. However, sometimes studies can be run in which participants are not given all of this information up front — either something is left out or there is actual deception. Such deception must be necessary and justified and any potential harmful consequences of the deception must be ameliorable.

In addition, IRBs must consider the research question and carefully weigh the potential risks and benefits of the study. To take an extreme example: An experiment with a new drug that might lead to permanent brain damage might be allowable if the new drug were a cure for patients in terminal stages of cancer, but not if it were a cure for ingrown toenails.

So, suppose you proposed one of the shows below to your IRB. You are willing to give the participants a consent form. Would the shows fly?

Two programs would probably get through mostly intact. The first is *American Idol*, in which ambitious young pop singers perform in front of a panel and are judged instantly and often harshly about their abilities.

In the consent form you would tell the participants that they would be singing in front of judges that might judge them harshly — and that they might be made fun of in front of lots of people. As long as no deception was involved — for example, as long as Simon Cowell (the most obnoxious judge) didn't criticize the good people and let the bad ones slide — there is no problem with the study. Informed participants could make the decision that it was worth it for their careers to receive feedback — even harsh feedback — on their singing. In many ways, what happens on *Idol* is not much different from what happens to any new singers trying to break into the field — it just happens more quickly and more publicly.

The problem with *Idol*, though, is: What exactly would the research question be?

Something like *Who's Your Daddy?* might also make the cut, because the research potential is good; however, the lying, deception, and sleaziness would probably have to be eliminated. On this show, a woman who was adopted as a young

5

10

girl must choose her real father from a dozen older men, all of whom claim to be her biological dad (one actually is). If she gets it right she gets $100,000. If she guesses wrong, the imposter who has fooled her gets the money.

The idea of the research — can people identify relatives — is interesting and possibly valuable. The argument against such research is that it could be traumatic for the participant. That is true, but the participant is over 18 and therefore (we assume) legally eligible to find out who her father is through other channels. The IRB would want to make sure the process is done in the least traumatic way possible and that psychological services are available, should they be necessary. The elements of lying would have to be eliminated. In addition, the IRB might want to cut the prize money from $100,000 to something smaller. Such a large amount might entice someone to do something against his or her best psychological interest.

This show, which was quickly cancelled, had an element of sleaze (so I'm told) in that it was always older men trying to dupe younger women. One could imagine, however, a non-deceptive study in which siblings separated at an early age tried to identify each other. Eliminating the lying, deception, sleaze, and big prize might get the show past the IRB; however, it probably wouldn't get the show past the network executives (who would worry that the eviscerated show would not have enough "juice" for the reality audience).

Too Much Psychological Risk

At the other extreme, there are two programs that could probably never make it through an IRB. The first is *Trading Spouses: Meet Your New Mommy*, in which wives swap homes for a short period of time and experience life in the new home with the other wife's partner, children, and pets.

The subtle problem with *Trading Spouses* is that there is no way to get true consent for or from any minors involved. Typically, consent has to be given by the parent — who is assumed to have the best interest of the child at heart. Also, typically, researchers get minors' "assent" — their agreement (behavioral or written, depending on age) to be in the study. An IRB would worry about real psychological risks to the children and that the children could not truly understand the potential dangers. With the lure of TV fame for the parents perhaps blinding their acknowledgment of potential risks to their children, there is no way that the parent's agreement on behalf of the minor would be seen as "objective."

On *The Swan*, women who believe themselves unattractive are offered complete, often full-body makeovers after a thorough "analysis" of their appearance by the show's plastic surgeons, dentists, etc. After the makeover, they enter a beauty contest with other made-over participants. An IRB would find here that the risks are far too great in proportion to the benefits for these activities to be allowed as research. There are not only physical risks in all of the medical procedures, but there are also great unknown psychological risks — not only for the surgery but also for the majority of participants who lose the after-makeover beauty contest. Those risks would not be perceived as outweighing the potential benefits (to either the individual or society).

Too Much Deception?

Sometimes deception is so great that there is no way to imagine that people would have agreed to be in the study had they known at the outset what the study was really about or would involve. For example, in *Joe Millionaire*, dozens of women compete for the hand of a supposed millionaire. When it turns out at the end that he's a minimum wage worker, they must decide whether to stay with him. This show exhibits the classic illegal action of "bait and switch" — entice someone to do something in order to receive a desirable good, then switch to a less desirable good. The very first rule of ethical research is: If it ain't legal then it ain't ethical.

Too Much Physical Risk?

It is hard to see how an IRB would approve of shows with real physical risks, such as *Fear Factor*, in which contestants compete for a cash prize by doing things their competitors might not do, such as eating ground-up rats, jumping off buildings, or laying in a coffin filled with worms. Is there any research question aside from how much physical/psychological pain will people endure for fame and/or money? As mentioned above, IRBs scrutinize excessive payments for research participation watching for potential coercion.

On *Survivor*, a dozen people are left on an island (or other exotic place). They are placed into teams and must compete against each other for food and other provisions. At the end of each show, one person (from the losing team) is voted off the island by his teammates, so backstabbing is prevalent. This scenario is a more interesting case than *Fear Factor* because there are some real possible research questions and because the physical dangers are not as immediate. With an appropriate consent form detailing the potential physical and psychological risks, strong assurances that one could quit the study without repercussion, and a re-worked payment scale, some version of *Survivor* might actually pass.

READING AND DISCUSSION QUESTIONS

1. What is an IRB, and what connection is Spellman trying to make between IRBs and reality shows?
2. How does Spellman answer the question that is her essay's title?
3. Why are examples essential to the success of her essay?
4. Why are researchers required to submit experiments to IRBs even when there is no physical threat?

WRITING SUGGESTIONS

5. Write an essay in which you discuss how some reality shows are like experiments in human behavior. Be sure to give specific examples.
6. Choose one reality show or one type of reality show and write an essay explaining why you think it is so popular.
7. Write an essay explaining what you think is wrong with reality shows. You can focus on one example or several.

A Movie, a Word, and My Family's Battle

PATRICIA E. BAUER

Margaret and I were lingering in front of the multiplex one evening last summer, a mom and her adult daughter laughing about the movie we'd just seen, when a gaggle of cute pre-teen girls sauntered past.

The one in the lead jerked a thumb in our direction and made a goofy face to her friend. "Look. Retard," we heard her say, and Margaret wilted. Her chin trembled. One by one, the other girls turned to look, nudging one another and whispering. The last girl spun all the way around as she slowly walked by, eyes fixed on my daughter.

In her size 6 jeans and Old Navy shirt, Margaret hadn't done anything to attract that unwanted attention. But then, my blond, blue-eyed daughter lives every day behind a face that can be a lightning rod for such talk. The beautiful face I've loved for 24 years displays some of the characteristic signs of Down syndrome, a chromosomal anomaly associated with varying degrees of cognitive impairment.

Last week lightning struck again, not just for Margaret, but for millions of Americans with intellectual disabilities. Ben Stiller's highly anticipated *Tropic Thunder* hit screens across the country. The film packs a powerful combination of explosions, irreverence, crudity, and political incorrectness. It also features many iterations of the word "retard."

With the film's release, the public has plunged headlong into an overheated   5
argument about the borders between comedy and hate speech, political correctness and oversensitivity. I know, because posts that I put on my blog, drawing attention to the movie's marketing and discussion of a character with an intellectual disability, have set off a firestorm in Hollywood and the disability community. Protesters picketed *Tropic Thunder*'s premiere last week, while the film's high-profile stars defended it as a parody aimed at the movie industry.

The film features Stiller, Robert Downey Jr., and Jack Black as unsavory actors who are thrust into a real conflict while filming a war movie. Stiller's character is an actor who previously sought Oscar glory by portraying Simple Jack, a man with an intellectual disability, a bowl haircut reminiscent of state institutions, and few relatable qualities. Cue the retard jokes.

The original marketing campaign, featured on a Web site that was taken down in response to complaints, included an image of Stiller as Simple Jack bearing the

---

Patricia E. Bauer, a former *Washington Post* reporter, edits patriciaebauer.com, a Web site of news and commentary on issues related to disability.

memorable tagline, "Once upon a time . . . There was a retard." Another marketed scene depicts Downey uttering the line that will undoubtedly launch a thousand T-shirts: "Never go full retard."

For years I've tried to figure out how to handle moments like these, when the word "retard" crash-lands at our feet, either aimed directly at Margaret or tossed around as an all-purpose weapon. It has become a routine epithet, used to describe something or someone stupid or worthless or pathetic. For my daughter and my family, it's more like a grenade, and we're the collateral damage. "It's not a good word," Margaret says. "It's mean, it's insulting, and it hurts people's feelings."

As the word has seemingly become increasingly pervasive in recent years, I've tried gently to let others know that it heaps scorn on people who are already stigmatized and may not be in a position to defend themselves. The responses I've gotten? *Gosh, everybody says it. It's just a joke.* Or: *I didn't mean it like that.* Or: *Lighten up. It doesn't mean anything.* People reacted as if I'd offended them when I told tell them that they were insulting my daughter and others like her; they would never insult such people, they said.

Discouraged, I started letting it pass, gritting my teeth, wishing it would go   10
away. Not everyone uses it, and sometimes I wonder whether I'm overreacting. But I hear it at every turn. A clerk in a store apologizes for being "such a retard" when she can't find an item for me. Ouch. Kids at the mall call one another "you big retard." Ouch. A friend tells a long, involved story at my dinner table about her recent fender bender, with a punchline about "some retard" who parked behind her. Ouch. Ouch. Ouch.

With each of these incidents, I hear what others perhaps don't hear. This word, derived from a clinical term used to describe people like my daughter, carries a cultural subtext so huge that we don't even notice it. By using it, we threaten years of progress toward a society that accepts and values all its citizens, including the 14.3 million with cognitive disabilities.

When I was young, kids like my daughter were kept at home or, worse, sent to institutions by the hundreds of thousands. They had no legally guaranteed right to an education.

A man my age who grew up in a small town in Georgia told me about a boy with Down syndrome who lived down the street. The boy wasn't allowed to go to school and was kept behind a board fence in the backyard; neighborhood kids used to climb a tree to spy on him. The man wept as he recalled the view from an overhanging branch.

Over the past 35 years, the legal landscape has been transformed. In 1975, the Individuals with Disabilities Education Act granted children with disabilities the right to a public education, and the federal government pledged to pay a substantial portion of local special-education costs. The Americans with Disabilities Act of 1990 prohibited discrimination against the disabled. A group of people who'd been invisible emerged to work toward taking their rightful place in society.

We've come a long way, but we still have far to go. There are still 38,000   15
people with intellectual and developmental disabilities housed in institutions nationwide. The federal government hasn't kept its promise to fund special

education, and millions of children across the country remain poorly served or not served at all.

Meanwhile, adults with intellectual disabilities are on waiting lists for independent living services all over the country; one recent report estimated more than 100,000 in Texas alone. These adults are largely unemployed and frequently live in poverty. Experts estimate that fewer than 20 percent of those of working age are employed, even though research shows that they are reliable and effective workers when given support and matched with appropriate jobs.

Without a coherent federal policy for providing community services and support, millions of families across the country are left to take care of their loved ones on their own. Parents have little assurance that their adult children will be cared for after they die. At last count, 715,000 people were residing with caregivers age 60 and older. As life expectancies increase, that number grows.

On top of all this is the problem of negative public attitudes. Recent research conducted by the University of Massachusetts found that, if given a choice, more than half of young people wouldn't spend time with a student with an intellectual disability. More than half of parents didn't want such students at their children's school. Almost half of the young people surveyed wouldn't sit next to a student like Margaret on a school bus.

I find these facts and statistics terrifying. My husband and I have spent much of the past two decades doing all we can to shield Margaret from the effects of what I've just described. With a lot of hard work on her part, and with the active support of family and friends, she's faring far better than doctors predicted when she was born. She's a high school graduate, works part-time at a Mediterranean restaurant, takes care of her own apartment, and volunteers at her local hospital and senior center. She's a regular at the gym. She has a lively social network, a cellphone, an e-mail address. That's not to say that her life is rosy all the time, but it seems to be working.

I'd like to hold on to the hope that Margaret's journey reflects our steady   20
national progress toward respecting and valuing all our citizens. But I'm stopped cold by the thought of a major studio constructing an ad campaign and film that prominently feature the word "retard" without a thought to the consequences.

According to the nonprofit Arc of the United States, people with developmental disabilities are 4 to 10 times more likely to be victims of violence than those without. There are always people looking to pick on other people. With the introduction of "Never go full retard" into the lexicon, I can't help thinking that those people have been handed both a weapon and a target.

DreamWorks and the actors in *Tropic Thunder* have already said that this is not their problem. They say that the movie targets Hollywood and seeks to criticize past exploitation of people with disabilities in stereotype-filled blockbusters such as *Rain Man* and *Forrest Gump*.

Such criticism is surely present, and it's not wide of the mark. The film is rated "R" for a reason. It's art, even if crude and distasteful, and it's entitled to this country's broad protections for freedom of speech and expression.

Yet *Tropic Thunder* provides another example of the unthinking acceptance of language that promotes oppression. Anticipating public scrutiny, the studio was careful to build nuance and subtlety into the film's racial humor. A white actor who uses blackface to portray a black character is countered at every turn by a black actor critiquing his actions. But there's no on-screen presence countering the Simple Jack portrayal, nor did the filmmakers consult people with intellectual disabilities or their families about the script.

It seems that the studio never considered that its portrayal of people with disabilities would touch a nerve farther below the skin than it would want to go. Again we hear: I didn't mean it like *that,* and lighten up. It doesn't mean anything.   25

For millions of Americans like Margaret and me, it does.

The Case Against Banning the Word "Retard"

CHRISTOPHER M. FAIRMAN

Does the word "retard" have less than three weeks to live? Long before Rahm Emanuel, Sarah Palin, and Rush Limbaugh made the word fodder for political controversy and late-night punch lines, a movement was underway to eliminate it from everyday conversation. Saying, irrefutably, that the word and its variations are hurtful to many, the Special Olympics is leading a campaign to end its use and is promoting a national awareness day on March 3. Nearly 60,000 people have signed on to the following promise on www.r-word.org: "I pledge and support the elimination of the derogatory use of the r-word from everyday speech and promote the acceptance and inclusion of people with intellectual disabilities."

I sympathize with the effort, but I won't be making that pledge. It's not that I've come to praise the word "retard"; I just don't think we should bury it. If the history of offensive terms in America shows anything, it is that words themselves are not the culprit; the meaning we attach to them is, and such meanings change dramatically over time and across communities. The term "mentally retarded" was itself introduced by the medical establishment in the 20th century to supplant other terms that had been deemed offensive. Similarly, the words "gay" and "queer" and even the N-word can be insulting, friendly, identifying, or academic in different contexts.

Christopher M. Fairman is a professor at the Moritz College of Law at Ohio State University. He is the author of a book subtitled *Word Taboo and Protecting Our First Amendment Liberties* (2009). This article appeared in the *Washington Post* on February 14, 2010.

The varied and evolving uses of such words ultimately render self-censorship campaigns unnecessary. And restricting speech of any kind comes with a potential price — needlessly institutionalized taboos, government censorship, or abridged freedom of expression — that we should be wary of paying.

The latest battle over the R-word kicked into high gear with a Jan. 26 *Wall Street Journal* report that last summer White House Chief of Staff Rahm Emanuel blasted liberal activists unhappy with the pace of health-care reform, deriding their strategies as "[expletive] retarded." Palin, the mother of a special-needs child, quickly took to Facebook to demand Emanuel's firing, likening the offensiveness of the R-word to that of the N-word. Limbaugh seized the low ground, saying he found nothing wrong with "calling a bunch of people who are retards, retards," and Palin rushed to his defense, saying Limbaugh had used the word satirically. Comedy Central's Stephen Colbert took her up on it, calling Palin an "[expletive] retard" and adding, with a smile: "You see? It's satire!"

Emanuel apologized and promised to take the Word.org pledge, but as March 3 nears, the word may already be an endangered species. Forty-eight states have voted to remove the term "mental retardation" from government agencies and state codes, and legislation is pending in Congress to strike it from any federal statutes that still use it, such as the Individuals With Disabilities Education Act. The largest advocacy group for the intellectually disabled, the Association for Retarded Citizens, is now simply the Arc. Similarly, the American Association of Mental Retardation is now the American Association on Intellectual and Developmental Disabilities. The Centers for Disease Control and Prevention now use "intellectual disability" in place of "mental retardation." The diagnostic manuals used by medical professionals also embrace "intellectual disability" as the official label. Behind the changes is the belief that "retardation" doesn't communicate dignity and respect.

The irony is that the use of "mental retardation" and its variants was originally an attempt to convey greater dignity and respect than previous labels had. While the verb "retard" — meaning to delay or hinder — has roots in the 15th century, its use in reference to mental development didn't occur until the late 19th and early 20th centuries, when medical texts began to describe children with "retarded mental development," "retarded children" and "mentally retarded patients." By the 1960s, "mental retardation" became the preferred medical term, gradually replacing previous diagnostic standards such as "idiot," "imbecile," and "moron" — terms that had come to carry pejorative connotations.

As I was growing up in the 1970s, my father worked for the Texas Department of Mental Health and Mental Retardation, one of the now-renamed state agencies. The term "retardation" was common in my home and life, but it was sterile and clinical. It is only in the past generation that the medical term turned into the slang "retard" and gained power as an insult. The shift is even apparent in popular movies. There was little public controversy when Matt Dillon tried to woo Cameron Diaz in the 1998 hit comedy *There's Something About Mary* by confessing his passion: "I work with retards." (Diaz's character, Mary, had a mentally disabled brother.) But 10 years later, in the comedy *Tropic Thunder*, Robert Downey Jr.'s use of the phrase "full retard" led to picketing and calls for a boycott.

What happened to make the word a target for extinction?

All cultures have taboos. Western culture, particularly in the United States, has several taboos surrounding sexuality, grounded largely in a subconscious fear of the parade of horribles — adultery, unwanted pregnancy, incest, venereal disease — that might befall us because of some sexual behaviors. Sometimes the taboo extends to even uttering the words that describe certain behaviors. You can see word taboo at work in the way Emanuel's blunder was reported: "[expletive] retarded." It's still okay to print the R-word. The F-word? Forget it.

For years, I've been researching taboo language and its interaction with the law, and I have written a law review article and recently a book, both titled with the unprintable four letter F-word. The resilience of word taboos, the multiple usages and meanings of a single word, the rise of self-censorship, and the risks of institutionalized taboo and ultimately censorship are all core issues surrounding the F-word, and they help explain what is happening — and may happen still — with the R-word.

Mental disorders also carry cultural taboos. For centuries, mental illness and disability were poorly understood; as recently as the 1800s, they were thought to be the work of devils and demons. Because the origins of mental illness were a mystery, fears that such conditions could be contagious led to isolation through institutionalization. Shame was often attached to individuals and their families, and the result was stigma.

Fortunately, we've come a long way from those days. It's precisely the new enlightenment and openness about mental disabilities that allow Palin to launch the controversy over "retard." But at a subconscious level, the underlying taboo may explain why we constantly seek new terms for this type of disability, new ways to avoid the old stigmas. Invariably, negative connotations materialize around whatever new word is used; "idiot" becomes an insult and gives way to "retardation," which in turn suffers the same fate, leading to "intellectual disability." This illustrates one of the recurring follies of speech restriction: While there may be another word to use, a negative connotation eventually is found. Offense — both given and taken — is inevitable.

Whatever future offensiveness may emerge, though, are we not better off by purging today's insulting language and making our discourse a little kinder? That is the argument of self-censorship advocates such as Palin, who draws parallels between the use of the R-word and the N-word — the most powerful and insulting of all racial epithets. In some respects, the comparison seems overblown. The N-word invokes some of the foulest chapters in our nation's history; "retard," however harsh, pales in comparison. But there still may be some guidance to be gleaned.

While the N-word endures as an insult, it is so stigmatized that its use is no longer tolerated in public discourse. This is a positive step for us all, of course, but its containment does not come without costs. As Harvard law professor Randall Kennedy described in his 2002 book on the subject, stigmatizing the word has

10

15

elicited new problems, including an overeagerness to detect insult where none is intended and the use of excessively harsh punishment against those who use the word wrongly.

I've coined a term for overzealous or extreme responses to insulting words: "word fetish." Those under the influence of word fetish aren't content to refrain from using a certain word; they are set on eradicating any use by others. A classic example was the plight of David Howard, a white employee in the D.C. mayor's office in 1999. Howard told staff members that because of budget cuts, he would have to be "niggardly" with available funds. Wrongly believing "niggardly" was a variation of the N-word, black subordinates lobbied for his resignation. Howard ultimately resigned after public protests, though he was soon reinstated. If the campaign against "retard" is successful, an identical risk of word fetish exists. (Imagine that Emanuel had spoken of "retarding the opposition" — would that be unacceptable?)

Like virtually every word in our language, the N-word has multiple uses. While its use as an insult has decreased, there has been a resurgence of the word as a term of identification, even affection, among some African Americans. But should certain groups of people, to the exclusion of others, be allowed to reclaim certain words? If "retard" or "retarded" were similarly restricted, could intellectually disabled individuals appropriate the term for self-identification, essentially reclaiming its original use or developing a new one?

Over time, word fetish can evolve into censorship among private organizations and ultimately direct government control of language and institutionalized word taboo. During the 1980s and 1990s, for example, many colleges and universities sought to reduce discrimination by developing speech codes, often targeting racial hate speech such as the N-word. Even with the most combustible insults, however, there must be some accommodation to their continued use; freedom of expression surely embraces unpopular, even insulting, speech. Luckily, speech codes that have been challenged in court have generally lost because they violated the First Amendment.

The risk of direct government censorship of the word "retard" is real. The New Zealand chapter of the Special Olympics is already calling on the country's Broadcasting Standards Authority (equivalent to our Federal Communications Commission) to deem the word "retard" unacceptable for broadcast. This plea is based upon a single incident involving New Zealand television personality Paul Henry, who described the runner-up in the *Britain's Got Talent* competition, Susan Boyle, as retarded. It is not difficult to imagine calls for a similar broadcast ban emerging here.

The current public awareness campaign surrounding the use of the word "gay" 20 offers better lessons and parallels for the R-word debate. Advocacy groups contend that the phrase "that's so gay" fosters homophobia and that anti-gay language is directly related to violence and harassment against homosexuals. At the same time, there is recognition that much anti-gay language is uttered carelessly and isn't necessarily intended as hurtful — as is probably the case with uses of "retard." The Ad Council and the Gay, Lesbian, and Straight Education Network have developed a Web site, ThinkB4YouSpeak.com, that, much like R-Word.org, encourages the public to sign a pledge to cease using the phrase. (The slogan: "Saying that's so gay is so yesterday.")

By increasing sensitivity and awareness, the campaign hopes to encourage people to think about the possible consequences of their word choices. Such reflection would presumably lead individuals to censor themselves once they understand that others can be hurt by their language.

Inherent in this idea is the realization that words have multiple meanings and that those meanings depend on the context and circumstances surrounding any particular statement. For example, "gay" is a term of identification for homosexuals, but it also can be used as an all-purpose put-down: "That's so gay." Those using it as an insult don't intend to say "that's so homosexual," nor do they necessarily make the conscious leap that homosexuality is bad. (Indeed, the success of the ThinkB4YouSpeak.com campaign depends on this distinction.)

Similarly, the R-word has multiple usages. When Emanuel calls fellow Democrats "retarded" for jeopardizing a legislative plan, the term is a stand-in for "stupid" or "misguided" or "dumb" — it obviously does not mean that they meet the IQ diagnostic standard for intellectual disability. It is quite another thing to look at a person with Down syndrome and call him or her a "retard." So, if there are readily identifiable alternate meanings, what is the reason for censorship?

Differing usages also give rise to reclaiming — when words that have an offensive meaning are deliberately given a new spin. The putative slur is captured, repurposed and owned by the target of insult. We see this when an African American uses the N-word as a term of identification for his friends, or when the word "queer" is reclaimed for TV shows such as *Queer Eye for the Straight Guy* and *Queer as Folk*, and for queer studies and queer theory in university courses. Reclaiming the word "retard" is an option that should involve no risk to freedom of expression.

If interest groups want to pour resources into cleaning up unintentional insults, more power to them; we surely would benefit from greater kindness to one another. But we must not let "retard" go without a requiem. If the goal is to protect intellectually disabled individuals from put-downs and prejudice, it won't succeed. New words of insult will replace old ones. 25

Words are ideas, and we should be reluctant to surrender any of them. Freedom of expression has come at a dear price, and it is not worth abridging, even so we can get along a little better. That's one F-word we really can't do without.

DISCUSSION QUESTIONS

1. Is it acceptable, in your opinion, to use the word "retard"? What if you are just among your friends?

2. In what contexts is Bauer opposed to the use of the word "retard"? Is her position justified? Explain your answer.

3. What claims does Bauer make about the harm that results from the use of "retard"?

4. What emotional appeals does Bauer make in her argument? How persuasive do you find them?

5. What is Fairman's position on the use of the word "retard"?

6. In paragraph 2 of Fairman's piece he cites a pledge from www.r-word.org. In that pledge, what does "derogatory use" mean? Why is that important?

7. Why won't Fairman be making the pledge?

8. Is Fairman making a claim of fact, value, or policy? Explain.

9. Who makes a more compelling case, Bauer or Fairman? Why?

Assignments for Analytical Writing

READING AND DISCUSSION QUESTIONS

1. Choose an editorial from your campus or local newspaper and evaluate it. How successful an argument does it make?

2. Which of the three analyses of reality television presented here provides the strongest argument? Defend your choice.

3. Do you agree with Ravitch's view of education as presented by Roger Kaplan?

4. Barbara Dafoe Whitehead argues that parents need help from the state in controlling their children's leisure activities. Charles Krauthammer (p. 39) argues that parents should not interfere with the way the state says that science should be taught in public schools. Who provides a more convincing argument?

WRITING SUGGESTIONS

5. Choose an editorial from your campus or local newspaper and write an objective analysis of it. Your thesis statement will be a claim of fact.

6. Locate two editorials or two articles that take different stands on the same controversial issue. Write an analysis in which you objectively compare the two as examples of argumentation.

7. Locate two editorials or two articles that take different stands on the same controversial issue. Write an essay in which you argue which of the two is a more effective argument and why.

8. Write an analysis of Eric Jaffe's "Reality Check" (p. 93) that supports a claim of value.

Research Readiness: Incorporating Quotations

What is the best way to include in your own writing what others have to say?

The Writer's Guide on page 88 illustrates three ways of incorporating direct quotations into your own text. The ability to work quotations smoothly into your writing gives it a sophistication that it otherwise would lack. One of the signs of an immature use of sources is having "floating quotations." That means that the writer moves from his or her own text into a direct quote with no specific connection having been made. Another is back-to-back quotations — two direct quotations with none of your own text in between.

Remember that you use quotations to support your ideas, not to replace them. And use them sparingly. Use summary or paraphrase when possible to incorporate another's ideas. Save direct quotations for those times when the wording is particularly important or striking.

ASSIGNMENT

Read each of the following passages. Then for each, write one or two sentences incorporating a quotation. Also incorporate in your sentence(s) the author's name and the title of the work. Choose a different way of incorporating the quote each time so that all three ways are represented: (1) as a grammatical part of your own sentence, (2) with a speech tag such as "he says" or "she writes," and (3) with a complete sentence and a colon.

Put the page number in parentheses and punctuate correctly according to MLA style.

PASSAGE 1

1. From page 158 of "Gay Marriage Shows Why We Need to Separate Church and State," by Howard Moody. So what is marriage? It depends on whom you ask, in what era, in what culture. Like all words or institutions, human definitions, whether religious or secular, change with time and history. When our beloved Constitution was written, blacks, Native Americans, and, to some extent, women were quasihuman beings with no rights or privileges, but today they are recognized as persons with full citizenship rights. The definition of marriage has been changing over the centuries in this nation, and it will change yet again as homosexuals are seen as ordinary human beings.

PASSAGE 2

2. From page 333 of "A New Look, an Old Battle" by Anna Quindlen. The catalytic issue is research on stem cells. These are versatile building blocks that may be coaxed into becoming any other type of cell type; they could therefore hold the key to endless mysteries of human biology, as well as someday help provide a cure for ailments as diverse as diabetes, Parkinson's, spinal-cord degeneration, and Alzheimer's. By some estimates, more than 100 million Americans have diseases that scientists suspect

could be affected by research on stem cells. Scientists hope that the astonishing potential of this research will persuade the federal government to help fund it and allow the National Institutes of Health to help oversee it. This is not political, researchers insist. It is about science, not abortion.

PASSAGE 3

3. From page 163 of "Will It Be Marriage or Civil Union?" by Jo Ann Citron. But let there be no mistake: Whatever happens in Massachusetts is absolutely critical to how the gay marriage question will be answered in the rest of the United States. What happens here is even more important than what happened in Vermont. Here's why. The next marriage case with a reasonable likelihood of success is working its way through the courts in New Jersey, a state with a history of progressive court decisions. New Jersey will be looking very carefully at the way Vermont and Massachusetts have addressed the marriage question. If the Massachusetts SJC [Supreme Judicial Court] ratifies its decision and mandates the issuance of marriage licenses, New Jersey will look at its predecessor states and see two alternative models, marriage and civil union. New Jersey will choose one or the other. But the SJC could fail to confirm its marriage decision and approve instead some form of civil union. Coupled with the Vermont ruling, this will create a critical mass in favor of civil union, an outcome that will make it far more likely that New Jersey will opt for civil union over marriage. After that, the rest of the states will almost certainly fall into line with civil unions, and that will spell the end of gay marriage, probably forever.

Analyzing the Elements

CHAPTER 4

Definition

The Purposes of Definition

Before we examine the other elements of argument, we need to consider definition, a component you may have to deal with early in writing an essay.

Arguments often revolve around definitions of crucial terms. For example, how does one define *democracy*? Does a democracy guarantee freedom of the press, freedom of worship, freedom of assembly, and freedom of movement? In the United States, we would argue that such freedoms are essential to any definition of *democracy*. But countries in which these freedoms are nonexistent also represent themselves as democracies or governments of the people. In the words of Senator Daniel P. Moynihan, "For years now the most brutal totalitarian regimes have called themselves 'people's' or 'democratic' republics." Rulers in such governments are aware that defining their regimes as democratic may win the approval of people who would otherwise condemn them. In his formidable attack on totalitarianism in *1984*, George Orwell coined the slogans "War Is Peace" and "Slavery Is Freedom," phrases that represent the corrupt use of definition to distort reality.

But even where there is no intention to deceive, the snares of definition are difficult to avoid. How do you define *abortion*? Is it "termination of pregnancy"? Or is it "murder of an unborn child"? During a celebrated trial in 1975 of a physician who performed an abortion and was accused of manslaughter, the prosecution often used the word *baby* to refer to the fetus, but the defense referred to "the products of conception." These definitions of *fetus* reflected the differing judgments of those on opposite sides. Not only do judgments create definitions; definitions influence judgments.

Definitions can indeed change the nature of an event or a "fact." How many farms are there in the state of New York? The answer to the question depends on the definition of *farm*. In 1979 the *New York Times* reported:

> Because of a change in the official definition of the word "farm," New York lost 20 percent of its farms on January 1, with numbers dropping from 56,000 to 45,000. . . .
>
> Before the change, a farm was defined as "any place from which $250 or more of agricultural products is sold" yearly or "any place of 10 acres or more from which $50 or more of agricultural products is sold" yearly. Now a farm is "any place from which $1,000 or more of agricultural products is sold" in a year.[1]

A change in the definition of *poverty* can have similar results. An article in the *New York Times*, whose headline reads, "A Revised Definition of Poverty May Raise Number of U.S. Poor," makes this clear:

> The official definition of *poverty* used by the Federal Government for three decades is based simply on cash income before taxes. But in a report to be issued on Wednesday, a panel of experts convened by the [National] Academy of Sciences three years ago at the behest of Congress says the Government should move toward a concept of poverty based on disposable income, the amount left after a family pays taxes and essential expenses.[2]

The differences are wholly a matter of definition. But such differences can have serious consequences for those being defined, most of all in the disposition of billions of federal dollars in aid of various kinds. In 1992 the Census Bureau classified 14.5 percent of Americans as poor. Under the new guidelines, at least 15 or 16 percent would be poor, and, under some measures recommended by a government panel, 18 percent would be so defined.

In fact, local and federal courts almost every day redefine traditional concepts that can have a direct impact on our everyday lives. The definition of *family*, for example, has undergone significant changes that acknowledge the existence of new relationships. In January 1990 the New Jersey Supreme Court ruled that a family may be defined as "one or more persons occupying a dwelling unit as a single nonprofit housekeeping unit, who are living together as a stable and permanent living unit, being a traditional family unit or the *functional equivalent* thereof" (italics for emphasis added). This meant that ten Glassboro State College students, unrelated by blood, could continue to occupy a single-family house despite the objection of the borough of Glassboro.[3] Even the legal definition of *maternity* has shifted. Who is the mother — the woman who contributes the egg or the woman (the surrogate) who bears the child? Several states, acknowledging the changes brought by medical technology, now recognize a difference between the birth mother and the legal mother.

[1]*New York Times*, March 4, 1979, sec. 1, p. 40.
[2]*New York Times*, April 10, 1995, sec. A, p. 1.
[3]*New York Times*, February 1, 1990, sec. B, p. 5.

Does this couple live on a farm? It depends on how you define the term.

Defining the Terms in Your Argument

In some of your arguments you will introduce terms that require definition. We've pointed out that a definition of *poverty* is crucial to any debate on the existence of poverty in the United States. The same may be true in a debate about the legality of euthanasia, or mercy killing. Are the arguers referring to passive euthanasia (the withdrawal of life-support systems) or to active euthanasia (the direct administration of drugs to hasten death)? It is not uncommon, in fact, for arguments about controversial questions to turn into arguments about the definition of terms.

An argument can end almost before it begins if writer and reader cannot agree on definitions of key terms. While clear definitions do not guarantee agreement, they do ensure that all parties understand the nature of the argument.

In the Rogerian approach to argumentation, negotiating a definition that all parties can accept is the starting point to resolving conflict.

Defining Vague and Ambiguous Terms

You will need to define other terms in addition to those in your claim. If you use words and phrases that have two or more meanings, they may appear vague and ambiguous to your reader. In arguments of value and policy abstract terms such as *freedom of speech, justice,* and *equality* require clarification. Despite their abstract nature, however, they are among the most important in the language because they represent the ideals that shape our laws. When conflicts arise, the courts must define these terms to establish the legality of certain practices. Is the Ku Klux Klan permitted to make disparaging public statements about ethnic and racial groups? That depends on the court's definition of *free speech*. Can execution for some crimes be considered cruel and unusual punishment? That, too, depends on the court's definition of *cruel and unusual punishment.*

Consider the definition of *race,* around which so much of American history has revolved, often with tragic consequences. Until recently, the only categories listed in the census were white, black, Asian-Pacific, and Native American, "with the Hispanic population straddling them all." But rapidly increasing intermarriage and ethnic identity caused a number of political and ethnic groups to demand changes in the classifications of the Census Bureau. Some Arab Americans, for example, prefer to be counted as "Middle Eastern" rather than white. Children of black-white unions are defined as black 60 percent of the time, while children of Asian-white unions are described as Asian 42 percent of the time. Research is now being conducted to discover how people feel about the terms being used to define them. As one anthropologist pointed out, "Socially and politically assigned attributes have a lot to do with access to economic resources."[4]

"Socially and politically assigned attributes" can also be the basis for judging others. The definition of *success,* for example, varies among social groups as well as among individuals within the group. One scientist has postulated five signs by which to measure success: wealth (including health), security (confidence in retaining the wealth), reputation, performance, and contentment.[5] Consider whether all of these are necessary to your own definition of *success*. If not, which may be omitted? Do you think others should be added? Notice that one of the signs — reputation — is defined by the community; another — contentment — can be measured only by the individual. The assessment of performance probably owes something to both the group and the individual.

Christopher Atkins, an actor, gave an interviewer an example of an externalized definition of success — that is, a definition based on the standards imposed by other people:

[4]*Wall Street Journal*, September 9, 1995, sec. B, p. 1.
[5]Gwynn Nettler, *Social Concerns* (New York: McGraw-Hill, 1976), pp. 196–97.

Success to me is judged through the eyes of others. I mean, if you're walking around saying, "I own a green Porsche," you might meet somebody who says, "Hey, that's no big deal. I own a green Porsche and a house." So all of a sudden, you don't feel so successful. Really, it's in the eyes of others.[6]

So difficult is the formulation of a universally accepted measure for success that some scholars regard the concept as meaningless. Nevertheless, we continue to use the word as if it represented a definable concept because the idea of success, however defined, is important for the identity and development of the individual and the group. It is clear, however, that when crossing subcultural boundaries, even within a small group, we need to be aware of differences in the use of the word. If contentment — that is, the satisfaction of achieving a small personal goal — is enough, then a person making a minimal salary but doing work that he or she loves may be a success. But you should not expect all your readers to agree that these criteria are enough to define *success*.

PRACTICE

1. Use one or more cases to illustrate how, in a court of law, guilt or innocence can hinge on a matter of definition.

2. Choose two terms that are sometimes confused and define them to make their differences clear. Some examples are *active euthanasia* and *passive euthanasia, psychologist* and *psychiatrist, manslaughter* and *murder, envy* and *jealousy, sympathy* and *pity,* and *liberal* and *radical*.

3. Many recent controversial movements and causes are identified by terms that have come to mean different things to different people. Define the following terms, considering any positive or negative connotations of each. Also consider whether there is a term with a similar meaning that has more positive or more negative connotations.

   a. abortion

   b. war on terror

   c. affirmative action

   d. assisted suicide

   e. undocumented workers

Methods for Defining Terms

Reading a dictionary definition is the simplest and most obvious way to learn the basic definition of a term. An unabridged dictionary is the best source because

[6]*New York Times*, August 6, 1982, sec. 3, p. 8.

it usually gives examples of the way a word can be used in a sentence; that is, it furnishes the proper context.

In many cases, the dictionary definition alone is not sufficient. It may be too broad or too narrow for your purpose. Suppose, in an argument about pornography, you wanted to define the word *obscene*. *Webster's New International Dictionary* (third edition, unabridged) gives the definition of *obscene* as "offensive to taste; foul; loathsome; disgusting." But these synonyms do not tell you what qualities make an object or an event or an action "foul," "loathsome," and "disgusting." In 1973 the Supreme Court, attempting to narrow the definition of *obscenity*, ruled that obscenity was to be determined by the community in accordance with local standards. One person's obscenity, as numerous cases have demonstrated, may be another person's art. The celebrated trials in the early twentieth century about the distribution of novels regarded as pornographic — D. H. Lawrence's *Lady Chatterley's Lover* and James Joyce's *Ulysses* — emphasized the problems of defining obscenity.

Another dictionary definition may strike you as too narrow. *Patriotism*, for example, is defined in one dictionary as "love and loyal or zealous support of one's country, especially in all matters involving other countries." Some readers may want to include an unwillingness to support government policies they consider wrong.

These limitations are the reason that opening an essay with a dictionary definition is often not a very effective strategy, although it is a strategy often used by beginning writers. In order to initiate the effective discussion of a key term, you should be able to define it in your own words.

Stipulation

In stipulating the meaning of a term, the writer asks the reader to accept a definition that may be different from the conventional one. He or she does this to limit or control the argument. A term like *national security* can be defined by a nation's leaders in such a way as to sanction persecution of citizens and reckless military adventures. Likewise, a term such as *liberation* can be appropriated by terrorist groups whose activities often lead to oppression rather than liberation.

Even the word *violence*, which the dictionary defines as "physical force used so as to injure or damage" and whose meaning seems so clear and uncompromising, can be manipulated to produce a definition different from the one normally understood by most people. Some pacifists refer to conditions in which "people are deprived of choices in a systematic way" as "institutionalized quiet violence." Even where no physical force is employed, this lack of choice in schools, in the workplace, in the black ghettos is defined as violence.[7]

---

[7]Newton Garver, "What Violence Is," in James Rachels, ed., *Moral Choices* (New York: Harper and Row, 1971), pp. 248–49.

A reader and an audience cannot agree on a solution to a problem if they cannot even agree on what they are talking about. Carl Rogers's advice applies here: Listen to how your audience defines a key term. Make clear how you define it. And then work from there toward a definition that you can stipulate as the agreed-upon definition that you will use as you move toward resolution.

In *Through the Looking-Glass* Alice asked Humpty Dumpty "whether you can make words mean so many different things."

> "When *I* use a word," Humpty Dumpty said scornfully, "it means just what I choose it to mean — neither more nor less."[8]

A writer, however, is not free to invent definitions that no one will recognize or that create rather than solve problems between writer and reader.

Negation

To avoid confusion it is sometimes helpful to tell the reader what a term is *not.* In discussing euthanasia, a writer might say, "By euthanasia I do not mean active intervention to hasten the death of the patient."

A negative definition may be more extensive, depending on the complexity of the term and the writer's ingenuity. The former Communist party member Whittaker Chambers, in a foreword to a book on the spy trial of Alger Hiss, defined *communism* this way:

> First, let me try to say what Communism is not. It is not simply a vicious plot hatched by wicked men in a subcellar. It is not just the writings of Marx and Lenin, dialectical materialism, the Politburo, the labor theory of value, the theory of the general strike, the Red Army secret police, labor camps, underground conspiracy, the dictatorship of the proletariat, the technique of the coup d'état. It is not even those chanting, bannered millions that stream periodically, like disorganized armies, through the heart of the world's capitals: Moscow, New York, Tokyo, Paris, Rome. These are expressions, but they are not what Communism is about.[9]

This, of course, is only part of the definition. Any writer beginning a definition in the negative must go on to define what the term *is.*

Examples

One of the most effective ways of defining terms in an argument is to use examples. Both real and hypothetical examples can bring life to abstract and

---

[8]Lewis Carroll, *Alice in Wonderland and Through the Looking-Glass* (New York: Grosset and Dunlap, 1948), p. 238.

[9]*Witness* (New York: Random House, 1952), p. 8.

ambiguous terms. The writer in the following passage defines *preferred categories* (classes of people who are meant to benefit from affirmative action policies) by invoking specific cases:

> The absence of definitions points up one of the problems with preferred categories. . . . These preferred categories take no account of family wealth or educational advantages. A black whose father is a judge or physician deserves preferential treatment over any nonminority applicant. The latter might have fought his way out of the grinding poverty of Appalachia, or might be the first member of an Italian American or a Polish American family to complete high school. But no matter.[10]

Extended Definition

When we speak of an extended definition, we usually refer not only to length but also to the variety of methods for developing the definition. Let's take the word *materialism*. A dictionary entry offers the following sentence fragments as definitions: "1. the doctrine that comfort, pleasure, and wealth are the only or highest goals or values. 2. the tendency to be more concerned with material than the spiritual goals or values." But the term *materialism* has acquired so many additional meanings, especially emotional ones, that an extended definition serves a useful purpose in clarifying the many different ideas surrounding our understanding of the term.

Below is a much longer definition of *materialism*, which appears at the beginning of an essay entitled "People and Things: Reflections on Materialism."[11]

> There are two contemporary usages of the term *materialism*, and it is important to distinguish between them. On the one hand we can talk about *instrumental materialism*, or the use of material objects to make life longer, safer, more enjoyable. By instrumental, we mean that objects act as essential means for discovering and furthering personal values and goals of life, so that the objects are instruments used to realize and further those goals. There is little negative connotation attached to this meaning of the word, since one would think that it is perfectly sensible to use things for such purposes. While it is true that the United States is the epitome of materialism in this sense, it is also true that most people in every society aspire to reach our level of instrumental materialism.
>
> On the other hand the term has a more negative connotation, which might be conveyed by the phrase *terminal materialism*. This is the sense critics use when they apply the term to Americans. What they mean is that we not only use our material resources as instruments to make life more manageable, but that we reduce our ultimate goals to the possession of things. They believe that we don't just use our cars to get from place

---

[10]Anthony Lombardo, "Quotas Work Both Ways," *U.S. Catholic*, February 1974, p. 39.
[11]Mihaly Csikszentmihalyi and Eugene Rochberg-Halton, "People and Things: Reflections on Materialism," *University of Chicago Magazine*, Spring 1978, pp. 7–8.

to place, but that we consider the ownership of expensive cars one of the central values in life. Terminal materialism means that the object is valued only because it indicates an end in itself, a possession. In instrumental materialism there is a sense of directionality, in which a person's goals may be furthered through the interactions with the object. A book, for example, can reveal new possibilities or widen a person's view of the world, or an old photograph can be cherished because it embodies a relationship. But in terminal materialism, there is no sense of reciprocal interaction in the relation between the object and the end. The end is valued as final, not as itself a means to further ends. And quite often it is only the status label or image associated with the object that is valued, rather than the actual object.

In the essay from which this passage is taken, the authors distinguish between two kinds of materialism and provide an extended explanation, using contrast and examples as methods of development. They are aware that the common perception of materialism — the love of things for their own sake — is a negative one. But this view, according to the authors, doesn't fully account for the attitudes of many Americans toward the things they own. There is, in fact, another more positive meaning that the authors call *instrumental materialism*. You will recognize that the authors are *stipulating* a meaning with which their readers might not be familiar. In their essay they distinguish between *terminal materialism*, in which "the object is valued only because it indicates an end in itself," and *instrumental materialism*, "the use of material objects to make life longer, safer, more enjoyable." Since *instrumental materialism* is the less familiar definition, the essay provides a great number of examples that show how people of three different generations value photographs, furniture, musical instruments, plants, and other objects for their memories and personal associations rather than as proof of the owners' ability to acquire the objects or win the approval of others.

The Definition Essay

The argumentative essay can take the form of an extended definition. An example of such an essay is the one from which we've just quoted, as well as the essays at the end of this chapter. The definition essay is appropriate when the idea under consideration is so controversial or so heavy with historical connotations that even a paragraph or two cannot make clear exactly what the arguer wants his or her readers to understand. For example, if you were preparing a definition of *patriotism*, you would probably use a number of methods to develop your definition: personal narrative, examples, stipulation, comparison and contrast, and cause-and-effect analysis.

Writer's Guide: Writing a Definition Essay

The following important steps should be taken when you write an essay of definition.

1. Choose a term that needs definition because it is controversial or ambiguous, or because you want to offer a personal definition that differs from the accepted interpretation. Explain why an extended definition is necessary. Or choose an experience that lends itself to treatment in an extended definition. One student defined *culture shock* as she had experienced it while studying abroad in Hawaii among students of a different ethnic background.

2. Decide on the thesis — the point of view you wish to develop about the term you are defining. If you want to define *heroism*, for example, you may choose to develop the idea that this quality depends on motivation and awareness of danger rather than on the specific act performed by the hero.

3. Distinguish wherever possible between the term you are defining and other terms with which it might be confused. If you are defining *love*, can you make a clear distinction between the different kinds of emotional attachments contained in the word?

4. Try to think of several methods of developing the definition — using examples, comparison and contrast, analogy, cause-and-effect analysis. However, you may discover that one method alone — say, use of examples — will suffice to narrow and refine your definition.

5. Arrange your supporting material in an order that gives emphasis to the most important ideas.

SAMPLE ANNOTATED ESSAY

The Definition of Terrorism

BRIAN WHITAKER

Decide for yourself whether to believe this, but according to a new report there were only 16 cases of international terrorism in the Middle East last year.

That is the lowest number for any region in the world apart from North America (where there were none at

This article was published May 7, 2001, in *Guardian Unlimited*, the daily online version of the British newspaper the *Guardian*. Whitaker is an editor on Comment Is Free, the *Guardian's* Web expansion.

all). Europe had 30 cases — almost twice as many as the Middle East — and Latin America came top with 193.

The figures come from the U.S. State Department's annual review of global terrorism, which has just been published on the Internet. Worldwide, the report says confidently, "there were 423 international terrorist attacks in 2000, an increase of 8% from the 392 attacks recorded during 1999."

No doubt a lot of painstaking effort went into counting them, but the statistics are fundamentally meaningless because, as the report points out, "no one definition of terrorism has gained universal acceptance."

That is an understatement. While most people agree that terrorism exists, few can agree on what it is. A recent book discussing attempts by the UN and other international bodies to define terrorism runs to three volumes and 1,866 pages without reaching any firm conclusion.

Using the definition preferred by the state department, terrorism is: "Premeditated, politically motivated violence perpetrated against noncombatant* targets by subnational groups or clandestine agents, usually intended to influence an audience." (The asterisk is important, as we shall see later.)

"International" terrorism — the subject of the American report — is defined as "terrorism involving citizens or the territory of more than one country."

The key point about terrorism, on which almost everyone agrees, is that it's politically motivated. This is what distinguishes it from, say, murder or football hooliganism. But this also causes a problem for those who compile statistics because the motive is not always clear — especially if no one has claimed responsibility.

So the American report states — correctly — that there were no confirmed terrorist incidents in Saudi Arabia last year. There were, nevertheless, three unexplained bombings and one shooting incident, all directed against foreigners.

Another essential ingredient (you might think) is that terrorism is calculated to terrorize the public or a particular section of it. The American definition does not mention spreading terror at all, because that would exclude attacks against property. It is, after all, impossible to frighten an inanimate object.

Among last year's attacks, 152 were directed against a pipeline in Colombia which is owned by multinational

Marginal notes:

Statistics on terrorism from before 9/11

Problems with attempts to define terrorism

U.S. State Department's definition

Definition of "international" terrorism

Main point of agreement is motivation

Example of incidents with no known motivation

Another part of the definition

5

10

oil companies. Such attacks are of concern to the United States and so a definition is required which allows them to be counted.

For those who accept that terrorism is about terrorizing people, other questions arise. Does it include threats, as well as actual violence? A few years ago, for example, the Islamic Army in Yemen warned foreigners to leave the country if they valued their lives but did not actually carry out its threat.

More recently, a group of Israeli peace activists were arrested for driving around in a loudspeaker van, announcing a curfew of the kind that is imposed on Palestinians. Terrifying for any Israelis who believed it, but was it terrorism?

Another characteristic of terrorism, according to some people, is that targets must be random — the intention being to make everyone fear they might be the next victim. Some of the Hamas suicide bombings appear to follow this principle but when attacks are aimed at predictable targets (such as the military) they are less likely to terrorize the public at large.

Definitions usually try to distinguish between terrorism and warfare. In general this means that attacks on soldiers are warfare and those against civilians are terrorism, but the dividing lines quickly become blurred.

15

The state department regards attacks against "noncombatant* targets" as terrorism. But follow the asterisk to the small print and you find that "noncombatants" includes both civilians and military personnel who are unarmed or off duty at the time. Several examples are

given, such as the 1986 disco bombing in Berlin, which killed two servicemen.

The most lethal bombing in the Middle East last year was the suicide attack on USS *Cole* in Aden harbor which killed 17 American sailors and injured 39 more.

As the ship was armed and its crew on duty at the time, why is this classified as terrorism? Look again at the small print, which adds: "We also consider as acts of terrorism attacks on military installations or on armed military personnel when a state of military hostilities does not exist at the site, such as bombings against U.S. bases."

A similar question arises with Palestinian attacks on quasi-military targets such as Israeli settlements. Many settlers are armed (with weapons supplied by the army) and the settlements themselves — though they contain civilians — might be considered military targets because they are there to consolidate a military occupation.

If, under the state department rules, Palestinian mortar attacks on settlements count as terrorism, it would be reasonable to expect Israeli rocket attacks on Palestinian communities to be treated in the same way — but they are not. In the American definition, terrorism can never be inflicted by a state. 20

Limitations of American definition

Israeli treatment of the Palestinians is classified as a human rights issue (for which the Israelis get a rap over the knuckles) in a separate state department report.

Denying that states can commit terrorism is generally useful, because it gets the U.S. and its allies off the hook in a variety of situations. The disadvantage is that it might also get hostile states off the hook — which is why there has to be a list of states that are said to "sponsor" terrorism while not actually committing it themselves.

Interestingly, the American definition of terrorism is a reversal of the word's original meaning, given in the Oxford English Dictionary as "government by intimidation." Today it usually refers to intimidation of governments.

The term's original meaning

Its history

The first recorded use of "terrorism" and "terrorist" was in 1795, relating to the Reign of Terror instituted by the French government. Of course, the Jacobins, who led the government at the time, were also revolutionaries and gradually "terrorism" came to be applied to violent revolutionary activity in general. But the use of "terrorist" in an anti-government sense is not recorded until 1866 (referring to Ireland) and 1883 (referring to Russia).

The difficulty of making laws against terrorism

In the absence of an agreed meaning, making laws against terrorism is especially difficult. The latest British anti-terrorism law gets round the problem by listing 21 international terrorist organizations by name. Membership of these is illegal in the UK. 25

There are six Islamic groups, four anti-Israel groups, eight separatist groups, and three opposition groups. The list includes Hizbullah, which though armed, is a legal political party in Lebanon, with elected members of parliament.

Among the separatist groups, the Kurdistan Workers Party — active in Turkey — is banned, but not the KDP or PUK, which are Kurdish organizations active in Iraq. Among opposition groups, the Iranian People's Muja- hedeen is banned, but not its Iraqi equivalent, the INC, which happens to be financed by the United States.

Issuing such a list does at least highlight the anom- alies and inconsistencies behind anti-terrorism laws. It also points toward a simpler — and perhaps more honest — definition: terrorism is violence committed by those we disapprove of.

This author's stipulated definition

Analysis

In the United States, terrorism has received unprecedented attention since the tragic events of September 11, 2001. You may have been surprised to learn that Whitaker's essay was written in May of that year, before planes crashing into the World Trade Center, the Pentagon, and a field in Pennsylvania forever gave the term new meaning for Americans. Just as the problem of terrorism has not yet been solved, however, the problem of defining terrorism remains unsolved as well. It is still true that "no one definition of terrorism has gained universal acceptance."

The essay starts on an unusual note: "Decide for yourself whether to believe this," referring to the low number of cases of international terrorism reported in the Middle East for 2000. That statement suggests that readers should approach the numbers with skepticism. Although the specific numbers cited in the essay are at first attributed only to "a new report," Whitaker goes on to indicate that his statistical support comes from the U.S. State Department. He acknowledges that "a lot of painstaking effort" went into counting the instances of terrorism, but goes on to declare the numbers "fundamentally meaningless" because of the lack of an agreed-upon definition of the term.

In paragraphs 6 and 7, Whitaker provides the State Department's definitions of terrorism and international terrorism. He then goes on to use a combination of types of support to back up his claim, as is common in writing an extended definition. In paragraphs 8, 10, and 14, he introduces three characteristics of terrorism — that it is politically motivated, that it "is calculated to terrorize the public or a particular section of it," and that its targets must be random. Throughout the body of the essay, he includes examples to illustrate his key points. In paragraph 15, Whitaker employs another technique used often in ex- tended definition: He tells what terrorism is not.

The last third of the essay deals in part with unanswered questions and the limitations of the State Department's definition, illustrating the complications involved in defining terrorism and in passing laws against it.

Only at the end does Whitaker stipulate his own definition of terrorism. He is not providing a technical definition or one that he believes will gain universal acceptance. What he offers is his honest assessment of what Americans really perceive terrorism to be: "violence committed by those we disapprove of."

READINGS FOR ANALYSIS

When Is a Cross a Cross?
STANLEY FISH

Also, when is a menorah a menorah, and when is a crèche a crèche, and when are the Ten Commandments directives given to the Jews by God on Mt. Sinai? These questions, which might seem peculiar in the real world, are perfectly ordinary in the wild and wacky world of Establishment Clause[1] jurisprudence, where in one case (*Lynch v. Donnelly*, 1984) the Supreme Court declared, with a straight judicial face, that a display featuring the baby Jesus, Mary, Joseph, and the wise men conveyed a secular, not a religious message.

In the latest chapter of this odd project of saving religion by emptying it of its content, Justice Anthony Kennedy, writing for a plurality in *Salazar v. Buono*, ordered a district court to reconsider a ruling that Congress had impermissibly promoted religion by devising a plan designed to prevent the removal of a cross standing in the Mojave National Preserve. The cross had originally been erected in 1934 by the Veterans of Foreign Wars to commemorate American soldiers who had died in World War I. In 2002, Frank Buono, a retired Park Service employee, filed suit alleging a violation of the Establishment Clause and "sought an injunction requiring the government to remove the cross."

In litigation unfolding in at least four stages, the District Court and the Appellate Court of the Ninth Circuit determined that "a reasonable observer would perceive a cross on federal land as governmental endorsement of religion." In response, Congress took several actions, including designating the cross and the

---

[1]The part of the First Amendment that states, "Congress shall make no law respecting an establishment of religion." — EDS.

Stanley Fish is a professor of humanities and law at Florida International University and dean emeritus of the College of Liberal Arts and Sciences at the University of Illinois at Chicago. His most recent book is *Save the World on Your Own Time* (2008), about higher education. This article appeared on the *New York Times* online commentary site, the Opinionator, on May 3, 2010.

adjoining land a national memorial and transferring ownership of the land in question to the V.F.W. in exchange for land located elsewhere in the preserve. Turning again to the courts, Buono asked for an injunction against the transfer; the District Court granted it, concluding that "the transfer was an attempt by the Government to keep the cross atop Sunrise Rock and so was invalid."

The issue was Congress's motive. The effect of what it had done was obvious: the cross now stood on private land, which meant, at least theoretically, that there was no longer an Establishment Clause violation because a private party, not the government, was speaking. But the question remained: did the transfer "cure" the violation or did it, as Justice John Paul Stevens contended in dissent, extend and re-perform it?

Now the fun and crazy stuff begins. Kennedy denies that the "emplacement" of the cross was accompanied by any intention "to promote a Christian message." It was "intended simply to honor our Nation's fallen soldiers." (At oral argument Peter Eliasberg, an ACLU lawyer, observed, "There is never a cross on a tombstone of a Jew.") Therefore, Kennedy reasoned, Congress had no "illicit" intention either; it merely sought a way to "accommodate" (a term of art in Establishment Clause jurisprudence) a "symbol often used to honor and respect those whose heroic acts, noble contributions and patient striving help secure an honored place in history for this Nation and its people."

Notice what this paroxysm of patriotism had done: it has taken the Christianity out of the cross and turned it into an all-purpose means of marking secular achievements. (According to this reasoning the cross should mark the winning of championships in professional sports.) It is one of the ironies of the sequence of cases dealing with religious symbols on public land that those who argue for their lawful presence must first deny them the significance that provokes the desire to put them there in the first place.

It has become a formula: If you want to secure a role for religious symbols in the public sphere, you must de-religionize them, either by claiming for them a non-religious meaning as Kennedy does here, or, in the case of multiple symbols in a park or in front of a courthouse, by declaring that the fact of many of them means that no one of them is to be taken seriously; they don't stand for anything sectarian; they stand for diversity. So you save the symbols by leeching the life out of them. The operation is successful, but the patient is dead.

The game being played here by Kennedy (and many justices before him) is "let's pretend." Let's pretend that a cross that, as Kennedy acknowledges, "has been a gathering place for Easter services since it was first put in place," does not breathe Christianity. Let's pretend that Congress, which in addition to engineering a land-swap for the purpose of keeping the cross in place attached a reversionary clause requiring that the "memorial" (no cross is mentioned) be kept as it is, did not have in mind the preservation of a religious symbol. Let's pretend that after all these machinations a "reasonable observer" who knew all the facts would not see the government's hand, but would only see the hands of private parties. (This is what I call the "look, ma, no hands" argument.) Let's pretend that there will be many who, if the cross were removed, would think that the government had con-

5

veyed "disrespect for those the cross was seen as honoring." (Stevens points out that Kennedy just made that one up without the support of "any legislative history or findings.")

The trouble with pretending is that it involves a strain; keeping the pretense going is hard, and the truth being occluded often peeks through, as it does when Kennedy protests that the Establishment Clause "does not require eradication of all religious symbols in the public realm" and adds that "the Constitution does not oblige government to avoid any public acknowledgment of religion's role in society."

But I thought that the cross was not, at least in this instance, a religious symbol and that the issue was not government acknowledging religion, but government honoring its dead. At moments like this, the mask slips and the plurality's real concern — "to foster the display of the cross" (Stevens) — is revealed for all (who had no doubt already spied it beneath the subterfuge) to see. The Christian and conservative Web sites that welcomed the decision as a blow for Christianity and against liberalism knew what they were looking at.

My distaste for Kennedy's opinion has nothing to do with its result. In general, and for the record, I have no problem with the state accommodating religious symbols and I am not bothered by the thought of a cross standing in a remote part of the Mojave desert even if the land it stands on is owned by the government. I do have a problem with reasoning that is patently dishonest and protests too much about its own motives and the motives of those it defends. But that is what the religion clause drives you to when in one of its clauses — the free exercise clause — it singles out religion for special positive treatment, and in the other clause — the Establishment Clause — it places a warning label (watch out for this stuff; it's trouble) on religion. It's no wonder that the justices who try to deal with this schizophrenia tie themselves in knots and produce opinions that are as unedifying as they are disingenuous.

READING AND DISCUSSION QUESTIONS

1. What is the Establishment Clause?
2. Why does Fish say that the Supreme Court delivered its findings on *Lynch v. Donnelly*, 1984, "with a straight judicial face" (paragraph 1)?
3. How did Congress try to avoid taking down the cross?
4. What are some of the ways that defenders of the cross have tried to deny its Christian symbolism? What is the irony of these arguments?
5. Explain what Fish means when he says, "The operation is successful, but the patient is dead" (paragraph 7).
6. Why does Fish call the government's handling of religious symbols "schizophrenia"?

WRITING SUGGESTIONS

7. Do you think it is possible to reconcile the two clauses to which Fish refers at the end of the essay: the free exercise clause and the Establishment Clause? Explain.

8. Write a Rogerian analysis of the conflict between those who think it is all right to place religious symbols on public land and those who do not.

9. Explain your observations of how public school students feel about the presence or absence of religious symbols — and of prayer — in school.

Faux Friendship

WILLIAM DERESIEWICZ

We live in an age when friendship has become both all and nothing at all. Already the characteristically modern relationship, it has in recent decades become the universal one: the form of connection in terms of which all others are understood, against which they are all measured, into which they have all dissolved. Romantic partners refer to each other as boyfriends and girlfriends. Spouses boast they are best friends. Parents urge their young children and beg their teenage ones to think of them as friends. Teachers, clergy, and even bosses seek to mitigate and legitimate their authority by asking those they oversee to regard them as friends. As the anthropologist Robert Brain has put it, we're friends with everyone now.

Yet what, in our brave new mediated world, is friendship becoming? The Facebook phenomenon, so sudden and forceful a distortion of social space, needs little elaboration. (If we have 768 "friends," in what sense do we have any?) Yet Facebook and MySpace and Twitter — and whatever we're stampeding for next — are just the latest stages of a long attenuation. They have accelerated the fragmentation of consciousness, but they didn't initiate it. They have reified the idea of universal friendship, but they didn't invent it. In retrospect, it seems inevitable that once we decided to become friends with everyone, we would forget how to be friends with anyone. We may pride ourselves today on our aptitude for friendship, but it's not clear that we still even know what it means.

How did we come to this pass? The idea of friendship in ancient times could not have been more different. Far from being ordinary and universal, friendship, for the ancients, was rare, precious, and hard-won. In a world ordered by relations of kin and kingdom, friendship's elective affinities were exceptional, even subversive. David loved Jonathan despite the enmity of Saul; Achilles' bond with

Essayist and critic William Deresiewicz is the author of *A Jane Austen Education: How Six Novels Taught Me about Love, Friendship, and the Things that Really Matter* (2011). This excerpt is from the December 6, 2009, *Chronicle Review* section of *The Chronicle of Higher Education*.

Patroclus outweighed his loyalty to the Greek cause. Friendship was a high calling, demanding extraordinary qualities of character, rooted in virtue and dedicated to the pursuit of goodness and truth.

The rise of Christianity put the classical ideal in eclipse — Christian thought discouraged intense personal bonds, for the heart should be turned to God. The classical notion of friendship, however, was revived by the Renaissance. Truth and virtue, again, above all: "Those who venture to criticize us perform a remarkable act of friendship," wrote Montaigne, "for to undertake to wound and offend a man for his own good is to have a healthy love for him."

Classical friendship, now called romantic friendship, persisted through the   5
18th and 19th centuries, giving us the great friendships of Goethe and Schiller, Byron and Shelley, Emerson and Thoreau. Wordsworth addressed his magnum opus to his "dear Friend" Coleridge. Meanwhile, the growth of commercial society was shifting the grounds of personal life toward the conditions essential for the emergence of modern friendship. Capitalism, said David Hume and Adam Smith, by making economic relations impersonal, allowed for private relationships based on nothing other than affection and affinity.

We don't know the people who make the things we buy and don't need to know the people who sell them. The ones we do know — neighbors, parishioners, people we knew in school, parents of our children's friends — have no bearing on our economic life. We are nothing to one another but what we choose to become, and we can unbecome it whenever we want.

Add to this the growth of democracy, an ideology of universal equality and interinvolvement. We are citizens now, not subjects, bound together directly rather than through allegiance to a monarch. But what is to bind us emotionally,

From the tomb of Niankhkhnum and Khnumhotep, Egypt, c. 2450 BCE

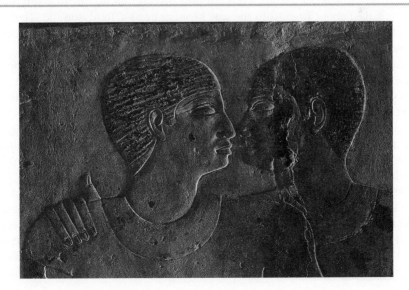

make us something more than an aggregate of political monads? One answer was nationalism, but another grew out of the 18th-century notion of social sympathy: friendship or, at least, friendliness.

It is no accident that *fraternity* made a third with *liberty* and *equality* as the watchwords of the French Revolution. Wordsworth in Britain and Whitman in America made visions of universal friendship central to their democratic vistas. For Mary Wollstonecraft, the mother of feminism, *friendship* was to be the key term of a new domestic democracy.

Now we can see why friendship has become the characteristically modern relationship. Modernity believes in equality, and friendships are egalitarian. Modernity believes in individualism. Friendships serve no public purpose and exist independent of all other bonds. Modernity believes in choice. Friendships, unlike blood ties, are elective. Modernity believes in self-expression. Friends, because we choose them, give us back an image of ourselves. Modernity believes in freedom. We can be friends with whomever we want, however we want, for as long as we want.

Social changes play into the question as well. As industrialization uprooted people from extended families and traditional communities and packed them into urban centers, friendship emerged to salve the anonymity and rootlessness of modern life. The process is virtually instinctive now: You graduate from college, move to New York or L.A., and assemble the gang that takes you through your 20s. Only it's not just your 20s anymore. We have yet to find a satisfactory name for that period of life, now typically a decade but often a great deal longer, between the end of adolescence and the making of definitive life choices. The one thing we know is that friendship is absolutely central to it.   10

Inevitably, the classical ideal has faded. The image of the one true friend, a soul mate rare to find but dearly beloved, has disappeared from our culture. We have our better or lesser friends, even our best friends, but no one in a very long time has talked about friendship the way Montaigne and Tennyson did. That glib neologism *bff* bespeaks an ironic awareness of the mobility of our connections: *Best friends forever* may not be on speaking terms by this time next month.

As for the moral content of classical friendship, its commitment to virtue and mutual improvement, that too has been lost. We have ceased to believe that a friend's highest purpose is to summon us to the good by offering moral advice and correction. We practice, instead, the nonjudgmental friendship of unconditional acceptance and support — "therapeutic" friendship, in sociologist Robert N. Bellah's scornful term. A friend fulfills her duty, we suppose, by taking our side — validating our feelings, supporting our decisions, helping us to feel good about ourselves. We're busy people; we want our friendships fun and friction-free.

Yet even as friendship became universal and the classical ideal lost its force, a new kind of idealism arose, a new repository for some of friendship's deepest needs: the group friendship or friendship circle. Companies of superior spirits go back at least as far as Pythagoras, but the culture of group friendship reached its apogee in the 1960s. Two of the counterculture's most salient and ideologically charged social forms were the commune — a community of friends in self-imagined retreat from a heartlessly corporatized society — and the rock 'n' roll "band," its name evoking Robin Hood's band of Merry Men, its great exemplar the Beatles.

Communes, bands, and other '60s friendship groups were celebrated as joyous, creative places of eternal youth. To go through life within one was the era's Utopian dream; it is no wonder the Beatles' breakup was received as a generational tragedy. It is also no wonder that '60s group friendship began to generate its own nostalgia as the baby boomers began to hit their 30s. *The Big Chill,* in 1983, depicted boomers attempting to recapture the magic of a late-'60s friendship circle. ("In a cold world," the movie's tagline reads, "you need your friends to keep you warm.") The TV series *Thirtysomething* certified group friendship as the new adult norm.

It was only in the 1990s that a new generation, remaining single well into adulthood, found its own images of group friendship in *Seinfeld, Sex and the City,* and, of course, *Friends.* By that point, however, the notion of friendship as a redoubt of moral resistance, a shelter from normative pressures and incubator of social ideals, had disappeared. Your friends didn't shield you from the mainstream, they were the mainstream. 15

And so we return to Facebook. With the social-networking sites of the new century — Friendster and MySpace were launched in 2003, Facebook in 2004 — the

Have social networking sites changed how we define "friend"?

friendship circle has expanded to engulf the whole of the social world, and in so doing has destroyed both its own nature and that of individual friendship itself. Facebook's very premise is that it makes our friendship circles visible. There they are, my friends, all in the same place. Except, of course, they're not in the same place, or, rather, they're not my friends. They're simulacra of my friends, little dehydrated packets of images and information, no more my friends than a set of baseball cards is the New York Mets.

I remember realizing a few years ago that most of the members of what I thought of as my "circle" didn't actually know one another. One I'd met in graduate school, another at a job, one in Boston, another in Brooklyn, one lived in Minneapolis now, another in Israel, so that I was ultimately able to enumerate some 14 people, none of whom had ever met any of the others. To imagine that they added up to a circle, an embracing and encircling structure, was a belief, I realized, that violated the laws of feeling as well as those of geometry.

Facebook, however, seduces us into exactly that illusion, inviting us to believe that by assembling a list, we have conjured a group. Visual juxtaposition creates the mirage of emotional proximity. "It's like they're all having a conversation," a woman I know once said about her Facebook page, full of comments from friends and friends of friends. "Except they're not."

Friendship is devolving, in other words, from a relationship to a feeling — from something people share to something we all hug privately to ourselves in the loneliness of our electronic caves. The same path was long ago trodden by community. As face-to-face community disappeared, we held on to what we had lost — the closeness, the rootedness — by clinging to the word. Now we speak of the Jewish "community" and the medical "community" and the "community" of readers, even though none of them actually is one. What we have instead is, if we're lucky, a "sense" of community — the feeling without the structure; a private emotion, not a collective experience.

Until a few years ago, you could share your thoughts with only one friend at 20 a time (on the phone, say), or maybe with a small group in person. And when you did, you were talking to specific people, and you tailored what you said, and how you said it, to who they were — their interests, their personalities, most of all, your degree of mutual intimacy. Now we're broadcasting our stream of consciousness to all 500 friends at once. We haven't just stopped talking to our friends as individuals, at such moments; we have stopped thinking of them as individuals.

It's amazing how fast things have changed. Not only don't we have Wordsworth and Coleridge anymore, we don't even have Jerry and George. Today, Ross and Chandler would be writing on each other's walls. If Carrie and the girls did manage to find the time for lunch, they'd be too busy checking their BlackBerrys to have a real conversation. *Sex* and *Friends* went off the air just six years ago, and already we live in a different world.

The new group friendship, already vitiated itself, is also cannibalizing our individual friendships as the boundaries between the two blur. The most disturbing thing about Facebook is the extent to which people are willing — are eager — to conduct their private lives in public: "hola cutie-pie! i'm in town on wednesday.

lunch?" "Julie, I'm so glad we're back in touch, xoxo." "Sorry for not calling, am going through a tough time right now."

Perhaps I need to surrender the idea that the value of friendship lies precisely in the space of privacy it creates: not the secrets that two people exchange so much as the unique and inviolate world they build up between them, the spider web of shared discovery they spin out, slowly and carefully, together.

But surely Facebook has its benefits. Long-lost friends can reconnect, far-flung ones can stay in touch. I wonder, though. Having recently moved across the country, I thought Facebook would help me feel connected to the friends I'd left behind. I find the opposite is true. Reading about the mundane details of their lives, a steady stream of trivia and ephemera, leaves me feeling both empty and unpleasantly full, as if I had just binged on junk food, and precisely because it reminds me of the real sustenance, the real knowledge, we exchange by e-mail or phone or face-to-face.

As for getting back in touch with old friends — yes, when they're people you   25
really love, it's a miracle. But most of the time, they're not. They're someone you knew for a summer in camp, or a midlevel friend from high school. They don't matter to you as individuals anymore; they matter because they made up the texture of your experience at a certain moment in your life. Tear them out of that texture — read about their brats, look at pictures of their vacation — and they mean nothing. Tear out enough of them and you ruin the texture itself, replace a matrix of feeling and memory, the deep subsoil of experience, with a spurious sense of familiarity.

Paul Gauguin, *Two Tahiti Women*, 1892.

In order to know people, you have to listen to their stories. E-mail, with its rapid-fire etiquette, already trimmed the letter to a certain acceptable maximum, perhaps 1,000 words. Now, with Facebook, the box is shrinking even more, leaving maybe a third of that as the conventional limit for a message, far less for a comment. (And we all know the deal on Twitter.) Posting information is like pornography, a slick, impersonal exhibition. Exchanging stories is like making love. It is mutual. It is intimate. It takes patience, devotion, sensitivity, subtlety, skill — and it teaches those qualities, too.

They call them social-networking sites for a reason. Networking once meant something specific: climbing the jungle gym of professional contacts in order to advance your career. The truth is that Hume and Smith were not completely right. Commercial society did not eliminate the self-interested aspects of making friends, it just changed the way we went about it. Now, in the age of the entrepreneurial self, even our closest relationships are being pressed onto this template.

A recent book on the sociology of modern science describes a networking event at a West Coast university: "There do not seem to be any singletons — disconsolately lurking at the margins — nor do dyads appear, except fleetingly." No solitude, no friendship, no space for refusal — the exact contemporary paradigm. At the same time, the author assures us, "face time" is valued in this "community" as a "high-bandwidth interaction," offering "unusual capacity for interruption, repair, feedback, and learning."

Actual human contact, rendered "unusual" and weighed by the values of a systems engineer. We have given our hearts to machines, and now we are turning into machines. The face of friendship in the new century.

READING AND DISCUSSION QUESTIONS

1. What are some of the points that Deresiewicz makes about the history of friendship?

2. Explain this quote by David Hume and Adam Smith: "Capitalism . . . by making economic relations impersonal, allowed for private relationships based on nothing other than affection and affinity" (paragraph 5).

3. Why has friendship become the characteristically modern relationship, according to Deresiewicz?

4. How has the duty of a friend changed from what Deresiewicz calls "classical friendship"?

5. How did friendship change in the 1960s? In the 1990s?

6. How has Facebook changed the nature of friendship?

WRITING SUGGESTIONS

7. Discuss the pros and cons of Facebook.

8. Explain whether or not you agree with Deresiewicz about how Facebook has changed the nature of friendship and why.

9. What are the potential dangers of Facebook or other social networking sites?

10. Has being active on Facebook or another social networking site changed your face-to-face relationships with friends? How?

Stop Calling Quake Victims Looters

GUY-URIEL CHARLES

To define someone as a looter is not simply to describe him, or her, through an act, it is to make a moral judgment. It is to characterize the person as lawless and criminal. It connotes someone who is without self-restraint; an animal; wanton and depraved.

It is a description that is void of empathy for someone who is consciously or subconsciously viewed as "the other." Tragically, it fits into the stereotype that many have about people of African descent, be they African Americans or Haitian Americans.

The news media have to stop describing starving Haitians who are simply trying to survive the earthquake and aftershocks that took their homes, their loved ones, and all their possessions by this highly derogatory term.

It's a lesson they should have learned covering the devastation wrought by Hurricane Katrina. I remember the news accounts then that described black residents of New Orleans as "looters," but used benign words to describe white residents engaged in the same action: "taking things."

Academics have found repeated instances of this in media content analyses after disasters. One example, widely disseminated on the Web post-Katrina, juxtaposed an Associated Press photo that showed a young black man wading through chest-high water "after looting a grocery store" (said the caption), with an AFP/Getty photo of a white woman in the same position, although the caption this time described her "finding" food "from a local grocery store." 5

It is time to put this practice to rest.

Put yourself in the position of the average Haitian in Port-au-Prince. One minute you were going about your business, the next minute the earth shook and literally your world crumbled all around you. But you were one of the lucky ones, you survived the earthquake. Injured? Yes. But alive.

Your first thought is to cry out for your family, especially your kids. But most of your family is buried under a rubble pile somewhere. You had four children but only one survived the earthquake. You have spent the last few days, along with your fellow survivors, digging through the rubble trying to find them.

Guy-Uriel Charles is a law professor at Duke Law School and founder of Duke's Center on Law, Race, and Politics. He is Haitian American. The article appeared on CNN.com January 21, 2010.

This photo was taken on January 18, 2010, in Port-au-Prince, Haiti, in the aftermath of a devastating earthquake.

It is now a week after the earthquake, and you have eaten little or nothing. You are hungry and thirsty, and while you hear rumors of aid coming, you have not seen any evidence of it.

You have not heard from the president and indeed you've heard rumors that his wife is dead. Perhaps he left the country; you would too, if you could. There is no police presence at all. No governmental authority to provide support. There are no markets.

The only money you have are the few gourdes (Haitian dollars) that you have in your pockets. The rest of your money is in the safe place you always kept it — but it is now buried with your food. The banks are not open. There is no one to borrow from; they are all in the same boat as you. There are no functioning institutions.

You have family in the United States and they are desperately trying to get you some help. They have contacted all of the big aid agencies, but those agencies have issues of their own. Some have lost staff members. They are doing the best they can, but they have no idea that you exist and you have no way of finding them. The roads are impassable, and they can't get clearance from whoever is in charge of the airport to land their planes, which bring much needed supplies.

They're afraid to go anywhere without security because they've heard that the people are becoming restless. Indeed, though you do not know this, the U.S. military is also worried that citizens will get violent and start stealing. The United Nations is waiting for more troops, and the doctors have stopped treating patients because of those same fears: violence, looting.

Under normal circumstances you would not think of taking food without paying for it. You are what other Haitians would call "bien eleve" not "mal eleve." By that they mean you were well-raised, with manners and dignity.

10

Haitians put a strong premium on dignity. To take something for which you   15
have not paid does not only offend your sense of legality but also your sense of
personhood. It is undignified. But not only are you starving, so is your only sur-
viving child. You would prefer to pay, but whom? What would you pay with?
You'd prefer to wait, but for whom? How long can you afford to wait?

You feel that your desperate state is evidence that you have been abandoned
by your family, your country, the international community, and Bondié (God).
(The Creole word for God literally means "good God.")

So you take. You take just enough for a couple of days and a couple of family
members. You take and you run to feed those for whom the only measure of for-
tune is survival in Haiti, post-earthquake. You take and you run.

Are you a looter? Try as we might to prevent it, the answer to that question is
inevitably racialized. We cannot separate the word looting from its racial implications or the supposed crime of looting from its racial origins. In the throes of the
civil rights movement in the United States, many states made looting a crime.
Almost all of these states were southern states that had a history of criminalizing
behavior that they associated more with African Americans than with whites.

Even so, the criminal law, for all of its shortcomings, is often more sophisticated than we are. It recognizes that context matters. It has been developed with
concepts — such as necessity and justification — to identify the circumstances under
which a person who would normally be held culpable can be held either less culpable or not at all culpable. Taking food is different than taking a television.

It is past time for our news media to develop similar sophistication. It is time   20
to stop characterizing black people trying to survive in dire circumstances as looters. Are they takers? Yes. Are they looters? Let's wait for a criminal conviction first.

READING AND DISCUSSION QUESTIONS

1. What is Charles's claim in the article?

2. How is what happened in Haiti after the earthquake similar to what happened in
   New Orleans after Hurricane Katrina?

3. What support does Charles offer for his contention that the answer to the question
   of whether or not a person is considered a looter "is inevitably racialized" (paragraph 18)?

4. Why is "looter" not an appropriate term to use to describe those in Haiti who took
   food and other goods without paying?

5. What does Charles mean when he says that criminal law "is often more sophisticated than we are" (paragraph 19)?

WRITING SUGGESTIONS

6. How would you evaluate the news coverage of the earthquake in Haiti? How do
   you think it compares with news coverage of other natural disasters?

7. Do you agree with Charles that news coverage of such disasters is "racialized"?
   Why, or why not?

DEBATE   Is the Definition of Marriage Changing?

Gay Marriage Shows Why We Need to Separate Church and State

HOWARD MOODY

If members of the church that I served for more than three decades were told I would be writing an article in defense of marriage, they wouldn't believe it. My reputation was that when people came to me for counsel about getting married, I tried to talk them out of it. More about that later.

We are now in the midst of a national debate on the nature of marriage, and it promises to be as emotional and polemical as the issues of abortion and homosexuality have been over the past century. What all these debates have in common is that they involved both the laws of the state and the theology of the church. The purpose of this writing is to suggest that the gay-marriage debate is less about the legitimacy of the loving relationship of a same-sex couple than about the relationship of church and state and how they define marriage.

In Western civilization, the faith and beliefs of Christendom played a major role in shaping the laws regarding social relations and moral behavior. Having been nurtured in the Christian faith from childhood and having served a lifetime as an ordained Baptist minister, I feel obligated first to address the religious controversy concerning the nature of marriage. If we look at the history of religious institutions regarding marriage we will find not much unanimity but amazing diversity — it is really a mixed bag. Those who base their position on "tradition" or "what the Bible says" will find anything but clarity. It depends on which "tradition" in what age reading from whose holy scriptures.

In the early tradition of the Jewish people, there were multiple wives and not all of them equal. Remember the story of Abraham's wives, Sara and Hagar. Sara couldn't get pregnant, so Hagar presented Abraham with a son. When Sara got angry with Hagar, she forced Abraham to send Hagar and her son Ishmael into the wilderness. In case Christians feel superior about their "tradition" of marriage, I would remind them that their scriptural basis is not as clear about marriage as we might hope. We have Saint Paul's conflicting and condescending words about the institution: "It's better not to marry." Karl Barth called this passage the Magna Carta of the single person. (Maybe we should have taken Saint Paul's advice more seriously. It might have prevented an earlier generation of parents from harassing, cajoling, and prodding our young until they were married.) In certain religious branches, the church doesn't recognize the licensed legality of marriage but requires that persons meet certain religious qualifications before the marriage is recognized by the church. For members of the Roman Catholic Church, a "legal

---

Reverend Howard Moody is minister emeritus of Judson Memorial Church in New York City. This article was published in July 2004 in the *Nation*.

divorce" and the right to remarry may not be recognized unless the first marriage has been declared null and void by a decree of the church. It is clear that there is no single religious view of marriage and that history has witnessed some monumental changes in the way "husband and wife" are seen in the relationship of marriage.

In my faith-based understanding, if freedom of choice means anything to individuals (male or female), it means they have several options. They can be single and celibate without being thought of as strange or psychologically unbalanced. They can be single and sexually active without being labeled loose or immoral. Women can be single with child without being thought of as unfit or inadequate. If these choices had been real options, the divorce rate may never have reached nearly 50 percent.

The other, equally significant choice for people to make is that of lifetime commitment to each other and to seal that desire in the vows of a wedding ceremony. That understanding of marriage came out of my community of faith. In my years of ministry I ran a tight ship in regard to the performance of weddings. It wasn't because I didn't believe in marriage (I've been married for sixty years and have two wonderful offspring) but rather my unease about the way marriage was used to force people to marry so they wouldn't be "living in sin."

The failure of the institution can be seen in divorce statistics. I wanted people to know how challenging the promise of those vows was and not to feel this was something they had to do. My first question in premarital counseling was, "Why do you want to get married and spoil a beautiful friendship?" That question often elicited a thoughtful and emotional answer. Though I was miserly in the number of weddings I performed, I always made exceptions when there were couples who had difficulty finding clergy who would officiate. Their difficulty was because they weren't of the same religion, or they had made marital mistakes, or what they couldn't believe. Most of them were "ecclesiastical outlaws," barred from certain sacraments in the church of their choice.

The church I served had a number of gay and lesbian couples who had been together for many years, but none of them had asked for public weddings or blessings on their relationship. (There was one commitment ceremony for a gay couple at the end of my tenure.) It was as though they didn't need a piece of paper or a ritual to symbolize their lifelong commitment. They knew if they wanted a religious ceremony, their ministers would officiate and our religious community would joyfully witness.

It was my hope that since the institution of marriage had been used to exclude and demean members of the homosexual community, our church, which was open and affirming, would create with gays and lesbians a new kind of ceremony. It would be an occasion that symbolized, between two people of the same gender, a covenant of intimacy of two people to journey together, breaking new ground in human relationships — an alternative to marriage as we have known it.

However, I can understand why homosexuals want "to be married" in the old-fashioned "heterosexual way." After all, most gays and lesbians were born of married parents, raised in a family of siblings; many were nourished in churches and synagogues, taught about a living God before Whom all Her creatures were equally loved. Why wouldn't they conceive their loving relationships in terms of marriage and family and desire that they be confirmed and understood as such? It follows that if these gays and lesbians see their relationship as faith-based, they would want a religious ceremony that seals their intentions to become lifelong partners, lovers and friends, that they would want to be "married."

Even though most religious denominations deny this ceremony to homosexual couples, more and more clergy are, silently and publicly, officiating at religious rituals in which gays and lesbians declare their vows before God and a faith community. One Catholic priest who defied his church's ban said: "We can bless a dog, we can bless a boat, but we can't say a prayer over two people who love each other. You don't have to call it marriage, you can call it a deep and abiding friendship, but you can bless it."

We have the right to engage in "religious disobedience" to the regulations of the judicatory that granted us the privilege to officiate at wedding ceremonies, and suffer the consequences. However, when it comes to civil law, it is my contention that the church and its clergy are on much shakier ground in defying the law.

In order to fully understand the conflict that has arisen in this debate over the nature of marriage, it is important to understand the difference between the religious definition of marriage and the state's secular and civil definition. The government's interest is in a legal definition of marriage — a social and voluntary contract between a man and woman in order to protect money, property, and children. Marriage is a civil union without benefit of clergy or religious definition. The state is not interested in why two people are "tying the knot," whether it's to gain money, secure a dynasty, or raise children. It may be hard for those of us who have a religious or romantic view of marriage to realize that loveless marriages are not that rare. Before the Pill, pregnancy was a frequent motive for getting married. The state doesn't care what the commitment of two people is, whether it's for life or as long as both of you love, whether it's sexually monogamous or an open marriage. There is nothing spiritual, mystical, or romantic about the state's license to marry — it's a legal contract.

Thus, George W. Bush is right when he says that "marriage is a sacred institution" when speaking as a Christian, as a member of his Methodist church. But as president of the United States and leader of all Americans, believers and unbelievers, he is wrong. What will surface in this debate as litigation and court decisions multiply is the history of the conflict between the church and the state in defining the nature of marriage. That history will become significant as we move toward a decision on who may be married.

After Christianity became the state religion of the Roman empire in A.D. 325, 15 the church maintained absolute control over the regulation of marriage for some 1,000 years. Beginning in the sixteenth century, English kings (especially Henry VIII, who found the inability to get rid of a wife extremely oppressive) and other monarchs in Europe began to wrest control from the church over marital regulations. Ever since, kings, presidents, and rulers of all kinds have seen how important the control of marriage is to the regulation of social order. In this nation, the government has always been in charge of marriage.

That is why it was not a San Francisco mayor licensing same-sex couples that really threatened the president's religious understanding of marriage but rather the Supreme Judicial Court of Massachusetts, declaring marriage between same-sex couples a constitutional right, that demanded a call for constitutional amendment. I didn't understand how important that was until I read an op-ed piece in the *Boston Globe* by Peter Gomes, professor of Christian morals and the minister of Memorial Church at Harvard University, that reminds us of a seminal piece of our history:

> The Dutch made civil marriage the law of the land in 1590, and the first marriage in New England, that of Edward Winslow to the widow Susannah White, was performed on May 12, 1621, in Plymouth by Governor William Bradford, in exercise of his office as magistrate.
>
> There would be no clergyman in Plymouth until the arrival of the Reverend Ralph Smith in 1629, but even then marriage would continue to be a civil affair, as these first Puritans opposed the English custom of clerical marriage as unscriptural. Not until 1692, when Plymouth Colony was merged into that of Massachusetts Bay, were the clergy authorized by the new province to solemnize marriages. To this day in the Commonwealth the clergy, including those of the archdiocese, solemnize marriage legally as agents of the Commonwealth and by its civil authority. Chapter 207 of the General Laws of Massachusetts tells us who may perform such ceremonies.

Now even though it is the civil authority of the state that defines the rights and responsibilities of marriage and therefore who can be married, the state is no more infallible than the church in its judgments. It wasn't until the mid-twentieth century that the Supreme Court declared antimiscegenation laws unconstitutional. Even after that decision, many mainline churches, where I started my ministry, unofficially discouraged interracial marriages, and many of my colleagues were forbidden to perform such weddings.

The civil law view of marriage has as much historical diversity as the church's own experience because, in part, the church continued to influence the civil law. Although it was the Bible that made "the husband the head of his wife," it was common law that "turned the married pair legally into one person — the husband," as Nancy Cott documents in her book *Public Vows: A History of Marriage and the Nation* (an indispensable resource for anyone seeking to understand the changing nature of marriage in the nation's history). She suggests that "the legal doctrine of marital unity was called coverture . . . [which] meant that the wife could not use legal avenues such as suits or contracts, own assets, or execute legal documents without her husband's collaboration." This view of the wife would not hold water in any court in the land today.

As a matter of fact, even in the religious understanding of President Bush and his followers, allowing same-sex couples the right to marry seems a logical conclusion. If marriage is "the most fundamental institution of civilization" and a major contributor to the social order in our society, why would anyone want to shut out homosexuals from the "glorious attributes" of this "sacred institution"? Obviously, the only reason one can discern is that the opponents believe that gay and lesbian people are not worthy of the benefits and spiritual blessings of "marriage."

At the heart of the controversy raging over same-sex marriage is the religious   20
and constitutional principle of the separation of church and state. All of us can
probably agree that there was never a solid wall of separation, riddled as it is
with breaches. The evidence of that is seen in the ambiguity of tax-free religious
institutions, "in God we trust" printed on our money and "under God" in the
Pledge of Allegiance to our country. All of us clergy, who are granted permission
by the state to officiate at legal marriage ceremonies, have already compromised
the "solid wall" by signing the license issued by the state. I would like to believe
that my authority to perform religious ceremonies does not come from the state
but derives from the vows of ordination and my commitment to God. I refuse to
repeat the words, "by the authority invested in me by the State of New York, I pro-
nounce you husband and wife," but by signing the license, I've become the state's
"handmaiden."

It seems fitting therefore that we religious folk should now seek to sharpen
the difference between ecclesiastical law and civil law as we beseech the state to
clarify who can be married by civil law. Further evidence that the issue of church
and state is part of the gay-marriage controversy is that two Unitarian ministers
have been arrested for solemnizing unions between same-sex couples when no
state licenses were involved. Ecclesiastical law may punish those clergy who dis-
obey marital regulations, but the state has no right to invade church practices and
criminalize clergy under civil law. There should have been a noisy outcry from all
churches, synagogues, and mosques at the government's outrageous contravention
of the sacred principle of the "free exercise of religion."

I come from a long line of Protestants who believe in a "free church in a
free state." In the issue before this nation, the civil law is the determinant of the
regulation of marriage, regardless of our religious views, and the Supreme Court
will finally decide what the principle of equality means in our Constitution in the
third century of our life together as a people. It is likely that the Commonwealth
of Massachusetts will probably lead the nation on this matter, as the State of New
York led to the Supreme Court decision to allow women reproductive freedom.

So what is marriage? It depends on whom you ask, in what era, in what culture. Like all words or institutions, human definitions, whether religious or secular,
change with time and history. When our beloved Constitution was written, blacks,
Native Americans, and, to some extent, women were quasi-human beings with no
rights or privileges, but today they are recognized as persons with full citizenship
rights. The definition of marriage has been changing over the centuries in this
nation, and it will change yet again as homosexuals are seen as ordinary human
beings.

In time, and I believe that time is now, we Americans will see that all the fears
foisted on us by religious zealots were not real. Heterosexual marriage will still
flourish with its statistical failures. The only difference will be that some homosexual couples will join them and probably account for about the same number
of failed relationships. And we will discover that it did not matter whether the
couples were joined in a religious ceremony or a secular and civil occasion for the
statement of their intention.

Will It Be Marriage or Civil Union?

JO ANN CITRON

This fall, while the right was still staggering from the U.S. Supreme Court's decision in *Lawrence v. Texas*,[1] Massachusetts dealt conservatives another body blow when its highest court legalized same-sex marriage. In a 4–3 ruling authored by Chief Justice Margaret Marshall, the Supreme Judicial Court (SJC) held that denying marriage to homosexuals violates the Massachusetts Declaration of Rights, the state constitution. To remedy the violation, the court changed the common-law definition of civil marriage to eliminate its opposite-sex requirement and to compel the issuance of marriage licenses to qualified persons of the same sex. Civil marriage in Massachusetts now means "the voluntary union of two persons as spouses, to the exclusion of all others." The legislature, which was directed to "take such action as it may deem appropriate in light of this opinion," has been running for cover ever since.[2]

A friend recently asked me how important the Massachusetts decision is in the struggle to achieve marriage equality in the United States. I was struck, first of all, by the terms of the question because "marriage equality" is not the same as "marriage." The issue all along has been whether gays will get marriage or some equivalent formality that will make them equal to their heterosexual counterparts. There are those who say that civil union is marriage equality. It's what Vermont said and what many Massachusetts legislators are saying in their desperate search for an escape route from the SJC ruling. It's also what William Eskridge claimed in his 2002 book, *Equality Practice: Civil Union and the Future of Gay Rights*, where he argues that, while there is no principled basis for withholding marriage from gays and lesbians, the gay community should bow to the political will of the majority and move slowly, accepting the equality of civil union now and pressing for marriage later when it becomes more palatable to the majority. Eskridge views *Baker v. State*, the Vermont civil union decision, as the equivalent of *Brown v. Board of Education*, the 1954 landmark civil rights decision that opened the way to racial integration in this country. Marriage activist Evan Wolfson, on the other hand, views *Baker* as the gay rights version of *Plessy v. Ferguson*, the railway carriage case that authorized "separate but equal" status for disfavored minorities.

[1] A 2003 case in which the Supreme Court declared unconstitutional a law that prohibited sexual intercourse between same-sex couples. — EDS.
[2] *Goodridge v. Department of Public Health.*

A former English professor at Bates College, Jo Ann Citron is now an attorney practicing in Boston, specializing in divorce and the ending of domestic partnerships. She has published widely on both literature and law and is currently working on a book, *The Gay Divorcée: How Same-Sex Couples Break Up*. This article was published in the *Gay and Lesbian Review Worldwide* in March–April 2004.

This essay is being written during the 180-day waiting period following the issuance of the decision, a period of either genuine confusion or deliberate obfuscation, depending on the degree of cynicism with which you view the political process. It might be useful at this point to summarize what the court said and how the legislature has responded. The court began by reminding everyone that the Massachusetts marriage statute is a licensing law. Because marriage has always been understood to mean the union of a man and a woman, the statute cannot be construed to authorize issuing a license to two people of the same sex. But to bar gay couples from all the benefits, protections, and obligations that accompany marriage violates the Massachusetts constitution, which means that the current marriage licensing law is unconstitutional. The remedy the court fashioned was to change the common law definition of civil marriage to eliminate its opposite-sex requirement, thereby removing the bar that excludes gay couples from obtaining marriage licenses.

Rather than declare that cities and towns must immediately begin to issue marriage licenses to gays, which would have created chaos, the court granted the legislature 180 days to revise state statutes so as to bring them into line with its ruling and to clean up a complicated domestic relations regulatory scheme that refers to husbands and wives. The court reminded the legislature that it retains "broad discretion to regulate marriage." This means that the Legislature can continue to impose certain restrictions upon persons who wish to marry. The legislature may refuse to authorize granting a marriage license to persons under a certain age, or to siblings, or to a parent and child. It may require a blood test or a birth certificate, or that applicants turn around three times and face north, or anything else that would be constitutional. But, as I read the decision, the legislature may not refuse to grant a license to otherwise qualified gay couples.

The SJC was perfectly clear in stating that the remedy for the constitutional violation was the reformulation of the definition of civil marriage. Yet many legislators, together with the current attorney general, want to take a different view of the matter. They have seized upon the "protections, benefits, and obligations" language in the opinion in the hope that, by providing the benefits that marriage yields in our society, they can avoid providing marriage itself. The legislature has asked the SJC to render an advisory opinion about a civil union bill, and the SJC has invited interested parties to submit briefs. Meanwhile, the Massachusetts constitutional convention is scheduled to meet on February 11, 2004, to vote on a Defense of Marriage Act or DOMA that, in its present form, would not only prevent gay marriage but would also outlaw domestic partner benefits. If the legislature passes the DOMA in a second convention, the measure would appear on the ballot in November of 2006 and voters could, by a simple majority, amend the state constitution to make gay marriage, civil union, and domestic partnerships illegal. The political reality is that such a DOMA will probably not garner the necessary votes either in the legislature or among voters; however, a simple DOMA limiting itself to marriage is more likely to succeed, especially in the face of the SJC decision, which presents the right with what it would call a "clear and present danger." This means that gay marriage could become legal in Massachusetts on May 18, 2004, via the SJC decision and illegal in Massachusetts on November 14, 2006, via a voter referendum. No one knows what will happen to gay couples who marry in the interim. Let the courts sort through that one!

Massachusetts has a good track record when it comes to gay families: It permits second-parent adoption; it allows two women to appear as "parent" on a child's birth certificate; it protects the relationship between a child and her non-biological parent. At the very least, *Goodridge* is going to yield "marriage equality" in some form of civil union. The problem, of course, is that there is no such thing as "marriage equality" for anyone who files federal income tax returns, bequeaths an estate, or travels outside of Massachusetts. When it comes to federal benefits or the tax-free transfer of marital property or the ability to have another state recognize your Massachusetts relationship, marriage is the only status that will do. This is why some are downplaying the SJC decision, pointing out that even if people are able to marry in Massachusetts, their status will not be recognized by the federal government or by any other state with a DOMA. In that respect, marriage is indeed no different from civil union. In fact, it might even be worse for a while. We're beginning to see judges in some states accept the validity of a Vermont civil union. Even in states with a DOMA, it will be possible to find a judge who would give full faith and credit to a civil union because most DOMA laws have nothing to say about civil unions. Not so with marriage. For the time being, a Massachusetts marriage will be even less portable than a Vermont civil union.

But let there be no mistake: Whatever happens in Massachusetts is absolutely critical to how the gay marriage question will be answered in the rest of the United States. What happens here is even more important than what happened in Vermont. Here's why. The next marriage case with a reasonable likelihood of success is working its way through the courts in New Jersey, a state with a history of progressive court decisions. New Jersey will be looking very carefully at the way Vermont and Massachusetts have addressed the marriage question. If the Massachusetts SJC ratifies its decision and mandates the issuance of marriage licenses, New Jersey will look at its predecessor states and see two alternative models, marriage and civil union. New Jersey will choose one or the other. But the SJC could fail to confirm its marriage decision and approve instead some form of civil union. Coupled with the Vermont ruling, this will create a critical mass in favor of civil union, an outcome that will make it far more likely that New Jersey will opt for civil union over marriage. After that, the rest of the states will almost certainly fall into line with civil unions, and that will spell the end of gay marriage, probably forever.

Ironically, it may also mean the end of marriage in its present form, the one that the right is working so hard to preserve. Conservatives Andrew Sullivan and David Brooks have argued that the best way to protect marriage would be to open it to anyone who wants to vow fidelity and is willing to forego an easy exit from a supposedly permanent relationship. Marriage is, after all, a conservative institution, and persons who enter it with the blessing of the state may not leave it without the state's permission. Already, as a result of the marriage cases and their surrounding discourse, the very term "marriage" is being qualified. We now speak of "civil marriage" to distinguish it from the religious ceremonies that are but one of its aspects. Insofar as material benefits are concerned, marriage is a civil institution. Those material benefits can attach just as easily to any civil institution the state cares to identify. This is, after all, the point of wanting to offer gays something called "union" rather than something called "marriage." Nothing but prejudice prevents state and federal governments from offering to partners in a civil union the identical benefits, protections, and obligations that the state now offers to spouses.

William Eskridge is wrong in thinking that civil union is a step on the path towards marriage. Civil union and marriage are not sequential; they are alternatives to one another. There is no reason to think that the country will permit civil union now and confer marriage later. In fact, the reality is likely to be quite the reverse. Because of equal protection considerations, the civil union alternative will have to be available to straights as well as gays. And if my analysis is correct, it will become more widely available to everyone in the coming years. At the moment, there is little incentive for marriage-eligible couples to elect a civil union. But this will change.

It is not difficult to imagine a tacit compromise in which the right is allowed   10 to maintain its stranglehold on marriage in exchange for allowing the material benefits now associated with it to break free and accompany civil union. This is another reason why the Massachusetts decision in favor of marriage is strategically important. As long as even a single state has legalized marriage, civil union becomes more attractive to the right. And the gay community can leverage those few gay marriage licenses into a demand that marriage benefits attach to civil unions.

In my view, this would be a good outcome. I say this as someone who views marriage as a regressive institution that has never been good to women, that insidiously creates insiders and outsiders, and, most importantly, that violates the separation of church and state at the heart of our form of government. The state should not be in the business of attaching material benefits to a religious institution. The right to social security death benefits, the right to favorable tax treatment, the right to take your formalized relationship with you when you travel, should be detached from marriage altogether and should be awarded according to some other equitable system. To the extent that this becomes so, there will eventually be no material difference between the old form of marriage and the new form of civil unions. Traditional marriage will endure as a religious institution. Already there are hundreds of clergy willing to perform marriage ceremonies for gay congregants and thousands of gay couples who have participated in these ceremonies whose benefits are wholly spiritual. Over time, civil union and civil marriage will ultimately come to mean much the same thing. Whether the SJC ratifies its original position or abandons it, *Goodridge* brings us closer to a consensus around civil union. It is time for the gay community to turn its attention to winning for civil union all the rights, benefits, protections, and obligations of marriage. That is the truly revolutionary project.

DISCUSSION QUESTIONS

1. Why is definition a critical element in Moody's argument? Why is it a critical element in Citron's? Do the two of them agree on a definition of marriage?

2. In the Rogerian approach to argumentation, what steps would Moody and Citron take to reconcile their differences?

3. What is Moody's attitude toward same-sex marriage? Why, in his opinion, do more serious problems arise when it comes to the laws of the state than the theology of the church?

4. Why does Moody believe that President Bush was wrong in saying, as president, that "marriage is a sacred institution"? Were you surprised by Moody's explanation of the history of marriage in the United States?

5. When Citron published her essay, the nation was awaiting Massachusetts's decision on the legality of same-sex marriages. What was her biggest fear about the future of the legal standing of same-sex relationships?

6. Analyze Citron's analogy between decisions regarding same-sex unions and two Supreme Court decisions regarding racial integration, *Plessy v. Ferguson* and *Brown v. Board of Education*.

7. What is the author's claim in each of the two essays?

Assignments for Understanding Definition

READING AND DISCUSSION QUESTIONS

1. Contrast the claims made by Jo Ann Citron in "Will It Be Marriage or Civil Union?" and Howard Moody in "Gay Marriage Shows Why We Need to Separate Church and State."

2. Who has the power to stipulate how a term is defined? The government? The media? Society in a broader sense? Where have you seen examples of each in the readings in this chapter?

WRITING SUGGESTIONS

3. Narrate an experience you have had in which you felt you were either aided or hindered by the fact that you were defined as a member of a specific group. It could be a group such as those defined by gender, race, religious affiliation, or membership on a team or in a club.

4. Would adoption at the state level of a policy prohibiting classifying people by race, color, ethnicity, or national origin be beneficial or pernicious for the individual and for society? In other words, what is good or bad about classifying people?

5. Find a subject in which definition is critical to how statistics are interpreted and which can be argued successfully in a 750- to 1,000-word paper. Your essay should provide proof for a claim.

WRITING ASSIGNMENTS

6. Write about an important or widely used term whose meaning has changed since you first learned it. Such terms often come from the slang of particular groups: drug users, rock music fans, musicians, athletes, computer programmers, or software developers.

7. Write an essay in which you explain how governments sometimes hide the full truth behind euphemisms and other careful word choices.

Research Readiness: Using Encyclopedias

Where can you look for more information about terms whose meanings are controversial?

When there is disagreement about the definition of a term, you may need more than a dictionary definition to clarify the points on which the disagreement is based. Often an encyclopedia will give you a much fuller discussion of the complexities of defining terms that defy simple, clear-cut definitions. The more specialized the encyclopedia, the more useful the information, unless it uses so much jargon that it is useful only to specialists.

For example, "abortion" is defined in the *Encyclopedia Britannica Online* like this:

> **Abortion** — the expulsion of a fetus from the uterus before it has reached the stage of viability (in human beings, usually about the 20th week of gestation). An abortion may occur spontaneously, in which case it is also called a miscarriage, or it may be brought on purposefully, in which case it is often called an induced abortion.

A specialized encyclopedia may provide more detailed information because it may discuss different positions in the debate for or against abortion. What follows is only a portion of an article from the *Encyclopedia of Philosophy*, which also includes a list of works cited that leads to other possible sources:

> The claims to which partisans on both sides of the "abortion" issue appeal seem, if one is not thinking of the abortion issue, close to self-evident, or they appear to be easily defensible. The case against abortion (Beckwith 1993) rests on the proposition that there is a very strong presumption that ending another human life is seriously wrong. Almost everyone who is not thinking about the abortion issue would agree. There are good arguments for the view that fetuses are both living and human. ("Fetus" is generally used in the philosophical literature on abortion to refer to a human organism from the time of conception to the time of birth.) Thus, it is easy for those opposed to abortion to think that only the morally depraved or the seriously confused could disagree with them.
>
> Standard pro-choice views appeal either to the proposition that women have the right to make decisions concerning their own bodies or to the proposition that fetuses are not yet persons. Both of these propositions seem either

to be platitudes or to be straightforwardly defensible. Thus, it is easy for pro-choicers to believe that only religious fanatics or dogmatic conservatives could disagree. This explains, at least in part, why the abortion issue has created so much controversy. The philosophical debate regarding abortion has been concerned largely with subjecting these apparently obvious claims to the analytical scrutiny philosophers ought to give to them.

Consider first the standard argument against abortion. One frequent objection to the claim that fetuses are both human and alive is that we do not know when life begins. The reply to this objection is . . . .

You may find that your library has a database like Gale Virtual Reference Library that lets you search a number of different encyclopedias at the same time. Just the first six entries from the list generated by that database lead to a range of different encyclopedias to investigate:

1. Abortion: I. Medical Perspectives. Allan Rosenfield, Sara Iden, and Anne Drapkin Lyerly. *Encyclopedia of Bioethics.* Ed. Stephen G. Post. Vol. 1. 3rd ed. New York: Macmillan Reference USA, 2004. p. 1–7.

2. Abortion. Menachem Elon. *Encyclopaedia Judaica.* Ed. Michael Berenbaum and Fred Skolnik. Vol. 1. 2nd ed. Detroit: Macmillan Reference USA, 2007. p. 270–273.

3. Abortion. Don Marquis. *Encyclopedia of Philosophy.* Ed. Donald M. Borchert. Vol. 1. 2nd ed. Detroit: Macmillan Reference USA, 2006. p. 8–10.

4. Abortion. *National Survey of State Laws.* Ed. Richard A. Leiter. 6th ed. Detroit: Gale, 2008. p. 339–371.

5. Abortion. *West's Encyclopedia of American Law.* Ed. Shirelle Phelps and Jeffrey Lehman. Vol. 1. 2nd ed. Detroit: Gale, 2005. p. 13–26.

6. Abortion. Mark R. Wicclair and Gabriella Gosman. *Encyclopedia of Science, Technology, and Ethics.* Ed. Carl Mitcham. Vol. 1. Detroit: Macmillan Reference USA, 2005. p. 1–6.

ASSIGNMENT

1. Find out what your library has to offer when it comes to encyclopedias. A librarian may be able to give you a list. Some may be in print and others online. If there is not a list, you can search under "encyclopedia" in the catalog and scan the list for relevant titles.

2. Now choose one of the controversial subjects listed below and investigate what you can learn about it from three different encyclopedias. Do not use more than one general encyclopedia. Cut, paste, and print; photocopy; or take notes on the three and be prepared to discuss what you found. One question you should consider is how useful each would be to a researcher.

Just war
Euthanasia
Same-sex marriage
Sexual harassment

CHAPTER 5

Claims

What are you trying to prove? Claims, or propositions, represent answers to this question. Although they are the conclusions you have reached about your subject, they often appear as thesis statements when you write about that subject. Claims can be classified as *claims of fact, claims of value,* and *claims of policy.*

Claims of Fact

Claims of fact assert that a condition has existed, exists, or will exist and that their support consists of factual information — information such as statistics, examples, and testimony that most responsible observers assume can be verified.

Many facts are not matters for argument: Our own senses can confirm them, and other observers will agree about them. We can agree that a certain number of students were in the classroom at a particular time, that the sun sets in the west, and that a new traffic light has been installed at the inter-section of Park and Main.

We can also agree about information that most of us can rarely confirm for ourselves — information in reference books, such as atlases, almanacs, and telephone directories; data from scientific resources about the physical world; and happenings reported in the media. We can agree on the reliabil-ity of such information if we trust the observers who report it.

However, the factual map is constantly being redrawn by new data in such fields as history and science that cause us to reevaluate our conclu-sions. For example, the discovery of the Dead Sea Scrolls in 1947 revealed that some books of the Bible — Isaiah, for one — were far older than we had thought. Recent research has proven that cervical cancer is caused by a virus and that a vaccination given early enough can possibly prevent it. DNA evidence has cleared individuals who served years in prison for crimes they did not commit.

In your conversations you probably generate claims of fact every day, some of which can be verified without much effort, others of which are more difficult to substantiate.

Claim: Most of the students in this class come from towns within fifty miles of Boston.

To prove this the arguer would need only to ask the students in the class where they come from.

Claim: More students entering this fall had AP credit for one or more courses than in any past year.

To prove this claim, the arguer would have to have access to entering students' records from the time Advanced Placement was first accepted to the present.

Claim: The Braves will win the pennant this year.

This claim is different from the others because it is an opinion about what will happen in the future. But it can be verified (in the future) and is therefore classified as a claim of fact.

More complex factual claims about political and scientific matters remain controversial because proof on which all or most observers will agree is difficult or impossible to obtain.

Claim: Bilingual programs have a lower success rate than English-only programs in preparing students for higher education.

Claim: The only life in the universe exists on this planet.

Not all claims are so neatly stated or make such unambiguous assertions. Because we recognize that there are exceptions to most generalizations, we often qualify our claims with words such as *generally, usually, probably,* and *as a rule.* It would not be true to state flatly, for example, "College graduates earn more than high school graduates." This statement is generally true, but we know that some high school graduates who are electricians or city bus drivers or sanitation workers earn more than college graduates who are schoolteachers or nurses or social workers. In making such a claim, therefore, the writer should qualify it with a word that limits the claim.

We have defined a fact as a statement that can be verified. An inference is "a statement about the unknown on the basis of the known."[1] The difference between facts and inferences is important to you as the writer of an argument because an inference is an *interpretation,* or an opinion reached after informed evaluation of evidence.

---

[1]S. I. Hayakawa, *Language in Thought and Action* (New York: Harcourt, Brace, Jovanovich, 1978), p. 35.

You have probably come across a statement such as the following in a newspaper or magazine: "Excessive television viewing has caused the steady decline in the reading ability of children and teenagers." Presented this way, the statement is clearly intended to be read as a factual claim that has been or can be proved. But it is an inference. The facts, which can be and have been verified, are (1) the reading ability of children and teenagers has declined and (2) the average child views television for six or more hours a day. (Whether this amount of time is "excessive" is also an opinion.) The cause-and-effect relation between the two facts is an interpretation of the investigator, who has examined both the reading scores and the amount of time spent in front of the television set and *inferred* that one is the cause of the other. The causes of the decline in reading scores are probably more complex than the original statement indicates. Since we can seldom or never create laboratory conditions for testing the influence of television separate from other influences in the family and the community, any statement about the connection between reading scores and television viewing can only be a guess.

By definition, no inference can ever do more than suggest probabilities. Of course, some inferences are much more reliable than others and afford a high degree of probability. Almost all claims in science are based on inferences, interpretations of data on which most scientists agree. Paleontologists find a few ancient bones from which they make inferences about an animal that might have been alive millions of years ago. We can never be absolutely certain that the reconstruction of the dinosaur in the museum is an exact copy of the animal it is supposed to represent, but the probability is fairly high because no other interpretation works so well to explain all the observable data — the existence of the bones in a particular place, their age, their relation to other fossils, and their resemblance to the bones of existing animals with which the paleontologist is familiar.

Inferences are profoundly important, and most arguments could not proceed very far without them. But an inference is not a fact. The writer of an argument must make it clear when he or she offers an inference, an interpretation, or an opinion that it is not a fact.

SAMPLE ESSAY   Claim of Fact

Picking Sides for the News

ROBERT J. SAMUELSON

We in the news business think we're impartial seekers of truth, but most Americans think otherwise. They view us as sloppy, biased, and self-serving.

Robert J. Samuelson, a contributing editor of *Newsweek*, has written a column for the *Washington Post* since 1977. This article appeared in *Newsweek* on June 28, 2004.

In 1985, 56 percent of the public felt news organizations usually got their facts straight, says the Pew Research Center. By 2002 that was 35 percent. In 1985 the public thought the media "moral" by 54 to 13 percent; by 2003 opinion was split 40 to 38 percent. Americans think the "media make news rather than just report it," says Pew's Andrew Kohut. The obsession with "scandal in high places" is seen as building audiences rather than advancing the public interest.

Still, the latest Pew survey confirms — with lots of numbers — something disturbing that we all sense: People are increasingly picking their media on the basis of partisanship. If you're Republican and conservative, you listen to talk radio and watch the Fox News Channel. If you're liberal and Democratic, you listen to National Public Radio and watch "NewsHour with Jim Lehrer." It's like picking restaurants: Chinese for some, Italian for others. And everyone can punch up partisan blogs — the fast food of the news business. What's disturbing is that, like restaurants, the news media may increasingly cater to their customers' (partisan) tastes. News slowly becomes more selective and slanted.

Rush Limbaugh has 14.5 million weekly listeners. By Pew, 77 percent are conservative, 16 percent moderate, and 7 percent liberal. Or take Fox's 1.3 million prime-time viewers: 52 percent are conservative, 30 percent moderate, and 13 percent liberal. By contrast, 36 percent of Americans are conservative, 38 percent moderate, and 18 percent liberal. The liberals' media favorites are slightly less lopsided. "NewsHour's" audience is 22 percent conservative, 44 percent moderate, and 27 percent liberal. NPR's audience is 31 percent conservative, 33 percent moderate, and 30 percent liberal. Of course, many news outlets still have broad audiences. Daily newspapers are collectively close to national averages; so is CNN.

But the partisan drift may grow because distrust is spreading. In 1988 Pew found that 58 percent of the public thought there was "no bias" in election coverage. Now that's 38 percent: 22 percent find a Democratic bias, 17 percent a Republican. Almost all major media have suffered confidence declines. Among Republicans, only 12 percent say they believe "all or most" of *Newsweek*; for Democrats the figure is twice that, 26 percent. In 1985 the overall figure was higher (31 percent), with little partisan gap. *Newsweek's* numbers typify mainstream media. Only 14 percent of Republicans believe "all or most" of the *New York Times*, versus 31 percent of Democrats.

What's going on? Why should we care?   5

Up to a point, conservative talk radio and Fox represent a desirable backlash against the perceived "liberal bias" of network news and mainstream media. I've worked in the mainstream press for 35 years. Editors and reporters reflexively deny a liberal bias, even though many ordinary people find it and mainstream newsrooms are politically skewed. Here are the latest Pew figures: 7 percent of national reporters and editors are conservative (a fifth the national rate), and 34 percent are liberal (almost twice the national rate). Most reporters I know believe fiercely in being fair and objective. Still, the debate over "what's news and significant?" is warped. Talk radio and Fox add other views.

But the sorting of audiences by politics also poses dangers — for the media and the country. We journalists think we define news, and from day to day, we do. Over the longer run, that's less true. All news organizations must satisfy their audiences. If they don't, they go out of business. "Media bias is product differen-tiation," says James T. Hamilton of Duke, whose book *All the News That's Fit to Sell* shows how economic forces powerfully shape news judgments. If liberals and con-servatives migrate to rival media camps, both camps may ultimately submit to the same narrow logic: like-minded editors and reporters increasingly feed like-minded customers stories that reinforce their world view.

Economic interests and editorial biases will converge. The *New York Times* is now a national paper; 49 percent of its daily circulation is outside the New York area, up from 38 percent five years ago. There's home delivery in 275 markets, up from 171 five years ago. But if the *Times* sells largely to upscale readers (average household income is $90,381, almost twice the national average) with vaguely liberal views, it risks becoming hostage to their sensibilities. No less does Fox risk becoming hostage to its base.

The worthy, if unattainable, ideals of fairness and objectivity will silently erode. Many forces push that way: new technologies (cable, the Internet); the blending of news and entertainment; the breakdown between "hard news" and interpretation; intense competition; changing news habits of the young. The dam-age will not just be to good journalism. Tom Rosenstiel of the Project for Excel-lence in Journalism notes that respected national media develop common facts and language that helps hold society together and solve common problems. It will be a sad day when we trust only the media that voice our views.

Claims of Value

Unlike claims of fact, which state that something is true and can be validated by reference to the data, claims of value **make a judgment**. They express approval or disapproval. They attempt to prove that some action, belief, or condition is right or wrong, good or bad, beautiful or ugly, worthwhile or undesirable.

Claim: Democracy is superior to any other form of government.

Claim: Killing animals for sport is wrong.

Claim: The Sam Rayburn Building in Washington is an aesthetic failure.

Some claims of value are simply expressions of taste, likes and dislikes, or preferences and prejudices. The Latin proverb *"De gustibus non est disputandum"* means that we cannot dispute taste. If you love the musical *Billy Elliot*, there is no way for anyone to prove you wrong.

Many claims of value, however, can be defended or attacked on the basis of standards that measure the worth of an action, a belief, or an object. As far as possible, our personal likes and dislikes should be supported by reference to these standards. Value judgments occur in any area of human experience, but whatever the area, the analysis will be the same. We ask the arguer who is defending a claim of value: *What are the standards or criteria for deciding that this action, this belief, or this object is good or bad, beautiful or ugly, desirable or undesirable? Does the thing you are defending fulfill these criteria?*

There are two general areas in which people often disagree about matters of value: aesthetics and morality.

Aesthetics is the study of beauty and the fine arts. Controversies over works of art — the aesthetic value of books, paintings, sculpture, architecture, dance, drama, and movies — rage fiercely among experts and laypeople alike. They may disagree on the standards for judging or, even if they agree about standards, may disagree about how successfully the art object under discussion has met these standards. The Rogerian approach to conflict resolution can be particularly useful in resolving disagreements over the standards for judging. Agreeing on those standards is the first step toward resolving the conflict and is a necessary step before seeking agreement on how well the standards have been met.

Consider a discussion about popular music. Hearing someone praise the singing of Manu Chao, a hugely popular European singer now playing to American crowds, you might ask why he is highly regarded. You expect Chao's fans to say more than "I like him" or "He's great." You expect them to give reasons to support their claims. They might show you a short review from a respected newspaper that says, "Mr. Chao's gift is simplicity. His music owes a considerable amount to Bob Marley . . . but Mr. Chao has a nasal, regular-guy voice, and instead of the Wailers' brooding, bass-heavy undertow, Mr. Chao's band delivers a lighter bounce. His tunes have the singing directness of nursery rhymes."[2] Chao's fans accept these criteria for judging a singer's appeal.

You may not agree that simplicity, directness, and a regular-guy voice are the most important qualities in a popular singer. But the establishment of standards itself offers material for a discussion or an argument. You may argue about the relevance of the criteria, or you may agree with the criteria but argue about the success of the singer in meeting them. Perhaps you prefer complexity to simplicity. Or even if you choose simplicity, you may not think that Chao has exhibited this quality to good effect.

It is probably not surprising then, that, despite wide differences in taste, professional critics more often than not agree on criteria and whether an art object has met the criteria. For example, almost all movie critics agree that *Citizen Kane* and *Gone with the Wind* are superior films. They also agree that *Plan 9 from Outer Space*, a horror film, is terrible.

Value claims about morality express judgments about the rightness or wrongness of conduct or belief. Here disagreements are as wide and deep as in the arts — and more significant. The first two examples on page 174 reveal how controversial such claims can be. Although you and your reader may share many values — among them a belief in democracy, a respect for learning, and a desire for peace — you may also disagree, even profoundly, about other values. The subject of divorce, for example, despite its prevalence in our society, can produce a conflict between people who have differing moral standards. Some people

[2]Jon Pareles, *New York Times*, July 10, 2001, p. B1.

may insist on adherence to absolute standards, arguing that the values they hold are based on immutable religious precepts derived from God and biblical scripture. Since marriage is sacred, divorce is always wrong, they say, whether or not the conditions of society change. Other people may argue that values are relative, based on the changing needs of societies in different places and at different times. Since marriage is an institution created by human beings at a particular time in history to serve particular social needs, they may say, it can also be dissolved when other social needs arise. The same conflicts between moral values might occur in discussions of abortion or suicide.

Nevertheless, even where people agree about standards for measuring behavior, a majority preference is not enough to confer moral value. If in a certain neighborhood a majority of heterosexual men decide to harass a few gay men and lesbians, that consensus does not make their action right. In formulating value claims, you should be prepared to ask and answer questions about the way in which your value claims and those of others have been arrived at. Lionel Ruby, an American philosopher, sums it up in these words: "The law of rationality tells us that we ought to justify our beliefs by evidence and reasons, instead of asserting them dogmatically."[3]

Of course, you will not always be able to persuade those with whom you argue that your values are superior to theirs and that they should therefore change their attitudes. What you can and should do, however, as Lionel Ruby advises, is give *good reasons* that you think one thing is better than another. If as a child you asked why it was wrong to take your brother's toys, you might have been told by an exasperated parent, "Because I say so." Some adults still give such answers in defending their judgments, but such answers are not arguments and do nothing to win the agreement of others.

SAMPLE ESSAY   Claim of Value

Crash

ROGER EBERT

Crash tells interlocking stories of whites, blacks, Latinos, Koreans, Iranians, cops and criminals, the rich and the poor, the powerful and powerless, all defined in one way or another by racism. All are victims of it, and all are guilty of it. Sometimes, yes, they rise above it, although it is never that simple. Their negative

---

Roger Ebert has been the film critic of the *Chicago Sun-Times* since 1967 and is the author of more than fifteen books about film. He appeared for years on a televised show about movies. He won the Pulitzer Prize for criticism in 1975, and his reviews are now syndicated in more than two hundred newspapers in the United States, Canada, England, Japan, and Greece.

[3]*The Art of Making Sense* (New York: Lippincott, 1968), p. 271.

impulses may be instinctive, their positive impulses may be dangerous, and who knows what the other person is thinking?

The result is a movie of intense fascination; we understand quickly enough who the characters are and what their lives are like, but we have no idea how they will behave because so much depends on accident. Most movies enact rituals; we know the form and watch for variations. *Crash* is a movie with free will, and anything can happen. Because we care about the characters, the movie is uncanny in its ability to rope us in and get us involved.

Crash was directed by Paul Haggis, whose screenplay for *Million Dollar Baby* led to Academy Awards. It connects stories based on coincidence, serendipity, and luck, as the lives of the characters crash against one another like pinballs. The movie presumes that most people feel prejudice and resentment against members of other groups, and observes the consequences of those feelings.

One thing that happens, again and again, is that people's assumptions prevent them from seeing the actual person standing before them. An Iranian (Shaun Toub) is thought to be an Arab, although Iranians are Persian. Both the Iranian and the white wife of the district attorney (Sandra Bullock) believe a Mexican-American locksmith (Michael Pena) is a gang member and a crook, but he is a family man.

A black cop (Don Cheadle) is having an affair with his Latina partner (Jennifer Esposito), but never gets it straight which country she's from. A cop (Matt Dillon) thinks a light-skinned black woman (Thandie Newton) is white. When a white producer tells a black TV director (Terrence Dashon Howard) that a black character "doesn't sound black enough," it never occurs to him that the director doesn't "sound black," either. For that matter, neither do two young black men (Larenz Tate and Ludacris), who dress and act like college students but have a surprise for us. 5

You see how it goes. Along the way, these people say exactly what they are thinking, without the filters of political correctness. The district attorney's wife is so frightened by a street encounter that she has the locks changed, then assumes the locksmith will be back with his "homies" to attack them. The white cop can't get medical care for his dying father, and accuses a black woman at his HMO with taking advantage of preferential racial treatment. The Iranian can't understand what the locksmith is trying to tell him, freaks out, and buys a gun to protect himself. The gun dealer and the Iranian get into a shouting match.

I make this sound almost like episodic TV, but Haggis writes with such directness and such a good ear for everyday speech that the characters seem real and plausible after only a few words. His cast is uniformly strong; the actors sidestep clichés and make their characters particular.

For me, the strongest performance is by Matt Dillon, as the racist cop in anguish over his father. He makes an unnecessary traffic stop when he thinks he sees the black TV director and his light-skinned wife doing something they really shouldn't be doing at the same time they're driving. True enough, but he wouldn't have stopped a black couple or a white couple. He humiliates the woman with an invasive body search, while her husband is forced to stand by powerless, because the cops have the guns — Dillon, and also an unseasoned rookie (Ryan Phillippe), who hates what he's seeing but has to back up his partner.

That traffic stop shows Dillon's cop as vile and hateful. But later we see him trying to care for his sick father, and we understand why he explodes at the HMO worker (whose race is only an excuse for his anger). He victimizes others by exercising his power and is impotent when it comes to helping his father. Then the plot turns ironically on itself, and both of the cops find themselves, in very different ways, saving the lives of the very same TV director and his wife. Is this just manipulative storytelling? It didn't feel that way to me because it serves a deeper purpose than mere irony: Haggis is telling parables, in which the characters learn the lessons they have earned by their behavior.

Other cross-cutting Los Angeles stories come to mind, especially Lawrence   10
Kasdan's more optimistic *Grand Canyon* and Robert Altman's more humanistic *Short Cuts*. But *Crash* finds a way of its own. It shows the way we all leap to conclusions based on race — yes, all of us, of all races, and however fair-minded we may try to be — and we pay a price for that. If there is hope in the story, it comes because as the characters crash into one another, they learn things, mostly about themselves. Almost all of them are still alive at the end and are better people because of what has happened to them. Not happier, not calmer, not even wiser, but better. Then there are those few who kill or get killed; racism has tragedy built in.

Not many films have the possibility of making their audiences better people. I don't expect *Crash* to work any miracles, but I believe anyone seeing it is likely to be moved to have a little more sympathy for people not like themselves. The movie contains hurt, coldness, and cruelty, but is it without hope? Not at all. Stand back and consider. All of these people, superficially so different, share the city and learn that they share similar fears and hopes. Until several hundred years ago, most people everywhere on earth never saw anybody who didn't look like them. They were not racist because, as far as they knew, there was only one race. You may have to look hard to see it, but *Crash* is a film about progress.

Claims of Policy

Claims of policy argue that certain conditions should exist. As the name suggests, they advocate adoption of policies or courses of action because problems have arisen that call for solution. Almost always *should* or *ought to* or *must* is expressed or implied in the claim.

> **Claim:** Voluntary prayer should be permitted in public schools.

> **Claim:** A dress code should be introduced for all public high schools.

> **Claim:** A law should permit sixteen-year-olds and parents to "divorce" each other in cases of extreme incompatibility.

> **Claim:** Mandatory jail terms should be imposed for drunk driving violations.

In defending such claims of policy you may find that you must first convince your audience that a problem exists. This will require that, as part of your longer argument, you make a factual claim, offering data to prove that present conditions are unsatisfactory. You may also find it necessary to refer to the values that support your claim. Then you will be ready to introduce your policy, to persuade your audience that the solution you propose will solve the problem. If you approach the problem from a Rogerian perspective, you will also point out what both conflicting sides could gain from it.

Consider this policy claim: "The time required for an undergraduate degree should be extended to five years." Immediate agreement with this policy among student readers would certainly not be universal. Some students would not recognize a problem. They would say, "The college curriculum we have now is fine. There's no need for a change. Besides, we don't want to spend more time in school." First, then, the arguer would have to persuade a skeptical audience that there is a problem — that four years of college is no longer enough because the stock of knowledge in almost all fields of study continues to increase. The arguer would provide data to show that students today have many more choices in history, literature, and science than students had in those fields a generation ago and would also emphasize the value of greater knowledge and more schooling compared to the value of other goods the audience cherishes, such as earlier independence. Finally, the arguer would offer a plan for implementing the policy. The plan would have to consider initial psychological resistance, revision of the curriculum, costs of more instruction, and costs of lost production in the workforce. Most important, this policy would point out the benefits for both individuals and society if it were adopted.

In this example, we assumed that the reader would disagree that a problem existed. In many cases, however, the reader may agree that there is a problem but disagree with the arguer about the way to solve it. Most of us, no doubt, agree that we want to reduce or eliminate the following problems: misbehavior and vandalism in schools, drunk driving, crime on the streets, child abuse, pornography, pollution. But how should we go about solving those problems? What public policy will give us well-behaved, diligent students who never destroy school property? Safe streets where no one is ever robbed or assaulted? Loving homes where no child is ever mistreated? Some members of society would choose to introduce rules or laws that punish infractions so severely that wrongdoers would be unwilling or unable to repeat their offenses. Other members of society would prefer policies that attempt to rehabilitate or reeducate offenders through training, therapy, counseling, and new opportunities.

A major mistake that one group can make is to ignore that other opinions even exist. You can only support the notion that your proposed solution is better if you can acknowledge that you are aware of and understand another's perspective. Rogerian analysis is one way of attempting to reconcile such differences of opinion. If one of the disagreeing parties has to state the other's position fairly before offering an opinion, it can be the first step toward a solution both can accept. The resulting claim may not advocate what either side considers the perfect solution, but it may keep the conversation going.

As you ponder what action or change in thought you are proposing as your claim of policy — what should or should not be done — you have to keep your audience in mind. Given their level of emotional involvement with the issue, what proposal might they be willing to consider? A vegetarian may argue that everyone should be a vegetarian but is much more likely to get a hearing if the argument is that every meat eater should learn about the health benefits of vegetarianism before rejecting it. A college student might argue that all general education requirements should be abolished but might be wiser to start with a less ambitious claim: High school and college math and science curricula should be coordinated so that the freshman year of college is not merely a repetition of the senior year in high school. You must also consider what, realistically, your audience can do about the situation. It is one thing to tell a group of parents that school resource officers should be better trained in interacting with students with disabilities. A more realistic solution would be to encourage the parents to write about this issue to the director of the state police training academy. At other times the most you might hope to accomplish is to get your readers to consider the situation from your perspective. Keep this question in mind as you arrive at your claim of policy: What do I want my readers to do or think?

SAMPLE ANNOTATED ESSAY   Claim of Policy

College Life Versus My Moral Code

ELISHA DOV HACK

Background that reveals his respect for Yale and his connection to it through his brother

How residency rules have changed

Many people envy my status as a freshman at Yale College. My classmates and I made it through some fierce competition, and we are excited to have been accepted to one of the best academic and extra-curricular programs in American higher education. I have an older brother who attended Yale, and I've heard from him what life at Yale is like.

He spent all his college years living at home because our parents are New Haven residents, and Yale's rules then did not require him to live in the dorms. But Yale's new regulations demand that I spend my freshman and sophomore years living in the college dormitories.

Elisha Dov Hack was a member of the Yale College freshman class of 1997. This article appeared on September 9, 1997, in the *New York Times*. The case brought by Hack and four other Jewish students remained in court until all but Hack had graduated. Hack went on to marry before his 2003 graduation in engineering sciences.

<table>
<tr><td>Establishes the problem</td><td></td></tr>
</table>

I, two other freshmen, and two sophomores have refused to do this because life in the dorms, even on the floors Yale calls "single sex," is contrary to the fundamental principles we have been taught as long as we can remember — the principles of Judaism lived according to the Torah and 3,000-year-old rabbinic teachings. Unless Yale waives its residence requirement, we may have no choice but to sue the university to protect our religious way of life.

Examples of affronts to his religious beliefs

Bingham Hall, on the Yale quadrangle known as the Old Campus, is one of the dorms for incoming students. When I entered it two weeks ago during an orientation tour, I literally saw the handwriting on the wall. A sign titled "Safe Sex" told me where to pick up condoms on campus. Another sign touted 100 ways to make love without having sex, like "take a nap together" and "take a steamy shower together."

Another example of accepted dorm standards

That, I am told, is real life in the dorms. The "freshperson" issue of the *Yale Daily News* sent to entering students contained a "Yale lexicon" defining *sexile* as "banishment from your dorm room because your roommate is having more fun than you." If you live in the dorms, you're expected to be part of the crowd, to accept these standards as the framework for your life.

Can we stand up to classmates whose sexual morality differs from ours? We've had years of rigorous religious teaching, and we've watched and learned from our parents. We can hold our own in the intellectual debate that flows naturally from exchanges during and after class. But I'm upset and hurt by this requirement that I live in the dorms. Why is Yale — an institution that professes to be so tolerant and open-minded — making it particularly hard for students like us to maintain our moral standards through difficult college years?

Challenges whether Yale should make it difficult for students to maintain their morals outside of class

We are not trying to impose our moral standards on our classmates or on Yale. Our parents tell us that things were very different in college dormitories in their day and that in most colleges in the 1950s students who allowed guests of the opposite sex into their dorm rooms were subject to expulsion. We acknowledge that today's morality is not that of the 50s. We are asking only that Yale give us the same permission to live off campus that it gives any lower classman who is married or at least twenty-one years old.

Tries to achieve middle ground by acknowledging that morality has changed but argues that exceptions to the policy are already made

5

Yale is proud of the fact that it has no "parietal rules" and that sexual morality is a student's own business. Maybe this is what Dean Richard H. Brodhead meant when he said that "Yale's residential colleges carry . . . a moral meaning." That moral meaning is, basically, "Anything goes." This morality is Yale's own residential religion, which it is proselytizing by force of its regulations.

Attacks the opposition by defining immorality as Yale's religion

We cannot, in good conscience, live in a place where women are permitted to stay overnight in men's rooms, and where visiting men can traipse through the common halls on the women's floors — in various stages of undress — in the middle of the night. The dormitories on Yale's Old Campus have floors designated by gender, but there is easy access through open stairwells from one floor to the next.

Floors designated by gender are not the solution

The moral message Yale's residences convey today is not one that our religion accepts. Nor is it a moral environment in which the five of us can spend our nights, or a moral surrounding that we can call home.   10

The source of conflict

Yale sent me a glossy brochure when it welcomed me as an entering student. It said, "Yale retains a deep respect for its early history and for the continuity that its history provides — a continuity based on constant reflection and reappraisal." Yale ought to reflect on and reappraise a policy that compels us to compromise our religious principles.

Uses Yale's own advertising against it

Claim of Policy: A university that espouses a willingness to reflect and reappraise should not compel Hack and the other Jewish students to compromise their principles.

Analysis

Notice that Hack's article originally appeared in the *New York Times*. Most would agree that it is unusual to see a piece written by a college freshman in such a prestigious publication, but the fact that he was accepted at Yale immediately establishes him as a member of an academically elite group, as Hack points out in his second sentence. He meets the possible objection that he does not yet know enough about what life at Yale is like by pointing out that his older brother went there. The crucial difference is that the university's rules have been changed in the interim. Where his older brother lived at home, Hack is required by university policy to live on campus his first two years. Therein lies the problem.

Hack most directly states his objection to Yale's residency requirement in his third paragraph — that life in the dorms "is contrary to the fundamental principles [he and four other Jewish students] have been taught as long as [they] can remember — "the principles of Judaism lived according to the Torah and 3,000-year-old rabbinic teachings." He also captures the intensity of his feelings on the subject by stating that he and the four other students who are in the same position "may have no choice but to sue the university to protect [their] religious way of life."

Hack supports his assertion that life in a Yale dormitory would pose a threat to his moral standards by citing examples of posters on dorm walls that advise safe sex and newspaper articles that joke about premarital sex. Hack feels that his religious training has prepared him to defend his moral principles, but he asks why an institution considered so tolerant cannot also be tolerant of those who want to maintain their conservative practices and beliefs: "Why is Yale — an institution that professes to be so tolerant and open-minded — making it particularly hard for students like us to maintain our moral standards through difficult college years?"

Hack heads off a possible objection to his argument by explaining that he and the other Jewish students are not trying to impose their moral standards on others. They simply don't want to have others' standards imposed on them. Some would argue that an assignment to a dorm that has floors designated by gender should be accommodation enough, but even those have open stairwells between floors. If exceptions are made for students who are married or who are twenty-one, why can an exception not be made for those who object to dorm life for religious reasons?

A characteristic of good arguers is that they know well their opponents' position. Hack acknowledges that he even knows well the language Yale uses in "selling" itself to new students. He quotes the brochure that Yale sent him: "Yale retains a deep respect for its early history and for the continuity that its history provides — a continuity based on constant reflection and reappraisal." His request and claim is that Yale should reappraise a position that compels him to compromise his religious principles.

What happened to the lawsuit to which Hack refers? It was tied up in court until 2001, when all of the students involved except Hack had graduated. The students lost the legal battle at all levels, primarily because their case depended on their proving that having to live in a residence hall constituted discrimination based on religion. The university successfully argued that the residence requirement was not discriminatory. Hack graduated from Yale in 2003. All five students chose to live in apartments during their first two years while paying full housing fees for dorm rooms they never occupied.

PRACTICE

Use the claim of policy on page 179: "The time required for an undergraduate degree should be extended to five years." Apply to it Hairston's five steps for Rogerian argumentation (p. 11). Support whichever side of the issue you agree with.

Supersize Your Child?

RICHARD HAYES

I n the late 1950s, soon after Watson and Crick had discovered DNA's structure, scientists began predicting that someday we'd be able to genetically engineer our children. We'd design them to be healthy, smart, and attractive, with life spans of 200 years, photographic memories, enhanced lung capacity for athletic endurance, and more. Our children would pass these modifications to their own children and add new ones as well. Humanity would take control of its own evolution and kick it into overdrive.

Few people took these speculations very seriously. Could this sort of genetic engineering really be done? Even if it could, would anyone really want to do it? If they did, wouldn't society step in and set limits? In any event, wouldn't it be decades before we'd have to worry about this?

Now it's 2004, and those decades have passed. The era of genetically modified humans is close upon us. Almost every day we read of new breakthroughs: cloning, artificial chromosomes and now high-tech sex selection. Scientists create genetically modified animals on an assembly-line basis. Biotech entrepreneurs discuss the potential market for genetically modified children at investors' conferences. For the most part, society has not stepped in and set limits.

Last year *Science* magazine reported that a variant of the human 5-HTT gene reduces the risk of depression following stressful experiences. Depression can be a devastating condition. Would it be wrong if a couple planning to start a family used in vitro fertilization procedures to have the 5-HTT gene variant inserted into the embryos of their prospective children? Taken as an isolated instance, many people would be hard-pressed to say that it was.

In 1993, University of California at San Francisco biochemist Dr. Cynthia Kenyon discovered a variant of the DAF-2 gene that doubles the two-week life span of nematode worms. The university filed for patents based on knowledge of the metabolic pathway regulated by the human version of the DAF-2 gene. In 1999, Kenyon and others founded Elixir Pharmaceuticals, a biotech firm. In early 2003, Elixir licensed the university's patent rights to Kenyon's discoveries and secured $17 million in private financing. In an earlier interview with *ABC News*, Kenyon said she saw no reason humans might not be able to achieve 200-year life spans.

5

Richard Hayes is the executive director of the Center for Genetics and Society, a California-based nonprofit organization working for the responsible governance of genetic technologies. This piece was published on the TomPaine.com Web site in February 2004.

"Post-human" Nature

Last June at Yale University, the World Transhumanist Association held its first national conference. The Transhumanists have chapters in more than 20 countries and advocate the breeding of "genetically enriched" forms of "post-human" beings. Other advocates of the new techno-eugenics, such as Princeton University professor Lee Silver, predict that by the end of this century, "All aspects of the economy, the media, the entertainment industry, and the knowledge industry [will be] controlled by members of the GenRich class . . . Naturals [will] work as low-paid service providers or as laborers . . . ."

What happens then? Here's Dr. Richard Lynn, emeritus professor at the University of Ulster, who, like Silver, supports human genetic modification: "What is called for here is not genocide, the killing off of the population of incompetent cultures. But we do need to think realistically in terms of the 'phasing out' of such peoples. . . . Evolutionary progress means the extinction of the less competent."

Notice that I've gone, in just four steps, from reducing susceptibility to depression, to extending the human life span, to the creation of a genetic elite, to proposals that genetically inferior people be "phased out."

When first presented with this scenario, people typically respond in one of two ways. Some say, "It's impossible." Others say, "It's inevitable." Notice what these otherwise diametrically different responses have in common: Both counsel passivity. If the "post-human future" is impossible, there's no need to try to prevent it. If it's inevitable, such efforts would be in vain.

Will it actually be possible to genetically engineer our children? Most scientists who have studied this question conclude that although the techniques need to be refined, there's no reason to believe it can't be done. Meanwhile, research on stem cells, cloning, artificial chromosomes, and more continues to refine those techniques.

Many people believe that to suggest that manipulating genes can affect behavioral and cognitive traits in humans is to indulge discredited ideologies of "genetic determinism." It's true that the crude sociobiology of the 1970s has been discredited, as have simplistic notions that there exist "I.Q. genes" or "gay genes" that determine one's intelligence or sexual orientation. But to say that genes have no influence over traits is equally simplistic. Some genes have minimal influence, others have greater influence. Some have influence in the presence of certain environmental factors but no influence otherwise. Few genes determine anything; most confer propensities.

Deepening Inequality

Suppose scientists found a gene giving male children a 15 percent greater chance of growing one inch taller than they would have grown without that gene, all else equal. If fertility clinics offered to engineer embryos to include this gene, would there be customers? Yes. Couples would say, "In this competitive world, I want to do anything I can that might give my child an edge."

Will genetic changes be part of human reproduction in future years?

Once we allow children to be designed through embryo modification, where would we stop? If it's acceptable to modify one gene, why not two? If two, why not 20? Or 200? There are some 30,000 genes in the human genome. Each contributes, in smaller or larger proportions, to some propensity. Where would we stop? On what grounds?

Some suggest we allow embryo modification for certified medical conditions and prohibit it for cosmetic or enhancement purposes. It's unlikely that this would succeed. Prozac, Viagra, and Botox were all developed for medical purposes but in the blink of an eye became hugely profitable cosmetic and enhancement consumer products.

Will the use of genetic engineering to redesign our children exacerbate inequality? Amazingly, the neo-eugenic advocates don't deny that it will. As good libertarians, they celebrate free markets and social Darwinism, and counsel us to accept a rising tide of genetically enhanced inequality as the inevitable result of human ingenuity and desire.

15

But couldn't this be prevented? Wouldn't society step in? Several years ago, a team of health policy academics examined a range of proposals, including systems of national health insurance making eugenic engineering available to all, or preferentially to the poor, or by lottery. Despite their best efforts, they couldn't identify any realistic set of policies that would prevent the new eugenic technologies, once allowed at all, from generating unprecedented inequality.

And consider the international implications. What happens when some country announces an aggressive program of eugenic engineering explicitly intended to create a new, superior, omni-competent breed of human? What does the rest of the world do then?

We need to take a deep breath and realize what is going on here. The birth of the first genetically modified child would be a watershed moment in human history. It would set off a chain of events that would feed back upon themselves in ways impossible to control.

Unnatural Selection

Everything we experience, everything we know, everything we do is experienced, known and done by a species — homo sapiens — which evolved through natural selection over hundreds of thousands of years. We differ as individuals, but we are a single human species with a shared biology so fundamental to what we are that we are not even conscious of it, or of the manifold ways it unites us. What happens if we begin changing that fundamental shared biology?

Three hundred years ago the scientific and political leaders of that era took as a self-evident fact the division of humanity into "superior" and "inferior" types, designed by Providence respectively as masters and slaves. Human beings were bred, bought and sold, like cattle or dogs. After three hundred years of struggle and bloodshed we are on the verge — barely — of putting this awful legacy behind us.

Or maybe not. If left uncontrolled, the new human genetic technologies could set us on a trajectory leading to a new Dark Age in which people are once again regarded as little better than cattle or dogs. Here is "bioethicist" Gregory Pence, who has testified in support of human cloning before the U.S. Congress and elsewhere:

> [M]any people love their retrievers and their sunny dispositions around children and adults. Could people be chosen in the same way? Would it be so terrible to allow parents to at least aim for a certain type, in the same way that great breeders . . . try to match a breed of dog to the needs of a family?

The common initial responses to the prospect of the new techno-eugenics — "It's impossible," and "It's inevitable" — are incorrect and unhelpful. The response we need to affirm is at once more realistic and more challenging: The techno-eugenic future certainly is possible, and is certainly not inevitable.

Road to Regulation

In 1997, the Council of Europe negotiated an important international agreement, the Convention on Biomedicine and Human Rights. Thus far, it has been signed by more than two-thirds of the council's 45 member countries. The convention draws the lines on human genetic modification in just the right ways. It allows medical research, including stem cell research, to continue, and does not restrict abortion rights, but it bans genetic modifications that would open the door to high-tech eugenic engineering. Many countries in Asia, Africa, and Latin America have likewise begun to address these issues through legislation.

These efforts are encouraging, but we have a long way to go before such policies are implemented, as they must be, worldwide. In some countries, notably the United States, the politics of the new genetic technologies have become polarized to the point of gridlock. The religious right insists on total bans on nearly all human embryo research, while bio-research interests and the biotech industry insist on nearly total freedom from any meaningful social oversight and accountability.

In other countries, and at the international level, the challenge of a new high-tech, free market eugenics, while worrisome, can seem remote in comparison with the real existing challenges of warfare, hunger, and disease.   25

What is to be done? More than anything, we need to realize the unprecedented nature of the challenges that the new human genetic technologies present. We need to distinguish benign applications of these technologies from pernicious ones, and support the former while opposing the latter. Concerned organizations and individuals need to engage these challenges and make their voices heard worldwide. National and international leaders in politics, the sciences and the arts need to declare that humanity is not going to let itself be split asunder by human genetic technology. The United Nations and other international bodies need to give these issues the highest attention. The hour is late. There is no greater challenge before us.

READING AND DISCUSSION QUESTIONS

1. Hayes alerts us that he is using the organization of his essay to help make his point. Explain where and how he does that. How does he appeal to his readers' need to feel secure? Why might his readers feel their sense of security being threatened?

2. Is Hayes supporting a claim of fact, value, or policy? Where does he state that claim most directly?

3. What types of support does Hayes offer to back up his opinion? How convincing do you find his support to be?

4. Can you identify the warrant underlying Hayes's argument? In order to accept his claim, what assumption of his must you agree with? Does he state his warrant explicitly anywhere in the essay?

WRITING SUGGESTIONS

5. Write an essay in which you either support or argue against Hayes's claim.

6. Write an essay in which you explain your own position on who should set limits on genetic engineering.

7. Choose an invention or scientific development that people once said was impossible and explain how those skeptics were proved wrong.

8. Choose an invention or scientific development and explain how it is now used, for good or ill, for purposes it was never intended to serve.

Saw Good at Tying Things in Knots

WESLEY MORRIS

All anybody should want from a horror movie is the steady tightening in the pit of your stomach. While the new sado-masochistic gross-out flick *Saw* often resembles the ghastliest editions yet of *Fear Factor* and *Survivor* and features some of the grodiest direction this side of *Project Greenlight*, it does manage at times to knead your tummy like dough, using real suspense for a rolling pin.

Most of it is generated from wondering whether the movie will deliver on the promise of one of its posters, which shows a foot severed from its leg. It's the kind of terror that really has nothing to do with the plot, which, by the time it's been fully carried out, is as twisted as your stomach.

A doctor (Cary Elwes) and a bratty young photographer (Leigh Whannell, the movie's writer) wake up on either side of the sort of big, grimy bathroom you see only in bad horror movies and good music videos. Each man's leg is chained to a pipe, and neither has any idea how he got there or what that male body is doing lying dead between them in its undies. There's a gun in one hand, a tape recorder in the other, and a pool of blood around the head.

After beginning the dopey dialogue (mostly from Elwes, who brings a dinner-theater zest to his predicament), both men discover personal notes that indicate what they have to do: One has to kill the other to survive. And while you wait for Joe Rogan or Jeff Probst to supervise the mayhem, the two men start following the series of clues, which have been left on cassette tapes and elsewhere by a sicko watching on a surveillance camera. The contestants (what else are they?) turn up a pair of hacksaws and immediately start using them in vain on their chains. Silly rabbits, hacksaws are for ankles.

By this point, the movie has likely won your dread. So rather than commence with the cutting, *Saw* takes a break, in order for the doctor to treat the photographer to the hunch he has about who might be behind this stunt. It's in these flashbacks that screenwriter Whannell and director James Wan are exposed as being under the dubious influence of every movie in the modern psychopath-movie liquor cabinet — and *The Usual Suspects*, too.

5

Wesley Morris is a film critic at the *Boston Globe* and formerly wrote film reviews and essays for the *San Francisco Examiner* and the *San Francisco Sun-Chronicle*. This review appeared on October 24, 2004, in the *Boston Globe*.

Someone has been rounding up people who've been "wasting their lives" and subjecting them to horrific tortures to prove how much they want to live. While the victims demonstrate this, the editing and photography go predictably nuts, running around them and deliriously speeding up their futile escapes. One man tried to crawl through a nest of barbed wire to freedom. Another was slathered in a flammable jelly and asked to crawl across a floor strewn with glass to decipher a code that would free him. He had to do this holding a candle. (He failed.) The sole "winner" was a woman who had to fish a key from a living man's stomach or her head would explode. Frankly, that looks comparatively easy.

Two detectives on the case — Ken Leung and a never nuttier Danny Glover — fingered the good doctor as the culprit. He was innocent of those crimes but guilty of a lesser one that makes a decent alibi. But the movie persists in dredging up more implausible mysteries and domestic drama, namely through some terribly handled scenes between the doctor and his soon-to-be-jeopardized family.

Eventually, it grows frustrating to watch the movie's puzzle assemble itself — even once it does, there are pieces still missing. Why, for instance, does Glover's freaky character love news clippings as much as the average serial killer? And are we really to believe the major curveball in the final scene?

Not really. But as long as *Saw* stays in that big, nasty bathroom, all we need to believe is the knot in our stomachs.

READING AND DISCUSSION QUESTIONS

1. Morris establishes immediately "[a]ll anybody should want from a horror movie." What is it that all viewers should want?

2. The reference in the first paragraph to the way the movie makes a viewer's stomach feel may not seem significant at first glance, but how does Morris follow through on this idea of a "gut-level" response to horror?

3. How does Morris manage to praise the movie in the first paragraph in spite of referring to it as a "sado-masochistic gross-out flick" with "grody" direction?

4. What other weakness does Morris see in the film?

5. What is Morris's ultimate judgment regarding the film? On what criteria does he base that judgment?

6. How effective is the support that Morris offers for his assessment?

WRITING SUGGESTIONS

7. Write an essay in which you explain your own criteria for evaluating horror films. Or choose another genre (romantic comedy, drama, or mocumentary, for example) and write evaluating criteria for it.

8. If you have seen *Saw*, write an essay explaining whether or not you agree with Morris's assessment of the film.

9. Write your own review of a recent movie, being sure to establish the criteria for evaluation on which you base your review. See Ebert's review of *Crash* earlier in this chapter for another example of a movie review.

Take This Internship and Shove It

ANYA KAMENETZ

My younger sister has just arrived in New Orleans for the summer after her freshman year at Yale. She will be consuming daily snowballs, the local icy treat, to ward off the heat, volunteering to help clean up neighborhoods damaged by Hurricane Katrina and working part time, for pay, at both a literary festival and a local restaurant. Meanwhile, most of her friends from college are headed for the new standard summer experience: the unpaid internship.

Instead of starting out in the mailroom for a pittance, this generation reports for business upstairs without pay. A national survey by Vault, a career information Web site, found that 84 percent of college students in April planned to complete at least one internship before graduating. Also according to Vault, about half of all internships are unpaid.

I was an unpaid intern at a newspaper from March 2002, my senior year, until a few months after graduation. I took it for granted, as most students do, that working without pay was the best possible preparation for success; parents usually agree to subsidize their offspring's internships on this basis. But what if we're wrong?

What if the growth of unpaid internships is bad for the labor market and for individual careers?

Let's look at the risks to the lowly intern. First there are opportunity costs. 5 Lost wages and living expenses are significant considerations for the two-thirds of students who need loans to get through college. Since many internships are done for credit and some even cost money for the privilege of placement overseas or on Capitol Hill, those students who must borrow to pay tuition are going further into debt for internships.

Second, though their duties range from the menial to quasi-professional, unpaid internships are not jobs, only simulations. And fake jobs are not the best preparation for real jobs.

Long hours on your feet waiting tables may not be particularly edifying, but they teach you that work is a routine of obligation, relieved by external reward, where you contribute value to a larger enterprise. Newspapers and business magazines are full of articles expressing exasperation about how the Millennial-generation employee supposedly expects work to be exciting immediately, wears flip-flops to the office, and has no taste for dues-paying. However true this stereotype may be, the spread of the artificially fun internship might very well be adding fuel to it.

Anya Kamenetz, a columnist for *The Village Voice,* is the author of *Generation Debt: How Our Future Was Sold Out for Student Loans, Credit Cards, Bad Jobs, No Benefits, and Tax Cuts for Rich Geezers — and How to Fight Back* (published in 2006 and reissued, with an additional chapter, in 2007).

Duties for an unpaid intern can range from menial to quasi-professional.

By the same token, internships promote over-identification with employers: I make sacrifices to work free, therefore I must love my work. A sociologist at the University of Washington, Gina Neff, who has studied the coping strategies of interns in communications industries, calls the phenomenon "performative passion." Perhaps this emotion helps explain why educated workers in this country are less and less likely to organize, even as full-time jobs with benefits go the way of the Pinto.

Although it's not being offered this year, the A.F.L.-C.I.O.'s Union Summer Internship program, which provides a small stipend, has shaped thousands of college-educated career organizers. And yet interestingly, the percentage of young workers who hold an actual union card is less than 5 percent, compared with an overall national private-sector union rate of 12.5 percent. How are twentysomethings ever going to win back health benefits and pension plans when they learn to be grateful to work for nothing?

So an internship doesn't teach you everything you need to know about coping in today's working world. What effect does it have on the economy as a whole?   10

The Bureau of Labor Statistics does not identify interns or track the economic impact of unpaid internships. But we can do a quick-and-dirty calculation: according to *Princeton Review*'s "Internship Bible," there were 100,000 internship positions in 2005. Let's assume that out of those, 50,000 unpaid interns are employed full time for 12 weeks each summer at an average minimum wage of $5.15 an hour. That's a nearly $124 million yearly contribution to the welfare of corporate America.

In this way, unpaid interns are like illegal immigrants. They create an over-supply of people willing to work for low wages, or in the case of interns, literally nothing. Moreover, a recent survey by Britain's National Union of Journalists found that an influx of unpaid graduates kept wages down and patched up the gaps left by job cuts.

There may be more subtle effects as well. In an information economy, productivity is based on the best people finding the jobs best suited for their talents, and interns interfere with this cultural capitalism. They fly in the face of meritocracy — you must be rich enough to work without pay to get your foot in the door. And they enhance the power of social connections over ability to match people with desirable careers. A 2004 study of business graduates at a large mid-Atlantic university found that the completion of an internship helped people find jobs faster but didn't increase their confidence that those jobs were a good fit.

With all this said, the intern track is not coming to an end any time soon. More and more colleges are requiring some form of internship for graduation. Still, if you must do an internship, research shows you will get more out of it if you find a paid one.

A 1998 survey of nearly 700 employers by the Institute on Education and the   15
Economy at Columbia University's Teachers College found: "Compared to unpaid internships, paid placements are strongest on all measures of internship quality. The quality measures are also higher for those firms who intend to hire their interns." This shouldn't be too surprising — getting hired and getting paid are what work, in the real world, is all about.

READING AND DISCUSSION QUESTIONS

1. What complaint does Kamenetz have against internships?
2. What two problems does Kamenetz see with unpaid internships?
3. What are the risks to the "lowly intern"?
4. Why is it, according to Kamenetz, better to wait tables than to have an unpaid internship at a prestigious firm? Do you agree?
5. Why does Kamenetz compare unpaid interns to illegal immigrants? Is it a valid comparison?
6. How do interns interfere with "cultural capitalism"?
7. Does your school require internships? If so, where would you like to intern and why? If not, do you plan to have an internship anyway?
8. Where does Kamenetz most clearly state her claim? What type of claim is it?

WRITING SUGGESTIONS

9. Write an essay in which you explain whether or not you agree with Kamanetz's argument against unpaid internships.
10. Write an essay in which you explain how effective Kamenetz is in defending her position.
11. Write an essay in which you argue why you think an internship is valuable for every student.
12. Write an essay in which you argue that internships should not be required at your school.
13. Write an essay in which you explain what you can do while in college to best prepare you for the career you plan to pursue or one that you might pursue. Be specific. Don't depend on the obvious, like "study hard."

DEBATE   What Is the Social Responsibility of Business?

Putting Customers Ahead of Investors

JOHN MACKEY

In 1970 Milton Friedman wrote that "there is one and only one social responsibility of business — to use its resources and engage in activities designed to increase its profits so long as it stays within the rules of the game, which is to say, engages in open and free competition without deception or fraud." That's the orthodox view among free market economists: that the only social responsibility a law-abiding business has is to maximize profits for the shareholders.

I strongly disagree. I'm a businessman and a free market libertarian, but I believe that the enlightened corporation should try to create value for all of its constituencies. From an investor's perspective, the purpose of the business is to maximize profits. But that's not the purpose for other stakeholders — for customers, employees, suppliers, and the community. Each of those groups will define the purpose of the business in terms of its own needs and desires, and each perspective is valid and legitimate.

My argument should not be mistaken for a hostility to profit. I believe I know something about creating shareholder value. When I co-founded Whole Foods Market 27 years ago, we began with $45,000 in capital; we only had $250,000 in sales our first year. During the last 12 months we had sales of more than $4.6 billion, net profits of more than $160 million, and a market capitalization over $8 billion.

But we have not achieved our tremendous increase in shareholder value by making shareholder value the primary purpose of our business. In my marriage, my wife's happiness is an end in itself, not merely a means to my own happiness; love leads me to put my wife's happiness first, but in doing so I also make myself happier. Similarly, the most successful businesses put the customer first, ahead of the investors. In the profit-centered business, customer happiness is merely a means to an end: maximizing profits. In the customer-centered business, customer happiness is an end in itself, and will be pursued with greater interest, passion, and empathy than the profit-centered business is capable of.

Not that we're only concerned with customers. At Whole Foods, we measure   5
our success by how much value we can create for all six of our most important stakeholders: customers, team members (employees), investors, vendors, communities, and the environment. . . .

John Mackey was the cofounder in 1980 of Whole Foods Market and is now its CEO. He supports free market economics and the movement for organic food. His article and T. J. Rodgers's, which follows, were part of a debate on the social responsibility of business that appeared in the October 2005 issue of *Reason* magazine.

There is, of course, no magical formula to calculate how much value each stakeholder should receive from the company. It is a dynamic process that evolves with the competitive marketplace. No stakeholder remains satisfied for long. It is the function of company leadership to develop solutions that continually work for the common good.

Many thinking people will readily accept my arguments that caring about customers and employees is good business. But they might draw the line at believing a company has any responsibility to its community and environment. To donate time and capital to philanthropy, they will argue, is to steal from the investors. After all, the corporation's assets legally belong to the investors, don't they? Management has a fiduciary responsibility to maximize shareholder value; therefore, any activities that don't maximize shareholder value are violations of this duty. If you feel altruism towards other people, you should exercise that altruism with your own money, not with the assets of a corporation that doesn't belong to you.

This position sounds reasonable. A company's assets do belong to the investors, and its management does have a duty to manage those assets responsibly. In my view, the argument is not wrong so much as it is too narrow.

First, there can be little doubt that a certain amount of corporate philanthropy is simply good business and works for the long-term benefit of the investors. For example: In addition to the many thousands of small donations each Whole Foods store makes each year, we also hold five 5% Days throughout the year. On those days, we donate 5 percent of a store's total sales to a nonprofit organization. While our stores select worthwhile organizations to support, they also tend to focus on groups that have large membership lists, which are contacted and encouraged to shop our store that day to support the organization. This usually brings hundreds of new or lapsed customers into our stores, many of whom then become regular shoppers. So a 5% Day not only allows us to support worthwhile causes, but is an excellent marketing strategy that has benefited Whole Foods investors immensely.

That said, I believe such programs would be completely justifiable even if they   10
produced no profits and no P.R. This is because I believe the entrepreneurs, not the current investors in a company's stock, have the right and responsibility to define the purpose of the company. It is the entrepreneurs who create a company, who bring all the factors of production together and coordinate it into viable business. It is the entrepreneurs who set the company strategy and who negotiate the terms of trade with all of the voluntarily cooperating stakeholders — including the investors. At Whole Foods we "hired" our original investors. They didn't hire us.

We first announced that we would donate 5 percent of the company's net profits to philanthropy when we drafted our mission statement, back in 1985. Our policy has therefore been in place for over 20 years, and it predates our IPO [Initial Public Offering] by seven years. All seven of the private investors at the time we created the policy voted for it when they served on our board of directors. When we took in venture capital money back in 1989, none of the venture firms objected to the policy. In addition, in almost 14 years as a publicly traded company, almost no investors have ever raised objections to the policy. How can Whole Foods' philanthropy be "theft" from the current investors if the original owners of the company unanimously approved the policy and all subsequent investors made their investments after the policy was in effect and well publicized?

The shareholders of a public company own their stock voluntarily. If they don't agree with the philosophy of the business, they can always sell their investment, just as the customers and employees can exit their relationships with the company if they don't like the terms of trade. If that is unacceptable to them, they always have the legal right to submit a resolution at our annual shareholders meeting to change the company's philanthropic philosophy. A number of our company policies have been changed over the years through successful shareholder resolutions.

Another objection to the Whole Foods philosophy is where to draw the line. If donating 5 percent of profits is good, wouldn't 10 percent be even better? Why not donate 100 percent of our profits to the betterment of society? But the fact that Whole Foods has responsibilities to our community doesn't mean that we don't have any responsibilities to our investors. It's a question of finding the appropriate balance and trying to create value for all of our stakeholders. Is 5 percent the "right amount" to donate to the community? I don't think there is a right answer to this question, except that I believe 0 percent is too little. It is an arbitrary percentage that the co-founders of the company decided was a reasonable amount and which was approved by the owners of the company at the time we made the decision. Corporate philanthropy is a good thing, but it requires the legitimacy of investor approval. In my experience, most investors understand that it can be beneficial to both the corporation and to the larger society.

That doesn't answer the question of why we give money to the community stakeholder. For that, you should turn to one of the fathers of free-market economics, Adam Smith. *The Wealth of Nations* was a tremendous achievement, but economists would be well served to read Smith's other great book, *The Theory of Moral Sentiments*. There he explains that human nature isn't just about self-interest. It also includes sympathy, empathy, friendship, love, and the desire for social approval. As motives for human behavior, these are at least as important as self-interest. For many people, they are more important.

When we are small children we are egocentric, concerned only about our own 15 needs and desires. As we mature, most people grow beyond this egocentrism and begin to care about others — their families, friends, communities, and countries. Our capacity to love can expand even further: to loving people from different races, religions, and countries — potentially to unlimited love for all people and even for other sentient creatures. This is our potential as human beings, to take joy in the flourishing of people everywhere. Whole Foods gives money to our communities because we care about them and feel a responsibility to help them flourish as well as possible.

The business model that Whole Foods has embraced could represent a new form of capitalism, one that more consciously works for the common good instead of depending solely on the "invisible hand" to generate positive results for society. The "brand" of capitalism is in terrible shape throughout the world, and corporations are widely seen as selfish, greedy, and uncaring. This is both unfortunate and unnecessary, and could be changed if businesses and economists widely adopted the business model that I have outlined here.

To extend our love and care beyond our narrow self-interest is antithetical to neither our human nature nor our financial success. Rather, it leads to the further fulfillment of both. Why do we not encourage this in our theories of business and economics? Why do we restrict our theories to such a pessimistic and crabby view of human nature? What are we afraid of?

Put Profits First

T. J. RODGERS

John Mackey's article attacking corporate profit maximization could not have been written by "a free market libertarian," as claimed. Indeed, if the examples he cites had not identified him as the author, one could easily assume the piece was written by Ralph Nader. A more accurate title for his article is "How Business and Profit Making Fit into My Overarching Philosophy of Altruism."

Mackey spouts nonsense about how his company hired his original investors, not vice versa. If Whole Foods ever falls on persistent hard times — perhaps when the Luddites are no longer able to hold back the genetic food revolution using junk science and fear — he will quickly find out who has hired whom, as his investors fire him.

Mackey does make one point that is consistent with, but not supportive of, free market capitalism. He knows that shareholders own his stock voluntarily. If they don't like the policies of his company, they can always vote to change those policies with a shareholder resolution or simply sell the stock and buy that of another company more aligned with their objectives. Thus, he informs his shareholders of his objectives and lets them make a choice on which stock to buy. So far, so good.

It is also simply good business for a company to cater to its customers, train and retain its employees, build long-term positive relationships with its suppliers, and become a good citizen in its community, including performing some philanthropic activity. When Milton Friedman says a company should stay "within the rules of the game" and operate "without deception or fraud," he means it should deal with all its various constituencies properly in order to maximize long-term shareholder value. He does not mean that a company should put every last nickel on the bottom line every quarter, regardless of the long-term consequences.

My company, Cypress Semiconductor, has won the trophy for the Second   5
Harvest Food Bank competition for the most food donated per employee in Silicon Valley for the last 13 consecutive years (1 million pounds of food in 2004). The contest creates competition among our divisions, leading to employee involvement,

---

Thurman John Rodgers is the founder and CEO of Cypress Semiconductor. He is a strong advocate of laissez-faire capitalism.

company food drives, internal social events with admissions "paid for" by food donations, and so forth. It is a big employee morale builder, a way to attract new employees, good P.R. for the company, and a significant benefit to the community — all of which makes Cypress a better place to work and invest in. Indeed, Mackey's own proud example of Whole Foods' community involvement programs also made a profit.

But Mackey's subordination of his profession as a businessman to altruistic ideals shows up as he attempts to negate the empirically demonstrated social benefit of "self-interest" by defining it narrowly as "increasing short-term profits." Why is it that when Whole Foods gives money to a worthy cause, it serves a high moral objective, while a company that provides a good return to small investors — who simply put their money into their own retirement funds or a children's college fund — is somehow selfish? It's the philosophy that is objectionable here, not the specific actions. If Mackey wants to run a hybrid business/charity whose mission is fully disclosed to his shareholders — and if those shareholder-owners want to support that mission — so be it. But I balk at the proposition that a company's "stakeholders" (a term often used by collectivists to justify unreasonable demands) should be allowed to control the property of the shareholders. It seems Mackey's philosophy is more accurately described by Karl Marx: "From each according to his ability" (the shareholders surrender money and assets); "to each according to his needs" (the charities, social interest groups, and environmentalists get what they want). That's not free market capitalism.

Then there is the arrogant proposition that if other corporations would simply emulate the higher corporate life form defined by Whole Foods, the world would be better off. After all, Mackey says corporations are viewed as "selfish, greedy, and uncaring." I, for one, consider free market capitalism to be a high calling, even without the infusion of altruism practiced by Whole Foods.

If one goes beyond the sensationalistic journalism surrounding the Enron-like debacles, one discovers that only about 10 to 20 public corporations have been justifiably accused of serious wrongdoing. That's about 0.1 percent of America's 17,500 public companies. What's the failure rate of the publications that demean business? (Consider the *New York Times* scandal involving manufactured stories.) What's the percentage of U.S. presidents who have been forced or almost forced from office? (It's 10 times higher than the failure rate of corporations.) What percentage of our congressmen have spent time in jail? The fact is that despite some well-publicized failures, most corporations are run with the highest ethical standards — and the public knows it. Public opinion polls demonstrate that fact by routinely ranking businessmen above journalists and politicians in esteem.

I am proud of what the semiconductor industry does — relentlessly cutting the cost of a transistor from $3 in 1960 to three-millionths of a dollar today. Mackey would be keeping his business records with hordes of accountants on paper ledgers if our industry didn't exist. He would have to charge his poorest customers more for their food, pay his valued employees less, and cut his philanthropy programs if the semiconductor industry had not focused so relentlessly on increasing its profits, cutting his costs in the process. Of course, if the U.S. semiconductor industry had been less cost-competitive due to its own philanthropy, the food industry simply would have bought cheaper computers made from Japanese and Korean silicon chips (which happened anyway). Layoffs in the nonunion semiconductor industry were actually good news to Whole Foods' unionized grocery store clerks. Where was Mackey's sense of altruism when unemployed semiconductor workers needed it? Of course, that rhetorical question is foolish, since he did exactly the right thing by ruthlessly reducing his recordkeeping costs so as to maximize his profits.

I am proud to be a free market capitalist. And I resent the fact that Mackey's   10
philosophy demeans me as an egocentric child because I have refused on moral grounds to embrace the philosophies of collectivism and altruism that have caused so much human misery, however tempting the sales pitch for them sounds.

DISCUSSION QUESTIONS

1. What does Mackey think the social responsibility of business should be? How does this differ from Milton Friedman's belief?
2. How does Whole Foods "create value for all of its constituencies"?
3. Why is Rodgers so vehemently opposed to Mackey's philosophy of the social responsibility of business?
4. How does Rodgers feel that his company aids society, not just its investors?
5. Which of the two do you feel presents a more convincing argument? Why?

Assignments for Understanding Claims

READING AND DISCUSSION QUESTIONS

1. Locate a movie review online or in hard copy that has a clear claim and is based on clear evaluative criteria. Choose a review that is an essay, not just a single paragraph. Bring it to class and share it with your class or group. By looking at a range of different reviews, come to some conclusions about the sort of criteria used in making judgment calls about movies and what sort of claims provide good thesis statements for reviews. What are some other characteristics that all or most good movie reviews share?
2. Consider one or more of your school's policies that you would like to see changed. In your opinion, what exactly is wrong with the policy as it currently exists? What exactly would you recommend be done to improve the situation?
3. Samuelson, in "Picking Sides for the News" (p. 172), argues that different news sources slant their news toward different audiences. Do you agree with his argument? Why, or why not? What examples can you provide in support of your opinion?

WRITING ASSIGNMENTS

4. Choose a controversial issue in the field in which you are majoring or one in which you might major. Practice differentiating among the three types of claims by writing a claim of fact, a claim of value, and a claim of policy on that issue.

5. Choose one of the three claims you wrote for assignment four above and write an essay supporting it.

6. Write an essay arguing that your school should or should not require internships. If your school has a school newspaper, you may choose to write a letter to the editor instead of an essay.

Research Readiness: Acknowledging Reliable Authorities

How can you let your readers know that your sources are reliable?

If you are conscientious in your research and documentation of sources, you need to be sure that your efforts pay off by communicating to your audience relevant information that will strengthen your argument. Not only do you need to know that you are drawing information from reliable authorities, but also your readers need to know that. Below are some quotations and the names of those who are quoted. Do some research and find out what gives the person quoted the authority to speak knowledgeably on the subject of the quotation. Then work the information you found into a lead-in to the quotation, as in the model.

EXAMPLE:

"We are promoting human rights by building homes for people who don't have them." — Jimmy Carter

"We are promoting human rights by building homes for people who don't have them," explains former president Jimmy Carter, who has been involved with Habitat for Humanity International since 1984 and who, with his wife, leads its Jimmy and Rosalynn Carter Work Project one week each year.

1. "[Operation Iraqi Children] is a beautiful way to begin a relationship with the future leaders of Iraq, Afghanistan and other war-torn nations. They have been forgotten for so long. Now there is a chance for them." — Gary Sinise

2. "Innovation has nothing to do with how many R&D dollars you have. When Apple came up with the Mac, IBM was spending at least 100 times more on R&D. It's not about money. It's about the people you have, how you're led, and how much you get it." — Steve Jobs

3. "If gun laws in fact worked, the sponsors of this type of legislation should have no difficulties drawing upon long lists of crime rates reduced by such legislation. That they cannot do so after a century and a half of trying — that they must sweep under the rug the southern attempts at gun control in the 1870–1910 period, the northeastern attempts in the 1920–1939 period, the attempts at both Federal and State levels in 1965–1976 — establishes the repeated, complete and inevitable failure of gun laws to control serious crime." — Orrin G. Hatch

4. "If we want our children to possess the traits of character we most admire, we need to teach them what those traits are and why they deserve both admiration and

allegiance. Children must learn to identify the forms and content of those traits."
— William J. Bennett

5. "The three major brain sciences, brain imaging, pharmacology, and genetics, can work together hand and glove, and when needed hand and glove and foot, to illuminate a mysterious disorder like depression." — J. Raymond DePaulo, Jr.

6. Of a plan by a Florida church to burn Qurans on the anniversary of 9/11 in 2010: "It is precisely the kind of action the Taliban uses and could cause significant problems. Not just here, but everywhere in the world we are engaged with the Islamic community." — General David Petraeus

CHAPTER 6

Support

Types of Support: Evidence and Appeals to Needs and Values

All the claims you make — whether of fact, of value, or of policy — must be supported. Sometimes you will use your own experience as support for a claim. At other times you may conduct interviews, field research, lab experiments, or surveys to obtain support for your position. For the majority of your assignments, you will most likely turn primarily to print and electronic sources.

Support for a claim represents the answer to the question "What have you got to go on?"[1] There are two basic kinds of support in an argument: evidence and appeals to needs and values. When you provide evidence, you use facts, including examples and statistics, and opinions, or interpretations of facts — both your own and those of experts. Another tactic is to appeal to readers' needs (that is, requirements for physical and psychological survival and well-being) and values (or standards for right and wrong, good and bad).

This chapter presents the different types of evidence and appeals you can use to support your claim and examines the criteria by which you can evaluate the soundness of that support.

[1]Stephen Toulmin, *The Uses of Argument* (Cambridge: Cambridge University Press, 1958), p. 98.

Evidence

Factual Evidence

In Chapter 5, we defined facts as statements possessing a high degree of public acceptance. Some facts can be verified by experience alone. Eating too much will make us sick; we can get from Hopkinton to Boston in a half hour by car; in the Northern Hemisphere it is colder in December than in July. The experience of any individual is limited in both time and space, so we must accept as fact thousands of assertions about the world that we ourselves can never verify. Thus we accept the report that human beings landed on the moon in 1969 because we trust those who can verify it. (Country people in Morocco, however, received the news with disbelief because they had no reason to trust the reporters of the event. They insisted on trusting their senses instead. One man said, "I can see the moon very clearly. If a man were walking around up there, wouldn't I be able to see him?")

Factual evidence appears most frequently as examples and statistics, which are a numerical form of examples.

Examples

Examples are the most familiar kind of factual evidence. In addition to providing support for the truth of a generalization, examples can enliven otherwise dense or monotonous prose.

In the following paragraph the writer supports the claim in the topic sentence by offering a series of specific examples.

> Americans expect the next century to bring some striking political and social changes, but people are discerning. Two-thirds believe gay marriages probably will be legal and over half think that fathers will spend as much time and energy with their kids as mothers. Half of the public also predicts that Social Security will probably die; that view is particularly prevalent among younger Americans. But a majority doubts that cigarette smoking will be illegal or that all racial and gender discrimination will disappear.[2]

Hypothetical examples, which create imaginary situations for the audience and encourage them to visualize what might happen under certain circumstances, can also be effective. The following paragraph illustrates the use of hypothetical examples. (The author is describing megaschools, high schools with more than two thousand students.)

> And in schools that big there is inevitably a critical mass of kids who are neither jocks nor artists nor even nerds, kids who are nothing at all,

---

[2]Elizabeth Crowley, "Putting Faith in Technology for Year 3000," *Wall Street Journal*, September 15, 2000, sec. A, p. 10.

nonentities in their own lives. . . . The creditable ballplayer who might have made the team in a smaller school is edged out by better athletes. The artist who might have had work hung in a smaller school is supplanted by abler talents. And the disaffected and depressed boy who might have found a niche, or a friend, or a teacher who noticed, falls between the cracks. Sometimes he quietly drops out. Sometimes he quietly passes through. And sometimes he comes to school with a gun.[3]

All claims about vague or abstract terms would be boring or unintelligible without examples to illuminate them. For example, if you claim that a movie contains "unusual sound effects," you will certainly have to describe some of the effects to convince the reader that your generalization can be trusted.

Statistics

Statistics express information in numbers. In the following example statistics have been used to express raw data in numerical form.

A study released by the Center for Media and Public Affairs in June 1999 states that though television shows a lot of violence, it rarely shows its outcome. "We found that despite the high volume of televised violence, viewers rarely see it causing adverse effects," states the report. The report found serious acts of violence — murder, rape, kidnapping, and assault with a deadly weapon — occurred once every four minutes on the major TV networks. However, it notes that "no physical harm was shown three quarters (75 percent) of the time violence occurred on broadcast series and over two-thirds (68 percent) of the time it occurred on cable programs. A mere 7 percent of violent acts on broadcast shows and 4 percent on cable resulted in fatalities."

The CMPA report notes that in its study, "serious violence was more likely to have tangible consequences, but a majority of even these more brutal acts had no direct harmful results. Fifty-nine percent of acts of serious violence on broadcast series and 54 percent on cable lacked negative consequences." Only in rare instances, about 10 percent, did violence result in some type of mental distress for the victim or another character. "Thus, fully 90 percent of violent acts on broadcast and 87 percent on cable proved psychologically painless," says the report.[4]

Statistics are more effective in comparisons that indicate whether a quantity is relatively large or small and sometimes even whether a reader should interpret the result as gratifying or disappointing. For example, if a novice gambler were told that for every dollar wagered in a state lottery, 50 percent goes back to the players as prizes, would the gambler be able to conclude that the percentage is

[3] Anna Quindlen, "The Problem of the Megaschool," *Newsweek*, March 26, 2001, p. 68.
[4] Ron Kaufman, "Filling Their Minds with Death: TV Violence and Children," *TurnOffYourTV.com*, 2004. August 1, 2010. http://turnoffyourtv.com/healtheducation/violencechildren/violencechildren.html.

high or low? Would he be able to choose between playing the state lottery and playing a casino game? Unless he had more information, probably not. But if he were informed that in casino games, the return to the players is over 90 percent and in slot machines and racetracks the return is around 80 percent, the comparison would enable him to evaluate the meaning of the 50 percent return in the state lottery and even to make a decision about where to gamble his money.[5]

Comparative statistics are also useful for measurements over time. For instance, the following statistics show what comparisons based on BMI or body mass index reveal about how Miss America contestants have changed over the years.

> Miss America contestants have become increasing thinner over the past 75 years. In the 1920s, contestants had BMIs in the normal range of 20–25. Since then, pageant winners' body weights have decreased steadily to a level about 12 percent below levels from the mid-1900s. Since 1970, nearly all of the winners have had BMIs below the healthy range, with some as low as 16.9, a BMI that would meet part of the diagnostic criteria for anorexia nervosa.[6]

Diagrams, tables, charts, and graphs can make clear the relations among many sets of numbers. Such charts and diagrams allow readers to grasp the information more easily than if it were presented in paragraph form.

The graphs that constitute Figures 1 and 2 on pages 206 and 207 summarize the information produced by polls about cancer care and cancer costs. The pie charts on page 208 (Figures 3 and 4) clarify coverage of Africa by two popular newsmagazines.

Opinions: Interpretations of the Facts

Opinions or interpretations about facts are the inferences discussed in Chapter 5. They are an indispensable source of support for your claims.

Opinions or interpretations of facts generally take four forms: (1) They may suggest the cause for a condition or a causal connection between two sets of data; (2) they may offer predictions about the future; (3) they may suggest solutions to a problem; (4) they may refer to the opinion of experts.

Causal Connection

A more common term than *causal connections* is *cause-effect relationships*. Here Phyllis Rose analyzes some opinions about what causes anorexia.

---

[5] Curt Suphee, "Lotto Baloney," *Harper's,* July 1983, p. 201.

[6] S. Rubenstein and B. Caballero, "Is Miss America an Undernourished Role Model?" *JAMA* (2000), p. 1569. Qtd. in Jillian Croll, "Body Image and Adolescents," *Guidelines for Adolescent Nutrition Services*, J. Stang and M. Story, eds. (2005). June 9, 2007. http://www.epi.umn.edu/let/pubs/adol_book.shtm.

FIGURE 1
Ratings of Health-Care System for Cancer Care
Note: Don't know and refused responses not shown.
Source: USA Today/Kaiser Family Foundation/Harvard School of Public Health, *National Survey of Households Affected by Cancer* (conducted Aug. 1–Sept. 14, 2006); Employee Benefit Research Institute, *Health Confidence Survey* (conducted June 30–Aug. 6, 2005).

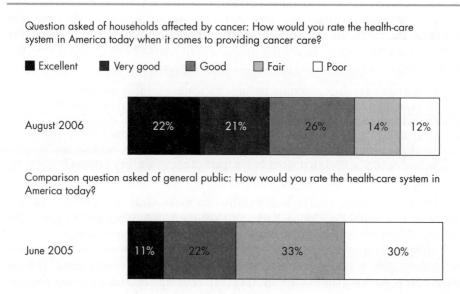

Question asked of households affected by cancer: How would you rate the health-care system in America today when it comes to providing cancer care?

■ Excellent   ■ Very good   ■ Good   ■ Fair   ☐ Poor

August 2006   22%   21%   26%   14%   12%

Comparison question asked of general public: How would you rate the health-care system in America today?

June 2005   11%   22%   33%   30%

Anorexia nervosa is a serious, sometimes fatal, disease characterized by self-starvation. It is found largely among young women. Physicians, psychologists, and social scientists have speculated about the causes, which remain unclear. A leading researcher in the field, Hilde Bruch, believes that food refusal expresses a desire to postpone sexual development. Another authority, Joan Blumberg, believes that one cause may be biological, a nervous dysfunction of the hypothalamus. Still others infer that the causes are cultural, a response to the admiration of the thin female body.[7]

Predictions

In the fall and winter of 1989 to 1990 extraordinary events shook Eastern Europe, toppling Communist regimes and raising more popular forms of government. Politicians and scholars offered predictions about future changes in the region. One expert, Zbigniew Brzezinski, former national security adviser under President Carter, concluded that the changes for the Soviet Union might be destructive.

[7] Phyllis Rose, "Hunger Artists," *Harper's,* July 1988, p. 82.

FIGURE 2

Financial Burden of Cancer Care by Insurance Status, Income, and Age

Source: USA Today/Kaiser Family Foundation/Harvard School of Public Health, *National Survey of Households Affected by Cancer* (conducted Aug. 1–Sept. 14, 2006).

Percent saying the cost of cancer care is a *major* burden on their family . . .

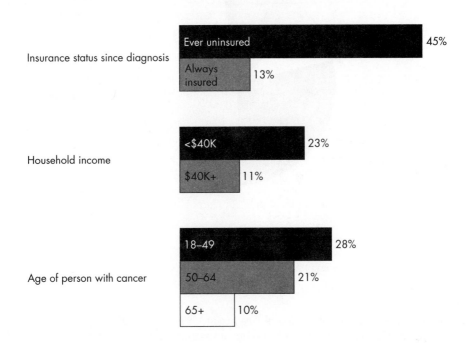

It would be a mistake to see the recent decisions as marking a break-
through for democracy. Much more likely is a prolonged period of democratizing chaos. One will see the rise in the Soviet Union of increasingly
irreconcilable conflicts between varying national political and social
aspirations, all united by a shared hatred for the existing Communist
nomenklatura. One is also likely to see a flashback of a nationalist type
among the Great Russians, fearful of the prospective breakup of the existing Great Russian Empire.[8]

Solutions to Problems

How shall we solve the problems caused by young people in our cities "who
commit crimes and create the staggering statistics in teenage pregnancies and
the high abortion rate"? The minister emeritus of the Abyssinian Baptist Church
in New York City proposes establishment of a national youth academy with

[8] *New York Times*, February 9, 1990, sec. A, p. 13.

FIGURE 3

Percentages of Five Story Topics about Africa in *Newsweek*, August 1989 to August 1991

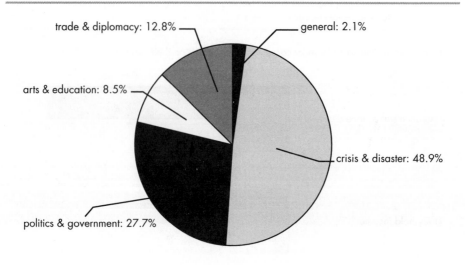

trade & diplomacy: 12.8%

general: 2.1%

arts & education: 8.5%

crisis & disaster: 48.9%

politics & government: 27.7%

FIGURE 4

Percentages of Five Story Topics about Africa in *Time*, August 1989 to August 1991

Source: Jerry Domatob, "Coverage of Africa in American Popular Magazines," *Issue: A Journal of Opinion*, 22 (Winter-Spring 1994): 25.

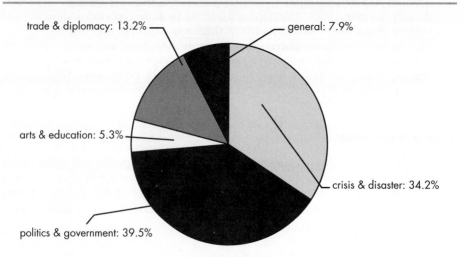

trade & diplomacy: 13.2%

general: 7.9%

arts & education: 5.3%

crisis & disaster: 34.2%

politics & government: 39.5%

fifty campuses on inactive military bases. "It is a 'parenting' institution. . . . It is not a penal institution, not a prep school, not a Job Corps Center, not a Civilian Conservation Camp, but it borrows from them." Although such an institution has not been tried before, the author of the proposal thinks that it would represent an effort "to provide for the academic, moral, and social development of young people, to cause them to become responsible and productive citizens."[9]

Expert Opinion

For many of the subjects you discuss and write about, you will find it necessary to accept and use the opinions of experts. Based on their reading of the facts, experts express opinions on a variety of controversial subjects: whether capital punishment is a deterrent to crime; whether legalization of marijuana will lead to an increase in its use; whether children, if left untaught, will grow up honest and cooperative; whether sex education courses will result in less sexual activity and fewer illegitimate births. The interpretations of the data are often profoundly important because they influence social policy and affect our lives directly and indirectly.

For the problems mentioned above, the opinions of people recognized as authorities are more reliable than those of people who have neither thought about nor done research on the subject. But opinions may also be offered by student writers in areas in which they are knowledgeable. If you were asked, for example, to defend or refute the statement that work has advantages for teenagers, you could call on your own experience and that of your friends to support your claim. You can also draw on your experience to write convincingly about your special interests.

One opinion, however, is not as good as another. The value of any opinion depends on the quality of the evidence and the trustworthiness of the person offering it.

PRACTICE

1. Choose either Figure 1, "Ratings of Health-Care System for Cancer Care" (p. 206), or Figure 2, "Financial Burden of Cancer Care by Insurance Status, Income, and Age" (p. 207). Consider the facts presented in the graph you chose. What is one conclusion you can draw based on those facts? Summarize that conclusion in one sentence and make it the topic sentence for a paragraph. Then use facts from the graph as specific support to complete the paragraph.

2. Do the same with Figure 3 and Figure 4 (p. 208), the pie charts about Africa, but this time consider both charts.

---

[9]Samuel D. Proctor, "To the Rescue: A National Youth Academy," *New York Times,* September 16, 1989, sec. A, p. 27.

3. Write two possible topic sentences supporting conclusions you were able to draw from the information in Figure 1, one a statement of fact and the other a statement of opinion. Do the same with Figure 2.

Research Skill: Evaluation of Evidence

Before you begin to write, you must determine whether the facts and opinions you have chosen to support your claim are sound. Can they convince your readers? A distinction between the evaluation of facts and the evaluation of opinions is somewhat artificial because many facts are verified by expert opinion, but for our analysis we discuss them separately.

Evaluation of Factual Evidence

As you evaluate factual evidence, you should keep in mind the following questions:

1. Is the evidence up to date? The importance of up-to-date information depends on the subject. If you are defending the claim that suicide is immoral, you will not need to examine new data. For many of the subjects you write about, recent research and scholarship will be important, even decisive, in proving the soundness of your data. "New" does not always mean "best," but in fields where research is ongoing — education, psychology, technology, medicine, and all the natural and physical sciences — you should be sensitive to the dates of the research.

In writing a paper a few years ago warning about the health hazards of air pollution, you would have used data referring only to outdoor pollution produced by automobile and factory emissions. But writing about air pollution today, you would have to take into account new data about indoor pollution, which has become a serious problem as a result of attempts to conserve energy. Because research studies in indoor pollution are continually being updated, recent evidence will probably be more accurate than past research.

2. Is the evidence sufficient? The amount of evidence you need depends on the complexity of the subject and the length of your paper. Given the relative brevity of most of your assignments, you will need to be selective. For the claim that indoor pollution is a serious problem, one example would obviously not be enough. For a 750- to 1,000-word paper, three or four examples would probably be sufficient. The choice of examples should reflect different aspects of the problem: in this case, different sources of indoor pollution — gas stoves, fireplaces, kerosene heaters, insulation — and the consequences for health.

Indoor pollution is a fairly limited subject for which the evidence is clear. But more complex problems require more evidence. A common fault in argument is generalization based on insufficient evidence. In a 1,000-word paper you could not adequately treat the causes of conflict in the Middle East; you could not develop workable proposals for health-care reform; you could not predict the development of education in the next century. In choosing a subject for a brief paper, determine whether you can produce sufficient evidence to convince a reader who may not agree with you. If not, the subject may be too large for a brief paper.

3. Is the evidence relevant? All the evidence should, of course, contribute to the development of your argument. Sometimes the arguer loses sight of the subject and introduces examples that are wide of the claim. In defending a national health-care plan, one student offered examples of the success of health maintenance organizations, but such organizations, although subsidized by the federal government, were not the structure favored by sponsors of the plan. The examples were interesting but irrelevant.

Also keep in mind that not all readers will agree on what is relevant. Is the unsavory private life of a politician relevant to his or her performance in office? If you want to prove that a politician is unfit to serve because of his or her private activities, you may first have to convince some members of the audience that private activities are relevant to public service.

4. Are the examples representative? This question emphasizes your responsibility to choose examples that are typical of all the examples you do not use. Suppose you offered Vermont's experience to support your claim that same-sex marriage should be legal. Is the experience of Vermont typical of what is happening or may happen in other states? Or is Vermont, a small, mostly rural New England state, different enough from other states to make the example unrepresentative?

5. Are the examples consistent with the experience of the audience? The members of your audience use their own experiences to judge the soundness of your evidence. If your examples are unfamiliar or extreme, they will probably reject your conclusion. Consider the following excerpt from Jacob Neusner's hypothetical commencement speech, "The Speech the Graduates Didn't Hear" (pp. 374–75), which is meant to represent a faculty member's response to student apathy.

> For years we have created an altogether forgiving world, in which whatever slight effort you gave was all that was demanded. When you did not keep appointments, we made new ones. When your work came in beyond the deadline, we pretended not to care.
>
> Worse still, when you were boring, we acted as if you were saying something important. When you were garrulous and talked to hear yourself talk, we listened as if it mattered. When you tossed on our desks writing upon which you had not labored, we read it and even responded, as though you earned a response. When you were dull, we pretended you were smart. When you were predictable, unimaginative, and routine, we listened as if to new and wonderful things. When you demanded free lunch we served it.

If most members of the audience find that such a description doesn't reflect their own attitudes or those of their friends, they will probably question the validity of the claim.

Evaluation of Statistics

The questions you must ask about examples also apply to statistics. Are they recent? Are they sufficient? Are they relevant? Are they typical? Are they consistent with the experience of the audience? But there are additional questions directed specifically to evaluation of statistics.

1. Do the statistics come from trustworthy sources? Perhaps you have read newspaper accounts of very old people, some reported to be as old as 135, living in the Caucasus or the Andes, nourished by yogurt and hard work. But these statistics are hearsay; no birth records or other official documents exist to verify them. Now two anthropologists have concluded that the numbers were part of a rural mythology and that the ages of the people were actually within the normal range for human populations elsewhere.[10]

Hearsay statistics should be treated with the same skepticism accorded to gossip or rumor. Sampling a population to gather statistical information is a sophisticated science; you should ask whether the reporter of the statistics is qualified and likely to be free of bias. Among the generally reliable sources are polling organizations such as Gallup, Roper, and Louis Harris and agencies of the U.S. government such as the Census Bureau and the Bureau of Labor Statistics. Other qualified sources are well-known research foundations, university centers, and insurance companies that prepare actuarial tables. Statistics from underdeveloped countries are less reliable for obvious reasons: lack of funds, lack of trained statisticians, lack of communication and transportation facilities to carry out accurate censuses.

2. Are the terms clearly defined? In an example in Chapter 4, the reference to poverty (p. 132) made clear that any statistics would be meaningless unless we knew exactly how *poverty* was defined by the user. *Unemployment* is another term for which statistics will be difficult to read if the definition varies from one user to another. For example, are seasonal workers employed or unemployed during the off-season? Are part-time workers employed? (In Russia they are unemployed.) Are workers on government projects employed? (During the 1930s they were considered employed by the Germans and unemployed by the Americans.) The more abstract or controversial the term, the greater the necessity for clear definition.

3. Are the comparisons between comparable things? Folk wisdom warns us that we cannot compare apples and oranges. Population statistics for the world's

---

[10]Richard B. Mazess and Sylvia H. Forman, "Longevity and Age Exaggeration in Vilcabamba, Ecuador," *Journal of Gerontology* (1979), pp. 94–98.

largest city, for example, should indicate the units being compared. Greater London is defined in one way, greater New York in another, and greater Tokyo in still another. The population numbers will mean little unless you can be sure that the same geographical units are being compared.

4. Has any significant information been omitted? *The Plain Truth,* a magazine published by the World-Wide Church of God, advertises itself as follows:

> *The Plain Truth* has now topped 5,000,000 copies per issue. It is now the fastest-growing magazine in the world and one of the widest circulated mass-circulation magazines on earth. Our circulation is now greater than *Newsweek.* New subscribers are coming in at the rate of around 40,000 per week.

What the magazine neglects to mention is that it is *free.* There is no subscription fee, and the magazine is widely distributed in drugstores, supermarkets, and airports. *Newsweek* is sold on newsstands and by subscription. The comparison therefore omits significant information.

Evaluation of Opinions

When you evaluate the reliability of opinions in subjects with which you are not familiar, you will be dealing almost exclusively with opinions of experts. Most of the following questions are directed to an evaluation of authoritative sources. But you can also ask these questions of students or of others with opinions based on their own experience and research. Keep them in mind when doing research on the Internet.

1. Is the source of the opinion qualified to give an opinion on the subject? The discussion of credibility in Chapter 1 (pp. 4–7) pointed out that certain achievements by the interpreter of the data — publications, acceptance by colleagues — can tell us something about his or her competence. Although these standards are by no means foolproof (people of outstanding reputations have been known to falsify their data), nevertheless they offer assurance that the source is generally trustworthy. The answers to questions you must ask are not hard to find: Is the source qualified by education? Is the source associated with a reputable institution — a university or a research organization? Is the source credited with having made contributions to the field — books, articles, research studies? Suppose that in writing a paper on organ transplants you came across an article by Peter Medawar. He is identified as follows:

> Sir Peter Medawar, British zoologist, winner of the 1960 Nobel Prize in Physiology or Medicine, for proving that the rejection by the body of foreign organs can be overcome; president of the Royal Society; head of the National Institute for Medical Research in London; a world leader in immunology.

These credentials would suggest to almost any reader that Medawar is a reliable source for information about organ transplants.

If the source is not so clearly identified, you should treat the data with caution. Such advice is especially relevant when you are dealing with popular works about such subjects as miracle diets, formulas for instant wealth, and sightings of monsters and UFOs. Do not use such data until you can verify them from other, more authoritative sources.

In addition, you should question the identity of any source listed as "spokesperson" or "reliable source" or "an unidentified authority." The mass media are especially fond of this type of attribution. Sometimes the sources are people in public life who plant stories anonymously or off the record for purposes they prefer to keep hidden.

Even when the identification is clear and genuine, you should ask if the credentials are relevant to the field in which the authority claims expertise. So specialized are areas of scientific study today that scientists in one field may not be competent to make judgments in another. William Shockley is a distinguished engineer, a Nobel Prize winner for his contribution to the invention of the electronic transistor. But when he made the claim, based on his own research, that blacks are genetically inferior to whites, geneticists accused Shockley of venturing into a field where he was unqualified to make judgments. Similarly, advertisers invite stars from the entertainment world to express opinions about products with which they are probably less familiar than members of their audience. All citizens have the right to express their views, but this does not mean that all views are equally credible or worthy of attention.

2. Is the source biased for or against his or her interpretation? Even authorities who satisfy the criteria for expertise may be guilty of bias. Bias arises as a result of economic reward, religious affiliation, political loyalty, and other interests. The expert may not be aware of the bias; even an expert can fall into the trap of ignoring evidence that contradicts his or her own intellectual preferences. A British psychologist has said:

> The search for meaning in data is bound to involve all of us in distortion to greater or lesser degree. . . . Transgression consists not so much in a clear break with professional ethics, as in an unusually high-handed, extreme or self-deceptive attempt to promote one particular view of reality at the expense of all others.[11]

Before accepting the interpretation of an expert, you should ask: Is there some reason why I should suspect the motives of this particular source?

Consider, for example, an advertisement claiming that sweetened breakfast cereals are nutritious. The advertisement, placed by the manufacturer of the cereal, provides impeccable references from scientific sources to support its claims. But since you are aware of the economic interest of the company in promoting sales, you may wonder if they have reproduced only facts that favor their claims. Are there other facts that might prove the opposite? As a careful

---

[11]Liam Hudson, *The Cult of the Fact* (New York: Harper and Row, 1972), p. 125.

researcher you would certainly want to look further for data about the advantages and disadvantages of sugar in our diets.

It is harder to determine bias in the research done by scientists and university faculty even when the research is funded by companies interested in a favorable review of their products. If you discover that a respected biologist who advocates the use of sugar in baby food receives a consultant's fee from a sugar company, should you conclude that the research is slanted and that the scientist has ignored contrary evidence? Not necessarily. The truth may be that the scientist arrived at conclusions about the use of sugar legitimately through experiments that no other scientist would question. But it would probably occur to you that a critical reader might ask about the connection between the results of the research and the payment by a company that profits from the research. In this case you would be wise to read further to find confirmation or rejection of the claim by other scientists.

The most difficult evaluations concern ideological bias. Early in our lives we learn to discount the special interest that makes a small child brag, "My mother (or father) is the greatest!" Later we become aware that the claims of people who are avowed Democrats or Republicans or supply-side economists or Yankee fans or zealous San Franciscans or joggers must be examined somewhat more carefully than those of people who have no special commitment to a cause or a place or an activity. This is not to say that all partisan claims lack support. They may, in fact, be based on the best available support. But whenever special interest is apparent, there is always the danger that an argument will reflect this bias.

3. Has the source bolstered the claim with sufficient and appropriate evidence? An author might claim, "Statistics show that watching violence on television leads to violent behavior in children." But if the author gave no further information — neither statistics nor proof that a cause-effect relation exists between televised violence and violence in children, the critical reader would ask, "What are the numbers? Who compiled them?"

Even those who are reputed to be experts in the subjects they discuss must do more than simply allege that a claim is valid or that the data exist. They must provide facts to support their interpretations.

When Experts Disagree

Authoritative sources can disagree. Such disagreement is probably most common in the social sciences. They are called the "soft" sciences precisely because a consensus about conclusions in these areas is more difficult to arrive at than in the natural and physical sciences. Consider the controversy over what determines the best interests of the child where both biological and foster parents are engaged in trying to secure custody. Experts are deeply divided on this issue. Dr. Daniel J. Cohen, a child psychologist and director of the Yale Child Study Center, argues that the psychological needs of the child should take precedence. If the child has a stable and loving relationship with foster parents, that is where

Experts disagree on some questions, such as the reason why dinosaurs became extinct.

he should stay. But Bruce Bozer and Bernadine Dohrn of the Children and Family Justice Center at Northwestern University Law School insist that "such a solution may be overly simplistic." The child may suffer in later life when he learns that he has been prevented from returning to biological parents "who fought to get him back."[12]

But even in the natural and physical sciences, where the results of observation and experiment are more conclusive, we encounter heated differences of opinion. A popular argument concerns the extinction of the dinosaurs. Was it the effect of an asteroid striking the earth? Or widespread volcanic activity? Or a cooling of the planet? All these theories have their champions among the experts.

Environmental concerns also produce lively disagreements. Scientists have lined up on both sides of a debate about the importance of protecting the tropical rain forest as a source of biological, especially mammalian, diversity. Dr. Edward O. Wilson, a Harvard biologist, whose books have made us familiar with the term *biodiversity*, says, "The great majority of organisms appears to reach maximum diversity in the rain forest. There is no question that the rain forests are the world's headquarters of diversity." But in the journal *Science* another biologist, Dr. Michael Mares, a professor of zoology at the University of Oklahoma, argues that "if one could choose only a single South American habitat in which to preserve the greatest mammalian diversity, it would be the dry lands. . . . The dry lands are very likely far more highly threatened than the largely inaccessible rain forests."[13] A debate of more immediate relevance concerns possible dangers in genetically modified foods, as distinguished from foods modified by traditional breeding practices. Dr. Louis Pribyl, a U.S. Food and Drug

---

[12] *New York Times,* September 4, 1994, sec. E, p. 3.
[13] *New York Times,* April 7, 1992, sec. C, p. 4.

Administration microbiologist, has accused the agency of claiming "that there are no unintended effects that raise the FDA's level of concern. But . . . there are no data to back up this contention." On the other hand, Dr. James Marjanski, the FDA's biotechnology coordinator, maintains that "as long as developers of these foods follow agency guidelines, genetically engineered foods are as safe as any on the market."[14]

How can you choose between authorities who disagree? If you have applied the tests discussed so far and discovered that one source is less qualified by training and experience or makes claims with little support or appears to be biased in favor of one interpretation, you will have no difficulty in rejecting that person's opinion. If conflicting sources prove to be equally reliable in all respects, then continue reading other authorities to determine whether a greater number of experts support one opinion rather than another. Although numbers alone, even of experts, don't guarantee the truth, nonexperts have little choice but to accept the authority of the greater number until evidence to the contrary is forthcoming. Finally, if you are unable to decide between competing sources of evidence, you may conclude that the argument must remain unsettled. Such an admission is not a failure; after all, such questions are considered controversial because even the experts cannot agree, and such questions are often the most interesting to consider and argue about.

Appeals to Needs and Values

Good factual evidence is usually enough to convince an audience that your factual claim is sound. Using examples, statistics, and expert opinion, you can prove, for example, that women do not earn as much as men for the same work. But even good evidence may not be enough to convince your audience that unequal pay is wrong or that something should be done about it. In making value and policy claims, an appeal to the needs and values of your audience is absolutely essential to the success of your argument. If you want to persuade the audience to change their minds or adopt a course of action — in this case, to demand legislation guaranteeing equal pay for equal work — you will have to show that assent to your claim will bring about what they want and care deeply about.

If the audience concludes that the things you care about are very different from what they care about, if they cannot identify with your goals and principles, they may treat your argument with indifference, even hostility, and finally reject it. But you can hope that decent and reasonable people will share many of the needs and values that underlie your claims. Finding these shared needs and values is what Carl Rogers was advocating when he said that the way to improved communication is to try to express your audience's position fairly and to look for common ground between their position and yours.

[14]*New York Times*, December 1, 1999, sec. A, p. 15.

Appeals to Needs

The most familiar classification of needs was developed by the psychologist Abraham H. Maslow in 1954.[15] These needs, said Maslow, motivate human thought and action. In satisfying our needs, we attain both long- and short-term goals. Because Maslow believed that some needs are more important than others, he arranged them in hierarchical order from the most urgent biological needs to the psychological needs that are related to our roles as members of a society.

PHYSIOLOGICAL NEEDS Basic bodily requirements: food and drink; health; sex

SAFETY NEEDS Security; freedom from harm; order and stability

BELONGINGNESS AND LOVE NEEDS Love within a family and among friends; roots within a group or a community

ESTEEM NEEDS Material success; achievement; power, status, and recognition by others

SELF-ACTUALIZATION NEEDS Fulfillment in realizing one's potential

For most of your arguments you won't have to address the audience's basic physiological needs for nourishment or shelter. The desire for health, however, now receives extraordinary attention. Appeals to buy health foods, vitamin supplements, drugs, exercise and diet courses, and health books are all around us. Many of the claims are supported by little or no evidence, but readers are so eager to satisfy the need for good health that they often overlook the lack of facts or authoritative opinion. The desire for physical well-being, however, is not so simple as it seems; it is strongly related to our need for self-esteem and love.

Appeals to our needs to feel safe from harm, to be assured of order and stability in our lives are also common. Insurance companies, politicians who promise to rid our streets of crime, and companies that offer security services all appeal to this profound and nearly universal need. (We say "nearly" because some people are apparently attracted to risk and danger.) At this writing those who monitor terrorist activity are attempting both to arouse fear for our safety and to suggest ways of reducing the dangers that make us fearful.

The last three needs in Maslow's hierarchy are the ones you will find most challenging to appeal to in your arguments. It is clear that these needs arise out of human relationships and participation in society. Advertisers make much use of appeals to these needs.

BELONGINGNESS AND LOVE NEEDS

"Whether you are young or old, the need for companionship is universal." (ad for dating service)

"Share the Fun of High School with Your Little Girl!" (ad for a Barbie doll)

---

[15] *Motivation and Personality* (New York: Harper and Row, 1954), pp. 80–92.

ESTEEM NEEDS

"Enrich your home with the distinction of an Oxford library."

"Apply your expertise to more challenges and more opportunities. Here are outstanding opportunities for challenge, achievement, and growth." (Perkin-Elmer Co.)

SELF-ACTUALIZATION NEEDS

"Be all that you can be." (former U.S. Army slogan)

"Are you demanding enough? Somewhere beyond the cortex is a small voice whose mere whisper can silence an army of arguments. It goes by many names: integrity, excellence, standards. And it stands alone in final judgment as to whether we have demanded enough of ourselves and, by that example, have inspired the best in those around us." (*New York Times*)

Of course, it is not only advertisers who use these appeals. We hear them from family and friends, from teachers, from employers, from editorials and letters to the editor, from people in public life.

Appeals to Values

Needs give rise to values. If we feel the need to belong to a group, we learn to value commitment, sacrifice, and sharing. And we then respond to arguments that promise to protect our values. It is hardly surprising that values, the principles by which we judge what is good or bad, beautiful or ugly, worthwhile or undesirable, should exercise a profound influence on our behavior. Virtually all claims, even those that seem to be purely factual, contain expressed or unexpressed judgments.

For our study of argument, we will speak of groups or systems of values because any single value is usually related to others. People and institutions are often defined by such systems of values. We can distinguish, for example, between those who think of themselves as traditional and those who think of themselves as modern by listing their differing values. One writer contrasts such values in this way:

> Among the values of traditionalism are merit, accomplishment, competition, and success; self-restraint, self-discipline, and the postponement of gratification; the stability of the family; and a belief in certain moral universals. The modernist ethos scorns the pursuit of success; is egalitarian and redistributionist in emphasis; tolerates or encourages sensual gratification; values self-expression as against self-restraint; accepts alternative or deviant forms of the family; and emphasizes ethical relativism.[16]

[16]Joseph Adelson, "What Happened to the Schools," *Commentary,* March 1981, p. 37.

Systems of values are neither so rigid nor so distinct from one another as this list suggests. Some people who are traditional in their advocacy of competition and success may also accept the modernist values of self-expression and alternative family structures. Values, like needs, are arranged in a hierarchy; that is, some are clearly more important than others to the people who hold them. Moreover, the arrangement may shift over time or as a result of new experiences. In 1962, for example, two speech teachers prepared a list of what they called "Relatively Unchanging Values Shared by Most Americans."[17] Included were "puritan and pioneer standards of morality" and "perennial optimism about the future." More than forty-five years later, an appeal to these values might fall on a number of deaf ears.

You should also be aware of not only changes over time but also different or competing value systems that reflect a multitude of subcultures in the United States. Differences in age, sex, race, ethnic background, social environment, religion, even in the personalities and characters of its members define the groups we belong to. Such terms as *honor, loyalty, justice, patriotism, duty, responsibility, equality, freedom,* and *courage* will be interpreted very differently by different groups.

All of us belong to more than one group, and the values of the several groups may be in conflict. If one group to which you belong — say, peers of your own age and class — is generally uninterested in and even scornful of religion, you may nevertheless hold to the values of your family and continue to place a high value on religious belief.

How can a knowledge of your readers' values enable you to make a more effective appeal? Suppose you want to argue in favor of a sex education program in the middle school you attended. The program you support would not only give students information about contraception and venereal disease but also teach them about the pleasures of sex, the importance of small families, and alternatives to heterosexuality. If the readers of your argument are your classmates or your peers, you can be fairly sure that their agreement will be easier to obtain than that of their parents, especially if their parents think of themselves as conservative. Your peers are more likely to value experimentation, tolerance of alternative sexual practices, freedom, and novelty. Their parents are more likely to value restraint, conformity to conventional sexual practices, obedience to family rules, and foresight in planning for the future.

Knowing that your peers share your values and your goals will mean that you need not spell out the values supporting your claim; they are understood by your readers. Convincing their parents, however, who think that freedom, tolerance, and experimentation have been abused by their children, will be a far more challenging task. In one written piece you have little chance of changing

---

[17]Edward Steele and W. Charles Redding, "The American Value System: Premises for Persuasion," *Western Speech,* 26 (Spring 1962), pp. 83–91.

their values, a result that might be achieved only over a longer period of time. So you might first attempt to reduce their hostility by suggesting that, even if a community-wide program were adopted, students would need parental permission to enroll. This might convince some parents that you share their values regarding parental authority and primacy of the family. Second, you might look for other values to which the parents subscribe and to which you can make an appeal. Do they prize maturity, self-reliance, responsibility in their children? If so, you could attempt to prove, with authoritative evidence, that the sex education program would promote these qualities in students who took the course.

But familiarity with the value systems of prospective readers may also lead you to conclude that winning assent to your argument will be impossible. It would probably be fruitless to attempt to persuade a group of lifelong pacifists to endorse the use of nuclear weapons. The beliefs, attitudes, and habits that support their value systems are too fundamental to yield to one or two attempts at persuasion.

Evaluation of Appeals to Needs and Values

If your argument is based on an appeal to the needs and values of your audience, the following questions will help you evaluate the soundness of your appeal.

1. Have the values been clearly defined? If you are appealing to the patriotism of your readers, can you be sure that they agree with your definition? Does patriotism mean "Our country, right or wrong!" or does it mean dissent, even violent dissent, if you think your country is wrong? Because value terms are abstractions, you must make their meaning explicit by placing them in context and providing examples.

2. Are the needs and values to which you appeal prominent in the reader's hierarchy at the time you are writing? An affluent community, fearful of further erosion of quiet and open countryside, might resist an appeal to allow establishment of a high-technology firm, even though the firm would bring increased prosperity to the area.

3. Is the evidence in your argument clearly related to the needs and values to which you appeal? Remember that the reader must see some connection between your evidence and his or her goals. Suppose you were writing an argument to persuade a group of people to vote in an upcoming election. You could provide evidence to prove that only 20 percent of the town voted in the last election. But this evidence would not motivate your audience to vote unless you could provide other evidence to show that their needs were not being served by such a low turnout.

Writer's Guide: Using Effective Support

1. In deciding how much support you need for your claim, it is always a good idea to assume that you are addressing an audience that may be at least slightly hostile to that claim. Those who already agree with you do not need convincing.

2. Keep a mental, if not a written, list of the different types of support you use in an essay. Few essays will use all of the different types of support, but being aware of all the possibilities will prevent you from forgetting to draw on one or more types of support that may advance your argument.

3. In that checklist of types of support, don't forget that there are two main categories: evidence and appeals to needs and values. Appeals to needs and values will generally need the reinforcement that comes from more objective forms of evidence, but the two in combination can often provide the strongest case for your claim. Aristotle explained that in an ideal world, arguers could depend on logic alone, but we live in a world that is far from ideal.

4. Use the following questions about the evaluation of evidence as a checklist to analyze the support you use in your argumentative essays:

Factual evidence:

- Is the evidence up to date?
- Is the evidence sufficient?
- Is the evidence relevant?
- Are the examples representative?
- Are the examples consistent with the experience of the audience?

Statistics:

- Do the statistics come from trustworthy sources?
- Are the terms clearly defined?
- Are the comparisons between comparable things?
- Has any significant information been omitted?

Opinion:

- Is the source of the opinion qualified to give an opinion on the subject?
- Is the source biased for or against his or her interpretation?
- Has the source bolstered the claim with sufficient and appropriate evidence?

5. Also check your essays against the list of questions regarding appeals to needs and values:

- Have the values been clearly defined?
- Are the needs and values to which you appeal prominent in the reader's hierarchy at the time you are writing?
- Is the evidence in your argument clearly related to the needs and values to which you appeal?

PRACTICE

1. Locate two advertisements from magazines or newspapers that appeal to needs or values or both. Be prepared to explain what needs and/or values the ads appeal to.

2. Share your ads with your classmates so that everyone can get an idea of the range of how ads appeal to needs and values.

3. Choose one of the ads your class compiled and write a paragraph analyzing its appeal to needs and/or values.

4. Write an essay in which you compare two ads for the same product or same type of product in terms of the types of appeal that they use.

SAMPLE ANNOTATED ESSAY

American Dream Is Elusive for New Generation

LOUIS UCHITELLE

Begins an extended example

After breakfast, his parents left for their jobs, and Scott Nicholson, alone in the house in this comfortable suburb west of Boston, went to his laptop in the living room. He had placed it on a small table that his mother had used for a vase of flowers until her unemployed son found himself reluctantly stuck at home.

The reference to his award appeals to those who value academic excellence.

The daily routine seldom varied. Mr. Nicholson, twenty-four, a graduate of Colgate University, winner of a dean's award for academic excellence, spent his mornings searching corporate Web sites for suitable job openings. When he found one, he mailed off a résumé and cover letter — four or five a week, week after week.

Over the last five months, only one job materialized. After several interviews, the Hanover Insurance Group in nearby Worcester offered to hire him as an associate claims adjuster, at $40,000 a year. But even before the formal offer, Mr. Nicholson had decided not to take the job.

His refusal to accept this job goes against the values of those who believe any job is better than none.

Rather than waste early years in dead-end work, he reasoned, he would hold out for a corporate position that would draw on his college training and put him, as he sees it, on the bottom rungs of a career ladder.

Louis Uchitelle worked as a reporter, a foreign correspondent, and the editor of the business news department at the Associated Press before joining the *New York Times* — the source of this article on July 6, 2010 — in 1980. He has taught journalism at Columbia University and is author of *The Disposable American: Layoffs and Their Consequences* (2006).

Scott Nicholson searches for a job while living in his parents' home.

"The conversation I'm going to have with my parents   5
now that I've turned down this job is more of a concern
to me than turning down the job," he said.

Generational conflict about values

He was braced for the conversation with his father in
particular. While Scott Nicholson viewed the Hanover
job as likely to stunt his career, David Nicholson, fifty-
seven, accustomed to better times and easier mobility,
viewed it as an opportunity. Once in the door, the father
has insisted to his son, opportunities will present themselves — as they did in the father's rise over thirty-five
years to general manager of a manufacturing company.

"You maneuvered and you did not worry what the
maneuvering would lead to," the father said. "You knew
it would lead to something good."

Complicating the generational divide, Scott's grandfather, William S. Nicholson, a World War II veteran and
a retired stockbroker, has watched what he described
as America's once mighty economic engine losing its
pre-eminence in a global economy. The grandfather has

Appeal to need for security

encouraged his unemployed grandson to go abroad — to
"Go West," so to speak.

"I view what is happening to Scott with dismay," said
the grandfather, who has concluded, in part from reading

Conflicts with U.S. value
system — the belief that U.S.
does everything better than
anyone else

the *Economist*, that Europe has surpassed America in offering opportunity for an ambitious young man. "We hate
to think that Scott will have to leave," the grandfather
said, "but he will."

The grandfather's injunction startled the grandson.   10
But as the weeks pass, Scott Nicholson, handsome as a
Marine officer in a recruiting poster, has gradually realized that his career will not roll out in the Greater Boston
area — or anywhere in America — with the easy inevitability that his father and grandfather recall, and that
Scott thought would be his lot, too, when he finished
college in 2008.

"I don't think I fully understood the severity of the
situation I had graduated into," he said, speaking in effect
for an age group — the so-called millennials, eighteen to

Another appeal to need for
security and esteem — it's
threatening for this generation to be compared to the
same age group during the
Depression.

twenty-nine — whose unemployment rate of nearly 14
percent approaches the levels of that group in the Great
Depression. And then he veered into the optimism that,
polls show, is persistently, perhaps perversely, characteristic of millennials today. "I am absolutely certain that my
job hunt will eventually pay off," he said.

For young adults, the prospects in the workplace, even
for the college-educated, have rarely been so bleak. Apart
from the 14 percent who are unemployed and seeking
work, as Scott Nicholson is, 23 percent are not even seek-

Statistical support

ing a job, according to data from the Bureau of Labor Statistics. The total, 37 percent, is the highest in more than
three decades and a rate reminiscent of the 1930s.

The college-educated among these young adults are
better off. But nearly 17 percent are either unemployed
or not seeking work, a record level (although some are

More statistical support

in graduate school). The unemployment rate for college-
educated young adults, 5.5 percent, is nearly double what
it was on the eve of the Great Recession, in 2007, and the
highest level — by almost two percentage points — since
the bureau started to keep records in 1994 for those with
at least four years of college.

Yet surveys show that the majority of the nation's millennials remain confident, as Scott Nicholson is, that they
will have satisfactory careers. They have a lot going for them.

"They are better educated than previous generations   15

Appeal to esteem needs

and they were raised by baby boomers who lavished a lot
of attention on their children," said Andrew Kohut, the
Pew Research Center's director. That helps to explain their
persistent optimism, even as they struggle to succeed.

So far, Scott Nicholson is a stranger to the triumphal stories that his father and grandfather tell of their working lives. They said it was connections more than perseverance that got them started — the father in 1976 when a friend who had just opened a factory hired him, and the grandfather in 1946 through an Army buddy whose father-in-law owned a brokerage firm in nearby Worcester and needed another stock broker.

Appeal to a need to belong to a community

From these accidental starts, careers unfolded and lasted. David Nicholson, now the general manager of a company that makes tools, is still in manufacturing. William Nicholson spent the next 48 years, until his retirement, as a stockbroker. "Scott has got to find somebody who knows someone," the grandfather said, "someone who can get him to the head of the line."

While Scott has tried to make that happen, he has come under pressure from his parents to compromise: to take, if not the Hanover job, then one like it. "I am beginning to realize that refusal is going to have repercussions," he said. "My parents are subtly pointing out that beyond room and board, they are also paying other expenses for me, like my cellphone charges and the premiums on a life insurance policy."

Appeal to the need for esteem — material success, status, etc.

Scott Nicholson also has connections, of course, but no one in his network of family and friends has been able to steer him into marketing or finance or management training or any career-oriented opening at a big corporation, his goal. The jobs are simply not there.

The Millennials' Inheritance

The Great Depression damaged the self-confidence of the young, and that is beginning to happen now, according to pollsters, sociologists and economists. Young men in particular lost a sense of direction, Glen H. Elder Jr., a sociologist at the University of North Carolina, found in his study, *Children of the Great Depression*. In some cases they were forced into work they did not want — the issue for Scott Nicholson.

Expert opinion

Military service in World War II, along with the G.I. Bill and a booming economy, restored well-being; by the 1970s, when Mr. Elder did his retrospective study, the hardships of the Depression were more a memory than an open sore. "They came out of the war with purpose in their lives, and by age forty most of them were doing well," he said, speaking of his study in a recent interview.

20

Appeal to the need for
security

The outlook this time is not so clear. Starved for jobs at adequate pay, the millennials tend to seek refuge in college and in the military and to put off marriage and child-bearing. Those who are working often stay with the jobs they have rather than jump to better paying but less secure ones, as young people seeking advancement normally do. And they are increasingly willing to forgo raises or to settle for small ones.

Expert opinion

"They are definitely more risk-averse," said Lisa B. Kahn, an economist at the Yale School of Management, "and more likely to fall behind."

Statistical support

In a recent study, she found that those who graduated from college during the severe early '80s recession earned up to 30 percent less in their first three years than new graduates who landed their first jobs in a strong economy. Even fifteen years later, their annual pay was 8 to 10 percent less.

Many hard-pressed millennials are falling back on their parents, as Scott Nicholson has. While he has no college debt (his grandparents paid all his tuition and board) many others do, and that helps force them back home.   25

In 2008, the first year of the recession, the percentage of the population living in households in which at least two generations were present rose nearly a percentage point, to 16 percent, according to the Pew Research Center. The high point, 24.7 percent, came in 1940, as the Depression ended, and the low point, 12 percent, in 1980.

Striving for Independence

Appeal to self-actualization
need

"Going it alone," "earning enough to be self-supporting" — these are awkward concepts for Scott Nicholson and his friends. Of the twenty college classmates with whom he keeps up, twelve are working, but only half are in jobs they "really like." Three are entering law school this fall after frustrating experiences in the work force, "and five are looking for work just as I am," he said.

Like most of his classmates, Scott tries to get by on a shoestring and manages to earn enough in odd jobs to pay some expenses.

Examples

The jobs are catch as catch can. He and a friend recently put up a white wooden fence for a neighbor, embedding the posts in cement, a day's work that brought Scott $125. He mows lawns and gardens for half a dozen clients in Grafton, some of them family friends. And he is an active volunteer firefighter.

"As frustrated as I get now, and I never intended to   30
live at home, I'm in a good situation in a lot of ways,"
Scott said. "I have very little overhead and no debt, and it
is because I have no debt that I have any sort of flexibility
to look for work. Otherwise, I would have to have a job,
some kind of full-time job."

That millennials as a group are optimistic is partly
because many are, as Mr. Kohut put it, the children of
doting baby boomers — among them David Nicholson
and his wife, Susan, fifty-six, an executive at a company
that owns movie theaters.

The Nicholsons, whose combined annual income is
north of $175,000, have lavished attention on their three
sons. Currently that attention is directed mainly at sus-
taining the self-confidence of their middle son.

Appeal to need for belongingness, love, and self-esteem

"No one on either side of the family has ever gone
through this," Mrs. Nicholson said, "and I guess I'm im-
patient. I know he is educated and has a great work ethic
and wants to start contributing, and I don't know what
to do."

Her oldest, David Jr., twenty-six, did land a good job.
Graduating from Middlebury College in 2006, he joined
a Boston insurance company, specializing in reinsurance,
nearly three years ago, before the recession.

Example

"I'm fortunate to be at a company where there is some   35
security," he said, adding that he supports Scott in his determination to hold out for the right job. "Once you start
working, you get caught up in the work and you have
bills to pay, and you lose sight of what you really want,"
the brother said.

He is earning $75,000 — a sum beyond Scott's reach
today, but not his expectations. "I worked hard through
high school to get myself into the college I did," Scott
said, "and then I worked hard through college to graduate with the grades and degree that I did to position
myself for a solid job." (He majored in political science
and minored in history.)

It was in pursuit of a solid job that Scott applied to
Hanover International's management training program.
Turned down for that, he was called back to interview for
the lesser position in the claims department.

"I'm sitting with the manager, and he asked me how
I had gotten interested in insurance. I mentioned Dave's
job in reinsurance, and the manager's response was, 'Oh,
that is about fifteen steps above the position you are

Appeal to the need for self-
esteem and self-actualization

interviewing for,'" Scott said, his eyes widening and his
voice emotional.

Scott acknowledges that he is competitive with his
brothers, particularly David, more than they are with
him. The youngest, Bradley, twenty-two, has a year to
go at the University of Vermont. His parents and grandparents pay his way, just as they did for his brothers in
their college years.

In the Old Days

Going to college wasn't an issue for grandfather Nicholson,   40
or so he says. With World War II approaching, he entered
the Army not long after finishing high school and, in
the fighting in Italy, a battlefield commission raised him
overnight from enlisted man to first lieutenant. That was

Appeal to values

"the equivalent of a college education," as he now puts it,
in an age when college on a stockbroker's resumé "counted
for something, but not a lot."

He spent most of his career in a rising market, putting
customers into stocks that paid good dividends and growing wealthy on real estate investments made years ago,
when Grafton was still semi-rural. The brokerage firm
that employed him changed hands more than once, but
he continued to work out of the same office in Worcester.

When his son David graduated from Babson College

Extended example

in 1976, manufacturing in America was in an early phase
of its long decline, and Worcester was still a center for
the production of sandpaper, emery stones, and other
abrasives.

He joined one of those companies — owned by the
family of his friend — and he has stayed in manufacturing, particularly at companies that make hand tools.
Early on, he and his wife bought the home in which
they raised their sons, a white colonial dating from the
early 1800s, like many houses on North Street, where the
grandparents also live, a few doors away.

David Nicholson's longest stretch was at the Stanley
Works, and when he left, seeking promotion, a friend at
the Endeavor Tool Company hired him as that company's
general manager, his present job.

In better times, Scott's father might have given his son   45
work at Endeavor, but the father is laying off workers,
and a job in manufacturing, in Scott's eyes, would be a
defeat.

"If you talk to twenty people," Scott said, "you'll find only one in manufacturing and everyone else in finance or something else."

The Plan

Scott Nicholson almost sidestepped the recession. His plan was to become a Marine Corps second lieutenant. He had spent the summer after his freshman year in "platoon leader" training. Last fall he passed the physical for officer training and was told to report on January 16.

If all had gone well, he would have emerged in ten weeks as a second lieutenant, committed to a four-year enlistment. "I could have made a career out of the Marines," Scott said, "and if I had come out in four years, I would have been incredibly prepared for the workplace."

It was not to be. In early January, a Marine Corps doctor noticed that he had suffered from childhood asthma. He was washed out. "They finally told me I could reapply if I wanted to," Scott said. "But the sheen was gone."

So he struggles to get a foothold in the civilian work force. His brother in Boston lost his roommate, and early last month Scott moved into the empty bedroom, with his parents paying Scott's share of the $2,000-a-month rent until the lease expires on August 31.   50

Concludes his extended example that begins the essay

And if Scott does not have a job by then? "I'll do something temporary; I won't go back home," Scott said. "I'll be a bartender or get work through a temp agency. I hope I don't find myself in that position."

SAMPLE ESSAY WITH ANALYSIS

At times, assignments may ask you to analyze or evaluate the evidence and appeals to needs and values offered in support of a claim. At other times, you will have to discover your own support for use in an argument that you are writing. After the following essay about sport utility vehicles and its reading and discussion questions, you will first find an example of an essay of the type you might write if you were asked to evaluate an author's use of support. It is followed by a student essay that illustrates effective use of support.

The True Costs of SUVs

HAL R. VARIAN

Traffic fatalities in the United States fell steadily from 54,600 in 1972 to 34,900 in 1992. But then they started to rise again, and by 2002 there were 38,300 traffic deaths a year.

Our performance compared with other countries has also deteriorated. America's ranking has fallen from first to ninth over the last thirty years, with Australia, Britain, and Canada all having better records.

A big part of the difference between the United States and other countries seems to be the prevalence of sport utility vehicles and pickups on American highways. Sales of light trucks — SUVs, pickups, and minivans — were about a fifth of total automobile sales thirty years ago. Now they account for more than half.

But aren't large vehicles supposed to be safer than small cars? Yes, they are safer for their occupants in collisions, but their design makes them all the more dangerous for anyone they hit.

Michelle White, an economist at the University of California, San Diego, estimates that for each fatality that light-truck drivers avoid for themselves and their passengers, they cause four fatalities involving car occupants, pedestrians, bicyclists, and motorcyclists. "Safety gains for those driving light trucks," Ms. White said, "come at an extremely high cost to others."

Being larger than ordinary vehicles, SUVs and light trucks cause more damage to upper bodies and heads in collisions. Furthermore, their bumpers do not always align with automobile bumpers, and their body structure is stiffer, transferring more force to other vehicles during impact.

A few weeks ago, the auto industry announced a voluntary plan to deal with some of these design problems. They intend to make side-impact airbags standard to help protect heads and upper bodies better in collisions, and they intend to standardize bumper heights.

These will no doubt be helpful improvements, but do they go far enough?

Recently Ms. White examined the econometrics of traffic accidents in an attempt to measure the benefits and costs of changing the number of light trucks on the road. . . .

Ms. White notes that changing average vehicle size could, in principle, increase or decrease the cost of accidents.

Suppose the cost of a small vehicle–large vehicle collision is $50, the cost of a small vehicle–small vehicle collision is $45, and the cost of a large vehicle–large vehicle collision is $40.

A professor emeritus in the School of Information Management and Systems at the University of California at Berkeley, Hal R. Varian has written economics textbooks as well as columns for the *New York Times*. He is currently chief economist at *Google*. This piece appeared in the *Times* as the "Economic Scene" article on December 18, 2003.

The results of an accident in New York involving a sport utility vehicle and a smaller car. Traffic fatalities are on the rise, apparently linked to the increase of SUVs.
G. Paul Burnett/*New York Times*

If all vehicles are small, and there are ten accidents a year, the total cost of the accidents is $450. But if 10 percent of the small vehicles are replaced by large ones, the average cost of collisions becomes $458.50, since more collisions will be between large and small vehicles. On the other hand, if 60 percent of the vehicles on the road are large, the average cost of a collision is only $456, since more collisions are between large vehicles.

Think about a safety-conscious soccer mom choosing a vehicle. If there are mostly small cars in her town, she can reduce the risk to her and her family in the event of a collision by buying an SUV.

The unfortunate side effect is that the large SUV would cause significant damage to smaller cars if she was involved in an accident.

The laudable private incentive to choose a safe vehicle could, perversely, reduce overall safety.

15

In addition, Ms. White finds that people involved in single-vehicle crashes are more likely to be killed or seriously injured if they are in SUVs or light trucks rather than cars. This may be a result of the increased likelihood of rollovers.

On the other hand, suppose everybody in town drives an SUV. Then the soccer mom will definitely want to purchase one for herself, since it would both increase her family's safety and reduce the overall costs of collisions.

In this case, private incentives and social incentives are aligned.

The dynamics involved is the same as that of an arms race: If other families buy bigger vehicles, then you will want to as well, if only in self-defense.

To see where we are in this arms race, Ms. White examined crash data maintained by the National Highway Safety Administration. . . .   20

Using this data, Ms. White was able to estimate how the probability of fatalities or serious injury varied with the types of vehicles involved in collisions.

For example, in a two-car accident, the probability of a fatality in the car is 38 percent less than in a car–light truck accident. However, in car–light truck accidents, the probability of fatalities in the light truck is 55 percent less than it would be in a truck–truck accident.

If a light truck hits a pedestrian or a cyclist, the probability of fatalities is about 82 percent greater than if a car is involved.

Ms. White then asked what the impact would be of replacing a million light trucks with cars. She considered two models for driver behavior. In the first, she assumed that the former drivers of light trucks would have the same number of accidents as they did when driving trucks. In the second, she assumed that the former drivers of light trucks would have the same accident probabilities as other car drivers.

Using conventional methods for value-of-life calculations, she finds that each   25
light-truck owner who switches to a car saves about $447 in total expected costs of accidents.

Ms. White examines various policies that might persuade drivers to adopt such changes, including changes in liability rules, traffic rules, and insurance rules.

Unfortunately, each of these policies has its problems, so there are no easy solutions.

One interesting way to reduce the arms race problem would be to link automobile liability insurance to gasoline taxes. This means drivers whose cars use more gasoline and those who drive a lot would pay more for their insurance — not unreasonable, since, on average, they impose more costs in accidents.

Aaron Edlin, a professor of economics and law at the University of California, Berkeley, has argued that such "pay at the pump" insurance premiums would have many other benefits (www.bepress.com/aaronedlin/contribution5/). So this type of payment scheme is worth considering for a variety of reasons.

READING AND DISCUSSION QUESTIONS

1. For the purposes of his article, how is Varian defining *light truck*?

2. What relationship does he see between light trucks and the number of traffic fatalities?

3. What type of support does Varian use in the three opening paragraphs? Does he use that type of support anywhere else in the essay?

4. What other types of support does Varian make use of in his essay? What types of support do you find most effective in making his argument? What types do you find least effective?

5. What claim is Varian supporting in the essay?

6. How does Varian document his sources? How does he try to establish that his sources are reliable?

The True Confusion About SUV Costs

BETHANY ROYCE

al R. Varian entitled his December 18, 2003, *New York Times* piece on sport utility vehicles "The True Costs of SUVs." A more accurate title might have been "The Confusing Costs of SUVs." While Varian turns to the right type of support for his subject — statistics — his use of that support is more confusing than enlightening.

Varian made a wise choice in appealing to his readers' need to feel safe and secure. His statistics are most appealing when he points out that for twenty years the number of traffic fatalities in our country went down and that parents can feel secure knowing that they can make their children safer by buying light trucks (SUVs, pickups, or minivans) instead of cars. In each case, however, there is a negative side. The number of fatalities started rising again between 1992 and 2002, in part because of the increase in the number of sales of light trucks during that time. And Varian tells us that in making their families safer by buying light trucks, they are increasing the risk of doing more harm to others should they be involved in accidents.

For the rest of his support, Varian draws primarily on research done by Michelle White, whom he identifies only as "an economist at the University of California, San Diego" (231). She may have done excellent work, but the way that Varian explains it is confusing and unconvincing. White tries to predict how the cost of accidents would change depending on the size of the vehicles involved. Instead of using realistic cost estimates, however, she arbitrarily assigns the cost of $50 to a small vehicle–large vehicle collision, the cost of $45 to a small vehicle–small vehicle collision, and the cost of $40 to a large vehicle–large vehicle collision. Varian summarizes what this hypothetical scenario reveals:

> If all vehicles are small, and there are ten accidents a year, the total cost of the accidents is $450. But if 10 percent of the small vehicles are replaced by large ones, the average cost of collisions becomes $458.50, since more collisions will be between large and small vehicles. On the other hand, if 60 percent of the vehicles on the road are large, the average cost of a collision is only $456, since more collisions are between large vehicles. (232)

Average Americans are left wondering what all of this means to them. The hypothetical situation cannot be easily applied to any individual driver and certainly not to any specific accident. How should a reader evaluate the information in attempting to make the decision regarding what size vehicle to buy? The driver who just paid $3000 in car repairs is going to find any of the numbers Varian cites attractive.

Bethany Royce teaches business courses and introductory economics at a two-year college in Florida and writes a consumer advice column for a local newspaper.

There are a lot of "ifs" in Varian's argument. If you live in a town with lots of SUVs, it is safer to drive one yourself. If you live in a town where there are few SUVs, you should drive a car so that you would not be as likely to hurt someone else in a wreck. If you have a single-vehicle accident in an SUV, you are more likely to be killed. If you hit a pedestrian while driving one, you are more likely to kill that person.

There are also few clear conclusions to be drawn from the support that Varian   5
offers. After Ms. White examines "various policies that might persuade drivers to adopt such changes, including changes in liability rules, traffic rules, and insurance rates," the unfortunate conclusion is that "each of these policies has its problems, so there are no easy solutions" [233]. The only solution that Varian advances as "worth considering" is one by a colleague of his at the University of California, Berkeley, that would link a vehicle owner's liability insurance to gas taxes [233]. Overall the article succeeds more in revealing the complexities involved in the increased use of SUVs than in clarifying any of those complexities.

SAMPLE STUDENT ESSAY

Safer? Tastier? More Nutritious? The Dubious Merits of Organic Foods

KRISTEN WEINACKER

Organic foods are attractive to some consumers because of the principles behind them and the farming techniques used to produce them. There is a special respect for organic farmers who strive to maintain the ecological balance and harmony that exist among living things. As these farmers work in partnership with nature, some consumers too feel a certain attachment to the earth (Wolf 1–2). They feel happier knowing that these foods are produced without chemical fertilizers, pesticides, and additives to extend their shelf life (Pickerell; Agricultural Extension Service 5). They feel that they have returned to nature by eating organic foods that are advertised as being healthy for maintaining a vigorous lifestyle. Unfortunately, research has not provided statistical evidence that organic foods are more nutritious than conventionally grown ones.

The debate over the nutritional benefits has raged for decades. Defenders of the nutritional value of organic foods have employed excellent marketing and sales strategies. First, they freely share the philosophy behind their farming and follow up with detailed descriptions of their management techniques. Second, organic farmers skillfully appeal to our common sense. It seems reasonable to believe that organic foods are more nutritious since they are grown without chemical

---

At the time she wrote this essay, Kristen Weinacker was an undergraduate at Clemson University.

fertilizers and pesticides. Third, since the soil in which these crops are grown is so rich and healthy, it seems plausible that these crops have absorbed and developed better nutrients. As Lynda Brown asserts in her book *Living Organic*, "Organic farmers believe that growing crops organically provides the best possible way to produce healthy food" (26). Brown provides beautifully illustrated and enlarged microscopic photographs to show the more developed structure of organic foods compared to conventional products to convince the consumer to believe that organic foods are more nutritious (27). Fourth, many consumers view the higher price tags on organic foods and assume that they must be more nutritious. Generalizations permeate the whole world of organic foods. These marketing strategies persuade the consumer that organic foods are healthier than conventional foods without providing any factual comparisons.

In their book *Is Our Food Safe?* Warren Leon and Caroline Smith Dewaal compare organic and conventionally produced foods. They strongly suggest that consumers buy organic foods to help the environment (68). They believe that organic foods are healthier than conventional ones. However, statistics supporting this belief are not provided. The authors even warn consumers that they need to read product labels because some organic foods may be as unhealthy as conventional ones (68–69). An interesting poll involving 1,041 adults was conducted by ABC News asking, "Why do people buy organic?" Analyst Daniel Merkle concluded that 45 percent of the American public *believes* that organic products are more nutritious than conventionally grown ones. Also, 57 percent of the population maintains that organic farming is beneficial for the environment. According to the pollsters, the primary reason why people bought organic foods is the belief that they are healthier because they have less pesticide residue. However, there has never been any link established between the nutritional value of organic foods and the residue found on them. Clever marketing strategies have made the need for concrete data really not of prime importance for the consumer to join the bandwagon promoting organic foods.

This pervasive belief among the American public that organic foods are probably healthier than conventionally grown foods was reiterated in my telephone interview with Mr. Joseph Williamson, an agricultural county extension agent working with Clemson University. When asked if organically grown foods are more nutritious than those grown conventionally, he replied that they probably were for two reasons. First, organic crops tend to grow more slowly. Therefore, the nutrients have more time to build up in the plants. Second, organic plants are usually grown locally. The fruits and vegetables are allowed to stay on the plants for a longer period of time. They ripen more than those picked green and transported across miles. He contends that these conditions promote a better nutrient buildup. Unfortunately, the extension agent acknowledges that statistical evidence is not available to support the claim that organic products are more nutritious.

An article entitled "Effects of Agricultural Methods in Nutritional Quality: A Comparison of Organic with Conventional Crops" reports on conclusions drawn by Dr. Virginia Worthington, a certified nutrition specialist. Worthington examines why it is so difficult to ascertain if organic foods are more nutritious. First, "the difference in terms of health effects is not large enough to be readily apparent." There is no concrete evidence that people are healthier eating organic foods

5

or, conversely, that people become more ill eating conventionally grown produce. Second, Dr. Worthington notes that variables such as sunlight, temperature, and amount of rain are so inconsistent that the nutrients in crops vary yearly. Third, she points out that the nutrient value of products can be changed by the way products are stored and shipped. After reviewing at least thirty studies dealing with the question if organic foods are more nutritious than conventionally grown ones, Dr. Worthington concludes that there is too little data available to substantiate the claim of higher nutritional value in organic foods. She also believes that it is an impossible task to make a direct connection between organic foods and the health of those people who consume them.

After being asked for thirty years about organic foods by her readers and associates, Joan Dye Gussow, writer for *Eating Well* magazine, firmly concludes that there is "little hard proof that organically grown produce is reliably more nutritious." Reviewing seventy years' worth of studies on the subject, Gussow has no doubt that organic foods should be healthier because of the way they are produced and cultivated. Gussow brings up an interesting point about chemical and pesticide residue. She believes that the fact that organic foods have been found to have fewer residues does not make them automatically more nutritious and healthier for the consumer. As scientific technologies advance, Gussow predicts that research will someday discover statistical data that will prove that organic foods have a higher nutritional value compared to conventionally grown ones.

In order to provide the public with more information about the nature of organic foods, the well-known and highly regarded magazine *Consumer Reports* decided to take a closer look at organic foods in their January 1998 magazine, in an article entitled "Organic Foods: Safer? Tastier? More nutritious?" By conducting comparison tests, their researchers discovered that organic foods have less pesticide residue, and that their flavors are just about the same as conventionally grown foods. These scientists came to the conclusion that the "variability within a given crop is greater than the variability between one cropping system and another." *Consumer Reports* contacted Professor Willie Lockeretz from the Tufts University School of Nutrition Science and Policy. He told researchers that "the growing system you use probably does affect nutrition. . . . But it does it in ways so complex you might be studying the problem forever." Keeping in mind these comments made by Dr. Lockeretz, *Consumer Reports* believes it would be an impossible task to compare the nutritional values of organic and conventional foods. Therefore, researchers at *Consumer Reports* decided not to carry out that part of their comparison testing.

Although statistical evidence is not available at this time to support the claim that organic foods are more nutritious than conventionally grown ones, there is a very strong feeling shared by a majority of the general public that they are. We are called back to nature as we observe the love that organic farmers have for the soil and their desire to work in partnership with nature. We are easily lured to the attractive displays of organic foods in the grocery stores. However, we must keep in mind the successful marketing techniques that have been used to convince us that organic foods are more nutritious than conventionally grown ones. Although common sense tells us that organic foods should be more nutritious, research has not provided us with any statistical data to prove this claim.

WORKS CITED

Agricultural Extension Service. *Organic Vegetable Gardening*. The University of Tennessee. PB 1391.

Brown, Lynda. *Organic Living*. New York: Dorling Kindersley Publishing, Inc., 2000.

Gussow, Joan Dye. "Is Organic Food More Nutritious?" *Eating Well* (May/June 1997). 27 March 2003. <http://www.prnac.net/rodmap-nutrition.html>.

"Effect of Agricultural Methods on Nutritional Quality: A Comparison of Organic with Conventional Crops." *Alternative Therapies* 4 (1998): 58–69. 18 Feb. 2003. <http://www.purefood.org/healthier101101.cfm>.

Leon, Warren, and Caroline Smith DeWaal. *Is Our Food Safe?* New York: Three Rivers Press, 2002.

Merkle, Daniel. "Why Do People Buy Organic?" ABCNews.com. 3 Feb. 2000. 27 March 2003.

"Organic Foods: Safer? Tastier? More Nutritious?" *Consumer Reports*. Jan. 1998. 24 Feb. 2003. <http://www.consumerreports.org/main/detailsv2.jsp?content%3%ecnt_id+18959&f>.

Pickrell, John. "Federal Government Launches Organic Standards." *Science News* 162.17 (Nov. 2002). <http://www.sciencenews.org/20021102/food.asp._17_March 2003>.

Williamson, Joseph. Telephone interview. 28 Feb. 2003.

Wolf, Ray, ed. *Organic Farming: Yesterday's and Tomorrow's Agriculture*. Philadelphia: Rodale Press, 1977.

READINGS FOR ANALYSIS

Connecting the Dots . . . to Terrorism

BERNARD GOLDBERG

Most of the time television is nothing more than a diversion — proof, as the old quip goes, that we would rather do anything than talk to each other. We'd also rather watch a bad sitcom than read a good book. Bad sitcoms get millions of viewers; good books get thousands. In an "entertainment culture," even the news is entertainment. Certainly too much local news has been pure fluff for some time now, with their Ken and Barbie anchors who have nothing intelligent to say but look great while they're saying it. And because network news is losing viewers every year, executives and producers are trying to figure out ways to hold on to the ones they still have. They think cosmetics will work, so they change the anchor desk or they change the graphics. They get the anchor to stand instead of sit. They feature more "news you can use." They put Chandra Levy[18] on all over

[18]*Chandra Levy*: A government intern whose disappearance was widely covered in the press in 2001. — EDS.

Bernard Goldberg was a reporter and producer for CBS for more than thirty years. He has won ten Emmy awards and was once rated by *TV Guide* as one of the ten most interesting people on television. This chapter is from his 2002 book *Bias: A CBS Insider Exposes How the Media Distort the News*, written after he left the network.

the place, hoping they can concoct a ratings cocktail by mixing one part missing intern with ten parts sex scandal.

And then something genuinely big and really important happens that shakes us to our core, and all those producers who couldn't get enough of Chandra are through with her. Only in the fickle world of television news can someone who has disappeared without a trace disappear a second time.

And it's when that history-making story comes along that Americans — no matter what their politics, religion, age, race, or sex — turn to television, not just for information, but also for comfort and for peace of mind. It doesn't happen often, but when it does, television becomes a lot more than just a diversion.

It happened when John Kennedy was assassinated. We all turned to Walter Cronkite and Huntley and Brinkley, not just for facts, but also for reassurance — that despite the terrible tragedy, America was going to be okay.

It happened when *Challenger* blew up. And it happened again on September 11, 2001, when a band of religious lunatics declared war on the United States of America to punish us for not wanting to dwell in the fourteenth century, where they currently reside, and, of course, to show the world that their intense hatred of Israel — *and of Israel's friends* — knows no bounds. On September 11, they not only killed as many innocent Americans as they could in the most dramatic way they knew how, but, as the *Wall Street Journal* put it, they also "wiped out any remaining illusions that America is safe from mass organized violence."

On that day we all turned to television. We turned to Dan Rather and Peter Jennings and Tom Brokaw and the others. And they did a fine job, as they often do when covering tragedy. They showed empathy. They were fair and accurate, and the information they passed along to us wasn't filtered through the usual liberal political and social sensibilities. They gave us the news on that day the way they should give us the news *all the time*, whether the story is about race or feminism or taxes or gay rights or anything else. *For a change, they gave it to us straight.*

On the night of September 11, 2001, Peter Jennings made a point about how, in times of danger and tragedy, television serves the function that campfires used to serve in the old days when Americans migrated westward in covered wagons. Back then, they would sit around the campfire and get the news from other travelers about what they should look out for down the road. "Some people pulled the wagons around," Peter said, "and discussed what was going on and tried to understand it." But the campfire was more than just a meeting place where families could pick up important information. The campfire also provided a sense of community, a sense that *we're all in this together*. That's what television was on September 11.

As I listened to Peter tell that story, I thought about another American tragedy that shocked us six years earlier, when Timothy McVeigh — another true believer who cared nothing about killing innocent Americans — blew up the federal building in Oklahoma City. I thought about how it took some of the media elites only a few days before they started to play one of their favorite games — connect the dots. What they found back then — or more accurately, what they convinced themselves they found — was a line stretching from Oklahoma City to the Republican Party to conservatives in general and finally to Rush Limbaugh.

5

Dan Rather said, "Even after Oklahoma City, you can turn on your radio in any city and still dial up hate talk: extremist, racist, and violent from the hosts and those who call in."

Time senior writer Richard Lacayo put it this way: "In a nation that has entertained and appalled itself for years with hot talk on radio and the campaign trail, the inflamed rhetoric of the '90s is suddenly an unindicted coconspirator in the blast."   10

Nina Easton wrote in the *Los Angeles Times*, "The Oklahoma City attack on federal workers and their children also alters the once-easy dynamic between charismatic talk show host and adoring audience. Hosts who routinely espouse the same antigovernment themes as the militia movement now must walk a fine line between inspiring their audience — and inciting the most radical among them."

On *Face the Nation*, Bob Schieffer asked this question: "Mr. Panetta, there's been a lot of antigovernment rhetoric, it comes over talk radio, it comes from various quarters. Do you think that that somehow has led these people to commit this act, do they feed on that kind of rhetoric, and what impact do you think it had?"

Carl Rowan, the late columnist, was quoted in a *Washington Post* story saying that, "Unless Gingrich and Dole[19] and the Republicans say 'Am I inflaming a bunch of nuts?' you know we're going to have some more events. I am absolutely certain the harsher rhetoric of the Gingriches and the Doles . . . creates a climate of violence in America."

And David Broder had this to say in the *Washington Post*: "The bombing shows how dangerous it really is to inflame twisted minds with statements that suggest political opponents are enemies. For two years, Rush Limbaugh described this nation as 'America held hostage' to the policies of the liberal Democrats, as if the duly elected president and Congress were equivalent to the regime in Tehran. I think there will be less tolerance and fewer cheers for that kind of rhetoric."

The message was clear: Conservative talk radio and conservative politicians   15 created an antigovernment atmosphere in America that spawned Timothy McVeigh and therefore were at least partially to blame for his terrorism. It's true, of course, that the atmosphere in which we live contributes to everything that happens in our culture. Calling people "kikes" or "niggers" makes it easier to see them as less than human and to treat them as something less than human. But to point fingers at talk radio for somehow encouraging Timothy McVeigh strikes me as a stretch at best; more likely it's just another opportunity for liberal journalists to blame conservatives for one more evil. And if this kind of connecting the dots is fair game, then should we also accuse Americans who spoke out loudly and forcefully against the war in Vietnam — including many journalists — of contributing to the 1972 bombing of the Pentagon and to other sometimes deadly terrorism, perpetuated by fanatics on the Left? According to the media elites' rulebook, when liberals rant it's called free speech; when conservatives rant it's called incitement to terrorism.

---

[19]*Gingrich and Dole*: Newt Gingrich (b. 1943) was Speaker of the House of Representatives from 1995 to 1999. Robert Dole (b. 1923) was a Senate majority leader and served in the Senate from 1968 to 1996. — EDS.

As I watched the coverage of the attacks on the Pentagon and the World Trade Center, I wondered why I hadn't seen more stories on television news, long before these zealots flew their hijacked planes into American buildings, about the culture of anti-American hate that permeates so much of the Middle East — stories that might help explain how little Arab children can grow up to become fanatical suicide bombers.

If the media found it so important to discuss the malignant atmosphere created by "hot" conservative talk radio, then why didn't they find it important to delve into this malignant atmosphere that seems to have bred such maniacal killers? Why would journalists, so interested in connecting the dots when they thought they led to Rush Limbaugh, be so uninterested in connecting the dots when there might actually be dots to connect — *from hateful, widely held popular attitudes in much of the Arab world straight to the cockpits of those hijacked jetliners?*

One of the networks put an American Muslim woman on the news who said that no one blamed Christianity when McVeigh killed all those people. Why blame Islam now? The reporter interviewing this woman let her have her say, never bothering to point out that Timothy McVeigh didn't kill all those people in the name of Christianity. Suicide airplane hijackers, on the other hand, are people who actually believe their murderous acts will earn them a one-way ticket to Paradise.

Was what happened on September 11 a subversion of Islam, as pundits and journalists on network and cable TV told us over and over again? Or was it the result of an *honest* reading of the Koran? It's true, of course, that if taken too literally by uncritical minds, just about any holy book can lead to bad things. Still, why are there no Christian suicide bombers, or Jewish suicide bombers, or Hindu suicide bombers, or Buddhist suicide bombers, but no apparent shortage of Muslim suicide bombers? If Islam is "a religion of peace" as so many people from President Bush on down were telling us (and, for what it's worth, I'm prepared to believe that it is), then what exactly is it in the Koran that so appeals to these Islamic fanatics? Don't look for that answer on the network news. A *Lexis-Nexis* search going back to 1991 linking the words "Koran" and "terrorist" produced absolutely nothing that told us what the Koran actually says which *might* encourage a Muslim, no matter how misguided, to commit acts of terrorism.

I understand that even to ask questions about a possible connection between   20
Islam and violence is to tread into politically incorrect terrain. But it seems to me that the media need to go there anyway. And any network that can put thousands of stories on the air about sex and murder should be able to give us a few on the atmosphere that breeds religious zealotry. It might have helped us see what was coming on September 11.

In fact, I learned much more about the atmosphere that breeds suicide bombers from one short article in *Commentary* magazine than I have from watching twenty years of network television news. In its September 2001 issue (which came out before the attack on America), there was an article by Fiamma Nirenstein, an Italian journalist based in Israel, entitled "How Suicide Bombers Are Made." In it, she tells about a "river of hatred" that runs through not just the most radical of Arab nations but also much of what we like to think of as the "moderate" Arab world.

She tells us about a series of articles that ran in the leading government-sponsored newspaper in Egypt, *Al Ahram*, about how Jews supposedly use the blood of Christians to make matzah for Passover.

She tells us about a hit song in Cairo, Damascus, and the West Bank with the catchy title "I Hate Israel."

Why didn't I know this? A computer check soon answered my question. On television, only CNN reported the "I Hate Israel" story. On radio, NPR did a piece. So did the *Christian Science Monitor* and the *Chicago Tribune*. The *Los Angeles Times* ran a short wire service story that said "'I Hate Israel' . . . made an overnight singing sensation of a working-class crooner."

Can you imagine if the big hit song in Israel was "I Hate Palestine" or "I Hate Arabs"? The *New York Times* would have put the story on page one and then run an editorial just to make sure we all got the message — that the song is indecent and contributes to an atmosphere of hate. And since the *Times* sets the agenda for the networks, Dan Rather, Tom Brokaw, and Peter Jennings would have all fallen into line and run big stories on their evening newscasts, too, saying the exact same thing. A week later, Mike Wallace would have landed in Tel Aviv looking absolutely mortified that those Jews would do such a thing.

And that's part of the problem. Despite the liberalism of the media, there is a subtle form of racism at work here. As Fiamma Nirenstein writes, "The Arabs, it is implicitly suggested, are a backward people, not to be held to civilized standards of the West." Of the Israelis, however, the American media expect much more. That is why a song called "I Hate Israel" becomes a big hit, and yet is not a news story. And it is why a series of stories in a government-sponsored newspaper — in a supposedly moderate country — about Jews killing Christians for their blood holds almost no interest for American journalists.

It's true that not long after the twin towers of the World Trade Center came tumbling down, the networks showed us pictures of Palestinians in East Jerusalem honking their horns, firing their guns into the air, and generally having a good old time celebrating the death of so many Americans in New York and Washington. They cheered "God is great" while they handed out candy, which is a tradition in the Arab world when something good happens.

It's not that there's been a total news blackout of anti-American hate in the Middle East — *Nightline* has done some good, intelligent work in this area — it's just that we need more than pictures of happy Palestinians reveling in the death of thousands of Americans. And we need more than what has become a staple of Middle East television news coverage: young children throwing stones at Israeli soldiers — the perfect made-for-television David and Goliath story. What we need are stories that connect the dots, not just back to Afghanistan and its backward and repressive Taliban government, but also between the fanatics in New York and Washington and a cultural environment in the Arab world where even "moderates" hand out candy to celebrate the massacre of Americans.

But here the media — apparently feeling squeamish about stories that put the "underdogs" in a bad light — keep us virtually in the dark. And it's not just little tidbits like "I Hate Israel" and articles about Jews taking Christian blood that I — and almost all Americans — knew nothing about. Here's a quick rundown of what goes on in much of the Middle East as reported by Ms. Nirenstein in *Commentary* — news that is virtually ignored on the big American TV networks:

> In Egypt and Jordan, news sources have repeatedly warned that Israel has distributed drug-laced chewing gum and candy, intended (it is said) to kill children and make women sexually corrupt. . . .
>
> [Palestinian television] recently asserted that, far from being extermination camps, Chelmo, Dachau, and Auschwitz were in fact mere "places of disinfection."
>
> On April 13 — observed in Israel as Holocaust Remembrance Day — the official Palestinian newspaper *Al-Hayat al-Jadida* featured a column . . . entitled "The Fable of the Holocaust."
>
> A columnist in Egypt's government-sponsored Al-Akhbar thus expressed his "thanks to Hitler, of blessed memory, who on behalf of the Palestinians took revenge in advance on the most vile criminals on the face of the earth. Still, we do have a complaint against [Hitler], for his revenge on them was not enough."

In addition to these examples, Ms. Nirenstein cites a textbook for Syrian tenth   30
graders which teaches them that "the logic of justice obligates the application of the single verdict [on the Jews] from which there is no escape: namely, that their criminal intentions be turned against them and that they be exterminated." And she notes that in June 2001, two weeks after the fatal collapse of a Jewish wedding hall in Jerusalem, Palestinian television broadcast a sermon by a Muslim imam praying that "this oppressive Knesset [Israel's parliament] will [similarly] collapse over the heads of the Jews."

I did not know any of that because it's simply not the kind of news that we normally get from the Middle East — certainly not from network evening newscasts or from *Dateline, 20/20*, or *48 Hours*, three news magazine programs that are usually too busy peddling the trivial and sensational to bother with more significant stories. And besides, that kind of news makes liberal journalists uneasy. After all, these are the same people who bend over backwards to find "moral equivalence" between Palestinian terrorists who blow up discos in Tel Aviv filled with teenagers, on the one hand, and Israeli commandos who *preemptively* kill terrorist ringleaders *before* they send their suicide bombers into Israel on a mission to kill Jews, on the other.

On September 11, right after the networks showed us the pictures of Palestinians celebrating American deaths, they also showed us Yasser Arafat expressing his condolences and giving blood for the American victims. This, in its way, represented a kind of moral equivalence: while some Palestinians celebrate, the news anchors were suggesting, their leader does not; he is somber and, we're led to believe, absolutely shocked. But we could have done with a little less moral equivalence on the part of the press and a little more tough journalism. Someone should have asked the leader of the Palestinian people if he understood that the cultures that he and other "moderate" Arab leaders preside over "carefully nurture and inculcate resentments and hatreds against America and the non-Arab world," as a *Wall Street Journal* editorial put it. And if that's asking too much of a field reporter covering a seemingly shaken and distraught Arafat in the wake of September 11, then an anchor back in New York should have wondered out loud about that very connection.

But to have asked such a question might have been viewed as anti-Arab (and therefore pro-Israeli), and reporters and anchors would rather be stoned by an angry mob in Ramallah than be seen in that light. So we didn't learn that day if Chairman Arafat quite understood his role in the celebration he so deplored. Nor did we get an explanation on the news about why there were not thousands of other Arabs in the streets — on the West Bank or in Jerusalem or in the "moderate" Arab countries — expressing their *condolences*. Was it because they are afraid to show support for American victims of terrorism? Or was it because they, like the Palestinians we saw with great big smiles, didn't feel that bad about what happened?

If the networks can give us months and months of Chandra and JonBenét and Lorena Bobbitt and Joey Buttafuoco,[20] then they can give us more than they do about the river of hatred that breeds suicide bombers.

But this is where journalists — given their liberal tendency to empathize with, and sometimes even root for, the "underdog" — run into a big problem: if they start to connect those ideological and religious dots, they may not like what they find. 35

American journalists who covered the civil rights struggle recognized the pathology of racism and rightly made no allowance for it. They understood that in order for evil to flourish in places throughout the South, all it took was a few fundamentally bad people — while everybody else sat around making believe it wasn't happening, either because they were afraid or because they just didn't want to get involved.

The Middle East, of course, is a place with a long and troubled history. But it should be obvious that a place that turns "I Hate Israel" into a hit, that runs stories in its most important newspaper about Jews killing Christians for their blood, that faults Hitler *only because he did not kill more Jews*, and that celebrates the murder of thousands of innocent Americans is a place populated by many nasty people. Perhaps it has many good people, too, who just don't want to get involved. The point is, a story about all of this is at least as important as a story about Anne Heche and her sex life, even if sex does better in the ratings than disturbing news about raw, ignorant hatred in the world of Islam.

None of this is an argument that the media are intentionally pro-Arab. Rather, like the U.S. State Department, they are pro "moral equivalence." If they connect the dots with stories on the news about hit songs called "I Hate Israel" and all the rest, the Arab world will accuse the "Jewish-controlled" American media of being sympathetic to "Israeli oppression." If journalists — who were so willing to connect the dots when there was a belief that they led to Rush Limbaugh — connected *these* dots, they might find that there are a lot fewer moderates in those moderate places than they keep telling us about.

So they look the other way, which, as Ms. Nirenstein tells us, is not that easy. One has to turn "a determinedly blind eye to this river of hatred . . . [and] to be persuaded that, after all, 'everybody' in the Middle East really wants the same thing."

Obviously, there are legitimate issues about which there are differing viewpoints in the Middle East: Should Israel blow up the houses that belong to the 40

[20]JonBenét and Lorena Bobbitt and Joey Buttafuoco: JonBenét Ramsey was a six-year-old beauty pageant contestant found murdered in the basement of her home in Boulder, Colorado, the day after Christmas 1996, whose case has never been solved. Lorena Bobbit cut off her husband's penis in 1993 allegedly because of long-term abuse. Joey Buttafuoco's under-aged lover, Amy Fisher, shot his wife in the face in 1992. — EDS.

families of terrorists? Should Israel allow the construction of new settlements on the West Bank? These are two that come quickly to mind.

But moral equivalence and the quest for evenhanded journalism should not stop the media from telling us more — much more in my view — about the kind of backwardness and hatred that is alive and well, *not just in places like Kabul and Baghdad*, but in "moderate" cities and villages all over the Arab world. Even if it means going against their liberal sensibilities and reporting that sometimes even the underdog can be evil.

READING AND DISCUSSION QUESTIONS

1. How does Goldberg support his claim that television draws Americans together in times of crisis?
2. How does he believe the news is different during times of crisis from how it usually is?
3. Explain the title that Goldberg chose for this piece. What does he claim the "media elites" have "connected the dots" to find?
4. What does Goldberg believe the news media are *not* telling Americans? What sort of support does he offer for that part of his argument?
5. What type or types of support that Goldberg uses do you find most effective? Why?

WRITING SUGGESTIONS

6. Analyze the types of support that Goldberg makes use of in his essay.
7. Evaluate the effectiveness of the major types of support that he uses in his essay.
8. Attack or defend the claim that Goldberg is advancing in his essay.
9. What is your personal opinion of the media coverage of the tragedies of September 11?
10. Do you believe that your education has exposed you to recent history as well as the more distant past? Explain.

Abolish the SAT

CHARLES MURRAY

For most high school students who want to attend an elite college, the SAT is more than a test. It is one of life's landmarks. Waiting for the scores — one for verbal, one for math, and now one for writing, with a possible 800 on each — is painfully suspenseful. The exact scores are commonly remembered forever after.

Charles Murray is the W. H. Brady Scholar at the American Enterprise Institute. This article appeared in the July/August 2007 issue of the institute's journal, *The American*.

So it has been for half a century. But events of recent years have challenged the SAT's position. In 2001, Richard Atkinson, president of the University of California, proposed dropping the SAT as a requirement for admission. More and more prestigious small colleges, such as Middlebury and Bennington, are making the SAT optional. The charge that the SAT is slanted in favor of privileged children — "a wealth test," as Harvard law professor Lani Guinier calls it — has been ubiquitous. I have watched the attacks on the SAT with dismay. Back in 1961, the test helped get me into Harvard from a small Iowa town by giving me a way to show that I could compete with applicants from Exeter and Andover. Ever since, I have seen the SAT as the friend of the little guy, just as James Bryant Conant, president of Harvard, said it would be when he urged the SAT upon the nation in the 1940s.

Conant's cause was as unambiguously liberal in the 1940s as income redistribution is today. Then, America's elite colleges drew most of their students from a small set of elite secondary schools, concentrated in the northeastern United States, to which America's wealthy sent their children. The mission of the SAT was to identify intellectual talent regardless of race, color, creed, money, or geography, and give that talent a chance to blossom. Students from small towns and from poor neighborhoods in big cities were supposed to benefit — as I thought I did, and as many readers of *The American* think they did.

But data trump gratitude. The evidence has become overwhelming that the SAT no longer serves a democratizing purpose. Worse, events have conspired to make the SAT a negative force in American life. And so I find myself arguing that the SAT should be ended. Not just deemphasized, but no longer administered. Nothing important would be lost by so doing. Much would be gained.

To clarify my terms: Here, "SAT" will always refer to the verbal and mathematics tests that you have in mind when you recall your own SAT scores. They, along with the writing test added in 2005, are now officially known as "reasoning tests" or SAT I (labels I will ignore). The College Board also administers one-hour achievement tests in English literature, United States history, world history, biology, chemistry, physics, two levels of math, Chinese, French, German, Hebrew, Italian, Japanese, Korean, Latin, and Spanish. These are now called "subject tests" or SAT II (more labels I will ignore).

I do not discuss the College Board's advanced placement (AP) tests that can enable students to get college credit because they cannot serve as a substitute for either the SAT or the achievement tests. Not all schools offer AP courses, and the AP's five-point scoring system conveys limited information.

Start with the proposition that nothing important would be lost by dropping the SAT. The surprising empirical reality is that the SAT is redundant if students are required to take achievement tests.

In theory, the SAT and the achievement tests measure different things. In the College Board's own words from its Web site, "The SAT measures students' verbal reasoning, critical reading, and skills," while the achievement tests "show colleges their mastery of specific subjects." In practice, SAT and achievement test scores are so highly correlated that SAT scores tell the admissions office little that it does not learn from the achievement test scores alone.

5

The pivotal analysis was published in 2001 by the University of California (UC), which requires all applicants to take both the SAT and achievement tests (three of them at the time the data were gathered: reading, mathematics, and a third of the student's choosing). Using a database of 77,893 students who applied to UC from 1996 to 1999, Saul Geiser and Roger Studley analyzed the relationship among high school grades, SAT scores, achievement test scores, and freshman grades in college. Here is what they found:

Achievement tests did slightly better than the SAT in predicting freshman 10
grades. High school grade point average, SAT scores, and achievement test scores were entered into a statistical equation to predict the grade point that applicants achieved during their freshman year in college. The researchers found that achievement tests and high school grade point each had about the same independent role — that is, each factor was, by itself, an equally accurate predictor of how a student will do as a college freshman.

But the SAT's independent role in predicting freshman grade point turned out to be so small that knowing the SAT score added next to nothing to an admissions officer's ability to forecast how an applicant will do in college — the reason to give the test in the first place. In technical terms, adding the SAT to the other two elements added just one-tenth of a percentage point to the percentage of variance in freshman grades explained by high school grade point and the achievement tests.

But what about the students we're most concerned about — those with high ability who have attended poor schools? The California Department of Education rates the state's high schools based on the results from its standardized testing program for grades K–12. For schools in the bottom quintile of the ratings — hard as I found it to believe — the achievement tests did slightly *better* than the SAT in predicting how the test-takers would perform as college freshmen.

What about students from families with low incomes? Children of parents with poor education? Here's another stunner: After controlling for parental income and education, the independent role of the SAT in predicting freshman grade point disappeared altogether. The effectiveness of high school grade point and of achievement tests to predict freshman grade point was undiminished.

All freshman grades are not created equal, so the UC study took the obvious differences into account. It broke down its results by college campus (an A at Berkeley might not mean the same thing as an A at Santa Cruz) and by freshman major (an A in a humanities course might not mean the same thing as an A in a physical science course). The results were unaffected. Again, the SAT was unnecessary; it added nothing to the forecasts provided by high school grades and achievement tests.

Thorough as the Geiser and Studley presentation was, almost any social science 15
conclusion can be challenged through different data or a different set of analyses. The College Board, which makes many millions of dollars every year from the SAT, had every incentive and ample resources to refute the UC results. But it could not.

In 2002, the College Board published its analysis, "The Utility of the SAT I and SAT II for Admissions Decisions in California and the Nation." The College Board's study disentangled some statistical issues that the UC study had not and used a different metric to express predictive validity, but its bottom line was effectively identical. Once high school grade point and achievement test scores are known, the incremental value of knowing the SAT score is trivially small.

Still reluctant to give up on the SAT, I wondered whether the College Board had been unwilling to make the best defense. Perhaps the SAT had made an important independent contribution to predicting college performance in earlier years, but by the time research was conducted in the last half of the 1990s, the test had already been ruined by political correctness. To see where this hypothesis comes from, a little history is required.

Originally, the point of the SAT — whose initials, after all, stood for Scholastic Aptitude Test — was to measure *aptitude*, defined by the dictionary as "inherent ability," rather than to measure academic achievement. But in the aftermath of the 1960s, the concept of aptitude became troublesome. The temper of the times meant that long-observed ethnic and class differences in mental test scores had to be interpreted as the fault of the tests that produced them. Like all other mental tests, the SAT persistently showed such differences; therefore, the SAT had to be a bad test, culturally biased in favor of upper-middle-class white kids.

The psychometricians at the College Board could provide ample data to refute the cultural bias charge, but the College Board was run by people who were eager to demonstrate their own progressive credentials. They ran from the concept of aptitude as the Florentines fled the plague. In the 1980s, the College Board tried to make a semantic case for a difference between scholastic aptitude and intelligence. This was unsuccessful for the good reason that, operationally, there isn't any difference. In 1993, the College Board abandoned aptitude altogether and changed the name of the SAT to "Scholastic Assessment Test." In 1994, it introduced major substantive changes to the SAT that were explicitly intended to link the test more closely to the curriculum.

Did the pre-1994 SAT measure something importantly different from what the post-1994 SAT had measured? Don't bother asking the College Board. The data for answering that question would require the College Board to reveal just how well the original and revised SATs measure the general mental factor g, the stuff of intelligence/aptitude, and the College Board does not want to acknowledge that the SAT measures g at all or, for that matter, that g even exists.

Seen from an outsider's perspective, the changes in 1993–1994 do not look particularly important. Twenty-five antonym items in the SAT Verbal were replaced with reading-comprehension items, on grounds that the antonym items could be compromised by students who memorized vocabulary lists. The math test saw some changes in the answer format. But samples of the new items appear to be plausible measures of g and not obviously inferior to the items they replaced.

Despite the College Board's rhetoric about revamping the SAT to reflect curriculum, the changes in the test in 1993–1994 probably did not have much effect on the SAT's power to measure g — in the jargon, its g-loading. (I would not make the same statement about today's SAT, which has eliminated the highly g-loaded analogy items and added a writing component that carries with it a multitude of scoring problems.)

If I am wrong, and the pre-1994 SAT measured *g* much better than the SAT used for the UC study, then I hope some disaffected College Board psychometrician leaks that news immediately. I will thereupon join a crusade to restore the old SAT. But given the available information, I think it is probable that even analyses conducted prior to the revisions in the test would not have shown a major independent role for the SAT after taking high school transcript and achievement test scores into account. To put it another way, those of us who thought that the SAT was our salvation were probably wrong. Even coming from mediocre high schools, our scores on achievement tests would have conveyed about the same picture to college admissions committees as our scores on the SAT conveyed.

I know how counterintuitive this sounds (I am presenting a conclusion I resisted as long as I could). But the truth about any achievement test, from an AP exam down to a weekly pop quiz, is that the smartest kids tend to get the highest scores. All mental tests are *g*-loaded to some degree. What was not realized until the UC study was just how high that correlation was for the SAT and the achievement tests.

Before, studies of the relationship had been based on self-selected samples of   25
students who chose to take achievement tests along with the SAT, and there was good reason to think those students were unrepresentative. But by requiring all applicants to take both the SAT and achievement tests, the University of California got rid of this problem — and the correlations were still very high.

After the College Board did all of its statistical corrections in its 2002 study and applied them to test-takers from California, it found, for example, that the correlation between the SAT Verbal and the Literature Achievement test was a very high 0.83 (a correlation of 1.0 represents a perfect direct relationship). The correlation between the SAT Math and the Math IC achievement test was 0.86. So I conclude that bright students who do not go to first-rate high schools will do fine without the SAT. Consider these scenarios:

Start with motivated, high-ability students who go to truly bad schools, meaning the worst schools in the inner cities. The bright students' achievement test scores are likely to be depressed by the schools' dreadfulness, but even scores that are just fair will get the attention of an admissions office if the transcript shows Ask and the recommendations are enthusiastic. The nation's top colleges desperately want to increase their enrollment of inner-city blacks and Hispanics, and are willing to make large allowances for bad schooling to do so.

Next, turn to the much larger number of high-ability students who are in schools that are not awful, but mediocre — the typical urban or small-town public school. The curriculum includes all the standard college-prep courses with standard textbooks. A few of the teachers are terrific, but most are no more than ordinary.

The high-ability students in such schools who are playing the game, studying hard, have no problem at all if the SAT is eliminated. They have nearly straight As on their transcripts, which most college admissions offices treat as the most important single source of information. Their letters of recommendation are afire with zeal on their behalf. These students also do well on the achievement tests. A hard-working, high-ability physics student is likely to absorb enough physics from the textbook to do well on the physics achievement test despite a so-so teacher.

In addition, high-ability kids who play the game have usually been reading vora-
ciously — and in the process picked up a great deal of knowledge about history,
literature, and culture on their own. This information has been gathered ineffi-
ciently, but high-ability students absorb knowledge like a sponge, no matter what
schools they attend.

Now consider high-ability students in mediocre schools who do *not* play the   30
classroom game. They are bored with their classes and sometimes get Bs and the
occasional C, but they have active minds and are looking for ways to occupy themselves. They spend all their time on the debate team or writing for the high school
newspaper, or in the drama department. By the end of high school, they have a
long list of accomplishments studding their applications. One way or the other,
by the end of high school, students in this category are very likely to have done
things that will catch the attention of an admissions officer. And again, their
achievement test scores are high. These students are at least as intellectually curious as those who play the game. Their Bs do not mean they didn't absorb the substance of the coursework, and they too have typically encountered and retained
large amounts of information outside school.

That leaves the worst case: high-ability students who are alienated by school
and perhaps by life. They don't study, don't go out for the debate team, don't read
on their own, don't even watch the Discovery Channel. It is possible for them
nonetheless to achieve a high score on an individually administered IQ test, despite being hostile and uninterested. Arthur Jensen relates the time he was testing
a sullen subject in a juvenile detention facility and came to the vocabulary item
"apocryphal." The boy answered, "How the hell should I know? I think the whole
Bible is [bunk]." In an individually administered IQ test, the examiner could score
his answer as correct, but that same alienated boy is unlikely to get a high score
on the SAT because no one, no matter how smart, gets a high score on the SAT
without concentrating and trying hard over the course of three stressful hours. So
keeping the SAT will not help most students in this category. They won't try hard,
and their SAT scores will be mediocre despite their ability.

That leaves an extremely odd set of high-ability students who will be harmed
by dropping the SAT — so alienated that they do nothing to express their ability
in school, so completely walled off from independent learning that they do poorly
on the achievement tests, and yet able to buckle down on the SAT and get a good
score. I am not sure that getting a good score under such circumstances is even
possible on the SAT Math — too many of the questions presuppose hard work in
algebra class — but perhaps it could be done on the SAT Verbal.

In any case, we are now talking about a very few students, and even for them
it is not clear whether dropping the SAT introduces an injustice. Should such a
student be given a slot that could have been filled by a less-talented student who
is eager to give a competitive college his best effort? Being forced to go to an un-
selective college instead could well be the better outcome for all concerned.

There is good reason to think that a world in which achievement tests have
replaced the SAT is not going to be a world in which motivated high-ability students from bad or mediocre schools have less opportunity to get into the college
where they belong. It may be a marginally worse world for a small number of

unmotivated high-ability students who want to attend selective colleges, but that outcome is not necessarily undesirable.

But why get rid of the SAT? If it works just about as well as the achievement   35
tests in predicting college success, what's the harm in keeping it?

The short answer is that the image of the SAT has done a 180-degree turn. No longer seen as a compensating resource for the unprivileged, it has become a corrosive symbol of privilege. "Back when kids just got a good night's sleep and took the SAT, it was a leveler that helped you find the diamond in the rough," Lawrence University's dean of admissions told the *New York Times* recently. "Now that most of the great scores are affluent kids with lots of preparation, it just increases the gap between the haves and the have-nots."

If you're rich, the critics say, you can raise your children in an environment where they will naturally acquire the information the SAT tests. If you're rich, you can enroll your children in Kaplan, or Princeton Review, or even get private tutors to coach your kids in the tricks of test-taking, and thereby increase their SAT scores by a couple of hundred points. If you're rich, you can shop around for a diagnostician who will classify your child as learning-disabled and therefore eligible to take the SAT without time limits. Combine these edges, and it comes down to this: If you're rich, you can buy your kids a high SAT score.

Almost every parent with whom I discuss the SAT believes these charges. In fact, the claims range from simply false, in the case of cultural bias, to not-nearly-as-true-as-you-think, in the case of the others. Take coaching as an example, since it seems to be so universally accepted by parents and has been studied so extensively.

From 1981 to 1990, three separate analyses of all the prior studies were published in peer-reviewed journals. They found a coaching effect of 9 to 25 points on the SAT Verbal and of 15 to 25 points on the SAT Math. In 2004, Derek Briggs, using the National Education Longitudinal Study of 1988, found effects of 3 to 20 points for the SAT Verbal and 10 to 28 points for the SAT Math. Donald Powers and Donald Rock, using a nationally representative sample of students who took the SAT after its revisions in the mid-1990s, found an average coaching effect of 6 to 12 points on the SAT Verbal and 13 to 18 points on the SAT Math. Many studies tell nearly identical stories. On average, coaching raises scores by no more than a few dozen points, enough to sway college admissions in exceedingly few cases.

I am not reporting a scholarly literature with a two-sided debate. No study   40
published in a peer-reviewed journal shows average gains approaching the fabled 100-point and 200-point jumps you hear about in anecdotes. While preparing this article, I asked Kaplan and Princeton Review for such evidence. Kaplan replied that it chooses not to release data for proprietary reasons. Princeton Review did not respond at all.

But the coaching business is booming, with affluent parents being the best customers. If the payoff is really so small, why has the market judged coaching to be so successful?

Most obviously, parents who pay for expensive coaching courses ignore the role of self-selection: the students who seem to profit from a coaching course tend to be those who, if the course had not been available, would have worked hard on their own to prepare for the test.

Then parents confuse the effects of coaching with the effect of the basic preparation that students can do on their own. No student should walk into the SAT
cold. It makes sense for students to practice some sample items, easily available
from school guidance offices and online, and to review their algebra textbook if it
has been a few years since they have taken algebra. But once a few hours have been
spent on these routine steps, most of the juice has been squeezed out of preparation
for the SAT. Combine self-selection artifacts with the role of basic preparation, and
you have the reason that independent studies using control groups show such small
average gains from formal coaching.

It makes no difference, however, that the charges about coaching are wrong,
just as it makes no difference that the whole idea that rich parents can buy their
children high SAT scores is wrong. One part of the indictment is true, and that
one part overrides everything else: the children of the affluent and well educated
really do get most of the top scores. For example, who gets the coveted scores of
700 and higher, putting them in the top half-dozen percentiles of SAT test-takers?
Extrapolating from the 2006 data on means and standard deviations reported by
the College Board, about half of the 700+ scores went to students from families
making more than $100,000 per year. But the truly consequential statistics are
these: Approximately 90 percent of the students with 700+ scores had at least one
parent with a college degree. Over half had a parent with a graduate degree.

In that glaring relationship of high test scores to advanced parental education,   45
which in turn means high parental IQ, lies the reason that the College Board, politically correct even unto self-destruction, cannot bring itself to declare the truth:
The test isn't the problem. The children of the well educated and affluent get most
of the top scores because they constitute most of the smartest kids. They are smart
because their parents are smart. The parents have passed their smartness along
through parenting practices that are largely independent of education and afflu-
ence, and through genes that are completely independent of them.

The cognitive stratification of American society — for that's what we're talking
about — was not a problem 100 years ago. Many affluent people were smart in
1907, but there were not enough jobs in which high intellectual ability brought
high incomes or status to affect more than a fraction of really smart people, and
most of the really smart people were prevented from getting those jobs anyway by
economic and social circumstances (consider that in 1907 roughly half the adults
with high intelligence were housewives).

From 1907 to 2007, the correlation between intellectual ability and socioeconomic status (SES) increased dramatically. The socioeconomic elite and the
cognitive elite are increasingly one. If you want the details about how this process
worked and how it is transforming America's class structure, I refer you to *The Bell
Curve* (1994), the book I wrote with the late Richard Herrnstein. For now, here's
the point: Imagine that, miraculously, every child in the country were to receive
education of equal quality. Imagine that a completely fair and accurate measure of
intellectual ability were to be developed. In that utopia, a fair admissions process
based on intellectual ability would fill the incoming classes of the elite colleges
predominantly with children of upper-middle-class parents.

In other words, such a perfect system would produce an outcome very much like the one we see now. Harvard offers an easy way to summarize the revolution that accelerated after World War II. As late as 1952, the mean SAT Verbal score of the incoming freshman class was just 583. By 1960, the mean had jumped to 678. In eight years, Harvard transformed itself from a college with a moderately talented student body to a place where the average freshman was intellectually in the top fraction of 1 percent of the national population. But this change did not mean that Harvard became more socioeconomically diverse. On the contrary, it became more homogeneous. In the old days, Harvard had admitted a substantial number of Boston students from modest backgrounds who commuted to classes, and also a substantial number of rich students with average intelligence. In the new era, when Harvard's students were much more rigorously screened for intellectual ability, the numbers of students from the very top and bottom of the socioeconomic ladder were reduced, and the proportion coming from upper-middle-class backgrounds increased.

The other high-ranking schools have similar stories to tell. In a sample of 11 of the most prestigious colleges studied by William Bowen and his colleagues between the mid-1970s and the mid-1990s, the proportion of students in the top SES quartile rose from about a third to a half of all students, while the share in the bottom quartile remained constant at one-tenth. And these were schools such as Princeton and Yale that get first chance to admit the scarce and sought-after candidates of high ability from poor backgrounds.

When, in 2003, Anthony Carnevale and Stephen Rose expanded the definition 50 of top-tier colleges to include 146 schools, fully 74 percent of the students came from families in the top SES quartile, while only 3 percent came from the bottom quartile. Ethnic diversity has increased during the last half century, but not socioeconomic diversity.

Because upper-middle-class families produce most of the smartest kids, there is no way to reform the system (short of disregarding intellectual ability altogether) to prevent their children from coming out on top. We can only make sure that high-ability students from disadvantaged backgrounds realize that the nation's best colleges yearn for their applications and that their chance of breaking out of their disadvantaged situations has never been better — in short, that the system is not rigged. Now, the widespread belief is that the system is rigged, and the SAT is a major reason for that belief. The most immediate effect of getting rid of the SAT is to remove an extremely large and bright red herring. But there are more good effects.

Getting rid of the SAT will destroy the coaching industry as we know it. Coaching for the SAT is seen as the teaching of tricks and strategies — a species of cheating — not as supplementary education. The retooled coaching industry will focus on the achievement tests, but insofar as the offerings consist of cram courses for tests in topics such as U.S. history or chemistry, its taint will be reduced.

A low-income student shut out of opportunity for an SAT coaching school has the sense of being shut out of mysteries. Being shut out of a cram course is less daunting. Students know that they can study for a history or chemistry exam on their own. A coaching industry that teaches content along with test-taking techniques will have the additional advantage of being much better pedagogically — at least the students who take the coaching courses will be spending some of their time learning history or chemistry.

The substitution of achievement tests for the SAT will put a spotlight on the quality of the local high school's curriculum. If achievement test scores are getting all of the parents' attention in the college admissions process, the courses that prepare for those achievement tests will get more of their attention as well, and the pressure for those courses to improve will increase.

The final benefit of getting rid of the SAT is the hardest to describe but is probably the most important. By getting rid of the SAT, we would be getting rid of a totem for members of the cognitive elite.

People forget achievement test scores. They do not forget cognitive test scores. The only cognitive test score that millions of people know about themselves is the SAT score. If the score is high, it is seen as proof that one is smart. If the score is not high, it is evidence of intellectual mediocrity or worse. Furthermore, it is evidence that cannot be explained away as a bad grade can be explained away. All who enter an SAT testing hall feel judged by their scores.

Worse yet, there are few other kinds of scores to counterbalance the SAT. Of the many talents and virtues that people possess, we have good measures for quantifying few besides athletic and intellectual ability. Falling short in athletic ability can be painful, especially for boys, but the domain of sports is confined. Intellectual ability has no such limits, and the implications of the SAT score spill far too widely. The 17-year-old who is at the 40th percentile on the SAT has no other score that lets him say to himself, "Yes, but I'm at the 99th percentile in working with my hands," or "Yes, but I'm at the 99th percentile for courage in the face of adversity."

Conversely, it seems to make no difference that high intellectual ability is a gift for which its recipients should be humbly grateful. Far too many students see a high score on the SAT as an expression of their own merit, not an achievement underwritten by the dumb luck of birth.

Hence the final reason for getting rid of the SAT: knowing those scores is too dispiriting for those who do poorly and too inspiriting for those who do well. In an age when intellectual talent is increasingly concentrated among young people who are also privileged economically and socially, the last thing we need are numbers that give these very, very lucky kids a sense of entitlement.

How are we to get rid of the SAT when it is such an established American institution and will be ferociously defended by the College Board and a large test-preparation industry?

Actually, it could happen quite easily. Admissions officers at elite schools are already familiar with the statistical story I have presented. They know that dropping the SAT would not hinder their selection decisions. Many of them continue to accept the SAT out of inertia — as long as the student has taken the test anyway, it costs nothing to add the scores to the student's folder.

In that context, the arguments for *not* accepting the SAT can easily find a receptive audience, especially since the SAT is already under such severe criticism for the wrong reasons. Nor is it necessary to convince everyone to take action at

55

60

the same time. A few high-profile colleges could have a domino effect. Suppose, for example, that this fall Harvard and Stanford were jointly to announce that SAT scores will no longer be accepted. Instead, all applicants to Harvard and Stanford will be required to take four of the College Board's achievement tests, including a math test and excluding any test for a language used at home. If just those two schools took such a step, many other schools would follow suit immediately, and the rest within a few years.

It could happen, and it should happen. There is poignance in calling for an end to a test conceived for such a noble purpose. But the SAT score, intended as a signal flare for those on the bottom, has become a badge flaunted by those on top. We pay a steep educational and cultural price for a test that no one really needs.

READING AND DISCUSSION QUESTIONS

1. What does Murray mean when he says that "data trump gratitude"?
2. What is his claim?
3. What types of support does Murray use? How convincing are they?
4. According to Murray, how is intellectual ability related to socioeconomic status?
5. What is Murray's specific suggestion as to what should be done about the SAT?

WRITING SUGGESTIONS

6. Based on your experience and that of people you know and on your reading, write an essay in which you either agree or disagree with Murray's suggestions.
7. Write an essay analyzing Murray's use of support in the essay.

Marriage-Plus
THEODORA OOMS

The public has been concerned about "family breakdown" for a long time, but it was not until the passage of welfare reform in 1996 that the federal government decided to get into the business of promoting marriage. Although it was little noticed at the time, three of the four purposes of the welfare legislation refer directly or indirectly to marriage and family formation. The law exhorts states to promote "job preparation, work, and marriage," to "prevent and reduce the incidence of out-of-wedlock pregnancies," and to "encourage the formation and maintenance of two-parent families."

Theodora Ooms is a senior consultant to the National Healthy Marriage Resource Center in Fairfax, Virginia. Her article is an annotated version of one that originally appeared in a special issue of *The American Prospect* on "The Politics of the American Family," April 8, 2002.

The Bush administration, as it contemplates this year's extension of welfare legislation, plans to make marriage even more central. The administration's re-authorization proposal, announced February 27, includes $300 million for demonstration grants to focus on promoting healthy marriages and reducing out-of-wedlock births.[21] Meanwhile, Oklahoma Governor Frank Keating has launched a $10 million, multisector marriage initiative, and other smaller-scale government-sponsored initiatives have been enacted in Arizona, Florida, Louisiana, Michigan, and Utah. The federal government is primarily concerned with reducing out-of-wedlock births, which it views as a principal cause of welfare dependency and a host of other social problems. By contrast, state marriage initiatives are most concerned about the effects of high divorce rates and father absence on children.[22]

This new emphasis on marriage as a panacea for social problems is troubling to many liberals. For one thing, it risks being dismissive of children who happen to find themselves in single-parent families. It also can be seen as disparaging single mothers and ignoring the fact that many women have left abusive marriages for good reasons.

That said, it's hard to dismiss an overwhelming consensus of social-science research findings that children tend to be better off, financially and emotionally, when their parents are married to each other. Around 50 percent of all first marriages are expected to end in divorce, and 60 percent of all divorces involve children. One-third of all births are out of wedlock, nearly 40 percent of children do not live with their biological fathers, and too many nonresident fathers neither support nor see their children on a regular basis.

Children living with single mothers are five times as likely to be poor as those in two-parent families. Growing up in a single-parent family also roughly doubles the risk that a child will drop out of school, have difficulty finding a job, or become a teen parent. About half of these effects appear to be attributable to the reduced income available to single parents, but the other half is due to non-economic factors.[23] It's not just the presence of two adults in the home that helps children, as some argue. Children living with cohabiting partners and in stepfamilies generally do less well than those living with both married biological parents.[24]

Marriage also brings benefits to husbands and wives. Married adults are more productive on the job, earn more, save more, have better physical and mental health, and live longer, according to an extensive review of research, conducted

[21]See *Working Toward Independence: The President's Plan to Strengthen Welfare Reform*, February 2002. http://www.whitehouse.gov/news/releases/2002/02/welfare-reform-announcement-book.pdf.

[22]Theodora Ooms, "The Role of the Federal Government in Strengthening Marriage," in *Virginia Journal of Social Policy and the Law*, Fall 2001. Available at www.clasp.org.

[23]Sara McLanahan and Julien Teitler, "The Consequences of Father Absence," in *Parenting and Child Development in "Non-Traditional" Families*, ed. Michael E. Lamb (Mahwah, NJ: Lawrence Erlbaum, 1998). Also see Sara McLanahan and Gary Sanderfur, *Growing Up with a Single Parent: What Hurts, What Helps* (Cambridge, MA: Harvard UP, 1994).

[24]See McLanahan and Teitler; Susan L. Brown, "Child Well-Being in Cohabiting Unions" and Wendy D. Manning, "The Implications of Cohabitation for Children's Well-Being," in *Just Living Together: Implications of Cohabitation for Children, Families, and Social Policy*, eds. Alan Booth and Ann C. Crouter (Mahwah, NJ: Lawrence Erlbaum, 2002).

by scholar Linda Waite. Although Waite admits that these findings partly reflect the selection of better-adjusted people into marriage, she finds that when people marry, they act in more health promoting and productive ways.[25]

Conservatives are prone to exaggerate these research findings and underplay the importance of economics. If married people are more likely (other things being equal) to produce thriving children, other things are not, in fact, equal. It's not just the case that single mothers find themselves poor because they are unmarried; they find themselves unmarried because they are poor. Successful marriages are more difficult when husbands and wives are poorly educated, lack access to jobs that pay decently, and cannot afford decent child care. Economic hardship and other problems associated with poverty can wreak havoc on couples' relationships.

The controversy mostly isn't about research, however, but about values.[26] Most people regard decisions to marry, divorce, and bear children as intensely private. Any policy proposals that hint at coercing people to marry, reinforcing Victorian conceptions of gender roles, or limiting the right to end bad marriages are viewed as counter to American values of individual autonomy and privacy. Some worry about the existence of hidden agendas that threaten to put women back into the kitchen, ignore domestic violence, and eliminate public assistance for low-income families. Others fear that holding out marriage as the ideal blames single parents, many of whom do a terrific job under difficult circumstances. Use of the term "illegitimate" is especially offensive because it stigmatizes children (and, in fact, is legally inaccurate, as children born outside of marriage now have virtually the same legal rights as those born within marriage).[27] And some worry that the pro-marriage agenda discriminates against ethnic and sexual minorities and their children, particularly gays and lesbians.

There are also more pragmatic concerns. Skeptics of the pro-marriage agenda observe that the decline in marriage is worldwide, a result of overwhelming social and economic forces that cannot be reversed. In their view, attempts to change family formation behavior are largely futile; we should instead just accept and help support the increasing diversity of family forms. For others, the concern is less about the value of promoting marriage and more about whether government, rather than individuals, communities, or faith institutions, should lead the charge.

Finally, marriage per se is too simplistic a solution to the complex problems of   10
the poor. Marrying a low-income, unmarried mother to her child's father will not magically raise the family out of poverty when the parents often have no skills, no jobs, terrible housing, and may be struggling with depression, substance abuse, or domestic violence. Advocates also worry that funds spent on untested marriage-promotion activities will be taken away from programs that provide desperately needed services for single parents, such as child care.

---

[25]Linda J. Waite and Maggie Gallagher, *The Case for Marriage: Why Married People Are Happier, Healthier, and Better Off Financially* (New York: Doubleday, 2000).

[26]Theodora Ooms, *Toward More Perfect Unions: Putting Marriage on the Public Agenda* (Washington, DC: Family Impact Seminar, 1998). Available from tooms@clasp.org.

[27]Ruth-Arlene W. Howe, "Legal Rights and Obligations: An Uneven Evolution," in *Young Unwed Fathers: Changing Roles and Emerging Policies*, eds. Robert I. Lerman and Theodora Ooms (Philadelphia: Temple UP, 1993), pp. 141–69.

In response to some of these concerns — as well as research showing that serious parental conflict harms children — some marriage advocates respond that marriage per se should not be the goal but rather voluntary, "healthy" marriages.[28] They also agree that protections should be built into programs to guard against domestic violence. But this only raises doubts about how "healthy" will be defined, and by whom, and whether we even know how to help people create better relationships.

There also are some plainly foolish ideas in the marriage movement. West Virginia currently gives married families an extra $100 a month in welfare payments as a "marriage incentive." Robert Rector of the Heritage Foundation has proposed giving a $4,000 government bounty to welfare recipients who marry before they have a child and stay married for two years.[29] Charles Murray wants to end public assistance altogether and has proposed eliminating all aid to *unmarried* mothers under 21 in one state to test the idea. This proposal is especially egregious and surely would harm children of single mothers.[30]

Progressives and others thus are placed in a quandary. They don't want to oppose marriage — which most Americans still value highly — but are skeptical of many pro-marriage initiatives. Given that healthy marriage is plainly good for children, however, one can envision a reasonable agenda — one that would gain broad support — that we might call marriage-plus. This approach puts the well-being of children first by helping more of them grow up in married, healthy, two-parent families. However, for many children, the reality is that marriage is not a feasible or even a desirable option for their parents. Thus, a secondary goal is to help these parents — whether unmarried, separated, divorced, or remarried — cooperate better in raising their children. These are not alternative strategies. Children need us to do both.

A marriage-plus agenda does not promote marriage just for marriage's sake. It acknowledges that married and unmarried parents, mothers and fathers, may need both economic resources and non-economic supports to increase the likelihood of stable, healthy marriages and better co-parenting relationships. In addition, a marriage-plus agenda focuses more on the front end — making marriage better to be in — rather than the back end — making marriage more difficult to get out of.

Here are some elements of this agenda.   15

Strengthen "fragile families" at the birth of a child. For many poor families, relationship-education programs may be helpful but not enough. A new national study finds that at the time of their child's birth, one-half of unmarried parents (so-called "fragile families") are living together, and another third are romantically

---

[28]See, for example, Robin Toner, "Welfare Chief Is Hoping to Promote Marriage," *New York Times*, February 19, 2002, sec. A, p. 1.

[29]Robert Rector, *A Plan to Reduce Illegitimacy*, memorandum handed out at a meeting on Capitol Hill in early 2001.

[30]Charles Murray, "Family Formation," in *The New World of Welfare*, eds. Rebecca M. Blank and Ron Haskins (Washington, DC: Brookings Institution Press, 2001), pp. 137–68.

attached but not cohabiting.[31] The majorities of these parents are committed to each other and to their child and have high hopes of eventual marriage and a future together — although these hopes too often are not realized. We should reach out to young parents to help them achieve their desire to remain together as a family. A helpful package of services to offer these young families might include a combination of "soft" services — relationship-skills and marriage-education workshops, financial-management classes, and peer-support groups — and "hard" services, such as job training and placement, housing, medical coverage, and substance-abuse treatment, if necessary. At present, all we do is get the father to admit paternity and hound him for child support.

Reduce economic stress by reducing poverty. Poverty and unemployment can stress couples' relationships to their breaking point. Results of a welfare-to-work demonstration program in Minnesota suggest that enhancing the income of the working poor can indirectly promote marriage. The Minnesota Family Investment Program (MFIP), which subsidized the earnings of employed welfare families, found that marriage rates increased for both single-parent long-term recipients and two-parent families. Married two-parent families were significantly more likely to remain married. MFIP also reduced the reported incidence of domestic abuse.[32]

Provide better-paying jobs and job assistance for the poor. The inability of low-skilled, unemployed men to provide income to their families is a major reason for their failure to marry the mothers of their children. Better employment opportunities help low-income fathers, and men in general, to become responsible fathers and, perhaps, more attractive and economically stable marriage partners.[33] There is also growing support for making changes in the child-support system to ensure that more support paid by fathers goes to the children (rather than being used to recoup government program costs).[34]

Invest more in proven programs that reduce out-of-wedlock childbearing. Teen pregnancy and birth rates have fallen by over 20 percent since the early 1990s, and there is now strong evidence that a number of prevention programs are effective. A related strategy is enforcement of child support. States that have tough, effective

[31]Sara McLanahan et al., *The Fragile Families and Child Wellbeing Study Baseline Report*, August 2001, http://crcw.princeton.edu/fragilefamilies/nationalreport.pdf; and Sara McLanahan, Irwin Garfinkel, and Ronald B. Mincy, "Fragile Families, Welfare Reform, and Marriage," *Welfare Reform and Beyond Policy Brief*, No. 10, November 2001. http://www.brookings.edu/dybdocroot/wrb/publications/pb/pb10.htm. For additional papers from the Fragile Families study, see http://crcw.princeton.edu/fragilefamilies/index.htm.

[32]Virginia Knox, Cynthia Miller, and Lisa A. Gennetian, *Reforming Welfare and Rewarding Work: A Summary of the Final Report on the Minnesota Family Investment Program* (New York: Manpower Demonstration Research Corporation, September, 2000).

[33]See Chapter 4, "The Fading Inner-City Family," in William Julius Wilson, *When Work Disappears: The World of the New Urban Poor* (New York: Alfred A. Knopf, 1996), pp. 87–110; Kathy Edin, "Few Good Men: Why Poor Mothers Don't Marry or Remarry," *The American Prospect*, January 3, 2000.

[34]See Vicki Turetsky, Testimony Given to the Social Security and Family Policy Subcommittee of the U.S. Senate Finance Committee, October 11, 2001; and Vick Turetsky, *What If All the Money Came Home?* (Washington, DC: Center for Law and Social Policy, June, 2000). Both available online at www.clasp.org.

child support systems have been found to have lower nonmarital birth rates, presumably because men are beginning to understand there are serious costs associated with fathering a child.[35]

Institute workplace policies to reduce work/family conflict and stress on couples. Stress in the workplace spills over into the home. Persistent overtime, frequent travel, and inflexible leave policies place great strain on couples at all income levels. Employers are increasingly demanding nonstandard work schedules. A recent study found that married couples with children who work night and rotating shifts are at higher risk of separation and divorce.[36] The absence of affordable and reliable child care forces many parents who would prefer a normal workday to working split shifts solely to make sure that a parent is home with the children.

Reduce tax penalties and other disincentives to marriage. There has always been strong support for reducing marriage tax penalties for many two-earner families. This is a complicated task because the majority of married couples, in fact, receive tax bonuses rather than penalties.[37] A positive step was taken in 2001 to reduce significantly the marriage penalty affecting low-income working families in the Earned Income Tax Credit program. While there is uncertainty about the extent to which these tax-related marriage penalties affect marital behavior, there is broad general agreement that government has a responsibility to "first do no harm" when it comes to marriage.

Similarly, there is near unanimous agreement that government should not make it harder for eligible two-parent families to receive welfare benefits and assistance. In the past, the old welfare program, Aid to Families with Dependent Children, was much criticized for offering incentives to break up families. At least 33 states already have removed the stricter eligibility rules placed on two-parent families,[38] and the president's welfare reauthorization proposal encourages the other states to do the same. In addition, it proposes to end the higher work participation rate for two-parent families, a federal rule that has been criticized widely by the states. Another needed reform would forgive accumulated child-support debt owed by noncustodial fathers if they marry the mothers of their children. (Currently, such debt is owed to the state if the mothers and children are receiving welfare benefits.)[39]

Educate those who want to marry and stay married about how to have healthy relationships and good marriages. A vast industry is devoted to helping couples plan a successful wedding day — wedding planners, 500-page bridal guides, specialty

20

[35] Robert D. Plotnick, Inhoe Ku, Irwin Garfinkel, and Sara S. McLanahan, *The Impact of Child Support Enforcement Policy on Nonmarital Childbearing.* Paper presented at the Association for Public Policy Analysis and Management, Year 2000 Research Conference in Seattle, WA.

[36] Harriet B. Presser, "Nonstandard Work Schedules and Marital Instability," *Journal of Marriage and the Family* (February 2000).

[37] Congressional Budget Office, *For Better or For Worse: Marriage and the Federal Income Tax* (Washington, DC: Congress of the United States, Congressional Budget Office, June 1997).

[38] Gene Falk and Jill Tauber, *Welfare Reform: TANF Provisions Related to Marriage and Two-Parent Families* (Washington, DC: Congressional Research Service, Library of Congress, October 30, 2001).

[39] Paul Roberts, *An Ounce of Prevention and a Pound of Cure: Developing State Policy on the Payment of Child Support Arrears by Low Income Parents.* (Washington, DC: Center for Law and Social Policy, May 2001). Available online at www.clasp.org.

caterers, the list goes on. But where do young people go to learn about how to sustain good, lifelong marriages? In fact, we now know a lot about what makes contemporary marriages work. With the transformation of gender roles, there now are fewer fixed rules for couples to follow, meaning they have to negotiate daily about who does what and when. In the absence of the legal and social constraints that used to keep marriages together, there's now a premium on developing effective relationship skills. Building on three decades of research, there are a small but rapidly growing number of programs (both religious and secular) that help people from high school through adulthood understand the benefits of marriage for children and for themselves, develop realistic expectations for healthy relationships, understand the meaning of commitment, and learn the skills and attitudes needed to make marriage succeed.[40] Other programs help married couples survive the inevitable ups and downs that occur in most marriages, and remarried couples with the additional challenges of step-parenting. Oklahoma, Utah, and Michigan have begun using government funds to make these relationship- and marriage-education programs accessible to low-income couples. The Greater Grand Rapids Community Marriage Policy initiative is urging area businesses to include marriage education as an Employee Assistance Program benefit, arguing that it's more cost-effective to prevent marital distress than incur the costs of counseling and lost productivity involved when employees' marriages break up.[41]

A marriage-plus agenda that includes activities such as these is not just the responsibility of government. Some of the strategies proposed here are being implemented by private and religious groups, some by governments, and some by partnerships between these sectors. The approach adopted in Oklahoma, Greater Grand Rapids, and Chattanooga, for example, mobilizes the resources of many sectors of the community — government, education, legal, faith, business, and media — in a comprehensive effort to create a more marriage-supportive culture and to provide new services to promote, support, and strengthen couples and marriage and reduce out-of-wedlock childbearing and divorce. This "saturation model" seems particularly promising because it takes into account the many factors that influence individuals' decisions to marry, to divorce, or to remain unmarried. We should proceed cautiously, trying out and evaluating new ideas before applying them widely.

Ironically, in the midst of this furor about government's role in marriage, it's worth noting that the federal government recently has begun to shirk a basic responsibility: counting the numbers of marriages and divorces in the United States. Since budget cuts in 1995, the government has been unable to report on marriage and divorce rates in the states or for the nation as a whole.[42] And, for the first time

25

[40]See Scott Stanley, "Making a Case for Premarital Education," in *Family Relations* (July 2001). Also see *Directory of Couples and Marriage Education Programs* at www.smartmarriages.com.

[41]Personal communication with Mark Eastburg, Ph.D., director of Pine Rest Family Institute, Grand Rapids, Michigan. See Web site for the Greater Grand Rapids Community Marriage Initiative, www.ggrcmarriagepolicy.org.

[42]Stephanie Ventura, "Vital Statistics from the National Center for Health Statistics," in *Data Needs for Measuring Family and Fertility Change after Welfare Reform*, ed. Douglas Besharov (College Park, MD: Maryland School of Public Affairs, Welfare Reform Academy).

in the history of the Census, Americans were not asked to give their marital status in the 2000 survey. What kind of pro-marriage message from the government is that?

If liberals and conservatives are serious about strengthening families for the sake of helping children, liberals ought to acknowledge that noncoercive and egalitarian approaches to bolstering marriage are sound policy. Conservatives, meanwhile, should admit that much of what it takes to make marriage work for the benefit of spouses and children is not just moral but economic.

READING AND DISCUSSION QUESTIONS

1. What does Ooms mean when she says in the first paragraph that in 1996 "the federal government decided to get into the business of promoting marriage"?

2. How does Ooms support her belief that children are better off in a two-parent home?

3. What type of support does she use in the sixth paragraph to argue that "[m]arriage also brings benefits to husbands and wives"?

4. What are some of the problems that arise when government gets involved in promoting marriage?

5. What claim is Ooms supporting? How effective is she in supporting that claim? Are some types of support that she uses more effective than others, in your opinion?

WRITING SUGGESTIONS

6. Write an essay in which you oppose or support Ooms's marriage-plus plan.

7. Analyze the primary types of support that Ooms uses. If you wish, you may go a step further and evaluate the effectiveness of her support.

DEBATE   Is Assuming the Role of Citizen Journalist Worth the Risk?

Praise for Student's Footage of Virginia Tech Mass Killing

LILY YULIANTI

On a CNN *Larry King Live* special report of the student massacre at Virginia Tech that saw thirty-three people killed, King praised Jamal Albarghouti, the Palestinian graduate student who took the eyewitness footage of the immediate aftermath on his cellphone.

At roughly 10 a.m. Albarghouti was at the Blacksburg, Virginia, campus to meet with his graduate adviser. He sensed that something terrible had just happened on

---

Lily Yulianti is a journalist and writer from Indonesia who works in Tokyo as an Indonesian language specialist and broadcaster for Radio Tokyo. As a citizen journalist herself, she posted this article on Korea's massive online outlet for citizen journalists, OhmyNews, on April 17, 2007.

campus, explaining, "Everyone [was] running and screaming. The situation was so frightening. I ran to a safe place and then decided to record the situation using my cellphone."

He then sent his video to CNN's *I-Report*, a citizen-reporter video blog site, which repeatedly used it to accompany its other reporting of the incident. This has been without doubt the worst mass shooting tragedy in U.S. history, and Albarghouti was the one to capture the incident for the world.

His footage, some of it shaky, set the scene inside the campus: an empty road outside a nearby building being approached by three police officers, then sounds of gunshots registering almost simultaneously, the last sounding like a bomb blast.

In the CNN interview with Larry King, Albarghouti explained how the scene   5 reminded him of his homeland of Palestine. King and another CNN news anchor tried to get at why Albarghouti decided not to dash for safety with other students and staffers but chose to stand fast and record the incident. "Weren't you scared? What sort of cellphone did you use? Did you think you were really safe at that time?"

His response was to demonstrate the value of a citizen reporter in providing an on-the-spot report of a history-making, traumatic event, in having the gadget at the ready to take the footage, and in having the presence of mind and the passion to play his historical role. He was not the only eyewitness but also stood his ground as a resourceful citizen reporter, taking the initiative to record the scene.

We can understand how CNN's professional journalists and a famous TV personality like Larry King could be so taken with Albarghouti's "journalism skill." Tempted to discount the capability of ordinary citizens in their chosen field of journalism, there are many well-trained professional journalists, proud of their skill and experience, who become intrigued whenever an unsung citizen reporter performs such a heroic act of historical reportage.

Apart from the unevenness of the footage he provided, Albarghouti showed that being confident in the use of his cellphone and uploading the resulting footage could be taken as matters of course. Above all, he provided King a clear and firm account of the situation, exactly in the manner of a professional TV journalist making a live report. What added special depth and human interest to this live report was his being reminded of the grievous situation in his own country when hearing the gunshots on campus. "I am quite familiar with the sound of gunshots, because they remind me of the situation in the West Bank and Gaza. But when I saw it was happening here, in a peaceful place like this, it was hard to believe."

Such was the personal background of a citizen-reporter that made Larry King say later, "What an irony . . .".

Again, Albarghouti and his cellphone video have shown the power of the or-   10 dinary citizen to capture a news event. Granted that the efforts of ordinary people as citizen journalists are a matter for debate, the traditional media still make a reflexively negative comparison between citizen journalism and that provided by their professionals. Interestingly, when presented with a citizen who sent an exclusive report to the mainstream media, as Albarghouti did to CNN's *I-Report*, they insist on wondering, in grudging amazement, "What made you record the event? How did you record it?"

Of course, the mainstream media should first of all be thankful, because there is a live video record from the site. The role of Albarghouti was not only that of eyewitness but also of a citizen reporter who in fact provided a high-quality report for CNN.

In raising questions like these, professionals in the media show a tendency to overlook the existence of many ordinary citizens out there who embrace the idea of participatory journalism, people who have shifted from being passive media consumers to active citizen reporters, believing they can create a better society if they get involved in conveying the news. They make videos, they write on various issues, and they raise their voices. As for the mainstream media, they have begun to open their doors to citizen reporters, seeing that their well-trained professionals cannot always respond quickly enough to reach the location of an epochal event.

Disaster Photos: Newsworthy or Irresponsible?

MARK MEMMOTT WITH ALAN LEVIN AND GREG LIVADAS

Photos taken by survivors of the London bombings[43] and Tuesday's plane crash in Toronto are prompting concerns by safety investigators and journalism scholars.

At issue: Whether as camera phones and digital cameras multiply, so do the odds that victims will put themselves and others at risk by pausing to snap pictures.

Questions are also being raised about whether the media may be encouraging risky behavior by broadcasting the images.

On the other side of the debate, such photos may aid investigators.

Within a few hours of the London attacks [on] July 7, photos taken by survivors with camera phones were ricocheting around the world on the Internet and on television.   5

Four photos taken Tuesday by Air France Flight 358 passenger Eddie Ho were broadcast later on several outlets, including ABC's *Good Morning America*, CNN, and NBC's *Today*. One was snapped inside the jet moments after it skidded to a halt in Toronto. It shows passengers heading to an exit. The others were taken outside the jet and show passengers fleeing the crippled fuselage.

---

[43]On two different dates in July 2005, London's bus and subway system was the target of a synchronized cluster of bombs. On July 7, fifty-two people were killed and 770 injured. On July 21, four devices were planted on three subways and one bus, as in the previous incident, but this time all failed to go off.

Mark Memmott worked for *USA Today* from 1984 to 2009 as a reporter and editor, and he has been a blogger for NPR since 2009. Alan Levin is a reporter for *USA Today* and Greg Livadas is a former reporter for the *Rochester Democrat and Chronicle* in New York. This article was published on August 4, 2005 on *USAToday.com*.

All three hundred nine people aboard survived.

Ho, nineteen, a South African attending college in Canada, said Thursday in a telephone interview with *USA Today* that his digital camera was in his pocket during the flight. He is an "airline enthusiast" who often takes pictures while flying. Ho sold the photos to two syndicates, which are now reselling them to the media.

Ho said he doesn't think he delayed his exit or anyone else's. "I was running and taking pictures," he said. "I just kept pressing the button." He said he would not have tried to retrieve his camera if it had been in a bag.

Still, a top accident investigation official in the USA strongly advises passengers not to do such things.   10

Mark Rosenker, acting chairman of the National Transportation Safety Board, said, "Your business is to get off the airplane. Your business is to help anybody who needs help." Taking photos is "irresponsible," he said.

Helen Muir, aerospace psychology professor at Cranfield University in Great Britain, said in most crashes "You only have two minutes from the first spark to conditions not being survivable in the cabin." Pausing even for a second "is just what we don't want people to do." But, Muir said, the pictures could be "very valuable to accident investigators." They contain clues to the jet's condition after the crash.

More such photos are inevitable. There are digital cameras in about half of U.S. households and camera phones in about 40 percent, the market research firm IDC estimates. About 92 million camera phones have been sold in the USA, IDC says.

Kelly McBride, who lectures about media ethics at the Poynter Institute for professional journalists, said the media have a responsibility "to refuse to publish photos taken (by amateurs) when someone was obviously risking his life or the lives of others."

McBride said journalists must "talk to the person about the circumstances under which he took the photos and share that information with the public."   15

Ben Sherwood, executive producer at *Good Morning America*, said there was no reason to think Ho had caused any problems at the scene. "From what we could tell" from the photos, Sherwood said, "one was taken (in the jet) during what appeared to be an orderly evacuation. The others were taken from outside, looking back."

Sherwood said *Good Morning America* "welcomes contributions from people who find themselves in the middle of news stories [but] would never encourage anyone to take an unnecessary risk."

Jonathan Klein, president of CNN/US, said his network "urges folks, on the air, not to take foolish risks." He doubts many survivors are thinking about the media when they pull out their cameras.

"They're taking (pictures) in order to satisfy that primordial urge to record one's history," Klein said.

Mark Glaser, a columnist at the USC Annenberg School of Journalism's *Online Journalism Review*, said, "Over time, people will recognize when it's the right time to use your camera in an emergency."   20

Unfortunately, he said, "it may take someone dying" because they stopped to take a picture before that "cultural norm" is reached.

DISCUSSION QUESTIONS

1. What, if any, events can you recall that had better or more complete coverage because of the presence of citizen journalists?

2. The South Korean online newspaper to which Yulianti submitted her article, OhmyNews, draws 80 percent of its content from reporters who are not professional journalists. What sort of assumptions would you make about the quality of the reporting you would find in it?

3. What did Larry King mean when he said that Albarghouti's situation was ironic?

4. What is your opinion about what Albarghouti did during the massacre at Virginia Tech?

5. What is your opinion about what Ho did during the evacuation of Air France Flight 358?

6. In general, do you believe that Yulianti or Memmott builds a more compelling case?

Assignments for Providing Support

READING AND DISCUSSION QUESTIONS

1. Consider what types of evidence you find most convincing in an argument. Is the best type of evidence dependent on the topic and the context? Explain.

2. Look for examples in the media of the misuse of evidence. Explain why the evidence is misleading.

3. Use examples to explain which news shows depend on factual evidence and which depend largely on opinion. Do both have a useful role to play in our society? Explain.

4. In the aftermath of the massacre at Virginia Tech, at least one state tried to pass a law allowing registered owners to carry their weapons on school and college campuses. What needs of the people were those who proposed the law appealing to? How could the opponents have used similar types of appeal to argue their case?

5. Consider presidential debates you have seen or other televised coverage of candidates during the months leading up to an election. What are some specific examples of how the candidates try to appeal to the voters' needs and values?

6. Bernard Goldberg argues in his essay, "Connecting the Dots . . . to Terrorism," that the average American citizen is usually ignorant of much of the reality of what goes on in the Arab world. When Americans take a stand on issues such as U.S. involvement in Iraq, to what extent do you believe they are basing that stand on solid supporting evidence?

WRITING ASSIGNMENTS

7. Using Bethany Royce's "The True Confusion about SUV Costs" as a model, write an essay evaluating the use of support in one of the Readings for Analysis.

8. Write an essay explaining the types of support used in one of the Readings for Analysis or comparing the use of support in two of them.

9. Write an essay explaining which of the two authors in the debate over citizen journalists you believe presents a more convincing argument, Lily Yulianti or Mark Memmott.

10. Analyze different television commercials for the same product or similar products. Write an essay supporting a conclusion you are able to draw about the types of appeal used in the commercials.

11. Write a letter about a problem on your campus to the person who is in a position to correct the problem. Provide convincing evidence that a problem exists and, in suggesting a solution to the problem, keep in mind the needs and values of your audience as well as those of others on campus.

Research Readiness: Using Books for Support

When should you turn to books for support, and how do you find them?

When you are writing about controversial issues, you will want to find the most up-to-date sources that you can. You don't want to write in support of a change that has already taken place. You don't want to miss significant developments in the situation you are writing about. If your audience knows more about the latest news regarding your subject than you do, you can look foolish or at least ill-prepared.

It is a fact of the publishing world that it takes considerable time for a new book to reach the shelves of libraries and bookstores, sometimes as much as a year from the time a manuscript is completed. That means that for the most recent news on developing stories and current issues, you may need to turn to magazines, newspapers, and well-maintained and reliable electronic sources.

There may be times, though, when a book will be just the source you need for some material you want to include in your paper. That doesn't mean that you will need to read books in their entirety in researching your topic, but it does mean that you should search out books on your topic and scan the table of contents and index for information on the specific part of the topic that you are writing about. If you find that the whole book seems relevant to your topic, your topic probably needs to be narrowed down. If you find a chapter or smaller segment of a book that is useful, you will cite the author of the book in your documentation if the whole book is by the same author. If the book is a collection of chapters or articles by different authors, you will cite the part you use by the author of that part. Make that distinction clear as you take notes.

Why would a book be useful in researching a current issue? Some problems, of course, have been around for a long time, and there has been ample time for books on them to be published. Also, you may want to research the history of a problem situation or solutions that have been tried in the past. You may also just need some background information on the subject.

Don't rule out books as sources just because they may not be as convenient as searching for sources online. Use either your library's card catalog or online catalog to search for your subject. Try searching by title and also by keyword. A quick search for books on autism, for example, produces 291 sources when searched by keyword and forty-nine when searched by title. Online, you will then usually have the option of limiting those results in various ways — by year, for example, or by linking your keyword with other words that rule out sources not relevant to your search. Doing an advanced search linking the keyword *autism* with *vaccines*, for example, narrows the possibilities to six.

You will also find bound periodicals listed in the card or online catalog, so if you need to find issues of a magazine or journal that are not on the shelf with current issues, you can look in the card catalog or online catalog under the title to find its location in the library.

ASSIGNMENT

1. Do your own search for books (not bound periodicals) on one of these topics.
   - The link between autism and vaccines
   - The link between cell phones and cancer
   - The movement to drop the SAT as a requirement for college admissions
   - The environmental impact of plastic water bottles
2. Create a Works Cited page for three sources that seem to be useful for information on the subject. Remember that on your Works Cited page you will list the whole book if it is the work of a single author.

   Kirby, David. *Evidence of Harm: Mercury in Vaccines and the Autism Epidemic: A Medical Controversy*. New York: St. Martin's Griffin, 2005.

   (Indicate in parenthetical documentation exactly what page you used.)

   The Vaccine Court established to compensate victims in cases of vaccine-related injury or death awards payments from an account funded by taxpayers, not the companies that produce the vaccines, and has a statute of limitations of three years (Kirby 2).

3. In a book that consists of chapters or articles by different authors, cite only the chapter or article that you are using. In that case, include in your Works Cited the page numbers for the whole chapter or article, even if you are not using every page.

   Miller, Kelli. "Hope Renewed." *Recovering Autistic Children*. Eds. Stephen M. Edelson and Bernard Rimland. San Diego: Autism Research Institute, 2003. 245–50.

4. If you need further help with the format for these citations, see Chapter 10.

CHAPTER 7

Warrants

What Are Warrants?

We now come to the third element in the structure of the argument — the warrant. Claim and support, the other major elements we have discussed, are more familiar in ordinary discourse, but there is nothing mysterious or unusual about the warrant. All our claims, both formal and informal, are grounded in warrants or assumptions that the audience must share with us if our claims are to prove to be acceptable.

The following exercise provides a good starting point for this chapter. Do the assigned task by yourself or in a small group.

PRACTICE

A series of environmental catastrophic events has virtually wiped out human life on Earth. The only known survivors in your vicinity are the eleven listed below. There are resources to sustain only seven. Choose seven of the following people to survive. List them in the order in which you would choose them and be prepared to explain the reasons for your selection: that is, why you chose these particular persons and why you placed them in this certain order.

- Dr. D. — thirty-seven, Ph.D. in history, college professor, in good health (jogs daily), hobby is botany, enjoys politics, married with one child (Bobby).
- Mrs. D. — thirty-eight, rather obese, diabetic, M.A. in psychology, counselor in a mental health clinic, married to Dr. D., has one child.
- Bobby D. — ten, mentally retarded with IQ of 70, healthy and strong for his age.
- Mrs. G. — twenty-three, ninth-grade education, cocktail waitress, worked as a prostitute, married at age sixteen, divorced at age eighteen, one son (Joseph).
- Joseph G. — three months old, healthy.
- Mary E. — eighteen, trade school education, wears glasses, artistic.

- Mr. N. — twenty-five, starting last year of medical school, music as a hobby, physical fitness buff.
- Mrs. C. — twenty-eight, daughter of a minister, college graduate, electronics engineer, single now after a brief marriage, member of Zero Population Growth.
- Mr. B. — fifty-one, B.S. in mechanics, married with four children, enjoys outdoors, much experience in construction, quite handy.
- Father Frans — thirty-seven, Catholic priest, active in civil rights, former college athlete, farming background, often criticized for liberal views.
- Dr. L. — sixty-six, doctor in general practice, two heart attacks in the past five years, loves literature and quotes extensively.

There may have been a great deal of disagreement over which survivors to select. If so, the reason for that disagreement was that in making their choices, different members of your group or of your class as a whole were operating under different assumptions or basing their decisions on different warrants. Some of you may have chosen not to let Mrs. G. survive because she seemed to have nothing particularly vital to offer to the survival of the group as a whole. Others of you may have felt that she should be allowed to survive along with her child, the infant in the group. Some of you, whether you acknowledge it or not, may have opposed letting Mrs. G. survive because she was once a prostitute. Think about the warrant that would underlie the claim that Mrs. G. should not be one of the seven allowed to survive. What assumption — what generalized principle — would a person who made that claim be accepting about women who were once prostitutes? What assumption would underlie the claim that she should be allowed to survive? What assumption would underlie the claim that Bobby D. should be allowed to live (or die)?

Obviously this is an exercise with no right answer. What it can teach us, however, is to consider the assumptions on which our beliefs are based. There are reasons you might have chosen certain individuals to survive that could be stated as general principles: Those who are in the best physical condition should be allowed to survive. Those with the most useful skills should be allowed to survive. Those who are mentally deficient should not be allowed to survive. Those who are most likely to reproduce should be allowed to survive.

Fortunately, this is merely an intellectual exercise. Whenever you take a stand in a real-life situation, though, you do so on the basis of certain general principles that guide your choices. Those general principles that you feel most strongly about exist as part of your intellectual and moral being because of what you have experienced in your life thus far. They have been shaped by your observations, your personal experience, and your participation in a culture. But because these observations, experiences, and cultural associations will vary, the audience may not always agree with the warrants or assumptions of the writer. The success of Rogerian argument depends on identifying at least one assumption, or warrant, that opposing sides share. The success of any argument depends on at least understanding your own warrants and those of your audience.

What does this have to do with your writing? Any time you support an argumentative claim, you have to analyze the assumptions behind the argument and consider whether the members of your audience share the same assumptions. Some warrants are so widely accepted that you do not need to state them or to offer any proof of their validity. If you argue that every new dorm on campus should have a sprinkler system, you probably do not even need to state your warrant. If you did, it would be something like this: Measures that would increase the likelihood that dorm residents would survive a fire should be implemented in all dorms.

What about claims that are more controversial? Why is it so difficult for those who oppose abortion, for example, to communicate with those who favor it and vice versa? Anyone who believes that abortion is the murder of an unborn child is basing that argument on the warrant that a fetus is a child from conception. Many on the other side of the debate do not accept that warrant and thus do not accept the claim. Obviously disagreements on such emotionally charged issues are very difficult to resolve because the underlying warrants are based on firmly held beliefs that are difficult to change. It is always better to be aware of your opponent's warrants, however, than to simply dismiss them as irrelevant.

The British philosopher Stephen Toulmin, who developed the concept of warrants, dismissed more traditional forms of logical reasoning in favor of a more audience-based, courtroom-derived approach to argumentation. He refers to warrants as "general, hypothetical statements, which can act as bridges" and "entitle one to draw conclusions or make claims."[1] The word *bridges* to denote the action of the warrant is crucial. One dictionary defines warrant as a "guarantee or justification." We use the word *warrant* to emphasize that in an argument it guarantees a connecting link — a bridge — between the claim and the support. This means that even if a reader agrees that the support is sound, the support cannot prove the validity of the claim unless the reader also agrees with the underlying warrant. Recall the sample argument outlined in Chapter 1 (p. 25):

Claim: Backscatter screening should be implemented in America's airports.

Support: Backscatter screening will make planes safer.

Warrant: Any screening technique that will make planes safer should be implemented.

Notice that the reader must agree with the assumption that safety is worth undergoing any screening technique, even one that some would consider an invasion of privacy. Simply providing evidence that a certain technique will make planes safer is not enough to convince all readers that backscatter screening should be implemented in America's airports.

The following dialogue offers another example of the relationship between the warrant and the other elements of the argument.

---

[1]Stephen Toulmin, *The Uses of Argument* (Cambridge: Cambridge University Press, 1958), p. 98.

"I don't think that Larry can do the job. He's pretty dumb."
"Really? I thought he was smart. What makes you say he's dumb?"
"Did you know that he's illiterate — can't read above third-grade level? In my
book that makes him dumb."

If we put this into outline form, the warrant or assumption in the argument becomes clear.

Claim: Larry is pretty dumb.

Support: He can't read above third-grade level.

Warrant: Anybody who can't read above third-grade level must be dumb.

We can also represent the argument in diagram form, which shows the warrant as a bridge between the claim and the support.

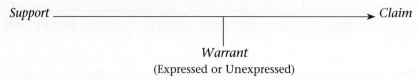

Warrant
(Expressed or Unexpressed)

The argument above can then be written like this:

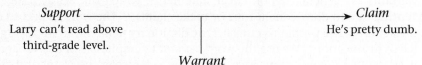

Warrant
Anybody who can't read above third-grade
level must be pretty dumb.

Is this warrant valid? We cannot answer this question until we consider the *backing*. Every warrant or assumption rests on something else that gives it authority; this is what we call backing. Backing or authority for the warrant in this example would consist of research data that prove a relationship between stupidity and low reading ability. This particular warrant, we would discover, lacks backing because we know that the failure to learn to read well may be due to a number of things unrelated to intelligence. So if the warrant is unprovable, the claim — that Larry is dumb — is also unprovable, even if the evidence is true. In this case, then, the evidence does not guarantee the soundness of the claim.

Now consider this example of a somewhat more complicated warrant: The beautiful and unspoiled Eastern Shore of Maryland is being discovered by thousands of tourists, vacationers, and developers who will, according to the residents, change the landscape and the way of life, which is now based largely on fishing and farming. In a few years the Eastern Shore may become a noisy, crowded string of resorts. Mrs. Walkup, the Kent County commissioner, says,

Catering to the wealthy puts property back on the tax rolls, but it's going
to make the Eastern Shore look like the rest of the country. Everything that

made our way of life so special is being eroded. We are a fragile area. The Eastern Shore is still special, but it is feeling pressure from all directions. Lots of people don't seem to appreciate the fact that God made us to need a little peace and quiet now and then.[2]

In simplified form the argument of those opposed to development would be outlined this way:

Claim: Development will bring undesirable changes to the present way of life on the Eastern Shore, a life of farming and fishing, peace and quiet.

Support: Developers will build express highways, condominiums, casinos, and nightclubs.

Warrant: A pastoral life of fishing and farming is superior to the way of life brought by expensive, fast-paced modern development.

Notice that the warrant is a broad generalization that can apply to a number of different situations, while the claim is about a specific place and time. It should be added that in other arguments the warrant may not be stated in such general terms. However, even in arguments in which the warrant makes a more specific reference to the claim, the reader can infer an extension of the warrant to other similar arguments. In the backscatter screening example outlined on page 271, the warrant mentions a specific screening technique. But it is clear that such warrants can be generalized to apply to other arguments in which we accept a claim based on an appeal to our very human need to feel secure.

To be convinced of the validity of Mrs. Walkup's claim, you must first find that the support is true, that the developers plan to introduce drastic changes that will destroy the pastoral life of the Eastern Shore. You may, however, believe that the support is not entirely sound, that the development will be much more modest than residents fear, and that the Eastern Shore will not be seriously altered. Next, you may want to see more justification for the warrant. Is pastoral life superior to the life that will result from large-scale development? Perhaps you have always thought that a life of fishing and farming means poverty and limited opportunities for the majority of the residents. Although the superiority of a way of life is largely a matter of taste and therefore difficult to prove, Mrs. Walkup may need to produce backing for her belief that the present way of life is more desirable than one based on developing the area for new residents and summer visitors. If you find either the support or the warrant unconvincing, you cannot accept the claim.

Remember that a claim is often modified by one or more qualifiers, which limit the claim. Mrs. Walkup might have said, "Development will *probably* destroy *some aspects of* the present way of life on the Eastern Shore." Warrants can also be modified or limited by *reservations*, which remind the reader that there are conditions under which the warrants will not be relevant. Mrs. Walkup

[2]Michael Wright, "The Changing Chesapeake," *New York Times Magazine,* July 10, 1983, p. 27.

might have added, "unless increased prosperity and exposure to the outside world brought by development improve some aspects of our lives." This is the sort of reservation that could be the means of reconciling two different points of view in Rogerian argument.

A diagram of Mrs. Walkup's argument shows the additional elements:

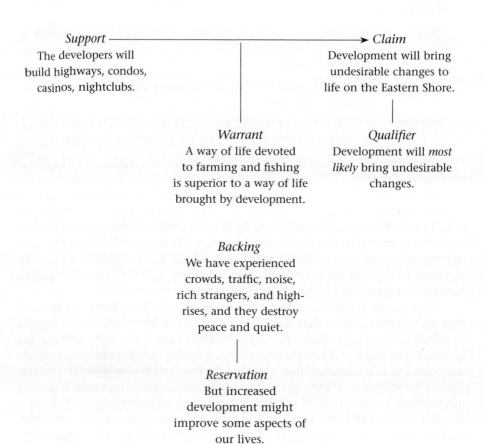

Support ————————————————→ *Claim*
The developers will   Development will bring
build highways, condos,   undesirable changes to
casinos, nightclubs.   life on the Eastern Shore.

Warrant   *Qualifier*
A way of life devoted   Development will *most*
to farming and fishing   *likely* bring undesirable
is superior to a way of life   changes.
brought by development.

Backing
We have experienced
crowds, traffic, noise,
rich strangers, and high-
rises, and they destroy
peace and quiet.

Reservation
But increased
development might
improve some aspects of
our lives.

Claim and support (or lack of support) are relatively easy to uncover in most arguments. One thing that makes the warrant different is that it is often unexpressed and therefore unexamined by both writer and reader because they take it for granted. In the argument about Larry's intelligence, the warrant was stated. But in the argument about development on the Eastern Shore, Mrs. Walkup did not state her warrant directly, although her meaning is perfectly clear. She probably felt that it was not necessary to be more explicit because her readers would understand and supply the warrant.

We can make the discovery of warrants even clearer by examining another argument, in this case a policy claim. We've looked at a factual claim (that Larry is dumb) and a value claim (that Eastern Shore development is undesirable). Now we examine a policy claim that rests on one expressed and one unexpressed warrant. Policy claims are usually more complicated than other claims because the statement of policy is preceded by an array of facts and values. In addition, such claims may represent chains of reasoning in which one argument is dependent on another. These complicated arguments may be difficult or impossible to summarize in a simple diagram, but careful reading, asking the same kinds of questions that the author may have asked about the claim, can help you to find the warrant or chain of warrants that must be accepted before evidence and claim can be linked.

In a familiar argument that appeared a few years ago,[3] the author argues for a radical reform in college sports — the elimination of subprofessional, intermural team sports, as practiced above all in football and basketball. The claim is clear, and evidence for the professional character of college sports not hard to find: the large salaries paid to coaches, the generous perquisites offered to players, the recruitment policies that ignore academic standing, the virtually full-time commitment of the players, the lucrative television contracts. But can this evidence support the author's claim that such sports do not belong on college campuses? Advocates of these sports may ask, "Why not?" In the conclusion of the article the author states one warrant or assumption underlying his claim.

> Even if the money to pay college athletes could be found, though, a larger question must be answered — namely, why should a system of professional athletics be affiliated with universities at all? For the truth is that the requirements of athletics and academics operate at cross purposes, and the attempt to play both games at once serves only to reduce the level of performance of each.

In other words, the author assumes that the goals of an academic education on the one hand and the goals of big-time college sports on the other hand are incompatible. In the article he develops the ways in which each enterprise harms the other.

But the argument clearly rests on another warrant that is not expressed because the author takes for granted that his readers will supply it: The academic goals of the university are primary and should take precedence over all other collegiate activities. This is an argument based on an authority warrant, the authority of those who define the goals of the university — scholars, public officials, university administrators, and others. (Types of warrants are discussed in the following section.)

This warrant makes clear that the evidence of the professional nature of college sports cited above supports the claim that they should be eliminated. If quasiprofessional college sports are harmful to the primary educational function of the college or university, then they must go. In the author's words, "The two are separate enterprises, to be judged by separate criteria. . . . For college

[3]D. G. Myers, "Why College Sports?" *Commentary*, December 1990, pp. 49–51.

sports, the university is not an educational institution at all; it is merely a locus, a means of coordinating the different aspects of the sporting enterprise."

This argument may be summarized in outline form as follows:

Claim: Intermural college team sports should be abolished.

Support: College sports have become subprofessional.

Warrant: The goals of an academic education and big-time college sports are incompatible.

Backing
For the
Warrant: Academic education is the primary goal of the college and must take precedence over athletic activity.

PRACTICE

Read the following argument by Robert A. Sirico. Then summarize the argument in a paragraph. Next, explain what the claim is, what types of support are used, and what the warrant is. Is the warrant one that you agree with? Explain.

An Unjust Sacrifice
ROBERT A. SIRICO

An appeals court in London has made a Solomonic ruling, deciding that eight-week-old twins joined at the pelvis must be separated. In effect, one twin, known as Mary, is to be sacrificed to save the other, known as Jodie, in an operation the babies' parents oppose.

The judges invoked a utilitarian rationale, justified on the basis of medical testimony. The specialists agreed that there is an 80 to 90 percent chance that the strong and alert Jodie could not survive more than a few months if she continued to support the weak heart and lungs of Mary, whose brain is underdeveloped.

This is a heartbreaking case, and the decision of the court was not arrived at lightly. But even the best of intentions, on the part of the state or the parents, is no substitute for sound moral reasoning. Utilitarian considerations like Mary's quality of life are not the issue. Nor should doctors' expert testimony, which is subject to error, be considered decisive.

Here, as in the case of abortion, one simple principle applies: There is no justification for deliberately destroying innocent life. In this case, the court has turned its back on a tenet that the West has stood by: Life, no matter how limited, should be protected.

While this case is so far unique, there are guidelines that must be followed. No human being, for instance, can be coerced into donating an organ — even if the individual donating the organ is unlikely to be harmed and the individual receiving the organ could be saved. In principle, no person should ever be forced to volunteer his own body to save another's life, even if that individual is a newborn baby.

Robert A. Sirico, a Roman Catholic priest, is president of the Acton Institute for the Study of Religion and Liberty in Grand Rapids, Michigan. This article appeared in the September 28, 2000, *New York Times*.

To understand the gravity of the court's error, consider the parents' point of view. They are from Gozo, an island in Malta. After being told of their daughters' condition, while the twins were in utero, they went to Manchester, England, seeking out the best possible medical care. Yet, after the birth on August 8, the parents were told that they needed to separate the twins, which would be fatal for Mary.

They protested, telling the court: "We cannot begin to accept or contemplate that one of our children should die to enable the other one to survive. That is not God's will. Everyone has a right to life, so why should we kill one of our daughters to enable the other one to survive?"

And yet, a court in a country in which they sought refuge has overruled their wishes. This is a clear evil: coercion against the parents and coercion against their child, justified in the name of a speculative medical calculus.

The parents' phrase "God's will" is easily caricatured, as if they believed divine revelation were guiding them to ignore science. In fact, they believe in the merit of science, or they would not have gone to Britain for help in the first place.

But utilitarian rationality has overtaken their case. The lawyer appointed by the court to represent Jodie insisted that Mary's was "a futile life." That is a dangerous statement — sending us down a slippery slope where lives can be measured for their supposed value and discarded if deemed not useful enough.

Some might argue that in thinking about the twins, we should apply the philosophical principle known as "double effect," which, in some circumstances, permits the loss of a life when it is an unintended consequence of saving another. But in this case, ending Mary's life would be a deliberate decision, not an unintended effect.

Can we ever take one life in favor of another? No, not even in this case, however fateful the consequences.

Arguers will often neglect to state their warrants for one of two reasons: First, like Mrs. Walkup, they may believe that the warrant is obvious and need not be expressed; second, they may want to conceal the warrant in the hope that the reader will overlook its weakness.

What kinds of warrants are so obvious that they need not be expressed? Here are a few that will probably sound familiar:

Mothers love their children.

The more expensive the product, the more satisfactory it will be.

A good harvest will result in lower prices for produce.

First come, first served.

These statements seem to embody beliefs that most of us would share and that might be unnecessary to make explicit in an argument. The last statement, for example, is taken as axiomatic, an article of faith that we seldom question in ordinary circumstances. Suppose you hear someone make the claim, "I deserve to get the last ticket to the concert." If you ask why he is entitled to a ticket that you also would like to have, he may answer in support of his claim, "Because I was here first." No doubt you accept his claim without further argument because you understand and agree with the warrant that is not expressed: "If you arrive first, you deserve to be served before those who come later." Your acceptance of the warrant probably also takes into account the unexpressed backing that is based on a belief in justice: "It is only fair that those who sacrifice time and comfort to be first in line should be rewarded for their trouble."

In this case it may not be necessary to expose the warrant and examine it. Indeed, as Stephen Toulmin tells us, "If we demanded the credentials of all warrants at sight and never let one pass unchallenged, argument could scarcely begin."[4]

But even those warrants that seem to express universal truths invite analysis if we can think of claims for which these warrants might not, after all, be relevant. "First in line," for example, may justify the claim of a person who wants a concert ticket, but it cannot in itself justify the claim of someone who wants a vital medication that is in short supply. Moreover, offering a rebuttal to a long-held but unexamined warrant can often produce an interesting and original argument. If someone exclaims, "All this buying of gifts! I think people have forgotten that Christmas celebrates the birth of Christ," she need not express the assumption — that the buying of gifts violates what ought to be a religious celebration. It goes unstated by the speaker because it has been uttered so often that she knows the hearer will supply it. But one writer, in an essay titled "God's Gift: A Commercial Christmas," argued that, contrary to popular belief, the purchase of gifts, which means the expenditure of time, money, and thought on others rather than oneself, is not a violation but an affirmation of the Christmas spirit.[5]

The second reason for refusal to state the warrant lies in the arguer's intention to disarm or deceive the reader, although the arguer may not be aware of this. For instance, failure to state the warrant is common in advertising and politics, where the desire to sell a product or an idea may outweigh the responsibility to argue explicitly. The following advertisement is famous not only for what it says but for what it does not say:

> In 1918 Leona Currie scandalized a New Jersey beach with a bathing suit cut above her knees. And to irk the establishment even more, she smoked a cigarette. Leona Currie was promptly arrested.
>   Oh, how Leona would smile if she could see you today.
>   You've come a long way, baby. *Virginia Slims*. The taste for today's woman.

What is the unstated warrant? The manufacturer of Virginia Slims hopes we will agree that being permitted to smoke cigarettes is a significant sign of female lib-

---

[4] *The Uses of Argument* (Cambridge: Cambridge University Press, 1958), p. 106.
[5] Robert A. Sirico, *Wall Street Journal*, December 21, 1993, sec. A, p. 12.

eration. But many readers would insist that proving "You've come a long way, baby" requires more evidence than women's freedom to smoke (or wear short bathing suits). The shaky warrant weakens the claim.

Politicians, too, conceal warrants that may not survive close scrutiny. In the 1983 mayoral election in Chicago, one candidate revealed that his opponent had undergone psychiatric treatment. He did not have to state the warrant supporting his claim. He knew that many in his audience would assume that anyone who had undergone psychiatric treatment was unfit to hold public office. This same assumption contributed to the withdrawal of a vice-presidential candidate from the 1972 campaign.

Types of Warrants

Arguments may be classified according to the types of warrants offered as proof. Because warrants represent the reasoning process by which we establish the relationship between support and claim, analysis of the major types of warrants enables us to see the whole argument as a sum of its parts.

Warrants may be organized into three categories: *authoritative, substantive*, and *motivational*.[6] The *authoritative warrant* is based on the credibility or trustworthiness of the source. If we assume that the source of the data is authoritative, then we find that the support justifies the claim. A *substantive warrant* is based on beliefs about reliability of factual evidence. In the example on page 272 the speaker assumes, although mistakenly, that the relationship between low reading level and stupidity is a verifiable datum, one that can be proved by objective research. A *motivational warrant*, on the other hand, is based on the needs and values of the audience. For example, the warrant about backscatter screening reflects a concern for safety, a value that would cause a reader who held it to agree that more rigid screening techniques are a good idea.

Each type of warrant requires a different set of questions for testing its soundness. The following list of questions will help you to decide whether a particular warrant is valid and can justify a particular claim.

1. *Authoritative* (based on the credibility of the sources)

    Is the authority sufficiently respected to make a credible claim?

    Do other equally reputable authorities agree with the authority cited?

    Are there equally reputable authorities who disagree?

2. *Substantive* (based on beliefs about the reliability of factual evidence)

    Are sufficient examples given to convince us that a general statement is justified? That is, are the examples given representative of the whole community?

---

[6]D. Ehninger and W. Brockriede, *Decision by Debate* (New York: Dodd, Mead, 1953).

If you have argued that one event or condition can bring about another (a cause-and-effect argument), does the cause given seem to account entirely for the effect? Are other possible causes equally important as explanations for the effect?

If you have used comparisons, are the similarities between the two situations greater than the differences?

If you have used analogies, does the analogy explain or merely describe? Are there sufficient similarities between the two elements to make the analogy appropriate?

3. *Motivational* (based on the values of the arguer and the audience)

Are the values ones that the audience will regard as important?

Are the values relevant to the claim?

SAMPLE ANNOTATED ESSAY

The Case for Torture

MICHAEL LEVIN

Introduction: statement of opposing view

It is generally assumed that torture is impermissible, a throwback to a more brutal age. Enlightened societies reject it outright, and regimes suspected of using it risk the wrath of the United States.

Claim of policy: rebuttal of opposing view

I believe this attitude is unwise. There are situations in which torture is not merely permissible but morally mandatory. Moreover, these situations are moving from the realm of imagination to fact.

Support: hypothetical example to test the reader's belief

Suppose a terrorist has hidden an atomic bomb on Manhattan Island which will detonate at noon on July 4 unless . . . (here follow the usual demands for money and release of his friends from jail). Suppose, further, that he is caught at 10 A.M. of the fateful day, but — preferring death to failure — won't disclose where the bomb is. What do we do? If we follow due process — wait for his lawyer, arraign him — millions of people will die. If the only way to save those lives is to subject the terrorist to the most excruciating possible pain, what grounds can

Michael Levin is a professor of philosophy at the City University of New York. This essay is reprinted from the June 7, 1982, issue of *Newsweek*.

there be for not doing so? I suggest there are none. In any case, I ask you to face the question with an open mind.

Torturing the terrorist is unconstitutional? Probably. But millions of lives surely outweigh constitutionality. Torture is barbaric? Mass murder is far more barbaric. Indeed, letting millions of innocents die in deference to one who flaunts his guilt is moral cowardice, an unwillingness to dirty one's hands. If *you* caught the terrorist, could you sleep nights knowing that millions died because you couldn't bring yourself to apply the electrodes?

Once you concede that torture is justified in extreme cases, you have admitted that the decision to use torture is a matter of balancing innocent lives against the means needed to save them. You must now face more realistic cases involving more modest numbers. Someone plants a bomb on a jumbo jet. He alone can disarm it, and his demands cannot be met (or if they can, we refuse to set a precedent by yielding to his threats). Surely we can, we must, do anything to the extortionist to save the passengers. How can we tell three hundred, or one hundred, or ten people who never asked to be put in danger, "I'm sorry, you'll have to die in agony, we just couldn't bring ourselves to . . ."

Here are the results of an informal poll about a third, hypothetical, case. Suppose a terrorist group kidnapped a newborn baby from a hospital. I asked four mothers if they would approve of torturing kidnappers if that were necessary to get their own newborns back. All said yes, the most "liberal" adding that she would administer it herself.

I am not advocating torture as punishment. Punishment is addressed to deeds irrevocably past. Rather, I am advocating torture as an acceptable measure for preventing future evils. So understood, it is far less objectionable than many extant punishments. Opponents of the death penalty, for example, are forever insisting that executing a murderer will not bring back his victim (as if the purpose of capital punishment were supposed to be resurrection, not deterrence or retribution). But torture, in the cases described, is intended not to bring anyone back but to keep innocents from being dispatched. The most powerful argument against using torture as a punishment or to secure confessions is that such

5

Margin notes:

Support: hypothetical example

Support: informal poll

Defense of the claim
a) Not punishment but protection of the innocent

practices disregard the rights of the individual. Well, if the individual is all that important — and he is — it is correspondingly important to protect the rights of individuals threatened by terrorists. If life is so valuable that it must never be taken, the lives of the innocents must be saved even at the price of hurting the one who endangers them.

b) Precedents for torture

Better precedents for torture are assassination and preemptive attack. No Allied leader would have flinched at assassinating Hitler, had that been possible. (The Allies did assassinate Heydrich.) Americans would be angered to learn that Roosevelt could have had Hitler killed in 1943 — thereby shortening the war and saving millions of lives — but refused on moral grounds. Similarly, if nation A learns that nation B is about to launch an unprovoked attack, A has a right to save itself by destroying B's military capability first. In the same way, if the police can by torture save those who would otherwise die at the hands of kidnappers or terrorists, they must.

c) Denial that terrorists have rights

There is an important difference between terrorists and their victims that should mute talk of the terrorists' "rights." The terrorist's victims are at risk unintentionally, not having asked to be endangered. But the terrorist knowingly initiated his actions. Unlike his victims, he volunteered for the risks of his deed. By threatening to kill for profit or idealism, he renounces civilized standards, and he can have no complaint if civilization tries to thwart him by whatever means necessary.

Just as torture is justified only to save lives (not extort confessions or recantations), it is justifiably administered only to those *known* to hold innocent lives in their hands. Ah, but how can the authorities ever be sure they have the right malefactor? Isn't there a danger of error and abuse? Won't We turn into Them?   10

Questions like these are disingenuous in a world in which terrorists proclaim themselves and perform for television. The name of their game is public recognition. After all, you can't very well intimidate a government into releasing your freedom fighters unless you announce that it is your group that has seized its embassy. "Clear guilt" is difficult to define, but when 40 million people see a group of masked gunmen seize an airplane on the evening news, there is not much question about who

d) Easy identification of terrorists

the perpetrators are. There will be hard cases where the situation is murkier. Nonetheless, a line demarcating the legitimate use of torture can be drawn. Torture only the obviously guilty, and only for the sake of saving innocents, and the line between Us and Them will remain clear.

There is little danger that the Western democracies will lose their way if they choose to inflict pain as one way of preserving order. Paralysis in the face of evil is the greater danger. Some day soon a terrorist will threaten tens of thousands of lives, and torture will be the only way to save them. We had better start thinking about this.

Conclusion warrant: "Paralysis in the face of evil is the greater danger."

Analysis

Levin's controversial essay attacks a popular assumption that most people have never thought to question — that torture is impermissible under any circumstances. Levin argues that in extreme cases torture is morally justified to bring about a greater good than the rights of the individual who is tortured.

Against the initial resistance that most readers may feel, Levin makes a strong case. Its strength lies in the backing he provides for the warrant that torture is sometimes necessary. This backing consists in the use of two effective argumentative strategies. One is the anticipation of objections. Unprecedented? No. Unconstitutional? No. Barbaric? No. Second, and more important, are the hypothetical examples that compel readers to rethink their positions and possibly arrive at agreement with the author. Levin chooses extreme examples — kidnapping of a newborn child, planting a bomb on a jumbo jet, detonating an atomic bomb in Manhattan — that draw a line between clear and murky cases and make agreement easier. And he bolsters his moral position by insisting that torture is not to be used as punishment or revenge but only to save innocent lives.

To support such an unpopular assumption the writer must convey the impression that he is a reasonable man, and this Levin attempts to do by a searching definition of terms, the careful organization and development of his argument, including references to the opinions of other people, and the expression of compassion for innocent lives.

Another strength of the article is its readability — the use of contractions, informal questions, conversational locutions. This easy, familiar style is disarming; the reader doesn't feel threatened by heavy admonitions from a writer who affects a superior, moral attitude.

> ## Writer's Guide: Recognizing Warrants
>
> 1. Locate in your essay the one sentence that best states your claim, or if there is no single sentence that does so, try to express your claim in a single sentence.
>
> 2. If you have not already done so, think about for what audience you are writing. How is that audience likely to respond to your claim? The most important question to ask about your audience regarding warrants is this one: What assumption or assumptions must my audience make to be able to accept my claim? The answer to that question will be the warrant or warrants on which your essay is based.
>
> 3. The support you offer will make it easier for your audience to accept your claim. Remember that the warrant is the link between claim and support. It may help to use the formula used in this chapter to think systematically through your argument. Ask yourself what the claim is, what support you are offering, and what warrant connects the two. Do that for each major supporting statement that you make.
>
> 4. You may not need to state your warrant directly if it is a universally accepted truth that most reasonable readers would agree with it. You should be able to do so, however, in order to check your own logic.
>
> 5. If you are asking the members of your audience to accept a warrant that they are not likely to accept, you must offer backing for that warrant or consider restating your claim in a way that does not ask them to agree to an assumption that they will not be willing to agree with.

READINGS FOR ANALYSIS

We're All Celebrities in Post-Privacy Age

ERIC AUCHARD

Move over, Paris Hilton. We all have celebrity issues in an age when anyone can create an online profile, post confessional videos on YouTube, or make snarky online comments about other people.

The latest generation of Web sites — which attract tens of millions of users daily to share words, photos, and videos about themselves and their friends — make a virtue of openness at the expense of traditional notions of privacy.

Eric Auchard is a columnist for Reuters, covering technology investment. This article appeared online on June 21, 2007.

"My grandparents would have had a different attitude about privacy," says Jeff Jarvis, a former critic for *TV Guide* turned top blogger and columnist for the *Guardian* in London.

"There is a different calculus now," he says.

Sites like Facebook, Photobucket, and Flickr are enjoying surging popularity   5
for allowing people to control their online identities in ways that make the danger of revealing too much information a constant worry — and all part of the game.

"Within the Web realm there is no private self," argues David Weinberger, author of a newly published book, *Everything Is Miscellaneous: The Power of the New Digital Disorder.*

"The closest you can mean is that you are with a small group behind some password-protected mechanism," he says.

The danger of such exposure is that it could affect careers when students seek jobs in the real world or private citizens seek public office.

George W. Bush and Bill Clinton might never have been elected president had sites like Google Inc.'s YouTube or News Corp.'s MySpace, the world's biggest online meeting places, existed to record the events of their younger years.

But while policy makers ponder how to bolster online anonymity, social net-   10
work users are more concerned about deciding what to reveal about themselves next.

Control, Community Trump Privacy

Most users of the new self-publishing tools report finding a stronger sense of community among friends, family, and random Web site visitors who share their interests.

Facebook, a site started by a Harvard University undergraduate as a way for students to get to know one another, has exploded in popularity among professional users in Britain and the United States since the site took steps to open up to people of all ages over the past year. It now claims 25 million active users, who like the control Facebook gives them over who they let into their network of online acquaintances.

"What Facebook does is it allows me to control my identity and my society — my group of friends," Jarvis says. "You can call it privacy or you can call it publicness. I am controlling both sides of that equation, together — that's the secret."

Highlighting his own change of thinking on the subject of privacy, Jarvis revealed last year in a blog post, entitled "My cheatin' heart," that he was suffering from a medical condition that slowed work on his widely read media criticism blog, *BuzzMachine* (http://www.buzzmachine.com/). Supportive comments, and advice about potential treatments, poured in.

"Revealing a little bit of yourself is the only way to make connections to other   15
people and that is how the Internet works," Jarvis says. "I couldn't have gotten that benefit unless I revealed the condition."

Caterina Fake, co-founder of popular photo sharing site Flickr, said recently that the defining moment for her start-up was when it decided all photos on the site would be public. Previously, photo sites had assumed users' photos should be private, unless deliberately published for public consumption.

Mena Trott, who, with her husband, Ben, developed Movable Type, a software system for publishing blogs, says "control" is a better word than "privacy" for defining oneself in different situations on the Web.

"We think blogging is sharing the stuff you care about with the people you care about," Trott says. "It comes down to control. They may or may not use it. But people want control."

Trott's company, Six Apart, makes publishing tools used by everyone from Hollywood gossip reporters to moms who seek to document their everyday lives, in private or semi-public mode.

"The Internet is often accused of leading to uncivil behavior," Jarvis says.   20
"Identity will lead to civility because we are being watched. It's like living in a small town again."

READING AND DISCUSSION QUESTIONS

1. What experience, if any, have you had with the sort of sites to which Auchard refers: for example, Facebook, Photobucket, and Flickr?

2. What are the pros and cons of posting to such social networking sites?

3. The heading halfway through the article reads, "Control, Community Trump Privacy." Explain what Auchard means by that.

4. What is Auchard's claim?

5. What types of support does he use?

6. What is his warrant?

7. Explain whether or not you accept his warrant.

WRITING SUGGESTIONS

8. Attack or defend this statement made by Auchard: "The danger of such exposure [on the Web] is that it could affect careers when students seek jobs in the real world or private citizens seek public office."

9. Write an essay in which you explain whether or not you believe that it is possible to achieve, on the Web, a balance between publicness and privacy.

10. What are the dangers of exposing personal information on the Internet?

11. Explain why you believe that sites like Facebook and MySpace are so popular.

What's Wrong with Price Gouging?

JEFF JACOBY

There wasn't much [Massachusetts Attorney General] Martha Coakley could do about the massive pipe break that left dozens of Greater Boston towns without clean drinking water over the weekend. So she kept herself busy instead lecturing vendors not to increase the price of the bottled water that tens of thousands of consumers were suddenly in a frenzy to buy.

"We have begun hearing anecdotal reports of the possible price gouging of store-bought water," Coakley announced Sunday. "Businesses and individuals cannot and should not take advantage of this public emergency to unfairly charge consumers . . . for water." Inspectors were being dispatched, "spot-checks" were being conducted, and "if we discover that businesses are engaging in price gouging," she warned, "we will take appropriate legal action."

Governor Deval Patrick got into the act, too. He ordered the state's Division of Standards to "closely monitor bottled water prices" in the area affected by the water emergency. "There is never an excuse for taking advantage of consumers," he intoned, "especially not during times like this."

It never fails. No sooner does some calamity trigger an urgent need for basic resources than self-righteous voices are raised to denounce the amazingly efficient system that stimulates suppliers to speed those resources to the people who need them. That system is the free market's price mechanism — the fluctuation of prices because of changes in supply and demand.

When the demand for bottled water goes through the roof — which is another way of saying that bottled water has become (relatively) scarce — the price of water quickly rises in response. That price spike may be annoying, but it's not nearly as annoying as being unable to find water for sale at any price. Rising prices help keep limited quantities from vanishing today, while increasing the odds of fresh supplies arriving tomorrow.   5

It is easy to demonize vendors who charge what the market will bear following a catastrophe. "After storm come the vultures" *USA Today* memorably headlined a story about the price hikes that followed Hurricane Charley in Florida in 2004. Coakley hasn't called anybody a vulture, at least not yet, but her office has dedicated a telephone hotline and is encouraging the public to drop a dime on "price gougers."

Before you drop that dime, though, consider who really serves the public interest — the merchant who boosts his price during a crisis, or the merchant who refuses to?

A thought experiment: A massive pipe ruptures, tap water grows undrinkable, and consumers rush to buy bottled water from the only two vendors who sell it.

Jeff Jacoby is a columnist for the *Boston Globe*, where this essay and the response that follows appeared on May 4, 2010.

In an emergency should merchants be allowed to charge high prices for water?

Vendor A, not wanting to annoy the governor and attorney general, leaves the price of his water unchanged at 69 cents a bottle. Vendor B, who is more interested in doing business than truckling to politicians, more than quadruples his price to $2.99.

You don't need an economics textbook to know what happens next.

Customers descend on Vendor A in droves, loading up on his 69-cent water. 10 Within hours his entire stock has been cleaned out, and subsequent customers are turned away empty-handed. At Vendor B's, on the other hand, sales of water are slower and there is a lot of grumbling about the high price. But even late-arriving customers are able to buy the water they need — and almost no one buys more than he truly *needs*.

When demand intensifies, prices rise. And as prices rise, suppliers work harder to meet demand. The same *Globe* story that reported yesterday on Coakley's "price-gouging" statement reported as well on the lengths to which bottlers and retailers were going to get more water into customers' hands.

"Suppliers worked overtime, pumping up production at regional bottling facilities and coordinating deliveries," reporter Erin Ailworth noted. Polar Beverages in Worcester, for example, "had emptied out its plant in the city last night and trucked in loads of water from its New York facility."

Letting prices rise freely isn't the only possible response to a sudden shortage. Government rationing is an option, and so are price controls — assuming you don't object to the inevitable corruption, long lines, and black market. Better by far to let prices rise and fall freely. That isn't "gouging," but plain good sense — and the best method yet devised for allocating goods and services among free men and women.

Response to Jacoby
BACKBAYALLTHEWAY

Your editorial urges the audience toward a horrendous logical fallacy. Using Micro101 you claim that a rise in prices should increase supply (true). You then use anecdotal evidence from Polar Beverages to claim that supply has increased (true). Early in your piece, however, you claim that increasing prices help increase supplies and keep water on the shelves. If we are to assume that government price controls have been relatively effective, there appears to be adequate financial incentive to increase water supply without price increases to consumers. This is especially true when considering that wholesale prices (bottlers to retailers) are probably the most heavily monitored and regulated. In the short run, larger payments to Poland Springs aren't going to increase supply beyond the maximum capacity that exists now.

In regards to allocation, your hypothesis is predicated on the idea that all individuals have a similar valuation of bottled water and that water is allocated based on need. Water, in general, is allocated based on ability to pay. If prices were to sky-rocket . . . who would be more likely to drink water straight out of the tap, a family in central Boston or a family in Newton?

To people who have never been exposed to low income areas, the possibility of taking a health risk to save money may seem completely foreign. To those families living paycheck to paycheck, the time/energy needed to boil water or the money needed to buy water can be a true economic hardship.

We all know that this water is *probably* safe to drink, but let's all lay our J.D. degrees on the table and really appreciate the families who have to consider if "probably" is worth the possibility of saving money and getting sick.

READING AND DISCUSSION QUESTIONS

1. Summarize Jacoby's argument as you understand it.
2. How does raising the cost of bottled water in this case compare with similar price gouging when there is a crisis of greater magnitude, affecting more people for a longer period of time? Does Jacoby's argument seem applicable to those cases?
3. How convincing did you find Jacoby's argument to be?
4. What is his warrant? Is it an assumption you can agree with?
5. Do you agree with BackBayalltheWay that Jacoby's argument is a "horrendous logical fallacy"? See the explanations of common fallacies on p. 308.
6. Whose argument do you find more acceptable, Jacoby's or BackBayalltheWay's? Why?

WRITING SUGGESTIONS

7. Write an evaluative essay analyzing Jacoby's essay.
8. Write an essay either agreeing with or arguing against Jacoby's thesis.

9. Write an essay explaining under what circumstances you feel the government —
   local, state, or federal — should step in and impose strict controls on the price of
   essential goods. (You will need to define what you mean by the term "essential
   goods.")

10. Write an essay explaining which of the two arguments about price gouging you
    think presents a better argument and why.

DEBATE   Is Recycling Plastic Good Stewardship or Bad Business?

Why Let Stewardship Get in the Way of a Quick Buck?

JOHN TROTTI

Send recycled plastic to China . . . four days later it's back as air pollution.
— UCLA PROFESSOR

It's time for us to take an honest look at recycling in the United States, focusing
attention on just what it is we're trying to accomplish in the light of environmental stewardship as well as societal needs. Allow me to air some thoughts here,
so you can decide whether this is a worthwhile subject for scrutiny.

It's becoming more and more apparent that many recycled materials have no
viable markets here — often, it is said, because of environmental concerns regarding their processing. And so instead of staying within our borders and under our
control, they are shipped abroad beyond the reach of our environmental regulations and/or permissible practices (WTE for instance[7]); thus their potential environmental impact is not mitigated but merely shifted overseas.

For example, discarded plastics are processed and then sold for around $0.21
per pound abroad, where routinely they are burned for their energy value in
combustors of dubious pollution prevention capability. Not surprisingly, there's
the small matter of air pollution borne on the north temperate zone's prevailing
west-to-east winds, in some cases coming to roost in its place of origin . . . a fitting
climax, all things considered.

This in itself would seem to be reason enough to question the wisdom of the
proposition, but wait . . . there's more.

---

[7]WTE stands for "Waste to Energy," and generally involves burning waste material to generate
electricity. Unregulated burning can provide toxic emissions. — EDS.

John Trotti is the editor of *MSW* [municipal solid waste] *Management* magazine. His article appeared in that publication in September 2008.

It takes about 12 barrels of oil to make one ton of polyethylene, which at to-   5
day's going rate amounts to something in the neighborhood of $115 each . . . so
let's do some math.

We take a commodity — oh, you don't like the word? — OK, a recycled material with a value on the local market of $1,380 and sell it abroad for $0.21 per
pound ($420 per ton). Does this sound a bit strange? Don't worry . . . it gets
stranger still.

After the discarded water- and pop bottles [on which advance disposal fees
were deposited at point-of-purchase] have been collected, sorted, compacted,
baled, and containerized at the ratepayers' expense, the freight is now moved by
surface transport to one of several seaports, where longshoremen stage and load it
aboard cargo vessels for shipment across the bounding main to customers whose
major challenge lies in how long it will take to off-load the recycled material and
commoditize it through the simple expedient of burning it for its caloric value.

Am I hallucinating this? Does the idea of giving up $960 worth of a valuable
commodity — one whose strategic significance ranks right up there with the proliferation of weapons of mass destruction — make sense somewhere or somehow?
Well, if you are so steeped in your belief that burning fuel for American energy
is bad, then shipping it to an economic competitor who intends to put it to the
torch with no pretense of environmental concern beyond a little rhetoric, makes
excellent sense.

Is this what you and I had in mind when we supported the rising tide of environmentalism back in the 1980s and '90s, or were we mistaken in viewing the
hierarchy as a means of forwarding and rewarding stewardship? I don't think so,
but let's look at where a decade-and-a-half has gotten us in terms of true stewardship. On the positive side of the ledger, we are diverting a far higher percentage of
our wastes away from our landfills, and we have seen a growing acceptance to the
use of recycled materials in a variety of products. So, too, have we seen an increase
in the public participation in recycling activities and the apparent success of recycling mandated targets. But are these the real measures of stewardship?

I don't know how much faith you and I should place in diversion figures from   10
around the nation, but supposing they're accurate, how germane are they if we've
relinquished the ability to participate responsibly in their return to the world of
commerce? To me that's the real issue, and I'm not sure those responsible for the
supposed success of recycling really want to know the answer.

DISCUSSION QUESTIONS

1. According to Trotti, what has happened to the "rising tide of environmentalism"
   that existed in the 1980s and 1990s?
2. What are his concerns about the way plastics are being disposed of?
3. Analyze his support. How convincing do you find it to be?
4. How convincing do you find his argument as a whole to be?
5. What is his warrant? Do you agree with it?

Argument for Recycling Is Strong

SHARON KNEISS

Recycling is an important and timely topic and a key contributor to a cleaner environment. We were disappointed to see that *MSW Management's* recent editorial oversimplified and overlooked many of the important gains that the US recycling industry has made in recent decades. Worse, the editorial may have left readers with a grossly inaccurate view of an industry with solid growth potential. The future of plastics recycling is actually quite bright. Here are the facts:

- The market for recycled plastic materials is strong.
- In order to increase recycling, we must work to increase collection opportunities.
- The export market is strong for recyclables based on pure economics.
- Seventy percent of plastics manufactured in the United States are made from natural gas.

Let's start with markets for recycled materials. In many cases, demand for recycled plastics has outpaced our ability to supply them. For almost fifteen years, there have been strong domestic markets to purchase recycled plastics, but the recycling industry has not been able to run at full capacity with limited quantities of collected materials. Today it is clearly the lack of supply of post-consumer plastics that keeps our markets from reaching their full potential.

With the current prices of recycled resins strong but still competitive with the prices of virgin resins, existing domestic markets could easily absorb an increase in supply — if we are able to boost the collection of post-consumer recycled materials. This is why the plastics industry is working aggressively to increase access to away-from-home recycling opportunities, boost municipal recycling of plastic bottles and non-bottle containers, and increase awareness through consumer education.

Despite strong domestic markets, about 50 percent of recovered PET and 20 percent of recovered HDPE is exported to China. Why? Simple economics — empty cargo ships headed back to China and a low wage rate make it difficult for domestic recyclers (particularly those on the West coast) to compete for the material. The important thing is that the materials are being purchased at a fair market price and recycled into useful new products.

But the most deeply concerning point in *MSW Management's* editorial is the suggestion that post-consumer plastics are exported to avoid the environmental impacts of recycling. The processes of cleaning, melting, and filtering post-consumer plastics are generally associated with very low levels of energy, minimal emissions, and tiny amounts of solid waste from labels, dirt, and other non-

5

Sharon Kneiss is vice president of the products divisions of the American Chemistry Council. Her response to Trotti appeared in the November–December 2008 edition of *MSW Management.*

recoverable components. In fact, the American Chemistry Council, Association of Postconsumer Plastics Recyclers, National Association for PET Container Resources, and the PET Resin Association are currently collaborating to generate life cycle inventory data to quantify these important environmental indicators for the plastics recycling industry. These data will be made publicly available as soon as they are complete.

The editorial also made a significant (but sadly common) mistake regarding energy used to produce plastics in the United States. Your column claims that "it takes about 12 barrels of oil to make one ton of polyethylene." Rather, it's barrels of oil equivalents — and the actual number is 10.2 barrels of oil equivalents. In the United States, 80 percent of polyethylene (and 70 percent of plastics overall) is made from domestic natural gas.

Finally, there is the issue of energy recovery, or waste-to-energy (WTE). We believe that *MSW Management*'s contention that plastics are sold abroad and "put to the torch" bears reconsidering because common sense suggests that in today's market it is unlikely that someone would pay a premium for recovered resins just to burn them. While these materials do have value as an energy source, that value is enhanced when recovered plastics are manufactured into useful and efficient new products.

The bottom line is that over the last two decades, plastics recycling has grown by leaps and bounds. Unlike the mixed streams that went straight into asphalt for pennies a pound, today's recovered plastics are sorted, cleaned, and processed to perform at levels competitive with virgin resins. We have versatile technologies, strong markets, and healthy demand both domestically and abroad. But our work is not finished. If the industry has an Achilles heel, it is collection. In our view, recovery is where we should be focusing our collective energies.

America's plastics producers are working to increase away-from-home recycling opportunities; to leverage our investments through creative new partnerships; and to increase the recycling of bottles, bags, rigid plastic containers, and even end-of-life vehicles. And above all, we are working to increase the collection of plastic through greater consumer education and awareness of recycling opportunities. We hope you will join us as we continue this industry's proud history of innovation by removing the remaining barriers to achieving our true recycling potential. Plastic is too valuable a resource to waste.

DISCUSSION QUESTIONS

1. How does Kneiss's view of the future of plastics recycling differ from Trotti's?
2. What does she see as the biggest obstacle to recycling at peak capacity?
3. What are the major flaws that Kneiss sees in Trotti's argument?
4. What suggestions does she have for improving plastics recycling?
5. How convincing is her support?
6. What warrant or warrants underlie her argument?
7. Which argument do you find more convincing, Trotti's or Kneiss's?

Assignments for Analyzing Warrants

READING AND DISCUSSION QUESTIONS

1. Should students be given a direct voice in the hiring of faculty members? On what warrants about education do you base your answer?

2. Discuss the validity of the warrant in this statement from the *Watch Tower* (a publication of the Jehovah's Witnesses) about genital herpes: "The sexually loose are indeed 'receiving in themselves the full recompense, which was their due for their error' (Romans 1:27)."

3. In 2010, a judge in Saudi Arabia had to make the decision whether or not a man could be intentionally paralyzed as punishment for having paralyzed another man in a fight. His victim had requested this punishment. What would the judge's warrant be if he chose to order the punishment? What would it be if he decided not to honor the victim's request?

4. In view of the increasing interest in health in general, and nutrition and exercise in particular, do you think that universities and colleges should impose physical education requirements? If so, what form should they take? If not, why not? What warrant underlies your position?

5. What are some of the assumptions underlying the preference for natural foods and medicines? Can *natural* be clearly defined? Is this preference part of a broader philosophy? Try to evaluate the validity of the assumption.

6. The author of the following passage, Katherine Butler Hathaway, became a hunchback as a result of a childhood illness. Here she writes about the relationship between love and beauty from the point of view of someone who is deformed. Discuss the warrants on which the author bases her conclusions.

   > I could secretly pretend that I had a lover . . . but I could never risk showing that I thought such a thing was possible for me . . . with any man. Because of my repeated encounters with the mirror and my irrepressible tendency to forget what I had seen, I had begun to force myself to believe and to remember, and especially to remember, that I would never be chosen for what I imagined to be the supreme and most intimate of all experience. I thought of sexual love as an honor that was too great and too beautiful for the body in which I was doomed to live.

WRITING ASSIGNMENTS

7. In "An Unjust Sacrifice," Robert A. Sirico presents a case in which he finds no justification for letting one Siamese twin die in order to save the other. His belief in the sanctity of human life appears to be absolute, even when it will most likely lead to the death of both twins. Write an essay in which you give examples of how your value system underlies your political views.

8. Write an essay explaining why you think either John Trotti or Sharon Kneiss make a better argument.

9. Both state and federal governments have been embroiled in controversies concerning the rights of citizens to engage in harmful practices. In Massachusetts, for

example, a mandatory seat-belt law was repealed by voters who considered the law an infringement of their freedom. (It was later reinstated.) Write an essay in which you explain what principles you believe should guide government regulation of dangerous practices.

10. Henry David Thoreau writes, "Unjust laws exist: Shall we be content to obey them, or shall we endeavor to amend them, and obey them until we have succeeded, or shall we transgress them at once?" Write an essay in which you explain under what circumstances you would feel compelled to break the law, or why you feel that you would never do so.

Research Readiness: Identifying Reliable Authorities

How can you tell which online information comes from reliable authorities?

In this chapter we have stressed the need for sufficient and appropriate data and reliable authorities. In Chapter 10 we will discuss, at length, how to research a topic and choose reliable sources for an independent research paper. Anytime you use someone else's words or ideas in your writing or formal speaking you should be aware who that person is; you can start now investigating the reliability of any sources you are thinking of quoting or paraphrasing.

We like to think that if information is in print, it is reliable. Unfortunately, that is not always the case. People with unjust biases and even those who want to sow hatred find their way into print. In general, works that appear in print go through a much more extensive vetting process than what appears online, but there are so-called vanity presses that will publish pretty much anything if the author will pay the cost. There are also all sorts of periodicals that express slanted — and often conflicting — points of view, some of them offensive to many of us. That's what comes of freedom of the press.

When you go online, how can you start to weed through a list of results to find reliable authorities? For one thing, you can learn to "read" the list of results you get from *Google* or other search engines.

ASSIGNMENT

1. Go to Google or another general search engine that you are familiar with. Do a search for either "autism and vaccines" or "cell phones and cancer." (You may have used one of these subjects for an earlier exercise.) Before you click on a link, examine the first ten to fifteen entries in the resulting list. Look at each URL and see what you can learn from it. Also notice any other information that might affect your opinion of the source's reliability or objectivity.

   - Are there sources that you immediately trust as reliable? Which ones, and why?

   - Are there any that you immediately assume will present a biased perspective? Which ones, and why?

   - Are there any that are completely unfamiliar to you? If so, choose two or three and speculate what type of source each might be.

2. Now click on a couple of the sources that you trusted as being reliable. Identify exactly who wrote the document that you have accessed. If you cannot find an author, what does that suggest? If there is an author, search that person's name and see if you find convincing credentials that support the assumption that he or she is qualified to write on the subject at hand.

3. Do the same with at least two sources that you predicted would be biased. Does further investigation support your assumption?

4. Go to at least one of the sources that were unfamiliar to you. Once you look more closely at the source, do you find any evidence of its reliability or lack thereof? Explain.

8

Logic

$\mathbf{T}$hroughout the book we have pointed out the weaknesses that cause arguments to break down. In the vast majority of cases these weaknesses represent breakdowns in logic or the reasoning process. We call such weaknesses *fallacies*, a term derived from Latin. Sometimes these false or erroneous arguments are deliberate; in fact, the Latin word *fallere* means "to deceive." But more often these arguments are either carelessly constructed or unintentionally flawed. Thoughtful readers learn to recognize them; thoughtful writers learn to avoid them.

The reasoning process was first given formal expression by Aristotle. In his famous treatises, he described the way we try to discover the truth — observing the world, selecting impressions, making inferences, generalizing. In this process Aristotle identified two forms of reasoning: *induction* and *deduction*. Both forms, he realized, are subject to error. Our observations may be incorrect or insufficient, and our conclusions may be faulty because they have violated the rules governing the relationship between statements. Induction and deduction are not reserved only for formal arguments about important problems; they also represent our everyday thinking about the most ordinary matters. As for the fallacies, they, too, unfortunately, may crop up anywhere, whenever we are careless in our use of the reasoning process.

In this chapter we examine some of the most common fallacies. First, however, a closer look at induction and deduction will make clear what happens when fallacies occur.

Induction

Induction is the form of reasoning in which we come to conclusions about the whole on the basis of observations of particular instances. If you notice that prices on the four items you bought in the campus bookstore are higher than similar items in the bookstore in town, you may come to the conclusion that the campus store is a more expensive place to shop. If you also noticed that most of the instructors you saw on the first day of school were wearing faded jeans and sandals, you might say that your school's teachers are generally informal in their dress. In both cases you have made an *inductive leap*, reasoning from what you have learned about a few examples to what you think is true of a whole class of things.

How safe are you in coming to these conclusions? The reliability of your conclusion depends on the quantity and quality of your observations. Were four items out of the thousands available in the campus store a sufficiently large sample? Would you come to the same conclusion if you chose fifty items? Might another selection have produced a different conclusion? As for the casually dressed instructors, perhaps further investigation would disclose that the teachers wearing jeans were all teaching assistants and that professors usually wore business clothes. Or the difference might lie in the academic discipline; anthropology teachers might turn out to dress less formally than business school teachers.

In these two situations, you could come closer to verifying your conclusions by further observation and experience — that is, by pricing more items at both stores over a longer period of time and by coming into contact with a greater number of teachers during a whole semester. Even without pricing every item in both stores or encountering every instructor on campus, you would be more confident of your generalization as the quality and quantity of your samples increased.

In some cases you can observe all the instances in a particular situation. For example, by acquiring information about the religious beliefs of all the residents of the dormitory, you can arrive at an accurate assessment of the number of Buddhists. But since our ability to make definitive observations about everything is limited, we must also make an inductive leap about categories of things that we ourselves can never encounter in their entirety. For some generalizations, as we have learned about evidence, we rely on the testimony of reliable witnesses who report that they have experienced or observed many more instances of the phenomenon. A television documentary may give us information about unwed teenage mothers in a city neighborhood; four girls are interviewed and followed for several days by the reporter. Are these girls typical of thousands of others? A sociologist on the program assures us that, in fact, they are. She herself has consulted with hundreds of other young mothers and can vouch for the fact that a conclusion about them, based on our observation of the four, will be sound. Obviously, though, our conclusion can only be probable, not certain. The sociologist's sample is large, but can account only for hundreds, not thousands, and there may be unexamined cases that will seriously weaken our conclusions.

In other cases, we may rely on a principle known in science as "the uniformity of nature." We assume that certain conclusions about oak trees in the temperate zone of North America, for example, will also be true for oak trees growing elsewhere under similar climatic conditions. We also use this principle in attempting to explain the causes of behavior in human beings. If we discover that institutionalization of some children from infancy results in severe emotional retardation, we think it safe to conclude that under the same circumstances all children would suffer the same consequences. As in the previous example, we are aware that certainty about every case of institutionalization is impossible. With rare exceptions, the process of induction can offer only probability, not certain truth.

SAMPLE ESSAY   An Inductive Argument

True or False: Schools Fail Immigrants

RICHARD ROTHSTEIN

Acommon indictment of public schools is that they no longer offer upward mobility to most immigrants. It is said that in the first half of the twentieth century, children learned English, went to college, and joined the middle class but that many of today's immigrants are more likely to drop out, take dead-end jobs, or end up in prison.

Many true accounts reinforce these beliefs. But less noticed are equally valid anecdotes pointing to an opposite claim.

Policy by anecdote is flawed because too often we notice only what confirms our preconceptions. California's recent experience with Mexican immigrants provides ample material for stories about school failure. But on a day to celebrate the American promise, we might also turn to anecdotes of another kind.

Recent college commencements across California featured many immigrants from impoverished families whose first language was Spanish, who came through much-maligned bilingual education programs, learned English, and now head for graduate schools or professions.

At California State University at Fresno, for example, about 700 of 4,000 gradu-   5 ates this spring were Latino, typically the first in their families to attend college. Top-ranked were Pedro Nava and Maria Rocio Magaña, Mexican-born children of farm laborers and cannery workers.

Mr. Nava did not settle in the United States until the third grade. Before that, he lived in migrant labor camps during harvests and in Mexico the rest of the year. His California schooling was in Spanish until the fifth grade, when he was moved to English instruction. Now, with a college degree, he has enrolled in management and teacher training courses.

Ms. Magaña did not place into English classes until the second half of the eleventh grade. Now fluent in both academic and conversational English, she will soon begin a Ph.D. program in anthropology at the University of Chicago.

Their achievements are not unique. Both credit success to their mothers' emphasis on education. Both mothers enrolled in English and high school equivalency courses at the local community college.

Richard Rothstein is a research associate of the Economic Policy Institute, a senior correspondent of the *American Prospect*, and the former national education columnist of the *New York Times*, where this article appeared on July 4, 2001. He is the author of *The Way We Were: Myths and Realities of America's Student Achievement* (1997), *All Else Equal: Are Public and Private Schools Different?* (2003), and *The Charter School Dust-Up* (2005).

Across California, these two-year institutions play an especially important role for immigrants.

Lourdes Andrade just finished her junior year at Brown University, having   10
transferred there after getting associate of arts degrees in history and liberal arts at Oxnard Community College, about forty miles northwest of Los Angeles.

Ms. Andrade arrived here at the age of four and all through elementary school worked with her mother making beds and cleaning bathrooms in hotels. Ms. Andrade, too, attributes her success to her mother's strong academic pressure and also to mentoring she received in a federally financed program to give extra academic support to migrant children.

The program's director, Lorenzo Moraza, also grew up speaking only Spanish. Now a school principal, Mr. Moraza estimates that about 30 percent of the immigrant children he has worked with acquired public school records that led them to college. Those who receive bachelor's degrees are many fewer, but Mr. Moraza says he thinks most drop out of college for economic reasons, not academic ones.

At the Fresno campus, nearly two-thirds of the immigrants and children of immigrants who enter as freshmen eventually graduate. The university operates special support services to help them do so.

You cannot spend time in California without noticing an extensive middle class of Latino schoolteachers, doctors, lawyers, and small-business people. Not all are recent immigrants, but many are. Some attended Catholic schools, but most are products of the public system. Many had bilingual education in the 1970s, 80s, and 90s. California has now banned such instruction, assuming it failed.

There are plenty of anecdotes to support a claim that schools fail immigrant   15
children or an equally persuasive claim that schools serve them well. Getting better statistics should be a priority. Government numbers do not distinguish between students who are immigrants (or whose parents immigrated) from Hispanics with American roots for several generations.

To help interpret California's experience, the best federal data tell only that in 1996, there were 100,000 college students nationwide who were American citizens born in Mexico. This is less than 1 percent of all college students. But uncounted are even larger numbers of those born here to recent migrants.

Even a balanced collection of anecdotes that include successes as well as failures cannot determine whether California schools are less effective than we should expect, and whether wholesale change is needed to move more immigrants to the middle class. But the answer is certainly more complex than the stereotypes of systematic failure that pervade most accounts.

Analysis

An inductive argument proceeds by examining particulars and arriving at a generalization that represents a probable truth. The author of this article arrives at the truth he will defend — that public schools have been more successful than is often acknowledged in moving many immigrants into the middle class — by offering statistical data and a number of stories about immigrants from poor families who have entered graduate school or one of the professions.

Rothstein begins, as many arguers do, with a brief summary of the popular position with which he disagrees. At the end of the third paragraph, he announces that he will provide examples that point to a different conclusion.

The reader should ask three questions of an inductive argument: Is the evidence sufficient? Is it representative? Is it up-to-date? The evidence that Rothstein assembles consists of a series of anecdotes and statistical data about the performance of immigrant students. The success stories of five real persons are impressive, despite limitations imposed by the brevity of the essay, in part because they offer vivid examples of struggle that appeal to our emotions and bring to life an issue with which some of us may not be familiar. But five stories are hardly enough to prove a case; perhaps they are not representative. Rothstein, therefore, adds other data about the rate at which immigrant students graduate and the growing number of Latino professionals and businesspeople.

Although the essay was published in 2001, his numbers are drawn from the 1990s and are thus a bit dated. A look at more recent data would reveal whether his conclusions remain valid.

The reader has some reason to believe that the facts are accurate. At the time this article was published, Rothstein wrote a regular column for a prestigious daily newspaper whose readers would have been quick to find errors in arguments of which they were critical. At the same time, he does not claim that his argument is beyond debate, since the data are incomplete. Even the title suggests that the issue is still unsettled. Modesty in the arguer is always welcome and disposes the reader to view the argument more favorably.

PRACTICE

Read Goldberg's essay "Connecting the Dots . . . to Terrorism" (p. 238). Explain how Goldberg uses inductive reasoning in the essay while not structuring the whole essay around it. What larger purpose does he have in the essay, and how does inductive reasoning help him achieve that purpose?

Deduction

While induction attempts to arrive at the truth, deduction guarantees sound relationships between statements. Unlike the conclusions from induction, which are only probable, the conclusions from deduction are certain. The simplest deductive argument consists of two premises and a conclusion. In outline such an argument looks like this:

Major Premise: All students with 3.5 averages and above for three years are invited to become members of Kappa Gamma Pi, the honor society.

Minor Premise:	George has had a 3.8 average for over three years.
Conclusion:	Therefore, he will be invited to join Kappa Gamma Pi.

This deductive conclusion is *valid*, or logically consistent, because it follows necessarily from the premises. No other conclusion is possible. Validity, however, refers only to the form of the argument. The argument itself may not be satisfactory if the premises are not true — if Kappa Gamma Pi has imposed other conditions or if George has only a 3.4 average. The difference between truth and validity is important because it alerts us to the necessity for examining the truth of the premises before we decide that the conclusion is sound.

One way of discovering how the deductive process works is to look at the methods used by Sherlock Holmes, that most famous of literary detectives, in solving his mysteries. His reasoning process follows a familiar pattern. Through the inductive process — that is, observing the particulars of the world — he came to certain conclusions about those particulars. Then he applied deductive reasoning to come to a conclusion about a particular person or event.

On one occasion Holmes observed that a man sitting opposite him on a train had chalk dust on his fingers. From this observation Holmes deduced that the man was a schoolteacher. If his thinking were outlined, it would take the form of the syllogism, the classic form of deductive reasoning:

Major Premise:	All men with chalk dust on their fingers are school-teachers.
Minor Premise:	This man has chalk dust on his fingers.
Conclusion:	Therefore, this man is a schoolteacher.

One dictionary defines *syllogism* as "a formula of argument consisting of three propositions." The major premise offers a generalization about a large group or class. This generalization has been arrived at through inductive reasoning or observation of particulars. The minor premise makes a statement about a member of that group or class. The third proposition is the conclusion, which links the other two propositions, in much the same way that the warrant links the support and the claim.

If we look back at the syllogism that summarizes Holmes's thinking, we see how it represents the deductive process. The major premise, the first statement, is an inductive generalization, a statement arrived at after observation of a number of men with chalk on their fingers. The minor premise, the second statement, assigns a particular member, the man on the train, to the general class of those who have dust on their fingers.

But although the argument may be logical, it is faulty. The deductive argument is only as strong as its premises. As Lionel Ruby pointed out, Sherlock Holmes was often wrong.[1] Holmes once deduced from the size of a large hat found in the street that the owner was intelligent. He obviously believed that

---

[1] *The Art of Making Sense* (Philadelphia: Lippincott, 1954), ch. 17.

a large head meant a large brain and that a large brain indicated intelligence. Had he lived one hundred years later, new information about the relationship of brain size to intelligence would have enabled him to come to a different and better conclusion.

In this case, we might first object to the major premise, the generalization that all men with chalk dust on their fingers are schoolteachers. Is it true? Perhaps all the men with dusty fingers whom Holmes had so far observed had turned out to be schoolteachers, but was his sample sufficiently large to allow him to conclude that all dust-fingered men, even those with whom he might never have contact, were teachers? Were there no other vocations or situations that might require the use of chalk? In Holmes's day draftsmen or carpenters or tailors might have had fingers just as white as those of schoolteachers. In other words, Holmes may have ascertained that all schoolteachers have chalk dust on their fingers, but he had not determined that *only* schoolteachers could be thus identified. Sometimes it is helpful to draw a Venn diagram, circles representing the various groups in their relation to the whole.

If a large circle (see the figure below) represents all those who have chalk dust on their fingers, we see that several different groups may be contained in this universe. To be safe, Holmes should have deduced that the man on the train *might* have been a schoolteacher; he was not safe in deducing more than that. Obviously, if the inductive generalization or major premise is false, the conclusion of the particular argument is also false or invalid.

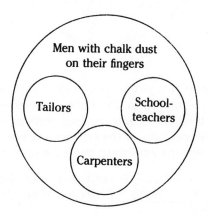

The deductive argument may also go wrong elsewhere. What if the minor premise is untrue? Could Holmes have mistaken the source of the white powder on the man's fingers? Suppose it was not chalk dust but flour or confectioner's sugar or talcum or heroin? Any of these possibilities would weaken or invalidate his conclusion.

Another example, closer to the kinds of arguments you will examine, reveals the flaw in the deductive process.

Major Premise:	All Communists oppose organized religion.
Minor Premise:	Robert Roe opposes organized religion.
Conclusion:	Therefore, Robert Roe is a Communist.

The common name for this fallacy is "guilt by association." The fact that two things share an attribute does not mean that they are the same thing. The following diagram makes clear that Robert Roe and Communists do not necessarily share all attributes. Remembering that Holmes may have misinterpreted the signs of chalk on the traveler's fingers, we may also want to question whether Robert Roe's opposition to organized religion has been misinterpreted.

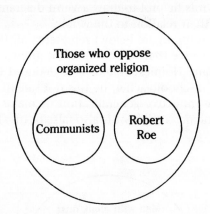

Some deductive arguments give trouble because one of the premises, usually the major premise, is omitted. As in the warrants we examined in Chapter 7, a failure to evaluate the truth of the unexpressed premise may lead to an invalid conclusion. When only two parts of the syllogism appear, we call the resulting form an *enthymeme.* Suppose we overhear the following snatch of conversation:

"Did you hear about Jean's father? He had a heart attack last week."
"That's too bad. But I'm not surprised. I know he always refused to go for his annual physical checkups."

The second speaker has used an unexpressed major premise, the cause-and-effect warrant "If you have annual physical checkups, you can avoid heart attacks." He does not express it because he assumes that it is unnecessary to do so. The first speaker recognizes the unspoken warrant and may agree with it. Or the first speaker may produce evidence from reputable sources that such a generalization is by no means universally true, in which case the conclusion of the second speaker is suspect.

A knowledge of the deductive process can help guide you toward an evaluation of the soundness of your reasoning in an argument you are constructing. The syllogism is often clearer than an outline in establishing the relations between the different parts of an argument.

Setting down your own or someone else's argument in this form will not necessarily give you the answers to questions about how to support your claim, but it should clearly indicate what your claims are and, above all, what logical connections exist between your statements.

SAMPLE ANNOTATED ESSAY   A Deductive Argument

It's All about Him

DAVID VON DREHLE

The author establishes his knowledge of mass murders, his "claim to authority."

M y reporter's odyssey has taken me from the chill dawn outside the Florida prison in which serial killer Ted Bundy met his end, to the charred façade of a Bronx nightclub where Julio Gonzalez incinerated eighty-seven people, to a muddy Colorado hillside overlooking the Columbine High School library, in which Eric Harris and Dylan Klebold wrought their mayhem. Along the way, I've come to believe that we're looking for why in all the wrong places.

I've lost interest in the cracks, chips, holes, and broken places in the lives of men like Cho Seung-Hui, the mass murderer of Virginia Tech. The pain, grievances, and self-pity of mass killers are only symptoms of the real explanation. Those who do these things share one common trait. They are raging narcissists. "I died — like Jesus Christ," Cho said in a video sent to NBC.

His thesis statement (and major premise): mass murderers are narcissists

Psychologists from South Africa to Chicago have begun to recognize that extreme self-centeredness is the forest in these stories, and all the other things — guns, games, lyrics, pornography — are just trees. To list the traits of the narcissist is enough to prove the point: grandiosity, numbness to the needs and pain of others, emotional isolation, resentment, and envy.

The traits of the narcissist

In interviews with Ted Bundy taped a quarter-century ago, journalists Stephen Michaud and Hugh Aynesworth

David von Drehle is editor-at-large for *Time* magazine. His most recent book is *Triangle: The Fire That Changed America* (2003). This article appeared in *Time* on April 30, 2007.

Major premise applied to
Ted Bundy

captured the essence of homicidal narcissism. Through
hour after tedious hour, a man who killed 30 or more
young women and girls preened for his audience. He
spoke of himself as an actor, of life as a series of roles,
and of other people as props and scenery. His desires
were simple: "control" and "mastery." He took whatever
he wanted, from shoplifted tube socks to human lives,
because nothing mattered beyond his desires. Bundy
said he was always surprised that anyone noticed his
victims had vanished. "I mean, there are so many
people," he explained. The only death he regretted was
his own.

Criminologists distinguish between serial killers like   5
Bundy, whose crimes occur one at a time and who try
hard to avoid capture, and mass killers like Cho. But the
central role of narcissism plainly connects them. Only
a narcissist could decide that his alienation should be
underlined in the blood of strangers. The flamboyant
nature of these crimes is like a neon sign pointing to
the truth. Charles Whitman playing God in his Texas
clock tower, James Huberty spraying lead in a California
restaurant, Harris and Klebold in their theatrical trench
coats — they're all stars in the cinema of their self-
absorbed minds.

Freud explained narcissism as a failure to grow up. All
infants are narcissists, he pointed out, but as we grow, we
ought to learn that other people have lives independent
of our own. It's not their job to please us, applaud for us,
or even notice us — let alone die because we're unhappy.

A generation ago, the social critic Christopher Lasch
diagnosed narcissism as the signal disorder of contemporary American culture. The cult of celebrity, the marketing of instant gratification, skepticism toward moral
codes, and the politics of victimhood were signs of a
society regressing toward the infant stage. You don't have
to buy Freud's explanation or Lasch's indictment, however, to see an immediate danger in the way we examine
the lives of mass killers. Earnestly and honestly, detectives and journalists dig up apparent clues and weave
them into a sort of explanation. In the days after Columbine, for example, Harris and Klebold emerged as alienated misfits in the jock culture of their suburban high
school. We learned about their morbid taste in music and
their violent video games. Largely missing, though, was
the proper frame around the picture: the extreme narcis-

Other examples of narcissistic
mass murderers

Freud said narcissists never
grow up. They put their happiness over others' lives.

Investigators have failed
to recognize narcissism as
the real motivation in mass
murder cases.

sism that licensed these boys, in their minds, to murder their teachers and classmates.

Major premise applied to Cho

Something similar is now going on with Cho, whose florid writings and videos were an almanac of gripes. "I'm so lonely," he moped to a teacher, failing to mention that he often refused to answer even when people said hello. Of course he was lonely.

In Holocaust studies, there is a school of thought that says to explain is to forgive. I won't go that far. But we must stop explaining killers on their terms. Minus the clear context of narcissism, the biographical details of these men can begin to look like a plausible chain of cause and effect — especially to other narcissists. And they don't need any more encouragement.

Outside the context of narcissism, the murderers' actions can seem too logical.

There's a telling moment in Michael Moore's film *Bowling for Columbine*, in which singer Marilyn Manson   10 dismisses the idea that listening to his lyrics contributed to the disintegration of Harris and Klebold. What the Columbine killers needed, Manson suggests, was for someone to listen to them. This is the narcissist's view of narcissism: Everything would be fine if only he received more attention. The real problem can be found in the killer's mirror.

The author reiterates that the killer's problem is not lack of attention but how the killer sees himself.

Analysis

Von Drehle wrote "It's All about Him" shortly after the 2007 massacre at Virginia Tech. Although we cannot know exactly how he arrived at the thesis, we can reasonably assume he went through something of an inductive process on the way to writing this deductive essay. Perhaps he read and watched enough about Cho, the shooter at Virginia Tech, to start to hypothesize about Cho's motivation. His earlier observations of other mass murderers led him to notice similarities among them. Once he arrived at a theory about what they had in common, he had the major premise for a deductive argument that he could test out on other mass murderers. He was able to construct an argument that could be summarized in syllogistic form:

Major Premise: Mass murderers are narcissistic.

Minor Premise: Cho was a mass murderer.

Conclusion: Cho was narcissistic.

In his essay he presents his major premise early and then applies it to other U.S. mass murderers: Ted Bundy, Charles Whitman, James Huberty, Eric Harris, and Dylan Klebold.

If von Drehle's major and minor premises are true, the conclusion, of necessity, must be true. That Cho was a mass murderer is an indisputable fact; thus the minor premise is true. But what of the major premise? If you applied the deduction that mass murderers are narcissistic to mass murderers not mentioned by von Drehle, would the conclusion be the same in each case? In other words, is it true that mass murderers are narcissistic?

Because it would be virtually impossible to apply von Drehle's deduction to all mass murderers, he would have built a more convincing case had he restricted his thesis statement with a word like *most* or *many*. That, however, would have invalidated the deductive logic that tells us that a syllogism's conclusion must be true. As it is, the examples he offers are not enough to convince all readers that his theory of narcissism is valid. Still, he offers a unique look at the motivation of mass murderers and one that makes it impossible for anyone else to be blamed for the crimes that these men and boys have committed. Behind his argument are his many years of journalistic experience and his opening revelation that he has been on the scene during the aftermath of many of the crimes to which he refers.

Common Fallacies

In this necessarily brief review it would be impossible to discuss all the fallacies listed by logicians, but we can examine the ones most likely to be found in the arguments you will read and write. Fallacies are difficult to classify, first, because there are literally dozens of systems for classifying, and second, because under any system there is always a good deal of overlap. Our discussion of the reasoning process, however, tells us where faulty reasoning occurs.

Inductive fallacies, as we know, result from the wrong use of evidence: That is, the arguer leaps to a conclusion on the basis of an insufficient sample, ignoring evidence that might have altered his or her conclusion. Deductive fallacies, on the other hand, result from a failure to follow the logic of a series of statements. Here the arguer neglects to make a clear connection between the parts of his or her argument. One of the commonest strategies is the introduction of an irrelevant issue, one that has little or no direct bearing on the development of the claim and serves only to distract the reader.

It's helpful to remember that, even if you cannot name the particular fallacy, you can learn to recognize it and not only refute it in the arguments of others but avoid it in your own as well.

Hasty Generalization

In Chapter 6 (see pp. 202–68) we discussed the dangers in drawing conclusions on the basis of insufficient evidence. Many of our prejudices are a result of hasty generalization. A prejudice is literally a judgment made before the facts are in. On the basis of experience with two or three members of an ethnic group, for example, we may form the prejudice that all members of the group share the characteristics that we have attributed to the two or three in our experience.

Superstitions are also based in part on hasty generalization. As a result of a very small number of experiences with black cats, broken mirrors, Friday the thirteenth, or spilled salt, some people will assume a cause-and-effect relation between these signs and misfortunes. *Superstition* has been defined as "a notion maintained despite evidence to the contrary." The evidence would certainly show that, contrary to the superstitious belief, in a lifetime hundreds of such "unlucky" signs are not followed by unfortunate events. To generalize about a connection is therefore unjustified.

Faulty Use of Authority

The use of authority — the attempt to bolster claims by citing the opinions of experts — was discussed in Chapter 6. Experts are a valuable source of information on subjects we have no personal experience with or specialized knowledge about. Properly identified, they can provide essential support. The faulty use of authority occurs when individuals are presented as authorities in fields in which they are not. An actor who plays a doctor on television may be hired to advertise the latest sleep medicine but actually has no more expertise with medications than the average consumer. The role that he plays may make him appear to be an authority but does not make him one. No matter how impressive credentials sound, they are largely meaningless unless they establish relevant authority. Both writers and readers need to be especially aware of the testimony of authorities who may disagree with those cited. In circumstances where experts disagree, you are encouraged to undertake a careful evaluation and comparison of credentials.

Post Hoc or Doubtful Cause

The entire Latin term for this fallacy is *post hoc, ergo propter hoc*, meaning, "After this, therefore because of this." The arguer infers that because one event follows another event, the first event must be the cause of the second. But proximity of events or conditions does not guarantee a causal relation. The rooster crows every morning at 5:00 and, seeing the sun rise immediately after, decides that his crowing has caused the sun to rise. A month after A-bomb tests are concluded, tornadoes damage the area where the tests were held, and residents decide that the tests caused the tornadoes. After the school principal suspends daily prayers in the classroom, acts of vandalism increase, and some parents are convinced that failure to conduct prayer is responsible for the rise in vandalism. In each of these cases, the fact that one event follows another does not prove a causal connection. The two events may be coincidental, or the first event may be only one, and an insignificant one, of many causes that have produced the second event. The reader or writer of causal arguments must determine whether another more plausible explanation exists and whether several causes have combined to produce the effect. Perhaps the suspension of prayer was only one of a number of related causes: a decline in disciplinary action, a relaxation of academic standards, a change in school administration, and changes in family structure in the school community.

In a previous section we saw that superstitions are the result not only of hasty generalization but also of the willingness to find a cause-and-effect connection in the juxtaposition of two events. A belief in astrological signs also derives from erroneous inferences about cause and effect. Only a very few of the millions of people who consult the astrology charts every day in newspapers and magazines have submitted the predictions to statistical analysis. A curious reader might try this strategy: Save the columns, usually at the beginning or end of the year, in which astrologers and clairvoyants make predictions for events in the coming year, allegedly based on their reading of the stars and other signs. At the end of the year evaluate the percentage of predictions that were fulfilled. The number will be very small. But even if some of the predictions prove true, there may be other less fanciful explanations for their accuracy.

In defending simple explanations against complex ones, philosophers and scientists often refer to a maxim called *Occam's razor,* a principle formulated by the medieval philosopher and theologian William of Occam. A modern science writer says this principle "urges a preference for the simplest hypothesis that does all we want it to do."[2] In other words, choose the simpler, more credible explanation wherever possible.

We all share the belief that scientific experimentation and research can answer questions about a wide range of natural and social phenomena: evolutionary development, hurricanes, disease, crime, poverty. It is true that repeated experiments in controlled situations can establish what seem to be solid relations suggesting cause and effect. But even scientists prefer to talk not about cause but about an extremely high probability that under controlled conditions one event will follow another.

In the social sciences cause-and-effect relations are especially susceptible to challenge. Human experiences can seldom be subjected to laboratory conditions. In addition, the complexity of the social environment makes it difficult, even impossible, to extract one cause from among the many that influence human behavior.

False Analogy

Many analogies are merely descriptive and offer no proof of the connection between the two things being compared. In recent years a debate has emerged between weight-loss professionals about the wisdom of urging overweight people to lose weight for health reasons. Susan Wooley, director of the eating disorders

---

[2]Martin Gardner, *The Whys of a Philosophical Scrivener* (New York: Quill, 1983), p. 174.

clinic at the University of Cincinnati and a professor of psychiatry, offered the following analogy in defense of her view that dieting is dangerous.

> We know that overweight people have a higher mortality rate than thin people. We also know that black people have a higher mortality rate than white people. Do we subject black people to torturous treatments to bleach their skin? Of course not. We have enough sense to know skin-bleaching will not eliminate sickle-cell anemia. So why do we have blind faith that weight loss will cure the diseases associated with obesity?[3]

But it is clear that the false analogy between black skin and excessive weight does not work. Bleaching one's skin does not eliminate sickle-cell anemia, but there is an abundance of proof that excess weight influences mortality.

Historians are fond of using analogical arguments to demonstrate that particular circumstances prevailing in the past are being reproduced in the present. They therefore feel safe in predicting that the present course of history will follow that of the past. British historian Arnold Toynbee argues by analogy that humans' tenure on earth may be limited.

> On the evidence of the past history of life on this planet, even the extinction of the human race is not entirely unlikely. After all, the reign of man on the Earth, if we are right in thinking that man established his present ascendancy in the middle paleolithic age, is so far only about 100,000 years old, and what is that compared to the 500 million or 900 million years during which life has been in existence on the surface of this planet? In the past, other forms of life have enjoyed reigns which have lasted for almost inconceivably longer periods — and which yet at last have come to an end.[4]

Toynbee finds similarities between the limited reigns of other animal species and the possible disappearance of the human race. For this analogy, however, we need to ask whether the conditions of the past, so far as we know them, at all resemble the conditions under which human existence on earth might be terminated. Is the fact that human beings are also members of the animal kingdom sufficient support for this comparison?

Ad Hominem

The Latin term *ad hominem* means "against the man" and refers to an attack on the person rather than on the argument or the issue. The assumption in such a fallacy is that if the speaker proves to be unacceptable in some way, his or her statements must also be judged unacceptable. Attacking the author of the statement is a strategy of diversion that prevents the reader from giving attention where it is due — to the issue under discussion.

---

[3] *New York Times,* April 12, 1992, sec. C, p. 43.
[4] *Civilization on Trial* (New York: Oxford University Press, 1948), pp. 162–63.

You might hear someone complain, "What can the priest tell us about marriage? He's never been married himself." This ad hominem accusation ignores the validity of the advice the priest might offer. In the same way an overweight patient might reject the advice on diet by an overweight physician. In politics it is not uncommon for antagonists to attack each other for personal characteristics that may not be relevant to the tasks they will be elected to perform. They may be accused of infidelity to their partners, homosexuality, atheism, or a flamboyant social life. Even if certain accusations should be proved true, voters should not ignore the substance of what politicians do and say in their public offices.

This confusion of private life with professional record also exists in literature and the other arts. According to their biographers, the American writers Thomas Wolfe, Robert Frost, and William Saroyan — to name only a few — and numbers of film stars, including Charlie Chaplin, Joan Crawford, and Bing Crosby, made life miserable for those closest to them. Having read about their unpleasant personal characteristics, some people find it hard to separate the artist from his or her creation, although the personality and character of the artist are often irrelevant to the content of the work.

Ad hominem accusations against the person do *not* constitute a fallacy if the characteristics under attack are relevant to the argument. If the politician is irresponsible and dishonest in the conduct of his or her personal life, we may be justified in thinking that the person will also behave irresponsibly and dishonestly in public office.

False Dilemma

As the name tells us, the false dilemma, sometimes called the *black-white fallacy,* poses an either-or situation. The arguer suggests that only two alternatives exist, although there may be other explanations of or solutions to the problem under discussion. The false dilemma reflects the simplification of a complex problem. Sometimes it is offered out of ignorance or laziness, sometimes to divert attention from the real explanation or solution that the arguer rejects for doubtful reasons.

You may encounter the either-or situation in dilemmas about personal choices. "At the University of Georgia," says one writer, "the measure of a man was football. You either played it or worshiped those who did, and there was no middle ground."[5] Clearly this dilemma — playing football or worshiping those who do — ignores other measures of manhood.

Politics and government offer a wealth of examples. In an interview with the *New York Times* in 1975, the Shah of Iran was asked why he could not introduce into his authoritarian regime greater freedom for his subjects. His reply was, "What's wrong with authority? Is anarchy better?" Apparently he considered that only two paths were open to him — authoritarianism or anarchy. Of course, democracy was also an option, which, perhaps fatally, he declined to consider.

[5] Phil Gailey, "A Nonsports Fan," *New York Times Magazine,* December 18, 1983, sec. 6, p. 96.

The fallacy of the false dilemma is when an argument presents only two choices.

Slippery Slope

If an arguer predicts that taking a first step will lead inevitably to a second, usually undesirable step, he or she must provide evidence that this will happen. Otherwise, the arguer is guilty of a slippery slope fallacy.

Predictions based on the danger inherent in taking the first step are commonplace:

> Legalization of abortion will lead to murder of the old and the physically and mentally handicapped.

> The Connecticut law allowing sixteen-year-olds and their parents to divorce each other will mean the death of the family.

> If we ban handguns, we will end up banning rifles and other hunting weapons.

Distinguishing between probable and improbable predictions — that is, recognizing the slippery-slope fallacy — poses special problems because only future developments can verify or refute predictions. For example, in 1941 the imposition of military conscription aroused some opponents to predict that the draft was a precursor of fascism in this country. Only after the war, when 10 million draftees were demobilized, did it become clear that the draft had been an insufficient sign for a prediction of fascism. In this case the slippery-slope prediction of fascism might have been avoided if closer attention had been paid to other influences pointing to the strength of democracy.

More recently, the debate about cloning has raised fears of creation of genetic copies of adults. The *New York Times* reported that

> Many lawmakers today warned that if therapeutic cloning went forward, scientists would step onto a slippery slope that would inevitably lead to cloning people.[6]

Most scientists, however, reject this possibility for the foreseeable future.

Slippery-slope predictions are simplistic. They ignore not only the dissimilarities between first and last steps but also the complexity of the developments in any long chain of events.

Begging the Question

If the writer makes a statement that assumes that the very question being argued has already been proved, the writer is guilty of begging the question. In a letter to the editor of a college newspaper protesting the failure of the majority of students to meet the writing requirement because they had failed an exemption test, the writer said, "Not exempting all students who honestly qualify for exemption is an insult." But whether the students are honestly qualified is precisely the question that the exemption test was supposed to resolve. The writer has not proved that the students who failed the writing test were qualified for exemption. She has only made an assertion *as if* she had already proved it.

Circular reasoning is an extreme example of begging the question: "Women should not be permitted to join men's clubs because the clubs are for men only." The question to be resolved first, of course, is whether clubs for men only should continue to exist.

Straw Man

The straw-man fallacy consists of an attack on a view similar to but not the same as the one your opponent holds. It is a familiar diversionary tactic. The name probably derives from an old game in which a straw man was set up to divert attention from the real target that a contestant was supposed to knock down.

---

[6]August 1, 2001, sec. A, p. 11.

A straw-man argument attempts to divert attention away from the real issue.

One of the outstanding examples of the straw-man fallacy occurred in the famous Checkers speech of Senator Richard Nixon. In 1952, during his vice-presidential campaign, Nixon was accused of having appropriated $18,000 in campaign funds for his personal use. At one point in the radio and television speech in which he defended his reputation, he said:

> One other thing I probably should tell you, because if I don't they will probably be saying this about me, too. We did get something, a gift, after the election.
>
> A man down in Texas heard Pat on the radio mention the fact that our two youngsters would like to have a dog, and, believe it or not, the day before we left on this campaign trip we got a message from Union Station in Baltimore saying they had a package for us. We went down to get it. You know what it was?
>
> It was a little cocker spaniel dog, in a crate that he had sent all the way from Texas, black and white, spotted, and our little girl, Tricia, the six-year-old, named it Checkers.

And, you know, the kids, like all kids, loved the dog, and I just want to say this, right now, that regardless of what they say about it, we are going to keep it.[7]

Of course, Nixon knew that the issue was the alleged misappropriation of funds, not the ownership of the dog, which no one had asked him to return.

Two Wrongs Make a Right

The two-wrongs-make-a-right fallacy is another example of the way in which attention may be diverted from the question at issue.

After President Jimmy Carter in March 1977 attacked the human rights record of the Soviet Union, Russian officials responded:

As for the present state of human rights in the United States, it is characterized by the following facts: millions of unemployed, racial discrimination, social inequality of women, infringement of citizens' personal freedom, the growth of crime, and so on.[8]

The Russians made no attempt to deny the failure of *their* human rights record; instead they attacked by pointing out that the Americans are not blameless either.

Non Sequitur

The Latin term *non sequitur,* which means "it does not follow," is another fallacy of irrelevance. An advertisement for a book, *Worlds in Collision,* whose theories about the origin of the earth and evolutionary development have been challenged by almost all reputable scientists, states:

Once rejected as "preposterous"! Critics called it an outrage! It aroused incredible antagonism in scientific and literary circles. Yet half a million copies were sold and for twenty-seven years it remained an outstanding bestseller.

We know, of course, that the popularity of a book does not bestow scientific respectability. The number of sales, therefore, is irrelevant to proof of the book's theoretical soundness — a non sequitur.

Other examples sometimes appear in the comments of political candidates. Donald Trump, the wealthy real-estate developer, in considering a run for president of the United States in 2000, told an interviewer:

My entire life, I've watched politicians bragging about how poor they are, how they came from nothing, how poor their parents and grandparents were. And I said to myself, if they can stay so poor for so many genera-

---

[7] Radio and television address of Senator Nixon from Los Angeles on September 23, 1952.
[8] *New York Times,* March 3, 1977, p. 1.

tions, maybe this isn't the kind of person we want to be electing to higher office. How smart can they be? They're morons. . . . Do you want someone who gets to be president and that's literally the highest paying job he's ever had?[9]

As a brief glance at U.S. history shows, it does not follow that men of small success in the world of commerce are unfit to make sound decisions about matters of state.

Ad Populum

Arguers guilty of the *ad populum* fallacy make an appeal to the prejudices of the people (*populum* in Latin). They assume that their claim can be adequately defended without further support if they emphasize a belief or attitude that the audience shares with them. One common form of ad populum is an appeal to patriotism, which may allow arguers to omit evidence that the audience needs for proper evaluation of the claim. In the following advertisement the makers of Zippo lighters made such an appeal in urging readers to buy their product.

> It's a grand old lighter. Zippo — the grand old lighter that's made right here in the good old U.S.A.
> We truly make an all-American product. The raw materials used in making a Zippo lighter are all right from this great land of ours.
> Zippo windproof lighters are proud to be Americans.

Appeal to Tradition

In making an appeal to tradition, the arguer assumes that what has existed for a long time and has therefore become a tradition should continue to exist *because* it is a tradition. If the arguer avoids telling his or her reader *why* the tradition should be preserved, he or she may be accused of failing to meet the real issue.

The following statement appeared in a letter defending the membership policy of the Century Club, an all-male club established in New York City in 1847 that was under pressure to admit women. The writer was a Presbyterian minister who opposed the admission of women.

> I am totally opposed to a proposal which would radically change the nature of the Century. . . . A club creates an ethos of its own over the years, and I would deeply deplore a step that would inevitably create an entirely different kind of place.
> A club like the Century should surely be unaffected by fashionable whims. . . .[10]

---

[9]*New York Times*, November 28, 1999, p. 11.
[10]David H. C. Read, letter to the *New York Times*, January 13, 1983, p. 14.

Emotional appeals may be fallacious.

Faulty Emotional Appeals

In some discussions of fallacies, appeals to the emotions of the audience are treated as illegitimate or "counterfeit proofs." All such appeals, however, are *not* illegitimate. As we saw in Chapter 6 on support, appeals to the values and emotions of an audience are an appropriate form of persuasion. You can recognize fallacious emotional appeals if (1) they are irrelevant to the argument or draw attention from the issues being argued or (2) they appear to conceal another purpose. Here we treat two of the most popular appeals — to pity and to fear.

Appeals to pity, compassion, and natural willingness to help the unfortunate are particularly hard to resist. The requests for aid by most charitable organizations — for hungry children, victims of disaster, stray animals — offer examples of legitimate appeals. But these appeals to our sympathetic feelings should not divert us from considering other issues in a particular case. It would be wrong, for example, to allow a multiple murderer to escape punishment because he or she had experienced a wretched childhood. Likewise, if you are asked to contribute to a charitable cause, you should try to learn how many unfortunate people or animals are being helped and what percentage of the contribution will be allocated to maintaining the organization and its officers. In some cases the financial records are closed to public review, and only a small share of the contribution will reach the alleged beneficiaries.

Writer's Guide: Avoiding Logical Fallacies

1. If you are making use of induction, that is, drawing a conclusion based on a number of individual examples, do you have enough examples with variety to justify the conclusion? In other words, will your readers be able to make the inductive leap from examples to the conclusion you are asking them to make?

2. If you are making use of deduction, is your conclusion a logical one based on the premises underlying it? To be sure, write out your argument in the form of a syllogism. Also avoid wording your thesis in absolute terms like *all*, *every*, *everyone*, *everybody*, and *always*.

3. It is relatively easy — and sometimes humorous — to notice other writers' logical fallacies. It is harder to notice your own. Use the list of fallacies in this chapter as a checklist as you read the draft of each of your essays with a critical eye, looking for any breakdown in logic. It may be useful to read your essay aloud to someone because if that listener cannot follow your logic, you may need to clarify your points.

Appeals to fear are likely to be even more effective. But they must be based on evidence that fear is an appropriate response to the issues and that it can move an audience toward a solution to the problem. (Fear can also have the adverse effect of preventing people from taking a necessary action.) Insurance companies, for example, make appeals to our fears of destitution for ourselves and our families as a result of injury, unemployment, sickness, and death. These appeals are justified if the possibilities of such destitution are real and if the insurance will provide relief. It would also be legitimate to arouse fear of the consequences of drunk driving, provided, again, that the descriptions were accurate. On the other hand, it would be wrong to induce fear that fluoridation of public water supplies causes cancer without presenting sound evidence of the probability.

An emotional response by itself is not always the soundest basis for making decisions. Your own experience has probably taught you that in the grip of a strong emotion like love or hate or anger you often overlook good reasons for making different and better choices. Like you, your readers want to be given the opportunity to consider all the available kinds of support for an argument.

PRACTICE

Decide whether the reasoning in the following examples is faulty. Explain your answers.

1. The presiding judge of a revolutionary tribunal, being asked why people are being executed without trial, replies, "Why should we put them on trial when we know that they're guilty?"

2. The government has the right to require the wearing of helmets while operating or riding on a motorcycle because of the high rate of head injuries incurred in motorcycle accidents.

3. Children who watch game shows rather than situation comedies receive higher grades in school. So it must be true that game shows are more educational than situation comedies.

4. The meteorologist predicted the wrong amount of rain for May. Obviously the meteorologist is unreliable.

5. Women ought to be permitted to serve in combat. Why should men be the only ones to face death and danger?

6. If Lady GaGa uses Truvia, it must taste better than Splenda.

7. People will gamble anyway, so why not legalize gambling in this state?

8. Because so much money was spent on public education in the last decade while educational achievement declined, more money to improve education can't be the answer to reversing the decline.

9. He's a columnist for a campus newspaper, so he must be a pretty good writer.

10. We tend to exaggerate the need for Standard English. You don't need much Standard English for most jobs in this country.

11. It's discriminatory to mandate that police officers must conform to a certain height and weight.

12. A doctor can consult books to make a diagnosis, so a medical student should be able to consult books when being tested.

13. Because this soft drink contains so many chemicals, it must be unsafe.

14. Core requirements should be eliminated. After all, students are paying for their education, so they should be able to earn a diploma by choosing the courses they want.

15. We should encourage a return to arranged marriages in this country since marriages based on romantic love haven't been very successful.

16. I know three redheads who have terrible tempers, and since Annabel has red hair, I'll bet she has a terrible temper, too.

17. Supreme Court Justice Byron White was an all-American football player while in college, so how can you say that athletes are dumb?

18. Benjamin H. Sasway, a student at Humboldt State University in California, was indicted for failure to register for possible conscription. Barry Lynn, president of Draft Action, an antidraft group, said, "It is disgraceful that this administration is embarking on an effort to fill the prisons with men of conscience and moral commitment."

19. James A. Harris, former president of the National Education Association: "Twenty-three percent of schoolchildren are failing to graduate and another large segment graduates as functional illiterates. If 23 percent of anything else failed — 23 percent of automobiles didn't run, 23 percent of the buildings fell down, 23 percent of stuffed ham spoiled — we'd look at the producer."

20. A professor at Rutgers University: "The arrest rate for women is rising three times as fast as that of men. Women, inflamed by the doctrines of feminism, are pursuing criminal careers with the same zeal as business and the professions."

21. Physical education should be required because physical activity is healthful.

22. George Meany, former president of the AFL-CIO, in 1968: "To these people who constantly say you have got to listen to these younger people, they have got something to say, I just don't buy that at all. They smoke more pot than we do and if the younger generation are the hundred thousand kids that lay around a field up in Woodstock, New York, I am not going to trust the destiny of the country to that group."

23. That candidate was poor as a child, so he will certainly be sympathetic to the poor if he's elected.

24. When the federal government sent troops into Little Rock, Arkansas, to enforce integration of the public school system, the governor of Arkansas attacked the action, saying that it was as brutal an act of intervention as Russia's sending troops into Hungary to squelch the Hungarians' rebellion. In both cases, the governor said, the rights of a freedom-loving, independent people were being violated.

25. Governor Jones was elected two years ago. Since that time constant examples of corruption and subversion have been unearthed. It is time to get rid of the man responsible for this kind of corrupt government.

26. Are we going to vote a pay increase for our teachers, or are we going to allow our schools to deteriorate into substandard custodial institutions?

27. You see, the priests were right. After we threw those virgins into the volcano, it quit erupting.

28. The people of Rome lost their vitality and desire for freedom when their emperors decided that the way to keep them happy was to provide them with bread and circuses. What can we expect of our own country now that the government gives people free food and there is a constant round of entertainment provided by television?

29. From Mark Clifton, "The Dread Tomato Affliction" (proving that eating tomatoes is dangerous and even deadly): "Ninety-two point four percent of juvenile delinquents have eaten tomatoes. Fifty-seven point one percent of the adult criminals in penitentiaries throughout the United States have eaten tomatoes. Eighty-four percent of all people killed in automobile accidents during the year have eaten tomatoes."

30. From Galileo, *Dialogues Concerning Two New Sciences*: "But can you doubt that air has weight when you have the clear testimony of Aristotle affirming that all elements have weight, including air, and excepting only fire?"

31. Robert Brustein, artistic director of the American Repertory Theatre, commenting on a threat by Congress in 1989 to withhold funding from an offensive art show: "Once we allow lawmakers to become art critics, we take the first step into the world of Ayatollah Khomeini, whose murderous review of *The Satanic Verses* still chills the heart of everyone committed to free expression." (The Ayatollah Khomeini called for the death of the author Salman Rushdie because Rushdie had allegedly committed blasphemy against Islam in his novel.)

On Nation and Race

ADOLF HITLER

There are some truths which are so obvious that for this very reason they are not seen or at least not recognized by ordinary people. They sometimes pass by such truisms as though blind and are most astonished when someone suddenly discovers what everyone really ought to know. Columbus's eggs lie around by the hundreds of thousands, but Columbuses are met with less frequency.

Thus men without exception wander about in the garden of Nature; they imagine that they know practically everything and yet with few exceptions pass blindly by one of the most patent principles of Nature's rule: the inner segregation of the species of all living beings on this earth.

Even the most superficial observation shows that Nature's restricted form of propagation and increase is an almost rigid basic law of all the innumerable forms of expression of her vital urge. Every animal mates only with a member of the same species. The titmouse seeks the titmouse, the finch the finch, the stork the stork, the field mouse the field mouse, the dormouse the dormouse, the wolf the she-wolf, etc.

Only unusual circumstances can change this, primarily the compulsion of captivity or any other cause that makes it impossible to mate within the same species. But then Nature begins to resist this with all possible means, and her most visible protest consists either in refusing further capacity for propagation to bastards or in limiting the fertility of later offspring; in most cases, however, she takes away the power of resistance to disease or hostile attacks.

This is only too natural.   5

Any crossing of two beings not at exactly the same level produces a medium between the level of the two parents. This means: The offspring will probably stand higher than the racially lower parent, but not as high as the higher one. Consequently, it will later succumb in the struggle against the higher level. Such mating is contrary to the will of Nature for a higher breeding of all life. The precondition for this does not lie in associating superior and inferior, but in the total victory of the former. The stronger must dominate and not blend with the weaker, thus sacrificing his own greatness. Only the born weakling can view this as cruel, but he after all is only a weak and limited man; for if this law did not prevail, any conceivable higher development of organic living beings would be unthinkable.

Adolf Hitler (1889–1945) became the Nazi dictator of Germany in the mid-1930s. "On Nation and Race" (editor's title) begins Chapter 11 of *Mein Kampf (My Struggle)*, vol. 1, published in 1925.

The consequence of this racial purity, universally valid in Nature, is not only the sharp outward delimitation of the various races, but their uniform character in themselves. The fox is always a fox, the goose a goose, the tiger a tiger, etc., and the difference can lie at most in the varying measure of force, strength, intelligence, dexterity, endurance, etc., of the individual specimens. But you will never find a fox who in his inner attitude might, for example, show humanitarian tendencies toward geese, as similarly there is no cat with a friendly inclination toward mice.

Therefore, here, too, the struggle among themselves arises less from inner aversion than from hunger and love. In both cases, Nature looks on calmly, with satisfaction, in fact. In the struggle for daily bread all those who are weak and sickly or less determined succumb, while the struggle of the males for the female grants the right or opportunity to propagate only to the healthiest. And struggle is always a means for improving a species' health and power of resistance and, therefore, a cause of its higher development.

If the process were different, all further and higher development would cease and the opposite would occur. For, since the inferior always predominates numerically over the best, if both had the same possibility of preserving life and propagating, the inferior would multiply so much more rapidly that in the end the best would inevitably be driven into the background, unless a correction of this state of affairs were undertaken. Nature does just this by subjecting the weaker part to such severe living conditions that by them alone the number is limited, and by not permitting the remainder to increase promiscuously, but making a new and ruthless choice according to strength and health.

No more than Nature desires the mating of weaker with stronger individuals,   10
even less does she desire the blending of a higher with a lower race, since, if she did, her whole work of higher breeding, over perhaps hundreds of thousands of years, might be ruined with one blow.

Historical experience offers countless proofs of this. It shows with terrifying clarity that in every mingling of Aryan blood with that of lower peoples the result was the end of the cultured people. North America, whose population consists in by far the largest part of Germanic elements who mixed but little with the lower colored peoples, shows a different humanity and culture from Central and South America, where the predominantly Latin immigrants often mixed with the aborigines on a large scale. By this one example, we can clearly and distinctly recognize the effect of racial mixture. The Germanic inhabitant of the American continent, who has remained racially pure and unmixed, rose to be master of the continent; he will remain the master as long as he does not fall a victim to defilement of the blood.

The result of all racial crossing is therefore in brief always the following:

(a) Lowering of the level of the higher race;

(b) Physical and intellectual regression and hence the beginning of a slowly but surely progressing sickness.

To bring about such a development is, then, nothing else but to sin against   15
the will of the eternal creator.

And as a sin this act is rewarded.

When man attempts to rebel against the iron logic of Nature, he comes into struggle with the principles to which he himself owes his existence as a man. And this attack must lead to his own doom.

Here, of course, we encounter the objection of the modern pacifist, as truly Jewish in its effrontery as it is stupid! "Man's role is to overcome Nature!"

Millions thoughtlessly parrot this Jewish nonsense and end up by really imagining that they themselves represent a kind of conqueror of Nature; though in this they dispose of no other weapon than an idea, and at that such a miserable one, that if it were true no world at all would be conceivable.

But quite aside from the fact that man has never yet conquered Nature in anything, but at most has caught hold of and tried to lift one or another corner of her immense gigantic veil of eternal riddles and secrets, that in reality he invents nothing but only discovers everything, that he does not dominate Nature, but has only risen on the basis of his knowledge of various laws and secrets of Nature to be lord over those other living creatures who lack this knowledge — quite aside from all this, an idea cannot overcome the preconditions for the development and being of humanity, since the idea itself depends only on man. Without human beings there is no human idea in this world; therefore, the idea as such is always conditioned by the presence of human beings and hence of all the laws which created the precondition for their existence. 20

And not only that! Certain ideas are even tied up with certain men. This applies most of all to those ideas whose content originates, not in an exact scientific truth, but in the world of emotion, or, as it is so beautifully and clearly expressed today, reflects an "inner experience." All these ideas, which have nothing to do with cold logic as such, but represent only pure expressions of feeling, ethical conceptions, etc., are chained to the existence of men, to whose intellectual imagination and creative power they owe their existence. Precisely in this case the preservation of these definite races and men is the precondition for the existence of these ideas. Anyone, for example, who really desired the victory of the pacifistic idea in this world with all his heart would have to fight with all the means at his disposal for the conquest of the world by the Germans; for, if the opposite should occur, the last pacifist would die out with the last German, since the rest of the world has never fallen so deeply as our own people, unfortunately, has for this nonsense so contrary to Nature and reason. Then, if we were serious, whether we liked it or not, we would have to wage wars in order to arrive at pacifism. This and nothing else was what Wilson, the American world savior, intended, or so at least our German visionaries believed — and thereby his purpose was fulfilled.

In actual fact the pacifistic-humane idea is perfectly all right perhaps when the highest type of man has previously conquered and subjected the world to an extent that makes him the sole ruler of this earth. Then this idea lacks the power of producing evil effects in exact proportion as its practical application becomes rare and finally impossible. Therefore, first struggle and then we shall see what can be done. Otherwise mankind has passed the high point of its development and the end is not the domination of any ethical idea but barbarism and consequently chaos. At this point someone or other may laugh, but this planet once moved through the ether for millions of years without human beings and it can do so again some day if men forget that they owe their higher existence, not to the ideas of a few crazy ideologists, but to the knowledge and ruthless application of Nature's stern and rigid laws.

Everything we admire on this earth today — science and art, technology and inventions — is only the creative product of a few peoples and originally perhaps of *one* race. On them depends the existence of this whole culture. If they perish, the beauty of this earth will sink into the grave with them.

However much the soil, for example, can influence men, the result of the influence will always be different depending on the races in question. The low fertility of a living space may spur the one race to the highest achievements; in others it will only be the cause of bitterest poverty and final undernourishment with all its consequences. The inner nature of peoples is always determining for the manner in which outward influences will be effective. What leads the one to starvation trains the other to hard work.

All great cultures of the past perished only because the originally creative race   25
died out from blood poisoning.

The ultimate cause of such a decline was their forgetting that all culture depends on men and conversely; hence that to preserve a certain culture the man who creates it must be preserved. This preservation is bound up with the rigid law of necessity and the right to victory of the best and stronger in this world.

Those who want to live, let them fight, and those who do not want to fight in this world of eternal struggle do not deserve to live.

Even if this were hard — that is how it is! Assuredly, however, by far the harder fate is that which strikes the man who thinks he can overcome Nature, but in the last analysis only mocks her. Distress, misfortune, and diseases are her answer.

The man who misjudges and disregards the racial laws actually forfeits the happiness that seems destined to be his. He thwarts the triumphal march of the best race and hence also the precondition for all human progress, and remains, in consequence, burdened with all the sensibility of man, in the animal realm of helpless misery.

It is idle to argue which race or races were the original representative of human   30
culture and hence the real founders of all that we sum up under the word *humanity*. It is simpler to raise the question with regard to the present, and here an easy, clear answer results. All the human culture, all the results of art, science, and technology that we see before us today, are almost exclusively the creative product of the Aryan. This very fact admits of the not unfounded inference that he alone was the founder of all higher humanity, therefore representing the prototype of all that we understand by the word *man*. He is the Prometheus of mankind from whose bright forehead the divine spark of genius has sprung at all times, forever kindling anew that fire of knowledge which illumined the night of silent mysteries and thus caused man to climb the path to mastery over the other beings of this earth. Exclude him — and perhaps after a few thousand years darkness will again descend on the earth, human culture will pass, and the world turn to a desert.

READING AND DISCUSSION QUESTIONS

1. Find places in the essay where Hitler attempts to emphasize the scientific objectivity of his theories.

2. Are some passages difficult to understand? (See, for example, para. 11.) How do you explain the difficulty?

3. In explaining his ideology, how does Hitler misinterpret the statement that "Every animal mates only with a member of the same species" (para. 3)? How would you characterize this fallacy?

4. Hitler uses the theory of evolution and his interpretation of the "survival of the fittest" to justify his racial philosophy. Find the places in the text where Hitler reveals that he misunderstands the theory in its application to human beings.

5. What false evidence about race does Hitler use in his assessment of the racial experience in North America? Examine carefully the last sentence of paragraph 11: "The Germanic inhabitant of the American continent, who has remained racially pure and unmixed, rose to be master of the continent; he will remain the master as long as he does not fall a victim to defilement of the blood."

6. What criticism of Jews does Hitler offer? How does this criticism help to explain Hitler's pathological hatred of Jews?

7. Hitler believes that pacifism is a violation of "Nature and reason" (para. 21). Would modern scientists agree that the laws of nature require unremitting struggle and conflict between human beings — until the master race conquers?

WRITING SUGGESTIONS

8. Use your responses to the Reading and Discussion Questions as the basis of an essay evaluating Hitler's logic in "On Nation and Race."

9. Do some research in early human history to discover the degree of truth in this statement: "All the human culture, all the results of art, science, and technology that we see before us today, are almost exclusively the creative product of the Aryan" (para. 30). You may want to limit your discussion to one area of human culture.

Teen Sex: The "Holy" vs. Humanistic Approach

LEON F. SELTZER AND DAVID NIOSE

With all the harsh rhetoric of the culture wars, it's easy to forget that secular humanists and conservative Christians share much common ground — even in the sensitive realm of parenting and education. After all, in one way or another, who *doesn't* want their kids to be well-adjusted, honest, and hard-working?

Leon F. Seltzer is a clinical psychologist and author of *Paradoxical Strategies in Psychotherapy* (1986). He coauthored this essay with David Niose, president of the American Humanist Association. It appeared on psychologytoday.com on August 5, 2010.

In some areas, however — such as the teaching of evolution, school prayer, and church-state separation — major ideological differences separate these two camps. And perhaps the most pointed example of this contrast involves premarital sex, particularly as it relates to teens.

The conservative Christian view on teen premarital sex is simple and straight-forward. It's wrong; sinful. And the unyielding nature of this approach explains why such Christians lobby incessantly against public school sex education that goes beyond teaching (preaching?) abstinence, despite all the studies now demon-strating that "abstinence-only" programs serve not to decrease but *increase* the risk of pregnancy and sexually transmitted diseases (STDs).

For example, a September 2009 study in the *Sexuality Research and Social Policy Journal* reported that most abstinence programs fail to delay sexual initiation, while more comprehensive programs show a positive impact, including postpon-ing sexual activity and increasing contraceptive use. Complementing these find-ings is a January 2007 study published in the *American Journal of Public Health* which concluded that declining teen pregnancy rates in the United States were primarily attributable to improved contraception (and not to abstinence-only education).

As opposed to conservative Christian beliefs about pre-marital sex, the secular   5
humanist view — which is atheistic or, better, non-theistic — doesn't start with "pre-ordained" assumptions about right and wrong but attempts to understand this basic libidinal drive holistically. By seeing sexuality not from the perspective of established religious dogma, but from a bio-socio-cultural vantage point, hu-manists endeavor to help young people better grasp the complex nature of sexual intimacy. To prompt them to consider the various ramifications — ethical and oth-erwise — of unrestrainedly letting loose their libido. And to have them question whether giving unmitigated expression to their erotic impulses is finally in their best interests.

These considerations don't necessarily mean waiting until marriage to (re-lationally, at least) express their sexuality. But hopefully, such self-scrutiny does mean that should they choose to become sexually active, their decision won't be purely emotional, or testosterone-driven; and that it won't, recklessly, put their healthy development or overall well-being at risk either.

Gloria Steinem (an American Humanist Association award winner) has ar-gued — similar to other humanists — for comprehensive sex education, stressing that abstinence-only-until-marriage programs fail to arm teenagers with the es-sential knowledge required to protect themselves against STDs and pregnancy. And Alice Walker (1997 AHA Humanist of the Year) echoed the view of humanists generally when she stated that sexuality should be acknowledged, affirmed — and even celebrated; and that the practice of punishing young women for enjoying sex is both damaging and counterproductive. Her position calls not for permissive-ness as such, but for a healthier understanding of sexuality as a natural phenome-non — not a double-edged "gift" from God, tempting us to stray even as it ensures procreation.

Humanists' respect for our basic nature (sexual or otherwise) leads them to search for solutions consonant with who we actually are — rather than prescribing artificially decreed, or "unnatural," code of conduct, which can bend us out of shape and eventuate in frustrating feelings of deprivation and unfulfillment. What humanists see as "naturalistic solutions" certainly consider the personal constraints requisite for maintaining a civilized society. But they also affirm that individual and social welfare are complementary, and that personal fulfillment (even while necessitating a certain amount of restraint and self-control) is best achieved through first understanding what is inherent about human nature. Not in a biblical sense, but scientifically. Solutions that result from such an approach are designed to affirm universal values — independent of custom and tradition, time and place.

Much conservative religious dogma approaches sexuality (especially unmarried, teenage sexuality) as inherently objectionable, base and ignoble. Humanists, however, avoid taking such unquestioned, categorical positions. What's ideal to them is that which — in a flexible, non-authoritarian way — complies with The Golden Rule (attempting to honor everyone, and shame no one). This fundamental, overarching ethical tenet — which transcends all historical, religious, and philosophical biases — aspires to integrate the pure with the pragmatic and, above all, "do no harm" to anyone (including one's self).

Moreover, not simply in matters of sexuality but in all areas of ethics and morality, humanism strives to put as few limits on personal freedom and self-expression as possible. At the same time, the positions taken by humanists (see http://www.americanhumanist.org/Who_We_Are/About_Humanism) are ever-mindful of the need to protect society from being trampled upon by rash or rampant hedonism — or anything else that doesn't sufficiently respect the humanity of all of us.

10

Perceiving human sexuality from a viewpoint grounded both in science and nature — as opposed, that is, to some pre-ordained, or "consecrated," fundamentalist Christian viewpoint — humanists search out all relevant information (and seek to verify it) before arriving at a decision. Ethical criteria are definitely part of the equation here — and perhaps the ultimate part at that. But such criteria are still considered in the context of undeniable human realities.

That said, let's look at the facts as they apply to the multiple issues surrounding teen sexuality. One anomalous characteristic of human society (at least in modern western culture) is that, for social reasons, we discourage mating until many years after our children reach the age of fertility. The very notion of an animal's reaching reproductive age but then being forced to wait — at minimum, six to ten years or more — before mating, is rarely, if ever, found elsewhere in nature (except where it's involuntary, due to competitive factors).

This counter-to-nature mating delay can best be understood as tied to the enormous social, economic, and technological changes that have taken place in our modern era. Before then, mating occurred "naturally" — at, or soon after, puberty. Only in modern industrial society do humans find themselves in cultures requiring an unnaturally extended period of sexual dormancy.

Think of it. What could be more antithetical to our nature?! Nonetheless, these facts aren't meant to imply that teen sex should be encouraged simply because that's what's natural. Acknowledging our inborn sexual proclivities hardly constitutes an endorsement of hedonistic romps. But such recognition does represent a good starting point for a productive — and compassionate — discussion of the many intricate issues linked to premarital sex.

We also need to consider, however, that as human animals we've developed technology that has completely transformed our environment. Not only have we constructed highly complex technological societies (with, as already mentioned, economic and social systems that encourage postponing sexual reproduction well into adulthood), we've also developed the remarkable ability to control our reproductive lives through reliable (and easily obtainable) birth control. As a consequence, many of us enjoy unprecedented material comfort and convenience — and, frankly, without the burden of undesired reproductive obligations.

But, alas, our advanced technology and material riches (comparatively speaking, at least) have hardly brought us a utopia. Perhaps because of the dominance of our economic, corporate, and media cultures, our fundamental nature — biological, psychological, and sexual — has in many respects not so much been nurtured as exploited. The same terms that provide unprecedented abundance can also rob us of what we most crave spiritually (or, as some humanists would prefer to put it, non-materially). And they can actually discourage us (and have discouraged us) from living our lives with intelligence and discernment — from acting in what, finally, is in our best interests.

This is nothing short of tragic. For in many ways contemporary society would seem to offer us the best opportunity to achieve personal fulfillment in so many areas of life (including sexual). Yet we seem to inhabit a socio-political environment that often fails to produce a population "adult enough" to seek such fulfillment — let alone achieve it. Attention spans get shorter, instant gratification predominates, intellectual inquiry is often downplayed (or even ridiculed), and meaningful relationships that might have been never really develop. Living in such a society, it's not at all surprising that for a great many individuals a mature understanding of intimacy is sadly lacking. Yet who would deny that being able to wisely mentor our children about how best to deal with their budding sexuality is crucial to good teen parenting?

Returning to the specific theme of this piece, few (if any!) humanist parents would jump for joy at the news that their fifteen-year-old had become sexually active. Their discomfort, however, would not at all relate to seeing their teenage child as having committed a mortal sin. No, their upset would be tied to the threat of their child's being saddled with an unwanted pregnancy — and how this might sabotage the child's future. And they'd certainly worry about their child's emotional readiness to be exploring their sexuality with another at such a tender age. If the relationship soured, would the child be mature enough to handle the fallout? Or might the relationship's "sexual chemistry" prompt the child to impulsively make a commitment oblivious to far more important areas of compatibility? Or, if the child had become indiscriminately sexual, how might that affect their academic performance and later social adjustment; or — more important still — their values and moral development? And what about the risks of an STD? and so on, and so on. . . .

In short, such parents would be examining the situation in a multi-faceted way: developmentally, psycho-socially, and ethically. Without adhering to any traditional faith, caring and responsible parents would yet have much to consider in talking with their child. But they wouldn't begin and end simply by condemning the child because they judged their behavior reprehensible, shameful, or "unholy."

Ironically, though from a different vantage point (and probably with greater   20
tolerance for some teen sexual experimentation), humanist parents would reach pretty much the same conclusion as would their conservative Christian counterparts. That is, both sets of parents would strongly prefer that their child wasn't sexually active. And, of course, that when they did express their sexuality, they did so prudently — and with a more grown-up understanding of what they were getting themselves into. Virtually all parents (whether they're able to articulate it or not) hope that their children will develop the ability to grasp the various ramifications not simply of sexual intimacy but of more general relational intimacy.

The difference, then, between the secular humanist and the conservative Christian viewpoint toward teen sexuality is not so much in the conclusions they arrive at, but in how these conclusions are reached. For secular humanists, matters of shame, divine judgment, or biblical reference do not enter into the deliberative process. Rather, questions of teen sexuality are investigated primarily from scientifically studying nature, with answers derived not from theology but the natural world. Basic human drives are recognized and respected. But in the end, all natural impulses (however strong, tempting, or erotic) are evaluated in the larger context of core individual and societal needs. And intellect — vs. faith — is employed to prepare them, as parents, to provide the best possible guidance for their children.

READING AND DISCUSSION QUESTIONS

1. What Rogerian strategy do Seltzer and Niose use in the first paragraph?
2. Summarize the differences that the authors see between the conservative Christian view of premarital sex and that of the secular humanists.
3. What types of support do Seltzer and Niose make use of in the essay? How effective are they?
4. What do these authors mean when they say that secular humanists advocate a "holistic" approach to understanding human sexuality?
5. Why do the authors feel that a secular humanist approach to sexuality is better for teens than a conservative Christian approach?
6. In what ways does the secular humanist's view of sexuality affirm universal values?
7. How have social, economic, and technological changes in society affected human sexuality?
8. Near the end of the essay, the authors once again try to establish common ground. How?
9. What fallacy does the last sentence illustrate?
10. How convincing do you find Seltzer and Niose's logical support for their position to be?

WRITING SUGGESTIONS

11. Write an essay explaining which points that Seltzer and Niose make in the essay would be acceptable to a conservative Christian audience. In other words, where is there common ground between conservative Christians and secular humanists?

12. Write an essay explaining how realistic you find the authors' suggestions for approaching human sexuality to be.

13. Write an essay expanding on the authors' point that the conservative Christian view of premarital sex is incompatible with the modern world.

Food for Thought (and for Credit)

JENNIFER GROSSMAN

Want to combat the epidemic of obesity? Bring back home economics. Before you choke on your 300-calorie, trans-fat-laden Krispy Kreme, consider: Teaching basic nutrition and food preparation is a far less radical remedy than gastric bypass surgery or fast-food lawsuits. And probably far more effective. Obesity tends to invite such drastic solutions because it is so frustratingly difficult to treat. This intractability, coupled with the sad fact that obese children commonly grow up to be obese adults, argues for a preventative approach. As the new school year begins, we need to equip kids with the skills and practical knowledge to take control of their dietary destinies.

Despite its bad rep as Wife Ed 101, home economics has progressive roots. At the turn of the century it "helped transform domesticity into a vehicle to expand women's political power," according to Sarah Stage in *Rethinking Home Economics: Women and the History of a Profession*. In time, focus shifted from social reform to the practical priorities of sanitation and electrification, and then again to an emphasis on homemaking after World War II — giving ammunition to later critics like Betty Friedan who charged home ec with having helped foster the "feminine mystique."

Banished by feminists, Becky Home-ecky was left to wander backwater school districts. For a while it seemed that mandating male participation might salvage the discipline while satisfying political correctness. By the late 1970s one-third of male high school graduates had some home-ec training, whereas they comprised a mere 3.5 percent of home-ec students in 1962. Since then, "home economics has moved

Jennifer Grossman is vice president of the Dole Nutrition Institute, which distributes health information to the public through lectures and publications. Formerly, she was director of Education Policy at the Cato Institute and a speechwriter for President George H. W. Bush. She has written editorials for the *New York Times*, where this column appeared on September 2, 2003; the *Wall Street Journal*; the *Los Angeles Times*; the *New York Post*; the *Weekly Standard*; the *National Review*; and the *Women's Quarterly*.

from the mainstream to the margins of American high school," according to the United States Department of Education, with even female participation — near universal in the 1950s — plummeting by 67 percent.

What has happened since? Ronald McDonald and Colonel Sanders stepped in as the new mascots of American food culture, while the number of meals consumed outside the home has doubled — from a quarter in 1970 to nearly half today. As a result, market economics has increasingly determined ingredients, nutrient content, and portion size. Agricultural surpluses and technological breakthroughs supplied the cheap sweeteners and hydrogenated oils necessary for food to survive indefinitely on store shelves or under fast-food heat lamps.

Unsurprisingly, the caloric density of such foods soared relative to those consumed at home. Good value no longer meant taste, presentation, and proper nutrition — but merely more-for-less. Thus, the serving of McDonald's French fries that contained 200 calories in 1960 contains 610 today. The lure of large was not limited to fast-food, inflating everything from snack foods to cereal boxes.   5

But the hunger for home economics didn't die with its academic exile. Martha Stewart made millions filling the void, vexing home-ec haters like Erica Jong for having "earned her freedom by glorifying the slavery of home." Home and Garden TV, the Food Network, and countless publications thrive on topics once taught by home ec.

All of which begs the question: If the free market has done such a good job of picking up the slack, why bring home ec back? Because much of the D.I.Y. (do-it-yourself) culture is divorced from the exigencies of everyday life. It's more like home rec: catering to pampered chefs with maids to clean up the kitchen.

The new home economics should be both pragmatic and egalitarian. Traditional topics — food and nutrition, family studies, home management — should be retooled for the twenty-first century. Children should be able to decipher headlines about the dangers of dioxin or the benefits of antioxidants. Subjects like home finance might include domestic problem-solving: How would you spend $100 to feed a family of four, including a diabetic, a nursing mother, and infant, for one week?

While this kind of training might most benefit those low-income minority children at highest risk of obesity, all children will be better equipped to make smart choices in the face of the more than $33 billion that food companies spend annually to promote their products. And consumer education is just part of the larger purpose: to teach kids to think, make, fix, and generally fend for themselves.

Some detractors will doubtless smell a plot to turn women back into stitching,   10 stirring Stepford Wives. Others will argue that schools should focus on the basics. But what could be more basic than life, food, home and hearth? A generation has grown up since we swept home ec into the dust heap of history and hung up our brooms. It's time to reevaluate the domestic discipline, and recapture lost skills.

READING AND DISCUSSION QUESTIONS

1. How would the students at the high school you attended have responded to a course such as the one Grossman describes?

2. Do you think that offering such a course would be a good idea? Why, or why not?

3. How convincing is Grossman's argument that there is a need for consumer education? How convincing is her argument that it should be offered in school?

4. Do you find any logical fallacies in her argument? If so, what type of fallacies are
   they?

WRITING SUGGESTIONS

5. Write a claim of policy essay arguing that the sort of course Grossman describes
   should be required of high school students.

6. Write an essay refuting what Grossman suggests.

7. Write an essay in which you argue that the majority of teenagers are responsible
   consumers or that they are not.

DEBATE   Should the Federal Government Fund
Embryonic Stem-Cell Research?

A New Look, an Old Battle

ANNA QUINDLEN

Public personification has always been the struggle on both sides of the abortion battle lines. That is why the people outside clinics on Saturday mornings
carry signs with photographs of infants rather than of zygotes, why they wear
lapel pins fashioned in the image of tiny feet and shout, "Don't kill your baby,"
rather than, more accurately, "Don't destroy your embryo." Those who support
the legal right to an abortion have always been somewhat at a loss in the face of
all this. From time to time women have come forward to speak about their decision to have an abortion, but when they are prominent, it seems a bit like grandstanding, and when they are not, it seems a terrible invasion of privacy when
privacy is the point in the first place. Easier to marshal the act of presumptive
ventriloquism practiced by the opponents, pretending to speak for those unborn
unknown to them by circumstance or story.

But the battle of personification will assume a different and more sympathetic
visage in the years to come. Perhaps the change in the weather was best illustrated
when conservative Senator Strom Thurmond invoked his own daughter to explain
a position opposed by the anti-abortion forces. The senator's daughter has diabetes. The actor Michael J. Fox has Parkinson's disease. Christopher Reeve is in a
wheelchair because of a spinal-cord injury, Ronald Reagan locked in his own devolving mind by Alzheimer's. In the faces of the publicly and personally beloved
lies enormous danger for the life-begins-at-conception lobby.

Anna Quindlen is a Pulitzer Prize–winning journalist and best-selling novelist. This piece appeared in the April 9, 2001, issue of *Newsweek* magazine.

The catalytic issue is research on stem cells. These are versatile building blocks that may be coaxed into becoming any other cell type; they could therefore hold the key to endless mysteries of human biology, as well as someday help provide a cure for ailments as diverse as diabetes, Parkinson's, spinal-cord degeneration, and Alzheimer's. By some estimates, more than 100 million Americans have diseases that scientists suspect could be affected by research on stem cells. Scientists hope that the astonishing potential of this research will persuade the federal government to help fund it and allow the National Institutes of Health to help oversee it. This is not political, researchers insist. It is about science, not abortion.

And they are correct. Stem-cell research is typically done by using frozen embryos left over from in vitro fertilization. If these embryos were placed in the womb, they might eventually implant, become a fetus, then a child. Unused, they are the earliest undifferentiated collection of cells made by the joining of the egg and sperm, no larger than the period at the end of this sentence. One of the oft-used slogans of the anti-abortion movement is "abortion stops a beating heart." There is no heart in this preimplantation embryo, but there are stem cells that, in the hands of scientists, might lead to extraordinary work affecting everything from cancer to heart disease.

All of which leaves the anti-abortion movement trying desperately to hold its hard line, and failing. Judie Brown of the American Life League can refer to these embryos as "the tiniest person," and the National Right to Life organization can publish papers that refer to stem-cell research as the "destruction of life." But ordinary people with family members losing their mobility or their grasp on reality will be able to be more thoughtful and reasonable about the issues involved.   5

The anti-abortion activists know this, because they have already seen the defections. Some senators have abandoned them to support fetal-tissue research, less promising than stem-cell work but still with significant potential for treating various ailments. Elected officials who had voted against abortion rights found themselves able to support procedures that used tissue from aborted fetuses; perhaps they were men who had fathers with heart disease, who had mothers with arthritis and whose hearts resonated with the possibilities for alleviating pain and prolonging life. Senator Thurmond was one, Senator McCain another. Former senator Connie Mack of Florida recently sent a letter to the president, who must decide the future role of the federal government in this area, describing himself "as a conservative pro-life now former member" of Congress, and adding that there "were those of us identified as such who supported embryonic stem-cell research."

When a recent test of fetal tissue in patients with Parkinson's had disastrous side effects, the National Right to Life Web site ran an almost gloating report: "horrific," "rips to shreds," "media cheerleaders," "defy description." The tone is a reflection of fear. It's the fear that the use of fetal tissue to produce cures for debilitating ailments might somehow launder the process of terminating a pregnancy, a positive result from what many people still see as a negative act. And it's the fear that thinking — really thinking — about the use of the earliest embryo for lifesaving research might bring a certain long-overdue relativism to discussions of abortion across the board.

The majority of Americans have always been able to apply that relativism to these issues. They are more likely to accept early abortions than later ones. They are more tolerant of a single abortion under exigent circumstances than multiple abortions. Some who disapprove of abortion in theory have discovered that they can accept it in fact if a daughter or a girlfriend is pregnant.

And some who believe that life begins at conception may look into the vacant eyes of an adored parent with Alzheimer's or picture a paralyzed child walking again, and take a closer look at what an embryo really is, at what stem-cell research really does, and then consider the true cost of a cure. That is what Senator Thurmond obviously did when he looked at his daughter and broke ranks with the true believers. It may be an oversimplification to say that real live loved ones trump the imagined unborn, that a cluster of undifferentiated cells due to be discarded anyway is a small price to pay for the health and welfare of millions. Or perhaps it is only a simple commonsensical truth.

The Misleading Debate on Stem-Cell Research

MONA CHAREN

Addressing the Democratic National Convention, Ron Reagan told the delegates that in the debate over funding research on embryonic stem cells, we face a choice between "the future and the past; between reason and ignorance; between true compassion and mere ideology." Not satisfied with that contrast, he elaborated that "a few of these folks (who oppose funding this research) are just grinding a political axe, and they should be ashamed of themselves."

It is Reagan who ought to be ashamed. As the mother of a ten-year-old with juvenile diabetes, I yearn more than most for breakthroughs in scientific research. My son takes between four and six shots of insulin daily and must test his blood sugar by pricking his finger the same number of times. This disease affects every major organ system in the body and places him in the high-risk category for more problems than I care to name. When he settles down to sleep at night, I can never be entirely sure that he won't slip into a coma from a sudden low blood sugar. How happily I would take the disease upon myself if I could only spare him! So please don't lecture me about grinding a political axe.

But like millions of others, I am troubled by the idea of embryonic stem-cell research. It crosses a moral line that this society should be loath to cross — even for the best of motives. Taking the stem cells from human embryos kills them. Before turning to the arguments of the pro-research side, permit a word about the pro-life

Mona Charen is a syndicated columnist and a political analyst. From 1984 to 1986, she worked at the White House as a speechwriter for Nancy Reagan and in the Public Affairs Office. This article appeared on townhall.com in August 2004.

position. Too many pro-life activists, it seems to me, have argued this case on the wrong grounds. My inbox is full of missives about the scientific misfires that stem-cell research has led to, as well as breathless announcements that adult stem cells actually hold more promise.

This is neither an honest nor a productive line of argument. The reason pro-lifers oppose embryonic stem-cell research is because they hold life sacred at all stages of development. They ought not to deny this or dress it up in a lab coat to give it greater palatability. The moral case is an honorable one. Leave it at that.

Proponents of embryonic stem-cell research point out that some of the em-   5
bryos currently sitting in freezers in fertility clinics around the world are going to be washed down the drain anyway — which surely kills them, and without any benefit to mankind. This is true. There are several answers to this. The first is that a society that truly honored each human life would take a different approach. Fertility clinics and the couples who use them would understand the moral obligation not to create more embryos than they can reasonably expect to transfer to the mother's uterus. In cases where this was impossible, the embryos could be placed for adoption with other infertile couples (this is already a widespread practice).

Once you begin to pull apart a human embryo and use its parts, you have thoroughly dehumanized it. You have justified taking one life to (speculatively) save another. Despite the rosy future painted by Ron Reagan and others, those of us who follow the field with avid interest have been disappointed by avenues of research that have failed, thus far, to pan out. Still, opponents of stem-cell re-search should not argue that the research is going to be fruitless. No one knows. The problem is that this kind of research is morally problematic. Germany, Italy, Portugal, Luxembourg, and Austria ban it. (The United States does not. We simply withhold federal funding.)

There is something else, as well. While the idea of growing spare parts — say, spinal nerves for a paraplegic — in a Petri dish seems wonderful, it may not be possible to do so from embryonic stem cells. As the *Wall Street Journal* reported on August 12 [2004], scientists have been frustrated by their inability to get stem cells to grow into endoderm (the cells that make up the liver, stomach, and pancreas), whereas they can coax them to become heart and nerve tissue.

"Scientists speculate," the *Journal* explained, "that might be because the em-bryo early on needs blood and nerve tissue to grow, while endoderm-based organs aren't needed until later." If we can use the stem cells of normal human embryos for research, by what logic would we shrink from allowing an embryo to reach a later stage of development in order to study better how endoderm forms?

These are treacherous moral waters we're setting sail in, and those who hesitate ought not to be scorned as ignorant, uncompassionate, or blinkered.

DISCUSSION QUESTIONS

1. Do both of these authors use evidence and appeal to needs and values? Explain. How is your reading of Charen's piece affected by her personal circumstances?

2. In what ways does Charen's choice of words affect her argument?

3. Where does each author most directly state the claim of her piece?

4. Charen makes the statement that embryonic stem-cell research "crosses a moral line that this society should be loath to cross — even for the best of motives" (para. 3). How might Quindlen respond?

5. Which of the two arguments do you find more convincing?

Assignments for Avoiding Flawed Logic

READING AND DISCUSSION QUESTIONS

1. Read through the draft of an essay that you are writing, looking for and correcting any logical fallacies that you find.

2. Compare the argument made to Congress by President Roosevelt on the day after the attack on Pearl Harbor in 1941 and the one made by President Bush after the attacks on the World Trade Center and the Pentagon in 2001.

WRITING ASSIGNMENTS

3. Write an essay explaining the logical fallacies in one of the essays from the Readings for Analysis portion of this chapter.

4. Explain in an essay whether you find Anna Quindlen's or Mona Charen's argument on stem-cell research more convincing, and why.

5. Find the printed text of a major political speech such as a State of the Union Address, a major political convention speech, or an inaugural address and analyze its logic. Does it use an inductive approach, a deductive approach, a combination? What types of support are used? Do you detect any logical fallacies? Write an essay about the speech that supports either a claim of fact or a claim of value.

Research Readiness: Using Up-to-Date Data

Where do I look for the most current data about an evolving issue?

The world of politics is a world of constant change. There is always another election around the corner. Officials grow in public esteem or fall out of favor. Response to natural disasters or environmental threats can make or break a politician's career. Relationships with other countries shift. Laws are passed or vetoed.

The social world changes as well. As individuals, as states, and as a nation, we have had to rethink the definition of marriage. We have had to deal with violence that has grown out of isolation for some of our teens. We see or read about the causes and effects of homelessness.

The world of science is ever evolving. New advances save and improve lives but may raise new ethical questions as well. We have the knowledge to perform transplants, but questions remain as to who gets the small number of organs available.

To write for and about anything less than a static world, you need to have the latest information possible. The challenge is where to find it.

Find the most recent information you can about each of the following and be prepared to discuss how and where you found it.

- The number of American troops in Iraq
- The legality of same-sex marriage
- The use of the SAT for college admissions
- The federal stance on human stem-cell research
- The number of Americans supporting the Tea Party
- The amount of federal funds being spent on space travel
- The status of construction at Ground Zero
- The feasibility of alternative automobile fuels

CHAPTER 9

Language

The Power of Words

Words play such a critical role in argument that they deserve special treatment. An important part of successful writers' equipment is a large and active vocabulary, but no single chapter in a book can give this to you; only reading and study can widen your range of word choices. Even in a brief chapter, however, we can point out how words influence the feelings and attitudes of an audience, both favorably and unfavorably.

One kind of language responsible for shaping attitudes and feelings is *emotive language,* language that expresses and arouses emotions. Understanding it and using it effectively are indispensable to the arguer who wants to move an audience to accept a point of view or undertake an action.

In one of the most memorable speeches in the history of America, President Franklin Delano Roosevelt asked the country both to accept a point of view and to prepare to take action. In his brief speech to Congress he captured some of the grief and the feeling of outrage Americans were experiencing. Except for the most famous phrase in the speech, in which he declares December 7, 1941, a "date which will live in infamy," most of the first portion of the speech establishes the facts. A turning point in the speech comes when he shifts from facts to implications. The speech then builds to its emotional climax in the next-to-last paragraph before he concludes with a declaration of war.

Address to Congress, December 8, 1941

FRANKLIN D. ROOSEVELT

Yesterday, December 7, 1941 — a date which will live in infamy — the United States of America was suddenly and deliberately attacked by naval and air forces of the Empire of Japan.

The United States was at peace with that nation, and, at the solicitation of Japan, was still in conversation with its government and its Emperor looking toward the maintenance of peace in the Pacific.

Indeed, one hour after Japanese air squadrons had commenced bombing in the American island of Oahu, the Japanese Ambassador to the United States and his colleague delivered to our Secretary of State a formal reply to a recent American message. And, while this reply stated that it seemed useless to continue the existing diplomatic negotiations, it contained no threat or hint of war or of armed attack.

It will be recorded that the distance of Hawaii from Japan makes it obvious that the attack was deliberately planned many days or even weeks ago. During the intervening time the Japanese Government has deliberately sought to deceive the United States by false statements and expressions of hope for continued peace.

The attack yesterday on the Hawaiian Islands has caused severe damage to American naval and military forces. I regret to tell you that very many American lives have been lost. In addition, American ships have been reported torpedoed on the high seas between San Francisco and Honolulu.   5

Yesterday the Japanese Government also launched an attack against Malaya. Last night Japanese forces attacked Hong Kong. Last night Japanese forces attacked Guam. Last night Japanese forces attacked the Philippine Islands. Last night the Japanese attacked Wake Island. And this morning the Japanese attacked Midway Island.

Japan has therefore undertaken a surprise offensive extending throughout the Pacific area. The facts of yesterday and today speak for themselves. The people of the United States have already formed their opinions and well understand the implications to the very life and safety of our nation.

As Commander-in-Chief of the Army and Navy I have directed that all measures be taken for our defense, that always will our whole nation remember the character of the onslaught against us.

No matter how long it may take us to overcome this premeditated invasion, the American people, in their righteous might, will win through to absolute victory.

I believe that I interpret the will of the Congress and of the people when I assert that we will not only defend ourselves to the uttermost but will make it very certain that this form of treachery shall never again endanger us.   10

Hostilities exist. There is no blinking at the fact that our people, our territory, and our interests are in grave danger.

President Roosevelt addresses Congress on December 8, 1941.

   With confidence in our armed forces, with the unbounding determination of our people, we will gain the inevitable triumph, so help us God.
   I ask that the Congress declare that since the unprovoked and dastardly attack by Japan on Sunday, December 7, 1941, a state of war has existed between the United States and the Japanese Empire.

Long before you thought about writing your first argument, you learned that words had the power to affect you. Endearments and affectionate and flattering nicknames evoked good feelings about the speaker and yourself. Insulting nicknames and slurs produced dislike for the speaker and bad feelings about yourself. Perhaps you were told, "Sticks and stones may break your bones, but words will never hurt you." But even to a small child it is clear that ugly words are as painful as sticks and stones and that the injuries are sometimes more lasting.

Nowhere is the power of words more obvious and more familiar than in advertising, where the success of a product may depend on the feelings that certain words produce in the prospective buyer. Even the names of products may have emotive significance. In recent years a new industry, composed of consultants who supply names for products, has emerged. Although most manufacturers agree that a good name won't save a poor product, they also recognize that the right name can catch the attention of the public and persuade people to buy a product at least once. According to an article in the *Wall Street Journal*, a product name not only should be memorable but also should "remind people of emotional or physical experiences."[1]

PRACTICE

Careful thought and extensive research go into the naming of automobiles, a "big ticket" item for most consumers. What reasoning might have gone into the naming of these models, old and new?

Aspen	Impala	Mustang	Rendezvous
Colorado	Infinity	Nova	Sequoia
Dart	Jaguar	Odyssey	Taurus
Eclipse	Liberty	Quest	Trailblazer
Electra	Malibu	Rainier	Viper
Grand Prix	Matrix	Regal	

What response do the names Mercedes-Benz and Rolls-Royce evoke?

Even scientists recognize the power of words to attract the attention of other scientists and the public to discoveries and theories that might otherwise remain obscure. A good name can even enable the scientist to visualize a new concept. One scientist says that "a good name," such as "quark," "black hole," "big bang," "chaos," or "great attractor," "helps in communicating a theory and can have substantial impact on financing."

It is not hard to see the connection between the use of words in conversation and advertising and the use of emotive language in the more formal arguments you will be writing. Emotive language reveals your approval or disapproval, assigns praise or blame — in other words, makes a judgment about the subject. Keep in mind that unless you are writing purely factual statements, such as scientists write, you will find it hard to avoid expressing judgments. Neutrality does not come easily, even where it may be desirable, as in news stories or reports of historical events. For this reason you need to attend carefully to the statements in your argument, making sure that you have not disguised judgments as statements of fact. In Rogerian argumentation, you need to remain neutral as you summarize your opponent's argument and your own.

Of course, in attempting to prove a claim, you will not be neutral. You will be revealing your judgment about the subject, first in the selection of facts and

---

[1] *Wall Street Journal*, August 5, 1982, p. 19.

opinions and the emphasis you give to them and second in the selection of words.

Like the choice of facts and opinions, the choice of words can be effective or ineffective in advancing your argument, moral or immoral in the honesty with which you exercise it. The following discussions offer some insights into recognizing and evaluating the use of emotive language in the arguments you read, as well as into using such language in your own arguments where it is appropriate and avoiding it where it is not.

Connotation

The connotations of a word are the meanings we attach to it apart from its explicit definition. Because these added meanings derive from our feelings, connotations are one form of emotive language. For example, the word *rat* denotes or points to a kind of rodent, but the attached meanings of "selfish person," "evil-doer," "betrayer," and "traitor" reflect the feelings that have accumulated around the word.

In Chapter 4 we observed that definitions of controversial terms, such as *poverty* and *unemployment*, may vary so widely that writer and reader cannot always be sure that they are thinking of the same thing. A similar problem arises when a writer assumes that the reader shares his or her emotional response to a word. Emotive meanings originate partly in personal experience. The word *home*, defined merely as "a family's place of residence," may suggest love, warmth, and security to one person; it may suggest friction, violence, and alienation to another. The values of the groups to which we belong also influence meaning. Writers and speakers count on cultural associations when they refer to our country, our flag, and heroes and enemies we have never seen. The arguer must also be aware that some apparently neutral words trigger different responses from different groups — words such as *cult, revolution, police,* and *beauty contest*.

Various reform movements have recognized that words with unfavorable connotations have the power not only to reflect but also to shape our perceptions of things. In 2007, the NAACP went so far as to hold a "funeral for the N — word." The women's liberation movement also insisted on changes that would bring about improved attitudes toward women. The movement condemned the use of *girl* for a female over the age of eighteen and the use in news stories of descriptive adjectives that emphasized the physical appearance of women. And the homosexual community succeeded in reintroducing the word *gay*, a word current centuries ago, as a substitute for words they considered offensive. Now *queer*, a word long regarded as offensive, has been adopted as a substitute for *gay* by a new generation of gays and lesbians, although it is still considered unacceptable by many members of the homosexual community.

Members of certain occupations have invented terms to confer greater respectability on their work. The work does not change, but the workers hope that public perceptions will change if janitors are called custodians, if garbage collectors are called sanitation engineers, if undertakers are called morticians, if people who sell makeup are called cosmetologists. Events considered unpleasant or unmentionable are sometimes disguised by polite terms, called *euphemisms*. During the 1992 to 1993 recession new terms emerged that disguised, or tried to, the grim fact that thousands of people were being dismissed from their jobs: *skill-mix adjustment, workforce-imbalance correction, redundancy elimination, downsizing, indefinite idling,* even a daring *career-change opportunity.* Many people refuse to use the word *died* and choose *passed away* instead. Some psychologists and physicians use the phrase *negative patient care outcome* for what most of us would call *death.* Even when referring to their pets, some people cannot bring themselves to say *put to death* but substitute *put to sleep* or *put down.* In place of a term to describe an act of sexual intercourse, some people use *slept together* or *went to bed together* or *had an affair.*

Polite words are not always so harmless. If a euphemism disguises a shameful event or condition, it is morally irresponsible to use it to mislead the reader into believing that the shameful condition does not exist. In his powerful essay "Politics and the English Language" George Orwell pointed out that politicians and reporters have sometimes used terms like *pacification* or *rectification of frontiers* to conceal acts that result in torture and death for millions of people. An example of such usage was cited by a member of Amnesty International, a group monitoring human rights violations throughout the world. He objected to a news report describing camps in which the Chinese were promoting "re-education through labor." This term, he wrote, "makes these institutions seem like a cross between Police Athletic League and Civilian Conservation Corps camps." On the contrary, he went on, the reality of "reeducation through labor" was that the victims were confined to "rather unpleasant prison camps." The details he offered about the conditions under which people lived and worked gave substance to his claim.[2]

Perhaps the most striking examples of the way that connotations influence our perceptions of reality occur when people are asked to respond to questions of poll-takers. Sociologists and students of poll-taking know that the phrasing of a question, or the choice of words, can affect the answers and even undermine the validity of the poll. In one case poll-takers first asked a selected group of people if they favored continuing the welfare system. The majority answered no. But when the poll-takers asked if they favored government aid to the poor, the majority answered yes. Although the terms *welfare* and *government aid to the poor* refer to essentially the same forms of government assistance, *welfare* has acquired for many people negative connotations of corruption and shiftless recipients.

In a *New York Times*/CBS poll conducted in January 1998, "a representative sample of Americans were asked which statement came nearer to their opinion: 'Is abortion the same thing as murdering a child, or is abortion not murder because the fetus really isn't a child?'" Thirty-eight percent chose "the fetus really isn't a child." But 58 percent, including a third of those who chose "abortion is

---

[2]Letter to the *New York Times,* August 30, 1982, p. 25.

the same thing as murdering a child," agreed that abortion "was sometimes the best course in a bad situation." The author of the report suggests an explanation of the fact that a majority of those polled seemed to have chosen "murder" as an acceptable solution to an unwanted pregnancy:

> These replies reveal, at least, a considerable moral confusion.
>
> Or maybe only verbal confusion? Should the question have asked whether abortion came closer, in the respondent's view, to "killing" rather than "murdering" a child? That would leave room for the explanation that Americans, while valuing life, are ultimately not pacifists: killing, they hold, may be justified in certain circumstances (self-defense, warfare, capital punishment).
>
> So one can challenge the wording of the question. Indeed, one can almost always challenge the wording of poll questions. . . . Poll takers themselves acknowledge the difficulty of wording questions and warn against relying too much on any single finding.[3]

This is also true in polls concerning rape, another highly charged subject. Dr. Neil Malamuth, a psychologist at the University of California at Los Angeles, says, "When men are asked if there is any likelihood they would force a woman to have sex against her will if they could get away with it, about half say they would. But if you ask them if they would rape a woman if they knew they could get away with it, only about 15 percent say they would." The men who change their answers aren't aware that "the only difference is in the words used to describe the same act."[4]

The wording of an argument is crucial. Because readers may interpret the words you use on the basis of feelings different from your own, you must support your word choices with definitions and with evidence that allows readers to determine how and why you made them.

Slanting

Slanting, says one dictionary, is "interpreting or presenting in line with a special interest." The term is almost always used in a negative sense. It means that the arguer has selected facts and words with favorable or unfavorable connotations to create the impression that no alternative view exists or can be defended. For some questions it is true that no alternative view is worthy of presentation, and emotionally charged language to defend or attack a position that is clearly right or wrong would be entirely appropriate. We aren't neutral, nor should we be, about the tragic abuse of human rights anywhere in the world or even about infractions of the law such as drunk driving or vandalism, and we should use strong language to express our disapproval of these practices.

---

[3]Peter Steinfels, "Beliefs," *New York Times,* January 24, 1998, sec. A, p. 15.
[4]*New York Times,* August 29, 1989, sec. C, p. 1.

Most of your arguments, however, will concern controversial questions about which people of goodwill can argue on both sides. In such cases, your own judgments should be restrained. Slanting will suggest a prejudice — that is, a judgment made without regard to all the facts. Unfortunately, you may not always be aware of your bias or special interest; you may believe that your position is the only correct one. You may also feel the need to communicate a passionate belief about a serious problem. But if you are interested in persuading a reader to accept your belief and to act on it, you must also ask: If the reader is not sympathetic, how will he or she respond? Will he or she perceive my words as "loaded" — one-sided and prejudicial — and my view as slanted?

R. D. Laing, a Scottish psychiatrist, defined *prayer* in this way: "Someone is gibbering away on his knees, talking to someone who is not there."[5] This description probably reflects a sincerely held belief. Laing also clearly intended it for an audience that already agreed with him. But the phrases "gibbering away" and "someone who is not there" would be offensive to people for whom prayer is sacred.

The following remarks by one writer attacking another appeared in *Salon,* an online magazine:

> Urging the hyperbolic *Salon* columnist David Horowitz to calm down and cite facts instead of spewing insults seems as pointless as asking a dog not to defecate on the sidewalk. In either instance, the result is always and predictably the same: Somebody has to clean up a stinking pile.[6]

An audience, whether friendly or unfriendly, interested in a discussion of the issues, would probably be both embarrassed and repelled by this use of language in a serious argument.

In the mid-1980s an English environmental group, London Greenpeace, began to distribute leaflets accusing the McDonald's restaurants of a wide assortment of crimes. The leaflets said in part:

> McDollars, McGreedy, McCancer, McMurder, McDisease, McProfits, McDeadly, McHunger, McRipoff, McTorture, McWasteful, McGarbage.
>
> This leaflet is asking you to think for a moment about what lies behind McDonald's clean, bright image. It's got a lot to hide. . . .
>
> McDonald's and Burger King are two of the many U.S. corporations using lethal poisons to destroy vast areas of Central American rain forest to create grazing pastures for cattle to be sent back to the States as burgers and pet food. . . .
>
> What they don't make clear is that a diet high in fat, sugar, animal products and salt . . . and low in fiber, vitamins and minerals — which describes an average McDonald's meal — is linked with cancers of the breast and bowel, and heart disease. . . .[7]

---

[5] "The Obvious," in David Cooper, ed., *The Dialectics of Liberation* (Penguin Books, 1968), p. 17.
[6] July 6, 2000.
[7] *New York Times,* August 6, 1995, sec. E, p. 7. In 1990 McDonald's sued the group for libel. In June 1997, after the longest libel trial in British history, the judge ruled in favor of the plaintiff, awarding McDonald's £60,000. In March 1999 an appeal partially overturned the verdict and reduced the damages awarded to McDonald's by approximately one-third.

Even readers who share the belief that McDonald's is not a reliable source of good nutrition might feel that London Greenpeace has gone too far, and that the name-calling, loaded words, and exaggeration have damaged the credibility of the attackers more than the reputation of McDonald's.

Selection, Slanting, and Charged Language

NEWMAN P. BIRK AND GENEVIEVE B. BIRK

A. The Principle of Selection

Before it is expressed in words, our knowledge, both inside and outside, is influenced by the principle of selection. What we know or observe depends on what we notice; that is, what we select, consciously or unconsciously, as worthy of notice or attention. As we observe, the principle of selection determines which facts we take in.

Suppose, for example, that three people, a lumberjack, an artist, and a tree surgeon, are examining a large tree in the forest. Since the tree itself is a complicated object, the number of particulars or facts about it that one could observe would be very great indeed. Which of these facts a particular observer will notice will be a matter of selection, a selection that is determined by his interests and purposes. A lumberjack might be interested in the best way to cut the tree down, cut it up, and transport it to the lumber mill. His interest would then determine his principle of selection in observing and thinking about the tree. The artist might consider painting a picture of the tree, and his purpose would furnish his principle of selection. The tree surgeon's professional interest in the physical health of the tree might establish a principle of selection for him. If each man were now required to write an exhaustive, detailed report on every thing he observed about the tree, the facts supplied by each would differ, for each would report those facts that his particular principle of selection led him to notice. . . .[1]

The principle of selection then serves as a kind of sieve or screen through which our knowledge passes before it becomes our knowledge. Since we can't notice everything about a complicated object or situation or action or state of our own consciousness, what we do notice is determined by whatever principle of selection is operating for us at the time we gain the knowledge. . . .

---

[1] Of course, all three observers would probably report a good many facts in common — the height of the tree, for example, and the size of the trunk. The point we wish to make is that each observer would give us a different impression of the tree because of the different principle of selection that guided his observation. [All notes are the authors'.]

This selection first appeared in *Understanding and Using English* (1972). Together, the Birks, specialists in English language and usage, also wrote *A Handbook of Grammar, Rhetoric, Mechanics, and Usage* (1976).

B. The Principle of Slanting

When we put our knowledge into words, a second process of selection, the process of slanting, takes place. Just as there is something, a rather mysterious principle of selection, which chooses for us what we will notice, and what will then become our knowledge, there is also a principle which operates, with or without our awareness, to select certain facts and feelings from our store of knowledge, and to choose the words and emphasis that we shall use to communicate our meaning.[2] Slanting may be defined as the process of selecting (1) knowledge — factual and attitudinal; (2) words; and (3) emphasis, to achieve the intention of the communicator. Slanting is present in some degree in all communication: one may *slant for* (favorable slanting), *slant against* (unfavorable slanting), or *slant both ways* (balanced shifting). . . .

C. Slanting by Use of Emphasis

Slanting by use of the devices of emphasis is unavoidable,[3] for emphasis is simply   5
the giving of stress to subject matter, and so indicating what is important and what is less important. In speech, for example, if we say that Socrates was *a wise old man,* we can give several slightly different meanings, one by stressing *wise,* another by stressing *old,* another by giving equal stress to *wise* and *old,* and still another by giving chief stress to *man.* Each different stress gives a different slant (favorable or unfavorable or balanced) to the statement because it conveys a different attitude toward Socrates or a different judgment of him. Connectives and word order also slant by the emphasis they give: Consider the difference in slanting or emphasis produced by *old but wise, old and wise, wise but old.* In writing, we cannot indicate subtle stresses on words as clearly as in speech, but we can achieve our emphasis and so can slant by the use of more complex patterns of word order, [by choice of connectives, by underlining heavily stressed words, and] by marks of punctuation that indicate short or long pauses and so give light or heavy emphasis. Question marks, quotation marks, and exclamation points can also contribute to slanting.[4] It is impossible either in speech or in writing to put two facts together without giving some slight emphasis or slant. For example, if we have in mind only two facts about a man, his awkwardness and his strength, we subtly slant those facts favorably or unfavorably in whatever way we may choose to join them.

---

[2]Notice that the "principle of selection" is at work as *we take in* knowledge, and that slanting occurs *as we express* our knowledge in words.

[3]When emphasis is present — and we can think of no instance in the use of language in which it is not — it necessarily influences the meaning by playing a part in the favorable, unfavorable, or balanced slant of the communicator. We are likely to emphasize by voice stress, even when we answer *yes* or *no* to simple questions.

[4]Consider the slanting achieved by punctuation in the following sentences: He called the Senator an honest man? *He* called the Senator an honest man? He called the Senator an honest man! He said one more such "honest" senator would corrupt the state.

More Favorable Slanting	*Less Favorable Slanting*
He is awkward and strong.	He is strong and awkward.
He is awkward but strong.	He is strong but awkward.
Although he is somewhat awkward, he is very strong.	He may be strong, but he's very awkward.

With more facts and in longer passages it is possible to maintain a delicate balance by alternating favorable emphasis and so producing a balanced effect.

All communication, then, is in some degree slanted by the *emphasis* of the communicator.

D. Slanting by Selection of Facts

To illustrate the technique of slanting by selection of facts, we shall examine three passages of informative writing which achieve different effects simply by the selection and emphasis of material. Each passage is made up of true statements or facts about a dog, yet the reader is given three different impressions. The first passage is an example of objective writing or balanced slanting, the second is slanted unfavorably, and the third is slanted favorably.

1. Balanced Presentation

> Our dog, Toddy, sold to us as a cocker, produces various reactions in various people. Those who come to the back door she usually growls and barks at (a milkman has said that he is afraid of her); those who come to the front door, she whines at and paws; also she tries to lick people's faces unless we have forestalled her by putting a newspaper in her mouth. (Some of our friends encourage these actions; others discourage them. Mrs. Firmly, one friend, slaps the dog with a newspaper and says, "I know how hard dogs are to train.") Toddy knows and responds to a number of words and phrases, and guests sometimes remark that she is a "very intelligent dog." She has fleas in the summer, and she sheds, at times copiously, the year round. Her blonde hairs are conspicuous when they are on people's clothing or on rugs or furniture. Her color and her large brown eyes frequently produce favorable comment. An expert on cockers would say that her ears are too short and set too high and that she is at least six pounds too heavy.

The passage above is made up of facts, verifiable facts,[5] deliberately selected and emphasized to produce a *balanced* impression. Of course not all the facts about the dog have been given — to supply *all* the facts on any subject, even such a comparatively simple one, would be an almost impossible task. Both favorable

---

[5] *Verifiable* facts are facts that can be checked and agreed upon and proved to be true by people who wish to verify them. That a particular theme received a failing grade is a verifiable fact; one needs merely to see the theme with the grade on it. That the instructor should have failed the theme is not, strictly speaking, a verifiable fact, but a matter of opinion. That women on the average live longer than men is a verifiable fact; that they live better is a matter of opinion, *a value judgment.*

Very different impressions of Toddy will be given depending on how the facts are presented.

and unfavorable facts are used, however, and an effort has been made to alternate favorable and unfavorable details so that neither will receive greater emphasis by position, proportion, or grammatical structure.

2. Facts Slanted Against

That dog put her paws on my white dress as soon as I came in the door, and she made so much noise that it was two minutes before she had quieted down enough for us to talk and hear each other. Then the gas man came and she did a great deal of barking. And her hairs are on the rug and on the furniture. If you wear a dark dress they stick to it like lint. When Mrs. Firmly came in, she actually hit the dog with a newspaper to make it stay down, and she made some remark about training dogs. I wish the Birks would take the hint or get rid of that noisy, shorteared, overweight "cocker" of theirs.

This unfavorably slanted version is based on the same facts, but now these facts have been selected and given a new emphasis. The speaker, using her selected

10

facts to give her impression of the dog, is quite possibly unaware of her negative slanting.

Now for a favorably slanted version:

3. Facts Slanted For

> What a lively and responsible dog! When I walked in the door, there she was with a newspaper in her mouth, whining and standing on her hind legs and wagging her tail all at the same time. And what an intelligent dog. If you suggest going for a walk, she will get her collar from the kitchen and hand it to you, and she brings Mrs. Birk's slippers whenever Mrs. Birk says she is "tired" or mentions slippers. At a command she catches balls, rolls over, "speaks," or stands on her hind feet and twirls around. She sits up and balances a piece of bread on her nose until she is told to take it; then she tosses it up and catches it. If you are eating something, she sits up in front of you and "begs" with those big dark brown eyes set in that light, buff-colored face of hers. When I got up to go and told her I was leaving, she rolled her eyes at me and sat up like a squirrel. She certainly is a lively and intelligent dog.

Speaker 3, like Speaker 2, is selecting from the "facts" summarized in balanced version 1, and is emphasizing his facts to communicate his impression.

All three passages are examples of *reporting* (i.e., consist only of verifiable facts), yet they give three very different impressions of the same dog because of the different ways the speakers slanted the facts. Some people say that figures don't lie, and many people believe that if they have the "facts," they have the "truth." Yet if we carefully examine the ways of thought and language, we see that any knowledge that comes to us through words has been subjected to the double screening of the principle of selection and the slanting of language. . . .

Wise listeners and readers realize that the double screening that is produced by the principle of selection and by slanting takes place even when people honestly try to report the facts as they know them. (Speakers 2 and 3, for instance, probably thought of themselves as simply giving information about a dog and were not deliberately trying to mislead.) Wise listeners and readers know too that deliberate manipulators of language, by mere selection and emphasis, can make their slanted facts appear to support almost any cause.

In arriving at opinions and values we cannot always be sure that the facts that   15
sift into our minds through language are representative and relevant and true. We need to remember that much of our information about politics, governmental activities, business conditions, and foreign affairs comes to us selected and slanted. More than we realize, our opinions on these matters may depend on what newspaper we read or what news commentator we listen to. Worthwhile opinions call for knowledge of reliable facts and reasonable arguments for and against — and such opinions include beliefs about morality and truth and religion as well as about public affairs. Because complex subjects involve knowing and dealing with many facts on both sides, reliable judgments are at best difficult to arrive at. If we want to be fairminded, we must be willing to subject our opinions to continual testing by new knowledge, and must realize that after all they *are* opinions, more

or less trustworthy. Their trustworthiness will depend on the representativeness of our facts, on the quality of our reasoning, and on the standard of values that we choose to apply.

We shall not give here a passage illustrating the unscrupulous slanting of facts. Such a passage would also include irrelevant facts and false statements presented as facts, along with various subtle distortions of fact. Yet to the uninformed reader the passage would be indistinguishable from a passage intended to give a fair account. If two passages (2 and 3) of casual and unintentional slanting of facts about a dog can give such contradictory impressions of a simple subject, the reader can imagine what a skilled and designing manipulation of facts and statistics could do to mislead an uninformed reader about a really complex subject. An example of such manipulation might be the account of the United States that Soviet propaganda has supplied to the average Russian. Such propaganda, however, would go beyond the mere slanting of the facts: It would clothe the selected facts in charged words and would make use of the many other devices of slanting that appear in charged language.

E. Slanting by Use of Charged Words

In the passages describing the dog Toddy, we were illustrating the technique of slanting by the selection and emphasis of facts. Though the facts selected had to be expressed in words, the words chosen were as factual as possible, and it was the selection and emphasis of facts and not of words that was mainly responsible for the two distinctly different impressions of the dog. In the passages below we are demonstrating another way of slanting — by the use of charged words. This time the accounts are very similar in the facts they contain; the different impressions of the subject, Corlyn, are produced not by different facts but by the subtle selection of charged words.

The passages were written by a clever student who was told to choose as his subject a person in action, and to write two descriptions, each using the "same facts." The instructions required that one description be slanted positively and the other negatively, so that the first would make the reader favorably inclined toward the person and the action, and the second would make him unfavorably inclined.

Here is the favorably charged description. Read it carefully and form your opinion of the person before you go on to read the second description.

Corlyn

Corlyn paused at the entrance to the room and glanced about. A well-cut black dress draped subtly about her slender form. Her long blonde hair gave her chiseled features the simple frame they required. She smiled an engaging smile as she accepted a cigarette from her escort. As he lit it for her she looked over the flame and into his eyes. Corlyn had that rare talent of making every male feel that he was the only man in the world.

She took his arm and they descended the steps into the room. She walked with an effortless grace and spoke with equal ease. They each took a cup of coffee and joined a group of friends near the fire. The flickering light danced across her face and lent an ethereal quality to her beauty. The good conversation, the crackling logs, and the stimulating coffee gave her a feeling of internal warmth. Her eyes danced with each leap of the flames.

Taken by itself this passage might seem just a description of an attractive girl.   20
The favorable slanting by use of charged words has been done so skillfully that it is inconspicuous. Now we turn to the unfavorably slanted description of the "same" girl in the "same" actions:

Corlyn

Corlyn halted at the entrance to the room and looked around. A plain black dress hung on her thin frame. Her stringy bleached hair accentuated her harsh features. She smiled an inane smile as she took a cigarette from her escort. As he lit it for her she stared over the lighter and into his eyes. Corlyn had a habit of making every male feel that he was the last man on earth.

She grasped his arm and they walked down the steps and into the room. Her pace was fast and ungainly, as was her speed. They each reached for some coffee and broke into a group of acquaintances near the fire. The flickering light played across her face and revealed every flaw. The loud talk, the fire, and the coffee she had gulped down made her feel hot. Her eyes grew more red with each leap of the flames.

When the reader compares these two descriptions, he can see how charged words influence the reader's attitude. One needs to read the two descriptions several times to appreciate all the subtle differences between them. Words, some rather heavily charged, others innocent-looking but lightly charged, work together to carry to the reader a judgment of a person and a situation. If the reader had seen only the first description of Corlyn, he might well have thought that he had formed his "own judgment on the basis of the facts." And the examples just given only begin to suggest the techniques that may be used in heavily charged language. For one thing, the two descriptions of Corlyn contain no really good example of the use of charged abstractions; for another, the writer was obliged by the assignment to use the same set of facts and so could not slant by selecting his material.

F. Slanting and Charged Language

. . . When slanting the facts, or words, or emphasis, or any combination of the three *significantly influences* feelings toward, or judgments about, a subject, the language used is charged language. . . .

Of course communications vary in the amount of charge they carry and in their effect on different people; what is very favorably charged for one person may have little or no charge, or may even be adversely charged, for others. It is sometimes hard to distinguish between charged and uncharged expression. But it is safe to say that whenever we wish to convey any kind of inner knowledge — feelings, attitudes, judgments, values — we are obliged to convey that attitudinal meaning through the medium of charged language; and when we wish to understand the inside knowledge of others, we have to interpret the charged language that they choose, or are obliged to use. Charged language, then, is the natural and necessary medium for the communication of charged or attitudinal meaning. At times we have difficulty in living with it, but we should have even greater difficulty in living without it.

Some of the difficulties in living with charged language are caused by its use in dishonest propaganda, in some editorials, in many political speeches, in most advertising, in certain kinds of effusive salesmanship, and in blatantly insincere, or exaggerated, or sentimental expressions of emotion. Other difficulties are caused by the misunderstandings and misinterpretations that charged language produces. A charged phrase misinterpreted in a love letter; a charged word spoken in haste or in anger; an acrimonious argument about religion or politics or athletics or fraternities; the frustrating uncertainty produced by the effort to understand the complex attitudinal meaning in a poem or play or a short story — these troubles, all growing out of the use of charged language, may give us the feeling that Robert Louis Stevenson expressed when he said, "The battle goes sore against us to the going down of the sun. . . ."

READING AND DISCUSSION QUESTIONS

1. How do the Birks distinguish between the process of selection and the process of slanting?
2. Explain the three types of slanting described by the Birks and illustrate each with examples from your own experience.
3. According to the Birks, why is charged language unavoidable — and ultimately desirable?

WRITING SUGGESTIONS

4. Choose a printed ad and analyze the use of language, applying the Birks' terminology.
5. Choose one or more editorials or letters to the editor and show how word choice reveals a writer's attitude toward a subject.

We find slanting everywhere, not only in advertising and propaganda, where we expect to find it, but in news stories, which should be strictly neutral in their recounting of events, and in textbooks. In the field of history, for example, it is often difficult for scholars to remain impartial about significant events. Like the rest of us, they may approve or disapprove, and their choice of words will reflect their judgments.

The following passage by a distinguished Catholic historian describes the events surrounding the momentous decision by Henry VIII, king of England, to break with the Roman Catholic Church in 1534, in part because of the Pope's refusal to grant him a divorce from the Catholic princess Catherine of Aragon so that he could marry Anne Boleyn.

> The *protracted* delay in receiving an annulment was very *irritating* to the *impulsive* English king. . . . Gradually Henry's former *effusive* loyalty to Rome gave way to a settled conviction of the tyranny of the papal power, and there *rushed* to his mind the recollections of efforts of earlier English rulers to restrict that power. A few *salutary* enactments against the Church might *compel* a favorable decision from the Pope.
>
> Henry seriously opened his campaign against the Roman Church in 1531, when he *frightened* the clergy into paying a fine of over half a million dollars for violating an *obsolete* statute . . . and in the same year he *forced* the clergy to recognize himself as supreme head of the Church. . . .
>
> His *subservient* Parliament then empowered him to stop the payments of annates to the Pope and to appoint bishops in England without recourse to the papacy. *Without waiting longer* for the decision from Rome, he had Cranmer, *one of his own creatures,* whom he had just named Archbishop of Canterbury, declare his marriage null and void. . . .
>
> Yet Henry VIII encountered considerable *opposition* from the *higher clergy,* from the monks, and from many *intellectual leaders.* . . . A *popular uprising* — the Pilgrimage of Grace — was *sternly* suppressed, and such men as the *brilliant* Sir Thomas More and John Fisher, the *aged* and *saintly* bishop of Rochester, were beheaded because they retained their former belief in papal supremacy.[8] [Italics added.]

In the first paragraph the italicized words help make the following points: that Henry was rash, impulsive, and insincere and that he was intent on punishing the church (the word *salutary* means healthful or beneficial and is used sarcastically). In the second paragraph the choice of words stresses Henry's use of force and the cowardly submission of his followers. In the third paragraph the adjectives describing the opposition to Henry's campaign and those who were executed emphasize Henry's cruelty and despotism. Within the limits of this brief passage the author has offered support for his strong indictment of Henry VIII's actions, both in defining the statute as obsolete and in describing the popular opposition. In a longer exposition you would expect to find a more elaborate justification with facts and authoritative opinion from other sources.

The advocate of a position in an argument, unlike the reporter or the historian, must express a judgment, but the preceding examples demonstrate how the arguer should use language to avoid or minimize slanting and to persuade readers that he or she has come to a conclusion after careful analysis. The careful arguer must not conceal his or her judgments by presenting them as if they were statements of fact, but must offer convincing support for his or her choice of words and respect the audience's feelings and attitudes by using temperate language.

Depending on the circumstances, *exaggeration* can be defined, in the words of one writer, as "a form of lying." An essay in *Time* magazine, "Watching Out

[8]Carlton J. H. Hayes, *A Political and Cultural History of Modern Europe,* vol. 1 (New York: Macmillan, 1933), pp. 172–73.

for Loaded Words," points to the danger for the arguer in relying on exaggerated language as an essential part of the argument.

> The trouble with loaded words is they tend to short-circuit thought. While
> they may describe something, they simultaneously try to seduce the mind
> into accepting a prefabricated opinion about the something described.[9]

PRACTICE

Locate specific examples of slanted language in the first of these two excerpts from the
debate later in the chapter. What effect does the word choice have in the first piece?
How does it compare to the word choice in the second passage, on the same topic?

> 1. Grandstanding politicians love to rail against the gun. Inanimate ob-
> jects are good targets to beat up on. That way, politicians do not have
> to address the real problems in our society. We pay a price for this cra-
> ven misdirection, though, in thousands of murders, muggings, rapes,
> robberies, and burglaries.
>
> Yet that is not the greatest danger we face. The Founding Fathers
> knew that *governments* could turn criminal. That is the principal reason
> they wanted every man armed: An armed citizenry militates against
> the development of tyranny. The Founding Fathers did not want every
> man armed in order to shoot a burglar, although they had nothing
> against doing so. The Founding Fathers did not want every man armed
> in order to shoot Bambi or Thumper, although they had nothing
> against doing so. The Founding Fathers wanted every man armed in
> order to shoot soldiers or police of tyrannical regimes who suppress the
> rights of free men. (McGrath 425)
>
> 2. Americans also have a right to defend their homes, and we need not
> challenge that. Nor does anyone seriously question that the Constitu-
> tion protects the right of hunters to own and keep sporting guns for
> hunting game any more than anyone would challenge the right to
> own and keep fishing rods and other equipment for fishing — or to
> own automobiles. To "keep and bear arms" for hunting today
> is essentially a recreational activity and not an imperative of survival,
> as it was 200 years ago; "Saturday night specials" and machine guns are
> not recreational weapons and surely are as much in need of regulation
> as motor vehicles.
>
> Americans should ask themselves a few questions. The Constitution
> does not mention automobiles or motorboats, but the right to keep
> and own an automobile is beyond question; equally beyond question
> is the power of the state to regulate the purchase or the transfer of such
> vehicle and the right to license the vehicle and the driver with reason-
> able standards. In some places, even a bicycle must be registered, as
> must some household dogs. (Burger 419)

---

[9] *Time,* May 24, 1982, p. 86.

Picturesque Language

Picturesque language consists of words that produce images in the mind of the reader. Students sometimes assume that vivid picture-making language is the exclusive instrument of novelists and poets, but writers of arguments can also avail themselves of such devices to heighten the impact of their messages.

Picturesque language can do more than render a scene. It shares with other kinds of emotive language the power to express and arouse deep feelings. Like a fine painting or photograph, it can draw readers into the picture where they partake of the writer's experience as if they were also present. Such power may be used to delight, to instruct, or to horrify. In 1741 the Puritan preacher Jonathan Edwards delivered his sermon "Sinners in the Hands of an Angry God," in which people were likened to repulsive spiders hanging over the flames of Hell to be dropped into the fire whenever a wrathful God was pleased to release them. The congregation's reaction to Edwards's picture of the everlasting horrors to be suffered in the netherworld included panic, fainting, hysteria, and convulsions. Subsequently Edwards lost his pulpit in Massachusetts, in part as a consequence of his success at provoking such uncontrollable terror among his congregation.

Language as intense and vivid as Edwards's emerges from very strong emotion about a deeply felt cause. In the following paragraph, Lavina Melwani uses picturesque language to call attention to some of the problems faced daily by undocumented workers.

> The rats — bold, tenacious, and totally fearless — are what bothered him the most. Prem, who requested his last name not be used, says the rodents have the run of the old apartment he shares in Baltimore City, Maryland, with five other Nepali men, most of them undocumented. "It is impossible to have beds for six people in two rooms," he says. "So we have small roll-out beds or mattresses on the floor. There are many rats running around the apartment and it's difficult to catch them. We can't complain. The landlord doesn't care. He knows we have to live here and have no choice."[10]

The rules governing the use of picturesque language are the same as those governing other kinds of emotive language. Is the language appropriate? Is it too strong, too colorful for the purpose of the message? Does it result in slanting or distortion? What will its impact be on a hostile or indifferent audience? Will they be angered, repelled? Will they cease to read or listen if the imagery is too disturbing?

[10]"No Roof No Roots No Rights." *Little India*, April 12, 2006, p. 42.

Concrete and Abstract Language

Writers of argument need to be aware of another use of language — the distinction between concrete and abstract. Concrete words point to real objects and real experiences. Abstract words express qualities apart from particular things and events. *Velvety, dark red roses* is concrete; we can see, touch, and smell them. *Beauty* in the eye of the beholder is abstract; we can speak of the quality of beauty without reference to a particular object or event. *Returning money found in the street to the owner, although no one has seen the discovery* is concrete. *Honesty* is abstract. In abstracting we separate a quality shared by a number of objects or events, however different from each other the individual objects or events may be.

Writing that describes or tells a story leans heavily on concrete language. Although arguments also rely on the vividness of concrete language, they use abstract terms far more extensively than other kinds of writing. Using abstractions effectively, especially in arguments of value and policy, is important for two reasons: (1) Abstractions represent the qualities, characteristics, and values that the writer is explaining, defending, or attacking; and (2) they enable the writer to make generalizations about his or her data. Equally important is knowing when to avoid abstractions that obscure the message.

You should not expect abstract terms alone to carry the emotional content of your message. The effect of even the most suggestive words can be enhanced by details, examples, and anecdotes. One mode of expression is not superior to the other; both abstractions and concrete detail work together to produce clear, persuasive argument. This is especially true when the meanings assigned to abstract terms vary from reader to reader.

In establishing claims based on the support of values, for example, you may use such abstract terms as *religion, duty, freedom, peace, progress, justice, equality, democracy,* and *pursuit of happiness.* You can assume that some of these words are associated with the same ideas and emotions for almost all readers; others require further explanation. Suppose you write, "We have made great progress in the last fifty years." One dictionary defines *progress* as "a gradual betterment," another abstraction. How will you define "gradual betterment" for your readers? Can you be sure that they have in mind the same references for progress that you do? If not, misunderstandings are inevitable. You may offer examples: supersonic planes, computers, shopping malls, nuclear energy. Many of your readers will react favorably to the mention of these innovations, which to them represent progress; others, for whom these inventions represent change but not progress, will react unfavorably. You may not be able to convince all of your readers that "we have made great progress," but all of them will now understand what you mean by "progress." And intelligent disagreement is preferable to misunderstanding.

Abstractions tell us what conclusions we have arrived at; details tell us how we got there. But there are dangers in either too many details or too many abstractions. For example, a writer may present only concrete data without telling readers what conclusions are to be drawn from them. Suppose you read the following:

> To Chinese road-users, traffic police are part of the grass . . . and neither they nor the rules they're supposed to enforce are paid the least attention. . . . Ignoring traffic-lights is only one peculiarity of Chinese traffic. It's normal for a pedestrian to walk straight out into a stream of cars without so much as lifting his head; and goodness knows how many Chinese cyclists I've almost killed as they have shot blindly in front of me across busy main roads.[11]

These details would constitute no more than interesting gossip until we read, "It's not so much a sign of ignorance or recklessness . . . but of fatalism." The details of specific behavior have now acquired a significance expressed in the abstraction *fatalism*.

A more common problem, however, in using abstractions is omission of details. Either the writer is not a skilled observer and cannot provide the details, or believes that such details are too small and quiet compared to the grand sounds made by abstract terms. These grand sounds, unfortunately, cannot compensate for the lack of clarity and liveliness. Lacking detailed support, abstract words may be misinterpreted. They may also represent ideas that are so vague as to be meaningless. Sometimes they function illegitimately as short cuts (discussed on pp. 360–65), arousing emotions but unaccompanied by good reasons for their use. The following paragraph exhibits some of these common faults. How would you translate it into clear English?

> We respectively petition, request, and entreat that due and adequate provision be made, this day and the date hereinafter subscribed, for the satisfying of these petitioners' nutritional requirements and for the organizing of such methods of allocation and distribution as may be deemed necessary and proper to assure the reception by and for said petitioners of such quantities of baked cereal products as shall, in the judgment of the aforesaid petitioners, constitute a sufficient supply thereof.[12]

If you had trouble decoding this, it was because there were almost no concrete references — the homely words *baked* and *cereal* leap out of the paragraph like English signposts in a foreign country — and too many long words or words of Latin origin when simple words would do: *requirements* instead of *needs*, *petition* instead of *ask*. An absence of concrete references and an excess of long Latinate words can have a depressing effect on both writer and reader. The writer may be in danger of losing the thread of the argument, the reader at a loss to discover the message.

The paragraph above, according to James B. Minor, a lawyer who teaches courses in legal drafting, is "how a federal regulation writer would probably write, 'Give us this day our daily bread.'" This brief sentence with its short,

[11]Philip Short, "The Chinese and the Russians," *The Listener,* April 8, 1982, p. 6.
[12]*New York Times,* May 10, 1977, p. 35.

familiar words and its origin in the Lord's Prayer has a deep emotional effect. The paragraph composed by Minor deadens any emotional impact because of its preponderance of abstract terms and its lack of connection with the world of our senses.

Finally, there are the moral implications of using abstractions that conceal a disagreeable reality. Consider this scenario:

> It has long been feared that a President could be making his fateful deci-
> sion while at a "psychological distance" from the victims of a nuclear
> barrage; that he would be in a clean, air-conditioned room, surrounded by
> well-scrubbed aides, all talking in abstract terms about appropriate military
> responses in an international crisis, and that he might well push to the
> back of his mind the realization that hundreds of millions of people would
> be exterminated.
>
> So Roger Fisher, professor of law at Harvard University, offers a simple
> suggestion to make the stakes more real. He would put the codes needed
> to fire nuclear weapons in a little capsule, and implant the capsule next
> to the heart of a volunteer, who would carry a big butcher knife as he
> accompanied the President everywhere. If the President ever wanted to
> fire nuclear weapons, he would first have to kill, with his own hands, that
> human being.
>
> He has to look at someone and realize what death is — what an inno-
> cent death is. "It's reality brought home," says Professor Fisher.[13]

The moral lesson is clear: It is much easier to do harm if we convince ourselves that the object of the injury is only an abstraction.

Short Cuts

Short cuts are arguments that depend on readers' responses to words. Short cuts, like other devices we have discussed so far, are a common use of emotive language but are often mistaken for valid argument.

Although they have power to move us, these abbreviated substitutes for argument avoid the hard work necessary to provide facts, expert opinion, and analysis of warrants. Even experts, however, can be guilty of using short cuts, and the writer who consults an authority should be alert to that authority's use of language. Two of the most common uses of short cuts are clichés and slogans.

Clichés

A cliché is an expression or idea grown stale through overuse. Clichés in language are tired expressions that have faded like old photographs; readers no lon-

---

[13] *New York Times*, September 7, 1982, sec. C, p. 1.

ger see anything when clichés are placed before them. Clichés include phrases like "cradle of civilization," "few and far between," "rude awakening," "follow in the footsteps of," "fly in the ointment."

But more important to recognize and avoid are *clichés of thought.* A cliché of thought may be likened to a formula, which one dictionary defines as "any conventional rule or method for doing something, especially when used, applied, or repeated without thought." Clichés of thought represent ready-made answers to questions, stereotyped solutions to problems, "knee-jerk" reactions. Two writers who call these forms of expression "mass language" describe it this way: "Mass language is language which presents the reader with a response he is expected to make without giving him adequate reason for having this response."[14] These clichés of thought are often expressed in single words or phrases.

Certain cultural attitudes encourage the use of clichés. The liberal American tradition has been governed by hopeful assumptions about our ability to solve problems. A professor of communications says that "we tell our students that for every problem there must be a solution."[15] But real solutions are hard to come by. In our haste to provide them, to prove that we can be decisive, we may be tempted to produce familiar responses that resemble solutions. All reasonable solutions are worthy of consideration, but they must be defined and supported if they are to be used in a thoughtful, well-constructed argument.

Although formulas change with the times, some are unexpectedly hardy and survive long after critics have revealed their weaknesses. Overpopulation is often cited as the cause of poverty, disease, and war. It can be found in the writing of the ancient Greeks 2,500 years ago. "That perspective," says the editor of *Food Monitor,* a journal published by World Hunger Year, Inc., "is so pervasive that most Americans have simply stopped thinking about population and resort to inane clucking of tongues."[16] If the writer offering overpopulation as an explanation for poverty were to look further, he or she would discover that the explanation rested on shaky data. Singapore, the second most densely populated country in the world (18,640 persons per square mile) is also one of the richest ($62,200 per capita income per year). Chad, one of the most sparsely populated (22 persons per square kilometer) is also one of the poorest ($1,900 per capita income per year).[17] Strictly defined, overpopulation may serve to explain some instances of poverty; obviously it cannot serve as a blanket to cover all or even most instances. "By repeating stock phrases," one columnist reminds us, "we lose the ability, finally, to hear what we are saying."

[14]Richard E. Hughes and P. Albert Duhamel, *Rhetoric: Principles and Usage* (Englewood Cliffs, N.J.: Prentice-Hall, 1962), p. 161.

[15]Malcolm O. Sillars, "The New Conservatism and the Teacher of Speech," *Southern Speech Journal* 21 (1956), p. 240.

[16]Letter to the *New York Times,* October 4, 1982, sec. A, p. 18.

[17]www.cia.gov; worldatlas.com.

Slogans

> I have always been rather impressed by those people who wear badges stat-
> ing where they stand on certain issues. The badges have to be small, and
> therefore the message has to be small, concise, and without elaboration.
> So it comes out as "I hate something" or "I love something," or ban this or
> ban that. There isn't space for argument, and I therefore envy the badge-
> wearer who is so clear-cut about his or her opinions.[18]

The word *slogan* has a picturesque origin. A slogan was the war cry or rallying cry of a Scottish or Irish clan. From that early use it has come to mean a
"catchword or rallying motto distinctly associated with a political party or other
group" as well as a "catch phrase used to advertise a product."

Slogans, like clichés, are short, undeveloped arguments. They represent abbreviated responses to often complex questions. As a reader you need to be
aware that slogans merely call attention to a problem; they cannot offer persuasive proof for a claim in a dozen words or less. As a writer you should avoid the
use of slogans that evoke an emotional response "without giving [the reader]
adequate reason for having this response."

Advertising slogans are the most familiar. Some of them are probably better known than nursery rhymes: "Got milk?" "L'Oréal, because I'm worth it,"
"Nike, just do it." Advertisements may, of course, rely for their effectiveness
on more than slogans. They may also give us interesting and valuable information about products, but most advertisements give us slogans that ignore
proof — short cuts substituting for argument.

The persuasive appeal of advertising slogans heavily depends on the connotations associated with products. In Chapter 6 (see p. 217, under "Appeals to
Needs and Values"), we discussed the way in which advertisements promise to
satisfy our needs and protect our values. Wherever evidence is scarce or nonexistent, the advertiser must persuade us through skillful choice of words and
phrases (as well as pictures), especially those that produce pleasurable feelings.
"Let it inspire you" is the slogan of a popular liqueur. It suggests a desirable state
of being but remains suitably vague about the nature of the inspiration. Another familiar slogan — "Noxzema, clean makeup" — also emphasizes a quality
that we approve of, but what is "clean" makeup? Since the advertisers are silent,
we are left with warm feelings about the word and not much more.

Advertising slogans are persuasive because their witty phrasing and punchy
rhythms produce an automatic *yes* response. We react to them as we might
react to the lyrics of popular songs, and we treat them far less critically than we
treat more straightforward and elaborate arguments. Still, the consequences of
failing to analyze the slogans of advertisers are usually not serious. You may be
tempted to buy a product because you were fascinated by a brilliant slogan, but
if the product doesn't satisfy, you can abandon it without much loss. However,

[18]Anthony Smith, "Nuclear Power — Why Not?" *The Listener,* October 22, 1981, p. 463.

Slogans are short, undeveloped arguments.

ignoring ideological slogans coined by political parties or special-interest groups may carry an enormous price, and the results are not so easily undone.

Ideological slogans, like advertising slogans, depend on the power of connotation, the emotional associations aroused by a word or phrase. In the 1960s and 1970s, a period of well-advertised social change, slogans flourished; they appeared by the hundreds of thousands on buttons, T-shirts, and bumper stickers. One of them read, "Student Power!" To some readers of the slogan, distrustful of young people and worried about student unrest on campuses and in the streets, the suggestion was frightening. To others, mostly students, the idea of power, however undefined, was intoxicating. Notice that "Student Power!" is not an argument; it is only a claim. (It might also represent a warrant.) As a claim, for example, it might take this form: Students at this school should have the power to select the faculty. Of course, the arguer would need to provide the kinds of proof that support his or her claim, something the slogan by itself cannot do. Many people, whether they accepted or rejected the claim, supplied the rest of the argument without knowing exactly what the issues were and how a developed argument would proceed. They were accepting or rejecting the slogan largely on the basis of emotional reaction to words.

American political history is, in fact, a repository of slogans. Leaf through a history of the United States and you will come across "Tippecanoe and Tyler, too," "manifest destiny," "fifty-four forty or fight," "make the world safe for democracy," "the silent majority," "the domino theory," "the missile gap," "the window of vulnerability." Each administration tries to capture the attention and allegiance of the public by coining catchy phrases. Roosevelt's New Deal in 1932 was followed by the Square Deal and the New Frontier. Today, slogans must be carefully selected to avoid offending groups that are sensitive to the ways in which words affect their interests. In 1983 Senator John Glenn, announcing his candidacy for president, talked about bringing "old values and new horizons" to the White House. "New horizons" apparently carried positive connotations. His staff, however, worried that "old values" might suggest racism and sexism to minorities and women.

Over a period of time, slogans, like clichés, can acquire a life of their own and, if they are repeated often enough, come to represent an unchanging truth we no longer need to examine. "Dangerously," says the writer quoted above, "policy makers become prisoners of the slogans they popularize."

Following are two examples. The first is part of the second inaugural address of George C. Wallace, governor of Alabama, in 1971. The second is taken from an article in the *Militia News,* the organ of a group that believed the U.S. government was engaged in a "satanic conspiracy" to disarm the American people and then enslave them. Timothy McVeigh, who blew up the Oklahoma City federal building in 1995, was influenced by the group.

> The people of the South and those who think like the South, represent the majority viewpoint within our constitutional democracy, but they are not organized and do not speak with a loud voice. Until the day arrives when the voice of the people of the South and those who think like us is, within the law, thrust into the face of the bureaucrats, only then can the "people's power" express itself legally and ethically and get results. . . . Too long, oh, too long, has the voice of the people been silenced by their own disruptive government — by governmental bribery in quasi- governmental handouts such as H.E.W. and others that exist in America today! An aroused people can save this nation from those evil forces who seek our destruction. The choice is yours. The hour is growing late![19]

> Every gun owner who is the least bit informed knows that those who are behind this conspiracy — who now have their people well placed in political office, in the courts, in the media, and in the schools, are working for the total disarming of the American people and the surrender of our nation and our sovereignty. . . . The time is at hand when men and women must decide whether they are on the side of freedom and justice, the American republic, and Almighty God, or if they are on the side of tyranny and oppression, the New World Order, and Satan.[20]

Whatever power these recommendations might have if their proposals were more clearly formulated, as they stand they are collections of slogans and loaded words. (Even the language falters: Can the voice of the people be "thrust into the face of the bureaucrats"?) We can visualize some of the slogans as brightly colored banners: "Dislodge Big Money!" "Power to the People!" "Save This

---

[19]Second Inaugural Address as governor of Alabama, January 18, 1971.
[20]Chip Berlet and Matthew N. Lyons, *Right-Wing Populism in America* (New York: Guildford Press, 2000), p. 301.

Nation from Evil Forces!" "The Choice Is Yours!" Do all the groups mentioned share identical interests? If so, what are they? Given the vagueness of the terms, it is not surprising that arguers on opposite sides of the political spectrum — loosely characterized as liberal and conservative — sometimes resort to the same clichés and slogans: the language of populism, or a belief in conspiracies against God-fearing people, in these examples.

Slogans have numerous shortcomings as substitutes for the development of an argument. First, their brevity presents serious disadvantages. Slogans necessarily ignore exceptions or negative instances that might qualify a claim. They usually speak in absolute terms without describing the circumstances in which a principle or idea might not work. Their claims therefore seem shrill and exaggerated. In addition, brevity prevents the sloganeer from revealing how he or she arrived at conclusions.

Second, slogans may conceal unexamined warrants. When Japanese cars were beginning to compete with American cars, the slogan "Made in America by Americans" appeared on the bumpers of thousands of American-made cars. A thoughtful reader would have discovered in this slogan several implied warrants: American cars are better than Japanese cars; the American economy will improve if we buy American; patriotism can be expressed by buying American goods. If the reader were to ask a few probing questions, he or she might find these warrants unconvincing.

Silent warrants that express values hide in other popular and influential slogans. "Pro-life," the slogan of those who oppose abortion, assumes that the fetus is a living being entitled to the same rights as individuals already born. "Pro-choice," the slogan of those who favor abortion, suggests that the freedom of the pregnant woman to choose is the foremost or only consideration. The words *life* and *choice* have been carefully selected to reflect desirable qualities, but the words are only the beginning of the argument.

Third, although slogans may express admirable sentiments, they often fail to tell us how to achieve their objectives. They address us in the imperative mode, ordering us to take an action or refrain from it. But the means of achieving the objectives may be nonexistent or very costly. If sloganeers cannot offer workable means for implementing their goals, they risk alienating the audience.

Sloganeering is one of the recognizable attributes of propaganda. Propaganda for both good and bad purposes is a form of slanting, of selecting language and facts to persuade an audience to take a certain action. Even a good cause may be weakened by an unsatisfactory slogan. The slogans of some organizations devoted to fundraising for people with physical handicaps have come under attack for depicting those with handicaps as helpless. According to one critic, the popular slogan "Jerry's kids" promotes the idea that Jerry Lewis is the sole support of children with muscular dystrophy. Perhaps increased sensitivity to the needs of people with disabilities will produce new words and new slogans. If you assume that your audience is sophisticated and alert, you will probably write your strongest arguments, devoid of clichés and slogans.

SAMPLE ANNOTATED ESSAY

President's Address to the Nation, September 11, 2006

GEORGE W. BUSH

Words like seared, barbarity, and murdered are examples of slanting used appropriately for the author's purpose.

Good evening. Five years ago, this date — September the 11th — was seared into America's memory. Nineteen men attacked us with a barbarity unequaled in our history. They murdered people of all colors, creeds, and nationalities — and made war upon the entire free world. Since that day, America and her allies have taken the offensive in a war unlike any we have fought before. Today, we are safer, but we are not yet safe. On this solemn night, I've asked for some of your time to discuss the nature of the threat still before us, what we are doing to protect our nation, and the building of a more hopeful Middle East that holds the key to peace for America and the world.

It is exaggeration to say that the acts described in this paragraph are distinctly American, but the concrete examples are effective for the author's purpose.

On 9/11, our nation saw the face of evil. Yet on that awful day, we also witnessed something distinctly American: ordinary citizens rising to the occasion, and responding with extraordinary acts of courage. We saw courage in office workers who were trapped on the high floors of burning skyscrapers — and called home so that their last words to their families would be of comfort and love. We saw courage in passengers aboard Flight 93, who recited the 23rd Psalm — and then charged the cockpit. And we saw courage in the Pentagon staff who made it out of the flames and smoke — and ran back in to answer cries for help. On this day, we remember the innocent who lost their lives — and we pay tribute to those who gave their lives so that others might live.

More concrete examples, with the first person I making it clear that Bush has shared moments of grief with the victims' families.

For many of our citizens, the wounds of that morning are still fresh. I've met firefighters and police officers who choke up at the memory of fallen comrades. I've stood with families gathered on a grassy field in Pennsylvania, who take bittersweet pride in loved ones who refused to be victims — and gave America our first victory in the war on terror. I've sat beside young mothers with children who are now five years old — and still long for the

For the second time Bush refers to a more hopeful world.

If the rest of the essay does not provide further explanation, this will be a cliché of thought.

Two of the strongest slanted words here are perverted and, in contrast to the reference to civilized nations, the implication that America's enemies are uncivilized.

On the other hand, to have a calling carries a positive slant, suggesting a religious or at least honorable sense of duty.

The allusion to the Cold War will evoke negative memories for some, depending on their age.

The reference to the war in Iraq as one that America didn't ask for suggests that it was imposed on an unwilling nation.

Suggesting what a loss would mean for America's children is an appeal to emotion.

daddies who will never cradle them in their arms. Out of this suffering, we resolve to honor every man and woman lost. And we seek their lasting memorial in a safer and more hopeful world.

Since the horror of 9/11, we've learned a great deal about the enemy. We have learned that they are evil and kill without mercy — but not without purpose. We have learned that they form a global network of extremists who are driven by a perverted vision of Islam — a totalitarian ideology that hates freedom, rejects tolerance, and despises all dissent. And we have learned that their goal is to build a radical Islamic empire where women are prisoners in their homes, men are beaten for missing prayer meetings, and terrorists have a safe haven to plan and launch attacks on America and other civilized nations. The war against this enemy is more than a military conflict. It is the decisive ideological struggle of the twenty first century, and the calling of our generation.

Our nation is being tested in a way that we have not been since the start of the Cold War. We saw what a handful of our enemies can do with box-cutters and plane tickets. We hear their threats to launch even more terrible attacks on our people. And we know that if they were able to get their hands on weapons of mass destruction, they would use them against us. We face an enemy determined to bring death and suffering into our homes. America did not ask for this war, and every American wishes it were over. So do I. But the war is not over — and it will not be over until either we or the extremists emerge victorious. If we do not defeat these enemies now, we will leave our children to face a Middle East overrun by terrorist states and radical dictators armed with nuclear weapons. We are in a war that will set the course for this new century — and determine the destiny of millions across the world.

For America, 9/11 was more than a tragedy — it changed the way we look at the world. On September the 11th, we resolved that we would go on the offense against our enemies, and we would not distinguish between the terrorists and those who harbor or support them. So we helped drive the Taliban from power in Afghanistan. We put al Qaeda on the run, and killed or captured most of those who planned the 9/11 attacks, including the man believed to be the mastermind, Khalid

5

Sheik Mohammed. He and other suspected terrorists have been questioned by the Central Intelligence Agency, and they provided valuable information that has helped stop attacks in America and across the world. Now these men have been transferred to Guantanamo Bay, so they can be held to account for their actions. Osama bin Laden and other terrorists are still in hiding. Our message to them is clear: No matter how long it takes, America will find you, and we will bring you to justice.

On September the 11th, we learned that America must confront threats before they reach our shores, whether those threats come from terrorist networks or terrorist states. I'm often asked why we're in Iraq when Saddam Hussein was not responsible for the 9/11 attacks. The answer is that the regime of Saddam Hussein was a clear threat. My administration, the Congress, and the United Nations saw the threat — and after 9/11, Saddam's regime posed a risk that the world could not afford to take. The world is safer because Saddam Hussein is no longer in power. And now the challenge is to help the Iraqi people build a democracy that fulfills the dreams of the nearly 12 million Iraqis who came out to vote in free elections last December.

Al Qaeda and other extremists from across the world have come to Iraq to stop the rise of a free society in the heart of the Middle East. They have joined the remnants of Saddam's regime and other armed groups to foment sectarian violence and drive us out. Our enemies in Iraq are tough and they are committed — but so are Iraqi and coalition forces. We're adapting to stay ahead of the enemy, and we are carrying out a clear plan to ensure that a democratic Iraq succeeds.

We're training Iraqi troops so they can defend their nation. We're helping Iraq's unity government grow in strength and serve its people. We will not leave until this work is done. Whatever mistakes have been made in Iraq, the worst mistake would be to think that if we pulled out, the terrorists would leave us alone. They will not leave us alone. They will follow us. The safety of America depends on the outcome of the battle in the streets of Baghdad. Osama bin Laden calls this fight "the Third World War" — and he says that victory for the terrorists in Iraq will mean America's "defeat and disgrace forever." If we yield Iraq to men like bin Laden, our enemies will

Side notes:

To be held to account for their actions is a cliché, one that may hide uncomfortable truths, given suspicions aroused about how the U.S. questions prisoners.

Another cliché of thought: a risk that the world could not afford to take.

References to democracy and free elections have positive connotations for most Americans.

The allusion to World War I and World War II by alluding to a Third World War, like the allusion to the Cold War, evokes memories, mostly negative, for older Americans.

Osama bin Laden's reference to America's defeat and disgrace forever is a verbal assault on national pride.

be emboldened; they will gain a new safe haven; they will use Iraq's resources to fuel their extremist movement. We will not allow this to happen. America will stay in the fight. Iraq will be a free nation, and a strong ally in the war on terror.

The primary slogan for the war in Iraq: the war on terror.

We can be confident that our coalition will succeed   10
because the Iraqi people have been steadfast in the face of unspeakable violence. And we can be confident in victory because of the skill and resolve of America's Armed Forces. Every one of our troops is a volunteer, and since the attacks of September the 11th, more than 1.6 million Americans have stepped forward to put on our nation's uniform. In Iraq, Afghanistan, and other fronts in the war on terror, the men and women of our military are making great sacrifices to keep us safe. Some have suffered terrible injuries — and nearly 3,000 have given their lives. America cherishes their memory. We pray for their families. And we will never back down from the work they have begun.

The enemy is guilty of unspeakable violence. The Iraqi people are steadfast. Our Armed Forces have exhibited skill and resolve, made great sacrifices.

We also honor those who toil day and night to keep our homeland safe, and we are giving them the tools they need to protect our people. We've created the Department of Homeland Security. We have torn down the wall that kept law enforcement and intelligence from sharing information. We've tightened security at our airports and seaports and borders, and we've created new programs to monitor enemy bank records and phone calls. Thanks to the hard work of our law enforcement and intelligence professionals, we have broken up terrorist cells in our midst and saved American lives.

Appeals to Americans' need for security.

Five years after 9/11, our enemies have not succeeded in launching another attack on our soil, but they've not been idle. Al Qaeda and those inspired by its hateful ideology have carried out terrorist attacks in more than two dozen nations. And just last month, they were foiled in a plot to blow up passenger planes headed for the United States. They remain determined to attack America and kill our citizens — and we are determined to stop them. We'll continue to give the men and women who protect us every resource and legal authority they need to do their jobs.

Slanted language: the enemy's ideology is hateful.

The use of the adjective legal to modify authority is loaded for those who believe Congress was rushed into passing laws that threaten Americans' right to privacy out of fear.

In the first days after the 9/11 attacks I promised to use every element of national power to fight the terrorists, wherever we find them. One of the strongest weapons

Many abstractions here that are clichés of thought if not supported: <u>power of freedom</u>, <u>clash of civilizations</u>, <u>struggle for civilization</u>, <u>way of life enjoyed by free nations</u>.

in our arsenal is the power of freedom. The terrorists fear freedom as much as they do our firepower. They are thrown into panic at the sight of an old man pulling the election lever, girls enrolling in schools, or families worshiping God in their own traditions. They know that given a choice, people will choose freedom over their extremist ideology. So their answer is to deny people this choice by raging against the forces of freedom and moderation. This struggle has been called a clash of civilizations. In truth, it is a struggle for civilization. We are fighting to maintain the way of life enjoyed by free nations. And we're fighting for the possibility that good and decent people across the Middle East can raise up societies based on freedom and tolerance and personal dignity.

We are now in the early hours of this struggle between tyranny and freedom. Amid the violence, some question whether the people of the Middle East want their freedom, and whether the forces of moderation can prevail. For 60 years, these doubts guided our policies in the Middle East. And then, on a bright September morning, it became clear that the calm we saw in the Middle East was only a mirage. Years of pursuing stability to promote peace had left us with neither. So we changed our policies, and committed America's influence in the world to advancing freedom and democracy as the great alternatives to repression and radicalism.

With our help, the people of the Middle East are now   15
stepping forward to claim their freedom. From Kabul to Baghdad to Beirut, there are brave men and women risking their lives each day for the same freedoms that we enjoy. And they have one question for us: Do we have the confidence to do in the Middle East what our fathers and grandfathers accomplished in Europe and Asia? By standing with democratic leaders and reformers, by giving voice to the hopes of decent men and women, we're offering a path away from radicalism. And we are enlisting the most powerful force for peace and moderation in the Middle East: the desire of millions to be free.

Across the broader Middle East, the extremists are fighting to prevent such a future. Yet America has confronted evil before, and we have defeated it — sometimes at the cost of thousands of good men in a single battle. When Franklin Roosevelt vowed to defeat two enemies across two oceans, he could not have foreseen D-Day and

The references to what our fathers and grandfathers did in Europe and Asia is an additional appeal to American pride. Only those who agree with America deserve the label <u>decent</u>.

Allusions to previous
American victories and former
presidents who led the nation
during World War II and the
Cold War.

Desert of despotism and
fertile gardens of liberty —
picturesque language used
for contrast.

A specific example that carries emotional impact.

Iwo Jima — but he would not have been surprised at
the outcome. When Harry Truman promised American
support for free peoples resisting Soviet aggression, he
could not have foreseen the rise of the Berlin Wall — but
he would not have been surprised to see it brought down.
Throughout our history, America has seen liberty challenged, and every time, we have seen liberty triumph
with sacrifice and determination.

At the start of this young century, America looks to the
day when the people of the Middle East leave the desert
of despotism for the fertile gardens of liberty, and resume
their rightful place in a world of peace and prosperity. We
look to the day when the nations of that region recognize
their greatest resource is not the oil in the ground, but
the talent and creativity of their people. We look to the
day when moms and dads throughout the Middle East
see a future of hope and opportunity for their children.
And when that good day comes, the clouds of war will
part, the appeal of radicalism will decline, and we will
leave our children with a better and safer world.

On this solemn anniversary, we rededicate ourselves
to this cause. Our nation has endured trials, and we face
a difficult road ahead. Winning this war will require the
determined efforts of a unified country, and we must put
aside our differences and work together to meet the test
that history has given us. We will defeat our enemies. We
will protect our people. And we will lead the twenty first
century into a shining age of human liberty.

Earlier this year, I traveled to the United States Military Academy. I was there to deliver the commencement
address to the first class to arrive at West Point after the
attacks of September the 11th. That day I met a proud
mom named RoseEllen Dowdell. She was there to watch
her son, Patrick, accept his commission in the finest
Army the world has ever known. A few weeks earlier,
RoseEllen had watched her other son, James, graduate
from the Fire Academy in New York City. On both these
days, her thoughts turned to someone who was not there
to share the moment: her husband, Kevin Dowdell. Kevin
was one of the 343 firefighters who rushed to the burning towers of the World Trade Center on September the
11th — and never came home. His sons lost their father
that day, but not the passion for service he instilled in
them. Here is what RoseEllen says about her boys: "As a

mother, I cross my fingers and pray all the time for their safety — but as worried as I am, I'm also proud, and I know their dad would be, too."

Our nation is blessed to have young Americans like these — and we will need them. Dangerous enemies have declared their intention to destroy our way of life. They're not the first to try, and their fate will be the same as those who tried before. Nine-Eleven showed us why. The attacks were meant to bring us to our knees, and they did, but not in the way the terrorists intended. Americans united in prayer, came to the aid of neighbors in need, and resolved that our enemies would not have the last word. The spirit of our people is the source of America's strength. And we go forward with trust in that spirit, confidence in our purpose, and faith in a loving God who made us to be free.

Thank you, and may God bless you.

20

A creative play on the two ways that people are brought to their knees.

Writer's Guide: Choosing Your Words Carefully

1. Be sure you have avoided language with connotations that might produce a negative reaction in your audience that would weaken your argument.
2. If you have used slanted language, consider whether it will advance your argument instead of weakening it.
3. Use picturesque language where appropriate for your purposes.
4. Replace abstract language with concrete language to be more effective.
5. Edit out any clichés or slogans from your early drafts.
6. Achieve a voice that is appropriate for your subject and audience.

Nobel Prize Acceptance Speech

WILLIAM FAULKNER

I feel that this award was not made to me as a man, but to my work — a life's work in the agony and sweat of the human spirit, not for glory and least of all for profit, but to create out of the materials of the human spirit something which did not exist before. So this award is only mine in trust. It will not be difficult to find a dedication for the money part of it commensurate with the purpose and significance of its origin. But I would like to do the same with the acclaim too, by using this moment as a pinnacle from which I might be listened to by the young men and women already dedicated to the same anguish and travail, among whom is already that one who will some day stand here where I am standing.

Our tragedy today is a general and universal physical fear so long sustained by now that we can even bear it. There are no longer problems of the spirit. There is only the question: When will I be blown up? Because of this, the young man or woman writing today has forgotten the problems of the human heart in conflict with itself which alone can make good writing because only that is worth writing about, worth the agony and the sweat.

He must learn them again. He must teach himself that the basest of all things is to be afraid; and, teaching himself that, forget it forever, leaving no room in his workshop for anything but the old verities and truths of the heart, the old universal truths lacking which any story is ephemeral and doomed — love and honor and pity and pride and compassion and sacrifice. Until he does so, he labors under a curse. He writes not of love but of lust, of defeats in which nobody loses anything of value, of victories without hope and, worst of all, without pity or compassion. His griefs grieve on no universal bones, leaving no scars. He writes not of the heart but of the glands.

Until he relearns these things, he will write as though he stood among and watched the end of man. I decline to accept the end of man. It is easy enough to say that man is immortal simply because he will endure: that when the last ding-dong of doom has clanged and faded from the last worthless rock hanging tideless in the last red and dying evening, that even then there will still be one more sound: that of his puny inexhaustible voice, still talking. I refuse to accept this. I believe that man will not merely endure: He will prevail. He is immortal, not because he alone among creatures has an inexhaustible voice, but because he has

William Faulkner was one of the dominant Southern novelists of the early twentieth century. He gave this speech at the Nobel Banquet at City Hall in Stockholm, Sweden, on December 10, 1950, when he accepted the Nobel Prize in Literature for 1949. Some minor revisions, included here, were made when the piece was prepared for publication in *The Faulkner Reader* (Random House, 1954).

a soul, a spirit capable of compassion and sacrifice and endurance. The poet's, the writer's, duty is to write about these things. It is his privilege to help man endure by lifting his heart, by reminding him of the courage and honor and hope and pride and compassion and pity and sacrifice which have been the glory of his past. The poet's voice need not merely be the record of man, it can be one of the props, the pillars to help him endure and prevail.

The Speech the Graduates Didn't Hear

JACOB NEUSNER

We the faculty take no pride in our educational achievements with you. We have prepared you for a world that does not exist, indeed, that cannot exist. You have spent four years supposing that failure leaves no record. You have learned at Brown that when your work goes poorly, the painless solution is to drop out. But starting now, in the world to which you go, failure marks you. Confronting difficulty by quitting leaves you changed. Outside Brown, quitters are no heroes.

With us you could argue about why your errors were not errors, why mediocre work really was excellent, why you could take pride in routine and slipshod presentation. Most of you, after all, can look back on honor grades for most of what you have done. So, here grades can have meant little in distinguishing the excellent from the ordinary. But tomorrow, in the world to which you go, you had best not defend errors but learn from them. You will be ill-advised to demand praise for what does not deserve it, and abuse those who do not give it.

For four years we created an altogether forgiving world, in which whatever slight effort you gave was all that was demanded. When you did not keep appointments, we made new ones. When your work came in beyond the deadline, we pretended not to care.

Worse still, when you were boring, we acted as if you were saying something important. When you were garrulous and talked to hear yourself talk, we listened as if it mattered. When you tossed on our desks writing upon which you had not labored, we read it and even responded, as though you earned a response. When you were dull, we pretended you were smart. When you were predictable, unimaginative, and routine, we listened as if to new and wonderful things. When you demanded free lunch, we served it. And all this why?

Despite your fantasies, it was not even that we wanted to be liked by you. It was that we did not want to be bothered, and the easy way out was pretense: smiles and easy Bs.

5

Formerly a professor at Brown University, Jacob Neusner is Distinguished Service Professor of the History and Theology of Judaism and Senior Fellow of the Institute of Advanced Theology at Bard College. His speech appeared in Brown's *Daily Herald* on June 12, 1983.

It is conventional to quote in addresses such as these. Let me quote someone you've never heard of: Professor Carter A. Daniel, Rutgers University (*Chronicle of Higher Education*, May 7, 1979):

> College has spoiled you by reading papers that don't deserve to be read, listening to comments that don't deserve a hearing, paying attention even to the lazy, ill-informed, and rude. We had to do it, for the sake of education. But nobody will ever do it again. College has deprived you of adequate preparation for the last fifty years. It has failed you by being easy, free, forgiving, attentive, comfortable, interesting, unchallenging fun. Good luck tomorrow.

That is why, on this commencement day, we have nothing in which to take much pride.

Oh, yes, there is one more thing. Try not to act toward your coworkers and bosses as you have acted toward us. I mean, when they give you what you want but have not earned, don't abuse them, insult them, act out with them your parlous relationships with your parents. This too we have tolerated. It was, as I said, not to be liked. Few professors actually care whether or not they are liked by peer-paralyzed adolescents, fools so shallow as to imagine professors care not about education but about popularity. It was, again, to be rid of you. So go, unlearn the lies we taught you. To Life!

READING AND DISCUSSION QUESTIONS

1. Neusner condemns students for various shortcomings. But what is he saying, both directly and indirectly, about teachers? Find places where he reveals his attitude toward them, perhaps inadvertently.

2. Pick out some of the language devices — connectives, parallel structures, sentence variety — that the author uses effectively.

3. Pick out some of the words and phrases — especially adjectives and verbs — used by Neusner to characterize both students and teachers. Do you think these terms are loaded? Explain.

4. Has the author chosen "facts" to slant his article? If so, point out where slanting occurs. If not, point out where the article seems to be truthful.

5. As a student you will probably object to Neusner's accusations. How would you defend your behavior as a student in answer to his specific charges?

WRITING SUGGESTIONS

6. Rewrite Neusner's article with the same "facts" — or others from your experience — using temperate language and a tone of sadness rather than anger.

7. Write a letter to Neusner responding to his attack. Support or attack his argument by providing evidence from your own experience.

8. Write your own short commencement address. Do some things need to be said that commencement speakers seldom or never express?

9. Write an essay using the same kind of strong language as Neusner uses about some aspect of your education of which you disapprove. Or write a letter to a teacher using the same form as "The Speech The Graduates Didn't Hear."

Driving Home Their Point

R. CORT KIRKWOOD

A recent story in the *Press-Enterprise* of Riverside, California, gives the lie to the notion that illegal aliens are just here "to do the jobs Americans won't do" and are largely a law-abiding class of the downtrodden, shifting where they can for work.

In May, the newspaper reported that "activists" warn illegal-alien drivers about sobriety checkpoints so they won't be stopped. That, you see, would mean losing their automobiles, the penalty in some benighted localities for driving without a valid driver's license.

The newspaper opened with the classic anecdotal lede:

> Adrianna Castellon, 16, stood on the sidewalk of a busy Moreno Valley street on a recent school night, yelling at cars rushing past.
>   "Checkpoint! Checkpoint ahead!" she screamed. "Turn back while you can!"
>   The high school student was among protesters hoping to help illegal immigrants whose vehicles were about to be impounded by police because they were driving without a license.

California, the paper reports, declared 2010 "the 'year of the checkpoint' and plans a record $8 million in checkpoint grants, up from $5 million in 2009." Unsurprisingly, "Latinos" rushed into action faster than Speedy Gonzalez, and not just because an illegal without a license can lose his car for a month.

They allege that police are "profiling" because they set up the checkpoints in   5
mostly "Hispanic" communities. Figures reported in the paper on the number and location of checkpoints prove it:

> A review of Riverside County Sheriff's Department figures shows that in 2009 Inland police in cities with larger percentages of Hispanic residents hosted more checkpoints.
>   For example, Temecula, a city of about 105,000 that's 22 percent Hispanic, had five. Riverside, which has 304,000 residents and a 48 percent Hispanic population, did 10. San Bernardino, a 205,000-person city with a 57 percent Hispanic community, had 14. Perris, a city of about 55,000 that's 70 percent Hispanic, had 13. Moreno Valley, where 53 percent of the city's 189,000 residents are Hispanic, held 20 checkpoints — more than any other city in Riverside County. . . .
>   In 2009 sheriff's stations in western Riverside County logged 70 vehicle tows in Temecula, 702 in Perris and 1,540 in Moreno Valley, where police impounded the most vehicles. Most belonged to drivers with no license or a suspended license.
>   Most Moreno Valley checkpoints have been in the most heavily Hispanic of the city's five voting districts. According to agency records, from 2007 to 2009,

---

R. Cort Kirkwood is a journalist who publishes frequently in *Chronicles: A Magazine of American Culture,* the source of this piece on August 16, 2010, and is the author of *Real Men: Ten Courageous Americans to Know and Admire* (2005).

police hosted a total of 36 checkpoints throughout three city districts where Hispanics are the largest ethnic group.

During the same two-year period police held a total of five checkpoints throughout two districts that are less densely populated and cover the largest area, where whites are the largest racial group.

With that kind of fascism afoot, what's a poor *campesino* to do?

Of course, police denied profiling Mexicans and claimed they "chose the busiest streets and relied on the same four or five spots because they have large areas to park tow trucks and other vehicles," the *Press-Enterprise* reported. So they "began this year spreading checkpoints across the entire city." This hasty admission proved the "Latinos" were right.

The better response would have been to tell the "Latinos" the checkpoints will stand as long as necessary, given this telling statistic, also from the newspaper account: Drivers without licenses account for 40 percent of the nation's hit-and-run crashes. The paper didn't report that statistics show a strong correlation between the number of illegals in a state and the number of unlicensed drivers involved in hit-and-run fatalities. Profiling used to be called good police work.

As reports about illegals go, this one seems ho-hum compared with the usual horror story about an unlicensed Mexican career criminal, hurtling down the street in a Chevy Suburban and killing a child eating ice cream at Baskin-Robbins. Except for one thing: the shift in what Latino "activists" implicitly claim by warning illegals about the checkpoints. In the past, they said illegals needed licenses because they must get to work. Now, licenses don't matter — because illegals must get to work.

And the "Latinos" — Mexicans — don't care who gets killed. Their activism   10
has gone beyond marching in the streets and shouting for open borders. Now it includes public obstruction of justice.

<hr>

DEBATE   Does the Government Have the Right to Regulate Guns?

The Right to Bear Arms

WARREN E. BURGER

Our metropolitan centers, and some suburban communities of America, are setting new records for homicides by handguns. Many of our large centers have up to ten times the murder rate of all of Western Europe. In 1988, there were 9,000 handgun murders in America. Last year, Washington, D.C., alone had more than 400 homicides — setting a new record for our capital.

<hr>

Warren E. Burger (1907–1995) was chief justice of the United States from 1969 to 1986. This article is from the January 14, 1990, issue of *Parade* magazine.

The Constitution of the United States, in its Second Amendment, guarantees a "right of the people to keep and bear arms." However, the meaning of this clause cannot be understood except by looking to the purpose, the setting, and the objectives of the draftsmen. The first ten amendments — the Bill of Rights — were not drafted at Philadelphia in 1787; that document came two years later than the Constitution. Most of the states already had bills of rights, but the Constitution might not have been ratified in 1788 if the states had not had assurances that a national Bill of Rights would soon be added.

People of that day were apprehensive about the new "monster" national government presented to them, and this helps explain the language and purpose of the Second Amendment. A few lines after the First Amendment's guarantees — against "establishment of religion," "free exercise" of religion, free speech and free press — came a guarantee that grew out of the deep-seated fear of a "national" or "standing" army. The same First Congress that approved the right to keep and bear arms also limited the national army to 840 men; Congress in the Second Amendment then provided:

> A well regulated Militia, being necessary to the security of a free State, the right of the people to keep and bear Arms, shall not be infringed.

In the 1789 debate in Congress on James Madison's proposed Bill of Rights, Elbridge Gerry argued that a state militia was necessary:

> to prevent the establishment of a standing army, the bane of liberty. . . . Whenever governments mean to invade the rights and liberties of the people, they always attempt to destroy the militia in order to raise an army upon their ruins.

We see that the need for a state militia was the predicate of the "right" guaranteed; in short, it was declared "necessary" in order to have a state military force to protect the security of the state. That Second Amendment clause must be read as though the word "because" was the opening word of the guarantee. Today, of course, the "state militia" serves a very different purpose. A huge national defense establishment has taken over the role of the militia of 200 years ago.   5

Some have exploited these ancient concerns, blurring sporting guns — rifles, shotguns, and even machine pistols — with all firearms, including what are now called "Saturday night specials." There is, of course, a great difference between sporting guns and handguns. Some regulation of handguns has long been accepted as imperative; laws relating to "concealed weapons" are common. That we may be "overregulated" in some areas of life has never held us back from more regulation of automobiles, airplanes, motorboats, and "concealed weapons."

Let's look at the history.

First, many of the 3.5 million people living in the thirteen original Colonies depended on wild game for food, and a good many of them required firearms for their defense from marauding Indians — and later from the French and English. Underlying all these needs was an important concept that each able-bodied man in each of the thirteen independent states had to help or defend his state.

The early opposition to the idea of national or standing armies was maintained under the Articles of Confederation; that confederation had no standing army and wanted none. The state militia — essentially a part-time citizen army, as in Switzerland today — was the only kind of "army" they wanted. From the time of the Declaration of Independence through the victory at Yorktown in 1781, George Washington, as the commander in chief of these volunteer-militia armies, had to depend upon the states to send those volunteers.

When a company of New Jersey militia volunteers reported for duty to Washington at Valley Forge, the men initially declined to take an oath to "the United States," maintaining, "Our country is New Jersey." Massachusetts Bay men, Virginians, and others felt the same way. To the American of the eighteenth century, his state was his country, and his freedom was defended by his militia.

The victory at Yorktown — and the ratification of the Bill of Rights a decade later — did not change people's attitudes about a national army. They had lived for years under the notion that each state would maintain its own military establishment, and the seaboard states had their own navies as well. These people, and their fathers and grandfathers before them, remembered how monarchs had used standing armies to oppress their ancestors in Europe. Americans wanted no part of this. A state militia, like a rifle and powder horn, was as much a part of life as the automobile is today; pistols were largely for officers, aristocrats — and dueling.

Against this background, it was not surprising that the provision concerning firearms emerged in very simple terms with the significant predicate — basing the right on the *necessity* for a "well regulated militia," a state army.

In the two centuries since then — with two world wars and some lesser ones — it has become clear, sadly, that we have no choice but to maintain a standing national army while still maintaining a "militia" by way of the National Guard, which can be swiftly integrated into the national defense forces.

Americans also have a right to defend their homes, and we need not challenge that. Nor does anyone seriously question that the Constitution protects the right of hunters to own and keep sporting guns for hunting game any more than anyone would challenge the right to own and keep fishing rods and other equipment for fishing — or to own automobiles. To "keep and bear arms" for hunting today is essentially a recreational activity and not an imperative of survival, as it was 200 years ago; "Saturday night specials" and machine guns are not recreational weapons and surely are as much in need of regulation as motor vehicles.

Americans should ask themselves a few questions. The Constitution does not mention automobiles or motorboats, but the right to keep and own an automobile is beyond question; equally beyond question is the power of the state to regulate the purchase or the transfer of such vehicle and the right to license the vehicle and the driver with reasonable standards. In some places, even a bicycle must be registered, as must some household dogs.

If we are to stop this mindless homicidal carnage, is it unreasonable:

1. to provide that, to acquire a firearm, an application be made reciting age, residence, employment, and any prior criminal convictions?

2. to require that this application lie on the table for ten days (absent a showing for urgent need) before the license would be issued?

3. that the transfer of a firearm be made essentially as that of a motor vehicle?

4. to have a "ballistic fingerprint" of the firearm made by the manufacturer and filed with the license record so that, if a bullet is found in a victim's body, law enforcement might be helped in finding the culprit?

These are the kinds of questions the American people must answer if we are to preserve the "domestic tranquility" promised in the Constitution.

A God-Given Natural Right

ROGER D. MCGRATH

I do not believe in unilateral disarmament: not for the nation; not for our citizens. Neither did the Founding Fathers. They were students of history, especially of classical antiquity. They knew the history of the Greek city-states and Rome as well as they knew the history of the American colonies. This led them to conclude that an armed citizenry is essential to the preservation of freedom and democracy. Once disarmed, populations either submit meekly to tyrants or fight in vain.

The ancient Greeks knew this. The Greek city-state of Laconia had a population that was five percent Spartan (the warrior aristocracy), one percent *perioeci* (small merchants and craftsmen), and 94 percent *helots* (serfs bound to the soil). It is no mystery how five percent of the population kept 94 percent of the people enslaved. The *helots* were kept disarmed and, if found in possession of a weapon, were put to death.

Meanwhile, most of the Greek city-states were bastions of democracy because they had developed strong middle classes of armed citizens known as *hoplites*. Supplying their own weapons and equipment, the *hoplites* went into battle not out of fear of punishment or in hopes of plunder and booty, as did subject peoples of the Oriental empires, but to defend their liberties and to protect hearth and home. They fought side by side with neighbors, brothers, fathers, sons, uncles, and cousins. They did their utmost to demonstrate courage, side by side with their comrades in arms. If they lost a battle to the armies of an Oriental despot, they stood

For fifteen years, Roger McGrath taught courses in the history of the American West, California, and the United States at UCLA and has also taught at California State University, Northridge. His articles have appeared in the *Wall Street Journal*, *American Guardian*, *Chronicles*, the *New York Times*, and *Harper's*. He is the author of *Gunfighters, Highwaymen, and Vigilantes* (1984) and coauthor of *Violence in America* (1989). This article appeared in the October 2003 issue of *Chronicles*.

to lose everything — property, freedom, democracy. A defeat for subject peoples usually meant nothing more than a change of rulers.

The ancient Romans also knew this. When Tarquin, the Etruscan king of Rome, issued an order — for the public good, for safety and security — that the Romans be disarmed, they rose in rebellion. Tarquin was driven from the city, and the early Roman Republic was established. For several hundred years, Rome was defended not by a professional army of mercenaries or subject peoples but by armed citizen-soldiers who left the farm from time to time to serve the republic. Once the system broke down, the Roman Republic was transformed into an empire similar to the despotic regimes of the East.

Death and destruction commonly followed disarmament. England did it to   5
the Gaels — the Irish and Scots — and the consequences beggar description. England had been fighting in Ireland for hundreds of years by the time the English got Irish leader Patrick Sarsfield to sign the Treaty of Limerick in 1691. The treaty guaranteed all Irish full civil, religious, and property rights. In return, it required that Sarsfield and more than 20,000 of his soldiers leave Ireland for the Continent.

With the armed defenders of Ireland overseas, England began to abrogate the rights supposedly guaranteed by the treaty. Beginning in 1709, England passed the statutes that collectively became known as the Penal Laws. One of the first of these laws declared that, for public safety, no Irish Catholic could keep and bear arms. Then the Irish Catholic was denied the right to an education, to enter a profession, to hold public office, to engage in trade or commerce, to own a horse of greater value than five pounds, to purchase or lease land, to vote, to attend the worship of his choice, to send his children abroad to receive an education. By the time the last of the Penal Laws was enacted, the Irish, although they were not chattel property, in many ways had fewer rights than black slaves in America. The Irish were kept on a near starvation diet, and their life expectancy was the lowest in the Western world.

Things were not much better in the Highlands of Scotland. England had subdued the Lowlands by the fourteenth century, but the Highlands, the truly Gaelic portion of Scotland, continued to be troublesome well into the eighteenth century. A major rebellion erupted in 1715; another, in 1745. The end for the Highlanders came at the Battle of Culloden in 1746. Following the battle, the English built a series of forts across the Highlands and passed laws for the Highlanders — who were originally Irish, of course — similar to the Penal Laws. England made it a crime for the Highlanders to wear kilts, play bagpipes, and keep and bear arms. A Highlander found with a claymore or any other kind of sword or arm was put to death. The English army, understanding that it is easier to starve a fierce enemy into submission than to fight him, eagerly slaughtered the cattle herds of the Highlands, precipitating a great starvation. Thousands of Highlanders died or fled. The English later engaged in the infamous "clearances" in which thousands more were driven from the land. Without arms, the Highlanders were helpless.

What the English did to the Irish and Scots was not lost on our Founding Fathers or on the colonists in general. More than a quarter of the colonists were Irish or Scottish or Scotch-Irish. When England tried to disarm the American colonists, all under the guise of preserving public order and peace, the colonists reacted violently. While it is rarely taught in schools today, the reason the British army marched to Lexington and Concord was to confiscate the arms caches of the local citizenry.

It is not by accident, then, that the Framers of the Constitution ensured that the government could not infringe on "the right of the people to keep and bear arms." It is important to understand that the Second Amendment grants no right to the people to keep and bear arms. This is a point misunderstood by most Americans today, even by most of those who are interested in keeping their guns.

The Second Amendment, like the First, recognizes a God-given, natural right   10 of the people and guarantees that the government not interfere with the exercise of that right. Note the wording of the amendment. Nowhere does it say, "This Constitution grants the people the right to . . ." Instead, it says "the right of the people . . . shall not be infringed." The right to keep and bear arms, like that of freedom of speech, is known, constitutionally, as an inherent right. By contrast, the Sixth Amendment right to be represented by an attorney in a criminal case is a derivative right — a right that comes from the Constitution.

To understand this is critical to all arguments about guns, or about freedom of speech, or religion, or the press. These freedoms were not given to us by the Founding Fathers. They were recognized by the Founding Fathers as God-given, natural rights that existed long before the establishment of our republic. These rights are not granted to men by a benevolent government but given to man by God. They are not to be destroyed, suppressed, or even compromised. When they are, it is the duty of the citizens to rise in revolt, overthrow the government, and establish a government that will protect these unalienable rights. Sound familiar? It should. This was the philosophy of our Founding Fathers.

The most basic of the natural rights of man is the right to self-preservation, the right to self-defense. No one would deny that we have such a right. In debates at universities and at other public forums, in debates on radio, in debates on television, I have never seen anyone deny that man has a natural right to self-defense. It follows that, if man has a natural right to self-defense, then he has a right to the arms necessary for that self-defense. The right to be armed is a logical and inescapable corollary of the right to self-defense. We cannot have one without the other.

If we do not have the right to the arms necessary for self-defense, then the right of self-defense is purely theoretical — something like having freedom of the press but not being allowed access to a printing press. Can you imagine the National Rifle Association telling the *New York Times* that it has freedom of the press but it may not have printing presses, or that the *Times* can purchase only one printing press per month, or that its writers must undergo background checks by the government, or that it cannot buy ink for the presses in New York City, or that its presses have limits on their speed and capacity, or that its presses must meet certain design requirements? If any of this were suggested, the *Times* would squeal like a stuck pig, and well it should.

Some people, presumably well intentioned, argue that the right to arms (and, thus, the right to self-defense) should be compromised — compromised further than it already has been — in an effort to make society safer. Such a position is ironic on two counts.

First, many of the same people who make gun-restriction arguments, such as   15
the ACLU, would be apoplectic if it were suggested that freedom of speech be curtailed to ensure greater public safety. For example, we could have a two-week waiting period on expressing an opinion after the opinion was duly registered with a government agency. That way, the government could screen the opinion to ensure that it was politically correct.

The compromise-your-rights-for-safety argument is also ironic because the thousands of gun laws on the books — municipal, county, state, and federal — have done nothing to stop crime. In fact, they have done the opposite. The laws, for the most part, have disarmed, or made access to guns more difficult for, the law-abiding, peaceable citizen. Criminals do not turn in their guns. Murderers, rapists, and robbers do not obey gun laws. However, they do calculate the risks involved in committing crime. If they can assume that potential victims are unarmed, they are emboldened and are more likely to attack.

John Lott, in *More Guns Less Crime*, an exhaustive county-by-county study of rates of gun ownership and crime, concludes that the counties with the highest rates of gun ownership have the least crime and that those with the lowest rates of gun ownership have the most crime. For years, this has been obvious when looking at cities. Washington, D.C., and New York City, for example, with the most restrictive gun laws in the nation, have, for a generation, been cesspools of crime. Criminals there know that they can count on their victims being unarmed.

I suspect that even deeply disturbed killers, such as the teenage boys in Littleton, Colorado, understood that they could kill with impunity in the disarmed environment of the high school. The presence of a highly trained, armed security guard, with a reputation as an expert marksman, may have deterred them. If not, then the guard might have granted them their suicidal wish before they were able to commit mass murder. One or two key teachers, trained and armed, might also have made a difference. Certainly, gun laws did nothing to stop the killers. The two boys violated more than a dozen different gun laws, including one of the oldest on the books — possession of a sawed-off shotgun. Gun laws promise much and deliver little, because they affect only the law abiding, something like sheep passing resolutions requiring vegetarianism while wolves circle the flock.

I grew up in Los Angeles when gun laws were few and crime was low. Nearly everyone I knew had a 30.06, a couple of .22s, a shotgun, and a revolver or two sitting around their house. We could buy guns mail-order and pick up our ammunition at the local grocery store. A gun was a common companion to the road maps in the glove compartment of the car. Did this cause crime? In 1952, there were 81 murders in Los Angeles. In 1992, forty years and many gun laws later, there were 1,092 murders. If the increase in murder had kept pace with the increase in population, there would have been 142 murders, a 75 percent increase. Instead, murder increased 1,350 percent. Other crimes had similar increases: robbery, 1,540 percent; auto theft, 1,100 percent.

The Los Angeles Police Department used to solve more than 90 percent of the murders committed in the city. Today, the figure is 60 percent. Detectives complain that the caseload is too great to conduct the kind of thorough investigations that were common in the '40s and '50s. It is far worse for lesser crimes. Merchants complain that customers brazenly walk out of their stores without paying for merchandise because they know that the police will not respond (at least in a timely fashion) to a call reporting shoplifting. Cars are stolen so often, some 200 per day, that the LAPD does nothing more than list the vehicle on a "hot sheet" and wish the victim good luck.

In the '50s, if your bicycle were stolen, the police would come out to your house and take a report. Try calling the LAPD today and telling them that your bike has been stolen! The police are simply overwhelmed by the sheer volume of crime and are kept fully occupied by murder, armed robbery, and rape — occupied, that is, by the aftermath of murder, armed robbery, and rape. When police arrive at the scene of a crime, the crime has already taken place — the victim has already been murdered, robbed, or raped.

"Carjacking" has become quite common in Los Angeles, because the carjackers know that California drivers cannot legally carry loaded firearms and will nearly always be unarmed. Occasionally, carjackers make poor choices. Three such carjackers followed my friend's son, Justin, as he drove home in his new car late one night. Little did they know that Justin was a reserve police officer. They did not know that he was well armed and an expert marksman.

When Justin pulled into the family driveway and got out of his car, one of the carjackers jumped out of his own vehicle and yelled at Justin, whose back was turned, "Freeze, motherf — er!" It was exactly what Justin had expected. Justin spun about and emptied the contents of his .45 into the carjacker. The carjacker's partners sped away as fast as their car would take them, leaving their good buddy very dead on my friend's front lawn.

Not long after Justin had sent the carjacker to the great salvage yard in the sky, I read of an off-duty police officer who had a similar encounter. On his way home and wearing plainclothes, he stopped to make a phone call. While he stood talking to his wife on an outdoor public phone, two muggers rushed up to him. One of them brandished a gun and said: "Your wallet!" Instead of pulling out his wallet, the cop drew a gun and sent the mugger to the morgue.

The *Los Angeles Times* noted that the mugger certainly picked on the wrong person. This is the same *Los Angeles Times* that regularly editorializes against an armed citizenry and has never seen a gun law that it did not like. Somehow, the newspaper thinks that disarming peaceable, law-abiding citizens will affect criminal behavior for the better. Disarming peaceable, law-abiding citizens *will* affect criminal behavior — but for the worse. Criminals will be emboldened because their chances of picking on the wrong person will be dramatically reduced. Shouldn't the opposite be the case? Shouldn't every person be the wrong person or, at least, potentially the wrong person?

Grandstanding politicians love to rail against the gun. Inanimate objects are good targets to beat up on. That way, politicians do not have to address the real problems in our society. We pay a price for this craven misdirection, though, in thousands of murders, muggings, rapes, robberies, and burglaries.

Yet that is not the greatest danger we face. The Founding Fathers knew that *governments* could turn criminal. That is the principal reason they wanted every man armed: An armed citizenry militates against the development of tyranny. The Founding Fathers did not want every man armed in order to shoot a burglar, although they had nothing against doing so. The Founding Fathers did not want every man armed in order to shoot Bambi or Thumper, although they had nothing against doing so. The Founding Fathers wanted every man armed in order to shoot soldiers or police of tyrannical regimes who suppress the rights of free men.

When governments become criminal, they disarm the populace. Then the numbers of deaths reach the tens of thousands, the hundreds of thousands, the millions. Can't happen? Ask the Irish and the Scots, or the Armenians, the Ukrainians, the Jews, the Chinese, the Cambodians.

In the Marine Corps, I was trained never to surrender my weapon. It was good advice then, and it is good advice now. I shall put my faith not in the goodwill of governments but in an armed citizenry — a band of brothers — steeped in the ideology of the Founding Fathers and the spirit of Patrick Henry, who said: "Is life so dear or peace so sweet as to be purchased at the price of slavery and chains? I know not what course others may take, but as for me, give me liberty or give me death."

DISCUSSION QUESTIONS

1. What does Burger understand the intent of the Second Amendment to have been, in context? How has history changed the way it should now be read?

2. What analogy does Burger make between guns and automobiles? Is his point a good one?

3. What questions does Burger believe Americans should be answering if we are to stop what he calls "this mindless homicidal carnage" (para. 16)?

4. Does McGrath make use of history in the same way and for the same purpose as Burger does? Explain.

5. What does McGrath mean when he says, "It is important to understand that the Second Amendment grants no right to the people to keep and bear arms" (para. 9)?

6. What is the warrant underlying Burger's essay? McGrath's?

7. What is McGrath's response to the claim that gun restrictions would make society safer?

8. Do you detect any logical fallacies in either essay?

9. Compare the authors' use of language. Do the authors use slanted or emotive language? Short cuts? Where in McGrath's essay is there a shift in the type of language used, and why?

Assignments for Choosing Fair and Precise Language

READING AND DISCUSSION QUESTIONS

1. Select one or two related bumper stickers visible in your town or city. Examine the hidden warrants on which they are based, and assess their validity.

2. For a slogan found on a bumper sticker or elsewhere, supply the evidence to support the claim in the slogan. Or find evidence that disproves the claim.

3. Examine a few periodicals from fifty or more years ago. Select either an advertising or a political slogan in one of them, and relate it to beliefs or events of the period. Or tell why the slogan is no longer relevant.

4. Discuss the origin of a cliché or slogan. Describe, as far as possible, the backgrounds and motives of its users.

5. Make up your own slogan for a cause that you support. Explain and defend your slogan.

6. Choose a cliché, and find evidence to support or refute it. *Examples:* People were much happier in the past. Mother knows best. Life used to be simpler. Money can't buy happiness.

7. In watching television dramas about law, medicine, or criminal or medical investigation, do you find that the professional language, some of which you may not fully understand, plays a positive or negative role in your enjoyment of the show? Explain your answer.

8. Listen to a radio or television report of a sports event. Do the announcers use a kind of language, especially jargon, that would not be used in print reports? One critic thinks that sports broadcasting has had a "destructive effect . . . on ordinary American English." Is he right or wrong?

9. Whose argument about the right to bear arms do you find more convincing, Burger's or McGrath's? Explain.

WRITING SUGGESTIONS

10. Write an essay analyzing either Neusner's language or Kirkwood's.

11. Choose a popular slogan from advertising or politics. Write an essay explaining how it appeals to needs and values.

12. Write an essay explaining which argument about the right to bear arms you find most convincing, Burger's or McGrath's.

13. Why are short cuts a natural result of ours being a technological age?

14. Analyze a presidential or other debate using some of the terms discussed in this chapter.

15. Locate a copy of President Bush's first speech after the attacks of 9/11 and compare it to Roosevelt's after the bombing of Pearl Harbor.

Research Readiness: Following a Research Trail

How can you investigate a source to determine if it is reliable?

One source that appeared on the results list when students searched "autism and vaccines" on Google for the Research Readiness exercise at the end of Chapter 6 was this one:

> *Vaccines* **don't cause** *autism*
> Sep 17, 2010 . . . The debate is essentially over and the final word is in: *vaccines* do not cause *autism*. The results of a rigorous study conducted over . . .
> *kottke.org/10/09/vaccines-dont-cause-autism* - Cached

The URL is probably not one that you would recognize. Follow the research trail to decide what you think about the reliability of this source.

A. Clicking on the title of the source leads to the following page. As you look it over, consider your initial response to this question: What can you conclude about who Jason Kottke is and where he got his information about autism and vaccinations?

Kottke.org is a weblog about the liberal arts 2.0 edited by Jason Kottke since March 1998 (archives). You can read about me and kottke.org here. If you've got questions, concerns, or interesting links, send them along.

VACCINES DON'T CAUSE AUTISM

The debate is essentially over and the final word is in: vaccines do not cause autism. The results of a rigorous study conducted over several years were just announced and they confirmed the results of several past studies.

> Basically, the final two groups that were studied consisted of 256 children with ASD [autism spectrum disorders] and 752 matched controls. One very interesting aspect that looks as though it were almost certainly placed into the experimental design based on concerns of anti-vaccine advocates like Sallie Bernard is a group of children who underwent regression. Basically, the study examined whether there was a correlation between ASD and TCV [thimerosal-containing vaccines, i.e. mercury-containing vaccines] exposure. It also examined two subsets of ASD, autistic disorder (AD) and ASD with regression, looking for any indication whether TCVs were associated with any of them. Regression was defined as:
>> "the subset of case-children with ASD who reported loss of previously acquired language skills after acquisition."
> Also, when adding up total thimerosal exposure, the investigators also included any thimerosal exposure that might have come prenatally from maternal receipt of flu vaccines during pregnancy, as well as immunoglobulins, tetanus toxoids, and diphtheria-tetanus. In other words, investigators tried to factor in all the various ideas for how TCVs might contribute to autism when designing this study.
> So what did the investigators find? I think you probably know the answer to that question. They found nothing. Nada. Zip. There wasn't even a

hint of a correlation between TCV exposure and either ASD, AD, or ASD with regression:

"There were no findings of increased risk for any of the 3 ASD outcomes. The adjusted odds ratios (95% confidence intervals) for ASD associated with a 2-SD increase in ethylmercury exposure were 1.12 (0.83–1.51) for prenatal exposure, 0.88 (0.62–1.26) for exposure from birth to 1 month, 0.60 (0.36–0.99) for exposure from birth to 7 months, and 0.60 (0.32–0.97) for exposure from birth to 20 months."

The last result is a bit of an anomaly in that it implies that exposure to TCVs from birth to 1 month and birth to 7 months actually protects against ASD. The authors quite rightly comment on this result thusly:

"In the covariate adjusted models, we found that an increase in ethylmercury exposure in 2 of the 4 exposure time periods evaluated was associated with decreased risk of each of the 3 ASD outcomes. We are not aware of a biological mechanism that would lead to this result."

So get your kids (and yourselves) vaccinated and save them & their playmates from this whooping cough bullshit, which is actually killing actual kids and not, you know, magically infecting them with autism. Vaccination is one of the greatest human discoveries ever — yes, Kanye, OF ALL TIME — has saved countless lives, and has made countless more lives significantly better. So: Buck. Up.

By Jason Kottke • Sep 17, 2010 at 11:48 am • autism medicine science vaccines
Source: http://kottke.org/10/09/vaccines-dont-cause-autism

B. Hyperlinks in Kottke's text are indicated in blue. You probably noticed that there is a hyperlink at the top of the page in the description of kottke.org from the words "read about me and kottke.org here." If you went online and clicked on that link, the following page would appear. What impression of Kottke do you start to draw from "The exciting About page"? What sort of ethos is he projecting?

C. You will also see that in the online version of Kottke's article "Vaccines Don't Cause Autism," there was a hyperlink from the words "vaccines do not cause autism" in the first sentence. If you clicked on that link, you would be directed to the article by David H. Gorski from which he drew his information.

Kottke.org is a weblog about the liberal arts 2.0 edited by Jason Kottke since March 1998 (archives). You can read about me and kottke.org here. If you've got questions, concerns, or interesting links, send them along.

THE EXCITING ABOUT PAGE

Hi, my name is Jason Kottke. I currently live in Manhattan with my wife Meg and son Ollie. For fun and income, I build web sites and edit kottke.org. My favorite font right now is Whitney by Hoefler & Frere-Jones. Being generally sober, level-headed, and trustworthy, I'm usually the guy who is chosen to drive. One of my favorite things is that, for a moment after you dip your toe in, you can't tell the difference between really hot water and really cold water.

I believe that when people talk about solving problems with technology, what they're usually talking about is solving problems with design . . . which is to say, the application of psychology in a visual & functional context. I prefer red wine to white, movies to films, jeans to khakis, vanilla to chocolate, Pixar to Dreamworks, the subway to taxis, nonfiction to fiction, and Safari to Firefox. I use a daily face wash in my "T-zone" area. I look like the guy in these photos. I find going to the dentist relaxing. I've lived in WI, IA, MO, MN, CA, NY, NH, and, briefly, France. I don't have a plan.

Need to reach me? Get in touch.

WHAT KOTTKE.ORG MIGHT BE, A LIST:

- The personal site of Jason Kottke. But also his full-time gig.
- A weblog, which is a frequently updated, chronologically ordered collection of hypertext fragments. You'll find the most recent posted stuff on the front page and many ways to get at the older posts on the archive page.
- My wunderkammer. Wunderkammer is a German word meaning, roughly, "cabinet of wonders" or "cabinet of curiousities." Julian Dibbell wrote about weblogs as wunderkammers for the dearly-departed Feed.
- Updated almost daily since March 1998.
- An attempt to track and make sense of "material that connects the insights of science and culture, rather than using one to dismantle the other" (as Steven Johnson puts it).
- Sheer egoism, aesthetic enthusiasm, historical impulse, and even a bit of political purpose. (after George Orwell)
- Small pieces, loosely joined (after David Weinberger's book of the same name).
- Chock full of "wussy PoMo Sedaris-wannabe attitude" (source)
- Speed 3: The Weblog. If I stop writing, the bus will blow up. (source)
- A giant RFC document.
- Not all that it could be.
- Slashdot for the literati (comment via AIM).

Source: http://kottke.org/about/

It's always a good idea to cite the original source of information if you can. There is no reason to cite Kottke instead of citing Gorski himself if you have access to Gorski's original article — especially if you have questions about Kottke's reliability and if he is not an expert who can add insight on the subject at hand. Also going to Gorski's article, which is entitled "The Final Nail in the Mercury-Autism hypothesis?", provides the quoted information in the context of the much longer article in which it originally appeared.

Kottke's whole article, except for the first two sentences and the last three, is a quote from Gorski. Did Kottke accurately and adequately document the fact that his information came from Gorski?

Source: sciencebasedmedicine.org/?p=6775

D. Search the publication in which Gorski's article appeared, *Science-Based Medicine,* and see what you can conclude about its reliability.

E. To be thorough in checking out your sources, if you do not recognize an author you are citing, you should check to see if he or she has a reputation relevant to the subject you are discussing. Gorski's name, where it is listed as author of the article that Kottke cited, is a hyperlink that leads to an interesting page. What is your response, as a researcher, to this page?

PART 3

Researching, Writing, and Presenting Arguments

CHAPTER **10**

The Argumentative Paper:
Planning and Research

By now you should be fairly adept at picking out claims, support, and warrants (explicit or unstated). The next step is to apply your skills to writing an argument of your own on a subject of your choice or for an assignment on a topic other than those covered in this text. Using what you have learned will enhance your ability to analyze critically the marketing efforts with which we are all bombarded every day. Mastering the writing of arguments also gives you a valuable tool for communicating with other people in school, on the job, and even at home.

In this chapter we move through the various stages involved in preparing to write an argumentative paper: choosing a topic, locating and evaluating sources, and taking notes. We will follow one student, Katie, as she goes through these stages.

Finding an Appropriate Topic

An old British recipe for jugged hare is said to begin, "First, catch your hare." To write an argumentative paper, you first must choose your topic. This is a relatively easy task for someone writing an argument as part of his or her job — a lawyer defending a client, for example, or an advertising executive presenting a campaign. For a student, however, it can be daunting. Which of the many ideas in the world worth debating would make a good subject?

Several guidelines can help you evaluate the possibilities. Perhaps your assignment limits your choices. If you have been asked to write a research paper, you obviously must find a topic on which research is available. If your assignment is more open-ended, you need a topic that is worth the time and effort you expect to invest in it. In either case, your subject should be one that interests you. Don't feel you have to write about what you know — very often finding out what you don't know will turn out to be more satisfying. You should, however, choose a subject that is familiar enough for you to argue about without fearing you're in over your head.

> In this chapter we will follow a student, Katie, who has been assigned a research paper for her first-year English class. In preparation for the assignment, the class has viewed the movie *Food, Inc.* This is the assignment that Katie must complete:
>
> The movie *Food, Inc.* raises a multitude of questions about food: the link between the corporate world and our food supply, organic foods, world hunger, alternative fuels, farm workers, childhood obesity. These are just a sampling of the issues raised. For your research essay, choose an argumentative topic related in some way to the issues discussed in the film. Your thesis should be either a claim of value or a claim of policy. Your essay should be 6–8 double-spaced pages and must use at least six sources. There should be some variety in type of sources — books, articles, electronic journals, etc. Use MLA guidelines for documentation.

Invention Strategies

As a starting point, think of conversations you've had in the past few days or weeks that have involved defending a position. Is there some current political issue you're concerned about? Some dispute with friends that would make a valid paper topic? One of the best sources is controversies in the media. Keep your project in mind as you watch TV, read print or online sources, or listen to the radio. You may even run into a potential subject in your course reading assignments or classroom discussions. Fortunately for the would-be writer, nearly every human activity includes its share of disagreement.

As you consider possible topics, write them down. One that looks unlikely at first glance may suggest others or may have more appeal when you come back to it later. Further, simply putting words on paper has a way of stimulating the thought processes involved in writing. Even if your ideas are tentative, the act of converting them into phrases or sentences can often help in developing them.

> With the assignment in hand, Katie starts to think about possible topics related to food. She knows that there is also a book called *Food, Inc.,* so she turns to her university library's online catalog and looks it up. She discovers that it is a collection of essays edited by Karl Weber. It looks like a source worth investigating, so she checks it out.
>
> The subtitle of the book is *How Industrial Food Is Making Us Sicker, Fatter, and Poorer — And What We Can Do about It.* That is in keeping with the focus of the film the students saw in class. Katie knows that she doesn't have time to read the whole book for this assignment, but she looks at the preface and table of contents to get ideas about how to find a subject narrow enough to write about. One interesting subject that she has heard about repeatedly on the news and has read

about in *Newsweek* is today's epidemic of childhood obesity, and she notices that one chapter in the part of the book that suggests solutions is called "Improving Kids' Nutrition: An Action Tool Kit for Parents." There is also another essay paired with that one and entitled "Childhood Obesity: The Challenge."

Skimming the latter of these two essays immediately gives her some impressive statistics about how bad the problem of childhood obesity is. She knows, though, that childhood obesity is too large a subject and that she has to come up with a thesis about her subject that is either a claim of value or a claim of policy. She has to do more than prove that a problem exists.

In the first of the two essays she runs across a term she is not familiar with: competitive foods. Katie now has the germ of an idea for a topic. She discovers that competitive foods are the "extras" sold to students in addition to or instead of the food served in the cafeteria. She thinks this must certainly be a controversial subject.

Evaluating Possible Topics

Your topic must interest your audience. Who is the audience? For a lawyer it is usually a judge or jury; for a columnist, anyone who reads the newspaper in which his or her column appears. For the student writer, the audience is to some extent hypothetical. You should assume that your paper is directed at readers who are reasonably intelligent and well informed, but who have no specific knowledge of the subject. It may be useful to imagine you are writing for a local or school publication.

Your thesis must be debatable. The purpose of an argument is to defend or refute a thesis, so choose a topic that can be seen from more than one perspective. In evaluating a subject that looks promising, ask yourself: Can a case be made for other views? If not, you have no workable ground for building your own case.

Your thesis must be neither too broad nor too narrow. Consider how long your paper will be, and whether you can do justice to your topic in that amount of space. For example, suppose you want to argue in favor of worldwide nuclear disarmament. Is this a thesis you can support persuasively in a short paper? One way to find out is by listing the potential issues or points about which arguers might disagree. Consider the thesis: "The future of the world is in danger as long as nuclear weapons exist." Obviously this statement is too general. You would have to specify what you mean by the future of the world (the continuation of human life? of all life? of the earth itself?) and exactly how nuclear weapons endanger it before the claim would hold up. You could narrow it down: "Human beings are error-prone; therefore as long as nuclear weapons exist there is the chance that a large number of people will be killed accidentally." Though this statement is more specific and includes an important warrant, it still depends on other unstated warrants: that one human being (or a small group) is in the position to discharge a nuclear weapon capable of killing a large number of people;

that such a weapon could, in fact, be discharged by mistake, given current safety systems. Can you expect to show sufficient evidence for these assumptions in the space available to you?

By now it should be apparent that arguing in favor of nuclear disarmament is too broad an undertaking. A more workable approach might be to defend or refute one of the disarmament proposals under consideration by the U.S. Congress, or to show that nuclear weapons pose some specific danger (such as long-term water pollution) that is sufficient reason to strive for disarmament.

Can a thesis be too narrow? Certainly. If you can prove your point convincingly in a paragraph, or even a page, you need a broader thesis.

At this preliminary stage, don't worry if you don't know exactly how to word your thesis. It's useful to write down a few possible phrasings to be sure your topic is one you can work with, but you need not be precise. The information you unearth as you do research will help you to formulate your ideas. Also, stating a thesis in final terms is premature until you know the organization and tone of your paper. If your topic or assignment does not require research, you may want to move ahead to Chapter 11.

> Katie has narrowed her topic from something related to the movie *Food, Inc.* to childhood obesity to competitive foods in schools. As she continues, she will have to keep asking herself if she can find enough authoritative sources to support her tentative claim — that competitive foods should not be allowed in schools.

Initiating Research

The success of any argument, short or long, depends in large part on the quantity and quality of the support behind it. Research, therefore, can be crucial for any argument outside your own experience. Most papers will benefit from research in the library and elsewhere because development of the claim requires facts, examples, statistics, and informed opinions that are available only from primary and secondary research sources. You should prepare for research by identifying potential resources and learning how they work. Make sure you know how to use the library's catalog and other databases available either in the library or through the campus network. For each database that looks useful, explore how to execute a subject search, how to refine a search, and how to print out or download results. Make sure you know how to find books, relevant reference materials, and journals. Find out whether interlibrary loan is an option and how long it takes. If you plan to use government publications, find out if your library is a depository for federal documents. Identify relevant organizations using the *Encyclopedia of Associations* and visit their Web sites. Finally, discuss your topic with a librarian at the reference desk to make sure you haven't overlooked anything.

Writer's Guide: Keeping Your Research on Track

1. Focus your investigation on building your argument, not merely on collecting information about the topic. Do follow any promising leads that turn up from the sources you consult, but don't be diverted into general reading that has no direct bearing on your thesis.

2. Look for at least two pieces of evidence to support each point you want to make. If you cannot find sufficient evidence, you may need to revise or abandon the point.

3. Use a variety of sources. Seek evidence from different kinds of sources (books, magazines, Web sites, government reports, even personal interviews with experts) and from different fields.

4. Be sure your sources are authoritative. Articles and essays in scholarly journals are more authoritative than articles in college newspapers or in magazines. Authors whose credentials include many publications and years of study at reputable institutions are probably more reliable than newspaper columnists and the so-called man in the street. However, we can judge reliability much more easily if we are dealing with facts and inferences than with values and emotions.

5. Don't let your sources' opinions outweigh your own. Your paper should demonstrate that the thesis and ideas you present are yours, arrived at after careful reflection and supported by research. The thesis need not be original, but your paper should be more than a collection of quotations or a report of the facts and opinions you have been reading.

6. Don't ignore information that opposes the position you plan to support. Your argument is not strengthened by pretending such information does not exist. You may find that you must revise or qualify your position based on what your research reveals. Your readers may be aware of other positions on the issue and may judge you to be unreliable, careless, or dishonest if you do not acknowledge them. It is far better to fairly summarize opposing arguments and refute them than to ignore them.

Mapping Research: A Sample Outline

To explore a range of research activities, let's suppose that you are preparing a research paper, six to ten pages long. You have chosen to defend the following thesis: *Even though thalidomide is infamous for causing birth defects in the 1960s, it has promise as a treatment for cancer and other diseases.* To keep your material under control and give direction to your reading, you would sketch a preliminary outline, which might look like this:

Thalidomide: Changing a Drug's Reputation

   I. Thalidomide's history: a promising drug but a medical nightmare
      A. Explain how drug was developed
      B. Explain the medical disaster it caused
  II. New look at thalidomide: its potential to effectively treat cancer and other diseases
      A. Discuss how it first worked to treat leprosy
      B. Support how it can treat cancer
      C. Support how it can treat other diseases
 III. Conclusion

Now you need to begin the search for the materials that will support your argument. There are two principal ways of gathering the materials — primary research and secondary research. Most writers will not want to limit themselves to one kind of research, but one method may work better than another for a particular project.

> At this point, Katie can sketch only a very rough outline of the shape her essay may take. She knows that her thesis and her outline may have to change as she continues her research.

Competitive Food in Schools

   I. The history of competitive food in schools
      A. Explain what competitive food is
      B. Explain why competitive food is allowed
  II. The dangers of competitive food in schools
      A. Explain the immediate effect on school performance
      B. Explain the long-term health effects
 III. Suggested solutions
 IV. Conclusion

Using Sources: Primary Research

Primary research involves looking for firsthand information. By *firsthand* we mean information taken directly from the original source, including field research (interviews, surveys, personal observations, or experiments). If your topic relates to a local issue involving your school or community, or if it focuses on a story that has never been reported by others, field research may be more valuable than anything available in the library. However, the library can be a source of firsthand information. Memoirs and letters written by witnesses to past events, photographs, contemporary news reports of historical events, or expert testimony presented at congressional hearings are all primary sources that may be available in your library. The Internet, too, can be a source of primary data. A discussion list, newsgroup, or chat room focused on your topic may give you a means to converse with activists and contact experts. Web sites of certain organizations provide documentation of their views, unfiltered by others' opinions. The text of laws, court opinions, bills, debates in Congress, environmental impact statements, and even selected declassified FBI files can be found through government-sponsored Web sites. Other sites present statistical data or the text of historical or political documents.

One of the rewards of primary research is that it often generates new information, which in turn produces new interpretations of familiar conditions. It is a favored method for anthropologists and sociologists, and most physical and natural scientists use observation and experiment at some point as essential tools in their research.

Consider the sample thesis that *even though thalidomide is infamous for causing birth defects in the 1960s, it has promise as a treatment for cancer and other diseases.* It is possible to go to primary sources in addition to or instead of consulting books. For example:

- Interview one or more physicians about current or potential uses of thalidomide.

- Interview someone locally who has had a family member affected by thalidomide.

- Read a first-person account by someone negatively affected by thalidomide use.

- Read a first-person account by someone positively affected by thalidomide use.

- Research newspaper reports from the time period regarding the birth defects caused by thalidomide before its dangers were known.

- Search the Web for reputable sources of information about thalidomide and the uses for which it is currently approved.

The information gleaned from primary research can be used directly to support your claim, or can provide a starting point for secondary research.

Katie and her classmates are not required to use primary sources, but she knows that they have the potential to add significant information to some arguments.

She roughs out a list of possible primary sources:

Interview with parents of school-aged children

Interview with students

Interview with school cafeteria workers/manager

Interview with school/district nutritionist

Printed regulations governing school lunches

Statistics about school nutrition

Statistics about competitive foods

Using Sources: Secondary Research

Secondary research involves locating commentary on and analysis of your topic. In addition to raw evidence found through primary research, secondary sources provide a sense of how others are examining the issues and can provide useful information and analysis. Secondary sources may be written for a popular audience, ranging from news coverage, to popular explanations of research findings, to social analysis, to opinion pieces. Or they may be scholarly publications — experts presenting their research and theories to other researchers. These sources might also come in the form of analytical reports written to untangle possible courses of action, such as a report written by staff members for a congressional committee or an analysis of an issue by a think tank that wants to use the evidence it has gathered to influence public opinion.

Whatever form it may take, be sure when you use a secondary source that you consider the author's purpose and the validity of the material presented to ensure that it is useful evidence for your argument. An opinion piece published in a small-town paper, for example, may be a less impressive source for your argument than an analysis written by a former cabinet member. A description of a scientific discovery published in a magazine will carry less weight as evidence than the article written by the scientists making the discovery presenting their research findings in a scientific journal.

The nature of your topic will determine which route you follow to find good sources. If the topic is current, you may find it more important to use articles than books and might bypass the library catalog altogether. If the topic has to do with social policy or politics, government publications may be particularly useful, though they would be unhelpful for a literary paper. If the topic relates to popular culture, the Internet may provide more information than more traditional publications. Consider what kinds of sources will be most useful as you choose your strategy. If you aren't certain which approaches fit your topic best, consult with a librarian at the reference desk.

Selecting and Searching Databases

You will most likely use one or more *databases* (online catalogs of reference materials) to locate books and articles on your topic. The library catalog is a database of books and other materials owned by the library; other databases may cover articles in popular or specialized journals and may even provide the full text of articles. Some databases may be available only in the library; others may be accessible all over campus. Here are some common features that appear in many databases.

Keyword or Subject Searching. You might have the option of searching a database by *keyword* — using the words that you think are most relevant to your search — or by subject. Typically, a keyword search will search for any occurrence of your search term in titles, notes, or the descriptive headings provided by database catalogers or indexers. The advantage to keyword searching is that you can use terms that come naturally to you to cast your net as widely as possible. The disadvantage is that there may be more than one way to express your topic and you may not capture all the relevant materials unless you use the right keywords.

With *subject searching*, you use search terms from a list of subject headings (sometimes called *descriptors*) established by the creators of the database. To make searching as efficient as possible, they choose one word or phrase to express a subject. Every time a new source is entered into the database, the indexers describe it using words from the list of subject headings: When you use the list to search the database, you retrieve every relevant source. You might find that a database lists these subject headings through a thesaurus feature. The sophisticated researcher will always pay attention to the subject headings or descriptors generally listed at the bottom of a record for clues to terms that might work best and for related terms that might be worth trying.

Searching for More Than One Concept. Most database searches allow you to combine terms using the connectors *and*, *or*, and *not*. These connectors (also known as *Boolean operators*) group search terms in different ways. If you search for zoos *and* animal rights, for example, the resulting list of sources will include only those that deal with both zoos and animal rights, leaving out any that deal with only one subject and not the other. If you connect terms with *or*, your list will contain sources that deal with either concept: A search for dogs or cats will create a list of sources that cover either animal. *Not* excludes concepts from a search. A search for animal rights *not* furs will search for the concept animal rights and then cut out any sources that deal with furs.

Limiting a Search. Most databases have some options for limiting a search by a number of variables, such as publication date, language, or format. If you find a large number of sources in a database search, you might limit your search to sources published in English in the past three years. If you need a visual aid for a presentation, you might limit a search of the library's catalog to videos, and so on.

Truncating Search Terms with Wild Cards. At times you will search for a word that has many possible endings. A wild card is a symbol that, placed at the end of a word root, allows for any possible ending for a word. For example, *animal** will allow a search for *animal* or *animals*.

Options for Saving Records. You may have the opportunity to print, download, or e-mail to yourself the citations you find in a database. Many databases have a feature for marking just the records you want so you save only those of interest.

Help Screens. Most databases offer some kind of online help that explains how to use the database effectively. If you invest five minutes getting familiar with the basics of a database, it may save you twenty minutes later.

Types of Databases

The Library Catalog. If you want to search for books, videos, or periodical publications, the library catalog is the database to search. Most libraries now have computerized catalogs, but some still have a card catalog. In either case, the type of information provided is the same. Every book in the library has an entry in the catalog that gives its author, title, publisher, date, length, and subject headings and perhaps some notes about its contents. It also gives the call number or location on the shelf and often some indication as to whether it is currently available. You can search the catalog for an author, title, subject, or keyword. Most online catalogs have ways of combining and limiting searches and for printing results. Remember when searching the catalog, though, that entries are created for whole books and not for specific parts of them. If you use too narrow search terms, you may not find a book that has a chapter that includes exactly what you are looking for. Use broad search terms, and check the subject headings for search terms that will work best. Plan to browse the shelves and examine the tables of contents of the books that you find through the catalog to see which, in fact, are most helpful for your topic.

General Periodical Databases. If you want to search for articles, you can find a number of options at your library. Most libraries have a generalized database of periodical articles that may include citations, citations with abstracts (brief summaries), or the entire text of articles. *EBSCOhost, Infotrac, Searchbank, Readers' Guide Abstracts*, and *ProQuest* are all online indexes of this type. Ask a librarian what is available in your library. These are particularly good for finding current information in fairly nonspecialized sources, though they may include some scholarly journals. If you are looking for articles published before the 1980s — say, for news accounts published when the atomic bomb was dropped on Hiroshima — you would most likely need to use a print index such as the *Readers' Guide to Periodical Literature*, which began publication in 1900.

Specialized Databases. In addition to these general databases, you may find you need to delve deeper into a particular subject area. Every academic discipline has some sort of in-depth index to its research, and though the materials they cover tend to be highly specialized, they can provide more substantial support for your claims because they tend to cover sources written by experts in their fields. These resources may be available in electronic or print form:

Art Index

Biological Abstracts (the online version is known as *Biosis*)

Business Periodicals Index

ERIC (focused on education research)

Index Medicus (*Medline* or *PubMed* online)

Modern Language Association International Bibliography (*MLA Bibliography* online)

Psychological Abstracts (*PsychInfo* or *PsychLit* online)

Sociological Abstracts (*Sociofile* online)

Check with a librarian to find out which specialized databases or indexes that relate to your topic are available in your library.

Database Services. In addition to individual databases, many libraries subscribe to database services that provide access to a number of databases from one search screen. *FirstSearch*, for example, provides access to a variety of subject-specific databases as well as *WorldCat*, a massive database of library catalogs. *LexisNexis* is a collection of databases to over a billion texts, most of them available in full text; it is a strong source for news coverage, legal research, and business information. These may be available to you through the Web anywhere on campus. Again, a visit with a librarian will help you quickly identify what your library has available.

> When Katie looks over the list of databases available through her campus library, she finds two general databases that she decides to start with.
>
> The first is Academic OneFile. She does a keyword search for "competitive foods" and gets 76 hits. She has the option to refine this search, so she adds the Boolean operator "AND" plus "school" and narrows the number of hits to 14. She skims these results and sees some titles that look useful. She checks the

Sample Online Catalog Record

You searched for the TITLE — animal rights movement

```
CALL #       Z7164.C45 M38 1994.
AUTHOR       Manzo, Bettina, 1943-
TITLE        The animal rights movement in the United States, 1975-
                1990 : an annotated bibliography / by Bettina Manzo.
IMPRINT      Metuchen, N.J. : Scarecrow Press, 1994.
PHYS DESCR   xi, 296 p. ; 23 cm.
NOTE         Includes indexes.
CONTENTS     Animal rights movement -- Activists and organizations --
                Philosophy, ethics, and religion -- Law and legislation
                --  Factory farming and vegetarianism -- Trapping and
                fur industry -- Companion animals -- Wildlife --
                Circuses, zoos, rodeos, dog
SUBJECT      Animal rights movement --United States --Bibliography.
             Animal rights --United States --Bibliography.
             Animal experimentation --United States --Bibliography.
OCLC #       30671149.
ISBN/ISSN    GB95-17241.
```

ones that seem most promising and prints up that narrowed list so that she can try to locate some of the articles later. She chooses the ones labeled "article" instead of ones labeled "report" because the titles of the reports suggest that they are much more technical.

The second general database she tries is EBSCOhost. This time she tries three words linked by the Boolean operator "and": "competitive" AND "food" AND "school." She gets 671 hits. She then tries "competitive food" AND "school" and finds a much more manageable 51. She tries one more refinement: She puts "competitive food" in quotation marks in the search box so that the system will search for those two words together. This produces a manageable 18 citations, so she selects the two that look most promising, chooses the option "add to folder," and then prints up the citations.

Katie decides to look for a specialized database. The one that seems to match her subject best is Food Science and Technology Abstracts. She discovers that this is a specialized EBSCOhost database, so she uses the same procedure that she used earlier, and this time she finds her hits are limited to just 8. She adds two to her folder and prints up the two citations.

When Katie tries to access some of her selected articles by clicking on the title, she finds she would have to pay to access the full text of the articles. She tries pasting the URL into Google, and is able to access the texts free.

Encyclopedias

General and specialized encyclopedias offer quick overviews of topics and easy access to factual information. They also tend to have excellent selective bibliographies, pointing you toward useful sources. You will find a wide variety of encyclopedias in your library's reference collection; you may also have an online encyclopedia, such as *Britannica Online*, available through the Web anywhere on campus. Some specialized encyclopedias include the following:

Encyclopedia of African American History and Culture

Encyclopedia of American Social History

Encyclopedia of Bioethics

Encyclopedia of Educational Research

Encyclopedia of Hispanic Culture in the United States

Encyclopedia of International Relations

Encyclopedia of Philosophy

Encyclopedia of Sociology

Encyclopedia of the United States in the Twentieth Century

Encyclopedia of World Cultures

International Encyclopedia of Communications

McGraw-Hill Encyclopedia of Science and Technology
Political Handbook of the World

Statistical Resources

Often statistics are used as evidence in an argument. If your argument depends on establishing that one category is bigger than another, that the majority of people hold a certain opinion, or that one group is more affected by something than another group, statistics can provide the evidence you need. Of course, as with any other source, you need to be sure that your statistics are as reliable as possible and that you are reporting them responsibly.

It isn't always easy to find things counted the way you want. If you embark on a search for numbers to support your argument, be prepared to spend some time locating and interpreting data. Always read the fine print that explains how and when the data were gathered. Some sources for statistics include these:

U.S. Bureau of the Census. This government agency produces a wealth of statistical data, much of it available on CD-ROM or through the Web at www.census .gov. A handy compilation of their most useful tables is found in the one-volume annual handbook, *Statistical Abstract of the United States*, which also includes statistics from other government sources.

Other Federal Agencies. Numerous federal agencies gather statistical data. Among these are the National Center for Education Statistics, the National Center for Health Statistics, the National Bureau of Labor Statistics, and the Federal Bureau of Investigation, which annually compiles national crime statistics. One handy place to find a wide variety of federal statistics is a Web site called *FedStats* at www.fedstats.gov.

United Nations. Compilations of international data published by the United Nations include the *Demographic Yearbook* and *Statistical Yearbook*. Some statistics are also published by U.N. agencies such as the Food and Health Organization. Some are available from the U.N. Web site at www.un.org.

Opinion Polls. Several companies conduct opinion polls, and some of these are available in libraries. One such compilation is the Gallup Poll series, which summarizes public opinion polling from 1935 to the present. Other poll results are reported by the press. Search a database that covers news publications by using your topic and *polls* as keywords to help you locate some summaries of results.

Government Publications

Beyond statistics, government agencies compile and publish a wealth of information. For topics that concern public welfare, health, education, politics, foreign relations, earth sciences, the environment, or the economy, government documents may provide just the information you need.

The U.S. federal government is the largest publisher in the world. Its publications are distributed free to libraries designated as document depositories across the country. If your library is not a depository, chances are there is a regional depository somewhere nearby. Local, state, and foreign governments are also potential sources of information.

Federal documents distributed to depository libraries are indexed in *The Monthly Catalog of U.S. Government Documents,* available in many libraries as an electronic database. These include congressional documents such as hearings and committee reports, presidential papers, studies conducted by the Education Department or the Centers for Disease Control, and so on. Many government documents are available through the Internet. If you learn about a government publication through the news media, chances are you will be able to obtain a copy at the Web site of the sponsoring agency or congressional body. In fact, government publications are among the most valuable of resources available on the Web because they are rigorously controlled for content. You know you are looking at a U.S. federal government site when you see the domain suffix *.gov* in the URL.

> Katie decides not to look for any more statistics or government documents because there are plenty of statistics in the articles from the book *Food, Inc.,* many of them drawn from federal sources.

Searching the Web

The World Wide Web is an increasingly important resource for researchers. It is particularly helpful if you are looking for information about organizations, current events, political debates, popular culture, or government-sponsored research and activities. It is not an especially good place to look for literary criticism, historical analysis, or scholarly research articles, which are still more likely to be published in traditional ways. Biologists reporting on an important experiment, for example, are more likely to submit an article about it to a prestigious journal in the field than simply post their results on the Web.

Because anyone can publish whatever they like on the Web, searching for good information can be frustrating. Search engines operate by means of automated programs that gather information about sites and match search terms to whatever is out there, regardless of quality. A search engine may locate thousands of Web documents on a topic, but most are of little relevance and dubious quality. The key is to know in advance what information you need and who might have produced it. For example, if your topic has to do with some aspect of free speech and you know that the American Civil Liberties Union is involved in the issue, a trip to the ACLU home page may provide you with a wealth of information, albeit from a particular perspective. If your state's pollution control agency just issued a report on water quality in the area, you may find the report published at their Web site or the e-mail address of someone who could send it to you. The more you know about your topic before you sit down to surf, the more likely you will use your time productively.

If you have a fairly broad topic and no specific clues about where it might be covered, you may want to start your search using a selective guide to good sites. For example, the University of Texas maintains an excellent directory to sites relating to Latin America. Subject guides that selectively list valuable sites can be found at the University of California's *Infomine* at http://infomine.ucr.edu and the *World Wide Web Virtual Library* project at www.vlib.org/Home.html. Reference librarians will also be able to point you to quality sites that relate to your topic.

If you have a fairly specific topic in mind or are looking for a particular organization or document on the Web, a search engine can help you find it. *Google* is one of the best. No matter what search engine you choose, find out how it works, how it ranks results, and how deeply it indexes Web pages. Some search engines will retrieve more results than others simply because of the way the program gathers information from sites. As with databases, there are usually ways to refine a search and improve your results. Many search engines offer an advanced search option that may provide some useful options for refining and limiting a search.

It is important to know what will not be retrieved by a search engine. Because publishing and transmitting texts on the Web is relatively easy, it is becoming more common for libraries to subscribe to databases and electronic journals that are accessed through a Web browser. You may have *Britannica Online* and *LexisNexis* as options on your library's home page. However, the contents of those subscriptions will be available only to your campus community and will not be searched by general Web search engines.

> When Katie turns to the Internet to do some additional searching for relevant material, she uses what she has learned in accessing sources in the databases. She searches for "competitive food" and "school," with "competitive food" in quotation marks in the search box. The search calls up over 15,000 entries, but she notices that the very first one is from the Centers for Disease Control, which she knows to be a reliable source. Within the first 10 she finds listings for articles from the California Department of Education, the federal General Accounting Office, the U.S. Department of Agriculture (USDA), the American Heart Association, and a few other organizations that she will have to investigate. She is pleased that she so easily found a number of authoritative sources. She can tell by the *.gov* at the end of some that they are government sources and that others are organizations (*.org*).
>
> One of the sources was published by healthiergeneration.org. Since she is not familiar with that organization, she calls up its Web site and discovers that it is the Alliance for a Healthier Generation, founded in 2005 by the American Heart Association and Bill Clinton to fight childhood obesity. That is enough information to reassure Katie that it is a reputable site, so she adds it to her list of sources to investigate further. Another listing leads her to FRAC, which proves to be the Food Research and Action Center. Its history indicates that it has an impressive record of fighting for food programs designed to serve the poor and the elderly, including breakfast programs for school children. Again, it seems a source worth pursuing.
>
> She looks up the Web site for the USDA and discovers a list of promising links, including one targeted at childhood obesity and one to a program called the HealthierUS School Challenge.

A quick look at the dates of the articles she is considering indicates that most were published in 2009 or 2010, but she will continue to check dates as she accesses other sources.

Katie feels that she is now ready to take a closer look at the sources she has been finding.

Evaluating Sources

When you begin studying your sources, read first to acquire general familiarity with your subject. Make sure that you are covering both sides of the question — in this case the negative as well as the positive aspects of the use of thalidomide — as well as facts and opinions from a variety of sources. In investigating this subject, you might examine data from doctors, victims of earlier thalidomide use, scientists studying the current uses of thalidomide, the manufacturer of the drug, and recent patients; their varied points of view will contribute to the strength of your claim.

As you read, look for what seem to be the major issues. They will probably be represented in all or most of your sources. Record questions as they occur to you in your reading. What went wrong when thalidomide was used in the 1960s? Why is it again receiving attention? What reasons are there for bringing back such a dangerous drug? Are there advantages that outweigh the dangers? What has changed that might make use of the drug safer today?

Evaluating Print Sources

The sources you find provide useful information that you need for your paper and help you support your claims. One key to supporting claims effectively is to make sure you have the best evidence available. It is tempting when searching a database or the Web to take the first sources that look good, print them or copy them, and not give them another thought until you are sitting down to compose your argument — only to discover that the sources aren't as valuable as they could be. Sources that looked pretty good at the beginning of your research may turn out to be less useful once you have learned more about the topic. And a source that seems interesting at first glance may turn out to be a rehash or digest of a much more valuable source, something you realize only when you sit down and look at it carefully.

To find the right stuff, be a critical thinker from the start of your research process. Scan and evaluate the references you encounter throughout your search. As you examine options in a database, choose sources that use relevant terms in their titles, seem directed to an appropriate audience, and are published in places that will look good in your Works Cited list. For example, a Senate Foreign Relations Committee report will be more impressive as a source than a comparable article in *Good Housekeeping*. An article from the scholarly journal *Foreign Affairs* will carry more clout than an article from *Reader's Digest*, even if they are on the same subject.

Skim and quickly evaluate each source that looks valuable.

- Is it relevant to your topic?
- Does it provide information you haven't found elsewhere?
- Can you learn anything about the author, and does what you learn inspire confidence?

As you begin to learn more about your topic and revise your outline as necessary, you can use sources to help direct your search. If a source mentions an organization, for example, you may use that clue to run a search on the Web for that organization's home page. If a newspaper story refers to a study published in a scientific journal, you may want to seek out that study to see the results of the research firsthand. And if you have a source that includes references to other publications, scan through them, and see which might also prove helpful to you. When you first started your research, chances are you weren't quite sure what you were looking for. Once you are familiar with your topic, you need to concentrate on finding sources that will best support the claims you want to make, and your increasing familiarity with the issue will make it easier to identify the best sources. That may mean a return trip to the library.

Once you have selected some useful sources to support your claims, make a more in-depth evaluation to be sure you have the best evidence available.

- Is it current enough? Have circumstances changed since this text was published?
- Is the author someone I want to call on as an expert witness? Does the author have the experience or credentials to make a solid argument that carries weight with my readers?
- Is it reliable information for my purposes? It may be highly opinionated, but are the basic facts it presents confirmed in other sources? Is the evidence presented in the text convincing?

These questions are not always easy to answer. In some cases, articles will include some information about the author, such as where he or she works. In other cases, no information or even an author's name is given. In that case, it may help to evaluate the publication and its reputation. If you aren't familiar with a publication and don't feel confident making your own judgment, see if it is described in Katz's *Magazines for Libraries*, which evaluates the reputation and quality of periodicals.

Evaluating Web Sources

Web sites pose challenges and offer unique opportunities for researchers, for one reason because they are part of a developing genre of writing. When evaluating a Web site, first examine what kind of site you are reading. Is the Web page selling or advertising goods or services (a business site)? Is it advocating a point of view (an advocacy site) or providing relatively neutral information, such as that found in the yellow pages (an informative or educational site)? Is the Web site addressing the interests of people in a particular organization or with common interests (an information-sharing site)? Is it reporting up-to-the-minute news (a news site) or appealing to some aspect of an individual's life and interests (a personal site)? Useful information for a research paper may be obtained from any of these kinds of Web pages, but it is helpful to know what the main purpose of the site is — and who its primary audience is — when determining how productive it will be for your research.

As you weigh the main purpose of the site, evaluate its original context. Does the site originate in a traditional medium, such as a print journal or an encyclopedia? Is the site part of an online journal, in which case its material had to go through a screening process? Or is the site the product of one individual's or organization's desire to create a Web page, which means the work may not have been screened or evaluated by any outside agency? In that case, the information may still be valuable, but you must be even more careful when evaluating it.

Answering preliminary questions like these helps you before you begin a more specific evaluation of the site's content. To find answers to many of these questions, make a brief overview of the site itself, by looking, for example, at the clues contained in the Web address. That is, .com in the address means a business or commercial site; .edu, a site sponsored by a university or college; .k12 is a site associated with a primary or secondary school; .gov indicates that the federal government sponsored the site; and .org suggests that the site is part of a nonprofit or noncommercial group. Sites originating outside the United States have URLs that end with a two-letter country abbreviation, such as .uk for United Kingdom. Although these address clues can reveal a great deal about the origins and purposes of a Web site, remember that personal Web sites may also contain some of these abbreviations. Institutions such as schools and businesses sometimes sponsor individuals' personal Web sites (which are often unscreened by the institution) as well as official institutional sites. One possible key to determining whether a Web site is a personal page, however, is to look for a tilde (~) plus a name or part of a name in the address. Finally, if you are unsure of the sponsoring organization of a page, try erasing all the information in the URL after the first slash (/) and pressing the "Enter" key. Doing so often brings you to the main page of the organization sponsoring the Web site.

Most Web sites include a way to contact the author or sponsoring organization of the site, usually through e-mail. This is often a quick and easy way to get answers to the preliminary questions. If the site contains an address or phone number as part of its contact information, this means the organization or individual is available and probably willing to stand behind the site's content. If you can't find contact information the site may not be suitable to use as a primary resource. The information is not necessarily invalid, but such clues should alert you that information found on that page needs to be verified.

For the next step — that of more closely evaluating the contents of any Web site — Web researchers generally agree on the importance of five criteria: the authority, accuracy, objectivity, currency, and coverage of the site.[1] These criteria are just as important in evaluating traditional print texts, but electronic texts require special care. To understand how these criteria work, let's look at a specific example.

Evaluating a Web Site: One Example

Assume that your observations have led you to conclude that high school students are largely apathetic about government and politics. As a likely future parent, you have decided to research ways of interesting teenagers in the political process. You hypothesize that students who take the whole cyberworld for granted as a part of everyday life might be attracted to an interactive Web site. You do a search on Google using different combinations of keywords, and one site you access looks promising. You want to be sure, however, that the site meets the tests of authority, accuracy, objectivity, currency, and coverage.

The site is Student Voices, designed to teach high school students about government and civic responsibility. Your first job is to evaluate the home page.

The home page design is simple but attractive, and the text is easy to read. There are a number of different features to explore, and the site is typical in that there is no set order for accessing the different links. It is clear from the buttons at the top of the page that the site is used in the context of classes because there are teacher resources as well as student ones.

Clicking on the Student Resources link leads to a useful video called *How to Use the Student Voices Web Site*. This ten-minute video introduces the resources the site offers students. The Teacher Resources page does the same for teachers. Teachers can get a password to the site that allows their students to interact with the material on the site.

The Student Resources page also includes links to a wealth of sources about government, including these:

- Encyclopedia entries on the U.S. president, U.S. senators, the federal government, and state government
- Official government sites, from the White House to the Library of Congress
- Sources that can be used for general research and constitutional research, and for access to voting/elections information
- Major newspapers from across the country and Web sites of the major television networks

---

[1] Wolfgram Memorial Library Web site.

The Student-voices.org home page

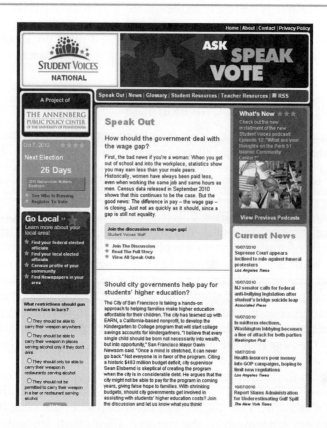

The video also explains the different ways that students can use the site interactively. Going back to the home page, you can see its major divisions:

- **Speak Out** is just that — a chance for students to speak out on current political issues. Every few weeks the topic on the home page changes, and the staff of Student Voices presents a brief summary of a "hot" issue such as eminent domain, illegal aliens, or wiretapping. Students can then respond to what they read, read Speak Out on other subjects, or read more on the topic.

- **Polls.** At any given time, there is one question on which students are being polled, plus access to previous polls.

- **What's New.** Clicking on this box takes students to information about what their representatives are voting on at the time.

- **Current News.** The national political news of the day.

The Student-voices.org Student Resources page

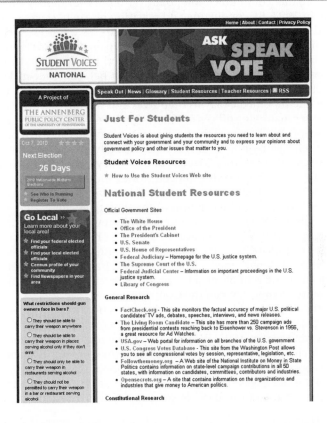

- **Go Local.** These links let the students discover who their local and federal elected representatives are, what their local newspapers are, and what the census reveals about their community.

- **Next Election.** This box is updated every day to reveal how many days until the next election, who is running, and how to register to vote.

The navigation bar also provides a link to a glossary of political terms.

Now that you have an overview of the site, consider whether it meets the criteria for a good source.

Authority. You decide to investigate who is behind this site. At the bottom of the home page is the information that the site is copyrighted by the Annenberg Public Policy Center. A quick check on Google leads you to this center's site, where you discover that the APPC is a part of the University of Pennsylvania. This is the way the center describes its mission:

The Annenberg Public Policy Center of the University of Pennsylvania has been the premier communication policy center in the country since its founding in 1993. By conducting and releasing research, staging conferences and hosting policy discussions, its scholars have addressed the role of communication in politics, adolescent behavior, child development, health care, civics and mental health, among other important arenas. The Center's researchers have drafted materials that helped policy-makers, journalists, scholars, constituent groups and the general public better understand the role that media play in their lives and the life of the nation. The Policy Center maintains offices in Philadelphia and Washington, D.C.

APPC's work has informed the policy debates around campaign finance, children's television, internet privacy, tobacco advertising and the tone of discourse in Washington. Scholars at the Policy Center have offered guidance to journalists covering difficult stories, including terrorist threats, suicide and mental health. The Center's discussions of key public policy issues have brought together industry representatives, advocates, government officials and the scholarly community. Its research has examined what messages work best to reduce the spread of HIV and drug use, how to improve candidate discourse and specific strategies for parents to use to monitor their children's media exposure. APPC has developed materials to help educators and schools do a better job of teaching youth about civic responsibility, democracy and the Constitution.

To further our mission, we are launching this new web site. It is designed to give scholars, the media and the general public expanded access to the work that we began in 1993. We intend to make that complete body of research, including extensive data sets and topline surveys, available as quickly as possible. If there are any questions about materials not yet posted on the site, please contact our Philadelphia office at the number listed at the bottom of this page, or send an email to [the address shown].

The fact that the Annenberg Public Policy Center is part of a reputable university tends to give the information it presents on the site credence. There also is an e-mail address by which to reach someone at Annenberg, which also suggests credibility. The biographies of the staff at Annenberg reveal that they are scholars and journalists with substantial experience in Washington D.C.

Accuracy. Much of the information on the site is factual. The site's affiliation with a major university and its well-qualified staff make a reader inclined to accept that the facts are accurately presented. Since the site is updated daily, news does not get old, as it can with sites that are not well maintained. Those parts of the site that elicit opinion are clearly that — an invitation for students to express their opinions, right or wrong. No one under the age of thirteen is allowed to participate in Speak Out, and those between thirteen and eighteen must have parental permission to participate or to send any personally identifying information. In fact, one other project of the APPC is FactCheck.org, a site that analyzes statements made to the media and points out inaccuracies. There is a link from the home page of Student Voices to FactCheck.org.

Objectivity. Again, it is easier to maintain objectivity when dealing with facts like the outcome of a vote in the Senate or the name of a local representative. Most of the links that provide information about government are linked directly to governmental sites — the House of Representatives, the Library of Congress, and the White House, for example. They are not to sites that present partisan views of the government. The links to broad categories such as U.S. presidents are to MSN's *Encarta*. The links to newspapers are to ones that are well established and well respected, such as the *New York Times* and the *Washington Post*, but they also show a range of possible slants on controversial issues. Included in the list, for example, is the *Christian Science Monitor*.

The factual nature of much of the information on the site increases the odds that the site is objective. The purpose of the whole site is to encourage students to discuss current political issues and to form their own opinions rather than to be presented with set notions as to what the "right" answer is. For those who want to read others' views, the analyses on FactCheck.org could be a starting point.

Currency. The site is updated every day. Although the Speak Out topic remains the same for a few weeks, that schedule allows students time to respond, and the national and state news is updated daily, as are the countdown to the next election and the What's New section.

Coverage. The site covers thoroughly much of the information that students need to learn about the political process on the national, state, and local levels. They can find in one place information that would be much more difficult and time-consuming to locate without its having been brought together in one place. Hypertext works well in such a context because the multiple links put masses of information at the students' fingertips. The Student Resources add great depth to the knowledge available on the home page, where there is also a link to another project of the APPC, Justice Learning, where students can go into more depth about some of the major issues of the day, should they want or need to.

Taking Notes

While everyone has methods of taking notes, here are a few suggestions that should be useful to research writers who need to read materials quickly, comprehend and evaluate the sources, use them as part of a research paper assignment, and manage their time carefully. If you need more detailed help with quoting, paraphrasing, and summarizing, review pages 86–89 in Chapter 3.

When taking notes from a source, summarize instead of quoting long passages. Summarizing as you read saves time. If you feel that a direct quote is more effective than anything you could write and provides crucial support for your argument, copy the material word for word. Leave all punctuation exactly as it appears and insert ellipsis points (". . .") if you delete material. Enclose all quotations in quotation marks and copy complete information about your source, including the author's name, the title of the book or article, the journal name if appropriate, page numbers, and publishing information. If you quote an article that appears in an anthology, record complete information about the book itself.

If you aren't sure whether you will use a piece of information later, don't copy the whole passage. Instead, make a note of its bibliographic information so that you can find it again if you need it. Taking too many notes, however, is preferable to taking too few, a problem that will force you to go back to the source for missing information.

Use the note-taking process as a prewriting activity. Often when you summarize an author's ideas or write down direct quotes, you see or understand the material in new ways. Freewrite about the importance of these quotes, paraphrases, or summaries, or at least about those that seem especially important. If nothing else, take a minute to justify in writing why you chose to record the notes. Doing so will help you clarify and develop your thoughts about your argument.

Taking this prewriting step seriously will help you analyze the ideas you record from outside sources. You will then be better prepared for the more formal (and inevitable) work of summarizing, paraphrasing, and composing involved in thinking critically about your topic and writing a research paper. Maybe most important, such work will help with that moment all writers face when they realize they "know what they want to say but can't find the words to say it." Overcoming such moments does not depend on finding inspiration while writing the final draft of a paper. Instead, successfully working through this common form of writer's block depends more on the amount of prewriting and thoughtful consideration of the notes done early in the research process.

As you take notes, also remember to refer to your outline to ensure that you are acquiring sufficient data to support all the points you intend to raise. Of course, you will be revising your outline during the course of your research as issues are clarified and new ideas emerge, but the outline will serve as a rough guide throughout the writing process. Keeping close track of your outline will also prevent you from recording material that is interesting but not relevant. It may help to label your notes with the heading from the outline to which they are most relevant.

Relying on the knowledge of others is an important part of doing research; expert opinions and eloquent arguments help support your claims when your own expertise is limited. But remember, this is *your* paper. Your ideas and insights into other people's ideas are just as important as the information you uncover at the library or through reputable online sources. When writing an argument, do not simply regurgitate the words and thoughts of others in your essay. Work to achieve a balance between providing solid information from expert sources and offering your own interpretation of the argument and the evidence that supports it. You are entering an ongoing conversation on your topic, not simply recording what others have already said.

Using word-processing software can invigorate the process of note taking and of outlining. Taking notes using a computer gives you more flexibility than using pen and paper alone. For example, you can save your computer-generated notes and your comments on them in numerous places (at home, school, or work, or on a disk); you can cut and paste the text into various documents; you can add to the notes or modify them and still revert to the originals with ease.

You can also link notes to background material on the Web that may be useful once you begin writing drafts of your paper. For example, you could create links to an author's Web page or to any of his or her other works published on the Web. You could create a link to a study or an additional source cited in your notes, or you could link to the work of other researchers who support or argue against the information you recorded.

Because you can record information in any number of ways on your computer, your notes act as tools in the writing process. One of the best ways to start is to open a file for each source; enter the bibliographic information; directly type into the file a series of potentially useful quotations, paraphrases, and summaries; and add your initial ideas about the source. (For each entry, note the correct page references as you go along and indicate clearly whether you are quoting, paraphrasing, or summarizing.) You can then use the capabilities of your computer to aid you in the later stages of the writing process. For example, you can collect all your research notes into one large file in which you group like sources, evaluate whether you have too much information about one issue or one side of an argument, or examine sources that conflict with one another. You can imagine various organizational schemes for your paper based on the central themes and issues of the notes you have taken, and you can more clearly determine which quotes and summaries are essential to your paper and which may not be needed.

When you're ready to begin your first draft, the computer allows you to readily integrate material from your source notes into your research paper by cutting and pasting, thus eliminating the need to retype and reducing the chance of error. You can also combine all the bibliographic materials you have saved in separate files and then use the computer to alphabetize your sources for your final draft.

Although taking notes on the computer does not dramatically change the research process, it does highlight the fact that taking notes, prewriting, drafting a paper, and creating a Works Cited page are integrated activities that should build from one another. When you take notes from a journal, book, or Web site, you develop your note-taking abilities so that they help with the entire writing process.

> Katie has decided to take notes on her sources on her computer. As this book suggests, she will start a new file for each source and compile all of the files into one folder. She does not start taking notes on a source until she looks it over and decides it is one that she will most likely use. At that point, she

puts at the top of the page the part of her outline the information will support. Then she puts in proper form at the top of the page the complete bibliographical information, using the rest of this chapter as a reference, so that when the time comes, she can simply alphabetize her sources and type them up for her Works Cited page.

She reminds herself to write down only what she needs so that she will not take notes that she will not use. She is also careful to put in quotation marks and in exact words any information taken directly from the source. That will remind her later that the notes not in quotation marks are in her own words. She writes down the page number for each idea because she will need that information for her parenthetical documentation. At times she makes notes to herself about why she is including certain information, such as who the author is and why that is important.

This is how a page of Katie's notes looks:

IIB—Long-term health effects

Robert Wood Johnson Foundation. "Childhood Obesity: The Challenge." *Food, Inc.: How Industrial Food Is Making Us Sicker, Fatter and Poorer — And What You Can Do about It.* Ed. Karl Weber. New York: PublicAffairs, 2009. 259–61. Print.

Link to Foundation: http://www.rwjf.org/

Might need to lead in to quotes: The Foundation is "the nation's largest philanthropy devoted exclusively to improving the health and health care of all Americans." 259

In three decades, the obesity rate has quadrupled for those aged 6–11. 259

"If we don't succeed in reversing this epidemic, we are in danger of raising the first generation of American children who will live sicker and die younger than their parents' generation." 259

Because of the difference between calorie intake and the physical activity needed to burn those calories, in ten years an adolescent could gain 58 pounds. 260

50% of children a generation ago walked to school. Now 90% ride. 260

"fewer than four percent of elementary schools provide daily physical education" 260

In some places where obesity is worst, the people can't afford healthy foods, there are convenience stores instead of grocery stores, and it is not safe for children to play outside. 261

Documenting Your Research (MLA SYSTEM)

One of the most effective ways to save yourself time and trouble when you are ready to write your research paper is to document your research as you go along. That way, when the time comes to create your Works Cited page, you will be ready to put the works you used in alphabetical order — or let your computer do it for you — and provide a list of those works at the end of your paper. Some instructors may require a bibliography, or a list of all of the works you consulted (sometimes called simply Works Consulted), but at a minimum you will need a Works Cited page. As that title indicates, the list will be only those works that you quote, paraphrase, or summarize in your paper.

Once you are fairly certain that you will use a certain source, go ahead and put it in proper bibliographic form. That way, if the citation form is complicated, you can look it up or ask your instructor before the last minute. Also, you will realize immediately if you are missing information required by the citation and can record it while the source is still at hand.

Following are examples of the citation forms you are most likely to need as you document your research. In general, for both books and magazines, information should appear in the following order: author, title, and publication information. Each item should be followed by a period. When using as a source an essay that appears in this book, follow the citation model for "Material reprinted from another source," unless your instructor indicates otherwise. Consult the *MLA Handbook for Writers of Research Papers*, Seventh Edition (New York: Modern Language Association of America, 2009) for other documentation models and a list of acceptable shortened forms of publishers.

Print Sources

A BOOK BY A SINGLE AUTHOR

Gubar, Susan. *Racechanges: White Skin, Black Face in American Culture*. New York: Oxford UP, 1997. Print.

TWO OR MORE BOOKS BY THE SAME AUTHOR OR AUTHORS

Gubar, Susan. *Judas: A Biography*. New York: Norton, 2009. Print.

---. *Race Changes: White Skin, Black Face in American Culture*. New York: Oxford UP, 1997. Print.

For the second and subsequent books by the same author, replace the author's name with three hyphens, followed by a period and the title.

AN ANTHOLOGY OR COMPILATION

Dark, Larry, ed. *Prize Stories 1997: The O. Henry Awards*. New York: Anchor, 1997. Print.

The Elements of Citation:
Book (MLA)

When you cite a book using MLA style, include the following:

1 Author

2 Title and subtitle

3 City of publication

4 Publisher

5 Date of publication

6 Medium

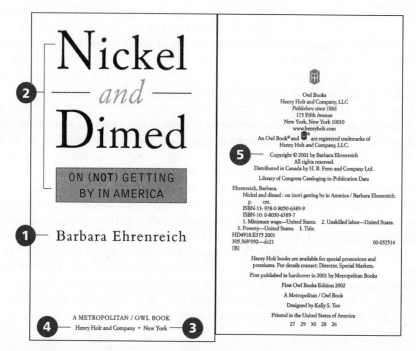

WORKS CITED ENTRY FOR A BOOK IN MLA STYLE

┌────── 1 ──────┐ ┌────────── 2 ──────────┐
Ehrenreich, Barbara. *Nickel and Dimed: On (Not) Getting by in America.*
┌─ 3 ─┐ ┌4┐ ┌ 5 ┐ ┌ 6 ┐
New York: Holt, 2001. Print.

A BOOK BY TWO AUTHORS

Alderman, Ellen, and Caroline Kennedy. *The Right to Privacy.* New York: Vintage, 1995.
Print.

NOTE: This form is followed even for two authors with the same last name.

Ehrlich, Paul, and Anne Ehrlich. *Extinction: The Causes and Consequences of the Disappearance of Species.* New York: Random, 1981. Print.

A BOOK BY TWO OR MORE AUTHORS

Heffernan, William A., Mark Johnston, and Frank Hodgins. *Literature: Art and Artifact*. San Diego: Harcourt, 1987. Print.

If there are more than three authors, name only the first and add "et al." (meaning "and others").

A BOOK BY A CORPORATE AUTHOR

Poets & Writers, Inc. *The Writing Business: A Poets & Writers Handbook*. New York: Poets & Writers, 1985. Print.

A WORK IN AN ANTHOLOGY

Head, Bessie. "Woman from America." *Wild Women: Contemporary Short Stories by Women Celebrating Women*. Ed. Sue Thomas. Woodstock: Overlook, 1994. 45-51. Print.

AN INTRODUCTION, PREFACE, FOREWORD, OR AFTERWORD

Callahan, John F. Introduction. *Flying Home and Other Stories*. By Ralph Ellison. Ed. John F. Callahan. New York: Vintage, 1996. 1–9. Print.

MATERIAL REPRINTED FROM ANOTHER SOURCE

Diffie, Whitfield, and Susan Landau. "Privacy: Protections and Threats." *Privacy on the Line: The Politics of Wiretapping and Encryption*. Cambridge, MA: MIT P, 1998. Rpt. in *Elements of Argument: A Text and Reader*. Annette T. Rottenberg and Donna Haisty Winchell. 8th ed. Boston: Bedford/St. Martin's, 2006. 601. Print.

A MULTIVOLUME WORK

Skotheim, Robert Allen, and Michael McGiffert, eds. *Since the Civil War*. Reading: Addison, 1972. Print. Vol. 2 of *American Social Thought: Sources and Interpretations*. 2 vols. 1972.

AN EDITION OTHER THAN THE FIRST

Charters, Ann, ed. *The Story and Its Writer: An Introduction to Short Fiction*. 8th ed. Boston: Bedford/St. Martin's, 2011. Print.

A TRANSLATION

Allende, Isabel. *The House of the Spirits*. Trans. Magda Bogin. New York: Knopf, 1985. Print.

A REPUBLISHED BOOK

Weesner, Theodore. *The Car Thief*. 1972. New York: Vintage-Random, 1987. Print.

NOTE: The only information about original publication you need to provide is the publication date, which appears immediately after the title.

A BOOK IN A SERIES

Eady, Cornelius. *Victims of the Latest Dance Craze*. Chicago: Omnation, 1985. Print.
Omnation Press Dialogues on Dance Ser. 5.

The series title goes after the publication information and the medium.

AN ARTICLE FROM A DAILY NEWSPAPER

Doctorow, E. L. "Quick Cuts: The Novel Follows Film into a World of Fewer Words."
New York Times 15 Mar. 1999, sec. B: 1+. Print.

AN ARTICLE FROM A MAGAZINE

Schulhofer, Stephen. "Unwanted Sex." *Atlantic Monthly* Oct. 1998: 55–66. Print.

AN UNSIGNED EDITORIAL

"Medium, Message." Editorial. *Nation* 28 Mar. 1987: 383–84. Print.

ANONYMOUS WORKS

"The March Almanac." *Atlantic Monthly* Mar. 1995: 20. Print.

Citation World Atlas. Maplewood: Hammond, 1999. Print.

AN ARTICLE FROM A JOURNAL WITH SEPARATE PAGINATION FOR EACH ISSUE

Brewer, Derek. "The Battleground of Home: Versions of Fairy Tales." *Encounter*
54.4 (1980): 52–61. Print.

AN ARTICLE IN A JOURNAL WITH CONTINUOUS PAGINATION THROUGHOUT
THE VOLUME

McCafferty, Janey. "The Shadders Go Away." *New England Review and Bread Loaf
Quarterly* 9 (1987): 332–42. Print.

MLA style is to include the issue number after the volume number, even though the volume has continuous pagination throughout the year. In this example, there is no issue number so only the volume number is included.

A REVIEW

Walker, David. Rev. of *A Wave*, by John Ashbery. *Field* 32 (1985): 63–71. Print.

AN ARTICLE IN A REFERENCE WORK

"Bylina." *The New Princeton Encyclopedia of Poetry and Poetics*. Ed. Alex Preminger
and T. V. F. Brogan. Princeton: Princeton UP, 1993. Print.

A GOVERNMENT DOCUMENT

United States. National Endowment for the Arts. *2006 Annual Report*. Washington:
Office of Public Affairs, 2007. Print.

Frequently the Government Printing Office (GPO) is the publisher of federal government documents.

AN UNPUBLISHED MANUSCRIPT

Leahy, Ellen. "An Investigation of the Computerization of Information Systems
in a Family Planning Program." MS thesis. U of Massachusetts, Amherst, 2010.

A LETTER TO THE EDITOR

Flannery, James W. Letter. *New York Times Book Review* 28 Feb. 1993: 34. Print.

PERSONAL CORRESPONDENCE

Bennett, David. Letter to the author. 3 Mar. 2010. TS.

Include the medium of the correspondence at the end of the entry. Use *TS* for
typescript and *MS* for manuscript (for handwritten letters).

A CARTOON

Henley, Marian. "Maxine." Comic strip. *Valley Advocate* 25 Feb. 2010: 39. Print.

Electronic Sources

A WEB SITE

Heiner, Heidi Anne. *SurLaLune Fairy Tales*. Heidi Anne Heiner, 3 Sept. 2009. Web.
9 Sept. 2010.

Include the name of the author or editor of the Web site, when this information is available; otherwise, begin the entry with the name of the Web site in
italics, followed by a period; the publisher or sponsor of the Web site (usually
found near the copyright information on the site's home page) followed by a
comma and the date of publication or last update. Then add the medium (Web),
a period, and the date you accessed the site.

A PAGE OR ARTICLE WITHIN A WEB SITE

Goodale, Wing, and Tim Divoll. "Birds, Bats and Coastal Wind Farm Development
in Maine: A Literature Review." *BioDiversity Research Institute*. BioDiversity Research Inst., 29 May 2009. Web. 25 Aug. 2010.

A BOOK AVAILABLE ON THE WEB

Kramer, Heinrich, and James Sprenger. *The Malleus Maleficarum*. Trans. Montague
Summers. New York, 1971. MalleusMaleficarum.org. Web. 14 Dec. 2010.

In this case the book had been previously published, and information about its
original publication was included at the site.

AN ARTICLE FROM AN ELECTRONIC JOURNAL

Minow, Mary. "Filters and the Public Library: A Legal and Policy Analysis." *First Mon-
day* 2.12 (1997): n. pag. Web. 28 Nov. 2010.

The Elements of Citation:
Article from a Web site (MLA)

When you cite a brief article from a Web site using MLA style, include the following:

1 Author

2 Title of work

3 Title of Web site

4 Sponsor of site

5 Date of publication or latest update

6 Medium (Web)

7 Date of access

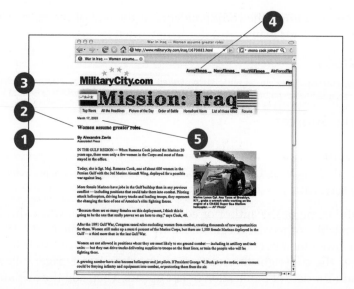

WORKS CITED ENTRY FOR A BRIEF ARTICLE FROM A WEB SITE IN MLA STYLE

    ━━ **1** ━━   ━━━━━ **2** ━━━━━   ━━ **3** ━━

Zavis, Alexandra. "Women Assume Greater Roles." *MilitaryTimes.com.*

    ━━━ **4** ━━━   ━━ **5** ━━ **6** ━━ **7** ━━

Army Times Publishing, 17 Mar. 2003. Web. 23 Aug. 2007.

AN ARTICLE FROM A FULL-TEXT DATABASE AVAILABLE THROUGH THE WEB

Warner, Marina. "Pity the Stepmother." *New York Times* 12 May 1991, late ed.: D17. *LexisNexis Universe.* Web. 12 Dec. 2010.

Gura, Mark. "The Gorgeous Mosaic." *School Arts* 93.2 (1993): 26–27. *General Reference Center Gold.* Web. 14 Dec. 2010.

Include the original source information and then add the name of the database in italics, the medium, and your date of access.

The Elements of Citation:
Article from a Database (MLA)

When you cite an article from a database using MLA style, include the following:

1 Author
2 Title of article
3 Title of periodical, volume and issue numbers
4 Date of publication

5 Inclusive pages
6 Name of database
7 Medium (Web)
8 Date of access

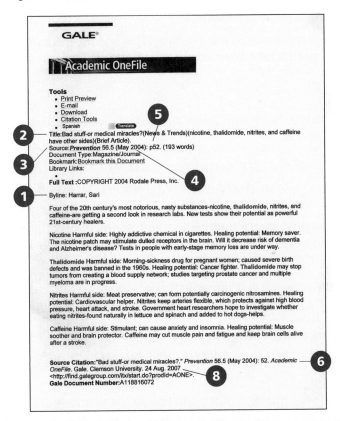

WORKS CITED ENTRY FOR AN ARTICLE FROM A DATABASE IN MLA STYLE

┌── 1 ──┐ ┌────── 2 ──────────┐ ┌── 3 ──┐ ┌ 4 ┐┌5┐
Harrar, Sari. "Bad Stuff — or Medical Miracles?" *Prevention* 56.5 (2004): 52.
      ┌───── 6 ─────┐ ┌7┐ ┌──8──┐
    Academic OneFile. Web. 24 Aug. 2007.

A REPORT FROM A DATABASE

Kassenbaum, Peter. *Cultural Awareness Training Manual and Study Guide*. 1992. ERIC.
Web. 14 Dec. 2010.

Treat educational resources and technical reports found on a database as you
would any other source from a database. Include the name of the database in
italics after the publication information, and then add the medium and your
date of access.

MATERIAL ACCESSED THROUGH A COMPUTER SERVICE

Boynton, Robert S. "The New Intellectuals." Atlantic Monthly Mar. 1995.
America Online. Web. 3 Mar. 2010.

Treat the computer service as the database, then add the medium and your date
of access. Do not include keywords or other information specific to the computer service.

A CD-ROM

Corcoran, Mary B. "Fairy Tale." *Grolier Multimedia Encyclopedia*. Danbury: Grolier,
1995. CD-ROM.

AN ARTICLE FROM A CD-ROM FULL-TEXT DATABASE

"Tribal/DNC Donations." *News from Indian Country* Dec. 1997. CD-ROM.
Ethnic Newswatch. Stamford: SoftLine. 12 Oct. 2007.

Include the original source information and the medium of publication (CD-
ROM), then add the name of the database, the publisher or vendor of the CD-
ROM, and the electronic publication data, if available.

AN ARTICLE FROM AN ELECTRONIC REFERENCE WORK

"Folk Arts." *Britannica*. Encyclopaedia Britannica, 2007. Web. 14 Dec. 2010.

A PERSONAL E-MAIL COMMUNICATION

Franz, Kenneth. "Re: Species Reintroduction." Message to the author. 12 Oct. 2010.
E-mail.

A POSTING TO A DISCUSSION LIST, WEB FORUM, OR NEWSGROUP

Lee, Constance. "Re: Mothers and Stepmothers." *Folklore Discussion List*. Texas A&M
U, 10 Sept. 2007. Web. 24 Oct. 2008.

House, Ron. "Wind Farms: Do They Kill Birds?" *Google Groups: Rec.Animals.Wildlife*.
Google, 7 Sept. 2009. Web. 14 Sept. 2010.

Treat these as short works from a Web site. Include the author of the posting
and the title or subject line of the posting in quotation marks (if there is no
title, use the designation "Online posting" without quotation marks). Then add

the name of the Web site, the sponsor of the site, the date of the posting, the medium, and your date of access.

Other Sources

A LECTURE

Calvino, Italo. "Right and Wrong Political Uses of Literature." Symposium on European Politics. Amherst College, Amherst. 25 Feb. 1976. Lecture.

A FILM

The Voice of the Khalam. Prod. Loretta Pauker. Perf. Leopold Senghor, Okara, Birago Diop, Rubadiri, and Francis Parkes. Contemporary Films/McGraw-Hill, 1971. Film.

Other pertinent information to give in film references, if available, is the writer and director (see model for radio/television program for style).

A TELEVISION OR RADIO PROGRAM

The Shakers: Hands to Work, Hearts to God. Narr. David McCullough. Dir. Ken Burns and Amy Stechler Burns. Writ. Amy Stechler Burns, Wendy Tilghman, and Tom Lewis. PBS. WGBY, Springfield, MA, 28 Dec. 1992. Television.

A VIDEOCASSETTE

Style Wars! Prod. Tony Silver and Henry Chalfont. New Day Films, 1985. Videocassette.

DVD

Harry Potter and the Order of the Phoenix. Prod. David Barron and David Heyman. Warner Bros., 2007. DVD.

A PERFORMANCE

Quilters: A Musical Celebration. By Molly Newman and Barbara Damashek. Dir. Joyce Devlin. Musical dir. Faith Fung. Mt. Holyoke Laboratory Theatre, South Hadley, MA. 26 Apr. 1991. Performance.

AN INTERVIEW

Hines, Gregory. Interview by D. C. Denison. *Boston Globe Magazine* 29 Mar. 1987: 2. Print.

NOTE: An interview conducted by the author of the paper would be documented as follows:

Hines, Gregory. Personal interview. 29 Mar. 1987.

A broadcast interview would be documented as follows:

Hines, Gregory. Interview by Charlie Rose. *Charlie Rose.* PBS. WGBH, Boston, 30 Jan. 2001. Television.

Exercise

We followed Katie as she located some possible sources for her research paper on competitive food in schools. She will examine more than the minimum of six sources required by her assignment, but for this exercise, assume the six that she uses in the final paper are the six listed below. The information from databases is listed as it appeared in the database, with some minor editing, and Katie accessed those sources online. For the date of access, use today's date.

Use the information to write Katie's Works Cited page for her, using MLA documentation.

"Are 'competitive foods' sold at school making our children fat?"
Detail: Larson N; Story M; Health Affairs, 2010 Mar; 29 (3): 430–5 (journal article - research, systematic review) ISSN: 0278-2715 PMID: 20194984 CINAHL AN: 2010589003
Database: CINAHL Plus with Full Text

Title: "The competitive food conundrum: can government regulations improve school food?"
Pub: *Duke Law Journal*
Detail: Ellen J. Fried and Michele Simon. 56.6 (April 2007): p1491(49). (19744 words)
Database: Academic OneFile

Food, Inc.: How Industrial Food Is Making Us Sicker, Fatter and Poorer—And What You Can Do about It
Editor: Karl Weber
Published in New York by PublicAffairs in 2009.
She will use two essays from the book: "Improving Kids' Nutrition: An Action Tool Kit for Parents" by the Center for Science in the Public Interest, pp. 227–57, and "Childhood Obesity: The Challenge" by the Robert Wood Johnson Foundation, pp. 259–61.

Title: *How Competitive Foods in Schools Impact Student Health, School Meal Programs, and Students from Low-Income Families*
Food Research and Action Center, Issue Briefs for Child Nutrition Reauthorization, Number 5. June 2010. 9 pages.

"The Economics of a Healthy School Meal"
Parke Wilde and Mary Kennedy
Choices (an online magazine), 3rd Quarter 2009 | 24(3)

Documenting Your Research (APA SYSTEM)

Following are examples of the bibliographical forms you are most likely to employ if you are using the American Psychological Association (APA) system for documenting sources. If you need the format for a type of publication not listed here, consult the *Publication Manual of the American Psychological Association, Sixth Edition* (2010).

If you are used to the Modern Language Association (MLA) system for documenting sources, take a moment to notice some of the key differences. In APA style, authors and editors are listed by last name and initials only, and the year comes immediately after the author's or editor's name instead of at or near the end of the entry. Titles in general are not capitalized in the conventional way. The overall structure of each entry, however, will be familiar: author, title, publication information.

Print Sources

A BOOK BY A SINGLE AUTHOR

Briggs, J. (1988). *Fire in the crucible: The alchemy of creative genius*. New York, NY: St. Martin's Press.

MULTIPLE WORKS BY THE SAME AUTHOR IN THE SAME YEAR

Gardner, H. (1982a). *Art, mind, and brain: A cognitive approach to creativity*. New York, NY: Basic Books.

Gardner, H. (1982b). *Developmental psychology: An introduction* (2nd ed.). Boston, MA: Little, Brown.

AN ANTHOLOGY OR COMPILATION

Gioseffi, D. (Ed.). (1988). *Women on war*. New York, NY: Simon & Schuster.

A BOOK BY TWO TO SEVEN AUTHORS OR EDITORS

Atwan, R., & Roberts, J. (Eds.). (1996). *Left, right, and center: Voices from across the political spectrum*. Boston, MA: Bedford Books.

Note: List the names of *all* the authors or editors, with an ampersand before the last one. For eight or more authors, list the first six authors followed by an ellipsis (three dots), and then list the last author's name. In these citations, there is no ampersand before the last author.

A BOOK BY A CORPORATE AUTHOR

International Advertising Association. (1977). *Controversy advertising: How advertisers present points of view on public affairs*. New York, NY: Hastings House.

The Elements of Citation:
Book (APA)

When you cite a book using APA style, include the following:

1 Author

2 Date of publication

3 Title and subtitle

4 City and state of publication

5 Publisher

REFERENCE LIST ENTRY FOR A BOOK IN APA STYLE

```
   ┌─1─┐ ┌─2─┐ ┌────────────────3────────────────┐
```
Bloom, H. (1994). *The western canon: The books and school of the ages.*
```
   ┌────4────┐ ┌─────5─────┐
```
New York, NY: Riverhead Books.

A WORK IN AN ANTHOLOGY

Mukherjee, B. (1988). The colonization of the mind. In D. Gioseffi (Ed.), *Women on war* (pp. 140–142). New York, NY: Simon & Schuster.

AN INTRODUCTION, PREFACE, FOREWORD, OR AFTERWORD

Hemenway, R. (1984). Introduction. In Z. N. Hurston, *Dust tracks on a road* (pp. ix–xxxix). Urbana: University of Illinois Press.

AN EDITION OTHER THAN THE FIRST

Gumpert, G., & Cathcart, R. (Eds.). (1986). *Inter/media: Interpersonal communication in a media world* (3rd ed.). New York, NY: Oxford University Press.

A TRANSLATION

Sartre, J. P. (1962). *Literature and existentialism* (B. Frechtman, Trans.). New York, NY: Citadel Press. (Original work published 1949)

A REPUBLISHED BOOK

James, W. (1969). *The varieties of religious experience: A study in human nature.* London, England: Collier Books. (Original work published 1902)

A BOOK IN A SERIES

Berthrong, D. J. (1976). *The Cheyenne and Arapaho ordeal: Reservation and agency life in the Indian territory, 1875–1907. Vol. 136. The civilization of the American Indian series.* Norman: University of Oklahoma Press.

A MULTIVOLUME WORK

Mussen, P. H. (Ed.). (1983). *Handbook of child psychology* (4th ed., Vols. 1–4). New York, NY: Wiley.

AN ARTICLE FROM A DAILY NEWSPAPER

Hottelet, R. C. (1990, March 15). Germany: Why it can't happen again. *Christian Science Monitor*, p. 19.

AN ARTICLE FROM A PERIODICAL

Gorriti, G. A. (1989, July). How to fight the drug war. *Atlantic Monthly*, 70–76.

AN ARTICLE IN A JOURNAL WITH CONTINUOUS PAGINATION THROUGHOUT THE VOLUME

Cockburn, A. (1989). British justice, Irish victims. *The Nation*, 249, 554–555.

AN ARTICLE FROM A JOURNAL WITH SEPARATE PAGINATION FOR EACH ISSUE

Mukerji, C. (1984). Visual language in science and the exercise of power: The case of cartography in early modern Europe. *Studies in Visual Communication*, 10(3), 30–45.

AN ARTICLE IN A REFERENCE WORK

Frisby, J. P. (1990). Direct perception. In M. W. Eysenck (Ed.), *Blackwell dictionary of cognitive psychology* (pp. 95–100). Oxford, England: Basil Blackwell.

A GOVERNMENT PUBLICATION

United States Dept. of Health, Education, and Welfare. (1973). *Current ethical issues in mental health.* Washington, DC: U.S. Government Printing Office.

AN ABSTRACT

Fritz, M. (1990/1991). A comparison of social interactions using a friendship awareness activity. *Education and Training in Mental Retardation, 25*, 352–359. Abstract retrieved (From *Psychological Abstracts*, 1991, 78, Abstract No. 11474)

When the dates of the original publication and of the abstract differ, give both dates separated by a slash.

AN ANONYMOUS WORK

The status of women: Different but the same. (1992–1993). *Zontian, 73*(3), 5.

A REVIEW

Harris, I. M. (1991). [Review of the book *Rediscovering masculinity: Reason, language, and sexuality*]. *Gender and Society, 5*, 259–261.

Give the author of the review, not the author of the book being reviewed. Use this form for a film review also. If the review has a title, place it before the bracketed material, and treat it like an article title.

A LETTER TO THE EDITOR

Pritchett, J. T., & Kellner, C. H. (1993). Comment on spontaneous seizure activity [Letter to the editor]. *Journal of Nervous and Mental Disease, 181*, 138–139.

PERSONAL CORRESPONDENCE

B. Ehrenreich (personal communication, August 7, 2010).

(B. Ehrenreich, personal communication, August 7, 2010.)

Cite all personal communications to you (such as letters, memos, e-mails, and telephone conversations) in text only, *without* listing them among the references. The phrasing of your sentences will determine which of the two above forms to use.

AN UNPUBLISHED MANUSCRIPT

McIntosh, P. (2008). *White privilege and male privilege: A personal account of coming to see correspondences through work in women's studies*. Working Paper 189. Unpublished manuscript, Wellesley College, Center for Research on Women, Wellesley, MA.

PROCEEDINGS OF A MEETING, PUBLISHED

Guerrero, R. (1972/1973). Possible effects of the periodic abstinence method. In W. A. Uricchio & M. K. Williams (Eds.), *Proceedings of a Research Conference on Natural Family Planning* (pp. 96–105). Washington, DC: Human Life Foundation.

If the date of the symposium or conference is different from the date of publication, give both, separated by a slash. If the proceedings are published annually, treat the reference like a periodical article.

Electronic Sources

AN ARTICLE FROM AN ONLINE PERIODICAL WITH A DOI

Chattopadhyay, P. (2003). Can dissimilarity lead to positive outcomes? The influence of open versus closed minds. *Journal of Organizational Behavior, 24,* 295–312. doi:10.1002/job.118

If the article duplicates the version which appeared in a print periodical, use the same basic primary journal reference. See "An Article from a Periodical." Some online articles have a "digital object identifier" (DOI.) Use the DOI at the end of the entry in place of the URL.

AN ARTICLE FROM AN ONLINE PERIODICAL WITHOUT A DOI

Riordan, V. (2001, January 1). Verbal-performance IQ discrepancies in children attending a child and adolescent psychiatry clinic. *Child and Adolescent Psychiatry On-Line.* Retrieved from http://www.priory.com/psych/iq.htm

If an article does not have a DOI, after the publication information add the exact URL for the article or the URL of the home page of the journal.

A NONPERIODICAL WEB DOCUMENT

Munro, K. (2001, February). *Changing your body image.* Retrieved from http://www.kalimunro.com/article_changing_body_image.html

In general, follow this format: author's name, the date of publication (if no publication date is available, use "n.d."), the title of the document in italics, and the source's URL.

A CHAPTER OR SECTION IN A WEB DOCUMENT

National Council of Welfare, Canada. (1998). Other issues related to poverty lines. In *A new poverty line: Yes, no or maybe?* (chap. 5). Retrieved from http://www.ncwcnbes.net/htmdocument/reportnewpovline/chap5.htm

AN E-MAIL

Do not include personal communications such as e-mails in your list of references. See "Personal Correspondence."

A MESSAGE POSTED TO A NEWSGROUP

Isaacs, K. (2008, January 20). Philosophical roots of psychology [Electronic newsgroup message]. Retrieved from news://sci.psychology.psychotherapy .moderated

Include an online posting in your reference list only if the posting is archived and is retrievable. Otherwise, cite an online posting as a personal communication and do not include it in the list of references. Care should be taken when citing electronic discussions. In general, they are not scholarly sources.

The Elements of Citation:
Article from a Web site (APA)

When you cite an article from a Web site using APA style, include the following:

1 Author

2 Date of publication or most recent update

3 Title of document on Web site

4 Title of section

5 Date of access (only if content is likely to change)

6 URL of document

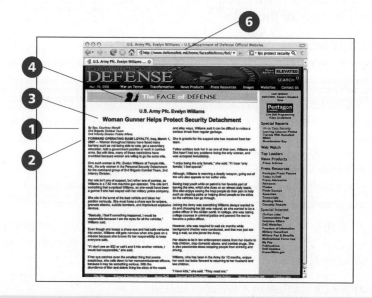

REFERENCE LIST ENTRY FOR A BRIEF ARTICLE FROM A WEB SITE IN APA STYLE

┌─**1**─┐ ┌───**2**───┐ ┌─────────────────**3**─────────────────┐
Marulli, C. (2007, March 1). Woman gunner helps protect security detachment.

┌──────**4**──────┐ ┌──────**6**──────────────
In *The Face of Defense*. Retrieved from http://www.defenselink.mil/home/

faceofdefense/fod/2007-03/f20070301a.html

AN ARTICLE FROM A DATABASE

Lopez, F. G., Melendez, M. C., Sauer, E. M., Berger, E., & Wyssmann, J. (1998).
Internal working models, self-reported problems, and help-seeking attitudes
among college students. *Journal of Counseling Psychology, 45,* 79–83.
Retrieved from http://www.apa.org/journals/cou

The Elements of Citation:
Article from a Database (APA)

When you cite an article from a database using APA style, include the following:

1 Author

2 Date of publication

3 Title of article

4 Name of periodical

5 Volume and issue numbers

6 Page numbers

7 DOI

8 URL for journal's home page (if no DOI)

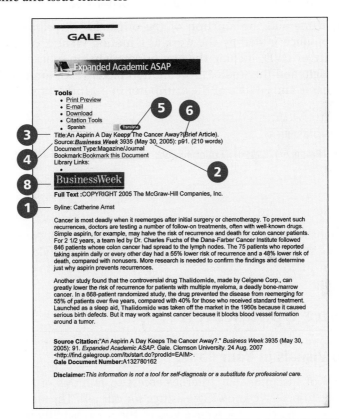

REFERENCE LIST ENTRY FOR AN ARTICLE FROM A DATABASE IN APA STYLE

```
 ┌─1─┐ ┌───2───┐ ┌───────────3───────────┐ ┌─4─
Arnst, C. (2005, May 30). An aspirin a day keeps the cancer away? Business
   ──┐ ┌5─┐┌6┐                    ┌────────8────────┐
Week 3935, 91. Retrieved from http://businessweek.com/
```

To cite material retrieved from a database, follow the format appropriate to the work retrieved. If the article has a DOI, include this at the end of the entry. If the article does not have a DOI, include the URL of the periodical's home page at the end of the entry.

Other Sources

A FILM

Wachowski, A., & Wachowski, L. (Writers/Directors). Silver, J. (Producer). (1999). *The matrix* [Motion picture]. United States: Warner Bros.

Include the name and the function of the originator or primary contributor (director or producer). Identify the work as a motion picture, or if you viewed a videocassette or DVD, include the appropriate label in brackets. Include the country of origin and the studio. If the motion picture is of limited circulation, provide the name and address of the distributor in parentheses at the end of the reference.

A TELEVISION SERIES

Jones, R. (Producer). (1990). *Exploring consciousness* [Television series]. Boston, MA: WGBH.

Exercise

Return to the six sources listed in the exercise on page 428. Now do a Works Cited page for those six sources using APA documentation style.

Wrapping Up Research

Including Visuals in Your Paper

In this world of instantaneous Internet access to millions of documents and sites, it is easy to perceive knowledge as free for our use. The fact that information is easy to access does not relieve you of the responsibility of giving credit to those who originated the ideas expressed there. In fact, the ease with which material can be posted to the Internet makes it even more difficult to separate valid information from that which is questionable at best.

Since the Internet is a world of images as well as words, it may give you ideas for livening up your own work with all sorts of visuals. Don't forget, though, that you are obligated to give credit to the source of your visuals along with the ideas and words that you use. A graph or chart may provide just the sort of statistical support that will make a key point in your argument, and it can be easily cut and pasted or scanned into your electronic text, but you must document that graph or chart just as you would text. You should acknowledge the location where you found the visual and as much information as is provided about who produced it. If you use copyrighted graphs or charts in work that you publish either in print or electronic form, you should seek permission for their use. The same is true for photographs and other illustrations, although some books and Web sites offer images that you can use free of charge. You may be surprised to find that something as common as your school's logo is copyrighted and cannot be used on your Web page, for example, without permission.

Keeping Research under Control

How do you know when you have done enough research? If you have kept your outline updated, you have a visual record of your progress. Check this against the guidelines on pages 397. Is each point backed by at least two pieces of support? Do your sources represent a range of authors and of types of data? If a large proportion of your support comes from one book, or if most of your references are to newspaper articles, you probably need to keep working. On the other hand, if your notes cite five different authorities making essentially the same point, you may have collected more data than you need. It can be useful to point out that more than one authority holds a given view and to make notes of examples that are notably different from one another. But it is not necessary to take down all the passages or examples expressing the same idea.

To This Point

Before you leave the library or your primary sources and start writing, check to make sure your research is complete.

1. Does your working outline show any gaps in your argument?
2. Have you found adequate data to support your claim?
3. Have you identified the warrants linking your claim with data and ensured that these warrants too are adequately documented?
4. If you intend to quote or paraphrase sources in your paper, do your notes include exact copies of all statements you may want to use and complete references?
5. Have you answered all the relevant questions that have come up during your research?
6. Do you have enough information about your sources to document your paper?

Compiling an Annotated Bibliography

An annotated bibliography is a list of sources that includes the usual bibliographic information followed by a paragraph describing and evaluating each source. Its purpose is to provide information about each source in a bibliography so that the reader has an overview of the resources related to a given topic.

For each source in an annotated bibliography, the same bibliographic information included in a Works Cited or References list is provided, alphabetized by author. Each reference also has a short paragraph that describes the work, its main focus, and, if appropriate, the methodology used in or the style of the work. An annotation might note special features such as tables or illustrations. Usually an annotation evaluates the source by analyzing its usefulness, reliability, and overall significance for understanding the topic. An annotation might include some information on the credentials of the author or the organization that produced it.

A SAMPLE ANNOTATION USING THE MLA CITATION STYLE

Warner, Marina. "Pity the Stepmother." *New York Times* 12 May 1991, late
    ed.: D17. *LexisNexis Universe*. Web. 12 Dec. 2010.

The author asserts that many fairy tales feature absent or cruel mothers, transformed by romantic editors such as the Grimm brothers into stepmothers because the idea of a wicked mother desecrated an ideal. She argues that figures in fairy tales should be viewed in their historical context and that social conditions often affected the way that motherhood figured in fairy tales. Warner, a novelist and author of books on the images of Joan of Arc and the Virgin Mary, writes persuasively about the social roots of a fairy-tale archetype.

APA style does not call for annotated citations. However, some instructors may require an annotated bibliography, so with either MLA or APA, follow your instructor's guidelines.

CHAPTER 11

The Argumentative Paper: Writing and Documentation

Chapter 10 discusses the planning of an argumentative paper and the process involved in researching topics that require support beyond what the writer knows firsthand. This chapter discusses moving from the planning and researching stage into the actual writing of the paper.

Making a preliminary outline before you conduct any needed research gives direction to your research. If your topic requires no research, a preliminary outline helps you to organize your own thoughts on the subject. Preliminary outlines can change, however, in the process of researching and writing the paper. As you begin drafting the paper, you will need to finalize your decisions about what issues you want to raise.

Once you are satisfied that you have identified all the issues that will appear in your paper, you should begin to determine what kind of organization will be most effective for your argument. Now is the time to organize the results of your thinking into a logical and persuasive form. If you have read about your topic, answered questions, and acquired some evidence, you may already have decided on ways to approach your subject. If not, you should look closely at your outline now, recalling your purposes when you began your investigation, and develop a strategy for using the information you have gathered to achieve those purposes.

Be mindful of the context in which the argument is taking place, and try this procedure for tackling the issues in any controversial problem.

1. Raise the relevant issues and omit those that would distract you from your purpose. Plan to devote more time and space to issues you regard as crucial.

2. Produce the strongest evidence you can to support your factual claims, knowing that the opposing side or critical readers may try to produce conflicting evidence.

3. Defend your value claims by finding support in the fundamental principles with which most people in your audience would agree.

4. Argue with yourself. Try to foresee what kinds of refutation are possible. Try to anticipate and meet the opposing arguments.

5. Consider the context in which your argument will be read and be sensitive to the concerns of your audience.

Organizing the Material

The first point to establish in organizing your material is what type of thesis you plan to present. Is your intention to make readers aware of some problem? To offer a solution to the problem? To defend a position? To refute a position held by others? The way you organize your material will depend to a great extent on your goal. With that goal in mind, look over your outline and reevaluate the relative importance of your issues. Which ones are most convincing? Which are backed up by the strongest support? Which ones relate to facts, and which concern values?

With these points in mind, let us look at various ways of organizing an argumentative paper. It would be foolish to decide in advance how many paragraphs a paper ought to have; however, you can and should choose a general strategy before you begin writing. If your thesis presents an opinion or recommends some course of action, you may choose simply to state your main idea and then defend it. If your thesis argues against an opposing view, you probably will want to mention that view and then refute it. Both these organizations introduce the thesis in the first or second paragraph (called the *thesis paragraph*). You may decide that two or more differing positions have merit and that you want to offer a compromise between or among positions. A fourth possibility is to start establishing that a problem exists and then introduce your thesis as the solution; this method is called *presenting the stock issues*. Although these four approaches sometimes overlap in practice, examining each one individually can help you structure your paper. Let's take a look at each arrangement.

Defending the Main Idea

All forms of organization will require you to defend your main idea, but one way of doing this is simple and direct. Early in the paper state the main idea that you will defend throughout your argument. You can also indicate here the two or three points you intend to develop in support of your claim; or you can raise these later as they come up. Suppose your thesis is that widespread vegetarianism would solve a number of problems. You could phrase it this way: "If the majority of people in this country adopted a vegetarian diet, we would see improvements in the economy, in the health of our people, and in moral sensitivity." You would then develop each of the claims in your list with appropriate data and warrants. Notice that the thesis statement in the first (thesis) paragraph has already outlined your organizational pattern. However, if you find that listing your two or three main ideas in the thesis leads to too much repetition later in the paper, you can introduce each one as it arises in your discussion of the topic. Your thesis would remain more general: "If the majority of people in this country adopted a vegetarian diet, there would be noticeable improvement."

Defending the main idea is effective for factual claims as well as policy claims, in which you urge the adoption of a certain policy and give the reasons for its adoption. It is most appropriate when your thesis is straightforward and can be readily supported by direct statements.

Refuting an Opposing View

Refuting an opposing view means to attack it in order to weaken, invalidate, or make it less credible to a reader. Since all arguments are dialogues or debates — even when the opponent is only imaginary — refutation of another point of view is always implicit in your arguments. As you write, keep in mind the issues that an opponent may raise. You will be looking at your own argument as an unsympathetic reader may look at it, asking yourself the same kinds of critical questions and trying to find its weaknesses in order to correct them. In this way every argument you write becomes a form of refutation.

How do you plan a refutation? Here are some general guidelines.

1. If you want to refute the argument in a specific essay or article, read the argument carefully, noting all the points with which you disagree. This advice may seem obvious, but it cannot be too strongly emphasized. If your refutation does not indicate scrupulous familiarity with your opponent's argument, he or she has the right to say, and often does, "You haven't really read what I wrote. You haven't really answered my argument."

2. If you think that your readers are sympathetic to an opposing view or are not familiar with it, summarize it at the beginning of your paper, providing enough information to give readers an understanding of exactly what you plan to refute. When you summarize, it's important to be respectful of the opposition's views. You don't want to alienate readers who might not agree with you at first.

3. If your argument is long and complex, choose only the most important points to refute. Otherwise the reader who does not have the original argument on hand may find a detailed refutation hard to follow. If the argument is short and relatively simple — a claim supported by only two or three points — you may decide to refute all of them, devoting more space to the most important ones.

4. Attack the principal elements in the argument of your opponent.

   a. Question the evidence. (See pp. 203–15 in the text.) Question whether your opponent has proved that a problem exists.

    b. Attack the warrants or assumptions that underlie the claim. (See pp. 279–80 in the text.)

    c. Attack the logic or reasoning of the opposing view. (Refer to the discussion of fallacious reasoning on pp. 308–19 in the text.)

    d. Attack the proposed solution to a problem, pointing out that it will not work.

5. Be prepared to do more than attack the opposing view. Supply evidence and good reasons in support of your own claim.

In Chapter 3 we saw a sentence form that can help shape this type of essay:

In his essay, X writes that _____. However, _____.

A sentence form that might help you write a thesis for this type of essay is this one:

On the topic of _____, X claims that _____. In contrast, Y argues that _____. However, _____.

See page 82 for additional sentence forms.

Finding the Middle Ground

Although an argument, by definition, assumes a difference of opinion, we know that opposing sides frequently find accommodation somewhere in the middle. As you mount your own argument about a controversial issue, you need not confine yourself to support of any of the differing positions. You may want to acknowledge that there is some justice on all sides and that you understand the difficulty of resolving the issue.

Consider these guidelines for an argument that offers a compromise between or among competing positions:

1. Early in your essay explain the differing positions. Make clear the major differences separating the two (or more) sides.

2. Point out, whenever possible, that the differing sides already agree to some exceptions to their stated positions. Such evidence may prove that the differences are not so extreme as their advocates insist. Several commentators, writing about the conflict between Democrats and Republicans over President Obama's health-care plan adopted this strategy, suggesting that compromise was possible because the differences were narrower than the public believed.

3. Make clear your own moderation and sympathy, your own willingness to negotiate. An example of this attitude appears in an essay on abortion in which the author infers how Abraham Lincoln might have treated the question of abortion rights.

In this debate I have made my own position clear. It is a pro-life
position (though it may not please all pro-lifers), and its model is
Lincoln's position on slavery from 1854 until well into the Civil
War: tolerate, restrict, discourage. Like Lincoln's, its touchstone
is the common good of the nation, not the sovereign self. Like
Lincoln's position, it accepts the legality but not the moral legitimacy of the institution that it seeks to contain. It invites argument
and negotiation; it is a gambit, not a gauntlet.[1]

4. If you favor one side of the controversy, acknowledge that opposing views
   deserve to be considered. For example, in another essay on abortion, the
   author, who supports abortion rights, says,

   Those of us who are pro-choice must come to terms with those
   thoughtful pro-lifers who believe that in elevating the right to privacy above all other values, the most helpless form of humanity is
   left unprotected and is, in fact, defined away. They deserve to have
   their views addressed with sympathy and moral clarity.[2]

5. Provide evidence that accepting a middle ground can offer marked advantages for the whole society. Wherever possible, show that continued
   polarization can result in violence, injustice, and suffering.

6. In offering a solution that finds a common ground, be as specific as possible, emphasizing the part that you are willing to play in reaching a
   settlement. In an essay titled "Pro-Life and Pro-Choice? Yes!" the author
   concludes with this:

   Must those of us who abhor abortion, then, reconcile ourselves to
   seeing it spread unchecked? By no means. We can refuse to practice
   it ourselves — or, if we are male, beseech the women who carry our
   children to let them be born, and promise to support them, and
   mean it and do it. We can counsel and preach to others; those of us
   who are religious can pray. . . . What we must not do is ask the state
   to impose our views on those who disagree.[3]

   On a different subject, a debate on pornography, the author, who is opposed to free distribution of obscene material, nevertheless refuses to
   endorse censorship.

---

[1] George McKenna, "On Abortion: A Lincolnian Position," *Atlantic Monthly,* September 1995,
p. 68. (A gauntlet or glove is flung down in order to challenge an opponent to combat; a gambit is the opening move in a chess game, or in the words of one dictionary, "a concession that
invites discussion." — EDS.)

[2] Benjamin C. Schwarz, "Judge Ginsburg's Moral Myopia," *New York Times,* July 30, 1993,
sec. A, p. 27.

[3] George Church, *Time,* March 6, 1995, p. 108.

I think that, by enlarging the First Amendment to protect, in effect, freedom of expression, rather than freedom of speech and of
the press, the courts made a mistake. The courts have made other
mistakes, but I do not know a better way of defining the interests
of the community than through legislation and through the courts.
So I am willing to put up with things I think are wrong in the hope
that they will be corrected. I know of no alternative that would
always make the right decisions.[4]

Presenting the Stock Issues

Presenting the stock issues, or stating the problem before the solution, is a type
of organization borrowed from traditional debate format. It works for policy
claims when an audience must be convinced that a need exists for changing the
status quo (present conditions) and for introducing plans to solve the problem.
You begin by establishing that a problem exists (need). You then propose a solution (plan), which is your thesis. Finally, you show reasons for adopting the
plan (advantages). These three elements — need, plan, and advantages — are
called the *stock issues*.

For example, suppose you wanted to argue that measures for reducing acid
rain should be introduced at once. You would first have to establish a need for
such measures by defining the problem and providing evidence of damage.
Then you would produce your thesis, a means for improving conditions. Finally
you would suggest the benefits that would follow from implementation of your
plan. Notice that in this organization your thesis paragraph usually appears
toward the middle of your paper, although it may also appear at the beginning.

A sentence form such as the following can guide you in writing an appropriate thesis:

_____ is a problem, but _____ can help resolve it.

For instance, "Childhood obesity is increasing at an alarming rate, but
schools can help by eliminating competitive foods."

Ordering Material for Emphasis

Whichever way you choose to work, you should revise your outline to reflect
the order in which you intend to present your thesis and supporting ideas. Not
only the placement of your thesis paragraph but also the wording and arrangement of your ideas will determine what points in your paper receive the most
emphasis.

Suppose your purpose is to convince the reader that cigarette smoking is a
bad habit. You might decide to concentrate on three unpleasant attributes of

---

[4]Ernest van den Haag, *Smashing Liberal Icons: A Collection of Debates* (Washington, D.C.:
Heritage Foundation, 1981), p. 101.

cigarette smoking: (1) It is unhealthy; (2) it is dirty; (3) it is expensive. Obviously, these are not equally important as possible deterrents. You would no doubt consider the first reason the most compelling, accompanied by evidence to prove the relationship between cigarette smoking and cancer, heart disease, emphysema, and other diseases. This issue, therefore, should be given greater emphasis than the others.

There are several ways to achieve emphasis. One is to make the explicit statement that you consider a certain issue the most important.

> Finally, and *most importantly,* human culture is often able to neutralize or reverse what might otherwise be genetically advantageous consequences of selfish behavior.[5]

This quotation also reveals a second way — placing the material to be emphasized in an emphatic position, either first or last in the paper. The end position, however, is generally more emphatic.

A third way to achieve emphasis is to elaborate on the material to be emphasized, treating it at greater length, offering more data and reasons for it than you give for the other issues.

Making Choices

With a working outline in hand that indicates the order of your thesis and claims, you are almost ready to begin turning your notes into prose. First, however, it is useful to review the limits on your paper to be sure your writing time will be used to the best possible advantage.

Scope

The first limit involves scope. As mentioned earlier, your thesis should introduce a claim that can be adequately supported in the space available to you. If your research has opened up more aspects than you anticipated, you may want to narrow your thesis to one major subtopic. Or you could emphasize only the most persuasive arguments for your position (assuming these are sufficient to make your case) and omit the others. In a brief paper (three or four pages), three issues are probably all you have room to develop. On the other hand, if you suspect your thesis can be proved in one or two pages, look for ways to expand it. What additional issues might be brought in to bolster your argument? Alternatively, is there a larger issue for which your thesis could become a supporting idea?

Style

Other limits on your paper are imposed by the need to make your points in a way that will be persuasive to an audience. The style and tone you choose

---

[5] Peter Singer, *The Expanding Circle* (New York: New American Library, 1982), p. 171.

depend not only on the nature of the subject but also on how you can best convince readers that you are a credible source. *Style* in this context refers to the elements of your prose — simple versus complex sentences, active versus passive verbs, metaphors, analogies, and other literary devices.

It is usually appropriate in a short paper to choose an *expository* style, which emphasizes the elements of your argument rather than your personality. You may want to appeal to your readers' emotions as well as their intellects, but keep in mind that sympathy is most effectively gained when it is supported by believable evidence. If you press your point stridently, your audience is likely to be suspicious rather than receptive. If you sprinkle your prose with jokes or metaphors, you may diminish your credibility by detracting from the substance of your case. Both humor and analogy can be useful tools, but they should be used with discretion.

You can discover some helpful pointers on essay style by reading the editorials in newspapers such as the *New York Times,* the *Washington Post,* or the *Wall Street Journal.* The authors are typically addressing a mixed audience comparable to the hypothetical readers of your own paper. Though their approaches vary, each writer is attempting to portray himself or herself as an objective analyst whose argument deserves careful attention.

Tone

Tone is the approach you take to your topic — solemn or humorous, detached or sympathetic. Style and tone together compose your voice as a writer. Many students assume that every writer has only one voice. In fact, a writer typically adapts his or her voice to the material and the audience. Perhaps the easiest way to appreciate this is to think of two or three works by the same author that are written in different voices. Or compare the speeches of two different characters in the same story, novel, or film. Every writer has individual talents and inclinations that appear in most or all of his or her work. A good writer, however, is able to amplify some stylistic elements and diminish others, as well as to change tone, by choice.

Again, remember your goals. You are trying to convince your audience of something; an argument is, by its nature, directed at people who may not initially agree with its thesis. Therefore, your voice as well as the claims you make must be convincing.

To This Point

The organizing steps that come between preparation and writing are often neglected. Careful planning at this stage, however, can save much time and effort later. As you prepare to start writing, you should be able to answer the following questions:

1. Is the purpose of my paper to persuade readers to accept a potentially controversial idea, to refute someone else's position, to find middle ground, or to propose a solution to a problem?

2. Can or should my solution also incorporate elements of compromise and negotiation?

3. Have I decided on an organization that is likely to accomplish this purpose?

4. Does my outline arrange my thesis and issues in an appropriate order to emphasize the most important issues?

5. Does my outline show an argument whose scope suits the needs of this paper?

6. What questions of style and tone do I need to keep in mind as I write to ensure that my argument will be persuasive?

Writing

Beginning the Paper

Having found a claim you can defend and the voice you will adopt toward your audience, you must now think about how to begin. An introduction to your subject should consist of more than just the first paragraph of your paper. It should invite the reader to give attention to what you have to say. It should also point you in the direction you will take in developing your argument. You may want to begin the actual writing of your paper with the thesis paragraph. It is useful to consider the whole paragraph rather than simply the thesis statement for two reasons. First, not all theses are effectively expressed in a single sentence. Second, the rest of the paragraph will be closely related to your statement of the main idea. You may show why you have chosen this topic or why your audience will benefit from reading your paper. You may introduce your warrant, qualify your claim, and in other ways prepare for the body of your argument. Because readers will perceive the whole paragraph as a unit, it makes sense to approach it that way.

Consider first the kind of argument you intend to present. Does your paper make a factual claim? Does it address values? Does it recommend a policy or action? Is it a rebuttal of some current policy or belief? The answers to those questions will influence the way you introduce the subject.

If your thesis makes a factual claim, you may be able to summarize it in one or two opening sentences. "Whether we like it or not, money is obsolete. The currency of today is not paper or coin, but plastic." Refutations are easy to introduce in a brief statement: "Contrary to popular views on the subject, the institution of marriage is as sound today as it was a generation ago."

A thesis that defends a value is usually best preceded by an explanatory introduction. "Some wars are morally defensible" is a thesis that can be stated as a simple declarative opening sentence. However, readers who disagree may not read any further than the first line. Someone defending this claim is likely to be more persuasive if he or she first gives an example of a situation in which war is or was preferable to peace or presents the thesis less directly.

One way to keep such a thesis from alienating the audience is to phrase it as a question. "Are all wars morally indefensible?" Still better would be to prepare for the question:

> Few if any of us favor war as a solution to international problems. We are too vividly aware of the human suffering imposed by armed conflict, as well as the political and financial turmoil that inevitably result. Yet can we honestly agree that no war is ever morally defensible?

Notice that this paragraph gains appeal from use of the first person *we*. The author implies that he or she shares the readers' feelings but has good reasons for believing those feelings are not sufficient grounds for condemning all wars. Even if readers are skeptical, the conciliatory phrasing of the thesis should encourage them to continue reading.

For any subject that is highly controversial or emotionally charged, especially one that strongly condemns an existing situation or belief, you may sometimes want to express your indignation directly. Of course, you must be sure that your indignation can be justified. The author of the following introduction, a physician and writer, openly admits that he is about to make a case that may offend readers.

> Is there any polite way to introduce today's subject? I'm afraid not. It must be said plainly that the media have done about as sorry and dishonest a job of covering health news as is humanly possible, and that when the media do not fail from bias and mendacity, they fail from ignorance and laziness.[6]

If your thesis advocates a policy or makes a recommendation, it may be a good idea, as in a value claim, to provide a short background. The following paragraph introduces an argument favoring relaxation of controls in high schools.

> "Free the New York City 275,000" read a button worn by many young New Yorkers some years ago. The number was roughly the total of students enrolled in the City's high schools.
>
> The condition of un-freedom which is described was not, however, unique to the schools of one city. According to the Carnegie Commission's comprehensive study of American public education, *Crisis in the Classroom,* public schools across the country share a common characteristic, namely, "preoccupation with order and control." The result is that students find themselves the victims of "oppressive and petty rules which give their schools a repressive, almost prison-like atmosphere."[7]

There are also other ways to introduce your subject. One is to begin with an appropriate quotation.

---

[6] Michael Halberstam, "TV's Unhealthy Approach to Health News," *TV Guide,* September 20–26, 1980, p. 24.

[7] Alan Levine and Eve Carey, *The Rights of Students* (New York: Avon Books, 1977), p. 11.

> "Reading makes a full man, conversation makes a ready man, and writing makes an exact man." So Francis Bacon told us around 1600. Recently I have been wondering how Bacon's formula might apply to present-day college students.[8]

Or you may begin with an anecdote. In the following introduction to an article about the relation between cancer and mental attitude, the author recounts a personal experience.

> Shortly after I moved to California, a new acquaintance sat in my San Francisco living room drinking rose-hip tea and chainsmoking. Like so many residents of the Golden West, Cecil was "into" all things healthy, from jogging to *shiatsu* massage to kelp. Tobacco didn't seem to fit, but he told me confidently that there was no contradiction. "It all has to do with energy," he said. "Unless you have a lot of negative energy about smoking cigarettes, there's no way they can hurt you; you won't get cancer."[9]

Finally, you may introduce yourself as the author of the claim.

> I wish to argue an unpopular cause: the cause of the old, free elective system in the academic world, or the untrammeled right of the undergraduate to make his own mistakes.[10]

> My subject is the world of Hamlet. I do not of course mean Denmark, except as Denmark is given a body by the play; and I do not mean Elizabethan England, though this is necessarily close behind the scenes. I mean simply the imaginative environment that the play asks us to enter when we read it or go to see it.[11]

You should, however, use such introductions with care. They suggest an authority about the subject that you shouldn't attempt to assume unless you can demonstrate that you are entitled to it. Some instructors do not allow the use of first person in argumentative essays, so check the written guidelines for your assignments or ask your instructor.

Guidelines for Good Writing

In general, the writer of an argument follows the same rules that govern any form of expository writing. Your style should be clear and readable, your organization logical, your ideas connected by transitional phrases and sentences, your paragraphs coherent. The main difference between an argument and expository writing, as noted earlier, is the need to persuade an audience to adopt a belief or take an action. You should assume your readers will be critical rather than

---

[8] William Aiken, "The Conversation on Campus Today Is, Uh . . . ," *Wall Street Journal,* May 4, 1982, p. 18.

[9] Joel Guerin, "Cancer and the Mind," *Harvard Magazine,* November–December 1978, p. 11.

[10] Howard Mumford Jones, "Undergraduates on Apron Strings," *Atlantic Monthly,* October 1955, p. 45.

[11] Maynard Mack, "The World of Hamlet," *Yale Review,* June 1952, p. 502.

neutral or sympathetic. Therefore, you must be equally critical of your own work. Any apparent gap in reasoning or ambiguity in presentation is likely to weaken the argument.

As you read the essays in this book and elsewhere, you will discover that good style in argumentative writing shares several characteristics:

- Variety in sentence structure: a mixture of both long and short sentences, different sentence beginnings
- Rich but standard vocabulary: avoidance of specialized terms unless they are fully explained, word choice appropriate to a thoughtful argument
- Use of details and examples to illustrate and clarify abstract terms, principles, and generalizations

You should take care to avoid the following:

- Unnecessary repetition: making the same point without new data or interpretation
- Exaggeration or stridency, which can create suspicion of your fairness and powers of observation
- Short paragraphs of one or two sentences, which are common in advertising and newspaper writing to get the reader's attention but are inappropriate in a thoughtful essay

In addition to these stylistic principles, seven general points are worth keeping in mind:

1. Although *you,* like *I,* should be used judiciously, it can be found even in the treatment of weighty subjects. Here is an example from an essay by the distinguished British mathematician and philosopher, Bertrand Russell.

   Suppose you are a scientific pioneer and you make some discovery of great scientific importance and suppose you say to yourself, "I am afraid this discovery will do harm": you know that other people are likely to make the same discovery if they are allowed suitable opportunities for research; you must therefore, if you do not wish the discovery to become public, either discourage your sort of research or control publication by a board of censors.[12]

2. Don't pad. This point should be obvious; the word *pad* suggests the addition of unnecessary material. Many writers find it tempting, however, to enlarge a discussion even when they have little more to say. It is never wise to introduce more words into a paper that has already made its point. If the paper turns out to be shorter than you had hoped, it may mean that you have not sufficiently developed the subject or that the subject was less

[12] "Science and Human Life," in James R. Newman, ed., *What Is Science?* (New York: Simon and Schuster, 1955), p. 12.

substantial than you thought when you selected it. Padding, which is easy to detect in its repetition and sentences empty of content, weakens the writer's credibility.

3. For any absolute generalization — a statement containing words such as *all* or *every* — consider the possibility that there may be at least one example that will weaken the generalization. Such a precaution means that you won't have to backtrack and admit that your generalization is not, after all, universal. A student who was arguing against capital punishment for the reason that all killing was wrong suddenly paused in her presentation and added, "On the other hand, if given the chance, I'd probably have been willing to kill Hitler." This admission meant that she recognized important exceptions to her rule and that she would have to qualify her generalization in some significant way.

4. When offering an explanation, especially one that is complicated or extraordinary, look first for a cause that is easier to accept, one that doesn't strain credibility. For example, years ago a great many people were bemused by reports about the mysterious Bermuda Triangle, which had apparently swallowed up ships and planes since the mid-nineteenth century. The forces at work were variously described as space-time warps, UFOs that transported earthlings to other planets, and sea monsters seeking revenge. But a careful investigation revealed familiar, natural causes. A reasonable person interested in the truth would have searched for more conventional explanations before accepting the bizarre stories of extraterrestrial creatures. He or she would also exercise caution when confronted by conspiracy theories that try to account for controversial political events, such as the assassination of John F. Kennedy.

5. Check carefully for questionable warrants. When necessary, these should be included in your paper to link claims with support. Many an argument has failed because it depended on an unstated warrant with which the reader did not agree. If you were arguing for a physical education requirement at your school, you might make a good case for all the physical and psychological benefits of such a requirement. But you would certainly need to introduce and develop the warrant on which your claim was based — that it is the proper function of a college or university to provide the benefits of a physical education. Many readers would agree that physical education is valuable, but they might question the assumption that an academic institution should introduce a nonintellectual enterprise into the curriculum. At any point where you draw a controversial or tenuous conclusion, be sure your reasoning is clear and logical.

6. Avoid conclusions that are merely summaries. Summaries may be needed in long technical papers, but in brief arguments they create endings that are without force or interest. In the closing paragraph you should find a new idea that emerges naturally from the development of the whole argument.

7. Strive for a paper that is unified, coherent, and emphatic where appropriate. A *unified* paper stays focused on its goal and directs each claim, warrant, and piece of evidence toward that goal. Extraneous information or unsupported claims impair unity. *Coherence* means that all ideas are fully explained and adequately connected by transitions. To ensure coherence, give especially close attention to the beginnings and ends of your paragraphs: Is each new concept introduced in a way that shows it following naturally from the one that preceded it? *Emphasis,* as we have mentioned, is a function partly of structure and partly of language. Your most important claims should be placed where they are certain of receiving the reader's attention: key sentences at the beginning or end of a paragraph, key paragraphs at the beginning or end of your paper. Sentence structure can also be used for emphasis. If you have used several long, complex sentences, you can emphasize a significant point by stating it briefly and simply. You can also create emphasis with verbal flags, such as "The primary issue to consider . . ." or "Finally, we cannot ignore. . . ."

All clear expository prose will exhibit the qualities of unity, coherence, and emphasis. But the success of an argumentative paper is especially dependent on these qualities because the reader may have to follow a line of reasoning that is both complicated and unfamiliar. Moreover, a paper that is unified, coherent, and properly emphatic will be more readable, the first requisite of an effective argument.

The MLA System for Citing Sources

As you write your paper, any time that you make use of the wording or ideas of one of your sources, you must document that use. One of the simplest methods of crediting sources is the Modern Language Association (MLA) in-text system, which is used in the research paper on competitive food in this chapter. In the text of your paper, immediately after any quotation, paraphrase, or idea you need to document, simply insert a parenthetical mention of the author's last name and the page number on which the material appears. You don't need a comma after the author's name or an abbreviation of the word *page* or *p.* For example, the following sentence appears in the sample paper:

> Although there are nutritious competitive options, those do not sell as well as the ones high in sugar, salt, and calories (Hartline-Grafton 2–3).

The parenthetical reference tells the reader that the information in this sentence came from pages of the book or article that appears in the Works Cited at the end of the paper. The complete reference on the Works Cited page provides all of the information readers need to locate the original source:

Hartline-Grafton, Heather. "How Competitive Foods in Schools Impact Student
    Health, School Meal Programs, and Students from Low-Income Families." Issue
    Briefs for Child Nutrition Reauthorization 5. Washington, D.C.: Food Research
    and Action Center, 2010. *EBSCOhost*. Web. 22 Sept. 2010.

If the author's name is mentioned in the same sentence, it is also acceptable to
place only the page numbers in parentheses; it is not necessary to repeat the
author's name. For example,

> According to Heather Hartline-Grafton, although there are nutritious competi-
> tive options, those do not sell as well as the ones high in sugar, salt, and calo-
> ries (2–3).

Remember, though, that a major reason for using qualified sources is that they
lend authority to the ideas expressed. The first time an author is mentioned in
the paper, he or she — or they — should be identified by full name and by claim
to authority:

> Parke Wilde and Mary Kennedy, both researchers in the Friedman School of Nutri-
> tion Science and Policy at Tufts University in Boston, explain some of the com-
> plexities in an article entitled "The Economics of a Healthy School Meal."

A last name and page number in parentheses do not carry nearly the same
weight as a full name and credentials. You should save the former for subsequent citations once the author has been fully identified. If more than one
sentence comes from the same source, you do not need to put parentheses
after each sentence. One parenthetical citation at the end of the material from
a source is enough if it is clear from the way you introduce the material where
your ideas end and the source's begin.

> According to the Robert Wood Johnson Foundation, a charitable organization
> whose goal is to improve the health of all Americans, the rate of obesity for
> those between the ages of six and eleven has quadrupled in three decades.
> Children are being diagnosed with what used to be considered adult diseases,
> like high blood pressure, adult-onset diabetes, and gallstones. The Foundation
> reports, "If we don't succeed in reversing this epidemic, we are in danger of
> raising the first generation of American children who will live sicker and die
> younger than their parents' generation" (259–60).

If you are using more than one work by the same author, you will need
to provide in the parentheses the title or a recognizable shortened form of the
title of the particular work being cited. If the author's name is not mentioned
in the sentence, you should include in parentheses the author's last name, the
title, and the page number, with a comma between the author's name and the
title. If both the author's name and the title of any work being cited are mentioned in the sentence, the parentheses will include only the page number. Had

two works by Hartline-Grafton been listed in the Works Cited, the first example above would have looked like this:

> Although there are nutritious competitive options, those do not sell as well as the ones high in sugar, salt, and calories (Hartline-Grafton, "How Competitive Foods" 2–3).

If there is more than one author, don't forget to give credit to all. Two or three authors are acknowledged by name in the parentheses if not in your own sentence: (Harmon, Livesy, and Jones 23). With four or more authors, use *et al.*, the Latin term for *and others*: (Braithwaite et al. 137).

Some sources do not name an author. To cite a work with an unknown author, give the title, or a recognizable shortened form, in the text of your paper. If the work does not have numbered pages, often the case in Web pages or non-print sources, do not include page numbers. For example,

> In some cases Sephardic Jews, "converted" under duress, practiced Christianity openly and Judaism in secret until recently ("Search for the Buried Past").

Direct quotations should always be introduced or worked into the grammatical structure of your own sentences. If you need help introducing quotations, refer to the Writer's Guide in Chapter 3 (pp. 88–89). Remember, however, that you need to provide parenthetical documentation not only for every direct quotation but also for every paraphrase or summary. Document any words or ideas that are not your own.

As a general rule, you cannot make any changes in a quotation. Two exceptions are clearly marked when they occur. At times you may use brackets to make a slight change that does not change the meaning of the quotation. For example, a pronoun may need to be replaced by a noun in brackets to make its reference clear. Or a verb tense may be changed and bracketed to make the quotation fit more smoothly into your sentence. An ellipsis (. . .) is used when you omit a portion of the quotation that does not change the essential meaning of the quote. You do not need to use ellipses at the beginning or end of a direct quotation. If the omitted portion included the end of one sentence and the beginning of another, there should be a fourth period (. . . .).

If a quotation is more than four typed lines long, it needs to be handled as a block quotation. A block quotation is usually introduced by a sentence followed by a colon. The quotation itself is indented one inch or ten spaces from the left margin. No quotation marks are necessary since the placement on the page informs the reader that it is a quotation. The only quotation marks in a block quotation would be ones copied from the original, as in dialogue. A paragraph break within a block quotation is indented an additional five spaces. The parenthetical citation is the same as with a quotation run into your text, but the period appears before the parenthesis.

With print sources in particular, you will often need to cite one work that is quoted in another or a work from an anthology. For the former, the parentheti-

Women in Combat 10

As the way we do battle continues to change, so will the roles of males and females; and the military will always have to come up with the best solution to accommodate these differences. As for now, the restrictions that are placed on women's assignments are based in sound reasoning. For the military's purposes, women do not have the physical abilities to fill combat oriented jobs, and the military does not have the resources to make these assignments available to them. The military needs to be aware of and most concerned with the effectiveness and readiness of its troops and figure out the best way to accomplish its mission and preserve America's freedom and sovereignty.

References

Baer, S. (2003, March 3). In Iraq war, women would serve closer to front lines than in past. *The Baltimore Sun*, p. 1A. Retrieved from http://www.baltimoresun.com

Dobbin, M. (2003, March 2). As war looms, women's role in U.S. military expands. *The Modesto Bee*, p. 3A. Retrieved from http://www.modbee.com

Gerber, R. (2002, September 23). Don't send military women to the back of the troop train. *USA Today*. Retrieved from http://www.usatoday.com

Layton, L. (2003, March 15). Navy women finding ways to adapt to a man's world. *The Washington Post*, p. A15. Retrieved from http://www.washingtonpost.com

Leo, J. (1997, August 11). A kinder, gentler army. *U.S. News and World Report*, 123(6), 14.

McDonough, S. (2003, February 10). More U.S. military women edging closer to combat positions in preparation for Iraq war. *The Associated Press*. Retrieved from http://www.ap.org/

Nath, C. (2002). *United States Air Force Leadership Studies*. Washington, DC: Air Education and Training Command, United States Air Force.

cal documentation provides name and page number of the source you actually used, preceded by the words "qtd. in":

> The National School Lunch Program has been in existence since 1946 "as a measure of national security, to safeguard the health and well-being of the Nation's children and to encourage the domestic consumption of nutritious agricultural commodities and other food" (qtd. in Center for Science 230).

A work in an anthology is cited parenthetically by the name of the author of the work, not the editor of the anthology: (Simkovich 3).

The list of Works Cited includes all material you have used to write your research paper. This list appears at the end of your paper and always starts on a new page. Center the title Works Cited, double-space between the title and the first entry, and begin your list, which should be arranged alphabetically by author. Each entry should start at the left margin; indent all subsequent lines of the entry five spaces or one-half inch. Number each page, and double-space throughout.

One more point: *Content notes*, which provide additional information not readily worked into a research paper, are also indicated by superscript numbers. Content notes are included on a Notes page before the list of Works Cited.

Revising

The final stage in writing an argumentative paper is revising. The first step is to read through what you have written for mistakes. Next, check your work against the guidelines listed under "Organizing the Material" and "Writing." Have you omitted any of the issues, warrants, or supporting evidence on your outline? Is each paragraph coherent in itself? Do your paragraphs work together to create a coherent paper? All the elements of the argument — the issues raised, the underlying assumptions, and the supporting material — should contribute to the development of the claim in your thesis statement. Any material that is interesting but irrelevant to that claim should be cut. Finally, does your paper reach a clear conclusion that reinforces your thesis?

Be sure, too, that the style and tone of your paper are appropriate for the topic and the audience. Remember that people choose to read an argument because they want the answer to a troubling question or the solution to a recurrent problem. Besides stating your thesis in a way that invites the reader to join you in your investigation, you must retain your audience's interest through a discussion that may be unfamiliar or contrary to their convictions. The outstanding qualities of argumentative prose style, therefore, are clarity and readability.

Style is obviously harder to evaluate in your own writing than organization. Your outline provides a map against which to check the structure of your paper. Clarity and readability, by comparison, are somewhat abstract qualities. Two procedures may be helpful. The first is to read two or three (or more) essays by authors whose style you admire and then turn back to your own writing. Awkward spots in your prose are sometimes easier to see if you get away from it and respond to someone else's perspective than if you simply keep rereading your own writing.

The second method is to read aloud. If you have never tried it, you are likely to be surprised at how valuable this can be. Again, start with someone else's work that you feel is clearly written, and practice until you achieve a smooth rhythmic delivery that satisfies you. And listen to what you are reading. Your objective is to absorb the patterns of English structure that characterize the clearest, most readable prose. Then read your paper aloud, and listen to the construction of your sentences. Are they also clear and readable? Do they say what you want them to say? How would they sound to a reader? According to one theory, you can learn the rhythm and phrasing of a language as you learn the rhythm and phrasing of a melody. And you will often *hear* a mistake or a clumsy construction in your writing that has escaped your eye in proofreading.

Preparing the Manuscript

Print your essay on one side of 8½-by-11-inch white computer paper, double-spacing throughout. Leave margins of 1 to 1½ inches on all sides, and indent each paragraph one-half inch or five spaces. Unless a formal outline is part of the paper, a separate title page is unnecessary. Instead, beginning about one inch from the top of the first page and flush with the left margin, type your name, the instructor's name, the course title, and the date, each on a separate line; then double-space and type the title, capitalizing the first letter of the words of the title except for articles, prepositions, and conjunctions. Double-space and type the body of the paper.

Number all pages at the top right corner, typing your last name before each page number in case pages are mislaid. If an outline is included, number its pages with lowercase roman numerals.

Writer's Guide: Checklist for Argumentative Papers

1. Present a thesis that interests both you and the audience, is debatable, and can be defended in the amount of space available.

2. Back up each statement offered in support of the thesis with enough evidence to give it credibility. Cite data from a variety of sources. Fully document all quotations and direct references to primary or secondary sources.

3. The warrants linking claims to support must be either specified or implicit in your data and line of reasoning. No claim should depend on an unstated warrant with which skeptical readers might disagree.

4. Present the thesis clearly and adequately introduce it in a thesis paragraph, indicating the purpose of the paper.

5. Organize supporting statements and data in a way that builds the argument, emphasizes your main ideas, and justifies the paper's conclusions.

6. Anticipate all possible opposing arguments and either refute or accommodate them.

7. Write in a style and tone appropriate for the topic and the intended audience. Your prose should be clear and readable.

8. Make sure your manuscript is clean, carefully proofed, and typed in an acceptable format.

Use the spell-check and grammar-check functions of your word-processing program, but keep in mind that correctness depends on context. A spell-check program will not flag a real word that is used incorrectly, such as the word *it's* used where the word *its* is needed. Also, a grammar-check function lacks the sophistication to interpret the meaning of a sentence and may flag as incorrect a group of words that is indeed correct while missing actual errors. It is ultimately up to you to proofread the paper carefully for other mistakes. Correct the errors, and reprint the pages in question.

Sample Research Paper (MLA Style)

Hedden 1

Kathleen Hedden
Mrs. Swanson
English 102-14
October 29, 2010

Competitive Foods and the Obesity Epidemic

It is difficult these days to watch television or read a newspaper without hearing about the problem of childhood obesity in the United States. Opinions differ as to the best solution for dealing with this problem that threatens the health of a rising generation, but few would deny that it is a problem.

Thomas R. Frieden, head of the Centers for Disease Control and Prevention in Atlanta and thus one of the leading health officials in the country, is among those who have used the term "epidemic" to describe what is happening: "What has changed, in just the course of a generation, is that childhood obesity has become an epidemic," he says. "In the 1960s, 5 percent of children were overweight. Today, nearly 20 percent are" (Frieden, Dietz, and Collins). Concern about obesity is not just concern for how our children — and our future adults — look, but for their present and future health. According to the Robert Wood Johnson Foundation, a charitable organization whose goal is to improve the health of all Americans, the rate of obesity for those between the ages of six and eleven has quadrupled in three decades. Children are being diagnosed with what used to be considered adult diseases, like high blood pressure, adult-onset diabetes, and gallstones. The Foundation reports, "If we don't succeed in reversing this epidemic, we are in danger of raising the first generation of American children who will live sicker and die younger than their parents' generation" (259–60).

The problem of childhood obesity will have to be attacked on several fronts. Parents and other caregivers have to be educated and motivated to control children's diet and physical activity. Because of the number of hours that

Frieden's name and position are used to introduce and lend authority to the quotation.

Article from a journal. Frieden is quoted, but all three authors need to be listed in parentheses. No page numbers because accessed online.

Foundation as author. Since it is mentioned in the text, all that is necessary in parentheses is the page number. The citation covers both paraphrased and quoted material.

Hedden 2

most children spend in school five days a week for a large
part of the year, however, the CDC's *Morbidity and Mortality
Weekly Report* has stated that "schools are in a unique position to help improve youth dietary behaviors and prevent
and reduce obesity" (Centers for Disease Control).

The federal government has long subsidized the nation's school lunch program. The National School Lunch
Program has been in existence since 1946 "as a measure of
national security, to safeguard the health and well-being of
the Nation's children and to encourage the domestic consumption of nutritious agricultural commodities and other
food" (qtd. in Center for Science 230).

One problem now is the sale of what are called
competitive foods, or those foods and beverages sold in
schools but outside of the meal program supported by the
federal government. They may be sold through vending
machines, snack bars, school stores, or in a la carte lines,
but they do not have to meet the nutrition standards that
must be met by cafeteria food. They are not supposed to
be available in the food service area during lunch, but they
sometimes are and in other cases are close by.

Dr. Heather Hartline-Grafton, Senior Nutrition Policy
Analyst for the Food Research and Action Center (FRAC),
explains how this competitive food contributes to the obesity epidemic:

> Competitive foods are often energy-dense, nutrient-
> poor items, and their availability at school undermines
> efforts to promote healthy diets and prevent obesity.
> Not only do the sales of competitive foods and bever-
> ages decrease participation in the school meal pro-
> grams, but the sales are often subsidized by school
> meal reimbursements. (1)

Competitive foods are a widespread presence in schools:
They are available in 73 percent of elementary schools, 97
percent of middle schools, and 100 percent of high schools,
most often in the form of vending machines and a la carte

The organization
is the author. No
page number
because ac-
cessed online.

One work
quoted in
another. The
citation is to
the work Katie
actually used.

Hedden 3

lines. Although there are nutritious competitive options, those do not sell as well as the ones high in sugar, salt, and calories (Hartline-Grafton 2–3).

Author not mentioned in text, so her name is included with page number in parentheses.

While the U.S. Department of Agriculture has the power to regulate the food served in the school lunch program, it currently has little power to regulate competitive foods. That power depends in part on what foods are defined as foods of minimal nutritional value (FMNVs). Hartline-Grafton explains:

> FMNVs are defined as foods providing less than five percent of recommended intakes for eight key nutrients. Examples include carbonated soda, gum, hard candies, and jelly beans. Other competitive foods, including candy bars, chips, and ice cream, are not considered FMNVs (and therefore not under USDA authority) and may be sold in the cafeteria during meal periods. In short, unlike the federal school lunch and breakfast programs, competitive foods are, for the most part, exempt from federal nutrition standards and regulation. (2)

Block quotation. Notice that the whole quotation is indented, there are no quotation marks, and the period comes before the parenthesis.

If it is obvious that many competitive foods are a danger to our children's health and well-being and that they are beyond the control of even the USDA's regulations, why are these foods not removed from schools?

One simple answer is because students like them and buy them. Most students are in the habit of eating fast food away from school and see no problem eating it at school. They like the high-fat, high-sugar foods that do not conform to the regulations that school cafeterias must follow.

If students are not willing to monitor their own food intake and the USDA cannot, why do schools continue to allow these foods lacking in nutritional value to be sold? Part of the answer is that some school districts in some states have chosen to regulate the competitive foods sold in the district or to eliminate them entirely. The economics of school meals, however, are much more complicated

Hedden 4

than one might think. Parke Wilde and Mary Kennedy, both
researchers in the Friedman School of Nutrition Science
and Policy at Tufts University in Boston, explain some of
the complexities in an article entitled "The Economics of a
Healthy School Meal." Schools are reimbursed a set amount
for each lunch subsidized by the federal government. Even
when better-off students pay for their lunch, the federal
government pays its part. Other students, depending on
their parents' income, pay a reduced rate or nothing at all.
Even that set formula, however, is affected by competitive
foods. Students and their parents are pushing for more nutritious foods than are required by the federal government,
and the districts must balance the money lost when students don't eat school lunches with that gained by selling
competitive foods. Wilde and Kennedy write,

> Any successful business must understand the economic
> interactions across its product lines, but these interac-
> tions are particularly intense for a school food service.
> A child who consumes a reimbursable lunch and break-
> fast will have lower demand for *a la carte* items, while
> a child who skips a real meal may be hungrier for a
> snack. This interaction means that school food service
> decisions about competitive foods strongly affect the
> federal school meals program, and vice versa.

No page num-
ber because
an electronic
source.

By that logic, if competitive foods were not available, students might opt for the healthier alternative of the school
meal.

In September 2010, Congress passed the Healthy,
Hunger-Free Kids Act of 2010, a huge step forward in
schools' ability to control the foods served at school.
The act will "commit an additional $4.5 billion to child-
nutrition programs over the next 10 years and implement
the most sweeping changes to those programs in decades."
In response to the problem of competitive foods, it "directs
the U.S. Department of Agriculture to set new nutrition
standards for all food served in schools, from lunchrooms
to vending machines" (Eisler).

Author not
identified in text.
No page number
because elec-
tronic source.

Hedden 5

Ironically, it is not a foregone conclusion that all schools will benefit from this new legislation. They have to adopt the new nutrition standards, which the Institute of Medicine will recommend and the U.S. Department of Agriculture will write. Schools that adopt the new nutrition requirements will get an increase of six cents per meal in their federal reimbursement rate, the first increase since 1973 and one that has long been needed (Eisler). Stipends are also available for those schools that need to upgrade their kitchens to accommodate preparing the more nutritious meals (Wilde and Kennedy).

It seems obvious that all school districts across the country should adopt the new nutritional standards that are being presented to them with the additional incentive of getting more money per meal for school lunches and breakfasts than they currently get. The new standards will remove from schools competitive foods that are particularly unhealthy and replace them with foods that fall under the nutrition guidelines of the new act. Students may not get all of the choices of foods that they would like, but parents, teachers, and school officials — and the students themselves — will know that schools are contributing less to the problem of childhood and adolescent obesity.

Hedden 6

Works Cited

Center for Science in the Public Interest. "Improving Kids'
    Nutrition: An Action Kit for Parents and Citizens."
    Food, Inc.: How Industrial Food Is Making Us Sicker,   A work in an
    Fatter and Poorer — And What You Can Do about It.   anthology
    Ed. Karl Weber. New York: PublicAffairs, 2009. 227–57.
    Print.

Centers for Disease Control and Prevention. "Competitive
    Foods and Beverages Available for Purchase in Second-   A journal article
    ary Schools---Selected Sites, United States, 2006."   accessed online
    MMWR Weekly 29 August 2008: 935–938. *EBSCOhost.*
    Web. 16 Sept. 2010.

Eisler, Peter. "Sweeping School Lunch Bill Clears Senate   A newspaper
    Panel." *usatoday.com.* USA Today, 24 March 2010. Web.   article accessed
                                                              online
    22 Sept. 2010.

Frieden, Thomas R., William Dietz, and Janet Collins. "Re-
    ducing Childhood Obesity Through Policy Change:
    Acting Now to Prevent Obesity." *Health Affairs* 29.3   A journal article
    (2010): 357–63. *EBSCOhost.* Web. 15 Sept 2010.   accessed online

Hartline-Grafton, Heather. "How Competitive Foods in
    Schools Impact Student Health, School Meal Programs,   A document ac-
    and Students from Low-Income Families." *Issue Briefs*   cessed online
    for Child Nutrition Reauthorization 5. Washington,
    D.C.: Food Research and Action Center, 2010.
    EBSCOhost. Web. 22 Sept. 2010.

Robert Wood Johnson Foundation. "Childhood Obesity: The
    Challenge." *Food, Inc.: How Industrial Food Is Making*   A work in an
    Us Sicker, Fatter and Poorer — And What You Can Do   anthology
    about It. Ed. Karl Weber. New York: PublicAffairs, 2009.
    259–61. Print.

Wilde, Parke, and Mary Kennedy. "The Economics of a   A journal article
    Healthy School Meal." *Choices* 24.3 (2009): n. pag.   accessed online
    EBSCOhost. Web. 21 Sept. 2010.

The APA System for Citing Sources

Instructors in the social sciences might prefer the citation system of the American Psychological Association (APA), which is used in the paper on women in the military in this chapter. Like the MLA system, the APA system calls for a parenthetical citation in the text of the paper following any quotations from your sources. The APA only recommends that page numbers be included for paraphrases or summaries, but you should provide page numbers for these anyway unless your instructor advises you that they are not necessary. In the text of your paper, immediately after any quotation, paraphrase, or idea you need to document, insert a parenthetical mention of the author's last name and the page number on which the material appears. Unlike the MLA system, the APA system also includes the year of publication in the parenthetical reference, using a comma to separate the items within the citation and using "p." or "pp." before the page number(s). Even if the source has a month of publication, only the year is included in the parenthetical citation. Here is an example:

> As of now, women are restricted from 30 percent of Army assignments and 1 percent of Air Force assignments (Baer, 2003, p. 1A).

The parenthetical reference tells the reader that the information in this sentence comes from page 1A of the 2003 work by Baer that appears on the References page at the end of the paper. The complete publication information that a reader would need to locate Baer's work will appear on the References page:

> Baer, S. (2003, March 3). In Iraq war, women would serve closer to front lines than in past. *The Baltimore Sun*, p. 1A.

If the author's name is mentioned in the same sentence in your text, the year in which the work was published follows it, in parentheses, and the page number only is placed in parentheses at the end of the sentence.

> According to Baer (2003) of the *Baltimore Sun*, as of now, women are restricted from 30 percent of Army assignments and 1 percent of Air Force assignments (p. 1A).

In the APA system, it is appropriate to include only the last name of the author unless you have more than one author with the same name in your list of references, in which case you would include the first initial of the author.

If your list of references includes more than one work written by the same author in the same year, cite the first work as "a" and the second as "b." For example, Baer's second article of 2003 would be cited in your paper like this: (Baer, 2003b).

If a work has two authors, list both in your sentence or in the parentheses, using "and" between them. In these examples from the women in combat paper, there is no page number because the source is a short work from a Web site:

> The fall 2000 suggestion from DACOWITS included a possible recruiting slogan: "A gynecologist on every aircraft carrier!" (Yoest & Yoest, 2001).

> Yoest and Yoest (2001) recall the fall 2000 suggestion from DACOWITS for a possible recruiting slogan: "A gynecologist on every aircraft carrier!"

If there are three to five authors, list them all by last name the first time they are referred to and, after that, by the last name of the first author and the term "et al." (meaning "and others"): (Sommers, Mylroie, Donnelly, & Hill, 2001); (Sommers et al., 2001). Also use the last name of the first author and "et al." when there are more than five authors, which is often the case in the sciences and social sciences.

If no author is given, use the name of the work where you would normally use the author's name, placing the names of short works in quotation marks and italicizing those of book-length works.

When using electronic sources, follow as much as possible the rules for parenthetical documentation of print ones. If no author's name is given, cite by the title of the work. If no date is given, use the abbreviation "n.d." instead. For a long work, if there are no page numbers, as is often the case with electronic sources, give paragraph numbers if the work has numbered paragraphs, or, if the work is divided into sections, the paragraph number within that section:

> Jamison (1999) warned about the moral issues associated with stem cell research, particularly the guilt that some parents felt about letting their children's cells be used (Parental Guilt section, para. 2).

Remember that the purpose of parenthetical documentation is to help a reader locate the information that you are citing.

At times you will need to cite one work that is quoted in another or a work from an anthology. For the former, the parenthetical documentation provides author's name, year of publication, and page number of the source you actually used, preceded by the words "as cited in":

> The female soldier "is, on the average, about five inches shorter than the male soldier, has half the upper body strength, lower aerobic capacity and 37 percent less muscle mass" (as cited in Owens, 1997, Anatomy section, para. 2).

A work in an anthology is cited parenthetically by the name of the author of the work, not the editor of the anthology.

Sample Research Paper (APA Style)

The following paper shows APA citations in the context of an actual text and the format for several different entries on the References page. Angela has used quotations sparingly and has instead made extensive use of summary and paraphrase. Often there is no page number in her parenthetical citations. That is because she was drawing from short online sources in which the paragraphs are not numbered but in which it is easy to find the material she refers to.

The format of the title page illustrates APA guidelines, as does the running head that is on each page.

Notice that Angela's thesis appears as the last sentence in her first paragraph. She carefully documents the restrictions on women that still exist in the U.S. military and argues why those restrictions are appropriate.

Women in Combat 1

The Controversy over Women in Combat

Angela Mathers
English 103-13
Ms. Carter
April 7, 2011

Women in Combat 2

Abstract

Women have served in the U.S. military since World War I. Although many barriers to their complete participation in all phases of military service have been broken, they are still appropriately restricted from direct ground combat assignments. Because women are held to a lower physical standard than men, men in their units cannot trust their ability to perform on the battlefield. One argument in favor of combat assignments for women has been that the lack of combat experience stands in the way of their progressing through the ranks. Such careerism, however, goes against a soldier's sworn duty, and there are ways to advance in the military other than combat service. The social and logistical problems created are an argument against women's serving in close quarters with men. Pregnancy among enlisted women is also inevitable and poses its own medical and logistical problems. Combat assignments for women would be a threat to the effectiveness and readiness of American troops.

Women in Combat 3

The Controversy over Women in Combat

Throughout the history of the military, the role of
women has changed and adapted as the needs of the country have. From Molly Pitcher to Rosie the Riveter, women
have always held a place in making the military what it is
today. Issues have surfaced in the modern military about
the current role of female service members with regard to
combat assignments. Positions on submarines, small destroyers, specialized combat teams, and a handful of other
assignments are restricted to men-only clubs. The factors
determining why women are restricted from these assignments include physical ability, deployability, the cost effectiveness of providing the facilities that women need,
and the effect on the overall readiness of the military.
Women who desire these assignments, and other opponents
of these restrictions, have retorted with reasons that they
should be included, the foremost being women's rights and
their desire to advance up the ranks of the military. However, women are rightly restricted from direct ground combat assignments to ensure the readiness of the military and
the effectiveness of these combat units.

Women were first recruited, and began serving, in the
military during World War I because they were needed to
fill the clerical, technical, and health care jobs that were
left vacant as more men were drafted. All these women,
however, were discharged as soon as the war ended. The
Women's Army Corps (WAC) was founded during World War
II and gave women their own branch of the military. They
served in the same jobs as they did in WWI but with the
addition of non-combatant pilot assignments. Women did
not get their permanent place in the ranks until 1948 when
the Women Armed Services Integration Act was passed
through Congress, allowing them to serve under the conditions that they were not to hold any rank above colonel,
were limited mostly to clerical or health care jobs, and
were not to make up more than 2 percent of the entire
military. They were still limited to their own female only

Overview of the controversy

Opposing view

Thesis

A history of women in the military from a source accessed through a sub-scription service

Women in Combat 4

corps until 1978, when the military was fully integrated and women were allowed to hold any assignment that their male counterparts could except for combat roles. The rules have been relaxed over the years as women have proven themselves in combat support missions, especially in the Persian Gulf War in 1991 ("Women," 2000). They continue to push to be allowed into every job that men hold, and the effect this is having on the military is a fiery issue.

The paren- thetical citation shows where paraphrase ends and her ideas begin

According to Baer (2003) of the *Baltimore Sun*, as of now, women are restricted from 30 percent of Army assign- ments, 38 percent of Marine assignments, and 1 percent of Air Force assignments. From the Navy, women are excluded from the special operations SEAL groups. These exclusions are from Military Occupational Specialities (MOS) "whose primary mission is ground combat" as defined by the Pen- tagon. They are also excluded from Navy submarines and small battleships that do not have the facilities to accom- modate women (p. 1A).

Source and year included in text

Page only in parentheses

There have been many advancements for combat seek- ing women since the Persian Gulf War. McDonough (2003), writing for the Associated Press, reports that females are now allowed to fly combat missions in fighter jets and bombers for the Air Force and Navy. They can serve in many combat support roles such as combat Military Police compa- nies. They can also be assigned to chemical specialist units that clean up contaminated areas on the battlefield, and to engineering units who build and repair bridges and runways in high risk areas. Women can also pilot the Army's Apache assault helicopters over the battlefield during high risk conditions, and pilot troop carrying helicopters onto the battlefield to deliver troops for a rescue mission during an assault. However, none of these MOSs are in selective spe- cial operations units such as Marine Force Recon or Army Airborne Rangers who serve as the "tip of the spear" in ground combat for missions like Operation Enduring Free- dom in Afghanistan or Operation Iraqi Freedom.

Author and year in text; no page number because electronic ver- sion

Women in Combat 5

The federal government and military have been under
pressure from several sides on the issue of women serving in combat roles in the military. There are those that
believe that all assignments, no matter how demanding
of time, body, talent, and mind should be open to women
as well as men. According to Gerber (2002) of the James   A Web site
MacGregor Burns Academy of Leadership, this is the general
consensus of the Defense Advisory Committee on Women
in the Services (DACOWITS). It was established in 1951 by
General George Marshall but was disbanded when Secretary
of Defense Donald Rumsfeld let its charter run out when it
came up for renewal in 2002. However, its motives could
be called into question as to whether it is rallying for the
good of the military and its purposes or pushing its own
platform that women should be integrated in all parts
just because they believe it is deserved. Former DACOWITS
Chairperson Vickie McCall even told the U.S. Air Force in
Europe News Service, "You have to understand. We don't
report facts, we report perception" (as qtd. in Yoest &   One source
Yoest, 2001). DACOWITS has often teamed up with other   quoted in an-
                                                              other; source
private women's rights activist groups that believe that the   with two au-
military should be an "equal opportunity employer" along   thors
with all other private and public employers.

     One cause of concern over women's inclusion in com-
bat units has been the rigorous physical standards these
troops must meet in training and in turn on the battlefield.
Many studies have been done to prove or disprove a distinction between men's and women's physical capabilities.
In the quest for evidence, Col. Patrick Toffler, Director of
the United States Military Office of Institutional Research,
reported that it had identified 120 physical differences
(Owens, 1997, p. 40). The female soldier "is, on the aver-   A journal pagi-
age, about five inches shorter than the male soldier, has   nated by issue
half the upper body strength, lower aerobic capacity and
37 percent less muscle mass" (as qtd. in Owens, 1997,
p. 38). Leo (1997) reports in *U.S. News and World Report*   A magazine

Women in Combat 6

that the way that the military accommodates for these differences is called "gender norming" and works by lowering the standards that women have to reach to pass the physical fitness tests. For instance, in the Marines, men are required to climb the length of a rope and females are only required to climb to a point below that marked with a yellow line (p. 14). These standards are mostly for people to enlist in the services; so the bar is significantly raised for those that choose to compete for a MOS in special operations or combat units. Females enrolled in Army Jump School to be paratroopers are still not required to run as far or do as many pushups or sit-ups as their male counterparts. When this double standard is employed in the military, it blurs the distinction as to which soldiers actually have the physical ability to perform on the battlefield.

When there is a question as to the physical abilities of a fellow soldier in a unit, there can be no guarantee that everyone can cover your back as well as you could for them. When there is no trust in a unit, it breaks down. Take, for example, the Marine ideology that no one is left behind on the battlefield. Imagine an officer trying to motivate his troops to jump out of a helicopter in the heat of battle. Some of the soldiers may doubt a female comrade's capability to carry them to safety should they be injured, because she does not have to meet the same physical standards as her male counterparts do. The training is not only meant to prepare the troops for war combat and to show the officers that they meet the physical requirements. It is also a time to begin to build the trust that binds the troop's lives together and prove to each other they have the physical and mental toughness to accomplish the mission and bring each other back safely. How can this trust be established when male soldiers witness some female soldiers being excused from throwing live grenades in practice because they cannot throw the dummy ones far enough to keep from being blown to shreds? "The military should be the real world," said Jeanne Holm, retired two-star General of the Air Force. "The name of the game is putting together a team that fits and works together. That is the top priority, not social experimentation" (as qtd. in Yoest & Yoest, 2001). The military studies prove that a female body is not equipped to perform the same physical rigors as the male body; therefore, they should not be put in the position where impossible war fighting demands are put on them.

One source quoted in another

When left out of selective combat positions, there is the possibility that women cannot advance up the ranks because they would not get ample opportunity to prove themselves on the battlefield and gain combat experience. This experience goes a long way because it stands to prove that an officer has the leadership ability to command troops under fire and accomplish the mission. Experience can be gained in many ways, though, since America is not always at war. All officer career fields are necessary to the overall success of the mission, and in order to be promoted every officer must pull his or her weight. Even though the proceedings of the promotion committees are supposed to be kept private, it is no secret that combat experience weighs heavily on promotion picks (Nath, 2002). In a military that is centered on the chain of command, seniority is the most valuable commodity for any member, especially officers. The practice of officers' jockeying for promotions to further their career, stature, and income is called "careerism" (Nath, 2002). This is supposedly prohibited under the Air Force's second core value of "Service Before Self," and similar pledges in the other branches. The argument lies in the conflict between the career ambition of female officers seeking a combat MOS and the needs of a ready military to support the mission.

No page number given

The truth is, however, that the United States Armed Forces is not an "equal opportunity employer" as many other public and private organizations are. The military is not out to make a profit, or provide a ladder to corporate success. Instead, military officers swear to "support and defend the Constitution of the United States against all

Women in Combat 8

enemies, foreign and domestic; that I will bear the true
faith and allegiance to the same" (Oath of Office, 2003).
This oath states they are to uphold the best interest of the
mission that the Commander in Chief charges them with.
Careerism is not an option under this oath because it is
only serving the individual's ambition, and not the mission
of the military. Elaine Donnelly, President of the Center for
Military Readiness, says, "Equal opportunity is important,
but the armed forces exist to defend the country. If there
is a conflict between career opportunities and military necessity, the needs of the military must come first" (as qtd.
in "Women," 2000).

　　Another concern with females in combat is their
deployability, or their availability to be deployed. Because
the very nature of combat units is being the "tip of the
spear" in battle, they are deployed and away from home
much of the year and are used for an indefinite period of
time during the war. Donnelly explains that "if you have
a pregnancy rate and it's constant, 10 or 15%, you know
that out of 500 women on a carrier at least 50 are going
to be unavailable before or during the six-month deployment" (Sommers, Mylroie, Donnelly, & Hill, 2001). This   First reference
pregnancy issue is not just applicable for conception before   to source with
the deployment, but during deployment, as is evident on   four authors
Navy aircraft carriers and destroyers that house women.
Even though fraternization, defined as "sexual relationships
between service members" (Nath, 2002), is illegal, many   Different parts
ships such as the U.S.S. *Lincoln* "report a dozen [pregnan-   of the same
cies] a month" (Layton, 2003). In a close quarters environ-   sentence cited
ment, where combat units are together every hour of the   to different
day, this kind of problem distracts from the mission. Also,   sources
sailors on submarines sleep in what they call "hot beds,"
which are rotating shifts for sleep in the few available
beds, and changing this system to accommodate separate
quarters for females would not be cost effective. Also,
pregnant females aboard aircraft carriers are being taken
from their duty, and they must be replaced, which is a

Women in Combat 9

costly endeavor for the military and throws off the working relationship between service members.

When men and women are put in close quarters, it is just human nature that sexual relationships will begin to develop. This fact has been proven all around the military from the pregnancies on board Naval ships all the way up to the Navy's "Tail Hook Convention," where in Las Vegas in 1991, dozens of female officers reported being openly sexually assaulted by male officers, both married and unmarried ("Women," 2000). If there was this kind of distraction within special operation ground combat units, the mission would suffer greatly because fraternization would become a huge issue, for favoritism would ensue. When the mission is not the first thing on these troops' minds, the morale, and most importantly, the trust breaks down.

Another very real barrier to the inclusion of women in these units and on small battleships and submarines is the medical needs of the female body. The fall 2000 suggestion from DACOWITS included as a possible recruiting slogan "A gynecologist on every aircraft carrier! (Yoest & Yoest, 2001). This is a possibility on every base and possibly on huge aircraft carriers, but these needs of women cannot be met in the field hospitals in the deserts of Iraq and Afghanistan where the only goal is to keep soldiers from dying long enough to get them to a base hospital. Another dilemma on forty to fifty person submarines is that if a woman were to get pregnant, as is the proven trend, the vessel would have to make a risky surface to get her off to be cared for and find a replacement for her job on board. DACOWITS also suggested to "ensure an adequate supply of hygiene products during deployment" (Yoest & Yoest, 2001), which is a far cry from reality when Marines who are currently in Iraq already march with a 130-pound rucksack holding their bare living necessities. The military certainly does not have the money to cover these hygiene and medical needs when in high risk areas simply because the resources must go to fulfilling the mission.

Women in Combat 11

Oath of office: U.S. federal and military oath of office. Retrieved from http://www.apfn.org/apfn/oathofoffice.htm

Owens, M. (1997, Spring). Mothers in combat boots: Feminists call for women in the military. *Human Life Review*, 23(2), 35–45.

Sommers, C., Mylroie, L., Donnelly, E., & Hill, M. (2001, October 17). IWF panel: Women facing war. *Independent Women's Forum*. Retrieved from RDS Contemporary Women's Issues.

Warrior women. (2003, February 16). *The New York Times*, sect. 6, p. 23. Retrieved from http://www.nytimes.com

Women in the military. (2000, September 1). *Issues and Controversies*. Retrieved from http://www.2facts.com

Yoest, C., & Yoest, J. (2002, Winter). Booby traps at the Pentagon. *Women's Quarterly*. Retrieved from http://www.bnet.com

CHAPTER 12

Oral Arguments

$\mathbf{A}$ classics scholar points out that the oratorical techniques we use today were "invented in antiquity and have been used to great effect ever since."[1] But history is not our only guide to the principles of public speaking. Much of what we know about the power of persuasive speech is knowledge based on lifelong experience — things we learn in everyday discourse with different kinds of people who respond to different appeals. Early in life you learned that you did not use the same language or the same approach to argue with your mother or your teacher as you used with your sibling or your friend. You learned, or tried to learn, how to convince people to listen to you and to trust you because you were truthful and knew what you were talking about. Although speeches to a larger, less familiar audience will require much more preparation, many of the rules of argument that guided you in your personal encounters can be made to work for you in more public arenas.

You will often be asked to make oral presentations in your college classes. Many jobs, both professional and nonprofessional, will call for speeches to groups of fellow employees or prospective customers, to community groups, and even government officials. Wherever you live, there will be controversies and public meetings about schooling and political candidates, about budgets for libraries and road repairs and pet control. The ability to rise and make your case before an audience is one that you will want to cultivate as a citizen of a democracy. Great oratory is probably no longer the most powerful influence in our society, and computer networks have usurped the role of oral communication in many areas of public life. But whether it's in person or on television there is still a significant role for a live presenter, a real human being to be seen and heard.

Some of your objectives as a writer will also be relevant to you as a speaker: making the appropriate appeal to an audience, establishing your credibility, find-

---

[1] Mary Lefkowitz, "Classic Oratory," *New York Times*, January 24, 1999, sec. W, p. 15.

ing adequate support for your claim. But other elements of argument will be different: language, organization, and the use of visual and other aids.

The Audience

Most speakers who confront a live audience already know something about the members of that audience. They may know why the audience is assembled to hear the particular speaker, their vocations, their level of education, and their familiarity with the subject. They may know whether the audience is friendly, hostile, or neutral to the views that the speaker will express. Analyzing the audience is an essential part of speech preparation. If speakers neglect it, both audience and speaker will suffer. At some time all of us have been trapped as members of an audience, forced to listen to a lecture, a sermon, an appeal for action when it was clear that the speaker had little or no idea what we were interested in or capable of understanding. In such situations the speaker who seems indifferent to the needs of the audience will also suffer because the audience will either cease to listen or reject his claim outright.

In college classes students who make assigned speeches on controversial topics are often encouraged to first survey the class. Questionnaires and interviews can give the speaker important clues to the things he should emphasize or avoid: They will tell him whether he should give both sides of a debatable question, introduce humor, use simpler language, and bring in visual or other aids.

When delivering a speech, it is helpful to know how your audience may react.

But even where such specific information is not immediately available, speakers are well advised to find out as much as they can about the beliefs and attitudes of their audience from other sources. They will then be better equipped to make the kinds of appeals — to reason and to emotion — that the audience is most responsive to.

If you know something about your audience, ask yourself what impression your clothing, gestures and bodily movements, voice, and general demeanor might convey. Make sure, too, that you understand the nature of the occasion — is it too solemn for humor? too formal for personal anecdotes? — and the purpose of the meeting, which can influence your choice of language and the most effective appeal.

Credibility

The evaluation of audience and the presentation of your own credibility are closely related. In other words, what can you do to persuade this particular audience that you are a reliable exponent of the views you are expressing? Credibility, as you learned in Chapter 1, is another name for *ethos* (the Greek word from which the English word *ethics* is derived) and refers to the honesty, moral character, and intellectual competence of the speaker.

Public figures, whose speeches and actions are reported in the media, can acquire (or fail to acquire) reputations for being endowed with those characteristics. And there is little doubt that a reputation for competence and honesty can incline an audience to accept an argument that would be rejected if offered by a speaker who lacks such a reputation. One study, among many that report similar results, has shown that the same speech will be rated highly by an audience that thinks the surgeon general of the United States has delivered it but treated with much less regard if they hear it delivered by a college sophomore.

How, then, do speakers who are unknown to the audience or who boast only modest credentials convince listeners that they are responsible advocates? From the moment the speaker appears before them, members of the audience begin to make an evaluation, based on external signs, such as clothing and mannerisms. But the most significant impression of the speaker's credibility will be based on what the speaker says and how. Does the speaker give evidence of knowing the subject? Of being aware of the needs and values of the audience? Especially if arguing an unpopular claim, does the speaker seem modest and conciliatory?

An unknown speaker is often advised to establish his credentials in the introduction to his speech, to summarize his background and experience as proof of his right to argue the subject he has chosen. A prize-winning and widely reprinted speech by a student begins with these words:

> When you look at me, it is easy to see several similarities between us. I
> have two arms, two legs, a brain, and a heart just like you. These are my
> hands, and they are just like yours. Like you, I also have wants and desires;
> I am capable of love and hate. I can laugh and I can cry. Yes, I'm just like
> you, except for one very important fact — I am an ex-con.[2]

This is a possibly risky beginning — not everybody in the audience will be
friendly to an ex-con — but it signifies that the speaker brings some authority
to his subject, which is prison reform. It also attests to the speaker's honesty
and may rouse sympathy among certain listeners. (To some in the audience,
the speaker's allusions to his own humanity will recall another moving defense,
the famous speech by Shylock, the Jewish moneylender, in Shakespeare's *The
Merchant of Venice*.)

Speakers will often use an admission of modesty as proof of an honest and
unassuming character, presenting themselves not as experts but as speakers well
aware of their limitations. Such an appeal can generate sympathy in the audience (if they believe the speaker) and a sense of identification with the speaker.

The professor of classics quoted earlier has analyzed the speech of a former
senator who defended President Clinton at his impeachment trial. She found
that the speaker "made sure his audience understood that he was one of them,
a friend, on their level, not above them. He denied he was a great speaker and
spoke of his friendship with Mr. Clinton." As the writer points out, this confes-
sion brings to mind the speech by Mark Antony in *Julius Caesar:*

> I am no orator, as Brutus is,
> But (as you know me all) a plain blunt man
> That loves my friend; (3.2.226–28)

The similarity of these attempts at credibility, separated by almost four hundred years (to say nothing of the fact that Aristotle wrote about *ethos* 2,500 years
ago) tells us a good deal about the enduring influence of *ethos* or character on
the speaker's message.

Organization

Look at the student speech on page 490. The organization of this short
speech — the usual length of speeches delivered in the classroom — is easily mas-
tered and works for all kinds of claims.

At the end of the first paragraph the speaker states what he will try to prove,
that a vegetarian diet contributes to prevention of chronic diseases. In the third
paragraph the speaker gives the four points that he will develop in his argument

---

[2] Richard M. Duesterbeck, "Man's Other Society," in Wil Linkugel, R. R. Allen, and Richard
Johannesen, eds., *Contemporary American Speeches* (Belmont, CA: Wadsworth, 1965), p. 264.

for vegetarianism. Following the development of these four topics, the conclusion urges the audience to take action, in this case, to stop eating meat.

This basic method of organizing a short speech has several virtues. First, the claim or thesis statement that appears early in a short speech, if the subject is well chosen, can engage the interest of the audience at once. Second, the list of topics guides the speaker in planning and developing his speech. Moreover, it tells the audience what to listen for as they follow the argument.

A well-planned speech has a clearly defined beginning, middle, and end. The beginning, which offers the introduction, can take a number of forms, depending on the kind of speech and its subject. Above all, the introduction must win the attention of the audience, especially if they have been required to attend, and encourage them to look forward to the rest of the speech. The authors of *Principles of Speech Communication* suggest seven basic attention-getters: (1) referring to the subject or occasion, (2) using a personal reference, (3) asking a rhetorical question, (4) making a startling statement of fact or opinion, (5) using a quotation, (6) telling a humorous anecdote, (7) using an illustration.[3]

The speeches by the ex-con and the vegetarian provide examples of two of the attention-getters cited above — using a personal reference and asking a rhetorical question. In another kind of argument, a claim of fact, the student speaker uses a combination of devices to introduce her claim that culturally deprived children are capable of learning:

> In Charles Schulz's popular cartoon depiction of happiness, one of his definitions has special significance for the American school system. The drawing shows Linus, with his eyes closed in a state of supreme bliss, a broad smile across two-thirds of his face and holding a report card upon which is a big bold "A." The caption reads: "Happiness is finding out you're not so dumb after all." For once, happiness is not defined as a function of material possessions, yet even this happiness is practically unattainable for the "unteachables" of the city slums. Are these children intellectually inferior? Are they unable to learn? Are they not worth the time and the effort to teach? Unfortunately, too many people have answered "yes" to these questions and promptly dismissed the issue.[4]

The middle or body of the speech is, of course, the longest part. It will be devoted to development of the claim that appeared at the beginning. The length of the speech and the complexity of the subject will determine how much support you provide. Some points will be more important than others and should therefore receive more extended treatment. Unless the order is chronological, it makes sense for the speaker to arrange the supporting points in emphatic order, that is, the most important at the end because this may be the one that listeners will remember.

---

[3] Bruce E. Gronbeck et al., *Principles of Speech Communication*, 13th Brief Ed. (New York: Longman, 1998), pp. 243–47.

[4] Carolyn Kay Geiman, "Are They Really 'Unteachables'?" in Linkugel, Allen, and Johannesen, p. 123.

The conclusion should be brief; some rhetoricians suggest that the ending should constitute 5 percent of the total length of the speech. For speeches that contain several main points with supporting data, you may need to summarize. Or you may return to one of the attention-getters mentioned earlier. One writer recommends this as "the most obvious method" of concluding speeches, "particularly appropriate when the introduction has included a quotation, an interesting anecdote, a reference to an occasion or a place, an appeal to the self-interest of the audience, or a reference to a recent incident."[5]

An example of such an ending appears in a speech given by Bruce Babbitt, Secretary of the Interior, in 1996. Speaking to an audience of scientists and theologians, the secretary defended laws that protected the environment. This is how the speech began:

> A wolf's green eyes, a sacred blue mountain, the words from Genesis, and the answers of children all reveal the religious values manifest in the 1977 Endangered Species Act.

(The children Babbitt refers to had written answers to a question posed at an "eco-expo" fair, "Why Save the Environment?")

And this is the ending of the speech:

> I conclude here tonight by affirming that those religious values remain at the heart of the Endangered Species Act, that they make themselves manifest through the green eyes of the grey wolf, through the call of the whooping crane, through the splash of the Pacific salmon, through the voices of America's children.
>
> We are living between the flood and the rainbow: between the threats to creation on the one side and God's covenant to protect life on the other.
>
> Why should we save endangered species?
>
> Let us answer this question with one voice, the voice of the child at that expo, who scrawled her answer at the very bottom of the sheet:
>
> "Because we can."[6]

The speaker must also ensure the smooth flow of argument throughout. Coherence, or the orderly connections between ideas, is even more important in speech than in writing because the listener cannot go back to uncover these connections. The audience listens for expressions that serve as guideposts — words, phrases, and sentences to indicate which direction the argument will take. The student speech on vegetarianism uses these words among others: *next, then, finally, here, first of all, whereas, in addition, secondly, in fact, now, in conclusion.* Other expressions can also help the listener to follow the development. Each of the following examples from real speeches makes a bridge from a previous idea

---

[5] James C. McCroskey, *An Introduction to Rhetorical Communication* (Englewood Cliffs, NJ: Prentice-Hall, 1968), p. 204.

[6] Calvin McLeod Logue and Jean DeHart, eds., *Representative American Speeches, 1995–1996* (New York: Wilson, 1996), p. 70ff.

to a new one: "Valid factual proof, right? No, wrong!" "Consider an illustration of this misinformation." "But there is another way." "Up to this point, I've spoken only of therapy." "And so we face this new challenge." "How do we make this clear?" "Now, why is this so important?"

Language

> It should be observed that each kind of rhetoric has its own appropriate style. That of written prose is not the same as that of spoken oratory.
> — Aristotle

In the end, your speech depends on the language. No matter how accurate your analysis of the audience, how appealing your presentation of self, how deep your grasp of the material, if the language does not clearly and emphatically convey your argument, the speech will probably fail. Fortunately, the effectiveness of language does not depend on long words or complex sentence structure; quite the contrary. Most speeches, especially those given by beginners to small audiences, are distinguished by an oral style that respects the rhythms of ordinary speech and sounds spontaneous.

The vocabulary you choose, like the other elements of spoken discourse we have discussed, is influenced by the kind of audience you confront. A student audience may be entertained or moved to identification with you and your message if you use the slang of your generation; an assembly of elderly church members at a funeral may not be so generous. Use words that both you and your listeners are familiar with, language that convinces the audience you are sharing your knowledge and opinions, neither speaking down to them nor over their heads. As one writer puts it, "You never want to use language that makes the audience appear ignorant or stupid."

Make sure, too, that the words you use will not be considered offensive by some members of your audience. Today we are all sensitive, sometimes hypersensitive, to terms that were once used freely if not wisely. One word, improperly used, can cause some listeners to reject the whole speech.

The short speeches you give will probably not be devoted to elaborating grand abstractions, but it is not only abstract terms that need definition. When you know your subject very well, you forget that others can be ignorant of it. Think whether the subject is one that the particular audience you are addressing is not likely to be familiar with. If this is the case, then explain even the basic terms. In one class a student who had chosen to discuss a subject about which he was extremely knowledgeable, betting on horse races, neglected to define clearly the words *exacta, subfecta, trifecta, parimutuel,* and others, leaving his audience fairly befuddled.

Wherever it is appropriate, use concrete language with details and examples that create images and cause the listener to feel as well as think. One student speaker used strong words to good effect in providing some unappetizing facts about hot dogs: "In fact, the hot dog is so adulterated with chemicals, so contaminated with bacteria, so puffy with gristle, fat, water, and lacking in protein, that it is nutritionally worthless."[7]

Another speech on a far more serious subject offered a personal experience with vivid details. The student speaker was a hemophiliac making a plea for blood donations.

> I remember the three long years when I couldn't even walk because repeated hemorrhages had twisted my ankles and knees to pretzel-like forms. I remember being pulled to school in a wagon while other boys rode their bikes and pushed to my table. I remember sitting in the dark empty classroom by myself during recess while the others went out in the sun to run and play. And I remember the first terrible day at the big high school when I came on crutches and built-up shoes carrying my books in a sack around my neck.[8]

As a rule, the oral style demands simpler sentences. That is because the listener must grasp the grammatical construction without the visual clues of punctuation available on the printed page. Simpler means shorter and more direct. Use subject-verb constructions without a string of phrases or clauses preceding the subject or interrupting the natural flow of the sentence. Use the active voice frequently. In addition to assuring clarity for the audience, such sentences are easier for the speaker to remember and to say. (The sentences in the paragraph above are long, but notice that the sentence elements of subject, verb, and subordinate clause are arranged in the order dictated by natural speech.)

Simpler, however, does not mean less impressive. A speech before any audience may be simply expressed without loss of emotional or intellectual power. One of the most eloquent short speeches ever delivered in this country is the surrender speech in 1877 by Chief Joseph of the Nez Percé Tribe, which clearly demonstrates the power of simple words and sentences.

> I am tired of fighting. Our chiefs are killed. Looking Glass is dead. Toohulsote is dead. The old men are all dead. It is the young men who say no and yes. He who led the young men is dead. It is cold and we have no blankets. The little children are freezing to death. My people, some of them, have run away to the hills and have no blankets, no food. No one knows where they are — perhaps they are freezing to death. I want to have time to look for my children and see how many of them I can find. Maybe I shall find them among the dead. Hear me, my chiefs. I am tired. My heart is sad and sick. From where the sun now stands I will fight no more forever.[9]

---

[7] Donovan Ochs and Anthony Winkler, *A Brief Introduction to Speech* (New York: Harcourt, Brace, Jovanovich, 1979), p. 74.

[8] Ralph Zimmerman, "Mingled Blood," in Linkugel, Allen, and Johannesen, p. 200.

[9] M. Gidley, *Kopet: A Documentary Narrative of Chief Joseph's Last Years* (Chicago: Contemporary Books, 1981), p. 31.

If you are in doubt about the kind of language in which you should express yourself, you might follow Lincoln's advice: "Speak so that the most lowly can understand you, and the rest will have no difficulty."

A popular stylistic device — repetition and balance or parallel structure — can emphasize and enrich parts of your message. Look back to the balanced sentences of the passage from the student speaker on hemophilia, sentences beginning with "I remember." Almost all inspirational speeches, including religious exhortation and political oratory, take advantage of such constructions, whose rhythms evoke an immediate emotional response. It is one of the strengths of Martin Luther King Jr.'s "I Have a Dream" speech. (See p. 492.) Keep in mind that the ideas in parallel structures must be similar and that, for maximum effectiveness, they should be used sparingly in a short speech. Not least, the subject should be weighty enough to carry this imposing construction.

Support

The support for a claim is essentially the same for both spoken and written arguments. Factual evidence, including statistics and expert opinion, as well as appeals to needs and values, is equally important in oral presentations. But time constraints will make a difference. In a speech the amount of support that you provide will be limited to the capacity of listeners to digest and remember information that they cannot review. This means that you must choose subjects that can be supported adequately in the time allotted. The speech by Secretary Babbitt, for example, on saving the environmental protection laws, developed material on animals, national lands, water, his own history, religious tradition, and the history of environmental legislation, to name only the most important. It would have been impossible to defend his proposition in a half-hour speech. Although his subject was far more limited, the author of the argument for vegetarianism could not do full justice to his claim for lack of time. Meat-eaters would find that some of their questions remain unanswered, and even those listeners friendly to the author's claim might ask for more evidence from authoritative sources.

While both speakers and writers use logical, ethical, and emotional appeals in support of their arguments, the forms of presentation can make a significant difference. The reasoning process demanded of listeners must be relatively brief and straightforward, and the supporting evidence readily assimilated. The ethical appeal or credibility of the speaker is affected not only by what is said but by the speaker's appearance, bodily movements, and vocal expressions. And the appeal to the sympathy of the audience can be greatly enhanced by the presence of the speaker. Take the excerpt from the speech of the hemophiliac. The written descriptions of pain and heartbreak are very moving, but place yourself in the audience, looking at the victim and imagining the suffering experienced by the human body standing in front of you. No doubt the effect would be deep and long-lasting, perhaps more memorable even than the written word.

Because the human instrument is so powerful, it must be used with care. You have probably listened to speakers who used gestures and voice inflections that had been dutifully rehearsed but were obviously contrived and worked, unfortunately, to undermine rather than support the speaker's message and credibility. If you are not a gifted actor, avoid gestures, body language, and vocal expressions that are not truly felt.

Some speech theorists treat support or proofs as *nonartistic* and *artistic*. The nonartistic support — factual data, expert opinion, examples — is considered objective and verifiable. Its acceptability should not depend on the character and personality of the speaker. It is plainly different from the artistic proof, which is subjective, based on the values and attitudes of the listener, and therefore more difficult for the speaker to control. This form of support is called artistic because it includes creative strategies within the power of the speaker to manipulate. In earlier parts of this chapter we have discussed the artistic proofs, ways of establishing credibility, and recognizing the values of the audience.

Presentation Aids

Charts, Graphs, Handouts

Some speeches, though not all, will be enhanced by visual and other aids: charts, graphs, maps, models, objects, handouts, recordings, and computerized images. These aids, however, no matter how visually or aurally exciting, should not overwhelm your own oral presentation. The objects are not the stars of the show. They exist to make your spoken argument more persuasive.

Charts and graphs, large enough and clear enough to be seen and understood, can illuminate speeches that contain numbers of any kind, especially statistical comparisons. You can make a simple chart yourself, on paper for use with an easel or on a computer to be projected or to be printed for presentation to an audience. Enlarged illustrations or a model of a complicated machine — say, the space shuttle — would help a speaker to explain its function. You already know that photographs or videos are powerful instruments of persuasion, above all in support of appeals for humanitarian aid, for both people and animals.

Court cases have been won or lost on the basis of diagrams or charts that purport to prove the innocence or guilt of a defendant. Such aids do not always speak for themselves. No matter how clear they are to the designer, they may be misinterpreted or misunderstood by a viewer. Some critics have argued that the jury in the O. J. Simpson case failed to understand the graphs of DNA relationships that experts for the prosecution displayed during the trial. Before you show

Presentation aids such as visuals can enhance your speech.

any diagrams or charts of any complexity to your audience, ask friends if they find them easy to understand.

The use of a handout also requires planning. It's probably unwise to put your speech on hold while the audience reads or studies a handout that requires time and concentration. Confine the subject matter of handouts to material that can be easily grasped as you discuss or explain it.

Audio

Audio aids may also enliven a speech or even be indispensable to its success. One student played a recording of a scene from *Romeo and Juliet*, spoken by a cast of professional actors, to make a point about the relationship between the two lovers. Another student chose to define several types of popular music, including rap, goth, heavy metal, and techno. But he used only words, and the lack of any musical demonstration meant that the distinctions remained unclear.

Video

With sight, sound, and movement, a video can illustrate or reinforce the main points of a speech. A speech warning people not to drink and drive will have a much greater effect if enhanced by a video showing the tragic and often gruesome outcome of car accidents caused by drunk driving. Schools that teach driver's education frequently rely on these bone-chilling videos to show their students that getting behind the wheel is a serious responsibility, not a game. If you want to use video, check to make sure that a computer, Blu-ray, or DVD player and television are available to you. Most schools have an audio-visual department that manages the delivery, setup, and return of all equipment.

Multimedia

Multimedia presentation software programs enable you to combine several different media such as text, charts, sound, and still or moving pictures into one unit. In the business world, multimedia presentations are commonly used in situations where you have a limited amount of time to persuade or teach a fairly large audience. For instance, the promotion director of a leading teen magazine is trying to persuade skeptical executives that a magazine Web site would increase sales and advertising revenue. Since the magazine is sold through newsstand and subscription, some executives question whether the cost of creating and maintaining a Web site outweighs the benefits. Using multimedia presentation software, the promotion director can integrate demographic charts and graphs showing that steadily increasing numbers of teenagers surf the Web, a segment from a television news program reporting that many teens shop online (an attraction for advertisers), and downloaded pages from a competitor's Web site to demonstrate that others are already reaping the benefits of the Internet. People today are increasingly "visual" in their learning styles, and multimedia software may be the most effective aid for an important presentation.

Though effective when done well, technically complicated presentations require large amounts of time and careful planning. First you must ensure that your computer is powerful enough to adeptly handle presentation software. Then you need to familiarize yourself with the program. Most presentation software programs come equipped with helpful tutorials. If the task of creating your own presentation from scratch seems overwhelming, you can use one of the many preformatted presentation templates: You will simply need to customize the content. Robert Stephens, the founder of the Geek Squad, a Minneapolis-based business that provides on-site emergency response to computer problems, gives the following tips for multimedia presentations:

1. In case of equipment failure, always bring two of everything.
2. Back up your presentation on CD-ROM or a Zip drive.
3. Avoid live visits to the Internet. Because connections can fail or be painfully slow, and sites can move or disappear, if you must visit the Internet in

your presentation, download the appropriate pages onto your hard drive ahead of time. It will still look like a live visit.

4. In the end, technology cannot replace creativity. Make sure that you are using multimedia to reinforce not replace your main points.[10]

Make sure that any necessary apparatus will be available at the right time. If you have never used the devices you need for your presentation, practice using them before the speech. Few things are more disconcerting for the speechmaker and the audience than a speaker who is fumbling with his materials, unable to find the right picture or to make a machine work.

Sample Persuasive Speech

The following speech was delivered by C. Renzi Stone to his public speaking class at the University of Oklahoma. Told to prepare a persuasive speech, Stone chose to speak about the health benefits of vegetarianism. Note his attention-grabbing introduction.

[10] Robert Stephens as paraphrased in "When Your Presentation Crashes . . . Who You Gonna Call?" by Eric Matson, *Fast Company*, February/March 1997, p. 130.

Live Longer and Healthier: Stop Eating Meat!

C. RENZI STONE

What do Steve Martin, Dustin Hoffman, Albert Einstein, Jerry Garcia, Michael Stipe, Eddie Vedder, Martina Navratilova, Carl Lewis, and twelve million other Americans all have in common? All of these well-known people were or are vegetarians. What do they know that we don't? Consuming a regimen of high-fat, high-protein flesh foods is a sure-fire prescription for disaster, like running diesel fuel through your car's gasoline engine. In the book *Why Do Vegetarians Eat Like That?* David Gabbe asserts that millions of people today are afflicted with chronic diseases that can be directly linked to the consumption of meat. Eating a vegetarian diet can help prevent many of those diseases.

In 1996, twelve million Americans identified themselves as vegetarians. That number is twice as many as in the decade before. According to a recent National Restaurant Association poll found in *Health* magazine, one in five diners say they now go out of their way to choose restaurants that serve at least a few meatless entrees. Obviously, the traditionally American trait of a meat-dominated society has subsided in recent years.

In discussing vegetarianism today, first I will tell how vegetarians are perceived in society. Next, I will introduce several studies validating my claim that a meatless diet is extraordinarily healthy. I will then show how a veggie diet can strengthen the immune system and make the meatless body a shield from unwanted diseases such as cancer and heart disease. Maintaining a strict vegetarian diet can also lead to a longer life. Finally, I will put an image into the audience's mind of a meatless society that relies on vegetables for the main course at breakfast, lunch, and dinner.

Moving to my first point, society generally holds two major misperceptions about vegetarians. First of all, society often perceives vegetarians as a radical group of people with extreme principles. In this view, vegetarians are seen as a monolithic group of people who choose to eat vegetables because they are opposed to the killing of animals for food. The second major misconception is that because vegetarians do not eat meat, they do not get the proper amounts of essential vitamins and minerals often found in meat.

Here is my response to these misconceived notions. First of all, vegetarians are not a homogeneous group of radicals. Whereas many vegetarians in the past did join the movement on the principle that killing animals is wrong, many join the movement today mainly for its health benefits. In addition, there are many different levels of vegetarianism. Some vegetarians eat nothing but vegetables. Others don't eat red meat but do occasionally eat chicken and fish.

5

Secondly, contrary to popular opinion, vegetarians get more than enough vitamins and minerals in their diet and generally receive healthier nourishment than meat eaters. In fact, in an article for *Health* magazine, Peter Jaret states that vegetarians actually get larger amounts of amino acids due to the elimination of saturated fats which are often found in meat products. Studies show that the health benefits of a veggie lifestyle contribute to increased life expectancy and overall productivity.

Hopefully you now see that society's perceptions of vegetarians are outdated and just plain wrong. You are familiar with many of the problems associated with a meat-based diet, and you have heard many of the benefits of a vegetarian diet. Now try to imagine how you personally can improve your life by becoming a vegetarian.

Can you imagine a world where people retire at age eighty and lead productive lives into their early 100s? Close your eyes and think about celebrating your seventieth wedding anniversary, seeing your great-grandchildren get married, and witnessing one hundred years of world events and technological innovations. David Gabbe's book refers to studies that have shown a vegetarian diet can increase your life expectancy up to fifteen years. A longer life is within your reach, and the diet you eat has a direct impact on your health and how you age.

In conclusion, vegetarianism is a healthy life choice, not a radical cult. By eliminating meat from their diet, vegetarians reap the benefits of a vegetable-based diet that helps prevent disease and increase life expectancy. People, take heed of my advice. There are many more sources of information available for those who want to take a few hours to research the benefits of the veggie lifestyle. If you don't believe my comments, discover the whole truth for yourself.

Twelve million Americans know the health benefits that come with being a   10
vegetarian. Changing your eating habits can be just as easy as making your bed in
the morning. Sure, it takes a few extra minutes and some thought, but your body
will thank you in the long run.

You only live once. Why not make it a long stay?

READING FOR ANALYSIS

I Have a Dream

MARTIN LUTHER KING JR.

Five score years ago, a great American, in whose symbolic shadow we stand, signed
the Emancipation Proclamation. This momentous decree came as a great beacon
light of hope to millions of Negro slaves who had been seared in the flames of wither-
ing injustice. It came as a joyous daybreak to end the long night of captivity.

But one hundred years later, we must face the tragic fact that the Negro is still
not free. One hundred years later, the life of the Negro is still sadly crippled by
the manacles of segregation and the chains of discrimination. One hundred years
later, the Negro lives on a lonely island of poverty in the midst of a vast ocean of
material prosperity. One hundred years later, the Negro is still languishing in the
corners of American society and finds himself an exile in his own land. So we have
come here today to dramatize an appalling condition.

In a sense we have come to our nation's capital to cash a check. When the
architects of our republic wrote the magnificent words of the Constitution and the
Declaration of Independence, they were signing a promissory note to which every
American was to fall heir. This note was a promise that all men would be guaranteed the unalienable rights of life, liberty, and the pursuit of happiness.

It is obvious today that America has defaulted on this promissory note insofar
as her citizens of color are concerned. Instead of honoring this sacred obligation,
America has given the Negro people a bad check; a check which has come back
marked "insufficient funds." But we refuse to believe that the bank of justice is
bankrupt. We refuse to believe that there are insufficient funds in the great vaults
of opportunity of this nation. So we have come to cash this check — a check that
will give us upon demand the riches of freedom and the security of justice. We
have also come to this hallowed spot to remind America of the fierce urgency of
now. This is no time to engage in the luxury of cooling off or to take the tranquil-

---

In the widely reprinted "I Have a Dream" speech, Martin Luther King Jr. appears as the charismatic leader of the civil rights movement. This inspirational address was delivered on August
28, 1963, in Washington, D.C., at a demonstration by two hundred thousand people for civil
rights for African Americans. From *A Testament of Hope* (1986).

izing drugs of gradualism. *Now* is the time to make real the promises of Democracy. *Now* is the time to rise from the dark and desolate valley of segregation to the sunlit path of racial justice. *Now* is the time to open the doors of opportunity to all of God's children. *Now* is the time to lift our nation from the quicksands of racial injustice to the solid rock of brotherhood.

It would be fatal for the nation to overlook the urgency of the moment and to underestimate the determination of the Negro. This sweltering summer of the Negro's legitimate discontent will not pass until there is an invigorating autumn of freedom and equality. Nineteen sixty-three is not an end, but a beginning. Those who hope that the Negro needed to blow off steam and will now be content will have a rude awakening if the nation returns to business as usual. There will be neither rest nor tranquillity in America until the Negro is granted his citizenship rights. The whirlwinds of revolt will continue to shake the foundations of our nation until the bright day of justice emerges.

But there is something that I must say to my people who stand on the warm threshold which leads into the palace of justice. In the process of gaining our rightful place we must not be guilty of wrongful deeds. Let us not seek to satisfy our thirst for freedom by drinking from the cup of bitterness and hatred. We must forever conduct our struggle on the high plane of dignity and discipline. We must not allow our creative protest to degenerate into physical violence. Again and again we must rise to the majestic heights of meeting physical force with soul force. The marvelous new militancy which has engulfed the Negro community must not lead us to a distrust of all white people, for many of our white brothers, as evidenced by their presence here today, have come to realize that their destiny is tied up with our destiny and their freedom is inextricably bound to our freedom. We cannot walk alone.

And as we walk, we must make the pledge that we shall march ahead. We cannot turn back. There are those who are asking the devotees of civil rights, "When will you be satisfied?" We can never be satisfied as long as the Negro is the victim of the unspeakable horrors of police brutality. We can never be satisfied as long as our bodies, heavy with the fatigue of travel, cannot gain lodging in the motels of the highways and the hotels of the cities. We cannot be satisfied as long as the Negro's basic mobility is from a smaller ghetto to a larger one. We can never be satisfied as long as a Negro in Mississippi cannot vote and a Negro in New York believes he has nothing for which to vote. No, no, we are not satisfied, and we will not be satisfied until justice rolls down like waters and righteousness like a mighty stream.

I am not unmindful that some of you have come here out of great trials and tribulations. Some of you have come fresh from narrow jail cells. Some of you have come from areas where your quest for freedom left you battered by the storms of persecution and staggered by the winds of police brutality. You have been the veterans of creative suffering. Continue to work with the faith that unearned suffering is redemptive.

Go back to Mississippi, go back to Alabama, go back to South Carolina, go back to Georgia, go back to Louisiana, go back to the slums and ghettos of our northern cities, knowing that somehow this situation can and will be changed. Let us not wallow in the valley of despair.

I say to you today, my friends, that in spite of the difficulties and frustrations 10 of the moment I still have a dream. It is a dream deeply rooted in the American dream.

I have a dream that one day this nation will rise up and live out the true meaning of its creed: "We hold these truths to be self-evident; that all men are created equal."

I have a dream that one day on the red hills of Georgia the sons of former slaves and the sons of former slaveowners will be able to sit down together at the table of brotherhood.

I have a dream that one day even the state of Mississippi, a desert state sweltering with the heat of injustice and oppression, will be transformed into an oasis of freedom and justice.

I have a dream that my four little children will one day live in a nation where they will not be judged by the color of their skin but by the content of their character.

I have a dream today. 15

I have a dream that one day the state of Alabama, whose governor's lips are presently dripping with the words of interposition and nullification, will be transformed into a situation where little black boys and black girls will be able to join hands with little white boys and white girls and walk together as sisters and brothers.

I have a dream today.

I have a dream that one day every valley shall be exalted, every hill and mountain shall be made low, the rough places will be made plain, and the crooked places will be made straight, and the glory of the Lord shall be revealed, and all flesh shall see it together.

This is our hope. This is the faith with which I return to the South. With this faith we will be able to hew out of the mountain of despair a stone of hope. With this faith we will be able to transform the jangling discords of our nation into a beautiful symphony of brotherhood. With this faith we will be able to work together, to pray together, to struggle together, to go to jail together, to stand up for freedom together, knowing that we will be free one day.

This will be the day when all of God's children will be able to sing with new 20 meaning

> My country, 'tis of thee,
> Sweet land of liberty,
>   Of thee I sing:
> Land where my fathers died,
> Land of the pilgrims' pride,
> From every mountain-side
>   Let freedom ring.

And if America is to be a great nation this must become true. So let freedom ring from the prodigious hilltops of New Hampshire. Let freedom ring from the mighty mountains of New York. Let freedom ring from the heightening Alleghenies of Pennsylvania!

Let freedom ring from the snowcapped Rockies of Colorado!

Let freedom ring from the curvaceous peaks of California!

But not only that; let freedom ring from Stone Mountain of Georgia!

Let freedom ring from Lookout Mountain of Tennessee!   25

Let freedom ring from every hill and molehill of Mississippi. From every mountainside, let freedom ring.

When we let freedom ring, when we let it ring from every village and every hamlet, from every state and every city, we will be able to speed up that day when all of God's children, black men and white men, Jews and Gentiles, Protestants and Catholics, will be able to join hands and sing in the words of the old Negro spiritual, "Free at last! free at last! thank God almighty, we are free at last!"

READING AND DISCUSSION QUESTIONS

1. What were the circumstances in which King delivered this speech? Of whom did the audience consist? How might the circumstances and the audience have affected decisions King made in composing the speech? Where in the speech does he most directly refer to his audience?

2. What sort of reputation had King established by the time he gave this speech in 1963? Are there ways in which he establishes his credibility through the speech itself? Explain.

3. How would you describe the organization of the speech?

4. Explain the metaphor of the check. Where else does King make use of metaphorical language?

5. How else does King's use of language lend power to his speech?

6. What allusions do you find in the speech?

WRITING SUGGESTIONS

7. Write an essay analyzing King's speech according to the elements of oral argument discussed in this chapter.

8. Write an essay analyzing King's language as a major source of the effectiveness of this historic speech.

Acknowledgments

Eric Auchard. "We're All Celebrities in Post-Privacy Age." From Reuters.com, June 21, 2007. All rights reserved. Republication or redistribution of Thomson Reuters content, including by framing or similar means, is expressly prohibited without the written consent of Thomson Reuters. Thomson Reuters and its logo are registered trademarks of the Thomson Reuters group of companies around the world. © Thomson Reuters 2007. Thomson Reuters journalists are subject to an Editorial Handbook which requires fair presentation and disclosure of relevant interests.

Response to Jacoby's "What's Wrong with Price Gouging?" by BackBayAlltheWay, May 4, 2010, as submitted and found on Response to Jacoby's "What's Wrong with Price Gouging?" (from *The Boston Globe*, May 4, 2010) by BackBayAlltheWay, May 4, 2010. Reprinted by permission.

Newman P. Birk and Genevieve B. Birk. "Selection, Slanting, and Charged Learning," from *Understanding and Using English.* Copyright © 1959 Newman P. Birk and Genevieve Birk.

Warren Burger. "The Right to Bear Arms." From *Parade Magazine*, January 14, 1990.

Mona Charen. "The Misleading Debate on Stem Cell Research." From Townhall.com, August 20, 2004. Copyright © 2004 by News America Syndicate. Reprinted by permission of Mona Charen and Creator's Syndicate, Inc.

Jo Ann Citron. "Will it be Marriage or Civil Union?" From *The Gay & Lesbian Review Worldwide*, March/April 2004, v. 11 i2, p. 10(2). Copyright © 2004 Jo Ann Citron. Reprinted by permission of the author and the Gay & Lesbian Review Worldwide.

William Deresiewicz. "Faux Friendship" by William Deresiewicz from *The Chronicle of Higher Education*, December 6, 2009. Reprinted by permission.

Alan M. Dershowitz. "Is There a Torturous Road to Justice?" From *The Los Angeles Times*, Commentary, November 8, 2001. Reprinted by permission of the author.

Roger Ebert. "Crash." Taken from the *Roger Ebert* column by Roger Ebert © 2005 The Ebert Company. Dist. By Universal Uclick. Reprinted by permission. All rights reserved.

Edward Jay Epstein. "Sex and the Cinema." From Slate.com, August 15, 2005. Reprinted by permission.

Christopher M. Fairman. "The Case Against Banning the Word 'Retard'" by Christopher M. Fairman from *The Washington Post*, February 14, 2010. Reprinted by permission of the author.

Stephanie Fairyington. Originally published as "Choice As Strategy: Homosexuality and the Politics of Pity," *Dissent* vol 57, no 1 (Winter 2010), pp. 7–10. Reprinted with permission of the University of Pennsylvania Press.

William Faulkner. "Nobel Prize Acceptance Speech." © The Nobel Foundation 1949. Reprinted by permission.

Seth Finkelstein. "Alan Dershowitz's Tortous Torturous Argument." From *Ethical Spectacle*, February 2002. Reprinted by permission of the author.

Stanley Fish. "When Is a Cross a Cross?" From *The New York Times*, May 3, 2010, © 2010 The New York Times. All rights reserved. Used by permission and protected by the Copyright Laws of the United States. The printing, copying, redistribution, or retransmission of this Content without express written permission is prohibited.

Bernard Goldberg. "Connecting the Dots to Terrorists." From *Bias* by Bernard Goldberg. Copyright © 2002. Published by Regnery Publishing, Inc. All rights reserved. Reprinted by special permission of Regnery Publishing Inc., Washington, D.C.

Jennifer Grossman. "Food for Thought (and for Credit)." From *The New York Times*, Sept. 2, 2003, p. 23, col. 1. Copyright © 2003 by Jennifer Grossman. Reprinted by permission of the author.

Elisha Dov Hack. "College Life Versus My Moral Code." From *The New York Times*, September 9, 1997. Reprinted by permission of the author.

Richard Hayes. "Supersize Your Child?" Originally entitled "Selective Science." From Tompaine.com, February 12, 2004. Copyright © 2004 by Tompaine.com. Reprinted by permission.

Adolf Hitler. "On Nation and Race" from *Mein Kampf* by Adolf Hitler, translated by Ralph Manheim and published by Pimlico. Copyright © 1943, © renewed 1971 by Houghton Mifflin Company. Reprinted by permission of Houghton Mifflin Harcourt Publishing Company and The Random House Group Ltd. All rights reserved.

Jeff Jacoby. "What's Wrong with Price Gouging?" by Jeff Jacoby from *The Boston Globe*, May 4, 2010, http://www.boston.com/bostonglobe/editorial_opinion/oped/articles/2010/05/04/whats_wrong_with_price_gouging/ Reprinted by permission.

Eric Jaffe. "Reality Check." From *APS Observer*, by American Psychological Society. Copyright

2005. Reproduced with permission of Association for Psychological Science in the format Textbook and Other book via Copyright Clearance Center.

Amy Kamenetz. "Take This Internship and Shove It." From *The New York Times*, May 30, 2006, © 2006 The New York Times. All rights reserved. Used by permission and protected by the Copyright Laws of the United States. The printing, copying, redistribution, or retransmission of this Content without express written permission is prohibited.

Roger Kaplan. "Enabling Ignorance." From *The American Spectator*, September 2010. Reprinted by permission.

Martin Luther King. "I Have a Dream." From *A Testament of Hope*. Copyright © 1963 by Martin Luther King, Jr. Copyright renewed 1991 by Coretta Scott King. Reprinted by arrangement with the Estate of Martin Luther King, Jr., c/o Writer's House, as agent for the proprietor.

Michael Kinsley. "Racial Profiling at the Airport: Discrimination We're Afraid to Be Against" by Michael Kinsley from *Slate*, September 28, 2001. http://www.slate.com/id/116347/ Reprinted by permission.

R. Cort Kirkwood. "Driving Home Their Point." From *Chronicles: A Magazine of American Culture*, August 2010. Reprinted by permission.

Sharon Kneiss. "Argument for Recycling Is Strong" from *MSW Management*, November–December 2008. Reprinted by permission.

Alfie Kohn. "No-Win Situations." Copyright © 1990 by Alfie Kohn. Reprinted from *Women's Sports & Fitness* with the author's permission. For more on this topic, please see www.alfiekohn.org or Kohn's book *No Contest: The Case Against Competition*.

Jason Kottke. "The Exciting About" page by Jason Kottke. From http://kottke.org. Reprinted by permission of the author. "Vaccines don't cause autism" by Jason Kottke. From http://kottke.org. Reprinted by permission of the author.

Charles Krauthammer. "Let's Have No More Monkey Trials." From *Time*, August 8, 2005. Reprinted by permission of the author.

Michael Levin. "The Case for Torture." Originally published in *Newsweek*, June 7, 1982. Copyright © 1982 by Michael Levin. Reprinted by permission of the author.

John Mackey. "Putting Customers Ahead of Investors" from *Reason* magazine and Reason.com, October 2005. Reprinted by permission.

Roger D. McGrath. "A God Given Natural Right 'Shall Not Be Infringed.'" From *Chronicles*, October 2003. Copyright © 2003. Reprinted by permission of the author.

Mark Memmott. "Disaster Photos: Newsworthy or Irresponsible?" From USAToday.com, August 4, 2005. Reprinted by permission.

Howard Moody. "Gay Marriage Shows Why We Need to Separate Church and State." Reprinted with permission from the July 5, 2004 issue of *The Nation*. For subscription information, call 1-800-333-8536. Portions of each week's Nation magazine can be accessed at http://www.thenation.com.

Wesley Morris. "'Saw' Good at Tying Things in Knots." From *Boston Globe*, October 29, 2004. Reprinted by permission.

Charles Murray. "Abolish the SAT" from *The American*, July/August, 2007. Reprinted by permission.

Jacob Neusner. "The Speech the Graduates Didn't Hear" from Brown University's *Daily Herald*, June 12, 1983. Reprinted by permission.

Theodora Ooms. "Marriage-Plus." Annotated and excerpted from a special issue of *The American Prospect* on "The Politics of the American Family," April 8, 2002. Copyright © 2002 by the American Prospect. Reprinted by permission of the author.

Anna Quindlen. "A New Look, an Old Battle." Published in *Newsweek*, April 9, 2001, pp. 72–73. Copyright © 2001 by Anna Quindlen. Reprinted by permission of International Creative Management, Inc.

T. J. Rodgers. "Put Profits First." From *Reason* magazine and Reason.com, October 2005. Reprinted by permission.

Richard Rothstein. "True or False: Schools Fail Immigrants." From *The New York Times*, July 4, 2001, © 2001 The New York Times. All rights reserved. Used by permission and protected by the Copyright Laws of the United States. The printing, copying, redistribution, or retransmission of the Material without express written permission is prohibited.

Robert J. Samuelson. "The Hard Truth of Immigration." From Newsweek.com, June 13, 2005. Copyright © 2005. The Newsweek/Daily Beast Company LLC. All rights reserved. Used by permission and protected by the Copyright Laws of the United States. The printing, copying, redistribution, or retransmission of the Material without express written permission is prohibited.

Robert J. Samuelson. "Picking Sides for the News." From *Newsweek*, June 28, 2004 © 2004. The Newsweek/Daily Beast Company LLC. All rights reserved. Used by permission and protected by the Copyright Laws of the United States. The printing, copying, redistribution, or retransmission of the Material without express written permission is prohibited.

Leon Seltzer and David Niose. "Teen Sex: The 'Holy' vs. Humanistic Approach" by Leon F.

Seltzer and David Niose from psychologytoday.com, August 5, 2010. By permission of the authors.

Joe Sharkey. "Airport Screeners Could Get X-Rated X-Rays." From *The New York Times*, May 24, 2005. Copyright © 2005 The New York Times. All rights reserved. Used by permission and protected by the Copyright Laws of the United States. The printing, copying, redistribution, or retransmission of the Material without express written permission is prohibited.

Noam Shpancer. "The Meaning of Reality (TV)" by Noam Shpancer from psychologytoday.com, August 10, 2010. Reprinted by permission of the author.

Robert A. Sirico. "An Unjust Sacrifice." From *The New York Times*, September 30, 2000, © 2000 The New York Times. All rights reserved. Used by permission and protected by the Copyright Laws of the United States. The printing, copying, redistribution, or retransmission of this Content without express written permission is prohibited.

Barbara A. Spellman. "Could Reality Shows Become Reality Experiments?" From *APS Observer*, by American Psychological Society. Copyright 2005. Reproduced with permission of Association for Psychological Science in the format Textbook and Other book via Copyright Clearance Center.

C. Renzi Stone. "Live Longer and Healthier: Stop Eating Meat!" Reprinted by permission of the author.

John Trotti. "Why Let Stewardship Get in the Way of a Quick Buck?" From *MSW Management*, September 2008. Reprinted by permission.

Louis Uchitelle. "American Dream Is Elusive for New Generation." From *The New York Times*, July, 6, 2010, © 2010 The New York Times. All rights reserved. Used by permission and protected by the Copyright Laws of the United States. The printing, copying, redistribution, or retransmission of this Content without express written permission is prohibited.

Hal Varian. "Economic Scene: Are Bigger Vehicles Safer? It Depends." From *The New York Times*, December 18, 2003. Copyright © 2003 by The New York Times Inc. All rights reserved. Used by permission and protected by the Copyright Laws of the United States. The printing, copying, redistribution, or retransmission of this Content without express written permission is prohibited.

David Von Drehle. "It's All About Him: We Should Stop Explaining Killers on Their Terms. It's Not About Guns or Culture. It's Narcissism." From *Time*, Thursday, April 19, 2007. Copyright © 2007 TIME INC. Reprinted by permission. TIME is a registered trademark of Time Inc. All rights reserved.

Brian Whitaker. "The Definition of Terrorism." From *The Guardian Unlimited*, May 7, 2001. Copyright Guardian News & Media Ltd 2001. Reprinted by permission.

Barbara Dafoe Whitehead. "Parents Need Help: Restricting Access to Video Games." From *Commonweal*, January 28, 2005, © 2010 Commonweal Foundation. Reprinted with permission.

Juan Williams. "Don't Mourn Brown v. Board of Education." From *The New York Times*, June 29, 2007, © 2007, The New York Times. All rights reserved. Used by permission and protected by the Copyright Laws of the United States. The printing, copying, redistribution, or retransmission of this Content without express written permission is prohibited.

Lily Yulianti. "Praise for Student's Footage of Virginia Tech Mass Killing." From Ohmynews.com, April 17, 2007. Copyright © 2007 Ohmynews. Reprinted by permission of the author.

PHOTO CREDITS

5 Imagno/Getty Images; **7** Ryan McVay/Getty Images; **9** Alex Wong/Getty Images; **12** Michael Rougier/Getty Images; **14** Colin Anderson/Getty Images; **22** Stephen Toulmin; **25** Chip Somodevilla; **44** Photofest; **52** Susanna Price/Getty Images; **63** AP Images/Dave Martin; Chris Gaythen/Getty Images; AP Images/Dave Martin; **66** Margaret Bourke White/Getty Images; Bruce Chambers/The Orange County Register; **94** Eamonn McCormack/Getty Images; **103** Altrendo Images/Getty Images; **111** OJO Images/Getty Images; **133** Sonya Farrell; **153** AKG Photos; **151** John Lund/Getty Images; **149** AKG Photos; **156** Gallo Images/Alamy; **186** Noel Hendrikson/Getty Images; **192** Leland Bobbel/Getty Images; **216** Roger Harris/SPL; **224** Matthew Cavanaugh/Redux; **232** G. Paul Burnett/The New York Times/Redux; **288** B2M Productions; **313** Steve Murrez/Getty Images; **315** Travel Ink/Getty Images; **318** Tara Moore/Getty Images; **341** MPI/Getty Images; **350** John Fletcher and Robert Sisson/Getty Images; **363** Jeff Coolidge/Getty

Images; **390** Science Based Medicine; **412** Student voice.org; **413** Student voice.org; **425** Screenshot from ACADEMIC ONEFILE c Gale , a part of Cengage Learning. Reproduced by permission www.cengage.com / permissions; **434** From www.defenselink.mil Article by Spc. Courtney Maurilli, 2nd Brigadire Combat Team, 2nd Infancy Division Public Affairs.; **435** From Gale: Screenshot from Thomson/Galegroup.com Expanded Academic ASAP. © Gale, a part of Cengage Learning, Inc. Reproduced by permission www.cengage.com/ permissions. Article reprinted from the May, 30, 2005 issue of *BusinessWeek* by permission. Copyright 2005 by The McGraw Hill Companies; **479** Jeff Mitchell/Getty Images; **488** Tetra Images

GLOSSARY

Abstract language: language expressing a quality apart from a specific object or event; opposite of *concrete language*

Ad hominem: "against the man"; attacking the arguer rather than the *argument* or issue

Ad populum: "to the people"; playing on the prejudices of the *audience*

Anecdotal evidence: stories or examples used to illustrate a *claim* but that do not prove it with scientific certainty

Appeal to tradition: a proposal that something should continue because it has traditionally existed or been done that way

Argument: a process of reasoning and advancing proof about issues on which conflicting views may be held; also, a statement or statements providing *support* for a *claim*

Aristotelian rhetoric: the approach to oral persuasion espoused by Aristotle (384 BC–322 BC) and used to shape school curricula well into the nineteenth century; a rhetorical theory based on using a combination of logos, ethos, and pathos to move an audience to a change in thought or action

Audience: those who will hear an *argument;* more generally, those to whom a communication is addressed

Authoritative warrant: a *warrant* based on the credibility or trustworthiness of the source

Backing: the assurances on which a *warrant* or assumption is based

Begging the question: making a statement that assumes that the issue being argued has already been decided

Claim: the conclusion of an argument; what the arguer is trying to prove

Claim of fact: a *claim* that asserts something exists, has existed, or will exist, based on data that the *audience* will accept as objectively verifiable

Claim of policy: a *claim* asserting that specific courses of action should be instituted as solutions to problems

Claim of value: a *claim* that asserts some things are more or less desirable than others

Cliché: a worn-out expression or idea, no longer capable of producing a visual image or provoking thought about a subject

Common ground: used in Rogerian argument to refer to any concept that two opposing parties agree on and that can thus be used as a starting point for negotiation

Concrete language: language that describes specific, generally observable, persons, places, or things; in contrast to *abstract language*

Connotation: the overtones that adhere to a word through long usage

Credibility: the audience's belief in the arguer's trustworthiness; see also *ethos*

Data: facts or figures from which a conclusion may be inferred; see *evidence*

Deduction: reasoning by which we establish that a conclusion must be true because the statements on which it is based are true; see also *syllogism*

Definition: an explanation of the meaning of a term, concept, or experience; may be used for clarification, especially of a *claim,* or as a means of developing an *argument*

Definition by negation: defining a thing by saying what it is not

Empirical evidence: *support* verifiable by experience or experiment

Enthymeme: a *syllogism* in which one of the premises is implicit

Ethos: the qualities of character, intelligence, and goodwill in an arguer that contribute to an *audience's* acceptance of the *claim*

Euphemism: a pleasant or flattering expression used in place of one that is less agreeable but possibly more accurate

Evidence: *facts* or opinions that support an issue or *claim;* may consist of *statistics,* reports of personal experience, or views of experts

Extended definition: a *definition* that uses several different methods of development

Fact: something that is believed to have objective reality; a piece of information regarded as verifiable

Factual evidence: *support* consisting of *data* that are considered objectively verifiable by the audience

Fallacy: an error of reasoning based on faulty use of *evidence* or incorrect *inference*

False analogy: assuming without sufficient proof that if objects or processes are similar in some ways, then they are similar in other ways as well

False dilemma: simplifying a complex problem into an either/or dichotomy

Faulty emotional appeals: basing an argument on feelings, especially pity or fear — often to draw attention away from the real issues or conceal another purpose

Faulty use of authority: failing to acknowledge disagreement among experts or otherwise misrepresenting the trustworthiness of sources

Hasty generalization: drawing conclusions from insufficient evidence

Induction: reasoning by which a general statement is reached on the basis of particular examples

Inference: an interpretation of the *facts*

Logos: argument based on reason

Major premise: see *syllogism*

Minor premise: see *syllogism*

MLA: the Modern Language Association, a professional organization for college teachers of English and foreign languages

Motivational appeal: an attempt to reach an *audience* by recognizing their *needs* and *values* and how these contribute to their decision making

Motivational warrant: a type of *warrant* based on the *needs* and *values* of an *audience*

Need: in the hierarchy of Abraham Maslow, whatever is required, whether psychological, or physiological, for the survival and welfare of a human being

Non sequitur: "it does not follow"; using irrelevant proof to buttress a *claim*

Paraphrase: to restate the content of an original source in your own words

Pathos: appeal to the emotions

Persuasion: the use of a combination of logos, ethos, and pathos to move an audience

Picturesque language: words that produce images in the minds of the *audience*

Plagiarism: the use of someone else's words or ideas without adequate acknowledgment

Policy: a course of action recommended or taken to solve a problem or guide decisions

Post hoc: mistakenly inferring that because one event follows another they have a causal relation; from *post hoc ergo propter hoc* ("after this, therefore because of this"); also called "doubtful cause"

Proposition: see *claim*

Qualifier: a restriction placed on the *claim* may not always be true as stated

Quote: to repeat exactly words from a printed, electronic, or spoken source

Referential relationship: the relationship between a writer and his or her subject

Referential summary: a summary that focuses on ideas rather than on the author's actions and decisions

Refutation: an attack on an opposing view to weaken it, invalidate it, or make it less credible

Reservation: a restriction placed on the *warrant* to indicate that unless certain conditions are met, the warrant may not establish a connection between the *support* and the *claim*

Rhetorical relationship: the relationship between writer and audience

Rhetorical summary: a condensation of passage in the writer's own words that stresses the author's decisions as a writer

Rogerian argument: a rhetorical theory based on the counseling techniques of Carl Rogers (1902–1987) that emphasizes a search for common ground that would allow two opposing parties to start negotiations

Slanting: selecting *facts* or words with *connotations* that favor the arguer's bias and discredit alternatives

Slippery slope: predicting without justification that one step in a process will lead unavoidably to a second, generally undesirable step

Slogan: an attention-getting expression used largely in politics or advertising to promote support of a cause or product

Statistics: information expressed in numerical form

Stipulative definition: a *definition* that makes clear that it will explore a particular area of meaning of a term or issue

Straw man: disputing a view similar to, but not the same as, that of the arguer's opponent

Style: choices in words and sentence structure that make a writer's language distinctive

Substantive warrant: a *warrant* based on beliefs about the reliability of *factual evidence*

Summary: a condensation of a passage into a shorter version in the writer's own words

Support: any material that serves to prove an issue or *claim;* in addition to *evidence,* it includes appeals to the *needs* and *values* of the *audience*

Syllogism: a formula of deductive *argument* consisting of three propositions: a major premise, a minor premise, and a conclusion

Thesis: the main idea of an essay

Toulmin model: a conceptual system of argument devised by the philosopher Stephen Toulmin; the terms *claim, support, warrant, backing, qualifier,* and *reservation* are adapted from this system

Two wrongs make a right: diverting attention from the issue by introducing a new point, e.g., by responding to an accusation with a counteraccusation that makes no attempt to refute the first accusation

Values: conceptions or ideas that act as standards for judging what is right or wrong, worthwhile or worthless, beautiful or ugly, good or bad

Warrant: a general principle or assumption that establishes a connection between the *support* and the *claim*

INDEX OF SUBJECTS

INDEX OF AUTHORS AND TITLES